# THE ROUTLEDGE COMPANION
# TO MUSIC COGNITION

*The Routledge Companion to Music Cognition* addresses fundamental questions about the nature of music from a psychological perspective. Music cognition is presented as the field that investigates the psychological, physiological, and physical processes that allow music to take place, seeking to explain how and why music has such powerful and mysterious effects on us. This volume provides a comprehensive overview of research in music cognition, balancing accessibility with depth and sophistication.

A diverse range of global scholars—music theorists, musicologists, pedagogues, neuroscientists, and psychologists—address the implications of music in everyday life while broadening the range of topics in music cognition research, deliberately seeking connections with the kinds of music and musical experiences that are meaningful to the population at large but are often overlooked in the study of music cognition. Such topics include:

- Music's impact on physical and emotional health
- Music cognition in various genres
- Music cognition in diverse populations, including people with amusia and hearing loss
- The relationship of music to learning and accomplishment in academics, sport, and recreation
- The broader sociological and anthropological uses of music

Consisting of over forty essays, the volume is organized by five primary themes. The first section, "Music from the Air to the Brain," provides a neuroscientific and theoretical basis for the book. The next three sections are based on musical actions: "Hearing and Listening to Music," "Making and Using Music," and "Developing Musicality." The closing section, "Musical Meanings," returns to fundamental questions related to music's meaning and significance, seen from historical and contemporary perspectives. *The Routledge Companion to Music Cognition* seeks to encourage readers to understand connections between the laboratory and the everyday in their musical lives.

**Richard Ashley** is Associate Professor of Music Theory and Cognition at Northwestern University, where he also holds appointments in Cognitive Science and Cognitive Neuroscience.

**Renee Timmers** is Reader in Psychology of Music at the Department of Music, The University of Sheffield, UK, where she directs the research center "Music, Mind, Machine in Sheffield," and teaches psychology of music at undergraduate and postgraduate level.

# THE ROUTLEDGE COMPANION TO MUSIC COGNITION

*Edited by*
*Richard Ashley and Renee Timmers*

LONDON AND NEW YORK

First published 2017
by Routledge

2 Park Square, Milton Park, Abingdon, Oxfordshire OX14 4RN
52 Vanderbilt Avenue, New York, NY 10017

*Routledge is an imprint of the Taylor & Francis Group, an informa business*

First issued in paperback 2019

*Library of Congress Cataloging-in-Publication Data*
Names: Ashley, Richard (Musicologist), editor. | Timmers, Renee, 1974– editor.
Title: The Routledge companion to music cognition / edited by Richard Ashley and Renee Timmers.
Description: New York : Routledge, 2017. | Includes bibliographical references and index.
Identifiers: LCCN 2016050960 (print) | LCCN 2016052264 (ebook) | ISBN 9781138721050 (hardback) | ISBN 9781315194738
Subjects: LCSH: Music—Psychological aspects. | Music—Physiological aspects. | Music—Performance—Psychological aspects. | Musical perception. | Music—Philosophy and aesthetics.
Classification: LCC ML3830 .R79 2017 (print) | LCC ML3830 (ebook) | DDC 781.1/1—dc23
LC record available at https://lccn.loc.gov/2016050960

ISBN: 978-1-138-72105-0 (hbk)
ISBN: 978-0-367-87655-5 (pbk)

Typeset in Bembo
by Apex CoVantage, LLC

# CONTENTS

**PART 3**
**Making and Using Music** 249

**PART 4**
**Developing Musicality** 389

# FIGURES AND TABLES

## Figures

## Tables

# NOTES ON CONTRIBUTORS

**Richard Ashley** is Associate Professor of Music, Cognitive Science, and Cognitive Neuroscience at Northwestern University. His research interests are in cognitive aspects of musical structure, musical memory, music and emotion, and expressive performance. A former president of the Society for Music Perception and Cognition, he remains active as a performer.

**Mylène Barbaroux** is a PhD student in Cognitive Neuroscience. She is working with Mireille Besson on the links between auditory perception and word learning in adults. Specifically, she is combining psychoacoustical training procedures with electoencephalographic measurements. To test for transfer effects on syllabic categorization and word learning.

**Fernando Benadon** is Associate Professor of Music at American University. His work explores rhythm and timing in jazz, popular music, speech, and global drumming traditions. An active composer, he has released two albums and was the recipient of a Guggenheim Fellowship.

**Tonya R. Bergeson,** PhD holds faculty positions at Butler University and Indiana University School of Medicine. Her research interests include the effects of early auditory experience on speech, language, and music development in infants and children with hearing loss who use hearing aids and cochlear implants.

**Mireille Besson** is Research Director at CNRS. Her research interests are centered on music, language, and the brain, mainly studying between domain transfer effects using electrophysiological methods. She is interested in the societal impact of music training, using music as an educational tool for childrens' development, and as a remediation tool for patients.

**Laura Bishop** is a Postdoctoral Researcher at the Austrian Research Institute for Artificial Intelligence (OFAI) in Vienna, Austria. She received her PhD in music cognition from the MARCS Institute, University of Western Sydney, Australia. Her research investigates audiovisual integration, visual communication, and coordination among ensemble musicians during creative collaboration.

**Ragnhild Brøvig-Hanssen** is Associate Professor in Popular Music Studies at the University of Oslo. She has published widely on music production, digital media, remix culture, and sound studies and is co-author of the book *Digital Signatures: The Impact of Digitization on Popular Music Sound* (MIT Press, 2016).

**Anne Caclin** holds a full-time INSERM research position within the "Brain Dynamics and Cognition" team of the Lyon Neuroscience Research Center. She completed a PhD and postdoctoral research in cognitive neuroscience.

**Elaine Chew** is Professor of Digital Media at Queen Mary University of London. A pianist (LTCL 1985, FTCL 1987) and operations researcher (PhD MIT 2000, SM MIT 1998) by training, her research centers on the mathematical and computational modeling of music structures and expressivity, including automated analysis and scientific visualization. She is the author of *Mathematical and Computational Modelling of Tonality: Theory and Applications* (Springer, 2014).

**Eric F. Clarke** is Heather Professor of Music at the University of Oxford. His books include *Ways of Listening, Music and Mind in Everyday Life*, and *Music and Consciousness*. He was Associate Director of the AHRC Centre for Musical Performance as Creative Practice (2009–14), and is a Fellow of the British Academy.

**Trevor de Clercq** is Assistant Professor in the Department of Recording Industry at Middle Tennessee State University in Murfreesboro, Tennessee, where he coordinates the musicianship curriculum and teaches coursework in audio technology. He holds a PhD in music theory from the Eastman School of Music in Rochester, New York.

**Annabel J. Cohen** (Ph.D. Queen's University; ARCT Voice Performance Royal Conservatory of Music) is Professor of Psychology at the University of Prince Edward Island, Fellow of the American and Canadian Psychological Associations, Editor of *Psychomusicology: Music, Mind & Brain*, and initiated and directs the AIRS (Advancing Interdisciplinary Research in Singing) SSHRC Major Collaborative Research Initiative.

**Anne Danielsen** is Professor of Musicology at the University of Oslo. Her field of research is rhythm, digital technology, and music production. Books include *Presence and Pleasure* (2006), the collection *Musical Rhythm in the Age of Digital Reproduction* (2010) and the co-authored *Digital Signatures: The Impact of Digitization on Popular Music Sound* (2016).

**Roger T. Dean** is a composer/improviser, and since 2007 a Research Professor in music cognition and computation at the MARCS Institute, Western Sydney University. He founded and directs the ensemble austraLYSIS, and performed as bassist, pianist, piano accompanist, and laptop computer artist in many other contexts. His current research is on affect in music, the role of acoustic intensity and timbre, and rhythm generation and perception. Previously he was foundation CEO of the Heart Research Institute, Sydney, researching in biochemistry, and then Vice-Chancellor and President of the University of Canberra.

**Nicola Dibben** is Professor in Music at the University of Sheffield, UK. She is former editor of the academic journals *Empirical Musicology Review* and *Popular Music*. Publications include the co-authored *Music and Mind in Everyday Life* (2010) and monograph *Björk* (2009), which lead to work on the multi-media app album, *Biophilia* (2011).

**Eva Dittinger** is a PhD student at the Brain and Language Research Institute (BLRI) under the supervision of Mireille Besson and Mariapaola D'Imperio. Her research is focused on transfer effects from music training to novel word learning in school-aged children, as well as in young and older adults.

**Zohar Eitan** is a Professor of Music Theory and Music Cognition at Tel Aviv University. Much of Eitan's research involves empirical investigation of crossmodal and cross-domain experience in musical contexts. His current research project examines the crossmodal correspondences implied by Western tonality. Eitan's recent work was published in *Cognition, JEP-HPP, Experimental Psychology,* and *Music Perception.*

**Dorottya Fabian** is Professor of Music at University of New South Wales, Sydney, Australia. Her research investigates the history and aesthetics of Western classical music performance as evidenced in sound recordings and written documents. Recently she published a new monograph, *A Musicology of Performance,* and an edited volume on style and expression in music performance.

**Jörg Fachner** is Professor of Music, Health, and the Brain at Anglia Ruskin University, Cambridge, UK. A specialist in translational issues of interdisciplinary research topics between medical, humanities, and music sciences, his research interests include music therapy and its applications in healing cultures, modern medicine and special education, biomarkers, and Kairological principles of music therapy processes and improvisation.

**Bruno Gingras** first completed an MSc in molecular biology before turning to music theory, graduating with a PhD from McGill University in 2008. He is currently a University Assistant at the Institute of Psychology of the University of Innsbruck. His research interests include biomusicology, music-induced emotions, and individuality in music performance.

**Robert O. Gjerdingen** teaches in the program of Music Theory and Cognition at Northwestern University. He is a former editor of *Music Perception* and a winner of the Wallace Berry Award given by the Society of Music Theory. His research concerns how music was taught to children in European conservatories in past centuries.

**Werner Goebl** is Associate Professor in the Department of Music Acoustics at the University of Music and Performing Arts in Vienna, Austria. His research focuses on motion analysis of musical behaviors, quantitative performance research, ensemble synchronization, and the acoustics of keyboard instruments. He co-chaired the 2013 International Symposium on Performance Science (ISPS) at his alma mater.

**Meghan Goodchild** received a PhD in music theory and a Master of Information Studies from McGill University. Her interdisciplinary research interests include orchestration, timbre perception, and music perception and cognition. She is currently the project manager for the Schulich School of Music's Orchestration and Perception project.

**Reyna L. Gordon,** PhD, is Assistant Professor of Otolaryngology at Vanderbilt University Medical Center, where she directs the Music Cognition Lab. She is also Associate Director of the program for Music, Mind, and Society at Vanderbilt. Dr. Gordon's research is focused on the role of rhythm in language development and disorders.

**Jessica A. Grahn** is an Associate Professor at the Brain and Mind Institute and Department of Psychology at the University of Western Ontario. She has degrees in neuroscience and piano performance from Northwestern University and a PhD from Cambridge University, England, in the neuroscience of music. She specializes in rhythm, movement, and cognition.

**Roni Granot** is a Senior Lecturer in the Musicology Department at the Hebrew University of Jerusalem. At the center of her research are questions related to our response to music, including how music is processed in the human brain, which cognitive processes are involved in these processes, and the relationship between these processes and music theory.

**Lucy Green** is Professor of Music Education at the UCL Institute of Education, London UK. Her research is in the sociology of music education, specializing in meaning, ideology, gender, informal learning and new pedagogies. She has written five books, and edited two, on music education. Her next one, co-authored with David Baker, is *Insights in Sound: The Lives and Learning of Visually Impaired Musicians*.

**Molly J. Henry** is a Postdoctoral Fellow in the Music and Neuroscience Lab at the University of Western Ontario. She completed her PhD in experimental psychology at Bowling Green State University. She studies how synchronization between brain rhythms and auditory rhythms affects human perception.

**Catherine Hirel** is full-time Neurologist at the Neurological Hospital in Lyon, France. She graduated with a master's degree in neuroscience at the Lyon Neuroscience Research Center.

**Rachael Frush Holt,** PhD, is Associate Professor of Speech and Hearing Science at Ohio State University. Her research interests include speech perception, language, and neurocognitive development in children with and without hearing loss, and the role of family environment in outcomes of children who use hearing aids and cochlear implants.

**Peter E. Keller**, B.Mus., B.A. (Psychology), PhD, is Professor of Cognitive Science and leader of the "Music Cognition and Action" research program in the MARCS Institute for Brain, Behaviour and Development at Western Sydney University, Australia. His research examines the behavioural and brain bases of human interaction in musical contexts.

**Morten L. Kringelbach** studies the functional neuroanatomy of pleasure using a range of behavioural, neuropsychological, neuroimaging, neurosurgical, and computational methods in his "Hedonia: Transnational Research Group," based at the Universities of Oxford and Aarhus. Professor Kringelbach is Principal Investigator in the centre for Music in Brain, Aarhus University.

**Alexandra Lamont** is Senior Lecturer at Keele University, and has just completed a five-year term as Editor of *Psychology of Music*. She is trained in the fields of music, education, and psychology, and her interests are diverse; among her research areas are musical development, music education, and the sociology and psychology of music consumption.

**Edward W. Large** directs the Music Dynamics Laboratory at University of Connecticut, where he is Professor of Psychological Sciences and Professor of Physics. His research interests include neural dynamics and embodied cognition, focusing on rhythm, tonality, pattern perception, learning and emotion.

**Kyung Myun Lee** is Assistant Professor in the School of Humanities and Social Sciences, Korea Advanced Institute of Science and Technology. Trained in music, psychology, and neuroscience, her research interests include neural processing of pitch and rhythm and meter perception. She has served as President of the Asia-Pacific Society for the Cognitive Sciences of Music.

**Yohana Lévêque** is a Lecturer in Cognitive Psychology at Lyon 1 University. She graduated from a speech therapy program and received a PhD in neurolinguistics. She is also affiliated with the Lyon Neuroscience Research Center.

**Psyche Loui** is Assistant Professor in the Department of Psychology and the program in neuroscience and behavior at Wesleyan University. She is director of the MIND Lab (Music, Imaging, and Neural Dynamics Laboratory) and enjoys asking questions about how the mind enables music, and what we can learn from musical functions of the brain. When not teaching and conducting research, she enjoys playing the violin.

**Cyrille L. Magne** is Associate Professor of Psychology at Middle Tennessee State University, where he is also a member of the interdisciplinary PhD program in Literacy Studies. His research interests include the neural basis of prosody sensitivity and the link between music aptitude and language comprehension skills.

**Elizabeth H. Margulis** is Professor and Director of the Music Cognition Lab at the University of Arkansas. Her 2014 book *On Repeat: How Music Plays the Mind* (Oxford University Press) won the Wallace Berry Award from the Society for Music Theory and the Deems Taylor/Virgil Thomson Award from ASCAP.

**Peter Martens** is Associate Professor at Texas Tech University, where he teaches specialized courses in music cognition, the history of music theory, and interdisciplinary arts. His research interests include the communication of musical time and emotional states between and among composers, performers, and listeners. He is also active as a translator and editor.

**Elizabeth West Marvin** is Professor of Music Theory at the Eastman School of Music, with a dual appointment in Brain and Cognitive Sciences at the University of Rochester. She is a past president of the Society for Music Theory and has published widely on music cognition and music theory pedagogy.

**Stephen McAdams** studied composition and theory before entering experimental psychology. He worked at IRCAM in Paris and was then a Research Scientist in the French CNRS before moving to the Schulich School of Music of McGill University to direct CIRMMT. He is Professor and Canada Research Chair in Music Perception and Cognition.

**Andrew McPherson** is a Reader (Associate Professor) in the Centre for Digital Music at Queen Mary University of London. Trained as a composer (PhD UPenn 2009) and an electrical engineer (MEng MIT 2005), his research focuses on augmented instruments, performer-instrument interaction and embedded hardware systems for musical applications.

**Nikki Moran** is Senior Lecturer in Music and programme director of Music—MA (Hons) at the Reid School of Music, University of Edinburgh. She specializes in the study of music as communication, through research and teaching projects that explore the relationship between musical performance and social interaction.

**Miriam A. Mosing** is Assistant Professor at the Neuroscience Department and the Department of Medical Epidemiology and Biostatistics at the Karolinska Institute Sweden. She completed her graduate and postgraduate research in the Netherlands and Australia. Her research investigates (1) expertise development and (2) quality of life throughout the lifetime and in the aged, using interdisciplinary approaches to quantify the interplay between genes and the environment.

**Susan A. O'Neill** is Professor in the Faculty of Education at Simon Fraser University in Canada. She is Director of MODAL (Multimodal Music Opportunities, Diversity and Learning) Research Group. In 2016, she became President-Elect of the International Society for Music Education. She has published widely in music psychology and music education.

**Emily Przysinda** is Research Assistant and Lab Coordinator for the MIND Lab at Wesleyan. A recent graduate from Skidmore College with a degree in neuroscience and music, she is excited to combine both of these passions through studying the perception and production of music along with its effects on cognition, personality, and creativity. Emily is also interested in the clinical applications of music cognition, as she plans to eventually pursue medical research. In her free time, Emily enjoys playing the flute, listening to classical music, and swimming.

Dr. **Suvi Saarikallio,** Docent of Music Psychology, works as a senior researcher at the University of Jyväskylä, Finland. Her research interests include music and emotion, especially mood regulation and emotional development, personality psychology, and well-being. Saarikallio actively publishes in the field of music psychology and has recently been running research projects involving music as part of everyday emotionality, youth emotional competence, and mental health.

**Rebecca S. Schaefer** has a background in clinical psychology, music cognition, and cognitive neuroscience. As an Assistant Professor in Health, Medical & Neuropsychology at Leiden University, The Netherlands, she focuses on health applications of musical interactions, specifically involving music imagery, perception, and moving to musical rhythm, using neuroimaging, behavioral and cognitive measures.

**Daniel Shanahan** is an Assistant Professor of Music Theory at Louisiana State University, where he is the founder and director of the Music Cognition and Computation Lab. He has a PhD from the University of Dublin, Trinity College, and is currently co-editor of *Empirical Musicology Review.*

**Tim Smart** is a PhD student at the UCL Institute of Education, London, UK. In addition, he is a professional trombone player. His current playing positions include the hit West End show, "The Book of Mormon," the iconic UK ska/punk band, The Specials, and a range of freelance and session work including the eclectic Heritage Orchestra.

**Siu-Lan Tan** is Professor of Psychology at Kalamazoo College, and holds a BA in Music and MA and PhD in Psychology. She is co-author of *Psychology of Music: From Sound to Significance* (Tan & Pfordresher, 2nd edition) published by Routledge, and co-editor of *The Psychology of Music in Multimedia* (Tan, Cohen, Lipscomb, Kendall) published by Oxford University Press. Another book, *The Oxford Handbook of Music and Advertising*, is currently in progress.

**David Temperley** is Professor of Music Theory at the Eastman School of Music in Rochester, NY. His books, *The Cognition of Basic Musical Structures* (2001) and *Music and Probability* (2007), explore the computational modeling of music cognition; his third book, *The Musical Language of Rock*, is forthcoming.

**William Forde Thompson** is Professor of Psychology and Director of the Music, Sound and Performance Lab at Macquarie University. His research concerns music and emotion, music and language, musical disorders, and music-based treatments for neurological disorders. He is the author of *Music, Thought, and Feeling: Understanding the Psychology of Music*, published by Oxford University Press.

**Barbara Tillmann** is holding a full-time CNRS research position in Lyon where she is directing the team "Auditory Cognition and Psychoacoustics" at the Lyon Neuroscience Research Center, following a PhD in cognitive psychology and postdoctoral research in cognitive neuroscience.

**Renee Timmers** is Reader in Psychology of Music at the Department of Music, The University of Sheffield where she directs the research center "Music, Mind, Machine in Sheffield". She obtained degrees in Musicology (MA) and Psychology (PhD) and continues to do interdisciplinary research. Her research interests concern meaning and emotion in music, musical expression, and timing and communication in solo and ensemble performance.

**Sandra E. Trehub** obtained her doctoral degree in psychology at McGill University in 1973. Since then, she has taught and conducted research at the University of Toronto, currently as Professor Emeritus. Her research is typically conducted in laboratory contexts, but she has travelled extensively to observe cross-cultural differences in musical interactions with infants.

**Fredrik Ullén** is Professor of Cognitive Neuroscience at Karolinska Institutet since 2010. His research focuses on the neuropsychology of expertise and creativity, primarily using music as a model domain. Professor Ullén is internationally active as a pianist, and a lifetime fellow of the Swedish Royal Academy of Music since 2007.

**Jonna K. Vuoskoski** (PhD) currently holds postdoctoral fellowships at the Universities of Oxford (UK) and Jyväskylä (Finland). Her research has been published in the leading journals of the field, including *Music Perception*, *Psychology of Music*, *Psychomusicology: Music Mind, and Brain*, *Psychology of Aesthetics, Creativity, the Arts*, and *Cortex*.

**Peter Vuust** is a brain scientist, jazz bassist, and composer. In addition to having performed on more than 85 records, he is Professor at both The Royal Academy of Music and Aarhus University, an internationally acknowledged brain scientist and the leader of the Danish National Research Foundation's Center of Excellence for Music in the Brain.

**Michael W. Weiss** (Ph.D., University of Toronto) is a Postdoctoral Fellow at the International Laboratory for Brain, Music, and Sound Research in Montréal. He studies adults' and children's memory for melodies, including differential processing of vocal and instrumental timbres. In his spare time, Michael builds synthesizers and records music.

**Clemens Wöllner** is Professor of Systematic Musicology at Universität Hamburg, Germany. His research focuses on performance, expert skills, multimodal perception and attention, employing a range of interdisciplinary methods including motion capture and physiological measures. He is currently editing a book entitled *Body, Sound and Space in Music and Beyond* (Routledge).

**Lawrence M. Zbikowski** is Professor of Music at the University of Chicago. His research focuses on the application of recent work in cognitive science to various problems confronted by music scholars. He is the author of *Conceptualizing Music: Cognitive Structure, Theory, and Analysis* and *Foundations of Musical Grammar*.

# FOREWORD

*Richard Ashley and Renee Timmers*

Music is an integral part of human life and society; written, oral, and anthropological records attest to music's ubiquity across time and space. Humans appear to have always and everywhere been a "musicking" species, and now as always human actions make, share, and comprehend music the world over. The last century and a half has brought changes to the music cultures of the world that are unprecedented in human history. Ever-changing technologies of music recording and dissemination have completely transformed not only *who* has access to music-as-sound, but also *when* this music can be heard. Analog and digital recordings, traditional broadcast media, and internet distribution of music have completely revolutionized the act of hearing music, removing the need for any listener to be physically co-present with performers. Dissolving the limitations of space and time, these technologies provide modern day listeners access to quite literally a world of music unimaginable at the dawn of the twentieth century. More recently, digital technologies have also impacted music composition, performance, and learning, allowing millions of people to make music in ways that are far less limited by one's formal training or skills with traditional instruments and notation.

With these changes in the nature of musical engagement with music comes renewed interest in questions about music's place in the life of humankind: How is music experienced not only by individuals, in brain and body, but also shared between and among people? How are musical skills developed? What biological markers or cognitive foundations are present for musicianship of various kinds to arise? Does technology fundamentally change the way music is heard and understood? In our present era, music and music-making are inevitably understood against the backdrop of science and culture: Music involves the brain, is shaped by culture, and raises fascinating questions about humankind's relationship to the other species with whom we share the planet. Westerners with no formal training in science, music, or both approach music with tacit or explicit beliefs that it can, at least to some degree, be understood and explained with the methods used by scientists to understand language, reasoning, and other cognitive phenomena. The explanation of musical thought and behavior from a scientific perspective is the domain of music cognition, one of the most exciting interdisciplinary fields of the early twenty-first century.

The aim of the *Routledge Companion to Music Cognition* is to introduce a broad range of topics and research in music cognition to a wide audience, including students in music and the cognitive sciences, as well as musicians and music lovers who are keen to look into music from a more academic and scientific point of view. We seek to provide our readers with an accurate and nuanced understanding of the goals, findings and limitations of research in music cognition, and to offer pathways into more in-depth study of the diverse subject areas that make up the field. Music cognition, drawing from the domains of music theory and history, psychology, neuroscience, education, ethnomusicology, and sociology is presented as the field that *investigates the psychological, physiological, and physical processes that allow music to take place*, and to explain how and why it has such powerful and mysterious effects on us, and perhaps other species as well.

The *Companion* builds on the foundation provided by multiple disciplines, including music theory, musicology, cognitive psychology, and neuroscience. In combining such approaches, it addresses fundamental questions of the nature of music. Our starting point is that music is not primarily an acoustical stimulus of patterned sound: rather, music is viewed as a collection of vital and essential *forms of human action*. Music is possible because humans have found varied and creative ways, in their differing physical and cultural contexts, to *use the human body and the physical world to organize sound* in ways that are emotionally moving, intellectually appealing, and socially powerful.

In dealing with these questions, we have brought together authors who are themselves researchers, coming from a variety of backgrounds, both musical and scientific. Some have conservatory degrees in music, whereas others have received scientific training in psychology or neuroscience; likewise, some make their academic homes in departments of music and others in laboratories—and one cannot always predict any of this from the topics on which a given author is writing! We sought a mix of established researchers, some of whom have investigated their topics for decades, alongside outstanding younger scholars who bring fresh perspectives to the field. Their diversity of backgrounds is reflected in the multiplicity of research methods discussed throughout the Companion: laboratory experiments using behavioral measures such as pressing a button or moving a slider while listening to music; measuring physiological responses, such as "chills" on the skin or activity in the brain; investigating musical structure through the analysis of individual works or large corpora; using motion capture or video to investigate performers' music-making; acoustic analysis of musical signals; and qualitative studies using *in vivo* observation, interviews, or questionnaires are all employed in the service of answering fundamental questions about the nature of music and musicality.

This *Companion* seeks to connect with readers in its breadth of topic and its explorations of diverse musical styles, genres, and repertoires. The music most central to research in music cognition has long been instrumental music from the Western art music or "classical" tradition. Within that tradition, the music most often chosen for study is typically "absolute", in that it is not related to a story of some kind; instrumental, in order to avoid additional and potentially complicating factors brought in by lyrics; and intended to be heard in isolation from other activities, in a mode of aesthetic contemplation. We have learned much from research based on these kinds of materials, but part of our aim in this *Companion* is to "problematize" this approach. To this end, you will see chapters dealing with the history of Western polyphony and rock chord progressions side by side, chapters dealing with music played from notation and music played by ear, and consideration of the musicality of those who have learned and developed their skills outside of formal musical education. We hope to encourage researchers to broaden the range of music systematically examined in music cognition studies and thus broaden the range of topics investigated in the field.

The volume is divided into five parts. Part 1, "Music from the Air to the Brain," begins with questions and answers about music and the brain, an area that has blossomed in recent years and received a surge of interest from academics and general public alike. You need not begin your reading of this book with these chapters, which are by necessity rather technical in nature, but you will find that they contain a wealth of information on the topics we find ourselves asked about so often. In this Part, our contributors introduce the methods of cognitive neuroscience and results from these methods that shed light on longstanding questions such as those about the relationship between language and music, and emotion and music. The initial chapters move from the peripheral auditory system—"the ear"—to the brain and body, exploring perception imagery (music "in the head"), memory, and rhythm and movement. The following chapters consider music's effects on the mind and body, including the impact of musical experience on other cognitive functions such as reading, mathematics, and executive function, mental and physical health, and therapeutic applications of music. The final chapter in this Part addresses a question familiar since Plato—why does music make us feel the ways we do?—from a modern, neurophysiological standpoint.

Bearing in mind the composer Charles Ives' famous question—"What has sound got to do with music?"—Part 2, "Hearing and Listening to Music," deals with the structure and materials of music viewed both from a physical standpoint (the nature of sound) and a creative standpoint (how the resources of sound are used for artistic purposes). We begin with time and rhythm, the foundation of all musical experience and structure, and proceed to timbre, or the qualities of musical sounds, alone and in combination. The next three chapters deal with pitch organization in Western tonal music, beginning with an introduction to the topics of tonality, melody, and harmony, and what we know of how they are perceived. This foundation is followed by chapters that deal in more detail with the materials of Western "classical" music and "rock," respectively. These chapters discuss the investigation of corpora—large datasets—as a research method in music cognition and present challenges to some assumptions about music theories as models for listening, suggesting new avenues for investigation. Following this, we present a chapter which deals with the perception and comprehension of longer spans of music and musical form, an understudied but important topic from both a musical and psychological standpoint. The remaining chapters in Part 2 put the perception of music into a variety of contexts. The first of these considers the impact of recording technology on how we comprehend music, now that most music is experienced via recordings. This is followed by a chapter dealing with the fascinating connections between music perception and perception using the other senses, and finally by chapters addressing special cases of music cognition: absolute ("perfect") pitch and amusia, the loss or absence of normal musical abilities.

Part 3, "Making and Using Music" begins with composition, central to music but curiously understudied from a cognitive standpoint, and segues to improvisation. These chapters consider cognitive resources for composition and improvisation, proposing reliance on more general abilities for creativity and critical revision for composition, and speech-like communication for improvisation. Three chapters on performance follow. These deal with score-based, oral, and technological contexts for music performance, giving a sense of the many factors involved in understanding cognition and music performance in the diverse contexts of the twenty-first century. Each chapter highlights different but equally relevant factors that inform performance related to the historical context, social and cultural environment, or technological innovation. Mindful that "musicking" is a broad concept indeed, our contributors explore collaborative music making in ensemble settings involving not only instrumentalists but also conductors, as well as considering the role of musicians' bodily movements in the creation and communication of expressive performances. Moving from performance to other musicking contexts, the remaining chapters of Part 3 consider the use of music in social settings: how music is used and understood in the context of film, every-day and advanced vocal musicianship, which addresses questions ranging from the processing of lyrics and music to benefits on wellbeing, and functions of music in the context of sport, work, and other daily pursuits. This Part of the *Companion* thus highlights not only skilled and expert music making, but also emphasizes the sophistication of everyday musical activities.

We consider musicality to be an essential part of what it means to be human, and so the *Companion's* Part 4, "Developing Musicality" deals with musical nurture and nature. We begin with a topic currently of much interest to researchers and laypeople alike: is music only a human activity, or do other animals also have music of some kind? Turning again to human musicking, the development of musical thought and involvement in childhood is surveyed, followed by a chapter engaging "nature and nurture" providing an overview of current findings and debates about the interrelationships between genetics and experience in the development of musicality. We would hold that almost all humans are musical—but only a minority develop their musicality through formal training in music; the next chapter describes music learning in the informal settings which facilitate musical growth for most people. The penultimate chapter in this Part discusses the musical lives of adolescents, the life-stage where music is so important, and so formative, to many. This leads to the final chapter of this Part, which examines individuals' personalized music choices and uses of music to address cognitive-emotional goals and needs in an individually appropriate manner.

Part 5 of the *Companion*, "Musical Meanings", may be the first destination for many readers, as the topics here are evergreen. We begin with a survey of approaches to music perception, from the ancient Greeks to the present, journeying from the music of the spheres to music in the brain. What and how music communicates, and the relationship between music and emotion, are discussed in our own chapters, before the *Companion* turns to questions of musical thought, the appreciation and value of music, and the varied meanings that we find and construct in our experiences with music. These chapters relate music to other human behavior and discuss processes of sense-making drawing relationships with interactions with our natural environment, social communication, neurophysiological responses, but also abstract and linguistic thought. Any or all of these topics could easily have introduced the volume, for the questions they engage continue to resist easy answers: What do we feel when we hear music? How and what does music communicate? Why do we care about music, and in the end, what does music mean? We cannot promise that the *Companion* answers these questions with any finality, but do guarantee that in these chapters every reader will find a greater understanding of, and appreciation for, the variety of human thought, creativity, and action which gives rise to music and wishes to share it with others.

# ACKNOWLEDGMENTS

The major contributors to this book are the authors of the chapters, who despite their many other responsibilities, both personal and professional, have given their best to make this *Companion* a success. We are immensely grateful for their dedication and enthusiasm and the outstanding quality of their contributions. We also gratefully acknowledge the assistance and insights of the reviewers who commented on first drafts of chapters; these included volume contributors and independent researchers. We are grateful to our student helpers: Caroline Curwen, Ioanna Filippidi, Tim Metcalfe, Nicola Pennill, and Shen Li, PhD students of the The University of Sheffield, who helped out with the checking of references of chapters, and Anjni Amin and Sarah Gates, PhD students of Northwestern University, who provided assistance with references and with the Glossary, a unique and helpful aspect of this volume.

Finally, this volume could not have been realized without the support and patience of our respective loving families. To Allison, Erwin, and Lidewij, we offer you our thanks—and the promise of more time together in the days to come!

# PART 1

# Music from the Air to the Brain

# 1

# MUSIC FROM THE AIR TO THE BRAIN AND BODY

*Edward W. Large*

What is music and why study the "cognition" of it? It is often claimed that music is universal, in the sense that all known human cultures practice some form of music. It is also commonly argued that music is unique to the human species. Therefore, like language, music displays two fundamental features that identify a high level cognitive capacity (see, e.g., Fitch, 2006; Patel, 2008). But music is also a physical process that takes place at an ecological scale. Musicians' bodies interact with instruments to create vibrations that travel through the air (see Bishop & Goebl, this volume). Once sounds reach a person's ear, they cause activation in the peripheral auditory system and the brain. Some sound sequences lead to visceral and emotional responses and forms of coordinated movement that we recognize as uniquely musical (Iyer, 2002; Leman & Maes, 2015). Thus, music may be a cognitive capacity but it is one that is embodied to an extent that seems qualitatively different from, say, writing an essay or solving a math problem.

The answer to the question of what music actually *is*, however, is not straightforward. Although often approached from the point of view of sound, it is not possible to adequately define music based solely on sound patterns (Cross, 2003). Music intrinsically involves qualitative experiences of the brain and body and its meaning depends on the social and cultural context that relates sound to experience (Iyer, 2002). Thus, musicality "is a property of communities rather than of individuals; and music is mutable in its specific significances or meanings" (Cross, 2003, p. 79). Nonetheless people can easily recognize the musical sounds of their native culture, and the study of musical sound is one of the oldest topics in Western science (Hunt, 1992).

## Early Musical Science

The study of musical sound in the West began with Pythagoras (ca. 570–497 B.C.) over twenty-five hundred years ago. The Pythagoreans were mystics who believed in secrecy and left virtually no writings, so what we know about their discoveries comes from followers writing after Pythagoras's death. However, historians generally attribute several important discoveries and inventions to Pythagoras (Hunt, 1992). Pythagoras discovered an inverse relationship between the length of a vibrating string and the pitch it produced. He may have invented the first experimental apparatus described in Western science, the monochord, to carry out pitch experiments. Most importantly, he observed that the perfect consonances[1]—the octave, fifth and fourth—correspond to pitches tuned in small integer frequency ratios—2:1, 3:2, and 4:3, respectively. Pythagoras and his successors invented small integer ratio systems for tuning musical instruments, the first known technological innovation in Western musical history.

Pythagorean ideas about tuning and arithmetic ratios dominated the study of musical sound for over two thousand years. However, Pythagoreans lost faith in perceptual experimentation, preferring to interpret phenomena such as musical consonance and dissonance as manifestations of pure mathematics (Hunt, 1992). Later philosophers, including Plato, Aristotle, and Aristoxenus, emphasized the importance not only of perception, but also emotional and physical experiences of music (Gracyk & Kania, 2011). However, the scientific study of the role of the brain and body in musical experience would have to wait for the advent of modern empirical methods.

## From the Air to the Brain and Body

Music—like all sound—is made up of waves. Complex sound waves, such as those made by vibrating strings or human voices, generally consist of a fundamental frequency, plus a number of other frequencies called harmonics, or overtones (see, e.g., Pierce, 1983; Goodchild & McAdams, this volume). Individual notes and chords occur in repeating patterns such as melodies, rhythms, and phrases. Musical sound patterns extend over many timescales, from the timescales of pitch and pitch combinations (from tens up to thousands of cycles per second, *cps*) to the timescales of tonality, rhythm, and form (from 8 or 10 *cps* down to fractions of one *cps*). Music engages the brain and body over this entire range through a phenomenon called *entrainment*, or *synchronization*, in which active, nonlinear processes in the nervous system resonate to quasi periodic temporal structures such as individual harmonics, complex pitches, beats, measures, phrases, and so on (Large, 2010).

Sound waves travel through the air and can be heard when they reach a person's ear. Sounds vibrate the structures of the outer and middle ear, which in turn cause vibrations in the fluid-filled, spiral-shaped hearing organ called the cochlea (see, e.g., Schnupp, Nelken, & King, 2011). Helmholtz (1885/1954) originally proposed that the cochlea decomposes complex sounds into individual frequency components. This hypothesis was confirmed by von Békésy (1960), who demonstrated that the cochlea carries out a frequency analysis of sound, resonating to different frequencies at different places along a structure called the basilar membrane. It soon came to be understood that cochlear resonance is not passive, like the reception of a microphone. Active cochlear processes amplify soft sounds, compress loud sounds (Eguíluz, Ospeck, Choe, Hudspeth, & Magnasco, 2000), and respond to signals from the brain that can tune the system depending on incoming sounds (Cooper & Guinan, 2006).

Auditory nerve fibers carry this signal to the brain in synchronized volleys of *action potentials*, fast electrical events that lead to the release of neurotransmitters. These volleys reflect the temporal structure of the sounds faithfully up to frequencies of several thousand *cps* (Langner, 1992), approximately the upper limit of pitch perception (Burns, 1999). In the auditory brain, time-locked signals interact with the intrinsic temporal dynamics of different types of neurons and networks to give rise to structured patterns of activity in multiple subcortical and cortical auditory areas (see Loui & Przysinda, this volume). Sound first reaches the auditory brainstem at the cochlear nucleus and travels up the subcortical pathway to the thalamus and then to primary and secondary auditory cortex. Brainstem responses to sound can be recorded non-invasively in humans using electroencephalography (EEG). EEG signals are synchronized up to one thousand *cps* or so (for a tutorial review, see Skoe & Kraus, 2010). Auditory brainstem processing is important in the perception of pitch (e.g., Wile & Balaban, 2007) and the perception of consonance and dissonance (e.g., Lee, Skoe, Kraus, & Ashley, 2009).

As the auditory pathway is ascended, synchronization to simple tones deteriorates at higher frequencies (Langner, 1992). However, in higher auditory areas *spatial maps of frequency* are preserved (Formisano et al., 2003) and synchronization to *amplitude modulation* emerges (Joris, Schreiner, & Rees, 2004). The auditory cortex is primarily sensitive to the amplitude modulations of sound at slower frequencies (less than about 10 *cps*), which is to say events such as musical notes. People synchronize rhythmic movements such as hand clapping, finger tapping, dancing, or swaying to the rhythms created by musical events (Iyer, 2002; Henry & Grahn, this volume). Interestingly, the cortex produces its own intrinsic rhythms, called oscillations (Buzsáki, 2006), and intrinsic neural oscillations synchronize with musical rhythms (e.g., Fujioka, Trainor, Large, & Ross, 2012; Henry & Grahn, this volume).

## Pitch and Consonance

Although the perception of pitch and consonance are among the oldest topics in Western science, they are still areas of active investigation. One fundamental issue in pitch perception surrounds the "missing fundamental." If the energy at the fundamental frequency is removed from a complex periodic sound, the perceived pitch remains unchanged (Seebeck, 1841). Helmholtz (1885/1954) proposed that a physical component at the missing fundamental frequency could be generated by nonlinear cochlear processes, while Seebeck (1841) favored a periodicity detection theory. Eventually, it became clear that pitch depends on central auditory processes. Recent theoretical explanations include autocorrelation (Cariani & Delgutte, 1996) and synchronization of oscillatory neurons (Meddis & O'Mard, 2006). However, complex pitch perception is still a matter of active debate among theorists (see Plack, Fay, Oxenham, & Popper, 2005).

Regarding consonance and dissonance, in the eighteenth century the mathematician Leonard Euler hypothesized that the mind directly perceives and aesthetically appreciates the purity of simple integer ratios, a psychological version of Pythagorean ideas (see Helmholtz, 1885/1954 for a discussion). Helmholtz strongly critiqued Euler's approach, and pointed out that mathematical purity could not explain the perception of consonance in equal tempered tuning systems, where pure integer ratios are approximated by irrational numbers. Instead, he proposed that as the cochlea analyses complex sounds, neighboring frequencies on the basilar membrane interfere with one another and produce a sensation of roughness, which he equated with dissonance. Because small integer ratios have more harmonics in common, fewer harmonics interfere, yielding a smoother, more consonant sound (e.g., Kameoka & Kuriyagawa, 1969). However, as with pitch, recent perceptual studies have implicated the central auditory system in consonance perception (Cousineau, McDermott, & Peretz, 2012). Two mechanisms, harmonicity and synchronization of neural oscillations, have been proposed (Tramo, Cariani, Delgutte, & Braida, 2001). Both theories relate consonance and dissonance to simple integer frequency ratios, and both have received support from auditory brainstem studies (e.g., Lee, et al., 2009; Lerud, Almonte, Kim, & Large, 2014). Thus, fundamental neural processes do seem to prefer simple integer ratios.

## Embodiment of Structure

Musical sounds do not consist merely of isolated pitches and intervals; they are complex sequences of sound events. A number of authors have suggested that the complexity of musical sound sequences implies the existence of a set of rules that govern musical structure, parallel to the rules of language (Bernstein, 1976; Lerdahl & Jackendoff, 1983; see Besson, Barbaroux, & Dittenger, this volume). Patel (2008) hypothesized that both language and music are processed syntactically, and these computations exploit the same neural resources. There is a great deal of evidence to suggest that the processing of music and language overlap in terms of functional activation of brain regions (e.g., Koelsch, Gunter, Cramon, & Zysset, 2002; Tillmann, Janata, & Bharucha, 2003; see also Jantzen, Large, & Magne, 2016). However, the spatial overlap of functional activation does not necessarily imply that music is processed computationally, as hypothesized by linguistic theory (e.g., Lerdahl & Jackendoff, 1983).

Iyer (2002) points out that linguistic paradigms treat neural and cognitive processes—including musical ones—as computations on abstract symbols. In other words, the brain transforms musical sounds into symbols whose meaning is unrelated to their sound. The comprehension of musical structure then depends on rule-based syntactic computation (Patel, 2008). However, with its deep connection to dance, movement, and other functions, much musical behavior appears to be essentially nonlinguistic in nature (Iyer, 2002; Leman & Maes, 2015; see chapters by Lamont, Tan, and Ashley [Communication], this volume). Important musical experiences, such as groove (Janata, Tomic, & Haberman, 2012), have no analogue in linguistic theory. Music has significant emotional and associative qualities as well (Burger, Saarikallio, Luck, Thompson, & Toiviainen, 2013), seeming to challenge traditional computational theories of mind. As Cross puts it, "music embodies, entrains and transposably intentionalises time in sound and action" (2003, p. 79). It has been argued that embodied (Rosch, Thompson, & Varela, 1992) and ecological (Gibson, 1966) approaches are required to understand these aspects of musical experience (Iyer, 2002). One intereting question is whether such approaches can handle the complexity of musical structure as well.

## Tonality and Meter

Two of the most universal and widely studied characteristics of musical structure are tonality and metricality. In its most general form, tonality is the means by which music creates feelings of tension and resolution (Lerdahl, 2001). In Western and non-Western tonal music, certain pitches are felt as more stable than others, providing a sense of completion. Less stable pitches are felt as points of tension; they function relative to the more stable ones and are heard to point toward or be attracted to them (Bharucha, 1984; Lerdahl, 2001). Stability and attraction are the properties that differentiate musical sound sequences from arbitrary sound sequences and are thought to enable simple sound patterns to carry meaning (Meyer, 1956). These musical qualia provide the fundamental elements of musical structure (Huron, 2006), leading to the feeling that some sound sequences make sense while others do not (e.g., Lerdahl & Jackendoff, 1983). The central question is what processes in the nervous system give rise to percepts of tension, resolution, and ultimately of musical pattern.

*Metricality* is the way in which musical rhythms create feelings of temporal regularity, directing our expectations for when future musical events will occur. *Groove* is a related feeling of wanting to move and synchronize with the rhythm of the music (Janata, Tomic, &

Haberman, 2012). In many Western and non-Western musical styles a perception of periodic or quasi periodic *beats* emerges (Clayton, Sager, & Will, 2004), and *meter* refers to a perceived pattern of stronger and weaker beats (Cooper & Meyer, 1960; Lerdahl & Jackendoff, 1983) The main beat, or *pulse*, of a rhythm is often defined as the frequency at which a listener will synchronize a periodic movement, such as toe tapping or hand clapping, with a rhythm (see, Large, 2008 and chapters by Henry & Grahn and Martens & Benadon, this volume). Pulse is mostly regular, but can exhibit temporally irregular patterns as well (London, 2004). The meaning of individual musical events is impacted by their timing in relation to this emergent pattern of metrical accent (Cooper & Meyer, 1960). Here we must also ask what processes in the nervous system give rise to these percepts.

## Computation, Learning, and Dynamics

One way in which music is similar to language is that different musical "languages" develop depending upon cultural and stylistic environments. Syntactic computation approaches have posited musical grammars, analogous to linguistic grammars, that successfully describe various aspects of basic musical structure (Lerdahl & Jackendoff, 1983; Temperley, 2001). However, such approaches either explicitly assume innate mechanisms (Bernstein, 1976) or simply decline to address the question of knowledge acquisition (Lerdahl & Jackendoff, 1983). Perhaps more importantly, even for language there exists an "ontological incommensurability" between the abstract symbols and rule-based computations of linguistic theories on the one hand, and observations of action potentials, synaptic plasticity, oscillations, and synchronization in the physical brain, on the other (Poeppel & Embick, 2005). Thus, questions of learning and neural "implementation" loom large for syntactic approaches.

It has been known for some time now that tonal perceptions such as stability and attraction correlate strongly with the statistics of tonal sequences (Krumhansl, 1990). Listeners develop sensitivity to the statistical and sequential structures consistent with their musical experience (Castellano, Bharucha, & Krumhansl, 1984; Loui, Wessel, & Kam, 2010). Metrical percepts also correlate with the statistics of rhythmic contexts (Palmer & Krumhansl, 1990) and depend on learning (Hannon & Johnson, 2005). Both tonal cognition and rhythmic abilities develop over the first years of life (Kirschner & Tomasello, 2009; Trainor & Trehub, 1994; see Trehub & Weiss, this volume). Information-processing theories have interpreted such evidence to mean that musical structure is internalized based on a form of statistical learning in which notes are treated as abstract symbols (Krumhansl, 2000; Pearce & Wiggins, 2012; Temperley, 2007).

However, an abstract-symbols and learning-only approach raises some perplexing questions. If notes are abstract symbols, why are small integer ratio tuning systems so pervasive across the world and so stable over time (Burns, 1999)? How did the statistics of tonal music arise in the first place, such that they appear to favor small integer frequency ratios across cultures (Large, Kim, Flaig, Bharucha, & Krumhansl, 2016)? Why are simple metric ratios found across the rhythms of the world (Savage, Brown, Sakai, & Currie, 2015)? In fact, why do so many musical features appear to be shared across the world's cultures (Savage, Brown, Sakai, & Currie, 2015)?

What seems to be needed is a theory that can take into account both the intrinsic dynamics of the brain and body, as well as the influences of culture-specific experience. The dynamical systems approach (Large, 2010) takes into account the intrinsic dynamics of movement coordination (Kelso, deGuzman, & Holroyd, 1990; Loehr, Large, & Palmer, 2011;

Treffner & Turvey, 1993) and the intrinsic dynamic patterns that play out in the neurons and networks of the brain (Large, 2010; Large & Snyder, 2009). The theory incorporates neural plasticity, which can, in principle, explain learning of different styles (Large, Kim, Flaig, Bharucha, & Krumhansl, 2016). One key prediction is that small integer frequency ratios produce more stable resonances (Large, 2010), at both tonal and rhythmic timescales (see, e.g., Razdan & Patel, 2016). Although it is a relatively new approach, it has shown to be sufficiently powerful to explain fundamental aspects of musical structure perception (Large, Herrera, & Velasco, 2015; Large, et al., 2016). Importantly, unlike linguistic theory, it makes predictions about physical processes, such as rhythmic synchronization, that can be directly observed in the brain and body (Large, Fink, & Kelso, 2002).

## Concluding Remarks

The fundamental questions posed by musical experience provide a unique window onto the question of what it means to be human. Approaches that treat bodies as robots and brains as computers packed with high-tech modules contrived to overcome specific obstacles (Pinker, 1997), do not offer meaningful insights into the ancient questions of musical experience. The study of music, among other things, suggests that the mind does not work that way (Fodor, 2001). Understanding the complex interplay of brain, body, and world may require more sophisticated tools and methods (e.g., Thompson & Varela, 2001); perhaps the brain and body literally resonate to music (Gibson, 1966; Iyer, 2002). Only in confronting these core issues will music cognition be able to adequately address the question of music's meanings, its origins, and its role in human life.

## Note

1. Consonance and dissonance are used here to refer to the perception of pleasantness or unpleasant-ness of isolated pitch intervals. These same terms are also used to refer to the perception of tension and resolution within a tonal context. Tonality will be discussed shortly.

## Core Reading

I have attempted to give a brief introduction to many of the core topics in music cognition with emphasis on their historical significance. Subsequent chapters will bring the reader up to date on research in these areas, and in areas it was not possible to even mention here. For the reader interested in pursuing these topics at a deeper level, this core reading list includes key books in music cognition and related areas, including some historical sources.

Bernstein, L. (1976). *The unanswered question: Six talks at Harvard.* Cambridge, MA: Harvard University Press.

Cooper, G., & Meyer, L. B. (1960). *The rhythmic structure of music.* Chicago, IL: University of Chicago Press.

Fodor, J. A. (2001). *The mind doesn't work that way: The scope and limits of computational psychology.* Cambridge, MA: MIT Press.

Helmholtz, H. L. F. (1885/1954). *On the sensations of tone as a physiological basis for the theory of music.* New York, NY: Dover Publications.

Hunt, F. V. (1992). *Origins in acoustics.* Woodbury, NY: Acoustical Society of America.

Huron, D. (2006). *Sweet anticipation: Music and the psychology of expectation.* Cambridge, MA: MIT Press.

Kameoka, A., & Kuriyagawa, M. (1969). Consonance theory part II: Consonance of complex tones and its calculation method. *The Journal of the Acoustical Society of America, 45*(6), 1460–1469.

Krumhansl, C. L. (1990). *Cognitive foundations of musical pitch.* New York, NY: Oxford University Press.

Lerdahl, F. (2001). *Tonal pitch space.* New York, NY: Oxford University Press.

Lerdahl, F., & Jackendoff, R. (1983). *A generative theory of tonal music.* Cambridge, MA: MIT Press.

Meyer, L. B. (1956). *Emotion and meaning in music.* Chicago, IL: University of Chicago Press.

Patel, A.D. (2008). *Music, language, and the brain.* Oxford: Oxford University Press.

Pinker, S. (1997). *How the mind works.* New York, NY: Norton.

Plack, C. J., Fay, R. R., Oxenham, A. J., & Popper, A. N. (Eds.). (2005). *Pitch: Neural coding and perception.* New York, NY: Springer.

Rosch, E., Thompson, E., & Varela, F. J. (1992). *The embodied mind: Cognitive science and human experience.* Cambridge, MA: MIT Press.

## Further References

Bharucha, J. J. (1984). Anchoring effects in music: The resolution of dissonance. *Cognitive Psychology, 16*, 485–518.

Burger, B., Saarikallio, S., Luck, G., Thompson, M. R., & Toiviainen, P. (2013). Relationships between perceived emotions in music and music-induced movement. *Music Perception, 30*(5), 517–533.

Burns, E. M. (1999). Intervals, scales, and tuning. In D. Deustch (Ed.), *The psychology of music* (pp. 215–264). San Diego, CA: Academic Press.

Buzsáki, G. (2006). *Rhythms of the brain.* New York, NY: Oxford University Press.

Cariani, P. A., & Delgutte, B. (1996). Neural correlates of the pitch of complex tones. I. Pitch and pitch salience. *Journal of Neurophysiology, 76*(3), 1698–1716.

Castellano, M. A., Bharucha, J. J., & Krumhansl, C. L. (1984). Tonal hierarchies in the music of North India. *Journal of Experimental Psychology: General, 113*(3), 394–412.

Clayton, M., Sager, R., & Will, U. (2004). In time with the music: The concept of entrainment and its significance for ethnomuiscology. *ESEM CounterPoint, 1*, 1–82.

Cooper, N. P., & Guinan, J. J. (2006). Efferent-mediated control of basilar membrane motion. *The Journal of Physiology, 576*(1), 49–54.

Cousineau, M., McDermott, J. H., & Peretz, I. (2012). The basis of musical consonance as revealed by congenital amusia. *Proceedings of the National Academy of Sciences, 109*(48), 19858–19863.

Cross, I. (2003). Music and evolution: Consequences and causes. *Contemporary Music Review, 22*(3), 79–89.

Eguìluz, V. M., Ospeck, M., Choe, Y., Hudspeth, A. J., & Magnasco, M. O. (2000). Essential nonlinearities in hearing. *Physical Review Letters, 84*(22), 5232.

Fitch, W. T. (2006). On the biology and evolution of music. *Music Perception, 24*(1), 85–88.

Formisano, E., Kim, D. S., Di Salle, F., van de Moortele, P. F., Ugurbil, K., & Goebel, R. (2003). Mirror-symmetric tonotopic maps in human primary auditory cortex. *Neuron, 40*(4), 859–869.

Fujioka, T., Trainor, L. J., Large, E. W., & Ross, B. (2012). Internalized timing of isochronous sounds is represented in neuromagnetic beta oscillations. *The Journal of Neuroscience, 32*(5), 1791–1802.

Gibson, J. J. (1966). *The senses considered as perceptual systems.* Boston, MA: Houghton Mifflin.

Gracyk, T., & Kania, A. (2011). *The Routledge companion to philosophy and music*: New York, NY: Routledge.

Hannon, E. E., & Johnson, S. P. (2005). Infants use meter to categorize rhythms and melodies: Implications for musical structure learning. *Cognitive Psychology, 50*(4), 354–377.

Iyer, V. (2002). Embodied mind, situated cognition, and expressive microtiming in African-American music. [10.1525/mp.2002.19.3.387]. *Music Perception 19*(3), 387–414.

Janata, P., Tomic, S. T., & Haberman, J. M. (2012). Sensorimotor coupling in music and the psychology of the groove. *Journal of Experimental Psychology-General, 141*(1), 54–75.

Jantzen, M. G., Large, E. W., & Magne, C. (Eds.). (2016). *Overlap of neural systems for processing language and music.* Lausanne: Frontiers Media.

Joris, P. X., Schreiner, C. E., & Rees, A. (2004). Neural processing of amplitude-modulated sounds. *Physiological Reviews, 84*(2), 541–577.

Kelso, J. A. S., deGuzman, G. C., & Holroyd, T. (1990). The self-organized phase attractive dynamics of coordination. In A. Babloyantz (Ed.), *Self- organization, emerging properties, and learning* (Vol. 260, pp. 41–62).

Kirschner, S., & Tomasello, M. (2009). Joint drumming: Social context facilitates synchronization in preschool children. *Journal of Experimental Child Psychology, 102*(3), 299–314.

Koelsch, S., Gunter, T. C., Cramon, D. Y., & Zysset, S. (2002). Bach speaks: A cortical "language-network" serves the processing of music. *NeuroImage 17*(2), 956–966.

Krumhansl, C. L. (2000). Tonality induction: A statistical approach applied cross-culturally. *Music Perception, 17*, 461–479.

Langner, G. (1992). Periodicity coding in the auditory system. *Hearing Research, 60*, 115–142.

Large, E. W. (2008). Resonating to musical rhythm: Theory and experiment. In S. Grondin (Ed.), *The Psychology of Time* (pp. 189–231). Cambridge: Emerald.

Large, E. W. (2010). Neurodynamics of music. In M. R. Jones, A. N. Popper & R. R. Fay (Eds.), *Springer handbook of auditory research, Vol. 36: Music perception* (pp. 201–231). New York, NY: Springer.

Large, E. W., Fink, P., & Kelso, J. A. S. (2002). Tracking simple and complex sequences. *Psychological Research, 66*, 3–17.

Large, E. W., Herrera, J. A., & Velasco, M. J. (2015). Neural networks for beat perception in musical rhythm. *Frontiers in Systems Neuroscience, 9*(224), 583. doi: papers2://publication/doi/10.1152/jn.00066.2009

Large, E. W., Kim, J. C., Flaig, N., Bharucha, J., & Krumhansl, C. L. (2016). A neurodynamic account of musical tonality. *Music Perception, 33*(3), 319–331.

Large, E. W., & Snyder, J. S. (2009). Pulse and meter as neural resonance. The neurosciences and music III—Disorders and plasticity. *Annals of the New York Academy of Sciences, 1169*, 46–57.

Lee, K. M., Skoe, E., Kraus, N., & Ashley, R. (2009). Selective subcortical enhancement of musical intervals in musicians. *Journal of Neuroscience, 29*(18), 5832–5840.

Leman, M., & Maes, P. J. (2015). The role of embodiment in the perception of music. *Empirical Musicology Review.* doi: papers2://publication/uuid/01F207EC-D624-4FDE-AF00-F530540D58D2

Lerud, K. D., Almonte, F. V., Kim, J. C., & Large, E. W. (2014). Mode-locking neurodynamics predict human auditory brainstem responses to musical intervals. *Hearing Research, 308*, 41–49.

Loehr, J., Large, E. W., & Palmer, C. (2011). Temporal coordination and adaptation to rate change in music performance. *Journal of Experimental Psychology: Human Perception and Performance, 37*(4), 1292–1309.

London, J. (2004). *Hearing in time: Psychological aspects of musical meter.* New York, NY: Oxford University Press.

Loui, P., Wessel, D. L., & Kam, C. L. H. (2010). Humans rapidly learn grammatical structure in a new musical scale. *Music Perception, 27*(5), 377–388.

Meddis, R., & O'Mard, L. P. (2006). Virtual pitch in a computational physiological model. *The Journal of the Acoustical Society of America, 120*(6), 3861–3869.

Palmer, C., & Krumhansl, C. L. (1990). Mental representations for musical meter. *Journal of Experimental Psychology: Human Perception & Performance, 16*(4), 728–741.

Pearce, M. T., & Wiggins, G. A. (2012). Auditory expectation: The information dynamics of music perception and cognition. *Topics in Cognitive Science, 4*(4), 625–652.

Pierce, J. R. (1983). *The science of musical sound.* Cambridge, MA: MIT Press.

Poeppel, D., & Embick, D. (2005). Defining the relation between linguistics and neuroscience. In A. Cutler (Ed.), *Twenty-first century psycholinguistics: Four cornerstones.* (pp. 103–118). Mahwah, NJ: Lawrence Erlbaum and Associates, Inc.

Razdan, A. S., & Patel, A. D. (2016). Rhythmic consonance and dissonance: Perceptual ratings of rhythmic analogs of pitch intervals and chords. *Proceedings of the 14th International Conference on Music Perception and Cognition* (pp. 807–812). Adelaide: Causal Productions.

Savage, P. E., Brown, S., Sakai, E., & Currie, T. E. (2015). Statistical universals reveal the structures and functions of human music. [10.1073/pnas.1414495112]. *Proceedings of the National Academy of Sciences USA, 112*(29), 8987–8992.

Schnupp, J., Nelken, I., & King, A. (2011). *Auditory neuroscience.* Cambridge, MA: MIT Press.

Seebeck, A. (1841). Beobachtungen über einige bedingungen der entstehung von tönen. *Annalen der Physik und Chemie, 53,* 417–436.

Skoe, E., & Kraus, N. (2010). Auditory brain stem response to complex sounds: A tutorial. *Ear and Hearing, 31*(3), 302–324.

Temperley, D. (2001). *The cognition of basic musical structures.* Cambridge, MA: MIT Press.

Temperley, D. (2007). *Music and probability.* Cambridge, MA: MIT Press.

Thompson, E., & Varela, F. J. (2001). Radical embodiment: Neural dynamics and consciousness. *Trends in Cognitive Science, 5*(10), 418–425.

Tillmann, B., Janata, P., & Bharucha, J. J. (2003). Activation of the inferior frontal cortex in musical priming. *Cognitive Brain Research, 16*(2), 145–161.

Trainor, L. J., & Trehub, S. E. (1994). Key membership and implied harmony in Western tonal music: Developmental perspectives. *Perception & Psychophysics, 56*(2), 125–132.

Tramo, M. J., Cariani, P. A., Delgutte, B., & Braida, L. D. (2001). Neurobiological foundations for the theory of harmony in western tonal music. *Annals of the New York Academy of Sciences, 930,* 92–116.

Treffner, P. J., & Turvey, M. T. (1993). Resonance constraints on rhythmic movement. *Journal of Experimental Psychology: Human Perception & Performance, 19,* 1221–1237.

Von Békésy, G. (1960). *Experiments in hearing* (Vol. 8). E. G. Wever (Ed.). New York, NY: McGraw-Hill.

Wile, D., & Balaban, E. (2007). An auditory neural correlate suggests a mechanism underlying holistic pitch perception. *PloS One, 2*(4), e369. doi: papers2://publication/doi/10.1371/journal.pone.0000369

# 2

# MUSIC IN THE BRAIN
## Areas and Networks

*Psyche Loui and Emily Przysinda*

## Introduction

Scientists and philosophers alike have long asked questions about the cerebral localization of the human faculties such as language and music. In recent years, however, human cognitive neuroscience has shifted from "blobology"—a dogmatic focus on identifying individual brain areas that subserved specific cognitive functions—to a more network-based approach. This sea change is aided by the development of sophisticated tools for sensing and seeing the brain, as well as more mature theories with which neuroscientists think about the relationship between brain and behavior. The newly developed tools include magnetic resonance imaging (MRI) and its many uses including functional (fMRI) as well as structural imaging, electroencephalography (EEG) and magnetoencephalography (MEG), and brain stimulation techniques (transcranial magnetic stimulation, or TMS, and transcranial direct current stimulation, or tDCS) with which it is possible to test the causal roles of specific targeted brain areas. Here, we review representative studies that use music as a domain for understanding specific brain regions, as well as studies that identify widespread networks of regions that enable specific aspects of musical experience. General anatomical locations of brain regions that will be highlighted are shown in Figure 2.1 below. For a more comprehensive review of brain anatomy including all its structures and functions, the reader is directed to more general cognitive neuroscience sources such as Purves, et al. (2013). In this chapter, we focus on brain areas and networks as they relate to specific aspects of musical experience.

Two main focus points may serve as guideposts for this chapter's wide-ranging discussions: First, there is no single region for music, as there is no single musical experience: Distributed areas of the brain form networks to give rise to different aspects of musical experience. Second, music offers an appropriate test case for existing hypotheses about how brain areas and networks enable human behavior.

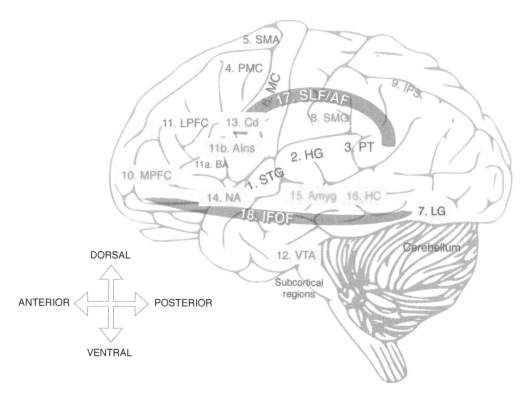

*Figure 2.1* Anatomical locations of some grey matter regions involved in music perception and cognition. Shaded grey regions represent mesial structures, i.e., areas that are seen in cross-section rather than in the present surface view of the brain. Shaded orange regions represent white matter pathways. Colors of text represent general areas of the brain: Blue = temporal lobe; red = frontal lobe; brown = occipital lobe; green = parietal lobe; pink and violet = subcortical structures. See insert for color figure.

1. STG: Superior temporal gyrus
2. HG: Heschl's gyrus
3. PT: Planum temporale
4. PMC: Premotor cortex
5. SMA: Supplementary motor area
6. MC: Motor cortex
7. LG: Lingual gyrus
8. SMG: Supramarginal gyrus
9. IPS: Intraparietal sulcus
10. MPFC: Medial prefrontal cortex
11. LPFC: Lateral prefrontal cortex

    a. BA: Broca's area
    b. AIns: Anterior insula

12. VTA: Ventral tegmental area
13. Cd: Caudate
14. NA: Nucleus accumbens
15. Amyg: Amygdala
16. HC: Hippocampus
17. SLF/AF: Superior Longitudinal Fasciculus/Arcuate Fasciculus
18. IFOF: Inferior Frontal-Occipital Fasciculus

## Understanding Areas and Networks

Inferring structure and function in the human brain is a science that dates back centuries. Renaissance scholars such as Leonardo Da Vinci believed that the soul was contained in the ventricles of the brain, whereas in the 1600s, Descartes believed that the soul was contained in the pineal gland (Purves, et al., 2013). More systematic study of brain-behavior relationships comes from neuropsychological findings from the nineteenth century onwards, where patients of stroke, tumor, and/or traumatic brain injury presented clinically with unique behavioral symptoms. Perhaps the best known of these cases was Monsieur LeBorgne, neurologist Paul Broca's famous patient "Tan," who, following a stroke-induced lesion to the left frontal lobe, suffered a complete loss of speech production other than the single syllable "Tan," but was nevertheless able to understand spoken sentences and was also able to sing. This paradoxical dissociation between music (singing ability) and language (spoken sentences) was a major step towards a fundamental postulate of cognitive neuroscience: That specific brain areas gave rise to specific mental functions such as language. Today, neuropsychological approaches still offer important insights on how specific brain areas may give rise to behaviors, by relating the presence of lesions in specific areas of the brain to disruptions in behavioral function.

At a fundamental level, neuroscience is based on the neuron doctrine: The idea that individual neurons communicate with each other to give rise to all behavior. Cell bodies of neurons and their supporting cells (glia) make up regions of grey matter, which perform many of the computations to enable neuronal signaling. In contrast to grey matter, white matter generally consists of myelin-sheathed axonal connections between neuronal cell bodies. Bundles of these axonal connections together constitute tracts and fasciculi, which are major white matter pathways that connect networks of regions in the brain, thus enabling neuronal communication.

Following the neuron doctrine, technological advances have enabled the sensing of the structure and activity of large groups of neurons, thus revolutionizing our understanding of the brain. Notably, the cognitive neuroscience of music has been facilitated by the invention in the 1920s of encephalography (EEG) from the recording of scalp electrical potentials, as well as the discovery of nuclear magnetic resonance, which first enabled structural and then functional magnetic resonance imaging (fMRI). EEG and fMRI are complementary methods that provide different types of information about the function of the brain. Since EEG captures the electrical fluctuations of large groups of neurons as they occur, it is a highly time-sensitive tool; however, with EEG we can only obtain readings from the surface of the head, which leads to less spatial sensitivity (e.g. less information about functions of structures deep within the brain). In contrast, fMRI uses changes in the oxygenation level of blood to provide information about *where* (as opposed to *when*) changes occur in the brain. This gives us higher spatial resolution, but poorer time resolution (due to the relatively slow process of blood flow changes as opposed to direct neuronal activity). Magnetoencephalography (MEG), which uses magnetic flux sensors to detect fluctuations of neural activity, is also increasingly a tool of choice, as it provides a reasonable tradeoff between its abilities to detect where and when changes occur in the brain.

In addition to functional neuroimaging, structural neuroimaging includes different methods of acquiring and analyzing MRI data: These methods are rapidly being developed to enable stronger inferences on brain structure and function and their relationship with behavior. One possible limitation of these techniques, however, is their reliance on *correlations* between brain and behavior, rather than *causal claims,* such as one that identifies a certain brain area as being necessary and sufficient for certain brain functions. Lesion methods (as mentioned above) and even open-brain recordings may provide more direct information about causality, but they are invasive for subjects and thus, for ethical reasons, they can only be naturally occurring or produced as a result of medical need (such as in open-brain recordings in patients undergoing brain surgery for epilepsy). Thus, in addition to being invasive for subjects, these studies also pose scientific difficulties, as they are difficult to control in an experimental setting.

To circumvent these difficulties, noninvasive brain-stimulation methods enable hypothesis testing through the creation of virtual (temporary) lesions in targeted regions of the brain. These methods include transcranial direct current stimulation (tDCS) and transcranial magnetic stimulation (TMS). tDCS stimulates specific regions of the brain by applying a low-voltage current through electrodes placed on the scalp over targeted brain regions. TMS stimulates the brain by inducing electrical current as a result of magnetic pulses that are applied via a magnetic coil placed over the head. Due to physical constraints of magnetic and electrical forces, TMS applies more focused stimulation (i.e. more targeted over specific areas) compared to tDCS; however, the use of the magnet in TMS can be mildly uncomfortable and emits sounds, which might add confounds to auditory studies. Despite these tradeoffs, TMS and tDCS both allow carefully controlled studies that can be used to gain a deeper understanding of specific roles of brain areas.

Today, these neuroimaging, neuropsychology, and brain-stimulation techniques are often used in combination, and novel techniques are rapidly being developed not only to localize specific brain functions, but also to understand the relationships and connections between specific brain areas and mental functions. Networks of brain areas give rise to all brain functions: from primary senses such as audition and vision, to motor functions, to association networks such as multisensory integration and spatial navigation, and to networks responsible for higher-level cognitive functions such as attention, working memory, and learning, all of which are required for intact musical functioning.

## Auditory Areas

Although much of the neuroimaging work in music and the brain focuses on the level of the auditory cortex and beyond, the pathway that sounds take from the air to the brain clearly includes many subcortical way stations. For a more comprehensive overview of the subcortical pathway that sound takes from the air to the brain, the reader is referred to the preceding chapter in this volume. Hereafter, we focus on responsiveness to musical sounds from the level of the auditory cortex and beyond.

Once auditory input reaches the primary auditory cortex, the pathways taken by neural impulses are relatively variable and involve distributed brain areas throughout the cortex. Very generally, cortical auditory processing begins at "core" areas and progresses towards "belt" and "parable" areas, which correspond to primary and secondary auditory cortices. These structures are collectively located in the superior temporal lobe. The primary auditory cortex is thought to be located in Heschl's gyrus, part of the superior temporal lobe. Posterior to Heschl's lies the superior temporal plane (planum temporale) and the rest of the superior temporal gyrus which, together with the upper bank of the superior temporal sulcus, constitute parts of the secondary auditory cortex.

A computational model derived from fMRI data suggests that the planum temporale may function as a computational hub that extracts spectrotemporal information to be routed to higher cortical areas for further processing (Griffiths & Warren, 2002). Anatomical MRIs have shown that the planum temporale is larger in the left hemisphere and is leftwardly asymmetric, especially more so among people with absolute pitch (AP) (Schlaug, Janacke, Huang, & Steinmetz, 1995). As AP entails superior categorization ability, these findings suggest that the planum temporale may extract pitch information for further categorization. More evidence for this role of the planum temporale comes from another study on people with AP, using diffusion tensor imaging (DTI) and diffusion tensor tractography, which are specialized MRI techniques for detecting white matter differences (Loui, Li, Hohmann, & Schlaug, 2011). AP possessors were shown, relative to non-AP possessors, to have higher volume of white matter connectivity from the left posterior superior temporal gyrus (STG) to the middle temporal gyrus, a region known to be involved in categorical perception. The posterior STG was also observed to be more functionally connected to the motor and emotional systems in the brain among AP possessors, a finding which again highlights the role of secondary auditory areas in sound extraction and categorization (Loui, Zamm, & Schlaug, 2012).

## Pathways Beyond Auditory Areas

### *Perisylvian Network*

Beyond the auditory cortices, musical sounds activate distributed grey matter throughout the brain. Researchers have proposed various functional networks or pathways beyond the level of the primary auditory cortex. These functional networks subserve language and generalized auditory processing as well as music. Language researchers describe a dual-stream pathway in speech and language processing. The two streams are dorsal and ventral: A dorsal stream projects from the superior temporal lobe (superior temporal gyrus and superior temporal sulcus) via the parietal lobe towards the inferior frontal gyrus and the premotor areas. In contrast, a ventral stream extends from the same superior temporal structures ventrally towards the inferior portions of the temporal lobe. The dorsal stream is involved in articulation and sensorimotor components of speech, and the ventral stream is implicated in lexical and conceptual representations (Hickok & Poeppel, 2007). These similar regions are also activated in musical tasks such as singing. Auditory researchers have also posited a ventral vs. dorsal distinction for the processing of complex sounds that involve most of the same brain areas, with the ventral stream allowing for auditory object recognition, while the dorsal stream enables sensorimotor integration (Rauschecker, 2012).

Although language, music, and auditory processing are ostensibly different neural functions, their underlying brain networks all share many overlapping areas in the brain (the chapter by Besson and colleagues in this volume discusses this matter from a functional as well as neurological perspective). Such overlapping areas include, but are not limited to, a perisylvian network: regions surrounding the sylvian fissure, which separates the temporal lobe from the parietal and frontal lobes. Notably, the superior longitudinal fasciculus is a major white matter pathway that includes the arcuate fasciculus, an arc-like structure that connects the frontal lobe and the temporal lobe. The importance of the arcuate fasciculus for language has been known since the nineteenth century, when it was observed that patients with conduction aphasia, who suffer lesions in the arcuate fasciculus, have trouble repeating sentences that are spoken to them. Due to its positioning as a connective pathway between auditory regions in the temporal lobe and motor regions in the frontal lobe, the arcuate fasciculus is hypothesized to play a key role in mapping sounds to motor movements (such as relating pitch to laryngeal tension). This auditory-motor mapping is a crucial process in speech and music.

To assess the relationship between auditory-motor connectivity and musical skills, we used DTI to compare people with tone-deafness (also known as congenital amusia, see Tillmann et al., this volume) against matched controls. Tone-deaf individuals showed decreased volume in the arcuate fasciculus. Furthermore, the volumes of specific branches of the arcuate fasciculus are correlated with pitch perception and production abilities: People with more accurate pitch discrimination ability had larger branches in their arcuate fasciculus (Loui, Alsop, & Schlaug, 2009). These findings dovetail with fMRI and structural MRI studies (Albouy et al., 2013) that showed grey matter differences in the temporal and frontal lobe areas, endpoints of the arcuate fasciculus, among tone-deaf individuals.

Further studies on the arcuate fasciculus also show larger volume in the left arcuate among singers compared to non-vocal instrumentalists, as well as larger right arcuate volume among singers as well as instrumentalists compared to non-musician controls (Halwani, Loui, Rüber, & Schlaug, 2011). In a combined behavioral and DTI study, participants were taught a novel, unfamiliar musical system, with pitch categories that differed from all existing musical scales. Learning success was significantly correlated with white matter in the turning point of the arcuate fasciculus in the right hemisphere: Better learners had higher connectivity in this white matter pathway (Loui, Li, & Schlaug, 2011). Taken together, these data patterns highlight individual differences in musical behaviors that are reflected by individual differences in brain anatomy, and these individual brain–behavior variations may fall along continua rather than belonging in discrete categories such as would arise from a rigid criterion defining tone-deafness. Rather than categorizing individuals into groups such as "tone-deaf" vs. "normal," it may be fruitful to identify continua of behavioral variations, as we see with many other kinds of neurobehavioral conditions.

## Areas of the Motor System

A major hub of the dorsal pathway in the perisylvian network is the premotor cortex, a region dorsal to the Broca's area. The premotor cortex is involved in action selection, such as in the identification and sequencing of rhythmic sequences (Janata & Grafton, 2003). It is also the site of the putative human mirror neuron system and is shown to respond to acquired actions such as learned melodies (Lahav, Saltzman, & Schlaug, 2007).

Posterior to the premotor areas are the motor cortices of the brain, which, in addition to enabling motor movements, are part of the perception-action network that is central to musical behaviors. Listening to metric rhythms is shown to activate motor cortices as well as the basal ganglia (Grahn & Brett, 2007). These studies, reviewed elsewhere in this volume (Henry & Grahn, this volume), together suggest that rhythm and timing prepares the motor system for response and action, which may explain why humans are so compelled to clap along with or move to the beat.

In addition to functional activity during rhythm perception, areas of the motor system are also sensitive to structural changes as a result of musical training. Bengtsson, et al. (2005) examined concert pianists via DTI and showed that white matter integrity in the motor system was associated with childhood practicing. This and other findings that relate musical training to microstructural changes are now being observed across many areas and networks of the brain. Such findings, reviewed elsewhere in this volume (see especially Gordon &

Magne, this volume), provide increasing support for structural neuroplasticity: the crucial notion that the brain structure changes as a result of experience.

## Multisensory Perception

Although the auditory modality is the primary pathway through which music is processed, much of musical experience includes more than auditory perception. The concurrent influence of visual information is verified by many behavioral studies in music perception and cognition (for a more thorough overview, refer to chapters by Eitan and by Tan, this volume). The underlying brain networks that subserve audiovisual integration appear to differ between musicians and nonmusicians: Network analysis of MEG data suggested that musicians rely more on auditory cues compared to nonmusicians (who rely more on visual cues) during the integration of audiovisual information (Paraskevopoulos, Kraneburg, Herholz, Bamidis, & Pantev, 2015), suggesting that long-term musical training can affect visual as well as auditory processing.

### *Enhanced Multisensory Perception*

While audiovisual integration is ubiquitous in everyday functioning, in the unique population of people with synesthesia, audiovisual or other cross-sensory experiences are enhanced. Synesthesia, the fusion of the senses, is a neurological phenomenon in which experienced sensations trigger concurrent sensations in a different modality. For instance, people with music–color synesthesia report seeing colors when they hear musical sounds, and this can be both bothersome to the synesthetes but also a source of artistic inspiration (Cytowic & Eagleman, 2009). Although the general reported incidence of synesthesia is between 1 and 4% of the population, it is reported to be eight times higher among people in the creative industries and possibly as frequent as 10% or higher for the visualization of overlearned sequences (such as seeing number lines or days of the week as being laid out in a specific manner). In a DTI study comparing music-color synesthetes and matched controls, a major white matter pathway known as the inferior frontal occipital fasciculus (IFOF) was found to be higher in fractional anisotropy (an index of white matter integrity) among the music-color synesthetes. Furthermore, the right hemisphere IFOF was correlated with the subjective report of consistency between musical stimuli (pitches, timbres, and chords) and color associations (Zamm, Schlaug, Eagleman, & Loui, 2013). As the IFOF connects the frontal lobe with areas important for visual perception in the occipital lobe, via auditory and categorization areas in the temporal lobe, this white matter pathway may act as a crucial highway of connectivity that holds together the network of areas necessary for multisensory integration.

### *Occipital Lobe*

The occipital lobe has long been known to be the seat of vision. Although the organization of visual structures in the occipital lobe is complex, it is sensitive to plastic changes as a function of experience from other senses. Many studies on blind subjects show that the occipital lobe may be taken over by auditory processing when deprived of visual experience (Voss & Zatorre, 2012). Occipital lobe regions are also activated during musical imagery

(Herholz, Halpern, & Zatorre, 2012; for more on musical imagery, see the next chapter in this volume; for more on cross modal connections, see Eitan, this volume). Studies with special populations are also informative: During a pitch memory task in an fMRI study, a blind AP musician activated visual association areas in the occipital lobe, whereas sighted AP musicians used more typical auditory regions in the superior temporal lobe (Gaab et al., 2006). Also interestingly, when music–color synesthetes listen to music, they activate color-sensitive areas in the lingual gyrus of the occipital lobe, in addition to classic auditory temporal lobe structures (Loui et al., 2012). These findings converge to show that areas classically viewed as visual cortex in the occipital lobe can be sensitive to nonvisual aspects of musical experience as well.

## Learning and Memory

Learning of and memory for music involve perceptual, motor, affective, and even autobiographical memory processes. The interaction of these processes poses a challenge for neuroscientists who must choose between different behavioral testing methods that may present conflicting results. For example, patients who have had a right temporal lobectomy were impaired in their retrieval of melodies, suggesting that the right temporal lobe stores long-term memories for musical melody (Samson & Zatorre, 1992). On the other hand, conflicting evidence comes from a report of a professional musician with severe amnesia (anterograde, interfering with new memory formation, and retrograde, involving loss of previous memories) who had lesions in most of the right temporal lobe, as well as large portions of the left temporal lobe and parts of left frontal and insular cortices, but who paradoxically had preserved memory for music (Finke et al., 2012). Furthermore, the left temporal pole (a most anterior portion of the temporal lobe) is also implicated in melodic identification, as patients with left temporal pole damage performed worse than a brain–damaged control group on melody naming but not in melody recognition (Belfi & Tranel, 2014). In contrast to neuropsychological studies, fMRI studies show a more distributed network for musical learning and memory, including bilateral superior temporal gyrus, as well as superior parietal regions and the supramarginal gyrus in the parietal lobe (Gaab, Gaser, Zaehle, Jancke, & Schlaug, 2003). Together these studies remind us that in the study of learning and memory, a search for a direct mapping between musical materials and its underlying brain substrates will probably remain elusive. Instead, results depend on the specific research question of each study, and the stimuli used. Results will also depend on task differences such as naming versus recognition, perception versus production, and task-dependent involvement of related cognitive processes such as attention and mental imagery. Nevertheless, here we review studies that very generally converge upon a frontoparietal network for learning and memory. Specifically, the supramarginal gyrus and intraparietal sulcus in the parietal lobe and the lateral prefrontal and medial prefrontal cortices in the frontal lobe show fairly consistent activity in various studies.

### *Parietal Lobe*

Classic parietal lobe functions include sensory integration, memory retrieval, and mental rotation. In the domain of music, these mental functions translate to cognitive and perceptual manipulations of musical materials, such as learning and memory of sequences of pitches and rhythms. The supramarginal gyrus, near the temporal-parietal junction, is a region within the parietal lobe that has appeared in several studies on learning and memory.

Activity in the supramarginal gyrus was significantly associated with memory performance, especially in musically trained subjects (Gaab et al., 2003). Other fMRI studies have refined our understanding of the role of the parietal lobe in music to cognitive operations on abstract musical materials. In one fMRI study, participants were given an encoding and retrieval task of unfamiliar microtonal compositions (i.e., using intervals smaller than those found in conventional Western music), and the right parietal lobe was activated during retrieval of these newly-encoded musical stimuli (Lee et al., 2011). Another fMRI study showed that the intraparietal sulcus, a parietal region dorsal to the supramarginal gyrus, was involved in melody transposition (Foster & Zatorre, 2010). White matter underlying the supramarginal gyrus was also correlated with individual differences in learning a grammar of musical pitches (Loui et al., 2011b). Finally, transcranial direct current stimulation (tDCS) and repetitive transcranial magnetic stimulation (rTMS) over the supramarginal gyrus modulated performance on pitch memory tasks (Schaal, Williamson, & Banissy, 2013).

Taken together, the role of the parietal lobe in music appears to encompass cognitive operations on musical materials: learning, memory, and mental transformations. Some of these operations will be addressed elsewhere in this volume (Schaefer, this volume).

## Prefrontal Cortex

Although debates are still ongoing regarding the optimal division of the prefrontal cortex, the majority of researchers agree on a functional division between lateral and medial prefrontal structures. In the musical domain, the medial prefrontal cortex is shown to track tonal structure (Janata et al., 2002) as well as autobiographical memories (Janata, 2009) and is also relatively active during free-form music making such as in jazz improvisation (Limb & Braun, 2008). Studies on emotional responses to music have also consistently activated the ventromedial prefrontal cortex as part of the reward network, which we will review in more detail in a later section (see also Granot, this volume). In contrast to the medial prefrontal cortex, the lateral prefrontal cortex plays roles in cognitive operations such as working memory and task-related attentional processing (Janata, Tillmann, & Bharucha, 2002). Notably, Broca's area lies within the lateral prefrontal cortex and has long been known to be crucial for language, but is sensitive to musical syntax as well (see Besson, Barbaroux, & Dittinger, this volume, for an in-depth review). Towards the midline of the brain from the Broca's area is the anterior insula, an area that predominantly activates in vocal tasks such as singing (Zarate, Wood, & Zatorre, 2010). Due to its role in vocal tasks and its proximity to other regions within the perisylvian network reviewed above, the anterior insula is frequently considered part of the dorsal sensorimotor network used in singing and speaking (Hickok & Poeppel, 2007). Taken together, the roles of the prefrontal cortex are many and complex, but very generally they fall under the categories of attention and memory, vocal-motor, and emotional and self-referential processing.

## Emotion and Reward

Music is widely reported as one of the most emotionally rewarding experiences in human experience. While other chapters in this Companion (Granot, this volume; Timmers, this volume) will give more specific overviews on emotion and pleasure, here we discuss briefly the brain areas and networks that enable the experience of emotion, which include the amygdala and hippocampus within the middle temporal lobe, insula and medial prefrontal cortex within the frontal lobe structures, and the reward network which is driven by the neurotransmitter dopamine.

The dopamine network includes the substantia nigra and ventral tegmental area in the brainstem, and the caudate and nucleus accumbens. Salimpoor et al. (2011) found temporally distinct activations between caudate and nucleus accumbens during the experience of intensely pleasurable moments in music: The caudate was more active during the anticipation of pleasurable moments, whereas the nucleus accumbens was active during the actual experience of pleasurable stimulus. This coupling between dopaminergic areas may give rise to reward processing of slightly unexpected events, consistent with the widely influential view that the systematic fulfillment and violation of expectations give rise to emotional arousal in music (Meyer, 1956).

Neuropsychological evidence shows the involvement of the amygdala in the medial temporal lobe in the fear responses to music. In Gosselin's (2005) study, for example, patients with lesions in the amygdala had trouble identifying specific emotional categories, such as "scary" music as being scary. Trost et al. (2012) completed an fMRI study to compare nine different emotions that varied in valence and arousal. They found that high-arousal emotions, such as power or joy, were associated with increased activation in the premotor and motor cortex, which suggests that these emotions might be the cause of an urge to move along to the beat or dance. Low arousal emotions such as tenderness, calm, and sadness showed activation in the medial prefrontal cortex (MPFC), which, as mentioned above, is often linked to autobiographical or self-referential processing. This finding is further validated by a study that showed increased connectivity between auditory areas and frontal lobe areas, including anterior insula and MPFC, in individuals who experience chills (Sachs, Ellis, Schlaug, & Loui, 2016). These results may suggest that music can evoke self-referential processing, i.e. the consideration of one's self relative to others, as part of its emotional influence. These findings suggest that social and emotional communications may serve as candidate evolutionary functions of music.

## Conclusions

The human experience of music requires multiple functions of the mind that engage distributed networks in the brain. While some of these networks may be defined by their anatomical relationships (e.g. perisylvian areas), more networks are defined by their functions (e.g. learning and memory, emotion and reward). Taken together, the results reviewed in this introductory chapter echo many findings from cognitive neuroscience more generally. They also expand our knowledge by enabling rigorous tests of neuroanatomical models that are offered by other studies outside the realm of music. The study of music and the brain is rapidly gaining in theoretical as well as empirical momentum, and it is clear that music can also be helpful to neuroscientists by supplying a rich source of stimulus materials with which to test out contemporary hypotheses with regard to regional and/or network views of the human brain.

## Core Reading

Janata, P. (2009). The neural architecture of music-evoked autobiographical memories. *Cerebral Cortex*, *19*(11), 2579–2594.

Loui, P., Alsop, D., & Schlaug, G. (2009). Tone deafness: A new disconnection syndrome? *Journal of Neuroscience*, *29*(33), 10215–10220.

Purves, D., Cabeza, R., Huettel, S. A., LaBar, K. S., Platt, M. L., & Woldorff, M. G. (2013). *Principles of cognitive neuroscience* (2nd Ed). Sunderland, MA: Sinauer Associates, Inc.

Salimpoor, V. N., Benovoy, M., Larcher, K., Dagher, A., & Zatorre, R. J. (2011). Anatomically distinct dopamine release during anticipation and experience of peak emotion to music. *Nature Neuroscience, 14*(2), 257–262.

Schlaug, G., Jancke, L., Huang, Y., & Steinmetz, H. (1995). In vivo evidence of structural brain asymmetry in musicians. *Science, 267*(5198), 699–701.

# Further References

Albouy, P., Mattout, J., Bouet, R., Maby, E., Sanchez, G., Aguera, P. E., Daligault, S, Delpeuch, C., Bertrand, O. Caclin, A., & Tillmann, B. (2013). Impaired pitch perception and memory in congenital amusia: The deficit starts in the auditory cortex. *Brain, 136*(Pt 5), 1639–1661.

Belfi, A.M., & Tranel, D. (2014). Impaired naming of famous musical melodies is associated with left temporal polar damage. *Neuropsychology, 28*(3), 429–435.

Bengtsson, S. L., Nagy, Z., Skare, S., Forsman, L., Forssberg, H., & Ullén, F. (2005). Extensive piano practicing has regionally specific effects on white matter development. *Nature Neuroscience, 8*(9), 1148–1150.

Cytowic, R. E., & Eagleman, D. M. (2009). *Wednesday is indigo blue: Discovering the brain of synesthesia.* Cambridge, MA: MIT Press.

Finke, C., Esfahani, N. E., & Ploner, C. J. (2012). Preservation of musical memory in an amnesic professional cellist. *Current Biology, 22*(15), R591–R592.

Foster, N. E. V., & Zatorre, R. J. (2010). A role for the intraparietal sulcus in transforming musical pitch information. *Cerebral Cortex, 20*(6), 1350–1359.

Gaab, N., Gaser, C., Zaehle, T., Jancke, L., & Schlaug, G. (2003). Functional anatomy of pitch memory—an fMRI study with sparse temporal sampling. *Neuroimage, 19*(4), 1417–1426.

Gaab, N., Schulze, K., Ozdemir, E., & Schlaug, G. (2006). Neural correlates of absolute pitch differ between blind and sighted musicians. *Neuroreport, 17*(18), 1853–1857.

Gosselin, N. (2005). Impaired recognition of scary music following unilateral temporal lobe excision. *Brain, 128*(3), 628–640.

Grahn, J. A., & Brett, M. (2007). Rhythm and beat perception in motor areas of the brain. *Journal of Cognitive Neuroscience, 19*(5), 893–906.

Griffiths, T. D., & Warren, J. D. (2002). The planum temporale as a computational hub. *Trends in Neurosciences, 25*(7), 348–353.

Halwani, G. F., Loui, P., Rüber, T., & Schlaug, G. (2011). Effects of practice and experience on the arcuate fasciculus: Comparing singers, instrumentalists, and non-musicians. *Frontiers in Psychology, 2*(July), 1–9.

Herholz, S. C., Halpern, A. R., & Zatorre, R. J. (2012). Neuronal correlates of perception, imagery, and memory for familiar tunes. *Journal of Cognitive Neuroscience, 24*(6), 1382–1397.

Hickok, G., & Poeppel, D. (2007). The cortical organization of speech processing. *Nature Reviews. Neuroscience, 8*(5), 393–402.

Janata, P., Birk, J. L., Van Horn, J. D., Leman, M., Tillmann, B., & Bharucha, J. J. (2002). The cortical topography of tonal structures underlying Western music. *Science, 298*(5601), 2167–2170.

Janata, P., & Grafton, S. T. (2003). Swinging in the brain: Shared neural substrates for behaviors related to sequencing and music. *Nature Neuroscience, 6*(7), 682–687.

Janata, P., Tillmann, B., & Bharucha, J. J. (2002). Listening to polyphonic music recruits domain-general attention and working memory circuits. *Cognitive, Affective, & Behavioral Neuroscience, 2*(2), 121–140.

Lahav, A., Saltzman, E., & Schlaug, G. (2007). Action representation of sound: Audiomotor recognition network while listening to newly acquired actions. *Journal of Neuroscience, 27*(2), 308–314.

Lee, Y.-S., Janata, P., Frost, C., Hanke, M., & Granger, R. (2011). Investigation of melodic contour processing in the brain using multivariate pattern-based fMRI. *NeuroImage, 57*(1), 293–300.

Limb, C. J., & Braun, A. R. (2008). Neural substrates of spontaneous musical performance: An fMRI study of jazz mprovisation. *PLoS ONE, 3*(2), e1679.

Loui, P., Li, H. C. C., Hohmann, A., & Schlaug, G. (2011). Enhanced cortical connectivity in absolute pitch musicians: A model for local hyperconnectivity. *Journal of Cognitive Neuroscience, 23*(4), 1015–1026.

Loui, P., Li, H. C., & Schlaug, G. (2011). White matter integrity in right hemisphere predicts pitch-related grammar learning. *NeuroImage, 55*(2), 500–507.

Loui, P., Zamm, A., & Schlaug, G. (2012). Enhanced functional networks in absolute pitch. *NeuroImage, 63*(2), 632–640.

Meyer, L. (1956). *Emotion and meaning in music.* Chicago, IL: University of Chicago Press.

Paraskevopoulos, E., Kraneburg, A., Herholz, S. C., Bamidis, P. D., & Pantev, C. (2015). Musical expertise is related to altered functional connectivity during audiovisual integration. *Proceedings of the National Academy of Sciences, 12*(40), 12522–12527.

Rauschecker, J. P. (2012). Ventral and dorsal streams in the evolution of speech and language. *Frontiers in Evolutionary Neuroscience, 4.* http://dx.doi.org/10.3389/fnevo.2012.00007

Sachs, M. E., Ellis, R. J., Schlaug, G., & Loui, P. (2016). Brain connectivity reflects human aesthetic responses to music. *Social, Cognitive, and Affective Neuroscience,* 1–6.

Samson, S., & Zatorre, R. J. (1992). Learning and retention of melodic and verbal information after unilateral temporal lobectomy. *Neuropsychologia, 30*(9), 815–826.

Schaal, N. K., Williamson, V. J., & Banissy, M. J. (2013). Anodal transcranial direct current stimulation over the supramarginal gyrus facilitates pitch memory. *European Journal of Neuroscience, 38*(February), 3513–3518.

Trost, W., Ethofer, T., Zentner, M., & Vuilleumier, P. (2012). Mapping aesthetic musical emotions in the brain. *Cerebral Cortex, 22*(12), 2769–2783.

Voss, P., & Zatorre, R. J. (2012). Organization and reorganization of sensory-deprived cortex. *Current Biology, 22*(5), R168–R173.

Zamm, A., Schlaug, G., Eagleman, D. M., & Loui, P. (2013). Pathways to seeing music: Enhanced structural connectivity in colored-music synesthesia. *NeuroImage, 74*, 359–366.

Zarate, J. M., Wood, S., & Zatorre, R. J. (2010). Neural networks involved in voluntary and involuntary vocal pitch regulation in experienced singers. *Neuropsychologia, 48*(2), 607–618.

# 3

# MUSIC IN THE BRAIN
## Imagery and Memory

*Rebecca S. Schaefer*

The experience of music, like many other perceptual and cognitive processes, can be argued to largely take place internally; air pressure waves are not necessarily music until they hit the ear, get processed in the brain and body, and are interpreted as music. A special but recognizable case of an internal musical experience is one we generate ourselves as a musical image in the absence of sound, either deliberately or spontaneously. The music in our heads can come from an effortfully initiated and sustained mental action, but often also arises automatically, either with or without some contextual link to other stimuli or situations we are exposed to, and in certain cases as part, and possibly in support, of other cognitive functions. In this chapter, I will discuss different types of imagery and their interactions with other cognitive functions, specifically aspects of memory, and their neural signatures. I will argue that a supportive (also termed *constructive*) form of imagery is of crucial importance to the generation of perceptual predictions, which can be considered to be central to the cognition of music listening. Finally, implications for future research are considered.

## Characteristics of Imagery

### Imagery Modality

A rich history of research focused on mental imagery has shown that when we imagine something, the related neural processes are at least partly shared with those of actually perceiving or performing the same stimulus or action (for an overview, see Kosslyn, Ganis, & Thompson, 2001). This means that depending on the sensory type, or *modality* of the imagery—referring to whether the imagined stimulus is visual, auditory, tactile, olfactory, or some sort of movement—the neural areas that are involved in that specific type of actual perception or action are often found to also be active during effortful mental imagery in that modality, albeit often to a lesser extent. Additionally, *modality-independent* neural activation patterns have also been identified that may be related to imagery vividness (e.g. Daselaar, Porat, Huijbers, & Pennartz, 2010), indicating that the task of initiating and sustaining a mental image also has commonalities between modalities.

Although some studies have found correlations between self-reported abilities across modalities, often visual and auditory, suggesting a general, modality-independent imagery ability (Gissurarson, 1992; Halpern, 2015), there are also clear indications that deliberate imagery abilities are increased generally in specific modalities with related expertise, such as auditory imagery (musical and non-musical) in musicians (e.g. Aleman, Nieuwenstein, Böcker, & De Haan, 2000), or movement imagery (Isaac & Marks, 1994) and spatial imagery (such as mental rotation, Ozel, Larue, & Molinaro, 2004) in trained athletes. It may also be the case that certain imagery modalities are more intricately related to each other than others. For instance, perceptual-imagery modalities may be more related to each other than to kinesthetic movement imagery, or certain modalities may share specific aspects (e.g., the time dimension necessarily present in both movement and auditory imagery; see Schaefer, 2014a for further discussion).

Reviewing the available experimental findings of imagery specific to varying kinds of musical stimuli, Hubbard (2010) concluded that many structural and temporal features of music appear to be preserved in musical images, and—importantly, in the context of the current discussion—can influence concurrent perception as well as expectations of upcoming stimuli. Crucially, the to-be-imagined stimuli need to be prescribed in experimental investigations of musical imagery quality in order to be able to make any kind of judgment about its structural properties, as improvised imagery is generally unpredictable and thus more difficult to evaluate in a lab setting.

## *Imagery Type*

Although researching mental imagery is in itself a complicated endeavor because of difficulties in experimental measurement of subjective experience, the effort of clarifying its mechanism is also sometimes hampered by varying use of similar terminology. The many activities or tasks that all may be called "imagery" in the scientific literature include generating a maximally vivid image, but also the ability to manipulate an image, or to compare it—while keeping it in working memory—with perceptual input. Other, somewhat more abstract types of imagery include sensory expectations of actions; mental rehearsal in experts; perceptual judgments that are thought to involve some sort of inner representations and many more. Specifically relating to music, imagery processes have been put forward as being crucial to active music listening (Hargreaves, 2012), arguing that inner representations play a central role in the experience of perceiving music. Moreover, imagery skills are often mentioned in the context of musical aptitude (Gordon, 1965). However, in this last case, as well as in music listening, it is not always clear which kind of imagery is meant; and it is likely that multiple aspects of imagery are relevant to both music perception and production (see for instance the imagery thought to be crucial in joint music making, cf. Keller, 2012).

One way to be more precise about the specific role of imagery in these functions is to make distinctions between different types of imagery, which could potentially apply to any sensory modality. Following a taxonomy based on Strawson's (1974) philosophical essay "Imagination and Perception," and further developed for music imagery specifically by Moore (2010), one can argue that the type of imagery most often investigated experimentally is *sensory* imagery, where someone deliberately imagines a sound (or some other sensory experience). Conversely, a different type of imagery, referred to as *constructive* imagery, does not take place deliberately, but functions more as a process of perceptual organization, and appears to be more in line with how imagery processes are thought to support music perception. The idea that something like imagery is inherently involved in any perceptual process that involves prediction of upcoming stimuli is not exclusive to music listening (cf. Clark, 2012), and also fits with the concept of modality-specific grounding of conceptual knowledge (cf. Barsalou, Simmons, Barbey, & Wilson, 2003). Given its hypothesized involvement in actual perception, constructive imagery has been put forward as a likely explanation for the shared aspects of perception and sensory imagery represented by overlapping neural activation patterns that have been identified between these two tasks through brain imaging findings (for further discussion of this idea, see Schaefer, 2014b). As the concept of constructive imagery needs further exploration, this assertion remains speculative for now, but it is clear that more insights from research into the different imagery types will not only inform our knowledge of music processing but of cognitive functioning more generally.

## *Imagery Content*

While the different modalities of imagery have long been distinguished, and the type of imagery is now also receiving more attention from researchers, the specific content of imagery itself within a certain modality is now also within reach of experimental paradigms, including those paradigms using brain measurements. Meticulous behavioral experiments have been able to isolate specific aspects of imagery content, for instance by looking specifically at pitch, contour, rhythm, timbre, loudness and so on in the context of music, either in isolation or combined, as a rich, holistic representation (cf. Hubbard, 2010). Using careful experimental design in combination with specific analysis methods that allow exploration of the information content of neural activity, we can now also distinguish brain activity patterns that are related to specific stimuli (or aspects of these stimuli) or actions. Examples come from different modalities, and include being able to distinguish between specific imagined visual images (e.g. cf. Cichy, Heinzle, & Haynes, 2012) or actions (Oosterhof, Tipper, & Downing, 2012), or isolating the neural activity related to specific melodic aspects of an imagined tune (e.g. Schaefer, Desain, & Suppes, 2009).

## *Spontaneous Imagery*

Even though most experimental evidence focuses on effortful, deliberate imagery, there are many ways in which a mental image can surface into consciousness spontaneously. In the musical domain, a significant body of work focuses on spontaneously experienced music (also termed "earworms," or INMI, for Involuntary Music Imagery), which has been investigated in a very large sample through a self-report questionnaire (Floridou, Williamson, Stewart, & Müllensiefen, 2015) and now also includes an exploration of brain differences for people who frequently experience spontaneous music imagery (Farrugia, Jakubowski, Cusack, & Stewart, 2015). Although early work on this phenomenon had already shown that music students experience music imagery more than a third of the time (Bailes, 2007), this experience is extremely widespread. In a sample of 2671 individuals, only 29 reported never experiencing INMI, giving an impression of the ubiquity of this experience. Unsurprisingly, INMI frequency was shown to correlate positively with musical behaviors (i.e. musical training, active engagement with music, perceptual and singing abilities, and emotional responses to music). Furthermore, INMI frequency showed substantial correlations with other kinds of spontaneous (or even intrusive) thought, such as mind wandering or daydreaming (Floridou et al., 2015).

Although there are indications that spontaneous imagery implicates similar brain areas as effortful imagery (Farrugia et al., 2015), it is likely that the cognitive aspects of involuntary imagery relate to low-attention states, and do not necessarily depend on deliberate concentration or attentional functions, or at least interact with these functions in a different way. Different aspects of the INMI experience, identified through the factor structure of the questionnaire created by Floridou et al. (2015), and found to have specific structural neural correlates (Farrugia et al., 2015), may also differentiate between the varying subjective experiences of INMI, from the annoyance of an unwanted song in your head to a helpful function that can support one's movements, reflections, or focus. Considering imagery more broadly, there are indications that individual differences in frequency of spontaneous imagery occur in visualization as well (Nelis, Holmes, Griffith, & Raes, 2014).

## Applications

When considering the potential applications of imagery, the most obvious areas of interest are clinical settings and pedagogy. In clinical settings, specifically visual imagery is increasingly utilized to achieve experiences that support healthy functioning, potentially through imagined rehearsal of that experience (for an overview, see Pearson, Naselaris, Holmes, & Kosslyn, 2015). Furthermore, there are indications that actively imagined music or singing may be useful in movement rehabilitation to regularize movement, effectively functioning as a self-generated movement cue (Satoh & Kazuhara, 2008; Schaefer, Morcom, Roberts & Overy, 2014).

Imagined rehearsal also supports learning in non-clinical settings, specifically acquiring motor skills such as those used in athletics and surgery (cf. Cocks, Moulton, Luu, & Cil, 2014), as well as music learning (cf. Holmes, 2005). Although the development of imagery techniques is not often explicitly taught in music pedagogy (Clark & Williamon, 2011), there are clear instances of expert musicians using, and benefiting from, imagery techniques that support memorization and performance (e.g. Davidson Kelly, Schaefer, Moran, & Overy, 2015). The way that imagery is approached in these applied settings— even though it does usually take the shape of deliberate, sensory imagery—differs from the way it is approached in most experimental research in several ways. Most saliently, it seems that in applied settings, rich, holistic, and thus multimodal images are encouraged, rather than focusing on a single stimulus aspect or modality. The goal of the strategy of employing rich images is to increase the effectiveness of the rehearsal method, thus directly tying in to learning and memory functions. The implication here is that the richer the image or rehearsed situation, the more effective the imagery intervention in terms of learning. As an example, consider the practice of creating a multimodal internal representation of a piano performance, which not only consists of an auditory memory of the piece but also includes visual aspects such as the score and the keyboard, and movement aspects of the actual performance. This approach, although requiring some extra memorization effort initially, can offer a much-reduced cognitive load to the pianist during performance, freeing up attentional resources for expressive communication, or other performance goals (Davidson Kelly et al., 2015).

Taken together, the main concepts to consider when discussing imagery are the sensory modality (or modalities) that are included in the image, the kind of imagery that is under discussion, and the content of the imagery, which is obviously related to the modality. These factors also determine the level of focus or engagement that is required to experience the imagined stimulus or action. Images can be made up of basic, low-level perceptual features up to complex, multimodal constructs or situations. Thus, imagery arguably does not exist as an isolated cognitive function, but is inherently related with other cognitive functions, as well as interrelated with perception and action.

## Imagery and Memory

As already suggested above, memory processes can be argued to be a part of imagery processes, as well as vice versa. The former appears intuitive; to actively call up a vivid image requires the preexisting knowledge of the to-be-imagined stimulus and the capacity to retrieve and (internally) reproduce it, even when producing it spontaneously. Moreover, both long-term memory and working memory function are suggested to contribute to imagery vividness through increased representation strength (Baddeley & Andrade, 2000; Navarro Cebrian & Janata, 2010).

The other direction, where memory depends on imagery, is somewhat less straightforward, but is arguably dependent on the type of imagery and the type of memory under consideration. Although imagery strategies can drive memory encoding processes (Alonso et al., 2016), and possibly enhance learning through mental rehearsal (cf. Davidson Kelly et al., 2015), the imagery necessarily involved in long-term memory may be restricted to the moment of recall (and possibly dependent on modality, cf. Greenberg & Rubin, 2003), but thought of as crucial to vivid remembering (Huijbers, Pennartz, Rubin, & Daselaar, 2011). Looking more broadly at holistic, multimodal scenarios, findings have been reported indicating that remembering the past and imagining the future lead to activation in comparable brain networks (e.g. Schacter, Addis, & Buckner, 2007), in line with the idea that both remembering and simulating an experience involve mechanisms related to sensory imagery.

The commonalities between deliberate sensory imagery and short-term or working memory[1] are further supported by more detailed research findings. For music specifically, similar neural activation features have been identified for effortful imagery and for modality-specific working memory in the electroencephalogram (EEG; cf. Schaefer, Vlek, & Desain, 2011) as well as in the brain responses measured by functional magnetic resonance imaging (fMRI; cf. Herholz, Halpern, & Zatorre, 2012). More recent results using visual and non-musical auditory stimuli indicate that the content of the memorized or imagined stimulus can be also detected from brain activity measurements (e.g. Linke & Cusack, 2015), although there appear to be differences in the extent to which low-level perceptual features are processed as compared to more abstract representations, with low-level features showing more overlap with actual perception than high-level features. This result is in line with an exploratory finding that the neural correlates for imagery of more complex musical material appear to overlap with perception of that same material to a lesser degree than for very simple stimuli (Schaefer, Desain, & Farquhar, 2013), suggesting that the more complex a stimulus is, the less its effortful imagination relies on the perceptual apparatus of the brain. Moreover, there are also distinct differences in neural activation patterns between imagery and short-term memory that indicate that, although there are great similarities in terms of the brain areas that are involved, there are also detectable differences between actively imagining a sound stimulus as vividly as possible, and keeping that stimulus in working memory for a change detection task (Linke & Cusack, 2015). Further investigations are necessary to better untangle the conceptual differences between active imagery and working memory, and to establish whether the same mechanisms apply to different modalities or complexity of imagery content.

## *Cognitive Overlap and Shared Brain Signatures*

Focusing specifically on short-term memory rehearsal and effortful sensory imagination, we can identify clear commonalities in their functions and features, centered mainly on the conscious inner experience of a specific stimulus. This experience may emerge because we deliberately imagine it or, alternately, because we need to keep the information or stimulus active for later use, such as when rehearsing a phone number, while performing some sort of change detection task, or while manipulating information (for example, doing mental arithmetic). The key difference appears to be that in the second case, the imagery is conjured in support of a goal beyond simply simulating an experience. As such, the internal percept that subserves a memory function tends to be spontaneous, but conscious, whereas in deliberate imagery it is more effortfully initiated. In either situation, the core of the percept may have modality-specific and amodal aspects, i.e. characteristics related to the type of sensory information (or action), or to the concept of the object itself.

Research into the neural activation patterns related to amodal conceptual information (i.e. lacking a specific sensory modality), reports temporal gyrus and precuneus activation that follows the structure of behavioral ratings of similarity between concepts (Fairhall & Caramazza, 2013). This, however, differs from the activation patterns that are related to modality-independent components of active imagery, seen in frontal (superior middle frontal gyrus and medial prefrontal cortex) and parietal areas (lateral parietal and posterior cingulate, Daselaar et al., 2010). Although these two studies approached the analyses of brain activation patterns in quite different ways, and more findings on these kinds of tasks are needed before being able to reach more robust conclusions, these results suggest that mentally activating a concept for manipulation (as in the similarity judgment task used by Fairhall & Caramazza, 2013) and deliberately imagining a maximally vivid sound or visual image (as was required in Daselaar et al., 2010) do not necessarily involve very similar neural processes. Thus, although the activation of amodal concepts must be part of imagining, there may be different timecourses of activation depending on the task. As neither of these studies used musical material, these findings make little suggestion as to how the amodal aspects of music (i.e. representations of semantic or emotional content, episodic knowledge related to the musical piece, etc.) are combined with the auditory (and other sensory or motor) aspects of the imagined stimulus.

Future work on how imagery processes may support other cognitive functions, for instance as described for different types of memory, should yield illuminating results concerning the role of attention or focus during spontaneous or deliberate internal experiences, and whether inter-individual differences in deliberate imagery ability or spontaneous imagery affect these functions. In particular, the idea that spontaneous music imagery or visualization may support other functions, such as personal reflection or focus during low-attention states (as reported by Floridou et al., 2105) is very interesting. Here, the spontaneous inner experience may speculatively be thought to be mediated by individual traits relating to tendencies for spontaneous simulation, degrees in which associated concepts may trigger one another, specific strategies that have been acquired over time, and so on.

Considering musical imagery specifically, much debate has surrounded the findings of activity in brain areas traditionally known as motor areas during active imagery. The relatively stable findings that, in addition to activating secondary auditory areas, music imagery leads to activation in (pre-)supplementary motor areas (SMA) and sometimes premotor areas and cerebellum (Halpern & Zatorre, 1999; Herholz et al., 2012), was initially interpreted as covert movement imagery (Zatorre & Halpern, 2005). However, rather than music imagery *necessarily* including some form of movement representation, this may actually reflect a much broader function related to timing and sequencing, which are increasingly seen as more prominent functions of these neural areas, thus expanding their status from "only" motor areas to areas involved in general temporal organization of sensory as well as motor processing, specifically timing processes (See Henry and Grahn, this volume; also Schwartze, Rothermich, & Kotz, 2012; Teki, Grube, & Griffiths, 2011). As such, these areas may mainly be involved in processing temporal information relating to an imagined sound or action (Schaefer, 2014a). Of course this does not preclude the possibility that many cases of musical imagery involve both motor and sound aspects, either deliberately and consciously, or passively through neural coactivation, as tends to develop in expert musicians. Aspects of music processing as a whole, and indeed music imagery processes specifically, often do include some representation of movement; however, when the assumption of covert motor imagery in the form of subvocalisation was specifically tested, results did not support this conclusion and instead support a broader role for SMA than pure motor processing (Halpern, Zatorre, Bouffard, & Johnson, 2004). Moreover, this music imagery-related SMA activation is seen additionally to activation related to actual movement when imagining music while performing a simple wrist flexions (Schaefer et al., 2014), suggesting that this imagery-related activation of SMA takes place independently from movement-related activation, supporting Halpern et al.'s (2004) finding.

When we consider other functions that might recruit SMA during music imagery, there is actually a range of functions in addition to those associated with movement that are reported to be related to SMA activity, including sensory processing, word generation, and even working memory (cf. Chung, Han, Jeong, & Jack, 2005). As our concept of working memory is also still changing from that of an item-holding storage to an increasingly flexible function that is more dependent on salience, attention, and quality of the representation than thought before (e.g Ma, Husain, & Bays, 2014), our ideas of how imagery and memory interact will certainly develop further. As such, it can be argued that research into the interactions between imagery and memory allows not only for a paradigm for the investigation of amodal and modality-specific conceptual knowledge, but also a way to increase our understanding of the brain systems relating action and perception to cognitive function.

## Mental Models and Perceptual Prediction

Predictive processes during music perception are thought to be at the core of our affective responses to music listening, and have enjoyed a rich history of theoretical development (cf. Meyer, 1956; Huron, 2006). The main concept which has been developed is that our expectations about where music may be going next—harmonically, melodically, rhythmically, etc.—relate directly to our emotional response to music, offering structure and regularity through predictable features, or surprise and potentially humor in more unpredictable transitions. More recent developments in thinking about predictive processing (or predictive coding) in the broader area of cognitive science (cf. Clark, 2013) can arguably be seen as an extension of these ideas, with specific implications for music processing (Schaefer, Overy, & Nelson, 2013).

At the basis of the framework of predictive coding as a theory of cognition, with clear parallels to the abovementioned ideas about music, lies the assumption that we create predictions, which are met or violated as new information comes in, which then lead to a response in the listener. In general perception, like in music, these predictions can be generated at multiple levels simultaneously, and vary greatly from low-level to high-level expectations. Arguably, a prediction can only be generated when an internal model exists, and while this internal model may be interpreted as constructive imagery (Schaefer, 2014b), there are many authors who frame this phenomenon as a learning mechanism, where statistical learning based on many stimuli creates a sense of what is predictable in the world around us and causes our predictions (musical and otherwise) to be based on what we have been exposed to before. Where deliberate, effortful imagery can be thought of as having direct commonalities with active working or short-term memory rehearsal, constructive imagery can be thought of as the outcome of statistical learning in the shape of internal models, on which perceptual predictions are based. Future investigations will have to further specify the potential differences between these functions, and the extent to which perceptual organization and statistical learning interact. However, the main implication is that imagery processes have been interpreted as impacting the same domains as not only explicit but also implicit memory and learning processes. Furthermore, the type of imagery considered to be crucial to the musical experience (cf. Hargreaves, 2012) can thus directly be interpreted as related to personal experience, mediated by all the associative processing gained through exposure to an auditory environment.

As mentioned previously, another way in which learning and memory functions may interact with implicit and explicit imagery processes is in specific types of expertise. As stated above, musical imagery abilities are often considered an important part of musicianship, and the relationship between modality-specific expertise and effortful imagery abilities also extends to other domains, such as athletics (cf. Ozel et al., 2004). When these findings on deliberate imagery are viewed as resulting from statistical learning (and potential concomitant increases in constructive imagery abilities), it may mean that constructive imagery and sensory imagery, although distinct functions, are actually part of the same system. From this perspective, the way that imagery is conceptualized and measured in an experiment becomes even more crucial in terms of interpreting the findings of effects of expertise on imagery abilities as result of a learning process. For instance, many musicians report that they imagine music while performing, and use this imagery as a guide for their performance, in terms of shaping their performance to produce a target sound, but also directing their attention to what is coming next, or to be aware of other parts performed by their collaborators (cf. Davidson Kelly et al., 2015; Keller, 2012). This imagery, which may have originated from deliberate practice, eventually happens spontaneously in experts, and supports expert performance.

## Conclusions and Future Research

In sum, the available literature shows us that not only the modality and content of imagery, but also the type of imagery may vary, and that imagery functions interact with other cognitive functions. There are strong cognitive parallels between imagery functions and memory functions, where specific types of imagery closely align with specific types of memory. Although considerable overlap between the functional neural activation of various types of imagery and memory can be found in the literature, the studies directly comparing imagery to memory are relatively sparse. And while an exhaustive review of this literature was not the aim of this chapter, a clear need has been demonstrated for studies that delve deeper into the mechanisms of imagery to better understand the different imagery types, their interactions with other cognitive functions, and their applications. Topics such as the individual differences in imagery ability and potential effects of aging, the effects of focus or attention on imagery quality as well as the interactions with expertise, the degree to which modality-specific and amodal aspects of a construct impact the learning effects of mental rehearsal, and a range of other questions need to be clarified through future research in order to fully make use of the potential of imagery strategies for learning purposes. Thus, we may learn more about the impact that our internal images can have, on our daily experiences more broadly, and on musical processing specifically. A broad range of musical activities – listening, performing and composing – inherently make use of rich internal representations, and thus a deeper understanding of imagery processes promises to yield crucial insights regarding musical perception, action, and cognition.

## Note

1.  The terms "short-term memory" and "working memory" here refer to the maintenance and the maintenance plus manipulation of information, respectively.

## Core Reading

Halpern, A. R., & Zatorre, R. J. (1999). When that tune runs through your head: A PET investigation of auditory imagery for familiar melodies. *Cerebral Cortex, 9*, 697–704.

Herholz, S. C., Halpern, A. R., & Zatorre, R. J. (2012). Neuronal correlates of perception, imagery, and memory for familiar tunes. *Journal of Cognitive Neuroscience, 24(6)*, 1382–1397.

Hubbard, T. L. (2010). Auditory imagery: Empirical findings. *Psychological Bulletin, 136*(2), 302–329.

Keller, P. E. (2012). Mental imagery in music performance: Underlying mechanisms and potential benefits. *Annals of the New York Academy of Sciences, 1252*, 206–213.

Schaefer, R. S. (2014b). Mental representations in musical processing and their role in action-perception loops. *Emprirical Musicology Review, 9*(3), 161–176.

## Further References

Aleman, A., Nieuwenstein, M. R., Böcker, K. B. E., & De Haan, E. H. F. (2000). Music training and mental imagery ability. *Neuropsychologia, 38*, 1664–1668.

Alonso, I., Davachi, L., Valabrègue, R., Lambrecq, V., Dupont, S., & Samson, S. (2016). Neural correlates of binding lyrics and melodies for the encoding of new songs. *NeuroImage, 127*, 333–345. http://doi.org/10.1016/j.neuroimage.2015.12.018

Baddeley, A. D., & Andrade, J. (2000). Working memory and the vividness of imagery. *Journal of Experimental Psychology. General, 129*(1), 126–45.

Bailes, F. (2007). The prevalence and nature of imagined music in the everyday lives of music students. *Psychology of Music, 35*, 555–570.

Barsalou, L. W., Simmons, W. K., Barbey, A. K., & Wilson, C. D. (2003). Grounding conceptual knowledge in modality-specific systems. *Trends in Cognitive Sciences, 7*(2), 84–91.

Chung, G. H., Han, Y. M., Jeong, S. H., & Jack, C. R. (2005). Functional heterogeneity of the supplementary motor area. *American Journal of Neuroradiology, 26*, 1819–1823.

Cichy, R. M., Heinzle, J., & Haynes, J. (2012). Imagery and perception share cortical representations of content and location. *Cerebral Cortex, 22*, 372–380.

Clark, A. (2012). Dreaming the whole cat: Generative models, predictive processing, and the enactivist conception of perceptual experience. *Mind, 121*(483), 753–771.

Clark, A. (2013). Whatever next? Predictive brains, situated agents, and the future of cognitive science. *The Behavioral and Brain Sciences, 36*(3), 181–204.

Clark, T., & Williamon, A. (2011). Imagining the music: Methods for assessing musical imagery ability. *Psychology of Music, 40*(4), 471–493.

Cocks, M., Moulton, C.-A., Luu, S., and Cil, T. (2014). What surgeons can learn from athletes: Mental practice in sports and surgery. *Journal of Surgical Education, 71*, 262–269.

Daselaar, S. M., Porat, Y., Huijbers, W., & Pennartz, C. M. A, (2010). Modality-specific and modality-independent components of the human imagery system. *NeuroImage, 52*(2), 677–85. http://doi.org/10.1016/j.neuroimage.2010.04.239

Davidson Kelly, K., Schaefer, R. S., Moran, N., & Overy, K. (2015). "Total Inner Memory": Deliberate uses of multimodal musical imagery during performance preparation. *Psychomusicology: Music, Mind, and Brain, 25*(1), 83–92.

Fairhall, S. L., & Caramazza, A. (2013). Brain regions that represent amodal conceptual knowledge, *Journal of Neuroscience 33*(25), 10552–10558.

Farrugia, N., Jakubowski, K., Cusack, R., & Stewart, L. (2015). Tunes stuck in your brain: The frequency and affective evaluation of involuntary musical imagery correlate with cortical structure. *Consciousness and Cognition, 35*, 66–77.

Floridou, G. A., Williamson, V. J., Stewart, L., & Müllensiefen, D. (2015). The Involuntary Musical Imagery Scale (IMIS). *Psychomusicology: Music, Mind and Brain, 25*, 28–36.

Gissurarson, L. R. (1992). Reported auditory imagery and its relationship with visual imagery. *Journal of Mental Imagery, 16*(3&4), 117–122.

Gordon, E. (1965). *Musical aptitude profile*. Boston, MA: Houghton Mifflin.

Greenberg, D. L., & Rubin, D. C. (2003). The neuropsychology of autobiographical memory. *Cortex, 39*(4–5), 687–728.

Halpern, A. R. (2015). Differences in auditory imagery self-report predict neural and behavioral outcomes. *Psychomusicology: Music, Mind, and Brain, 25*(1), 37–47.

Halpern, A. R., Zatorre, R. J., Bouffard, M., & Johnson, J. A. (2004). Behavioral and neural correlates of perceived and imagined musical timbre. *Neuropsychologia, 42*(9), 1281–1292.

Hargreaves, D. J. (2012). Musical imagination: Perception and production, beauty and creativity. *Psychology of Music, 40*(5), 539–557.

Holmes, P. A. (2005). Imagination in practice: A study of the integrated roles of interpretation, imagery and technique in the learning and memorisation processes of two experienced solo performers. *British Journal of Music Education, 22*, 217–235.

Huijbers, W., Pennartz, C. M. a, Rubin, D. C., & Daselaar, S. M. (2011). Imagery and retrieval of auditory and visual information: Neural correlates of successful and unsuccessful performance. *Neuropsychologia, 49*(7), 1730–40.

Huron, D. (2006). *Sweet anticipation: Music and the psychology of expectation*. Cambridge, MA: MIT Press.

Isaac, A. R., & Marks, D. F. (1994). Individual differences in mental imagery experience: Developmental changes and specialization. *British Journal of Psychology, 85*, 479–500.

Kosslyn, S. M., Ganis, G., & Thompson, W. L. (2001). Neural foundations of imagery. *Nature Reviews Neuroscience, 2*, 635–642.

Linke, A. L., & Cusack, R. (2015). Flexible information coding in human auditory cortex during perception, imagery, and STM of complex sounds. *Journal of Cognitive Neuroscience, 27*(7), 1322–1333.

Ma, W. J., Husain, M., & Bays, P. M. (2014). Changing concepts of working memory. *Nature Neuroscience, 17*(3), 347–356. http://doi.org/10.1038/nn.3655

Meyer, L. B. (1956). *Emotion and meaning in music.* Chicago IL: Unversity of Chicago Press.

Moore, M. E. (2010). Imagination and the mind's ear. (Doctoral dissertation). Available from Pro-Quest Dissertations & Theses Global. (Accession Order No. 758295222).

Navarro Cebrian, A., & Janata, P. (2010). Influences of multiple memory systems on auditory mental. *Journal of the Acoustical Society of America, 127*(5), 3189–3202.

Nelis, S., Holmes, E. A., Griffith, J. W., & Raes, F. (2014). Mental imagery during daily life: Psychometric evaluation of the Spontaneous Use of Imagery Scale (SUIS). *Psychologica Belgica, 54*(1), 19–32.

Oosterhof, N. N., Tipper, S. P., & Downing, P. E. (2012). Visuo-motor imagery of specific manual actions: A multi-variate pattern analysis fMRI study. *NeuroImage, 63*(1), 262–71. http://doi.org/10.1016/j.neuroimage.2012.06.045

Ozel, S., Larue, J., & Molinaro, C. (2004). Relation between sport and spatial imagery: Comparison of three groups of participants. *The Journal of Psychology, 138*(1), 49–63.

Pearson, J., Naselaris, T., Holmes, E. A., & Kosslyn, S. M. (2015). Mental imagery: Functional mechanisms and clinical applications. *Trends in Cognitive Sciences, 19*(10), 590–602.

Satoh, M., and Kuzuhara, S. (2008). Training in mental singing while walking improves gait disturbance in Parkinson's disease patients. *European Neurology, 60,* 237–243 http://doi.org/10.1159/000151699

Schacter, D. L., Addis, D. R., & Buckner, R. L. (2007). Remembering the past to imagine the future: The prospective brain. *Nature Reviews. Neuroscience, 8*(9), 657–661. http://doi.org/10.1038/nrn2213

Schaefer, R. S. (2014a). Images of time: Temporal aspects of auditory and movement imagination. *Frontiers in Psychology, 5,* 877. http://doi.org/10.3389/fpsyg.2014.00877

Schaefer, R. S., Desain, P., & Farquhar, J. (2013). Shared processing of perception and imagery of music in decomposed EEG. *NeuroImage, 70,* 317–326. http://doi.org/10.1016/j.neuroimage.2012.12.064

Schaefer, R. S., Desain, P., & Suppes, P. (2009). Structural decomposition of EEG signatures of melodic processing. *Biological Psychology, 82,* 253–259.

Schaefer, R. S., Morcom, A. M., Roberts, N., & Overy, K. (2014). Moving to music: Effects of heard and imagined musical cues on movement-related brain activity. *Frontiers in Human Neuroscience, 8,* 774. http://doi.org/10.3389/fnhum.2014.00774

Schaefer, R. S., Overy, K., & Nelson, P. (2013). Affect and non-uniform characteristics of predictive processing in musical behaviour. *Behavioral and Brain Sciences, 36*(3), 46–47.

Schaefer, R. S., Vlek, R. J., & Desain, P. (2011). Music perception and imagery in EEG: Alpha band effects of task and stimulus. *International Journal of Psychophysiology, 82*(3), 254–259.

Schwartze, M., Rothermich, K., & Kotz, S. A. (2012). Functional dissociation of pre-SMA and SMA-proper in temporal processing. *NeuroImage, 60*(1), 290–298. http://doi.org/10.1016/j.neuroimage.2011.11.089

Strawson, P. F. (1974). Imagination and perception. In *Freedom and resentment* (pp. 50–72). London: Methuen.

Teki, S., Grube, M., & Griffiths, T. D. (2011). A unified model of time perception accounts for duration-based and beat-based timing mechanisms. *Frontiers in Integrative Neuroscience, 5,* 90. http://doi.org/10.3389/fnint.2011.00090

Zatorre, R. J., & Halpern, A. R. (2005). Mental concerts: Musical imagery and auditory cortex. *Neuron, 47,* 9–12.

# 4

# MUSIC IN THE BRAIN
## Music and Language Processing

*Mireille Besson, Mylène Barbaroux, and Eva Dittinger*

## Introduction

Music and language[1] produce phenomenologically different experiences and require different abilities (for example, playing the violin is not speaking). However, they also share interesting commonalities: Both are formed of structured sequences of auditory events that unfold in time and they rely on the same acoustic parameters (frequency, duration, intensity, and timbre). These similarities have opened the intriguing possibility that musical training, by enhancing sensitivity to aspects that are common to music and language, positively influences language processing (the "cascade" hypothesis). As described below, such transfer effects have indeed been demonstrated from musical training to different levels of language processing.[2] Importantly, however, recent results have shown that musical training also influences cross-modal integration (Paraskevopoulos, Kraneburg, Herholz, Bamidis, & Pantev, 2015) and higher-order cognitive functions such as attention, working memory, short and long-term memory, and executive functions that are of primary importance to processing language (the multi-dimensional hypothesis). As a consequence, a currently debated issue is whether improvements in these cognitive functions are mediating the impact of musical training on language processing. However, as we will argue below, these two interpretations are probably best considered as complementary.

## Transfer Effects from Music to Language

Below we review evidence for the influence of musical training and musical abilities on different aspects of language processing and executive functions. Results were obtained using different methodologies that provide relevant information on behavior (percent correct and reaction times, RTs), on the time-course of information processing (event-related potentials, ERPs) and on the activation of brain structures (functional magnetic resonance imaging, fMRI).

*At the segmental level* (consonants, vowels, and syllables), musical training is positively correlated to the processing of brief speech sounds at multiple stages of the auditory system, from the brainstem (Wong, Skoe, Russo, Dees, & Kraus, 2007) to cortical regions (Chobert, Francois, Velay, & Besson, 2014; Elmer, Meyer, & Jancke, 2012). Musical training also enhances the discrimination of Mandarin tones in native English-speakers (Bidelman, Gandour, & Krishnan, 2011) and of lexical tones in Italian speakers (Delogu, Lampis, & Belardinelli, 2010). By recording ERPs, Marie et al. (2011) showed that both tone discrimination and higher-order decision processes were more efficient in musicians than in non-musicians. By contrast, the automatic orientation of attention was not different in the two groups.

***Categorical perception*** is fundamental to speech perception by allowing listeners to categorize continuous acoustic changes in the speech signal into discrete phonetic categories. Interestingly, Bidelman and Alain (2015) demonstrated an influence of musical training, in both younger and older musicians, on the categorical perception of speech sounds (vowels) by recording both brainstem and cortical evoked responses. Thus, increased auditory sensitivity may be one of the driving forces behind enhanced categorical perception and enhanced speech processing in musicians.

***At the supra-segmental level (words, sentences, discourse)***, early research has shown that adult musicians and children with musical training are more sensitive than non-musicians to linguistic prosody (e.g., final pitch rise in sentences; see Besson, Chobert, & Marie, 2011 for review; Gordon & Magne, this volume) and to emotional prosody (Lima & Castro, 2011). Since most of these findings were obtained from cross-sectional studies, it is possible that genetic predispositions for music and musical abilities were influencing the results. To determine whether improvements in linguistic pitch processing were causally linked to musical training, Moreno and colleagues (2009) compared non-musician children (8–12 years old) before and after six months of music or painting training. Enhanced perception of prosodic intonation was found only in the music group, together with better reading abilities of complex words, providing evidence that musical training was directly related to these improvements.

***At the phonological level***, there is evidence that musical abilities are predictive of phonological skills in children (Anvari, Trainor, Woodside, & Levy, 2002) and in adults (Slevc & Miyake, 2006). Moreover, musical training positively influences phonological and reading abilities in dyslexic children (Habib et al., 2016). These results from cross-sectional studies are in line with those of a longitudinal study with 6–7 year-old children showing that two months of rhythm-based training produced roughly comparable enhancements on a variety of standardized tests of phonological processing than an equivalent amount of training of phonological skills (Bhide, Power, & Goswami, 2013). They are also in line with the conclusions of an interesting meta-analysis of longitudinal studies recently conducted by Gordon et al. (2015), showing that musical training significantly improves phonological awareness skills, even if the effect sizes are small. By contrast, these analyses also showed that the evidence for an impact of musical training on reading has not yet been convincingly demonstrated.

***Speech segmentation*** is necessary for speech comprehension as is clearly exemplified when learning a foreign language that is first perceived as a continuous stream of nonsense words. François and colleagues (2013) used a longitudinal approach over two school-years with 8 year-old children to examine the impact of training in music, compared to painting, on the ability to extract "words" from a continuous stream of meaningless sung syllables. Implicit recognition of meaningless words steadily increased over the two years of music—but not of painting training—and this was associated with modulations of a fronto-central negative component.

***Syntactic processing:*** Since both music and language are structured sequences of events that unfold in time and since both syntax and harmony may rely on similar processing principles, several studies have investigated the influence of musical training on syntactic processing. Jentschke and Koelsch (2009) reported that violations of harmonic structure elicited larger cortical responses in musically trained children than in controls, possibly because the former made better use of the prosodic and rhythmic cues that constrain syntactic constructions (Cason & Schön, 2012). Recent results by Gordon, Fehd, and McCandliss (2015) are in line with this hypothesis by showing that children with stronger rhythmic abilities also showed higher grammatical competence, as measured by their ability to produce sentences with relevant grammatical constructions.

***Executive functions:*** What is meant by "executive functions and cognitive control" (generally concerned with top-down processes that control behavior) is currently debated in the literature (Diamond, 2013). Following Miyake and collaborators (2000), executive functions are linked to cognitive flexibility, inhibitory control, and working memory. However, executive functions are difficult to disentangle from one another as well as from short-term and long-term memory,[3] and contrastive results have been reported in the literature. For instance, results of several experiments showed that adult musicians outperformed non-musicians in working memory tasks based on musical and verbal stimuli (George & Coch, 2011; Schulze, et al., 2011). However, it is still debated whether these findings reflect music-related improvements in working memory, short-term or long-term verbal memory, the influence of enhanced selective attention and cognitive control or the use of different strategies. Inconsistent findings have also been reported in children (Degé, Kubicek, & Schwarzer, 2011; Schellenberg, 2011).

Recently, Zuk, et al. and collaborators (2014) tested both adult and children musicians and non-musicians, selected according to strict criteria, and used a large standardized battery of executive functions. Adult musicians outperformed non-musicians on tests of cognitive flexibility and working memory, but not on tests of inhibitory control and processing speed. Children with musical training also differed from those without musical training on verbal fluency and trail making but not on tests of working memory and inhibitory control. By contrast, results of longitudinal studies showed larger improvements in verbal intelligence and inhibitory control in children from kindergarten involved in an intensive and interactive computer-based musical training program for 20 days compared to children involved in visual arts training (Moreno et al., 2011). Moreover, Roden and collaborators (2012) reported improved verbal memory in children who followed 45 minutes of weekly musical training during 18 months compared to children involved in natural science training or in no training. Finally, in a longitudinal study including a wide age-range (6 to 25 years old) and a large number of participants (N=352), Bergman Nutley and collaborators (2014) showed that musical training was positively associated with spatial and verbal working memory as well as with processing speed and general reasoning.

Clearly more experiments are needed to better understand the influence of musical training on executive functions as well as short-term and long-term memory by testing groups of participants with a wide range of musical abilities, by using standardized tests when they are available and by trying to control for the effects of the many different factors that can influence the results (socio-economic status, bilingualism, etc.).

***Word learning:*** Learning the meaning of new words is a multi-dimensional task that requires both perceptive and higher-order cognitive abilities. Since there is evidence that musicians show improved auditory perception and attention together with enhanced working and verbal memory, they should be at an advantage learning new words in a foreign language like Thai, for example, in which both tones (i.e., patterns of rising and/or falling pitch) and vowel length contrasts change the meaning of a word.[4] Support for this hypothesis was provided by Wong and Perrachione (2007) and by Cooper and Wang (2012) who showed that both tone pitch identification and musical aptitudes were significantly correlated with word learning success in adult English native speakers.

Recently, we conducted a series of experiments (see Figure 4.1A) to further examine the influence of professional musical training on word learning (Dittinger et al., 2016). Participants performed a series of experiments, including phonological categorization, learning the meaning of monosyllabic words through picture-word associations, a matching task, and a semantic task to test for learning and for semantic generalization, respectively. Musicians outperformed non-musicians when phonological categorization was most difficult because it involved phonetic contrasts that belonged to the Thai but not to the French phonemic repertoire. In the learning phase, the N400 component, taken as an index that words had acquired meaning (Mestres-Misse, Rodriguez-Fornells, & Munte, 2007), developed after only 3 minutes of learning thereby reflecting fast brain plasticity in adults. Importantly, this N400 developed faster in musicians than in non-musicians (see Figure 4.1B). Moreover, in both the matching and semantic tasks, the N400 effect (i.e., the difference between mismatching/semantically unrelated and matching/related words) was larger in musicians than in non-musicians (see Figure 4.1C). The N400 effect was larger over centro-parietal regions in musicians and more frontally distributed in non-musicians, which was taken as evidence that musicians were more efficient at integrating the meaning of novel words into semantic networks. Finally, musicians were better than non-musicians at maintaining these novel words in long-term memory (tested five months later).

### *How can we account for these effects and more generally for the influence of musical training at various levels of language processing?*

Two main interpretations, the cascade and multi-dimensional interpretations, can account for the results reviewed above. In the cascade interpretation (bottom-up), increased sensitivity to low-level acoustic parameters such as pitch or duration, that are common to music and speech, drives the influence of musical training at different levels of language processing (e.g., phonetic, phonologic, prosodic, syntactic, and semantic; Besson et al., 2011; Cooper & Wang, 2012; Wong & Perrachione, 2007). In other words, because musicians perceive speech sounds better than non-musicians, they are more sensitive to prosodic cues such as pitch and rhythm and they form more accurate phonological representations. This cascades upward, facilitating the construction of more stable lexical representations as well as higher levels of language processing (e.g., syntactic structures, word learning, and semantic processing). By contrast, in the multi-dimensional interpretation (top-down), both language and music are processed in interaction with other cognitive, emotional, and motor functions that are enhanced by musical training (similar to the OPERA hypothesis proposed by Patel, 2014). Indeed, playing a musical instrument proficiently is a multi-dimensional ability requiring auditory and visual perception, auditory-visuo-motor integration, selective and divided attention, motor control, memory, cognitive control, and emotion.

In sum, it may come as no surprise that extensive training of these different abilities in musicians, from auditory perception to cognitive control, facilitate various levels of language processing (Kraus, Strait, & Parbery-Clark, 2012). In this respect the cascade and multi-dimensional hypotheses are complementary with both bottom-up and top-down processes

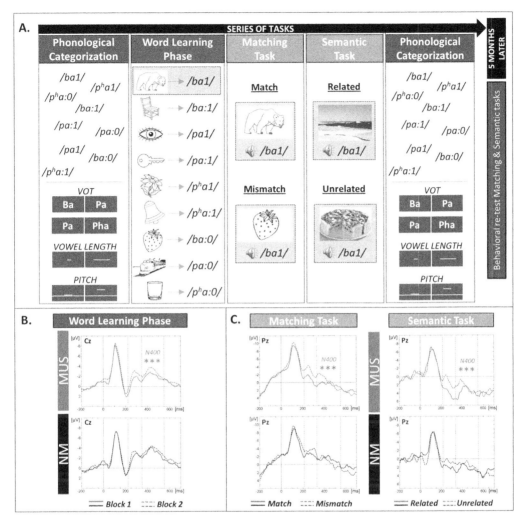

*Figure 4.1* (A) Illustration of the series of tasks used in the experiment. Phonological categorization task of mono-syllabic words based on pitch, vowel length, and voice-onset-time (VOT). In the word learning phase, participants learned the meaning of new words through picture-word associations. In the matching task, participants were asked to decide whether picture-word pairs matched or mismatched those from the learning phase and, in the semantic task, if novel pictures were semantically related or unrelated to the newly learned words. Finally, the matching and semantic tasks were performed again five months later in a subset of participants to test for long-term memory. (B) The increase in N400 amplitude from the first to the second part of the learning phase (block 1 vs. block 2) was larger in musicians than in non-musicians. (C) The differences between match/semantically related and mismatch/semantically unrelated words were also larger in musicians than in non-musicians. See insert for color figure.

probably at play to various degrees in most experimental designs. Moreover, the complementarity of the cascade and multi-dimensional interpretations is also illustrated by the results of neuro-imaging experiments investigating the neural basis of music and speech processing, a topic to which we now turn.

## Shared vs. Distinct Neural Networks for Music and Speech

Whether similar levels of processing in language and music activate similar brain regions, and whether musical expertise influences brain structures considered as speech-specific, are important issues for our understanding of the anatomo-functional organization of the brain.

### Broca's Area: From Speech Production and Syntax to Executive Functions

It has long been considered that the region of Broca, in the left inferior frontal cortex, was specific to speech production and to processing of syntactic structures. However, results of early experiments using fMRI showed that Broca's area was also activated when processing musical structures (Maess, Koelsch, Gunter, & Friederici, 2001). These results led to the conclusion that Broca's area was involved in the processing of syntax, defined as the rules that structure sequences of events that unfold in time, independently of whether these events form linguistic sentences or musical phrases. However, there is now evidence that Broca's area is also activated by the processing of phonological, lexical, and semantic information (Sahin, Pinker, Cash, Schomer, & Halgren, 2009), thereby calling into question its syntax-specificity and the idea that syntactic constructions are processed independently from lexico-semantic information. Finally, and in line with the multi-dimensional view that language, like music, is processed in interaction with other cognitive functions, results also point to the activation of parts of Broca's areas in tasks requiring verbal and non-verbal working memory and/ or executive functions (Schulze et al., 2011). Thus, although the functional role of Broca's area is still under debate, current evidence suggests that it may be part of a large prefrontal network, that includes language-specific as well as general cognitive functions (Fedorenko, Duncan, & Kanwisher, 2012; Hagoort, 2014; Schulze et al., 2011).

### Wernicke's Area: From Language Comprehension to the Fine Temporal Structure of Speech

The same general picture emerges when considering Wernicke's area [part of the planum temporale (PT) in the left superior temporal gyrus (STG)], that was initially taken to play a major role in language comprehension. There is indeed clear evidence that temporal regions are crucial for speech processing. At the same time, there is also growing evidence for the functional diversity of these brain regions, with sub-areas sub-serving both linguistic and non-linguistic functions (see Liebenthal, Desai, Humphries, Sabri, & Desai, 2014 for results of a large meta-analysis). Directly related to our concerns, recent results have highlighted the influence of musicianship on various regions of the temporal lobe that are involved in speech processing.

Jäncke and collaborators (2002) showed that the left PT is specialized for decoding phonetic features, in particular the fine-grained temporal structure of speech such as voice-onset-time. Interestingly, subsequent research revealed that the left PT is similarly activated both by speech and by non-speech sounds (Zaehle, Wüstenberg, Meyer, & Jäncke, 2004) and more activated in professional musicians than in non-musicians when the phonetic categorization task is difficult (Elmer, Meyer, & Jäncke, 2012). Moreover, enhanced phonetic discrimination in musicians was correlated with enhanced cortical surface area of the left PT (Elmer, Hänggi, Meyer, & Jäncke, 2013) and with increased structural connectivity between the right and left PT (Elmer, Hänggi, & Jäncke, 2016), providing evidence that long-term intensive musical training is associated with anatomical and functional changes in speech-specific brain regions such as the PT.

This is not to say, however, that the PT or, more generally, the superior temporal lobe is only involved in temporal speech processing. For instance, results of intra-cranial recordings in epileptic patients (Sammler et al., 2013) revealed activation of the left and right superior temporal lobes in response to violations of syntactic structures in both music and speech. Thus, while these data again provided evidence for shared neuroanatomical regions for syntactic processing in both domains, they were also somewhat surprising in showing a predominance of frontal regions for music harmonic processing and of temporal regions for linguistic syntax processing.

## Temporal Processing in Music and Speech

Results of two recent studies are revealing regarding the issue of shared vs. distinct neural substrates in music and speech (Abrams et al., 2011; Rogalsky, Rong, Saberi, & Hickok, 2011). In both experiments, results of fMRI data showed similar activations of frontal and temporal regions of both hemispheres when processing the temporal structure of sentences and melodies, thereby arguing against a simple dichotomy between the left hemisphere for language and the right hemisphere for music and providing support for shared neural resources between music and speech. However, as noted by Rogalsky and collaborators (2011), "[A]ctivation overlap does not necessarily imply computational overlap or even the involvement of the same neural systems at a finer-grained level of analysis" (p. 3846; see also Peretz, Vuvan, Lagrois, & Armony, 2015). Indeed, results using a finer-grained approach based on multivariate pattern analysis showed that the two types of stimuli elicited different patterns of spatial activity in music and speech. Thus, the authors concluded that temporal structure is encoded differently within the two domains and that distinct cortical networks are activated.

However, while both experiments examined the processing of temporal structures in music and speech, results were quite different in the two studies. In Abrams et al. (2011), activations in response to natural music and speech stimuli were found in Broca's and surrounding areas as well as in the left superior and middle temporal gyri, but the pattern of activation associated with temporal disruptions was different for music and speech. By contrast, using different rates of presentation of melodic phrases and jabberwocky sentences, Rogalsky et al. (2011) found no activation of Broca's area but increased activity in the temporal lobe, with some differences for melodic phrases and for jabberwocky sentences. Thus, confronting these results clearly showed that differences in task design and in participants (non-musicians in Abrams et al., 2011 vs. participants with different amount of musical training in Rogalsky et al., 2011), as well as differences in stimuli (e.g., sentences had a semantic content in the Abrams et al., 2011 study but not in Rogalsky et al., 2011) led to notable differences in the processing of temporal structures in music and speech.

## Music-Specific Brain Regions?

Some answers to this question can be found in a recent experiment by Angulo-Perkins and collaborators (2014). These authors used fMRI, different types of natural stimuli (speech, human vocalizations (non-speech), musical excerpts played at the violin, at the piano and at the synthetic piano, environmental sounds, and monkey vocalizations) and a task that was irrelevant to the aims of the study (detect the presentation of pure tones) to determine whether listening to music activates specific areas of the temporal lobe. Based on the results of a subsidiary analysis showing larger activation in the right planum polare for the violin excerpts than for speech, the authors concluded that "the planum polare may be involved in the processing of specific temporal characteristics that are inherent to music" (p. 136). However, the evidence for music-specific regions in this study was quite weak first because no region showed stronger activation for music than for speech in the main analysis (i.e., when considering both violin and piano musical excerpts and excluding non-speech vocalizations) and second because the bilateral anterior regions of the superior temporal gyrus (aSTG) responded similarly to music and human vocalizations (speech and non-speech) compared to environmental sounds and monkey vocalizations.

Nevertheless, it is interesting that converging results (music activating the planum temporale and planum polare bilaterally) were very recently reported by Norman-Haignere, Kanwisher, & McDermott (2015) when non-musician participants performed a task that, as in Angulo-Perkins, et al. (2014), was irrelevant to the goal of the study (i.e., to detect changes in sound level). Moreover, these authors tried to overcome limitations of previous studies by using a large number of stimuli (165 sounds) that varied along different dimensions (speech, environmental sounds, guitar, pop or rock songs). Results showed that six components explained 80% of the variance in the data. Most importantly, while components 1 to 4 responded to all sound categories, component 5 (located in the STG) responded to sounds categorized as speech and component 6 (located in the planum temporale and planum polare) to sounds categorized as music. These results thus provided evidence for distinct regions involved in some aspects of speech and music processing with a nice fit with previous findings of Angulo-Perkins et al. (2014). However, results again showed weak music selectivity, possibly because the neural populations involved in music processing overlapped with the other neuronal populations identified by components 1 to 5. In sum, results of these two studies again provided evidence for both shared and distinct neural substrates for music and speech.

## Interim Summary

The literature comparing the brain structures involved in music and language processing is very rich and we have only reviewed a few recent examples. However, we hope that these examples clearly illustrate that what we currently know is both complex and exciting. The complexity comes from behavioral and anatomical variability (within and between subjects), from the diversity of tasks and stimuli used to compare similar levels of processing in music and language (and how this similarity is defined), and from using diverse experimental methods (e.g., behavior, brainstem or cortical evoked potentials, intra-cranial recordings, fMRI) and procedures for data analysis.

These results are exciting because they strongly contribute to our understanding of how language and music are implemented in the human brain. Importantly, when considered in detail, results of each one of the experiments reported above (Abrams et al., 2011; Angulo-Perkins et al., 2014; Norman-Haignere et al., 2015; Rogalsky et al., 2011) showed evidence for both shared and distinct neural networks involved in music and speech processing depending upon the level and type of analysis. These results are thus compatible with the proposed complementarity of the previously described cascade and multi-dimensional interpretations.

## General Conclusion

Taken together, experimental results related to transfer effects contribute to the evolution of our understanding of human cognition. Theoretically, they demonstrate that the computations necessary for language and music processing are not performed independently from other cognitive functions and that language and music are not modular and encapsulated systems (Fodor, 1983). In line with current views in the neuroscience of language (Friederici & Singer, 2015), one way to reconcile the seemingly contradictory findings reported above is to consider the brain as a dynamic system (see also Loui & Przysinda, this volume) in which "the functionality of a region is co-determined by the network of regions in which it is embedded at particular moments in time" (p. 136; Hagoort, 2014), this being determined by the stimuli, the task demands, and the cognitive, emotional, and motivational state of the individual. Such a dynamic view of the brain functional organization is based on the idea that neuronal networks can be "coordinated anew on each occasion" (p. 331; Friederici & Singer, 2015).

Pragmatically, evidence that long-term intensive musical training is associated with anatomical and functional changes in various brain regions involved in speech processing (e.g., left planum temporale; Elmer et al., 2012; right planum temporale and bilateral planum polare, Angulo-Perkins et al., 2014; Norman-Haignere et al., 2015) should encourage the use of musical training in the classroom and of music therapy as a remediation method for patients with language deficits. More generally, if common activation for music and speech also reflects the activity of higher-order cognitive networks sustaining attention, memory (working memory, short-term, and long-term memory), executive functions (inhibition, updating, and switching), emotion and motivation, musical training can also be beneficial for patients with attention and memory problems.

In sum, cognitive neuroscience is a very dynamic field and a lot of data are accumulating that sometimes show converging evidence on the functional specialization of brain regions for music and language processing and sometimes show diverging results. The field may be soon ready for a paradigmatic revolution in the Kuhnian sense (Kuhn, 1970), from current static localized networks to dynamic size-varying networks underlying brain high-level functioning.

## Acknowledgments

We would like to thank Eduardo Martinez-Montès for relevant comments on this chapter and the Labex Brain and Language Research Institute (BLRI; ANR-11-LABX-0036) for continuous support. ED is supported by a doctoral fellowship from the BLRI and MBa by a doctoral fellowship from the French Ministry of Research and Education.

## Notes

1. We use language as a general term, but most of the time we refer to speech.
2. See Asaridou and McQueen (2013) for the influence of language experience on music abilities.
3. Different tasks are typically used to test for cognitive flexibility (e.g., switching task), inhibitory control (e.g., Stroop task, Simon task; Flanker task; Go/No-Go tasks, and stop-signal task), working memory (e.g., backward digit task; n-back task), short-term memory (forward digit span; non-word repetition) and long-term memory (delayed recognition, cued-recall, or free recall tests).
4. For instance, /pa1/ low tone with a short vowel means "to find" and /pa:1/ low tone with a long vowel means "forest."

# Core Reading

Diamond, A. (2013). Executive functions. *Annual Review of Psychology, 64*, 135–168.

Dittinger, E., Barbaroux, M., D'Imperio, M., Jäncke, L., Elmer, S., & Besson, M. (2016). Professional music training and novel word learning: From faster semantic encoding to longer-lasting word representations. *Journal of Cognitive Neuroscience 28*:10, pp. 1584–1602.

Friederici, A. D., & Singer, W. (2015). Grounding language processing on basic neurophysiological principles. *Trends in Cognitive Sciences, 19*(6), 329–338.

Gordon, R. L., Fehd, H. M., & McCandliss, B. D. (2015). Does music training enhance literacy skills? A meta-analysis. *Frontiers in Psychology, 6*. doi:10.3389/fpsyg.2015.01777

Norman-Haignere, S., Kanwisher, N. G., & McDermott, J. H. (2015). Distinct cortical pathways for music and speech revealed by hypothesis-free voxel decomposition. *Neuron, 88*(6), 1281–1296.

# Further References

Abrams, D. A., Bhatara, A., Ryali, S., Balaban, E., Levitin, D. J., & Menon, V. (2011). Decoding temporal structure in music and speech relies on shared brain resources but elicits different fine-scale spatial patterns. *Cerebral Cortex (New York, NY: 1991), 21*(7), 1507–1518.

Angulo-Perkins, A., Aubé, W., Peretz, I., Barrios, F. A., Armony, J. L., & Concha, L. (2014). Music listening engages specific cortical regions within the temporal lobes: Differences between musicians and non-musicians. *Cortex; a Journal Devoted to the Study of the Nervous System and Behavior, 59*, 126–137.

Anvari, S. H., Trainor, L. J., Woodside, J., & Levy, B. A. (2002). Relations among musical skills, phonological processing, and early reading ability in preschool children. *Journal of Experimental Child Psychology, 83*(2), 111–130.

Asaridou, S. S., & McQueen, J. M. (2013). Speech and music shape the listening brain: Evidence for shared domain-general mechanisms. *Frontiers in Psychology, 4*. 4. doi:10.3389/fpsyg.2013.00321

Bergman Nutley, S., Darki, F., & Klingberg, T. (2014). Music practice is associated with development of working memory during childhood and adolescence. *Frontiers in Human Neuroscience, 7*. doi:10.3389/fnhum.2013.00926

Besson, M., Chobert, J., & Marie, C. (2011). Transfer of training between music and speech: Common processing, attention, and memory. *Frontiers in Psychology, 2*. doi:10.3389/fpsyg.2011.00094

Bhide, A., Power, A., & Goswami, U. (2013). A rhythmic musical intervention for poor readers: A comparison of efficacy with a letter-based intervention. *Mind, Brain, and Education, 7*(2), 113–123.

Bidelman, G. M., & Alain, C. (2015). Musical training orchestrates coordinated neuroplasticity in auditory brainstem and cortex to counteract age-related declines in categorical vowel perception. *The Journal of Neuroscience: The Official Journal of the Society for Neuroscience, 35*(3), 1240–1249.

Bidelman, G. M., Gandour, J. T., & Krishnan, A. (2011). Musicians and tone-language speakers share enhanced brainstem encoding but not perceptual benefits for musical pitch. *Brain and Cognition, 77*(1), 1–10.

Cason, N., & Schön, D. (2012). Rhythmic priming enhances the phonological processing of speech. *Neuropsychologia, 50*(11), 2652–2658.

Chobert, J., Francois, C., Velay, J.-L., & Besson, M. (2014). Twelve months of active musical training in 8- to 10-year-old children enhances the preattentive processing of syllabic duration and voice onset time. *Cerebral Cortex, 24*(4), 956–967.

Cooper, A., & Wang, Y. (2012). The influence of linguistic and musical experience on Cantonese word learning. *The Journal of the Acoustical Society of America, 131*(6), 4756–4769.

Degé, F., Kubicek, C., & Schwarzer, G. (2011). Music lessons and intelligence: A relation mediated by executive functions. *Music Perception* (2), 195.

Delogu, F., Lampis, G., & Belardinelli, M. O. (2010). From melody to lexical tone: Musical ability enhances specific aspects of foreign language perception. *European Journal of Cognitive Psychology, 22*(1), 46–61.

Elmer, S., Hänggi, J., & Jäncke, L. (2016). Interhemispheric transcallosal connectivity between the left and right planum temporale predicts musicianship, performance in temporal speech processing, and functional specialization. *Brain Structure and Function, 221*(1), 331–344.

Elmer, S., Hänggi, J., Meyer, M., & Jäncke, L. (2013). Increased cortical surface area of the left planum temporale in musicians facilitates the categorization of phonetic and temporal speech sounds. *Cortex, 49*(10), 2812–2821.

Elmer, S., Meyer, M., & Jancke, L. (2012). Neurofunctional and behavioral correlates of phonetic and temporal categorization in musically trained and untrained subjects. *Cerebral Cortex, 22*(3), 650–658.

Fedorenko, E., Duncan, J., & Kanwisher, N. (2012). Language-selective and domain-general regions lie side by side within Broca's area. *Current Biology: CB, 22*(21), 2059–2062.

Fodor, J. A. (1983). *The modularity of mind: An essay on faculty psychology.* Cambridge, MA: MIT press.

Francois, C., Chobert, J., Besson, M., & Schon, D. (2013). Music training for the development of speech segmentation. *Cerebral Cortex, 23*(9), 2038–2043.

George, E. M., & Coch, D. (2011). Music training and working memory: An ERP study. *Neuropsychologia, 49*(5), 1083–1094.

Habib, M., Lardy, C., Desiles, T., Commeiras, C., Chobert, J., & Besson, M. (2016). Music and dyslexia: A new musical training method to improve reading and related disorders. *Frontiers in Psychology,* 7. doi:10.3389/fpsyg.2016.00026

Hagoort, P. (2014). Nodes and networks in the neural architecture for language: Broca's region and beyond. *Current Opinion in Neurobiology, 28,* 136–141.

Jäncke, L., Wüstenberg, T., Scheich, H., & Heinze, H.-J. (2002). Phonetic perception and the temporal cortex. *NeuroImage, 15*(4), 733–746.

Jentschke, S., & Koelsch, S. (2009). Musical training modulates the development of syntax processing in children. *NeuroImage, 47*(2), 735–744.

Kraus, N., Strait, D. L., & Parbery-Clark, A. (2012). Cognitive factors shape brain networks for auditory skills: Spotlight on auditory working memory. *Annals of the New York Academy of Sciences, 1252*(1), 100–107.

Kuhn, T. S. (1970). *The structure of scientific revolutions.* Chicago, IL: University of Chicago Press.

Liebenthal, E., Desai, R. H., Humphries, C., Sabri, M., & Desai, A. (2014). The functional organization of the left STS: A large scale meta-analysis of PET and fMRI studies of healthy adults. *Frontiers in Neuroscience,* 8. doi:10.3389/fnins.2014.00289

Lima, C. F., & Castro, S. L. (2011). Speaking to the trained ear: Musical expertise enhances the recognition of emotions in speech prosody. *Emotion (Washington, D.C.), 11*(5), 1021–1031.

Maess, B., Koelsch, S., Gunter, T. C., & Friederici, A.D. (2001). Musical syntax is processed in Broca's area: An MEG study. *Nature Neuroscience, 4*(5), 540–545.

Marie, C., Delogu, F., Lampis, G., Belardinelli, M. O., & Besson, M. (2011). Influence of musical expertise on segmental and tonal processing in Mandarin Chinese. *Journal of Cognitive Neuroscience, 23*(10), 2701–2715.

Mestres-Misse, A., Rodriguez-Fornells, A., & Munte, T. F. (2007). Watching the brain during meaning acquisition. *Cerebral Cortex, 17*(8), 1858–1866.

Miyake, A., Friedman, N. P., Emerson, M. J., Witzki, A. H., Howerter, A., & Wager, T. D. (2000). The unity and diversity of executive functions and their contributions to complex "Frontal Lobe" tasks: A latent variable analysis. *Cognitive Psychology, 41*(1), 49–100.

Moreno, S., Bialystok, E., Barac, R., Schellenberg, E. G., Cepeda, N. J., & Chau, T. (2011). Short-term music training enhances verbal intelligence and executive function. *Psychological Science, 22*(11), 1425–1433.

Moreno, S., Marques, C., Santos, A., Santos, M., Castro, S. L., & Besson, M. (2009). Musical training influences linguistic abilities in 8-year-old children: More evidence for brain plasticity. *Cerebral Cortex, 19*(3), 712–723.

Paraskevopoulos, E., Kraneburg, A., Herholz, S. C., Bamidis, P. D., & Pantev, C. (2015). Musical expertise is related to altered functional connectivity during audiovisual integration. *Proceedings of the National Academy of Sciences, 112*(40), 12522–12527.

Patel, A.D. (2014). Can nonlinguistic musical training change the way the brain processes speech? The expanded OPERA hypothesis. *Hearing Research, 308*, 98–108.

Peretz, I., Vuvan, D., Lagrois, M.-E., & Armony, J.L. (2015). Neural overlap in processing music and speech. *Philosophical Transactions of the Royal Society B: Biological Sciences, 370*(1664), 20140090–20140090.

Roden, I., Kreutz, G., & Bongard, S. (2012). Effects of a school-based instrumental music program on verbal and visual memory in primary school children: A longitudinal study. *Frontiers in Psychology, 3.* doi:10.3389/fpsyg.2012.00572

Rogalsky, C., Rong, F., Saberi, K., & Hickok, G. (2011). Functional anatomy of language and music perception: Temporal and structural factors investigated using functional magnetic resonance imaging. *The Journal of Neuroscience, 31*(10), 3843–3852.

Sahin, N. T., Pinker, S., Cash, S. S., Schomer, D., & Halgren, E. (2009). Sequential processing of lexical, grammatical, and phonological information within Broca's area. *Science, 326*(5951), 445–449.

Sammler, D., Koelsch, S., Ball, T., Brandt, A., Grigutsch, M., Huppertz, H.-J., Knoesch, T. R., Wellmer, J., Widman, G., Eljer, C. E., Friederici, A. D., & Schulze-Bonhage, A. (2013). Co-localizing linguistic and musical syntax with intracranial EEG. *NeuroImage, 64*, 134–146.

Schellenberg, E. G. (2011). Examining the association between music lessons and intelligence. *British Journal of Psychology (London, England: 1953), 102*(3), 283–302.

Schulze, K., Zysset, S., Mueller, K., Friederici, A. D., & Koelsch, S. (2011). Neuroarchitecture of verbal and tonal working memory in nonmusicians and musicians. *Human Brain Mapping, 32*(5), 771–783.

Slevc, L. R., & Miyake, A. (2006). Individual differences in second-language proficiency does musical ability matter? *Psychological Science, 17*(8), 675–681.

Wong, P. C. M., & Perrachione, T. K. (2007). Learning pitch patterns in lexical identification by native English-speaking adults. *Applied Psycholinguistics, 28*(4).

Wong, P. C. M., Skoe, E., Russo, N. M., Dees, T., & Kraus, N. (2007). Musical experience shapes human brainstem encoding of linguistic pitch patterns. *Nature Neuroscience, 10*(4), 420–422.

Zaehle, T., Wüstenberg, T., Meyer, M., & Jäncke, L. (2004). Evidence for rapid auditory perception as the foundation of speech processing: a sparse temporal sampling fMRI study. *European Journal of Neuroscience, 20*(9), 2447–2456.

Zuk, J., Benjamin, C., Kenyon, A., & Gaab, N. (2014). Behavioral and neural correlates of executive functioning in musicians and non-musicians. *PLOS ONE, 9*(6) e99868. doi:10.1371/journal.pone.0099868

# 5

# MUSIC AND THE BRAIN
## Music and Cognitive Abilities

*Reyna L. Gordon and Cyrille L. Magne*

## Introduction

Several decades of neuroscience and psychology research have deepened the knowledge base surrounding the old aphorism that "music makes you smarter." This notion particularly gained a surge in popularity following the results of a study by Rauscher and collaborators (Rauscher, Shaw, & Ky, 1993) showing that participants who listened to a Mozart sonata (K. 448) for 10 minutes performed better on visuospatial tasks than participants who listened to relaxation instructions or silence during the same amount of time. The effect, however, was shown to be only temporary (dissipating after 15 minutes), and follow-up attempts to replicate this initial finding were met with mixed results. A recent meta-analysis conducted on 39 studies (a combined total of 3109 participants) found evidence for a small "Mozart effect," but similar in size to the effect of listening to other pieces of music or nonmusical stimuli, and at least partially attributed to the arousing nature of the auditory stimulus (Pietschnig, Voracek, & Formann, 2010).

Regardless of whether or not the "Mozart effect" is indeed real, the initial study and its successors certainly sparked an interest in exploring the link between musical experience and cognitive abilities in more depth. Since then, researchers have explored this issue using a variety of cross-sectional and longitudinal approaches. Cross-sectional studies usually compare performances of musicians and non-musicians on a variety of musical, linguistic, and/or cognitive tasks; alternatively, they can examine correlations between participants' individual outcomes on these tasks and their level of music aptitude or years of music experience. While cross-sectional approaches can be useful for investigating potential associations between music and cognitive abilities, a longitudinal randomized trial approach remains the only way to examine potential transfer of learning (i.e., causality) between the two domains. Randomized trial studies on this topic assign non-musicians participants randomly to a music education program (varying in range from a couple of weeks to several years), a non-musical control activity or no activity, and use a pre-training/post-training comparison approach.

This chapter is focused on recent research exploring the relationship between music and other cognitive abilities, with emphases on language skills, mathematical and visuospatial abilities, executive function, auditory perception, and IQ. Both correlational and causal evidence are reported, such that we rigorously consider abundant findings in favor of (and against) associations between individual differences in music aptitude (defined as "the potential for someone to succeed at music training"; Schellenberg, 2015) or musical expertise (acquired through musical training) and cognitive abilities, as well as the small number of studies that have tested causal *transfer* (i.e., achievement of skills in a different context than the original learning situation) from music activities to gains in cognition. We refer to *near transfer* as an influence of music training on auditory or music skills, whereas a *far transfer* would be an influence of music training on non-musical domains, such as language or IQ.

## Music and Language Skills

The relation between music training and language skills has been well-documented using both cross-sectional studies and longitudinal studies (Jantzen, Large, & Magne, 2016). Recent studies have proposed that one of the possible drivers of this association may be enhanced sensitivity to the prosodic cues of spoken language. Prosody corresponds to the intonational and rhythmic patterns that characterize spoken language. Like music, prosody is expressed through a combination of acoustic variations in frequency, intensity, duration, and spectral characteristics. The information conveyed by prosody extends over the combination of multiple speech units within words, and across phrases and sentences; sensitivity to prosodic cues may be a foundational aspect of spoken language acquisition from infancy through adulthood. For instance, prosody may facilitate language acquisition in infants by providing cues about boundaries between words (e.g., Jusczyk, Cutler, & Redanz, 1993). Children's development of phonemic awareness (i.e., the ability to recognize and manipulate the smallest units of speech sounds, known as phonemes) may also be dependent on the child's sensitivity to rhythmic structure and stress cues in speech (e.g., Goswami, 2011). Below, we review evidence supporting the influence of musical aptitude and/or musical training on different aspects of prosody perception. In addition, we discuss how positive effects of music on prosody sensitivity may be driving enhancement in other language-related skills such as grammatical and reading abilities.

### *Intonation*

When you speak, the pitch of your voice rises and falls, thus forming an intonation pattern that can convey emotions or distinguish whether you are asking a question or making a statement. Cross-sectional studies comparing musicians and non-musicians revealed that children and adults with at least four years of formal music education were better at detecting violations of sentence-final pitch contour than non-musicians (Magne, Schön, & Besson, 2006; Schön, Magne, & Besson, 2004). Using the event-related potential (ERP) method, a neuroscientific technique that allows experimenters to record brain activity time-locked to the presentation of a specific stimulus, these studies also showed that this behaviorally measured prosodic acuity was accompanied by larger negative ERP components and earlier positive ERP components in musicians than non-musicians. These findings were interpreted as reflecting potential experience-dependent plasticity in the auditory neural pathways of musicians. Using a design similar to those in the two previously discussed studies, two longitudinal studies (4 weeks and 6 months in length, respectively) using random group assignments to music instruction point to a causal link between music training and enhanced sensitivity to pitch variations underlying intonation patterns in spoken language (See Besson, Schön, Moreno, Santos, & Magne, 2007 for a review). Data in a large sample of adults with a wide range of musical abilities also suggest robust associations between speech pitch perception and musical rhythm perception skills regardless of general cognitive abilities (Morrill, McAuley, Dilley, & Hambrick, 2015).

### Speech Rhythm

A relationship between musical abilities and prosody sensitivity has also been found for the perception of the rhythmic cues afforded by the pattern of stressed and unstressed syllables in the speech signal. For instance, adult musicians are better than non-musicians at detecting words pronounced with an incorrect stress pattern (Marie, Magne, & Besson, 2011). This behavioral advantage was accompanied by an increased P200 component in the ERPs, which was interpreted as reflecting enhanced sensitivity to acoustic cues that underlie perception of temporal properties of the speech signal and associated stress patterns. Similarly, we recently found that differences in brain sensitivity to speech rhythm variations could be explained by variance in musical aptitude, even in individuals with less than two years of musical training (Magne, Jordan, & Gordon, 2016), where aptitude was assessed using a standardized measure of musical abilities. In our experiment, participants listened to sequences consisting of four bisyllabic words for which the stress pattern of the final word either matched or mismatched the stress pattern of the preceding words. Words with mismatching stress patterns elicited an increased negative ERP component (See Figure 5.1A). In addition, for the mismatching words stressed on the second syllable (i.e., the less common type of stress pattern in English), participants' musical rhythm aptitude significantly correlated with the size of the negative effect (See Figure 5.1B). Thus, this shared variability between musical rhythm and speech rhythm sensitivity supports domain-general neurocognitive resources for rhythm processing, applied both to music and to speech.

### Grammatical Skills

Sensitivity to rhythm and pitch appear to be particularly important for grammatical processing.[1] Prosodic fluctuations such as pauses and final lengthening provide important cues to linguistic events (e.g., grammatically relevant phrase boundaries). Prosody also facilitates grammar learning and perception of grammatical structures throughout development. For instance, final lengthening of phrases provides acoustic cues to the boundaries between clauses; these cues aid the listener in parsing complex sentences (Fernald & McRoberts, 1996). One study produced ERP findings showing that grammatical violations are more easily detected in sentences with very predictable timing (Schmidt-Kassow & Kotz, 2008). Interestingly, rhythm is not only important for grammar when speech timing varies: Listening to musical rhythms can also influence the way that children perform on grammar tasks (Przybylski, et al., 2013). In this study, the ability to detect grammatical errors in spoken sentences was enhanced in blocks of trials that followed periods of listening to musical sequences with rhythmically regular, beat-based musical rhythms, compared to periods of listening to rhythmically irregular rhythms where the beat is less clear. This finding may imply shared neural resources recruited for beat-based musical rhythms and grammatical processing in the brain.

This evidence for online influence of rhythm on grammatical processing is complemented by recent work showing associations between rhythm abilities and grammar skills. Gordon et al. (2015) used an individual differences approach to study the relation of rhythm perception abilities and grammar skills in 25 children with typical language development who

A. ERPs to Iambic Words

B. Correlation between Musical Rhythm Aptitude and Speech Rhythm Sensitivity

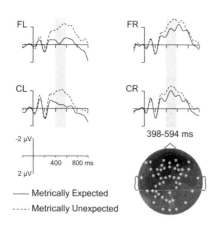

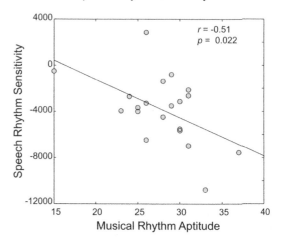

*Figure 5.1* (A) Grand-average ERPs recorded for iambic critical words. The top panel represents the averaged waveforms for metrically expected words (solid line) and metrically unexpected words (dashed line) at four selected electrodes (FL = frontal left, FR = frontal right, CL = central left, CR = central right). The latency range of the significant clusters is indicated in gray. Negative amplitude values are plotted upward. The bottom panel represents the topographic maps of the mean difference in scalp amplitudes in the latency range of the significant clusters (electrodes belonging to the cluster are indicated with a white asterisk). (B) Correlation between musical rhythm aptitude and speech rhythm sensitivity as indexed by the negative cluster sum (in microvolts) for unexpected iambic words. Lower values thus indicate larger ERPs and better speech rhythm sensitivity.

Adapted from Magne et al., 2016. Reproduced with permission from Elsevier.

had little or no musical training. Musical rhythm perception was tested with same-different discrimination tasks on short musical sequences. Spoken grammar was assessed through a task in which children were shown pictures and asked questions designed to elicit specific grammatical constructions (e.g., prepositions or the present progressive tense). The results showed a surprisingly large correlation (0.70), given the differences in task requirements and the fact that non-verbal IQ, music activities, and socio-economic status were controlled in the analysis.

Further analysis revealed that performance on the rhythm perception tasks accounted for individual differences in children's production of complex sentence structures (complex syntax and transformation/reorganization; Gordon, Jacobs, Schuele, & McAuley, 2015). Thus, children who had more fine-tuned perception and discernment of musical rhythms were also more likely to have stronger expressive language skills, and in particular were better able to produce complex sentence structures. These findings converged with prior work showing the influence of rhythmic listening on grammar performance (Przybylski et al., 2013) and with evidence reviewed above on the importance of temporal cues for the perception of grammatical variations. Moreover, shared neural resources between rhythm and grammar learning may be driving difficulties in language acquisition in children with language impairments (Cumming, Wilson, Leong, Colling, & Goswami, 2015).

Further converging evidence for shared resources between grammar and rhythm comes from data in adults showing that the number of hours of prior musical practice is significantly predictive of the ability to learn grammar in an artificial language (Brod & Opitz, 2012). Given the strong association between musical rhythm perception skills and speech rhythm sensitivity shown by Magne et al. (2016), it is theoretically possible that individuals who possess both heightened musical and speech rhythm sensitivity have an advantage during language acquisition due to enhanced sensitivity to prosodic cues to grammar. The individual differences approach holds promise as a potential tool to predict language development based on variations in early-developed or even innate musical abilities, and can provide complementary knowledge to that gained from cross-sectional work comparing children with and without musical training.

### Reading Abilities

Prosody sensitivity also plays an important role in the acquisition of reading skills. For instance, sensitivity to the rhythmic stress patterns in speech is a strong predictor of later reading abilities (e.g., Holliman, Wood, & Sheehy, 2010). Children with dyslexia may have deficits in perceiving speech rhythm cues as well as difficulties in processing musical rhythm (Huss, Verney, Fosker, Mead, & Goswami, 2011), suggesting a more general underlying rhythmic processing deficit. Together, these results point to the potential for music training to make an impact on language skills beyond speech perception, and suggest that music-based interventions could be used to target reading-related skills in both children with typical development and children with reading disabilities.

A recent meta-analysis (Gordon, Fehd, & McCandliss, 2015) compiled and reviewed evidence on the influence of musical training programs on a variety of literacy skills. Studies were included in the meta-analysis if they met the following criteria: they had to include a control group; test literacy outcomes (phonological awareness and reading fluency) pre- and post-music training (or control); and keep the amount of reading training constant across groups. Components of training programs and duration/intensity of training varied substantially across the thirteen studies, with eleven on typically developing children and two studies on children with atypical reading development. The meta-analysis results revealed that music-training programs consisting of at least forty cumulative hours were associated with gains in a subset of phonological outcomes corresponding to rhyming skills, with small effect sizes ($d = 0.2$). Interestingly, the small number of studies that included reading fluency outcomes did not show an aggregate transfer effect. The authors discuss possible confounding variables (SES, IQ, lack of random assignment, lack of suitable control interventions) that should be taken into consideration in future studies that seek to assess a transfer from music training to reading skills. At present, evidence in favor of an influence of music training on reading-related skills is modest at best.

### Mathematical and Visuospatial Abilities

Evidence for transfer between music training and mathematical skills remains somewhat mixed. Vaughn (2000) conducted two separate meta-analyses, one on 20 correlational studies and another on six experimental studies with a music training component. In both cases, she found significant positive correlations between musical expertise and mathematical skills. However, the mean effects sizes were rather small ($r = .15$ and $r = .13$, respectively). In another study not part of this meta-analysis, a correlation between music aptitude and mathematic skills was found in children at 4 years of age, but not in 5-year-olds (Anvari,

Trainor, Woodside, & Levy, 2002). A recent study examined two hundred and fifty 6–7 year-old Chinese elementary students for 11 consecutive semesters (Yang, Ma, Gong, Hu, & Yao, 2014). Academic performance in their native language, second language (English), and mathematics were compared between children who received out-of-school music training and those who received out-of-school painting lessons. Music training correlated with children's academic achievement in the second language, but not with their native language or mathematic abilities. In sum, the evidence for a benefit of music training on mathematical skills is sparse and requires further study.

Another cognitive domain which may be connected to music is spatial cognition, as seen before in the initial "Mozart Effect" study. Spatial and musical thought may be be connected in varied ways, for example in visual representation of music. In modern Western musical notation, pitches are visually represented using symbols located on, or between, lines on a five-line staff. Given the visual components of musical notation and their representation of corresponding spatial dimensions of sound generators for music production, it is thus not surprising that a number of studies have also examined the relationship between music training and visuospatial skills. Hetland (2000) conducted a meta-analysis of 15 experimental studies including 3–7 year-old children and music instruction ranging from six weeks to two years, and found a significant association between music training and spatial performance on a variety of spatial outcome measures, including some forms of mental rotation without the help of a physical model. In adults, several cross-sectional studies have also shown an association between musical expertise and visuospatial abilities. For instance, musicians were found to be faster than non-musicians at identifying on which side of a vertical or horizontal line a dot was flashed (Brochard, Dufour, & Despres, 2004). In an fMRI study, orchestral musicians were found to have better performance than non-musicians on a three-dimensional mental rotation task (Sluming, Brooks, Howard, Downes, & Roberts, 2007). In addition, while both musicians and non-musicians showed activation in the classic visuospatial brain networks during task performance (visual associative, premotor and superior parietal areas), musicians also showed increased activation in Broca's area. However, in one longitudinal study, performance enhancements did not persist through the end of the three-year training period (Costa-Giomi, 1999) and several others failed to find any significant improvements in spatial skills after short periods of musical training (e.g., Forgeard, Winner, Norton, & Schlaug, 2008; Mehr, Schachner, Katz, & Spelke, 2013). Different factors have been put forth to explain this discrepancy, such as the variety of tasks used to measure visuospatial outcomes and in some studies, the lack of a control measure to account for potential difference in general intellectual ability (Weiss, Biron, Lieder, Granot, & Ahissar, 2014), as well as the time at which individuals started taking music lessons during their childhood (Schellenberg & Weiss, 2013).

## Musical Abilities, Auditory Perception, and Executive Function

Since music and speech are expressed through variations of the same acoustic features, it may not come as a surprise that music training would be associated with benefits in language skills. Compared to non-musicians, musicians do show both functional and structural differences in cortical regions associated with auditory perception (for a review, see Barrett, Ashley, Strait, & Kraus, 2013). Differences between musicians and non-musicians can be seen in the subcortical regions of the auditory pathway as well, and more specifically in the brainstem response to acoustically complex sounds (cABR). Recordings of cABR have been used as a tool to measure participants' neural encoding of the specific characteristics of sound. Research using this method has consistently found that musicians have faster and more precise cABR for both music and speech (even if the language is foreign to the listener), as well as better neural encoding of speech embedded in background noise (for a review, see Strait & Kraus, 2014). Enhanced perceptual processes, however, do not fully explain why music training has also been associated with improved abilities in other non-auditory domains such as mathematical skills (e.g., Vaughn, 2000) and visuospatial abilities (e.g., Rauscher & Zupan, 2000), and more broadly with higher IQ (e.g., Schellenberg, 2015).

Recent findings suggest that such an association between music expertise and various cognitive abilities could be, at least partially, mediated by a positive effect of musical training on executive functions (e.g., Degé, Kubicek, & Schwarzer, 2011). In line with this view, it has also been proposed that enhancement of auditory perception skills, as observed in the cABR findings previously discussed, results from the strengthening of top-down influences between cognitive and sensory systems (e.g., Patel, 2011; Strait & Kraus, 2014). Likewise, Weiss and collaborators proposed that superior visuo-spatial skills observed in musicians may be the result of enhanced domain-general aspects of working memory rather than spatial ability per se (Weiss et al., 2014).

*Executive function* is an umbrella term referring to high-level processes that play an important role in the regulation of many of our daily activities. Defining the cognitive constructs underlying executive functions has been quite a challenge, and there are many influential models available in the literature (Jurado & Rosselli, 2007). In the discussion below, we will thus focus on the executive function subcomponents that have been most commonly investigated in the context of music training: Inhibitory control (i.e., ability to suppress conflicting responses); working memory (i.e., ability to temporarily store and manipulate information); attentional control (i.e., ability to select relevant information, while ignoring information deemed irrelevant); and cognitive flexibility (i.e., ability to quickly switch thinking or attention in order to adapt to new situations). Given that music training relies on many, if not all, of these executive function skills (Hannon & Trainor, 2007), it may not come as a surprise that musicians have been found to outperform non-musicians on many tasks tapping into executive function skills. However, as shown in the literature reviewed below, not all executive function abilities may be equally affected by, or associated with, music training.

Regarding inhibitory control, musicians outperformed non-musicians on a task involving spatial conflicts between a visual cue (i.e., an arrow pointing in a given direction) and its position on a screen, as well as on a task involving an auditory Stroop task between a word (*high/low*) and its pitch (Bialystok & Depape, 2009). Musical expertise has also been related to better performance on tasks of verbal and auditory working memory capacity, perhaps reflecting musicians' superior ability to sustain cognitive control during task performance (e.g., Pallesen et al., 2010), as well as the recruitment of additional neural resources not observed in non-musicians (Schulze & Koelsch, 2012). However, whether this advantage transfers to the visual modality remains a matter of debate. For instance, one study found both behavioral and neural evidence for improved visual working memory in musicians compared to non-musicians (George & Coch, 2011). Another study followed 6-to-25-year-old individuals' working memory performances on verbal and visuospatial tasks over the course of four years, and found an association between working memory capacity and the time spent practicing music (Bergman Nutley, Darki, & Klingberg, 2014). By contrast, two other studies failed to find difference in visual memory skills between musicians and non-musicians (e.g., Ho, Cheung, & Chan, 2003; Rodrigues, Loureiro, & Caramelli, 2014).

Similarly, results of studies investigating attentional control show somewhat mixed findings. There is ample evidence that auditory attention is enhanced in musicians (e.g., Strait & Kraus, 2014). However, musicians' visual attention is reported to be improved in some studies (e.g., Rodrigues et al., 2014) but not others (e.g., Strait, Kraus, Parbery-Clark, & Ashley, 2010; Martens, Wierda, Dun, de Vries, & Smid, 2015).

Cross-sectional studies also showed better performance in musicians than non-musicians on dual tasks and switching tasks, suggesting a correlation between music training and cognitive flexibility (Schroeder, Marian, Shook, & Bartolotti, 2016; Zuk, Benjamin, Kenyon, & Gaab, 2014). In line with these findings, older adults randomly assigned to a six-month period of individualized piano instruction showed improved cognitive flexibility compared to a control group, though it should be noted that this difference could be due to general mental stimulation since the control group did not receive any control activity during the same period (Bugos, Perlstein, McCrae, Brophy, & Bedenbaugh, 2007).

A few of the aforementioned studies have also utilized brain imaging methods in conjunction with standardized assessments of executive functions. When enhanced executive

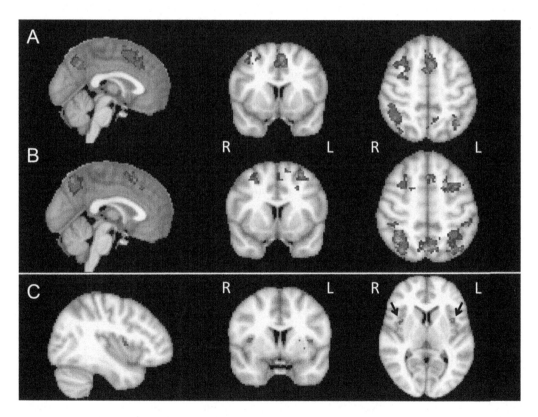

*Figure 5.2* Brain activation during task-switching in (A) musically trained and (B) musically untrained children, and (C) comparison between musically trained and untrained children. Children with music training showed greater activation in the ventro-lateral prefrontal cortex of both hemispheres (black arrows), a region classically associated with executive function.

Adapted from Zuk et al., 2014. Originally published under the Creative Commons Attribution (CC BY) license.

function skills were observed in musicians, they were associated with increased activity in brain regions classically associated with executive function, such as the prefrontal cortex and anterior cingulate cortex (e.g., Pallesen et al., 2010; Zuk et al., 2014).

In summary, there is some support for a positive effect of music training on executive functions, but the findings appear to be dependent on both the type of executive function components and the sensory modality being tested. A very recent study directly addressed this issue by investigating conflict monitoring, working memory, and cognitive flexibility in both visual and auditory modalities (Slevc, Davey, Buschkuehl, & Jaeggi, 2016). The results showed the strongest association between music ability and executive function was for performance on working memory tasks in both visual and auditory modalities (even after controlling for other possible confounds such as age, bilingualism experience, and socio-economic status). Thus, taken together, research findings to date argue for a combination of both domain-general and process-specific influence of music training on executive functions.

## Further Explanations for Transfer and Cognitive Enhancements

The wide body of evidence in favor of shared neural resources for music and other cognitive abilities stands in contrast to the small amount of evidence supporting a *causal* transfer from music training to other skills. It is entirely possible that pre-existing, innate differences, rather than musical training *per se*, are actually driving many of the reported effects of overlap between music and cognitive abilities, such that individuals who were born with enhanced musical, cognitive, and language potential are more likely to practice more and attain higher levels of achievement in these domains (Schellenberg, 2015; Thompson, Mosing, & Ullén, this volume). New insight on this question can be gleaned from recent studies that have used large-scale twin studies to examine the respective contributions of genetics and environment to musical achievement.

A series of studies by Mosing, Ullén, and colleagues have primarily used two genetic models to investigate the relationship between music abilities, music practice, cognitive abilities, and personality traits in a large cohort of Swedish twins. The authors employ a bivariate genetic model to discern environmental (practice) and genetically heritable influences. They also use an intra-pair difference model to test correlations between traits (e.g., practice hours versus IQ) within identical (monozygotic) twin pairs.

Mosing, Madison, Pedersen, Kuja-Halkola, and Ullén (2014) explored the relationship between music practice and music abilities, using self-reported estimates of lifetime musical practice and testing correlations with musical ability. Their results showed that total hours of lifetime practice were significantly heritable. In addition, contrary to hypotheses, the intrapair difference model revealed no further association of musical practice on music abilities after controlling for genetic influence. These results coincide with findings on heritable effects of both musical practice and musical achievement reported by Hambrick and Tucker-Drob (2015) on the National Merit Twin Study. Interestingly, these findings call into question conventional wisdom that extensive practice is uniquely responsible for musical expertise, and instead suggests that it is genetic predisposition that leads certain individuals to practice more and achieve more in the musical domain. Other recent work suggests that heritable and/or parental personality traits predict who will sign up for and stick with music lessons (Butkovic, Ullén, & Mosing, 2015; Corrigall & Schellenberg, 2015).

Mosing, Madison, Pedersen, and Ullén (2016) went on to investigate a far transfer of music practice to cognitive skills in the Swedish twin cohort. According to hypotheses set forth in the intra-twin pair difference model, a causal transfer in the subset of monozygotic twins would be demonstrated if the degree to which one twin practiced more than their co-twin was correlated with difference in IQ scores between the two twins. Although the authors did replicate previous findings of an association between music practice and IQ, they did not find support for the co-twin control hypothesis: Results showed that an individual who practiced more than their identical twin was not more likely to have a higher IQ. Furthermore, they reported that the association between music practice and IQ was attributable to genetic influences. In other words, they did not find evidence for a causal transfer of musical training on IQ, once genetics were factored out. These results stand in contrast to those from a study by Schellenberg (2004) in which children were randomly assigned to music lessons (keyboard or vocal performance), drama lessons or no lesson for 36 weeks. Pre-training vs. post-training comparison revealed a significantly larger increase in IQ for the music lesson groups than the drama and no-lesson groups. The discrepancy between the findings of these two studies, however, could be at least partially due to the fact that Mosing et al. (2016) used a non-verbal IQ measure whereas Schellenberg (2004) used a full-scale IQ measure. In addition, the age of the participants was different (average of 40.7 years for the former, and 6 years for the latter), and baseline (pre-musical-training) IQ in the adult study was not available. Further work is thus needed to better understand how gene-experience interactions at different phases of development contribute to the relation between music training and other cognitive abilities.

## Conclusion

In conclusion, there is a well-documented body of correlational evidence between musical training and cognitive enhancements, as well as between music aptitude and cognition, especially in the case of a near transfer from music to auditory expertise. Individual differences in speech sound sensitivity, grammar, and reading-related skills, also appear to be related to music skills, with recent findings of causal transfer in some of these aspects of language. The case for a causal far transfer from musical training to executive function is more variable, with findings varying across studies and for the type of executive function task. Twin studies and some related work on individual and familial personality traits have challenged previously held assumptions about far transfer and open up the possibility that music abilities and some of the associated cognitive benefits may be heritable and do not necessarily indicate casual effects of music training on other cognitive abilities. Future randomized trials and complex multi-factorial gene/environment modeling are needed to better understand the potential for far transfer from music training to non-musical cognitive skills.

## Note

1. Grammar refers to the set of rules governing the structure of a language, and in the context of the studies reviewed in this section, the definition of the term is limited to syntax and morphology.

## Core Reading

Gordon, R. L., Fehd, H. M., & McCandliss, B. D. (2015). Does music training enhance literacy skills? A meta-analysis. *Frontiers in Psychology, 6*, 1777. doi:10.3389/fpsyg.2015.01777
Gordon, R. L., Shivers, C. M., Wieland, E. A., Kotz, S. A., Yoder, P. J., & McAuley, J. D. (2015). Musical rhythm discrimination explains individual differences in grammar skills in children. *Developmental Science, 18*(4), 635–644.

Magne, C., Jordan, D. K., & Gordon, R. L. (2016). Speech rhythm sensitivity and musical aptitude: ERPs and individual differences. *Brain and Language, 153–154*, 13–19.

Mosing, M. A., Madison, G., Pedersen, N. L., & Ullén, F. (2016). Investigating cognitive transfer within the framework of music practice: Genetic pleiotropy rather than causality. *Developmental Science, 19*(3), 504–512.

Zuk, J., Benjamin, C., Kenyon, A., & Gaab, N. (2014). Behavioral and neural correlates of executive functioning in musicians and non-musicians. *PLoS ONE, 9*(6), e99868. doi:10.1371/journal. pone.0099868

## Further References

Anvari, S. H., Trainor, L. J., Woodside, J., & Levy, B. A. (2002). Relations among musical skills, phonological processing, and early reading ability in preschool children. *Journal of Experimental Child Psychology, 83*(2), 111–130.

Barrett, K. C., Ashley, R., Strait, D. L., & Kraus, N. (2013). Art and science: How musical training shapes the brain. *Frontiers in Psychology, 4*, 713. doi:10.3389/fpsyg.2013.00713

Bergman Nutley, S., Darki, F., & Klingberg, T. (2014). Music practice is associated with development of working memory during childhood and adolescence. *Frontiers in Human Neuroscience, 7*, 926. doi:10.3389/fnhum.2013.00926

Besson, M., Schön, D., Moreno, S., Santos, A., & Magne, C. (2007). Influence of musical expertise and musical training on pitch processing in music and language. *Restorative Neurology and Neuroscience, 2007*(25), 399–410.

Bialystok, E., & Depape, A. M. (2009). Musical expertise, bilingualism, and executive functioning. *Journal of Experimental Psychology: Human Perception and Performance, 35*(2), 565–574.

Brandt, A., Gebrian, M., & Slevc, L. R. (2012). Music and early language acquisition. *Frontiers in Psychology, 3*, 327. doi:10.3389/fpsyg.2012.00327

Brochard, R., Dufour, A., & Despres, O. (2004). Effect of musical expertise on visuospatial abilities: Evidence from reaction times and mental imagery. *Brain and Cognition, 54*(2), 103–109.

Brod, G., & Opitz, B. (2012). Does it really matter? Separating the effects of musical training on syntax acquisition. *Frontiers in Psychology, 3*, 543. doi: 10.3389/fpsyg.2012.00543

Bugos, J. A., Perlstein, W. M., McCrae, C. S., Brophy, T. S., & Bedenbaugh, P. H. (2007). Individualized piano instruction enhances executive functioning and working memory in older adults. *Aging and Mental Health, 11*(4), 464–471.

Butkovic, A., Ullén, F., & Mosing, M. A. (2015). Personality related traits as predictors of music practice: Underlying environmental and genetic influences. *Personality and Individual Differences, 74*, 133–138.

Corrigall, K. A., & Schellenberg, E. G. (2015). Predicting who takes music lessons: Parent and child characteristics. *Frontiers in Psychology, 6*, 282. doi: 10.3389/fpsyg.2015.00282

Costa-Giomi, E. (1999). The effects of three years of piano instruction on children's cognitive development. *Journal of Research in Music Education, 47*(3), 198–212.

Cumming, R., Wilson, A., Leong, V., Colling, L. J., & Goswami, U. (2015). Awareness of rhythm patterns in speech and music in children with specific language impairments. *Frontiers in Human Neuroscience, 9*, 672.

Degé, F., Kubicek, C., & Schwarzer, G. (2011). Music lessons and intelligence: A relation mediated by executive functions. *Music Perception, 29*, 195–201.

Fernald, A., & McRoberts, G. (1996). Prosodic bootstrapping: A critical analysis of the argument and the evidence. In J. L. Morgan & K. Demuth (Eds.), *Signal to syntax: Bootstrapping from speech to grammar in early acquisition* (pp. 365–388). Mahwah, NJ: Lawrence Erlbaum Associates, Inc.

Forgeard, M., Winner, E., Norton, A., & Schlaug, G. (2008). Practicing a musical instrument in childhood is associated with enhanced verbal ability and nonverbal reasoning. *PLoS ONE, 3*(10), e3566. doi:10.1371/journal.pone.0003566.

George, E. M., & Coch, D. (2011). Music training and working memory: An ERP study. *Neuropsychologia, 49*(5), 1083–1094.

Gordon, R. L., Jacobs, M. S., Schuele, C. M., & McAuley, J. D. (2015). Perspectives on the rhythm-grammar link and its implications for typical and atypical language development. *Annals of the New York Academy of Sciences, 1337*, 16–25.

Goswami, U. (2011). A temporal sampling framework for developmental dyslexia. *Trends in Cognitive Sciences, 15*(1), 3–10.

Hambrick, D. Z., & Tucker-Drob, E. M. (2015). The genetics of music accomplishment: Evidence for gene-environment correlation and interaction. *Psychonomic Bulletin & Review, 22*(1), 112–120.

Hannon, E. E., & Trainor, L. J. (2007). Music acquisition: Effects of enculturation and formal training on development. *Trends in Cognitive Sciences, 11*(11), 466–472.

Hetland, L. (2000). Learning to make music enhances spatial reasoning. *Journal of Aesthetic Education, 34*(3/4), 179–238.

Ho, Y. C., Cheung, M. C., & Chan, A. S. (2003). Music training improves verbal but not visual memory: Cross-sectional and longitudinal explorations in children. *Neuropsychology, 17*(3), 439–450.

Holliman, A. J., Wood, C., & Sheehy, K. (2010). Does speech rhythm sensitivity predict children's reading ability 1 year later? *Journal of Educational Psychology, 102*(2), 356–366.

Huss, M., Verney, J. P., Fosker, T., Mead, N., & Goswami, U. (2011). Music, rhythm, rise time perception and developmental dyslexia: Perception of musical meter predicts reading and phonology. *Cortex, 47*(6), 674–689.

Jantzen, K. J., Large, E. W., & Magne, C. (Eds.) (2016). *Overlap of neural systems for processing language and music.* Frontiers Media: Lausanne. doi:10.3389/978–2–88919–911–2.

Jurado, M. B., & Rosselli, M. (2007). The elusive nature of executive functions: A review of our current understanding. *Neuropsychology Review, 17*(3), 213–233.

Jusczyk, P. W., Cutler, A., & Redanz, N. J. (1993). Infants' preference for the predominant stress patterns of English words. *Child Development, 64*(3), 675–687.

Magne, C., Schön, D., & Besson, M. (2006). Musician children detect pitch violations in both music and language better than nonmusician children: Behavioral and electrophysiological approaches. *Journal of Cognitive Neuroscience, 18*(2), 199–211.

Marie, C., Magne, C., & Besson, M. (2011). Musicians and the metric structure of words. *Journal of Cognitive Neuroscience, 23*(2), 294–305.

Martens, S., Wierda, S. M., Dun, M., de Vries, M., & Smid, H. G. (2015). Musical minds: Attentional blink reveals modality-specific restrictions. *PLoS ONE, 10*(2), e0118294. doi:10.1371/journal.pone.0118294.

Mehr, S. A., Schachner, A., Katz, R. C., & Spelke, E. S. (2013). Two randomized trials provide no consistent evidence for nonmusical cognitive benefits of brief preschool music enrichment. *PLoS ONE, 8*(12), e82007.

Morrill, T. H., McAuley, J. D., Dilley, L. C., & Hambrick, D. Z. (2015). Individual differences in the perception of melodic contours and pitch-accent timing in speech: Support for domain-generality of pitch processing. *Journal of Experimental Psychology General, 144*(4), 730–736.

Mosing, M. A., Madison, G., Pedersen, N. L., Kuja-Halkola, R., & Ullén, F. (2014). Practice does not make perfect: No causal effect of music practice on music ability. *Psychological Science, 25*(9), 1795–1803.

Pallesen, K. J., Brattico, E., Bailey, C. J., Korvenoja, A., Koivisto, J., Gjedde, A., & Carlson, S. (2010). Cognitive control in auditory working memory is enhanced in musicians. *PLoS ONE, 5*(6), e11120. doi:10.1371/journal.pone.0011120.

Patel, A. D. (2011). Why would musical training benefit the neural encoding of speech? The OPERA hypothesis. *Frontiers in Psychology, 2*, 142.

Pietschnig, J., Voracek, M., & Formann, A. K. (2010). Mozart effect–shmozart effect: A meta-analysis. *Intelligence, 38*(3), 314–323.

Przybylski, L., Bedoin, N., Krifi-Papoz, S., Herbillon, V., Roch, D., Leculier, L., . . . Tillmann, B. (2013). Rhythmic auditory stimulation influences syntactic processing in children with developmental language disorders. *Neuropsychology, 27*(1), 121–131.

Rauscher, F. H., Shaw, G. L., & Ky, C. N. (1993). Music and spatial task performance. *Nature, 365*(6447), 611–611.

Rauscher, F. H., & Zupan, M. A. (2000). Classroom keyboard instruction improves kindergarten children's spatial-temporal performance: A field experiment. *Early Childhood Research Quarterly, 15*(2), 215–228.

Rodrigues, A. C., Loureiro, M., & Caramelli, P. (2014). Visual memory in musicians and non-musicians. *Frontiers in Human Neuroscience, 8.* doi: doi.org/10.3389/fnhum.2014.00424

Schellenberg, E. G. (2004). Music lessons enhance IQ. *Psychological Science, 15*(8), 511–514.

Schellenberg, E. G. (2015). Music training and speech perception: A gene-environment interaction. *Annals of the New York Academy of Sciences, 1337,* 170–177.

Schellenberg, E. G., & Weiss, M. (2013). Music and cognitive abilities. In D. Deutsch (Ed.), *The psychology of music (3rd Ed.)* (pp. 499–550). San Diego, CA: Academic Press.

Schmidt-Kassow, M., & Kotz, S. A. (2008). Entrainment of syntactic processing? ERP-responses to predictable time intervals during syntactic reanalysis. *Brain Research, 1226,* 144–155.

Schön, D., Magne, C., & Besson, M. (2004). The music of speech: Music training facilitates pitch processing in both music and language. *Psychophysiology, 41*(3), 341–349.

Schroeder, S. R., Marian, V., Shook, A., & Bartolotti, J. (2016). Bilingualism and Musicianship Enhance Cognitive Control. *Neural Plasticity,* vol. 2016, Article ID 4058620, 11 pages, 2016. doi:10.1155/2016/4058620

Schulze, K., & Koelsch, S. (2012). Working memory for speech and music. *Annals of the New York Academy of Sciences, 1252,* 229–236.

Slevc, L. R., Davey, N. S., Buschkuehl, M., & Jaeggi, S. M. (2016). Tuning the mind: Exploring the connections between musical ability and executive functions. *Cognition, 152,* 199–211.

Sluming, V., Brooks, J., Howard, M., Downes, J. J., & Roberts, N. (2007). Broca's area supports enhanced visuospatial cognition in orchestral musicians. *Journal of Neuroscience, 27*(14), 3799–3806.

Strait, D. L., & Kraus, N. (2014). Biological impact of auditory expertise across the life span: Musicians as a model of auditory learning. *Hearing Research, 308,* 109–121.

Strait, D. L., Kraus, N., Parbery-Clark, A., & Ashley, R. (2010). Musical experience shapes top-down auditory mechanisms: Evidence from masking and auditory attention performance. *Hearing Research, 261*(1–2), 22–29.

Vaughn, K. (2000). Music and mathematics: Modest support for the oft-claimed relationship. *Journal of Aesthetic Education, 34*(3–4), 149–166.

Weiss, A. H., Biron, T., Lieder, I., Granot, R. Y., & Ahissar, M. (2014). Spatial vision is superior in musicians when memory plays a role. *Journal of Vision, 14*(9).

Yang, H., Ma, W., Gong, D., Hu, J., & Yao, D. (2014). A longitudinal study on children's music training experience and academic development. *Scientific Reports, 4,* 5854.

# 6

# MUSIC, BRAIN, AND MOVEMENT

## Time, Beat, and Rhythm

*Molly J. Henry and Jessica A. Grahn*

## Introduction

When we listen to musical rhythm, we are often compelled to spontaneously tap our hands or feet, nod our heads, sway our bodies, or even dance to the beat. Movement along with a beat in musical rhythms seems to emerge automatically and at a very young age. Indeed, children as young as 5 months old move their bodies rhythmically in response to music (although their movements are not always synchronized with the music; Zentner & Eerola, 2010). One potential reason for this automatic, and sometimes uncontrollable, urge to move along with the beat in musical rhythms is that listening to rhythms (even without actually moving) activates motor areas of the brain, including the supplementary motor area, premotor cortex, basal ganglia, and cerebellum (Grahn & Brett, 2007). Moreover, listening to beat-based auditory rhythms increases communication, or "connectivity," between auditory and motor regions (Chen, Penhune, & Zatorre, 2008b; Grahn & Rowe, 2009; see also Loui & Przysinda, this volume). Thus, automatic activation of motor regions and connectivity between auditory and motor regions during rhythm listening might underlie the tight connection between rhythm and movement. The goal of this chapter will be to explore the link between musical rhythm and movement. We will first review functional brain imaging work, revealing the motor system's involvement in the perception of rhythm and beat. Then, we will describe how moving along with a rhythm actually improves perception of that rhythm. We will suggest that neural oscillations in the delta (0.5–4 Hz) and beta (~13–30 Hz) frequency bands might constitute a mechanism supporting auditory–motor connectivity, thereby allowing for anticipation and better perception of the events that comprise musical rhythms. Finally, we will suggest that the rising popularity of noninvasive brain stimulation paradigms that probe motor system excitability will provide another angle from which we can gain insight about why we move to the beat.

## Functional Imaging Work Reveals Activation of Motor Areas During Rhythm and Beat Perception

Perceiving musical rhythms, even in the absence of overt movement, activates brain areas including the supplementary motor area, premotor cortex, cerebellum, and basal ganglia, all of which are traditionally associated with overt movement and motor functions (Bengtsson, et al., 2009; Chen, Penhune, & Zatorre, 2008a; Grahn & Brett, 2007; Grahn & Rowe, 2013; Schubotz & Von Cramon, 2001). Rhythms that are composed of intervals that are *integer ratios* of one another (for example, 250ms:500ms = 1:2), and have *accents* (emphases by loudness or other means) occurring at regular intervals, tend to elicit the perception of a regular, salient beat. Such rhythms are thus termed "*beat-based rhythms.*" In particular, the basal ganglia and supplementary motor area are more active during the perception of rhythms that induce a beat compared to rhythms that do not (Grahn & Brett, 2007; Grahn & Rowe, 2009; Teki, Grube, Kumar, & Griffiths, 2011).

Rhythms that do not induce a beat *("non-beat-based rhythms")* rely instead on *absolute timing* mechanisms, where event durations are measured in real-time units rather than as ratios related to other events. Perception of non-beat-based rhythms is more strongly associated with the cerebellum (Grube, Cooper, Chinnery, & Griffiths, 2010; Grube, Lee, Griffiths, Barker, & Woodruff, 2010; Teki, Grube, Kumar, et al., 2011).

Neuropsychological work supports this dissociation: Compromised basal ganglia function in patients with Parkinson's disease results in a selective deficit in discriminating subtle changes in beat-based rhythms but not in non-beat-based rhythms in a same–different rhythm comparison task (Grahn & Brett, 2009). Conversely, patients with cerebellar degeneration have a selective deficit for non-beat-based timing, but not for beat-based timing; these patients performed as well as controls on tasks that involved comparing rhythms, but were impaired on tasks that required comparing the durations of isolated intervals (Grube, Cooper, et al., 2010). This dissociation, along with behavioral and imaging data from healthy participants, has led to suggestions that "beat-based" versus "interval-based" (Grahn & McAuley, 2009), or "beat-based" (i.e., relative) versus "duration-based" (i.e., absolute) timing mechanisms (Grube, Cooper et al., 2010; Teki, Grube, & Griffiths, 2011; Teki, Grube, Kumar et al., 2011) rely on different neural circuitry and may be used to different extents by healthy participants. For example, Grahn and McAuley (2009) made use of a tempo-judgment task and a specially designed ambiguous rhythm that could be perceived in two different ways. Individuals that heard the rhythm as "speeding up" were assumed to measure the final sequence interval with respect to a pulse induced by the rhythm, and were therefore considered to be making use of a *beat-based timing* strategy. Conversely, individuals that heard the same rhythm as "slowing down" were assumed to compare the final sequence interval to the individual intervals making up the rhythm, and were thus considered to be making use of an *interval-based timing* strategy. They found that individuals who were more likely to use a beat-based timing strategy to classify the ambiguous rhythm relied more on the supplementary motor area (midline surface anterior to primary motor cortex), frontal regions including left premotor cortex and left inferior frontal gyrus, as well as the left insula (within the lateral sulcus separating the temporal and frontal cortices). On the other hand, individuals who were more likely to use an interval-based strategy to classify the same rhythm more strongly activated the left superior temporal gyrus (located laterally) and right premotor cortex (Grahn & McAuley, 2009). Similarly, Teki and colleagues (2011) asked participants to judge the duration of the final interval of an isochronous sequence or jittered sequence relative to the immediately preceding interval. They reasoned that a jittered context would force participants to use an absolute, duration-based timing strategy. As such, they observed activation in the cerebellum and inferior olive (subcortical brain structures located at the back of the brain). They also assumed that an isochronous context would promote use of a relative, beat-based timing strategy, which activated a network comprising the basal ganglia and thalamus (both subcortical midline structures), supplementary motor area, premotor cortex, prefrontal cortex, and super temporal gyrus. Taken together, these studies suggest that different neural areas underlie beat-based and non-beat-based timing.

During rhythm and beat perception, brain regions do not act in isolation, but rather, in concert as functional networks. The relationships between activation in different brain regions are often assessed by measures of connectivity, which measure correlations in activity between two brain areas over time (functional connectivity) and how the strength of those correlations is altered by stimulus features, task conditions, etc. The degree of connectivity between brain areas is modulated by rhythmic features. For example, listening to beat-based rhythms, as compared to non-beat-based rhythms, increased connectivity between the basal ganglia and supplementary motor, premotor, and auditory cortical areas (Grahn & Rowe, 2009), as measured in this case using a technique referred to as *psychophysiological interaction*, PPI. This was especially the case when beat locations were physically accented by an increase in intensity or duration. Thus, beat and meter not only activate auditory and motor areas, but also increase communication within and between auditory and motor networks.

*[handwritten margin note: brain areas experience connectivity when work together]*

## Movement Alters Perception of and Brain Responses to Rhythms

Not only does listening to rhythms activate motor areas of the brain, but in turn, movement changes perception of, and brain responses to, rhythms. For example, Phillips-Silver and Trainor (2005, 2007) bounced babies (or had adults bounce) along with an ambiguous rhythm—one group was bounced in a way that was consistent with a binary-grouping interpretation of the ambiguous rhythm, while another group was bounced in a way that was consistent with a ternary-grouping interpretation of the same ambiguous rhythm. When infants and adults were later presented with physically accented versions of the rhythm, both infants and adults were biased to recognize a binary or ternary accented version of the rhythm as familiar, respectively (adults explicitly indicated recognition, while infants listened longer to rhythms that were congruent with the way they had been bounced). This is despite the original auditory presentation being physically unaccented and metrically ambiguous. Rhythmic movement along with rhythms—for example, tapping a finger along with the sound—can also influence sensitivity to rhythm, and in particular participants' abilities to detect subtle timing deviations (Manning & Schutz, 2013). In this study, participants tapped in time with an isochronous sequence—a sequence comprised solely of a series of equally spaced events—then judged whether a probe tone that was presented after a brief pause occurred "on time" or not. Finger tapping along with the sequence improved participants' timing judgments, specifically of probe tones that were presented late, as long as the participants tapped to keep time through the pause. Engaging in movement therefore appears to alter rhythm perception and improve timing accuracy.

Another approach to understanding rhythm in the neural system is to record the brain's electrical activity using a method called electroencephalography, or EEG, while listening to rhythm. EEG records electrical signals from electrodes on the scalp, and the signals obtained in this way can be analyzed with an eye towards neural "signatures" of perception, cognition, or movement. For example, responses that are time- and phase-locked to the onsets of stimuli are referred to as *evoked responses* or *event-related potentials* (ERPs). Components of ERPs are given names according to their timing and polarity. A P300 is a positive-going electrical deflection, taking place around 300ms after the onset of the triggering stimulus.

The P300 ERP component is often interpreted as an index of attentional allocation, so modulations of the P300 by movement can be interpreted as evidence that movement in time with a rhythm may improve allocation of attention to time points at which events are expected to occur. Indeed, pedaling an ergometer in time with isochronous tone sequences increased the magnitude of the P300 component of event-related potentials in response to oddball tones, events which were unpredictable or "out of place" in their surrounding sequences (Schmidt-Kassow, Heinemann, Abel, & Kaiser, 2013). Moreover, individuals exhibiting more accurate synchronization performance had larger-amplitude P300s, suggesting that their attentional focus to on-the beat pedal strokes was greater than that at other points in time. Such changes in the P300 are in line with the predictions of dynamic attending theory, which hypothesizes that attention waxes and wanes coupled to the rhythmic structure of events in a sequence (Henry & Herrmann, 2014; Jones, 1976, 2004). Further support for movement improving attentional allocation to expected time points (at the expense of unexpected time points) comes from a recent study in which participants attended a sequence of target tones while simultaneously ignoring a sequence of interleaved distractor tones (Morillon, Schroeder, & Wyart, 2014). Participants had to integrate pitch information across all target tones, judging their mean pitch against the pitch of a reference tone. This paradigm allowed the authors to use modeling techniques in order to quantify the contribution of each individual target and distractor tone to the final decision (referred to as the "sensory gain" of each tone). When participants tapped their finger in time with the target tones, sensory gain was increased for target tones and decreased for distractor tones, demonstrating increased attention to the target tones. Moreover, sensory gain was highest for individual target tones for which finger taps were most precisely aligned with the auditory stimulus.

Taken together, these studies demonstrate that rhythmic movement in time with isochronous sequences improves perception of the individual events making up those sequences, potentially by improving attentional allocation to expected time points. However, a major caveat is that most studies use isochronous sequences with little or no metrical structure—no hierarchical grouping of tones (see Martens & Benadon, this volume)—so it's not clear whether these studies inform us about *beat perception* (as opposed to tracking sequences in which the regularity and the presence of sequence tones are one and the same), which happens in response to many nonisochronous sequences. In order to examine this question, one study (Su & Pöppel, 2012) examined the effects of movement on beat finding in "metrically complex" rhythms. Such rhythmic sequences (as defined in Grahn & Brett, 2007), are composed of intervals that are integer ratios of one another, and thus "make sense" in terms of the durational relationships of notes to one another—but which nonetheless do not give rise to a strong sense of the beat, as the particular serial arrangement of the intervals makes the beat difficult to find. Initially, during the "beat-finding" period, participants either simultaneously heard and moved along with the sequence (whether the movement was finger tapping, foot tapping, or head nodding was left up to the participant) or only heard the sequence and were not permitted to move. Then, during the "beat-production" period, all participants moved along with the beat (once they had discovered it). Movement during beat finding led to more stable beat production (i.e., more trials with <10% *coefficient of variation*, a measure of how consistent or variable the produced intervals are; a lower CoV means a more stable set of produced intervals, and thus better beat production). This was true for both musicians and nonmusicians. Thus, movement along with nonisochronous, metrically complex rhythms leads to a more stable beat percept later on. This finding has important implications for making use of finger-tapping tasks to measure beat perception in rhythms that vary in complexity, as movement in time with complex rhythms actually strengthens the sense of the beat compared to listening alone.

## Neuronal Synchronization as a Mechanism for Auditory–Motor Coupling

The empirical work reviewed thus far strongly suggests interaction between auditory and motor brain regions during rhythm and beat perception. Long-range communication between brain regions is hypothesized to be supported by synchronization of neural oscillations (Fries, 2015; see also Loui & Przysinda, this volume). Of special interest in the context of beat perception are neural oscillations with frequencies corresponding to the stimulus (beat) rate, most likely in the delta frequency band (0.5–4 Hz/250–2000 ms, or 240 to 60 beats per minute, which encompasses the range of rates within which a sense of "the beat" is felt; Parncutt, 1994). Neural oscillations in the beta band (~13–30 Hz) are also likely to be important, as they are associated with the motor system (Engel & Fries, 2010) and synchronize across relatively long distances across the brain (Kopell, Ermentrout, Whittington, & Traub, 2000). Moreover, beta oscillations become pathological in Parkinson's disease (Hammond, Bergman, & Brown, 2007), a disorder which is characterized by motor system dysfunction and difficulty discriminating changes in beat-based rhythms. We will briefly review the current state of knowledge on beta oscillations and stimulus-rate entrainment, and suggest that delta–beta phase–amplitude coupling across auditory–motor regions might provide the mechanism underlying our desire to move to the beat in musical rhythms and the perceptual enhancements associated with the satisfaction of temporal predictions.

Neural oscillations can be measured intra-cortically as local field potentials (LFPs) or at the scalp using EEG or a related method, magnetoencephalography (MEG). These methods are used in studies of neural oscillations to record and analyze the various frequencies of brain activity in terms of their strengths (or amplitudes) and phase relations to stimulus rhythms. These oscillations are understood to reflect coordinated cyclic fluctuations of neuronal excitability (Buzsaki & Draguhn, 2004) that influence both *psychophysical performance*—performance on a task which is designed to measure perceptual thresholds or to maintain near-threshold performance (Busch & VanRullen, 2010; Henry & Obleser, 2012)—and the probability of neuronal firing (Lakatos, Karmos, Mehta, Ulbert, & Schroeder, 2008). That is, stimulus events coinciding with the excitable phase of neural oscillations are more likely to be detected, are more quickly responded to, and elicit larger evoked responses than events co-occurring with an inhibitory neural phase (see Fig. 6.1). Neural oscillations synchronize with external (exogenous) stimulus rhythms through a process called *entrainment* (Thut, Schyns, & Gross, 2011), bringing excitable phases of the neural oscillation into line with temporally expected stimulus events (Schroeder & Lakatos, 2009). In turn, stimulus events are better perceived when they occur at an expected time relative to an unexpected time (for a review, see Henry & Herrmann, 2014). Moreover, synchronization of neural oscillations across disparate brain regions provides a means for neuronal communication; signals from a sending brain region are more likely to be received when they coincide with high-excitability phases in the target brain region. Restated, communication requires *coherence*, synchrony between two or more continuous time series of brain activity (Fries, 2015).

Low-frequency, delta-band neural oscillations (0.5–4 Hz) in sensory cortices are entrained by rhythmic structure not only for auditory stimuli but also in the visual modality (Schroeder & Lakatos, 2009). For beat-based auditory rhythms, neural entrainment occurs at multiple distinct frequencies, most importantly at the beat rate (Nozaradan, Peretz, Missal, & Mouraux, 2011). Indeed, it has been hypothesized that perception of a beat might result from *nonlinear resonance* of a neural oscillatory system at the beat rate, causing enhanced oscillation strength at a subharmonic of the base inter-onset-interval, where the subharmonic corresponds to the beat frequency (Large, 2010; Large, this volume). Thus, beat-rate entrainment of delta oscillations to auditory rhythms would result in alignment of excitable neural phases with expected beat locations, leading to augmented neural responses and better perceptual sensitivity for events occurring at on-beat relative to off-beat locations (Bolger, Coull, & Schön, 2014; Jones & Pfordresher, 1997).

Higher-frequency, beta-band oscillations (~13–30 Hz) often originate in motor brain regions (Engel & Fries, 2010) and are modulated by both executed and imagined movement (Schnitzler, Salenius, Salmelin, Jousmäki, & Hari, 1997). Beta synchronization increases in anticipation of a sensory event, and beta power in motor/premotor regions is modulated in anticipation of an upcoming action (Engel & Fries, 2010). Beta-band responses reflect feedback from higher-order to more basic sensory brain regions (Fontolan, Morillon, Liegeois-Chauvel, & Giraud, 2014) and may index "error corrections" in response to violations of expectations (Arnal & Giraud, 2012). As such, in cognitive tasks, beta oscillations (measured from various brain regions including frontal and parietal cortices) are thought to reflect a top-down neural signal, often described as being related to updating predictions about the world (Arnal & Giraud, 2012; Engel & Fries, 2010; Fontolan, et al., 2014).

With respect to rhythm and beat perception, modulations of beta power have been associated with temporal prediction. In the context of listening to isochronous sequences at different tempi, Fujioka and colleagues (2012) observed a desynchronization of beta oscillations and a concomitant power reduction—a reduction in the strength of beta-band oscillations—following auditory events, followed by an *anticipatory* "beta rebound" (i.e., an increase in beta power) that peaked just prior to the onset of the subsequent (expected) tone. These fluctuations in beta power were tempo specific (i.e., the rebound rate was proportionate to stimulus tempo) and were absent when the sequence timing was made random. MEG source localization techniques, used to assess where in the brain some activity occurs, revealed that this beta power originated in bilateral auditory cortices, as well as in motor brain regions including premotor cortex, supplementary motor area, and cerebellum. Returning to the idea that beta oscillations reflect top-down processes, Iversen, Repp, and Patel (2009) observed increased beta power associated with imagined accents in nonisochronous rhythms. Participants listened to repeating sequences of two tones followed by a silence (in a xxoxxo pattern), and imagined accents on either the first (XxoXxo) or second tone (xXoxXo). Beta power was stronger in response to tones that were imagined as accented, despite all the tones being acoustically identical. Similarly, Fujioka, Ross, and Trainor (2015) asked participants to imagine either a binary (XxXxXx) or ternary (XxxXxx) accent structure during listening to isochronous sequences, and observed differences in the degree of beta desynchronization following tones with and without imagined accents. Finally, beta power recorded directly from human primary motor cortex of epilepsy patients using electrocorticography (ECOG), where electrodes are placed directly on the surface of the brain, was found to fluctuate in time with the temporal structure of a rhythm. In this ECOG study, participants waited for the presentation of a specific cue stimulus at one of two serial positions. Beta power ceased to track temporal structure after presentation of the cue stimulus, that is, when participants no longer had to attend to the stimulus, fluctuations in beta power no longer related to the structure of the stimulus. Thus, the findings are consistent with a tight link between beta oscillations and top-down attention (Saleh, Reimer, Penn, Ojakangas, & Hatsapoulos, 2010).

Interestingly, beta oscillations originating in the basal ganglia become pathological with Parkinson's disease (see Fachner, this volume). LFP recordings can be made in human basal ganglia during surgery for implantation of deep brain stimulators, used to help modulate brain activity so as to alleviate the abnormal brain signals present in Parkinson's disease. These LFP recordings reveal increased beta-band power and (pathological) increased synchronization between the basal ganglia and cortex (Hammond et al., 2007). Medications such as Levodopa, which synthesizes into dopamine, an important neurotransmitter in the brain (see Granot, this volume) suppress beta power and lead to clinical improvements. Thus,

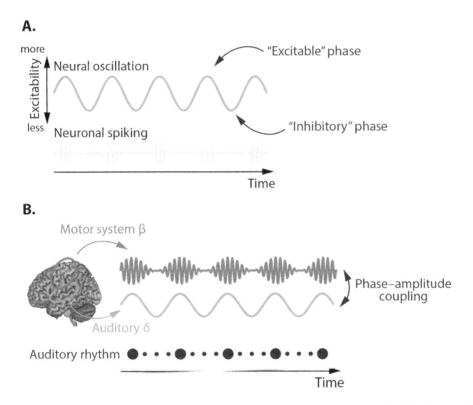

*Figure 6.1* (A) Neural oscillations reflect excitability fluctuations. During periods of high excitability ("excitable" phases, plotted up in the figure), neuronal spiking is more likely and psychophysical performance is better. During periods of low excitability ("inhibitory" phases, plotted down in the figure), neuronal spiking is less likely and psychophysical performance is worse. (B) Hypothetical scheme for auditory–motor interaction during rhythm and beat perception. Low-frequency delta oscillations (light gray) originating from sensory (auditory) areas are entrained by the temporal structure of an auditory rhythm (black). Power fluctuations of higher-frequency beta oscillations (dark gray) originating from motor regions are nested within auditory–delta oscillations. Thus, auditory–motor interaction during rhythm and beat perception is accomplished via delta–beta phase–amplitude coupling.

the pathological enhancement of beta power that arises from dopamine depletion disrupts motor function (Engel & Fries, 2010). We suggest that the deficits observed for Parkinson's patients in discriminating changes in beat-based rhythms (Grahn & Rowe, 2009) might be due in part to these pathological beta oscillations produced by the basal ganglia.

To summarize, neural oscillations in both the delta and beta frequency bands have been linked to rhythm and beat perception. We hypothesize that synchronization of neural oscillations across auditory and motor brain regions provides a means for neuronal communication during rhythm and beat processing (Large, Herrera, & Velasco, 2015). Fujioka et al. (2012) suggested that functional auditory–motor coupling might occur via beta-band neural synchronization. Here, we suggest that interactions between delta and beta frequency bands occur via *phase–amplitude coupling*, where the amplitude fluctuations of a relatively high-frequency neural oscillation align with the phase of a relatively low-frequency neural oscillation. Phase–amplitude coupling might provide another mechanism for auditory–motor interactions (see Figure 6.1B). That is, beta power modulations would be nested within lower-frequency (delta) excitability fluctuations entrained at the beat rate of a rhythm (Arnal, Doelling, & Poeppel, in press; Figure 6.1B). Such a mechanism would allow for communication between auditory and motor brain regions. Moreover, top-down beta signals increase entrainment precision in the delta band (Saleh et al., 2010). Since the delta phase modulates psychophysical performance, increasing entrainment precision effectively translates to increased precision of temporal expectations and perceptual sensitivity to events presented at expected times (e.g., on the beat).

## Non-Invasive Brain Stimulation Provides a New window onto the Role of the Motor System in Rhythm and Beat Perception

MEG/EEG recordings performed on humans, and invasive intracortical recordings in patients and non-human animals, allow for the measurement of neural oscillations, and thus for the inference of the momentary excitability of a particular brain region. Transcranial magnetic stimulation (TMS), a noninvasive brain stimulation technique, provides an alternative means to estimate momentary excitability of the corticospinal motor system. Briefly, TMS involves passing a magnetic field through the skull, inducing a temporary, focal electrical pulse in the underlying cortex (O'Shea & Walsh, 2007). For the purposes of this literature review, we will only discuss single-pulse TMS (as opposed to repetitive TMS, or rTMS), which, when applied over primary motor cortex, elicits a motor evoked potential (MEP) (i.e., a muscle twitch). MEP magnitude (measured, for example, from the hand or forearm) scales with motor system excitability, allowing the experimenter to infer corticospinal motor system excitability.

The large literature implicating the motor system in rhythm and beat perception suggests that motor system excitability, and thus MEP magnitude, should be modulated during listening to auditory rhythms. Indeed, larger MEPs have been measured during listening to beat-based compared to non-beat-based rhythms (Cameron, Stewart, Pearce, Grube, & Muggleton, 2012). Moreover, high-groove music (i.e., music that strongly induces the desire to move (Janata, Tomic, & Haberman, 2012) is associated with increased MEP magnitude relative to low-groove music, at least for musicians (Stupacher, Hove, Novembre, Schütz-Bosbach, & Keller, 2013). In addition, differences in MEP magnitude between high- and low-groove music were observed specifically for on-beat events; MEPs did not differ between high- and low-groove music when TMS pulses were applied off beat.

Although the literature using TMS to relate motor system excitability to rhythm and beat processing is sparse, this area is ripe for future work. Exciting research questions made tractable by the use of TMS will further delineate the motor system's role in beat perception and include: (1) What is the time course of motor system excitability during rhythm listening, and how is it modulated by the presence of a beat or, put another way, how does excitability differ between beat-based vs. non-beat-based rhythms (Cameron et al., 2012)? (2) Does excitability reflect the degree to which a musical rhythm makes the listener *want* to move (Stupacher et al., 2013)? (3) How do individual differences such as preferred tempo (Michaelis, Wiener, & Thompson, 2014) or beat perception ability relate to motor system excitability? Moreover, TMS provides a potentially useful tool to examine motor excitability in Parkinson's patients in the context of rhythm and beat perception without relying on invasive recordings that are made prior to or during surgery (and therefore only in relatively severe disease states). Understanding the nature of motor system excitability changes in Parkinson's patients will pave the way for developing ideas about the relationships between rhythm and beat on the one hand, and the motor system on the other.

## Conclusions

Listening to musical rhythm gives rise to an automatic, early developing, and sometimes uncontrollable urge to move our bodies. Functional imaging work suggests that this desire might arise, at least in part, from activation of motor brain regions and increased functional coupling between auditory and motor regions while listening to musical rhythm, even in the absence of overt movement. In this chapter, we have explored the tight link between rhythm, beat, and movement by reviewing behavioral work demonstrating that, not only does rhythm affect movement, but the reverse is also true—moving along with a rhythm changes our perception of that rhythm, increasing perceptual sensitivity to time and pitch and solidifying our sense of the beat. We have also suggested that neural synchrony between auditory and motor brain regions in the form of delta–beta phase–amplitude coupling might constitute a mechanism for functional auditory–motor coupling, and ultimately our desire to move to the beat in musical rhythm. Future work using noninvasive brain stimulation techniques will further clarify the time course of motor system involvement in rhythm and beat perception, and how the motor system's role might change depending on the nature of the stimulus, individual abilities, or disease.

## Core Reading

Cameron, D. J., Stewart, L., Pearce, M. T., Grube, M., & Muggleton, N. G. (2012). Modulation of motor excitability by metricality of tone sequences. *Psychomusicology: Music, Mind, and Brain, 22*, 122–128.

Fujioka, T., Trainor, L. J., Large, E. W., & Ross, B. (2012). Internalized timing of isochronous sounds is represented in neuromagnetic Beta oscillations. *Journal of Neuroscience, 32*, 1791–1802.

Grahn, J. A., & Brett, M. (2007). Rhythm and beat perception in motor areas of the brain. *Journal of Cognitive Neuroscience, 19*(5), 893–906.

Grahn, J. A., & Rowe, J. B. (2009). Feeling the beat: Premotor and striatal interactions in musicians and nonmusicians during beat perception. *Journal of Neuroscience, 29*, 7540–7548.

Henry, M. J., & Herrmann, B. (2014). Low-frequency neural oscillations support dynamic attending in temporal context. *Timing & Time Perception 2*, 62–86.

Iversen, J. R., Repp, B. H., & Patel, A. D. (2009). Top-down control of rhythm perception modulates early auditory responses. *Annals of the New York Academy of Sciences, 1169*, 58–73.

Phillips-Silver, J., & Trainor, L. J. (2005). Feeling the beat: Movement influences infant rhythm perception. *Science, 308,* 1430.

Su, Y.-H., & Pöppel, E. (2012). Body movement enhances the extraction of temporal structures in auditory sequences. *Psychological Research, 76,* 373–382.

## Further References

Arnal, L. H., Doelling, K. B., & Poeppel, D. (in press). Delta–beta coupled oscillations underlie temporal prediction accuracy. *Cerebral Cortex.* doi:10.1093/cercor/bhu103

Arnal, L. H., & Giraud, A.-L. (2012). Cortical oscillations and sensory predictions. *Trends in Cognitive Sciences, 16,* 390–398.

Bengtsson, S. L., Ullen, F., Ehrsson, H., Hashimoto, T., Kito, T., Naito, E., & Sadato, N. (2009). Listening to rhythms activates motor and premotor cortices. *Cortex, 45,* 62–71.

Bolger, D., Coull, J. T., & Schön, D. (2014). Metrical rhythm implicitly orients attention in time as indexed by improved target detection and left inferior parietal activation. *Journal of Cognitive Neuroscience, 26,* 593–605.

Busch, N. A., & vanRullen, R. (2010). Spontaneous EEG oscillations reveal periodic sampling of visual attention. *Proceedings of the National Academy of Sciences USA, 109,* 16048–16053.

Buzsaki, G., & Draguhn, A. (2004). Neuronal oscillations in cortical networks. *Science, 25,* 1926–1929.

Chen, J. L., Penhune, V. B., & Zatorre, R. J. (2008a). Listening to musical rhythms recruits motor regions of the brain. *Cerebral Cortex, 18,* 2844–2854.

Chen, J. L., Penhune, V. B., & Zatorre, R. J. (2008b). Moving on time: Brain network for auditory-motor synchronization is modulated by rhythm complexity and musical training. *Journal of Cognitive Neuroscience, 20,* 226–239.

Engel, A. K., & Fries, P. (2010). Beta-band oscillations—signalling the status quo? *Current Opinion in Neurobiology, 20,* 156–165.

Fontolan, L., Morillon, B., Liegeois-Chauvel, C., & Giraud, A.-L. (2014). The contribution of frequency-specific activity to hierarchical information processing in the human auditory cortex. *Nature Communications, 5,* 4694. doi:10.1038/ncomms5694

Fries, P. (2015). Rhythms for cognition: Communication through coherence. *Neuron, 88,* 220–235.

Fujioka, T., Ross, B., & Trainor, L. J. (2015). Beta-band oscillations represent auditory beat and its metrical hierarchy in perception and imagery. *The Journal of Neuroscience, 35,* 15187–15198.

Grahn, J. A., & Brett, M. (2009). Impairment of beat-based rhythm discrimination in Parkinson's disease. *Cortex, 45,* 54–61.

Grahn, J. A., & McAuley, J. D. (2009). Neural bases of individual differences in beat perception. *NeuroImage, 47,* 1894–1903.

Grahn, J. A., & Rowe, J. B. (2013). Finding and feeling the musical beat: Striatal dissociations between detection and prediction of regularity. *Cerebral Cortex, 23,* 913–921.

Grube, M., Cooper, F. E., Chinnery, P. F., & Griffiths, T. D. (2010). Dissociation of duration-based and beat-based auditory timing in cerebellar degeneration. *Proceedings of the National Academy of Sciences USA, 107,* 11597–11601.

Grube, M., Lee, K. H., Griffiths, T. D., Barker, A. T., & Woodruff, P. (2010). Transcranial magnetic theta-burst stimulation of the human cerebellum distinguishes absolute, duration-based from relative, beat-based perception of subsecond time intervals. *Frontiers in Psychology, 1,* 171. doi: 10.3389/fpsyg.2010.00171

Hammond, C., Bergman, H., & Brown, P. (2007). Pathological synchronization in Parkinson's disease: Networks, models and treatments. *Trends in Neurosciences, 30,* 357–364.

Henry, M. J., & Obleser, J. (2012). Frequency modulation entrains slow neural oscillations and optimizes human listening behavior. *Proceedings of the National Academy of Sciences USA, 109,* 20095–20100.

Janata, P., Tomic, S., & Haberman, J. M. (2012). Sensorimotor coupling in music and the psychology of the groove. *Journal of Experimental Psychology: General, 141,* 54–75.

Jones, M. R. (1976). Time, our lost dimension: Toward a new theory of perception, attention, and memory. *Psychological Review, 83*(5), 323–355.

Jones, M. R. (2004). Attention and timing. In J. G. Neuhoff (Ed.), *Ecological psychoacoustics* (pp. 49–85). San Diego, CA: Elsevier, Inc.

Jones, M. R., & Pfordresher, P. Q. (1997). Tracking melodic events using joint accent structure. *Canadian Journal of Experimental Psychology, 51*, 271–291.

Kopell, N. J., Ermentrout, B., Whittington, M. A., & Traub, R. D. (2000). Gamma rhythms and beta rhythms have different synchronization properties. *Proceedings of the National Academy of Sciences USA, 97*, 1867–1872.

Lakatos, P., Karmos, G., Mehta, A.D., Ulbert, I., & Schroeder, C. E. (2008). Entrainment of neuronal oscillations as a mechanism of attentional selection. *Science, 320*, 110–113.

Large, E. W. (2010). Neurodynamics of music. In M. R. Jones (Ed.), *Music perception* (pp. 201–231). New York, NY: Springer.

Large, E. W., Herrera, J. A., & Velasco, M. J. (2015). Neural networks for beat perception in musical rhythm. *Frontiers in Systems Neuroscience, 9*, 159. doi:10.3389/fnsys.2015.00159

Manning, F., & Schutz, M. (2013). "Moving to the beat" improves timing perception. *Psychonomic Bulletin & Review, 20*, 1133–1139.

Michaelis, K., Wiener, M., & Thompson, J. C. (2014). Passive listening to preferred motor tempo modulates corticospinal excitability. *Frontiers in Human Neuroscience, 8*, 252. doi:10.3389/fnhum.2014.00252

Morillon, B., Schroeder, C. E., & Wyart, V. (2014). Motor contributions to the temporal precision of auditory attention. *Nature Communications, 5*, 5255. doi:10.1038/ncomms6255

Nozaradan, S., Peretz, I., Missal, M., & Mouraux, A. (2011). Tagging the neuronal entrainment to beat and meter. *The Journal of Neuroscience, 31*, 10234–10240.

O'Shea, J., & Walsh, V. (2007). Transcranial magnetic stimulation. *Current Biology, 17*, R196–R199.

Parncutt, R. (1994). A perceptual model of pulse salience and metrical accents in musical rhythms. *Music Perception, 11*, 409–464.

Phillips-Silver, J., & Trainor, L. J. (2007). Hearing what the body feels: Auditory encoding of rhythmic movement. *Cognition, 105*(3), 533–546.

Saleh, M., Reimer, J., Penn, R., Ojakangas, C. L., & Hatsapoulos, N. G. (2010). Fast and slow oscillations in human primary motor cortex predict oncoming behaviorally relevant cues. *Neuron, 65*, 461–471.

Schmidt-Kassow, M., Heinemann, L. V., Abel, C., & Kaiser, J. (2013). Auditory-motor synchronization facilitates attention allocation. *NeuroImage, 82*, 101–106.

Schnitzler, A., Salenius, S., Salmelin, R., Jousmäki, V., & Hari, R. (1997). Involvement of primary motor cortex in motor imagery: A neuromagnetic study. *NeuroImage, 6*, 201–208.

Schroeder, C. E., & Lakatos, P. (2009). Low-frequency neuronal oscillations as instruments of sensory selection. *Trends in Neurosciences, 32*, 9–18.

Schubotz, R. I., & Von Cramon, D. Y. (2001). Interval and ordinal properties of sequences are associated with distinct premotor areas. *Cerebral Cortex, 11*, 210–222.

Stupacher, J., Hove, M. J., Novembre, G., Schütz-Bosbach, S., & Keller, P. E. (2013). Musical groove modulates motor cortex excitability: A TMS investigation. *Brain and Cognition, 82*, 127–136.

Teki, S., Grube, M., & Griffiths, T. D. (2011). A unified model of time perception accounts for duration-based and beat-based timing mechanisms. *Frontiers in Integrative Neuroscience, 5*, 90. doi: 10.3389/fnint.2011.00090

Teki, S., Grube, M., Kumar, S., & Griffiths, T. D. (2011). Distinct neural substrates of duration-based and beat-based auditory timing. *The Journal of Neuroscience, 31*, 3805–3812.

Thut, G., Schyns, P., & Gross, J. (2011). Entrainment of perceptually relevant brain oscillations by non-invasive rhythmic stimulation of the human brain. *Frontiers in Psychology, 2*, 170. doi: 10.3389/fpsyg.2011.00170

Zentner, M., & Eerola, T. (2010). Rhythmic engagement with music in infancy. *Proceedings of the National Academy of Sciences USA, 107*, 5768–5773.

# 7

# MUSIC AND HEALTH
## Physical, Mental, and Emotional

*Suvi Saarikallio*

### The Music and Health Framework

Music and health is one of the most rapidly growing research areas in music cognition. Scholars in psychology, neuroscience, psychoneuroendocrinology, and public health have taken a serious interest in investigating cultural activities such as music as a source of health, healing, and wellbeing. In 2012, the OUP volume *Music, Health & Wellbeing* (Eds. MacDonald, Kreutz, & Mitchell) brought together experts on music therapy, music medicine, public health, community music, and music education in a first step towards synthesizing our current understandings of how music connects to health and wellbeing. The realm of music and health is a vast one, touching on all aspects of human life. Therefore, this chapter begins with a presentation of a framework that provides an overall picture of the main factors involved (Figure 7.1). In this framework *health* and healing are conceptualized as covering the entire continuum from recovery and treatment to health promotion and health-beneficial growth. As illustrated in the figure, the framework further emphasizes the fact that musical healing always occurs in a certain context and is essentially a music-related act, performed and impacted by the individuals who engage with the music.

### The Contexts of Healing

The major contextual dimension in musical healing differentiates the professional/clinical use of music in therapy and medicine from the potentially self-therapeutic engagement with music in everyday life. This dimension particularly involves differences in how consciously the health-relevant goals of the musical activity are laid down, and whether these goals are set solely by the individual him/herself or together with health professionals such as therapists, physicians, or social workers. In between clinical care and daily music listening, there also exists a variety of contexts, such as community music therapy and community work, use of music at work places, and music in educational settings (MacDonald, Kreutz, & Mitchell, 2012). Another major, and closely related, contextual dimension concerns treatment versus prevention, distinguishing between situations where music is particularly used for recovery and rehabilitation, and situations where music acts to promote resilience, mental wellbeing, personal resources, and adaptive development. The way in which a musical act relates

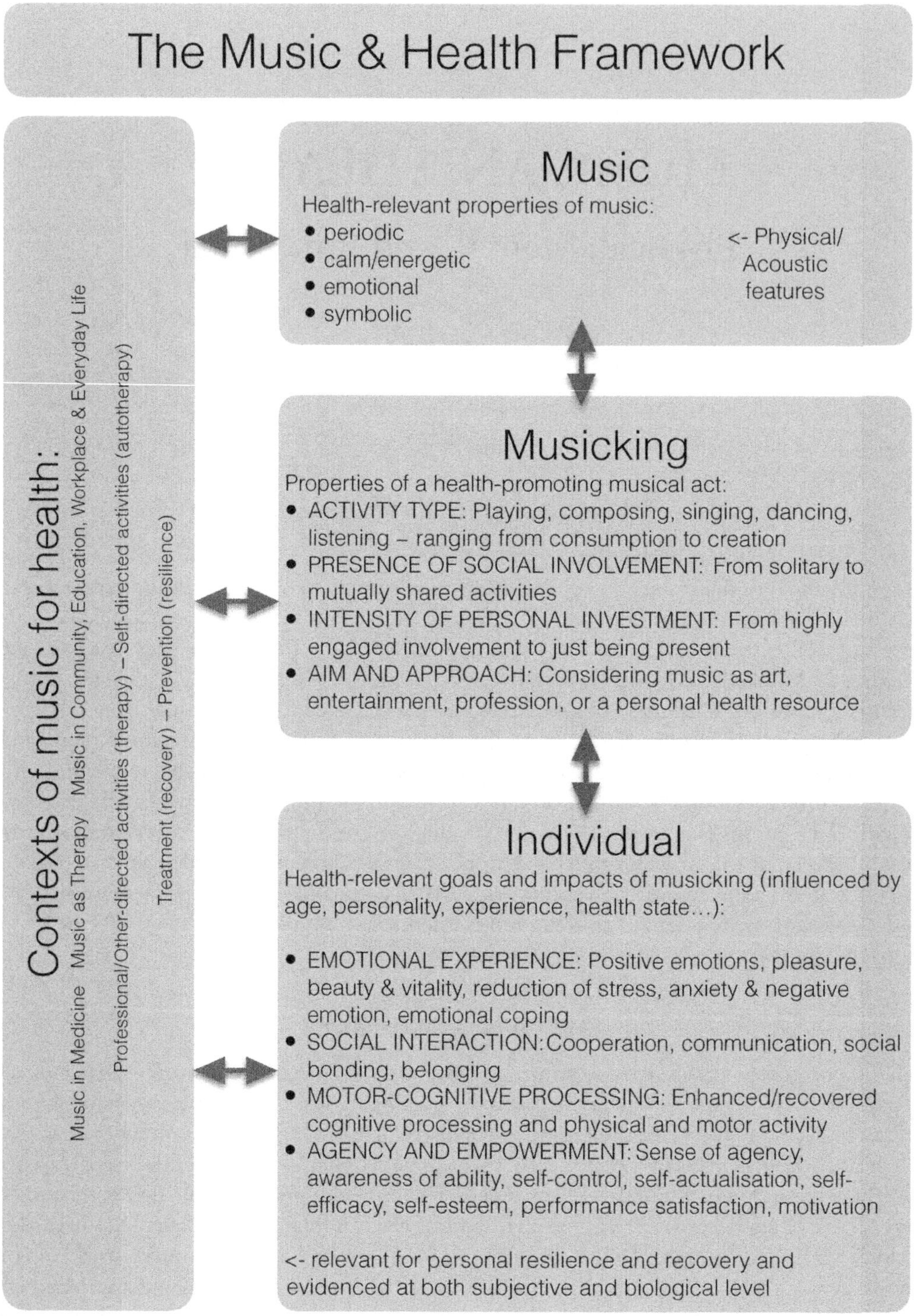

# The Music & Health Framework

## Music

Health-relevant properties of music:
- periodic
- calm/energetic
- emotional
- symbolic

<- Physical/ Acoustic features

## Musicking

Properties of a health-promoting musical act:
- ACTIVITY TYPE: Playing, composing, singing, dancing, listening – ranging from consumption to creation
- PRESENCE OF SOCIAL INVOLVEMENT: From solitary to mutually shared activities
- INTENSITY OF PERSONAL INVESTMENT: From highly engaged involvement to just being present
- AIM AND APPROACH: Considering music as art, entertainment, profession, or a personal health resource

## Individual

Health-relevant goals and impacts of musicking (influenced by age, personality, experience, health state...):

- EMOTIONAL EXPERIENCE: Positive emotions, pleasure, beauty & vitality, reduction of stress, anxiety & negative emotion, emotional coping
- SOCIAL INTERACTION: Cooperation, communication, social bonding, belonging
- MOTOR-COGNITIVE PROCESSING: Enhanced/recovered cognitive processing and physical and motor activity
- AGENCY AND EMPOWERMENT: Sense of agency, awareness of ability, self-control, self-actualisation, self-efficacy, self-esteem, performance satisfaction, motivation

<- relevant for personal resilience and recovery and evidenced at both subjective and biological level

## Contexts of music for health:

Music in Medicine   Music as Therapy   Music in Community, Education, Workplace & Everyday Life

Professional/Other-directed activities (therapy) – Self-directed activities (autotherapy)

Treatment (recovery) – Prevention (resilience)

*Figure 7.1* The music and health framework.

to these dimensions determines some of the characteristics and health-goals of the activity. However, despite varying on these major premises, the contexts of musical healing often appear to be characterized by highly similar health-impacts. For instance, stress reduction and the induction of positive moods has been systematically observed as a result of both music-based treatment interventions (Clark & Harding, 2012; Erkkilä et al. 2011; Field, Martinez, Nawrocki, et al. 1998; Maratos, Gold, Wang, & Crawford 2008; Menon & Levitin, 2005; Pelletier, 2004), and self-directed daily music engagement (Saarikallio & Erkkilä, 2007; Chin & Rickard, 2013; Van den Tol & Edwards, 2015). Some underlying similarities across contexts can therefore be assumed.

## Music and Musicking as the Forum for Healing

In explaining the linkage of music to health, the elaboration of the specific musical characteristics involved is of particular importance for understanding the special nature of music as a health resource, compared to other resources. Music as a physical and auditory phenomenon contains acoustic and perceptual properties, related to features like time, sound quality, and loudness, which form the basis of its health-relevant affordances. For instance, the rhythmic framework of musical expression enables entrainment and mutual synchronization between music and the individual, and between individuals, activating body movement and providing opportunities for social and cooperative acts and rewards (e.g. Thaut, 2005). The varying levels and degrees of qualities like tempo and sound volume impact the perception of music as calm or energetic, offering possibilities for influencing the energy levels of individuals. Consistent links have been demonstrated between a variety of acoustic features and the perception of music as expressive of a range of basic emotions (Gabrielsson & Lindström, 2001; Juslin & Laukka, 2003, 2004; Juslin & Timmers, 2010), providing resources for the emotional uses of music. Finally, the nature of music as a symbolic expression of various mental processes (Langer, 1942) and social identities (Frith, 2004) allows highly personalized and customized usage of music in music therapy. Such therapy may focus on personal identity, with both internal contemplation and interpersonal expression as therapeutic components (to read more about music as a symbolic process in a therapy context, see Fachner, this volume).

Despite the fact that music contains highly relevant characteristics for impacting human health, music itself is not considered in the present framework as the reason, but rather as the forum for healing. That is, health-related musical engagement is conceptualized first and foremost as an activity of an individual, in line with the ideas that underlie the notion of "musicking" (Small, 1998), which presents music as a process rather than an object. While the activities of singing, playing, composing, improvising, or dancing can easily be seen as acts, the consumption of music through listening can also fundamentally be considered as an engaged act, into which the listener brings his or her personal goals and attitudes.

The act of musicking can thus consist of a wide continuum of behaviors that range from the consumption of to the creation of musical material. Furthermore, these activities can be characterized by a variety of properties that play a role regarding the act's health-impact. For instance, the activity can range from a solitary engagement to an intrinsically social act, whether it be group drumming, participation in a concert with a thousand fans, listening to a favorite song with a group of friends, performing to strangers, improvising with a therapist, singing in a choir, or dancing intimately with a partner (cf. Lamont, this volume).

Another relevant element is the intensity of personal involvement. Sometimes musicking means merely to be present in a situation where there is music, without much personal interest or even attention. Sometimes, in contrast, the involvement is passionate, personal, and intensive, whether it is because of the love for the type of music being listened to, because of the social character of the situation, or because of a process of externalizing some deeply personal content to a musical form. Studies have shown that in the context of daily music listening clear differences exist between highly engaged and non-engaged listeners and that the amount of engagement is linked with the amount of personal and purposeful mood and activity supporting uses of music (Greasley & Lamont, 2011). The intensity of personal investment also involves issues of focused attention and flow, states that are linked with high personal satisfaction and subjective wellbeing (Csíkszentmihályi, 1990, 2014). Finally, the act of musicking is fundamentally grounded in the personal attitude and understanding of the very meaning of the act, ranging from considering the act as an art experience to daily entertainment and from a professional act to using music as a personal health-resource, such as listening to "my comfort music." With these considerations expressed, it is clear that the act of musicking consists of an immensely complex entity of factors that are likely to be influential upon the observed healing-effects of music and that the current research has only grasped the surface of their interactive influences.

## The Elements of Healing in the Individual

In this section of the chapter we discuss the individual level of musical healing, focusing on the different elements that broadly constitute healing within an individual. This again is a broad topic, since health itself is a vast area of interrelated elements that range from motor behavior to socio-emotional behavior and from understanding disorders and their treatments to the nature and encouragement of human flourishing. The first element to be discussed is emotion, which possibly is the most evident aspect of the health-relevance of music, and, as stated before, is widely evidenced in both clinical and everyday life contexts. The impact of music on emotion appears central for why music is relevant for both physical and mental health (MacDonald, Kreutz, & Mitchell, 2012), observed across cultures (Saarikallio, 2012), and involving processes that range from an increased awareness of emotion to the ability of managing them: inducing pleasurable emotions and adaptively regulating the avoidable ones (Saarikallio, 2016). The efficacy of music in evoking positive emotions has been indexed by self-reports (Juslin & Laukka, 2004; Scherer & Zentner, 2008); brain activation in areas connected to motivation, pleasure, and reward, including the ventral striatum, dorsomedial midbrain, amygdala, hippocampus, insula, cingulate cortex, and orbitofrontal cortex (cf. Granot, this volume; see also Blood & Zatorre, 2001; Koelsch, 2014; Menon & Levitin, 2005); shifts of frontal brain activity towards the left hemisphere (Field, Martinez, Nawrocki, et. al, 1998; Schmidt & Trainor 2001); and a variety of other physiological indicators of positive affect involving heart rate, respiration, blood pressure, skin conductivity, and biochemical responses (Bartlett, 1996).

In addition to such physiological markers, more centrally mental and emotional effects have been documented. Interventions with depressed individuals serve as a particularly illustrative example of the positive impact of music on mood (Erkkilä, Punkanen, Fachner, & Gold 2011; Field, Martinez, Nawrocki, et al. 1998; Maratos, Gold, Wang, & Crawford 2008). The impacts of music on reducing stress and anxiety have widely been evidenced through research on the endocrine system. These effects particularly involve the hypothalamic-pituitary-adrenocortical axis (HPA), a central hormone of which is cortisol, and decreases of cortisol levels have been systematically observed in relation to music listening tasks, singing, play-ing, and music therapy interventions (for a review, see Koelsch & Stegemann, 2012; Kreutz, Quiroga Murcia, & Bongard, 2012). Other systematically observed hormonal changes indica-tive of the reduced stress levels in relation to music engagement include increases of oxytocin and β-endorphin (Kreutz et al., 2012).

Finally, the efficiency of music in pain management has been shown in a variety of experimental studies (Mitchell & MacDonald, 2012) and music has been efficiently used to alleviate preoperative anxiety and stress, and to function as a non-pharmacological pain man-agement tool in medical operations and surgery (Bernatzky, Strickner, Presch, Wendtner, & Kullich, 2012; Spintge, 2012). Considering the strong and widely evidenced impact of music on emotion (Timmers, this volume), it is no surprise that experiences related to the induc-tion and regulation of emotional valence and arousal are a major reason for engaging in music in daily life (Juslin & Laukka, 2004), a major component of why music is rewarding (Mas-Herrero, Marco-Pallares, Lorenso-Seva, Zatorre, & Rodriguez-Fornells, 2013), and a characterizing element of musical coping and mental health maintenance (Miranda, Gaudrea, Debrosse et al., 2012).

Another major area of the health-relevance of music involves social interaction. The evo-lutionary significance of music is likely to be grounded in the ability of music to strengthen social bonding and cooperation (Clayton, 2009; Cross, 2014, 2016; Mithen, 2005). Many philosophical approaches to music embrace it fundamentally as a socially embedded and interactive act (Elliott, & Silverman, 2012) and the social dimension of music is considered as a core feature of its health-impact regardless of cultural context (Saarikallio, 2012). The use of musical elements for socio-emotional bonding and communication emerges early in mother-infant interaction, being an important part of learning emotional communication and forming a secure attachment (Malloch, 1999; Trevarthen, 1999, 2002; Trehub, Unyk, & Trainor, 1993; Oldfield, 1993; Trainor & Cirelli, 2015).

Later in development, engagement in joint musical activity encourages prosocial coopera-tive behavior in 4 year-olds (Kirschner & Tomasello, 2012). Studies on group singing and dancing also indicate clear connections of musical activity to increased experiences of social communication and bonding (Davidson & Emberly, 2012; Clift, 2012; Quiroga Murcia & Kreutz, 2012). As a medium for communication, music functions at a deep level of affective, amodal, and symbolic expression (Stern, 2010) and can therefore serve the human interac-tion even when language fails, such as with autistic patients (Ockelford, 2012). While the social affordances of music are highly relevant for all musical contexts from education to group therapy, they are perhaps most pronounced and elaborated in the context of com-munity music therapy, a rapidly growing field of practice and research, which is grounded on the idea of using music for empowering people through increased social participation, identification, and interaction with their community (Ansdell & DeNora, 2012; Murray & Lamont, 2012; Ruud, 2012).

The multifaceted nature of music as a social resource is illustrated with a list of "seven Cs" by Koelsch and Stegemann (2012): making *contact* with others, understanding others through social *cognition*, feeling *co-pathy* for the feelings of others, *communicating* emotional informa-tion, *coordinating* action through synchronized movement, *cooperating* for a shared musical goal, and feeling social *cohesion* and belonging to others. Koelsch and Stegemann particularly discuss the physiological correlates of these experiences at the levels of neural, hormonal, and immune system activity, showing how the impact of music has been widely evidenced also through physiological reactions, not only the ones linked with increased positive affect and stress reduction as discussed above but also the ones more directly linked with social bonding, such as release of oxytocin.

The impact of music on cognitive and motor behavior forms yet another major healing-relevant area. Music training and music listening have been systematically connected with improved cognitive functioning involving, for instance, spatial-temporal processing and concentration (Schellenberg, 2012; Costa-Giomi, 2012). In particular, the long-term dedicated commitment to learning a musical instrument appears to have positive impacts on children's cognitive development (Costa-Giomi, 2012).

The ability of music to activate motor-cognitive processing can be used for healing purposes in a variety of different contexts that range from a systematic use of music in therapy and rehabilitation with cognitively impaired individuals (e.g. Ockelford & Markou, 2012) to community activities with elderly people who naturally face reduction of motor-cognitive functioning (Gembris, 2012). Recent studies show promising results in all of these areas: music therapy work with cognitively impaired children (e.g. Ockelford & Markou, 2012), hospital settings where music listening is enhancing cognitive recovery after stroke (Särkämö et al., 2008), and everyday musical hobbies functioning as a protection against dementia in old age (Gembris, 2012). To read more about the clinical/therapeutic use of music for improving motor-cognitive behavior see Fachner (this volume) and Henry and Grahn (this volume). Different musical activities also appear to rely on different underlying impact mechanisms. With regards to music listening, the most plausible mechanism explaining improved cognitive processing appears to be the mood and arousal hypothesis: Cognitive performance becomes improved because music helps to achieve an optimal arousal and mood state (Schellenberg, 2012). Meanwhile, the various forms of music making and musical learning involve a wide combination of mechanisms with differing impacts from the rudimental training of motor-cognitive skills to the more executive level of learning concentrated goal-orientation for achievement. For example, the activity of dancing—fundamentally bodily movement—has been linked with fitness indicators such as aerobic capacity, balance, coordination, elasticity, muscle strength, kinesthetic awareness, and body control (Quiroga Murcia & Kreutz, 2012). Engagement in musical hobbies in general provides a forum for learning to merge pleasure with goal-oriented hard work through the experiences of deep concentration and flow (Csíkszentmihályi & Larson, 1984). Overall, the impact of music on improved cognitive and motor behavior is also strongly linked with the socio-emotional aspects that make music engagement a particularly motivating and enjoyable form of motor-cognitive training.

The final, more meta-level element of musical healing could be labeled as agency and empowerment, an element that partly arises as a constitution of the abovementioned elements. "Sense of agency" is a concept that refers to the subjective awareness of being the person who is initiating, executing, and controlling one's own actions, bodily movement, and thoughts—taking ownership of one's behavior (Jeannerod, 2003). The sense of agency relates to experiencing oneself as an independent self, and is reflected in the brain by activation of particular cortical networks, impairments of which relate to pathological conditions such as schizophrenia (Farrer, et. al., 2004). It is closely linked to concepts such as internal locus of control (Rotter, 1966) and self-efficacy (Bandura, 1977), which both are highly relevant for health and wellbeing (Roddenberry & Renk, 2010) and further link to experiences of self-esteem (Judge, Erez, Bono, & Thoresen, 2002). Ruud (1997) connects the sense of agency to health resources as defined by Aaron Antonovsky: Feeling that life is comprehensible (predictable), manageable (conceivable), and meaningful. Ruud shows that music can serve as a fundamental daily resource for such experiences by achieving a greater awareness of one's own possibilities of action and providing feelings of mastery, achievement, and empowerment.

The ability of music to promote self-agency is a core element in understanding how music supports adolescents' healthy psychosocial development (Laiho, 2004; Gold, Saarikallio & McFerran, 2011) and the increased experience of personal empowerment is a fundamental reason for why music is important for persons with long-term illnesses (Batt-Rawden, et al., 2005). The empowering capacity of music ranges from the mundane situations of providing personalization to daily activities through music listening choices (Sloboda & O'Neill, 2001) to music-induced feelings of self-control serving as the mediator for the ability to manage pain. Recent findings show that the feeling of empowerment is a core constituent of why music is considered pleasurable in daily life (Maksimainen & Saarikallio, 2015). The health-relevance of personal agency in music engagement is also illustrated by situations where agency is lacking: Adolescents who were receiving support for depression, anxiety, or emotional and behavioral problems appeared relatively unable, in comparison to their healthy peers, to identify, take responsibility for, and change their maladaptive patterns of music use towards more healthy patterns (McFerran & Saarikallio, 2013). Overall, the ability of music to empower individuals is an understudied and vaguely conceptualized topic, compared to emotion, social interaction, and motor-cognitive behavior, but should definitely be considered as a fundamental part of understanding how music functions to promote health and in developing resilience and wellbeing.

### The Interactive Nature of the Framework

In the framework presented above, healing is not purely seen as a result of music engagement by a person, but rather as an act that is fundamentally initiated and directed by that very person. The impacts of musical healing are therefore seen as closely intertwined with personal goals and reasons for musical engagement, and are fundamentally rooted in individual factors such as personality, age, and mental health state. This line of thinking is strongly supported by the distinct individual differences observed in musical engagement, even with the very same musical material. Certain types of individuals appear to be more likely to gain certain types of benefits from music: Music listening, for instance, effectively reduces stress levels, particularly in non-musicians (VanderArk & Eli, 1993), adolescents, and females (Pelletier, 2004).

These differences in impact are partly based on the varied ways in which people approach and experience music. Personality traits impact musical experience at the level of perceiving music in a certain way: Extraversion, openness, and agreeableness correlate with a bias for perceiving higher amounts of positive and lower amounts of negative emotions in music, while neuroticism relates to an opposite pattern (Vuoskoski & Eerola, 2011; for more about personality traits and music, see Vuoskoski, this volume).

Mental health states also bias music perception: Clinical depression (Punkanen, Eerola, & Erkkilä, 2011) and negative mood (Vuoskoski & Eerola, 2011a) correlate with a bias for higher ratings for perceived negative and lower ratings for perceived positive emotion in music. These trait and state congruent biases and other individual differences thus already exist at the fundamental level of perception and approach towards music, and they further impact the ways in which music may be used as a health resource. For instance, the emotional use of music for mood regulation is more typical for females than males (e.g., Wells & Hakanen, 1991; Chamorro-Premuzic et al., 2009b), for people who engage with music informally, not formally (Saarikallio, Nieminen, & Brattico, 2013), and for individuals high in neuroticism (Chamorro-Premuzic et al., 2009a, 2009b). Furthermore, from the healing perspective it is essential also to take a deeper look at the characteristics of musical engagement. That is, in emotion regulation, it is not the amount of regulation *per se* that makes a difference, but rather that the engagement patterns can be considered health-beneficial or even harmful. Indeed, depressed individuals have been shown to engage in patterns of emotional music use that can be considered maladaptive, such as rumination and avoidance (Garrido, Schubert, & Bangert, 2016; McFerran & Saarikallio, 2013; Miranda & Claes, 2009; Saarikallio, Gold, & McFerran, 2015). Similarly, anxiety and neuroticism relate to another undesirable strategy, using music for venting negative emotion (Carlson et al., 2015). Meanwhile, the ability to shift attention from negative thoughts and emotions towards positive ones through aesthetic pleasure (Van Den Tol & Edwards, 2015), dancing (Chin & Rickard, 2013), or regulatory strategies of positive reappraisal and distraction (Chin & Rickard, 2013; Van Den Tol, & Edwards, 2015) relates to positive health outcomes.

Differential impact of these music engagement patterns on emotional processing has also recently been evidenced at the level of brain activation: Males who typically use music for venting and discharging negative emotion show lower activation in medial prefrontal cortex (mPFC) as a response to emotion-evoking music, while females who typically engage in music for diverting away from negative thoughts show an increase in the mPFC activation, as a response to the same music (Carlson, et al., 2015). Striking differences exist in an individual's ability to become aware and take agency in actively modifying personal music engagement towards health-beneficial outcomes: Healthy adolescents efficiently use various techniques—even sad music listening and negative emotion processing—as steps towards mood improvement and healing (Saarikallio & Erkkilä, 2007), while vulnerable and depressed adolescents allow music to reinforce and fuel their negative emotions, ruminative tendencies, and feelings of social isolation (McFerran & Saarikallio, 2013).

The above-mentioned examples concern the emotional use of music, but the same principle applies to the other elements of healing: Individuals are likely to differ in their ability to use music to foster social interaction, motivate motor-cognitive behavior, and encourage personal empowerment. Research on music and health should be able to identify the personal capacity of different individuals for the health-beneficial use of music and possibilities for building such capacity could then subsequently be targeted at interventions, involving not only music therapeutic practice and recovery, but also preventive endeavors for promoting wellbeing, resilience, and personal growth. The Healthy-Unhealthy-Music Scale (HUMS) is a pioneering instrument for such purposes, specifically designed for identifying music use that is reflective of a risk for adolescent depression and to be used as a guide for preventive work with such individuals (Saarikallio, Gold, & McFerran, 2015).

## Concluding Words

The music and health framework presented in this chapter provides an overall map for comprehending the different elements that play a role in understanding musical health and healing. New research is rapidly emerging about the impacts of various forms of musicking on the different psychological, physiological, and social aspects of health and wellbeing. The role of individual factors in understanding these impacts is also receiving increased attention and, in the same way that the daily music use has become an individualized act, so should interventions be customized to foster individualized needs of particular target groups. Awareness of the interactive nature of the various individual, contextual, and musical elements is a fundamental starting point for situating particular healing interventions and experimental studies in their broader context, and for considering possible confounding and mediating factors. A more comprehensive understanding of this broader picture helps both researchers and practitioners to make grounded decisions about choosing particular elements as the focus of single studies or interventions: The context of the healing activity (e.g. prevention or rehabilitation), as well as the targeted element of psychopathology (e.g. stress or depression), particularly motor-cognitive challenge (e.g. memory loss or speech problem), or a social-emotional goal (e.g. fostering pro-social development), as well as a range of other individual factors (e.g. gender, mental health state) play a role in determining optimal requirements for the musical material and the musicking activity. They should also be carefully considered when choosing which self-reported, observed, and physiological outcome measures should be used for assessing whether desired health-outcomes have been reached. Research in this field is growing quickly, and the future is likely to provide better identification of various optimal and customized combinations regarding the different elements that best foster musical healing at the levels of individual and social recovery and growth.

## Core Reading

Koelsch, S., & Stegemann, T. (2012). The brain and positive biological effects in healthy and clinical populations. In R. MacDonald, G. Kreutz, & L. Mitchell (Eds.), *Music, health, and wellbeing* (pp. 436–456). Oxford: Oxford University Press.

Kreutz, G., Quiroga Murcia, C., & Bongard, S. (2012). Psychoneuroendocrine research on music and health: An overview. In R. MacDonald, G. Kreutz, & L. Mitchell (Eds.), *Music, health, and wellbeing* (pp. 457–476). Oxford: Oxford University Press.

Menon, V., & Levitin, D. (2005). The rewards of music listening: Response and physiological connectivity of mesolimbic system. *Neuroimage, 28*, 175–184.

Saarikallio. S. (2012). Cross-cultural approaches to music and health. In R. MacDonald, G. Kreutz, & L. Mitchell (Eds.), *Music, health, and wellbeing* (pp. 477–490). Oxford: Oxford University Press.

Saarikallio, S., & Erkkilä, J. (2007). The role of music in adolescents' mood regulation. *Psychology of Music, 35*(1), 88–109.

## Further References

Ansdell, G., & DeNora, T. (2012). Musical flourishing: Community music therapy, controversy, and the cultivation of wellbeing. In R. MacDonald, G. Kreutz, & L. Mitchell (Eds.), *Music, health, and wellbeing* (pp. 97–112). Oxford: Oxford University Press.

Bandura, A. (1977). Self-efficacy: Toward a unifying theory of behavioral change. *Psychological Review, 84*(2), 191 215.

Bartlett, D. L. (1996). Physiological responses to music and sound stimuli. In D. A. Dodges (Ed.), *Handbook of music psychology* (pp. 343–385). 2nd ed. San Antonio, TX: IMR.

Batt-Rawden, K. B., DeNora, T., & Ruud, E. (2005). Music listening and empowerment in health promotion: A study of the role and significance of music in everyday life of the long-term ill. *Nordic Journal of Music Therapy, 14*(2), 120–136.

Bernatzky, G., Strickner, S., Presch, M., Wendtner, F., & Kullich, W. (2012). Music as non-pharmacological pain management in clinics. In R. MacDonald, G. Kreutz, & L. Mitchell (Eds.), *Music, health, and wellbeing* (pp. 257–275). Oxford: Oxford University Press.

Blood, A. J., & Zatorre, R. J. (2001). Intensely pleasurable responses to music correlate with activity in brain regions implicated in reward and emotion. *Proceedings of the National Academy of Sciences, 98*(20), 11818–11823.

Carlson, E., Saarikallio, S., Toiviainen, P., Bogert, B. Kliuchko, M., & Brattico, E. (2015). Maladaptive and adaptive emotion regulation through music: A behavioral and neuroimaging study of males and females. *Frontiers in Human Neuroscience, 9*, 466. doi:10.3389/fnhum.2015.00466

Chamorro-Premuzic, T., Gomi-Freixanet, M., Furnham, A., & Muro, A. (2009a). Personality, self-estimated intelligence, and uses of music: A Spanish replication and extension using structural equation modeling. *Psychology of Aesthetics, Creativity, and the Arts, 3*(3), 149–155.

Chamorro-Premuzic, T., Swami, V., Furnham, A., & Maakip, I. (2009b). The big five personality traits and uses of music. A replication in Malaysia using structural equation modeling. *Journal of Individual Differences, 30*(1), 20–27.

Chin, T., & Rickard, N. S. (2013). Emotion regulation strategy mediates both positive and negative relationships between music uses and well-being. *Psychology of Music, 42*(5), 92–713.

Clark, I., & Harding, K. (2012). Psychosocial outcomes of active singing interventions for therapeutic purposes: A systematic review of the literature. *Nordic Journal of Music Therapy, 21*(1), 80–98.

Clayton, Martin (2009). The social and personal functions of music in cross-cultural perspective. In Hallam, S., Cross, I., & Thaut, M. (Eds.), *The Oxford handbook of music psychology* (pp. 35–44). Oxford: Oxford University Press.

Clift, S. (2012). Singing, wellbeing & health. In R. MacDonald, G. Kreutz, & L. Mitchell (Eds.), *Music, health, and wellbeing* (pp. 113–124). Oxford: Oxford University Press.

Costa-Giomi, E. (2012). Music instruction and children's intellectual development: The educational context of music participation. In R. MacDonald, G. Kreutz, & L. Mitchell (Eds.), *Music, health, and wellbeing* (pp. 339–355). Oxford: Oxford University Press.

Cross, I. (2014). Music and communication in music psychology. *Psychology of Music, 42*(6), 808–819.

Cross, I. (2016). The nature of music and its evolution. In S. Hallam, I. Cross, and M. Thaut (Eds.) *Oxford handbook of music psychology* (pp. 3–18). 2nd ed. Oxford: Oxford University Press.

Csikszentmihalyi, M. (1990). *Flow: The psychology of optimal experience.* New York, NY: Harper and Row.

Csikszentmihalyi, M. (2014). *Flow and the foundations of positive psychology: The collected works of Mihaly Csikszentmihalyi.* Dordrecht: Springer, 2014.

Csikszentmihalyi, M., & Larson, R. (1984). *Being adolescent: Conflict and growth in the teenage years.* New York, NY: Basic Books.

Davidson, J., & Emberly, A. (2012). Embodied musical communication across cultures: Singing and dancing for quality of life and wellbeing benefit. In R. MacDonald, G. Kreutz, & L. Mitchell (Eds.), *Music, health, and wellbeing* (pp. 136–149). Oxford: Oxford University Press.

Elliott, D. J., & Silverman, M. (2012). Why music matters: Philosophical and cultural foundations. In R. MacDonald, G. Kreutz, & L. Mitchell (Eds.), *Music, health, and wellbeing* (pp. 25–39). Oxford: Oxford University Press.

Erkkilä, J., Punkanen, M., Fachner, J., Ala-Ruona, E., Pöntiö, I., Tervaniemi, M., . . . Gold, C. (2011). Individual music therapy for depression: Randomized controlled trial. *The British Journal of Psychiatry, 199*(2), 132–139.

Farrer, C., Franck, N., Frith, C. D., Decety, J., Damato, T., & Jeannerod, M. (2004). Neural correlates of action attribution in schizophrenia. *Psychiatry Research: Neuroimaging, 131*, 31–44.

Field, T., Martinez, A., Nawrocki, T., et al. (1998). Music shifts frontal EEG in depressed adolescents. *Adolescence, 33*, 109–116.

Frith, S. (2004). *Popular music: Critical concepts in media and cultural studies. Volume 4 Music and identity.* London: Routledge.

Gabrielsson, A., & Lindström, E. (2001). The influence of musical structure on emotional expression. In P. N. Juslin, & J. A. Sloboda (Eds.), *Music and emotion: Theory and research* (pp. 223–248). New York, NY: Oxford University Press.

Garrido, S., Schubert, E., & Bangert, D. (2016). Musical prescriptions for mood improvement: An experimental study. *The Arts in Psychotherapy, 51*, 46–53.

Gembris, H. (2012). Music-making as a lifelong development and resource for health. In R. MacDonald, G. Kreutz, & L. Mitchell (Eds.), *Music, health, and wellbeing* (pp. 367–382). Oxford: Oxford University Press.

Gold, C., Saarikallio, S. H., & McFerran, K. (2011). Music therapy. In R.J. Levesque (Ed.), *Encyclopedia of adolescence* (pp. 1826–1834). New York, NY: Springer.

Greasley, A. E., & Lamont, A. (2011). Exploring engagement with music in everyday life using experience sampling methodology. *Musicae Scientiae, 15*(1), 45–71.

Jeannerod, M. (2003). The mechanism of self-recognition in human. *Behavioral Brain Research*, 142, 1–15.

Judge, T. A, Erez, A., Bono, J. E., & Thoresen, C. J. (2002). Are measures of self-esteem, neuroticism, locus of control, and generalized self-efficacy indicators of a common core construct? *Journal of Personality and Social Psychology, 83*(3), 693–710.

Juslin, P. N., & Laukka, P. (2003). Communication of emotions in vocal expression and music performance: Different channels, same code? *Psychological Bulletin, 129,* 770–814.

Juslin, P. N., & Laukka, P. (2004). Expression, perception, and induction of musical emotions: A review and a questionnaire study of everyday listening. *Journal of New Music Research, 33*(3), 217–238.

Juslin, P. N., & Timmers, R. (2010). Expression and communication of emotion in music. In P. N. Juslin & J. Sloboda (Eds.), *Handbook of music and emotion: Theory, research, applications* (pp. 453–92). Oxford: Oxford University Press.

Kirschner, S., & Tomasello, M. (2012). Joint music making promotes prosocial behavior in 4-year-old children. *Evolution and Human Behavior, 31*, 354–364.

Koelsch, S. (2014). Brain correlates of music-evoked emotions. *Nature Reviews Neuroscience, 15*, 170–180 doi:10.1038/nrn3666

Laiho, S. (2004). The psychological functions of music in adolescence. *Nordic Journal of Music Therapy, 13*(1), 49–65.

Langer, S. (1942). *Philosophy in a new key: A study in the symbolism of reason, rite, and art.* Cambridge, MA: Harvard University Press.

MacDonald, R., Kreutz, G., & Mitchell, L. (Eds.), *Music, health, and wellbeing.* Oxford: Oxford University Press.

Malloch, S. N. (1999). Mothers and infants and communicative musicality. *Musicae Scientiae, 3*(1), 29–57.

Maksimainen, J., & Saarikallio, S. (2015). Affect from art: Subjective constituents of everyday pleasure of music and pictures: Overview and early results. Paper presented at the Ninth Triennial Conference of the European Society for the Cognitive Sciences of Music, Manchester, UK.

Maratos, A., Gold, C., Wang, X., & Crawford, M. (2008). Music therapy for depression. *Cochrane Database Systematic Reviews*, 2008(1), CD004517.

Mas-Herrero, E., Marco-Pallares, J., Lorenso-Seva, U., Zatorre, R., & Rodriguez-Fornells, A. (2013). Individual differences in music reward experiences. *Music Perception, 31*(2), 118–138.

McFerran, K., & Saarikallio, S. (2013). Depending on music to feel better: Being conscious of responsibility when appropriating the power of music, *The Arts in Psychotherapy, 41*(1), 89–97.

Miranda, D., & Claes, M. (2009). Music listening, coping, peer affiliation and depression in adolescence. *Psychology of Music, 37*, 215–233.

Miranda, D., Gaudrea, P., Debrosse, R., Morizot, J. & Kirmayer., L. (2012). Music listening and mental health: Variations on internalizing psychopathology. In R. MacDonald, G. Kreutz, & L. Mitchell (Eds.), *Music, health, and wellbeing* (pp. 513–529). Oxford: Oxford University Press.

Mithen, S. (2005). *The singing Neanderthals. The origins of music, language, and body.* London: Weidenfeld and Nicholson.

Murray, M., & Lamont, A. (2012). Community music and social/health psychology: Linking theoretical and practical concerns. In R. MacDonald, G. Kreutz, & L. Mitchell (Eds.), *Music, health, and wellbeing* (pp. 76–86). Oxford: Oxford University Press.

Ockelford, A. (2012). Songs without words: Exploring how music can serve as a proxy language in social interaction with autistic children. In R. MacDonald, G. Kreutz, & L. Mitchell (Eds.), *Music, health, and wellbeing* (pp. 289–323). Oxford: Oxford University Press.

Ockelford, A., & Markou, K. (2012). Music education and therapy for children and young people with cognitive impairments: Reporting on a decade of research. In R. MacDonald, G. Kreutz, & L. Mitchell (Eds.), *Music, health, and wellbeing* (pp. 383–402). Oxford: Oxford University Press.

Oldfield, A. (1993). *Interactive music therapy in child and family psychiatry. Clinical practice, research, and teaching.* London: Jessica Kingsley Publishers.

Pelletier, C. L. (2004). The effect of music on decreasing arousal due to stress: A meta-analysis. *Journal of Music Therapy, 16*(3), 192–214.

Punkanen, M., Eerola, T., & Erkkilä, J. (2011). Biased emotional recognition in depression: Perception of emotions in music by depressed patients. *Journal of Affective Disorders, 13*(1), 118–126.

Quiroga Murcia, C., & Kreutz, G. (2012). Dance and health: Exploring interactions and implications. In R. MacDonald, G. Kreutz, & L. Mitchell (Eds.), *Music, health, and wellbeing* (pp. 125–135). Oxford: Oxford University Press.

Roddenberry, A., & Renk, K. (2010). Locus of control and self-efficacy: Potential mediators of stress, illness, and utilization of health services in college students. *Child Psychiatry & Human Development, 41*(4), 353–370.

Rotter, J. B. (1966). Generalized expectancies for internal versus external control of reinforcement. *Psychological Monographs: General & Applied, 80*(1), 1–28.

Ruud, E. (1997). Music and the quality of life. *Nordic Journal of Music Therapy, 6*(2), 86–97.

Ruud, E. (2012). The new health musicians. In R. MacDonald, G. Kreutz, & L. Mitchell (Eds.), *Music, health, and wellbeing* (pp. 87–96). Oxford: Oxford University Press.

Saarikallio, S. (2016). Musical identity in fostering emotional health. In. R. MacDonald, D. Hargreaves, & D. Miell (Eds). *Handbook of musical identities.* Oxford: Oxford University Press.

Saarikallio, S., Gold, C., & McFerran, K. (2015). Development and validation of the Healthy-Unhealthy Music Scale (HUMS). Development and validation of the Healthy-Unhealthy Music Scale. *Child and Adolescent Mental Health, 20*(4), 210–217. doi:10.1111/camh.12109

Saarikallio, S., Nieminen, S., & Brattico, E. (2013). Affective reactions to musical stimuli reflect emotional use of music in everyday life. *Musicae Scientiae, 17*(1), 27–39.

Särkämö, T., Tervaniemi, M., Laitinen, S., Forsblom, A., Soinila, S., Mikkonen, M., . . . & Peretz, I. (2008). Music listening enhances cognitive recovery and mood after middle cerebral artery stroke. *Brain, 131*(3), 866–876.

Schellenberg, E. G. (2012). Cognitive performance after listening to music: A review of the Mozart Effect. In R. MacDonald, G. Kreutz, & L. Mitchell (Eds.), *Music, health, and wellbeing* (pp. 324–338). Oxford: Oxford University Press.

Scherer, K., & Zentner, M. (2008). Music evoked emotions are different – more often aesthetic than utilitarian. *Behavioral and Brain Sciences, 31*(5), 595–596.

Schmidt, L. A., & Trainor, L. J. (2001). Frontal brain electrical activity (EEG) distinguishes valence and intensity of musical emotions. *Cognition & Emotion, 15*(4), 487–500.

Sloboda, J. A., & O'Neill, S. A. (2001). Emotions in everyday listening to music. In Juslin, P. N., & Sloboda, J. A. (Eds.), *Music and emotion: Theory and research* (pp. 415–429). New York, NY: Oxford University Press.

Small, C. (1998). *Musicking: The meanings of performing and listening.* Hanover, NH: University Press of New England.

Spintge, R. (2012). Clinical use of music in operating theatres. In R. MacDonald, G. Kreutz, & L. Mitchell (Eds.), *Music, health, and wellbeing* (pp. 276–286). Oxford: Oxford University Press.

Stern, D. (2010). *Forms of vitality. Exploring dynamic experience in psychology, the arts, psychotherapy, and development.* London: Oxford University Press.

Thaut, M. H. (2005). Rhythm, human temporality and brain function. In D. Miell, R. MacDonald, & D. J. Hargreaves (Eds). *Musical communication* (pp. 171–192). New York, NY: Oxford University Press.

Trainor, L. J., & Cirelli, L. (2015). Rhythm and interpersonal synchrony in early social development: Interpersonal synchrony and social development. *Annals of the New York Academy of Sciences,* March 2015.

Trehub, S. E., Unyk, A. M., & Trainor, L. J. (1993). Maternal singing in cross-cultural perspective. *Infant Behavior and Development, 16*(3), 285–295.

Trevarthen, C. (1999). Musicality and the intrinsic motive pulse: Evidence from human psychobiology and infant communication. *Musicae Scientiae, 3*(1 suppl), 157–213.

Trevarthen, C. (2002). Origins of musical identity: Evidence from infancy for musical social aware-ness. In R. MacDonald, D. J. Hargreaves, & D. Miell (Eds.), *Musical identities* (pp. 21–38). Oxford: Oxford University Press.

Van den Tol, A. J., & Edwards, J. (2015). Listening to sad music in adverse situations: How music selection strategies relate to self-regulatory goals, listening effects, and mood enhancement. *Psychology of Music, 43*(4), 473–494.

VanderArk, S. D., & Ely, D. (1993). Cortisol, biochemical, and galvanic skin responses to music stimuli of different preference values by college students in biology and music. *Perceptual and Motor Skills, 77*(1), 227–234.

Vuoskoski, J. K., & Eerola, T. (2011). Measuring music-induced emotion. A comparison of emotion models, personality biases, and intensity of experiences. *Musicae Scientiae, 15*(2), 159–173.

Wells, A., & Hakanen, E. A. (1991). The emotional use of popular music by adolescents. *Journalism & Mass Communication Quarterly, 68*(3), 445–454.

# 8

# MUSIC, MOMENTS, AND HEALING PROCESSES

## Music Therapy

*Jörg Fachner*

## Introduction

Music has been used for healing purposes since ancient times. Healing rituals through-out human history have included music accompanying ceremonies and serving to signify important parts and events within these culturally diverse healing practices. The use of music as a part of healing continues today, including, specifically, music therapy. Music therapy (to be abbreviated "MT" in this chapter) is the systematic use of music and its elements by trained music therapists in an interactive therapeutic context to restore, maintain, and increase emotional, physical, and mental health. Modern music therapy

> . . . uses music and its elements as an intervention in medical, educational, and everyday environments with individuals, groups, families, or communities who seek to optimize their quality of life and improve their physical, social, communicative, emotional, intellectual, and spiritual health and wellbeing.
>
> *(WFMT, 2011)*

We differentiate MT approaches in which we actively make music (*active* MT), such as improvising, singing, or composing together from approaches in which we focus on listen-ing to music (*receptive* MT). Both methods utilize music as "an art beyond words" for heal-ing purposes (Bunt & Stige, 2014). This chapter will focus on current research into musical communication in clinical improvisation as a core ingredient of human interaction in music therapy practice. A vital aspect of this practice is the recognition of *kairological moments*, i.e. important episodes of the music therapy process that indicate and promote change in therapy. How to document, recognize, and analyze such moments is one of the major chal-lenges in understanding why music seems to work in healing processes.

## Basic Categories of Music Therapy

The 1999 triannual World Congress of Music Therapy in Washington, DC, focused on five major models of music therapy: 1. Analytical MT, 2. Benenzon MT, 3. Guided Imag-ery in Music (GIM), 4. Nordoff/Robbins MT, and 5. Behavioral MT. The first three approaches to MT may be labeled psychodynamic, in contrast to the final two approaches, which may be called music-centered. In psychodynamic approaches music is used *in* therapy to evoke psychic material, whereby in music-centered approaches music is used *as* therapy and symbolic interpretations and verbalization are avoided (Bruscia, 1987). The first two models, Analytical and Benenzon, adhere to a psychodynamic model, in which music is used *in* therapy (including psychotherapy) and verbalizations, and observed psychic processes and symbolizations are interpreted from a variety of psychotherapeutic—mainly psychoanalytic—frameworks, such as those of Freud, Jung, Adler, Frankl, or Perls (Bruscia, 1998; Bunt & Stige, 2014; De Backer & Sutton, 2014; Erkkilä, Ala-Ruona, Punkanen, & Fachner, 2012). The first two models make use of musical improvisation and verbal therapy; in contrast, Guided Imagery in Music focuses on music listening and psychotherapeutic interaction based on the imagery evoked during and verbalized along with the listening process (Grocke, 2009). The music-centered Nordoff/Robbins approach (Nordoff & Robbins, 2007) sees the act of making and gradually improving music *as* therapy, compared to the Behavioral MT model, which is based on the idea that music listening can be used as a medicine and that we can measure the effect of music with distinct bodily responses, independent of psychotherapeutic frameworks (Spintge & Droh, 1992).

## Healing Settings

MT is a discipline which has evolved out of utilizing music for therapeutic purposes and is aimed at the needs of the patient and his/her specific illness, behavior, personality, and biography. Doing MT is based on an interaction between a patient and a therapist. As with any other therapy, the reason for MT is that people need and seek help from a qualified person (WFMT, 2011). This relationship of a "healing contract" distinguishes clinical improvisation, singing, moving, and imagery related to music listening from other situations involving music making and listening (Brown & Pavlicevic, 1996; De Backer & Sutton, 2014). MT happens at a specified place in a healing setting—for example, a hospital, hospice, private practice, special school, or even a prison—and the purpose of the meeting will be connected to a shared experience of listening to or making music.

Since its beginnings, MT has been influenced by other disciplines like medicine, psychology, pedagogics, anthropology, philosophy, and the sciences of music. In parts of the theoretical discourse in MT, its roots are traced back to shamanic healing practices (Hanser, 2009), at the core of which are a variety of techniques, such as drumming, dance, and music; these are used to alter consciousness, in order to change the focus of attention and cognition (Fachner, 2011). Techniques that alter the focus of attention offer a way to "empty" the contents of memory, allowing new information to enter. Such processes are safely accompanied and guided by a therapist, who may, for example, help a patient to focus on the imagery that may arise when listening to music together and in analyzing such associations and images, as practiced in the Bonny Method of Guided Imagery in Music (Grocke, 2009).

The practice of MT with a client is always unique for each patient's situation. This might explain why various models based on single case study designs have been employed in MT research in order to contextualize the complex and situated healing phenomena which arise. Similarly, case studies with multiple baselines across differing conditions and behaviors—for example, when analyzing different individual responses to MT in a class of autistic children

(Kern & Aldridge, 2006)—and mixed methods utilizing qualitative and quantitative research measures have dominated MT research (Wheeler & Murphy, 2016).

Over the last few decades, a growing number of studies have provided empirical and scientific evidence for the positive effects of MT, transforming it into a more evidence-based treatment. With the implementation of evidence-based research, the idea of a goal-driven and manual-based practice has entered the discussion on MT approaches. For example, treatments that sequence musical activities for training to overcome specific physical limitations due to stroke are now being based on neurological research outcomes (Street, Magee, Odell-Miller, Bateman, & Fachner, 2015). The Cochrane Library of Systematic Reviews has published promising reviews of music therapy as applied to autism spectrum disorder, depression, schizophrenia, and acquired brain injury; as of this writing, 920 MT controlled trial study results are currently registered. Among these, we see that studies utilizing randomized controlled trials report reductions of depression and anxiety (Erkkilä, et al., 2011) and also indicate reductions of dementia symptoms (Ridder, Stige, Qvale, & Gold, 2013; Schall, Haberstroh, & Pantel, 2015). Various systematic reviews indicate MT benefits for end-of-life patients, cancer, coronary heart disease, pain, serious mental disorders, pediatric clients, asthma, premature infants, and several reports on dementia (see Bradt, 2016, pp. 628–629).

Evolving from such empirical evidence, one approach to understanding the action mechanism which underlies effective MT is to take a detailed look at cases in which change occurred, and how that change evolved in specific moments and timeframes that were important and meaningful in the overall development of the therapy sessions (Amir, 1996; Fachner, 2014).

## Healing Processes—Therapeia, Symbols, and Consciousness

Music therapists use music to accompany people, making use of the temporal nature of music to and work with the emotions, imagery, and thoughts evoked by both clients and therapists when doing music together. They are working with aesthetics and with art as they work with patients in processes of healing as therapists, in the original Greek sense of the word. The term "therapy," as Plato used it, is "therapeia" (θεραπεία), meaning "to accompany patients on their way" into, through, and out of the unknown of their illnesses (Fachner, 2014).

This original connotation stresses a temporal understanding of the process of doing therapy with a guiding, nurturing and serving therapist ("therapon"—θεράπων). Illness is a "journey into the unknown" (Aldridge, 1990, p. 178) that contains a patient's continuous fear of loss of reality, whereby symptoms signify the struggle for expression of the unknown, inner reality; art has the mission to "confront us with something we have not realized before" (Aldridge, 1990) and therefore becomes an indicative means of objectification of subjective reality. Music or art in general not only stimulates feelings but facilitates expression of the unknown, but what may be heard in the MT process is not necessarily a "message *from* the subconscious" (Aldridge, 1990, p. 181).

Joint clinical improvisation produces audible information about the unknown and allows us to reveal symbols, images, and thoughts of the client's inner world with a therapist accompanying and sharing the client's journey into the unknown. However, how to interpret and handle what happens depends on the MT approach of the therapist. Music-centered approaches do not refer to a theoretical system of the psyche (such as those of Freud or

Jung), but focus on the development of the co-created musical material as the driving force of healing. Contrastingly, psychodynamic approaches are convinced that each therapeutic interaction will sooner or later face the interactional dynamics and patterns that were learned in the child–parent interaction and that each kind of playing is connected to the state of being a child. Thus, some MT theorists describe the clients' experiences in improvisation as *proto-symbolic* (De Backer & Sutton 2014), referring to Winnicott's (1968) ideas about transitional space and transitional object when interpreting certain musical phenomena—such as the appearance of a melody in improvisation—as not yet being a symbol as such, but a symbol in pre-state.

> When considering clinical improvisation from psychoanalytic perspective, its role is to activate the symbolic process, and let the improviser act creatively on the domain of non-verbal experiences, i.e. on a pre-conscious level, and thus bring out primary process orientated material to be dealt with verbally.
>
> *(Erkkilä et al., 2012, p. 416)*

## Change Processes, Health Beliefs, and Meaning

Bruscia (1998) defines clinical improvising in MT as "playing around with sounds until they form whatever patterns, shapes, or textures one wants them to have, or until they mean whatever one wants them to mean" (p. 5). In healing processes, it is of the utmost importance to consider the patient's individual health beliefs; such individual opinions on the symbolic significance of illness contribute to the cognitive management of illness and therapy. Meaning is created when we relate observation, statements, or behavior to an individual continually developing a "framework of fundamentals" (Aldridge, 1990, p. 179). In the therapy process, a patient's framework of fundamentals, representing the patient's limitations, experiences, cognition, and related health beliefs, are addressed and updated when his/her internal unknown elements are made known through the objectivation of a jointly produced "work of art" (Aldridge 1990, p. 180). In an artistically oriented therapy process, the act of creation transforms the negative sign of the illness into a socially positive sign as a potential for healing. This change in meaning—specifically if such meanings symbolize something personal or social—appears to be a basic element of healing processes.

Such a change in meaning may then become an initial moment of change in illness. For example, if a patient suffering from spasticity experiences that his involuntary body movements can make rhythmical sense in clinical improvisation, and that in this specific context an ability to create and shape the music arises which can be directed with the patient's own ideas and intentions, then this will result in a positive body experience and a different recognition of the patient's abilities, which may transfer to other areas. Here, consciousness is and becomes a creative act, an expression of "I am able" as an important part of intentionality, which is made audible in therapy. If illness in general is accompanied by loss of individual performance, then it is a reflexive limitation of consciousness that leads to limitations of individual perspective regarding possible action patterns. This suggests that consciousness is a creative act in itself and depends on action, intention, reflection, and the experience of the conscious individual.

> Music and consciousness are things we do. . . . Achieving consciousness, from the Latin *con* (with) and *scire* (to know), is the central activity of human knowledge.

At the heart of the word is a concept of mutuality, knowing with others. Our consciousness is a mutual activity; it is performed.

*(Aldridge & Fachner, 2006, p. 10)*

## *Kairos* and Situated Cognition

In the fairy tales of *1001 Nights* the uniqueness of the moment that changes the whole story is the focus of most storylines. Very often, the story describes a specific situation, a specific *plot* at a moment in which the protagonist is lucky to grab a chance to change his or her fortune. The Greek term *kairos*, meaning the "right moment", refers also to the ability to seize the moment, to recognize the opportunity to act and decide on something, based on an individual's experiences in the "here and now" (Aldridge, 1996, p. 37). *Kairos* seems to be a more appropriate time concept for music therapy than time as *chronos,* or "clock" time. Rather than looking at the chronological order of parts in a piece of music, as successive elements of the piece as a whole, the *kairos*-focus is on situational relationship to the music and how the perceived musical elements interact with the client's experience of the music in an interactive setting of therapy.

> Communication in music therapy needs to be seen through the lens of "situated cognition," in which meaning, knowing and learning are generated in the situation of doing something bound to a [temporal] social, cultural and physical context (Smith & Semin, 2004). Communication in music therapy is thus dependent on contextual developments and not on a plan made like a scene-play; the music is temporal and emotions signifying meaning are evoked through the interplay of music and the people who do the music.
>
> *(Fachner, 2014, pp. 792–3)*

Time processes are related to the events and the personal meanings and experience of these events in the music, rather than the music's inherent logic.

In order to apply quantitative methods in researching the time-course of changes brought about through music therapy, one recent music therapy study used time series analysis for the study of dementia treatment (Schall, Haberstroh, & Pantel, 2015). Analyzing excerpts (30 sec) of nine clients' session videos ratings, the "trend types" (p. 117) of the time series data showed statistically significant positive effects, suggesting that effects of music therapy are "situational rather than being cumulative" (p. 118).

## Focus Point: Important Moments in Therapy and Improvisation

The core ingredient of an active MT session is the interaction between a patient and a therapist, often engaged in dyadic improvisation. Regarding the action mechanisms of MT, one research focus is on the (micro)-analysis of pivotal MT episodes (Wosch & Wigram, 2007), i.e. important moments signifying turning points during the time-course of MT, in particular in clinical improvisation. Analysis of moment-to-moment interactions has been the subject of many MT case studies and different studies have expressed this variously, describing "meaningful moments" (Amir, 1996), "pivotal moments" (Grocke, 1999) "significant moments" (Trondalen, 2005), or "present moments" (Ansdell et al., 2010).

However, the basic feature such moments of interest have in common is that they are chosen time frames from the MT sessions in which change—in the sense of a turning point in therapy development—was recognized from the therapist and from the client (Fachner, 2014). This may be either in the situation whilst doing MT, or in retrospect when indexing the events in the session. Nevertheless, to understand the process of MT properly, one has to follow it through an extended and sometimes gradual series of changes; to focus only on highlights or pivotal moments will not suffice to understand the process and its development (Nordoff & Robbins, 2007, pp. xxii–xxiv). For example, a client responded to certain melodic motifs that have been used in several sessions—but in one session when these motifs were fitting together to become a song, the moment in which the song evolved became indicative for change.

Further, such moments may represent "good musical practice" in *clinical improvisation*—which is not necessarily the same as in art improvisation—and indicate moments of personal change, possibly linked to symptom decrease (Erkkilä, 2014). Good musical practice may be an ingredient of important moments in clinical improvisation but this is not necessarily the case; for example, when improvising with a depressed musician good art improvisation may happen very often during MT and thus, may not be of significance for the therapeutic process.

> In [art improvisation], "supporting" is equivalent to being "in background musically," and "leading" is equivalent to being "in foreground," where leading has the stronger focus musically. In [clinical improvisation], to think of supporting as only meaning background is not enough . . . [supporting] might require initiative, guiding, helping out—the equivalent to leading in [art improvisation] . . . [Furthermore a reversal of musical roles in clinical improvisation, whilst acceptable in art improvisation] would not be considered good therapeutic practice, maybe implying the therapist inserting her own issues, thus clouding her receptivity to the client's needs.
>
> *(Brown & Palicevic, 1996, p. 403, cited in Darnley-Smith, 2014, p. 64)*

## Capturing and Analyzing Important Moments

MT consists of interacting in or about music; this happens together with a therapist using a variety of musical instruments or listening and recording devices. Audiovisual recording devices are mostly used to capture the therapy sessions in order to revisit parts of the sessions and to analyze the musical, verbal, or gestural interactions. Magee (2014) offers a broad overview on how we can use music technology as an aid in therapy as well as to document and analyze the sessions. Audiovisual and MIDI data from clinical improvisation can be used to analyze dyadic processes in important therapeutic moments. The MATLAB based Music Therapy Toolbox (Erkkilä, 2014) allows a researcher to describe the pitch, density, velocity (loudness), and other acoustic features of selected musical parts using techniques of music information retrieval, and also allows a researcher to describe degrees of synchronization in dyadic playing.

*Microanalysis* focuses on selected segments in verbal, bodily, and musical interaction. Microanalytic techniques, such as the pioneering frame-by-frame analysis to show the interactive nature of bodies synchronizing to speech (Condon & Sander, 1974) have been applied often in music therapy (Wosch & Wigram, 2007). Microanalysis is a detailed analysis of moments, events, and episodes within a session to document the "moment-by moment experienced change" (Wosch & Wigram, 2007, p. 22). Wosch and Wigram's book on microanalysis describes several studies utilizing this approach to describe the relationship between musical features and clinical outcomes. Video analysis methods and motion capture methods may also be utilized to describe moment-to-moment interactions and how gestures and movements synchronize (Wosch & Wigram 2007; Street, et al., 2015).

Music therapists may want to contextualize brain activity during important moments in MT sessions, in order to see how brains process shared information, but attempts to capture practical MT in a laboratory setting often impair the authenticity of the situation (Fachner & Stegemann, 2013). Body movement, especially of the head, is restricted and subjects have to adapt to the brain recording machine. Thus, the recording instruments must be adjusted as closely as possible to everyday practice in order to generate context-sensitive authentic data. Recent developments in wireless EEG hardware have made it possible to use portable EEG units to record data during music performance, and so forth. Wireless data transmission and wearability is an important advancement, as most stationary EEG recording systems require one to sit quietly. When studying brain activity during improvisation in music therapy, where patients should be moving freely, however, the methods employed in sports and movement sciences need to be considered. There is no current *in situ* neurophysiological study of active MT and thus, the underlying neurodynamics of clinical improvisation remain unknown although recent hyperscanning research (involving scanning two or more brains at once in order to study brain-to-brain-coupling) offers a paradigm to simultaneously study interactive brain processes in social contexts (Fachner, 2014).

## Investigating Musical Communication in Important Moments

To understand musical communication (see Ashley [Communication], this volume) synchronization and entrainment, as indicators of enhanced musical communication, have been the focus of several investigations (Hari, Himberg, Nummenmaa, Hämäläinen, & Parkkonen, 2013). One means of acquiring an understanding of what happens when individuals create music together is to analyze electrophysiologically the synchronization patterns of brain waves and heart beat during interactive music making. Such analysis of synchronous brain activity can be realized with two (or more) synchronized machines recording MEG or EEG and/or two corresponding electrocardiographic (ECG) recording systems. We now turn to some uses of such methods to better understand the workings of MT.

Neugebauer and Aldridge (1998) studied cardiac synchronization between two musicians improvising in a MT context. Before analyzing the physiological data of the participants, an index of therapeutic events which took place during the session was created. This evaluation was done in keeping with standards of good practice in Nordoff-Robbins MT: "criteria for the judgment of musical relevance were concerned either with communicative interaction and/or musical events such as moments of musical interrelation, initiatives for musical change, mutual changes in the playing, changes of tempo, dynamic and mood" (Neugebauer & Aldridge 1998, p. 47). The therapeutic events identified in this manner were compared to the corresponding events identified on the timeline of the ECG. An analysis of participants' heart rate patterns revealed a convergence of activity within dialogical events represented as parallel or opposite heart rates and simultaneous or alternating peaks indicating action-specific synchrony patterns of coordinated activity, indicating how the musical dialogue was accompanied by converging HR measures.

Pioneering music performance research examining two people playing a short guitar melody in unison (Lindenberger, Li, Gruber, & Muller, 2009) or four people playing saxophone (C. Babiloni et al., 2011) has shown how physiological functions synchronize in a coherent manner during the production of a social product—a piece of music performed together. For the guitarists this was observed "during the periods of (i) preparatory metronome tempo setting and (ii) coordinated play onset" (Lindenberger et al., 2009, p. 1). Both were adhering to a short series of metronome clicks (i) and a start signal (ii) before playing a melody in unison (see video supplement of Lindenberger et al. 2009). Playing the melody together led to synchronous activity in frontal and central brain areas, indicating time-locked synchronization of planning and the creation of a shared activity. When playing non-unison melodies, findings were consistent with Lindenberger et al. (2009) but the authors noticed increasing phase synchronization between the brains during more challenging musical phrases that required increased coordination between the guitarists (Sänger, Müller, & Lindenberger, 2012). Another study described theta and delta brain frequency connections (oscillatory coupling) in dyadic improvisation between guitarists (Müller, Sänger, & Lindenberger, 2013).

Bablioni et al. (2011) recorded EEG data from musicians while playing together. Their findings indicate power-related differences in alpha frequency amplitudes, which were localized through sLORETA (low resolution electromagnetic tomography) source estimation. Studying the differences between performing a piece in a more improvised and in a composed fashion, Dolan and colleagues (2013) reported different responses from performers and listeners regarding activation of cortical areas. Differences between pre-composed and improvisation conditions were located via sLORETA in Brodman Area 9 (dorso-lateral prefrontal cortex) within the alpha range indicating less involvement of sustained attention, working memory in the improvised condition, implying a different brain working mode during improvisation (indicating less mental workload) then during playing the pre-composed condition (Dolan et al., 2013).

## Future Directions

The previously mentioned "hyperscanning" method in the field of social neuroscience tries to trace how brain-to-brain coupling functions in social interaction (F. Babiloni & Astolfi, 2014). How brain-to-brain coupling aligns with body posture and movement (Hari, et al., 2013), how the temporal dynamics of musical emotions create moments of similar brain activity in listeners (Trost, Frühholz, Cochrane, Cojan, & Vuilleumier, 2015), and how brain processes between music listeners synchronize when listening to longer pieces of music are topics of vital interest in the field of MT (Fachner, 2014; Fachner & Stegemann, 2013). Neugebauer and Aldridge's 1998 study was based on clinical scenarios as they happen in everyday clinical situations. However, determining how much of the brain coupling identified so far is applicable to clinical improvisation requires further experimental investigation.

Future studies may apply such physiological measurements and biomarkers for investigating more closely the workings of MT. Tracking therapy processes utilizing wearable measuring devices will allow capturing the *in situ* physiological signatures of important moments in therapy by integrating biomarkers into our clinical settings. Dual *in situ* recordings of therapist–client dyads might be submitted to a complex hyperscanning analysis based on a therapist's usual post-session analysis. Following selection (by the therapist or others) of important therapeutic moments over the time course of MT sessions, we may seek to analyze the physiological interplay of a micro-analytic event structure (see Wosch & Wigram, 2007). Such case studies may help to identify how brains synchronize and bodies entrain in music therapy processes, and help to explain how MT works and may allow prediction of specific disease treatment response and effectiveness.

## Core Reading

Aldridge, D. (1996). *Music therapy and research in medicine—from out of the silence*. London: Jessica Kingsley Publishers.

Babiloni, F., & Astolfi, L. (2014). Social neuroscience and hyperscanning techniques: Past, present and future. *Neuroscience and Biobehavioral Reviews, 44*, 76–93. doi:10.1016/j.neubiorev.2012.07.006

De Backer, J., & Sutton, J. P. (2014). *The music in music therapy: Psychodynamic music therapy in Europe: Clinical, theoretical and research approaches*. London: JKP.

Fachner, J. (2014). Communicating change—meaningful moments, situated cognition and music therapy – a reply to North (2014). *Psychology of Music, 42*(6), 791–799.

Wheeler, B., & Murphy, K. (Eds.) (2016). *Music therapy research* (3d ed.). Gilsum, NH: Barcelona Publishers.

## Further References

Aldridge, D. (1990). Meaning and expression: The pursuit of aesthetics in research. *Holistic Medicine, 5*, 177–186.

Aldridge, D., & Fachner, J. (Eds.). (2006). *Music and altered states: Consciousness, transcendence, therapy and addictions*. London: Jessica Kingsley.

Amir, D. (1996). Experiencing music therapy: Meaningful moments in the music therapy process. In M. Langenberg, K. Aigen, & J. Frommer (Eds.), *Qualitative music therapy research* (pp. 109–130). Phoenixville, PA: Barcelona Publishers.

Ansdell, G., Davidson, J., Magee, W. L., Meehan, J., & Procter, S. (2010). From "this f★★★ing life" to "that's better". . . in four minutes: An interdisciplinary study of music therapy's "present moments" and their potential for affect modulation. *Nordic Journal of Music Therapy, 19*(1), 3–28 26p.

Babiloni, C., Vecchio, F., Infarinato, F., Buffo, P., Marzano, N., Spada, D., . . . Perani, D. (2011). Simultaneous recording of electroencephalographic data in musicians playing in ensemble. *Cortex: A journal devoted to the study of the nervous system and behavior, 47*(9), 1082–1090.

Bradt, J. (2016). Systematic review and meta-analysis. In B. Wheeler & K. Murphy (Eds.), *Music Therapy Research* (3rd ed., pp. 622–634). Dallas, TX: Barcelona Publishers.

Brown, S., & Pavlicevic, M. (1996). Clinical improvisation in creative music therapy: Musical aesthetic and the interpersonal dimension. *The Arts in Psychotherapy, 23*(5), 397–405. doi:http://dx.doi.org/10.1016/S0197-4556(96)00033-0

Bruscia, K. E. (1987). *Improvisational models of music therapy*. Springfield, IL.: C.C. Thomas.

Bruscia, K. E. (1998). *The dynamics of music psychotherapy*. Gilsum, NH: Barcelona Publishers.

Bunt, L., & Stige, B. (2014). *Music therapy: An art beyond words* (2nd ed.). New York, NY: Routledge.

Condon, W. S., & Sander, L. W. (1974). Synchrony demonstrated between movements of the neonate and adult speech. *Child Development, 45*(2), 456–462.

Darnley-Smith, R. (2014). The role of ontology in music therapy. In J. de Backer & J. Sutton (Eds.), *The music in music therapy: Psychodynamic music therapy in Europe: Clinical, theoretical and research approaches* (pp. 58–70). London: Jessica Kingsley Publishers.

Dolan, D., Sloboda, J. A., Jensen, H. J., & Cruts, B. (2013). The improvisatory approach to classical music performance. *Music Performance Research, 6*, 1–38.

Erkkilä, J. (2014). Improvisational experiences of psychodynamic music therapy for people with depression. In J. D. Backer & J. Sutton (Eds.), *The music in music therapy: Psychodynamic music therapy in Europe: Clinical, theoretical and research approaches* (pp. 260–281). London: Jessica Kingsley Publishers.

Erkkilä, J., Ala-Ruona, E., Punkanen, M., & Fachner, J. (2012). Perspectives on creativity in improvisational, psychodynamic music therapy. In D. Hargreaves, D. Miell, & R. MacDonald (Eds.), *Musical Imaginations: Multidisciplinary perspectives on creativity, performance and perception* (pp. 414–428). Oxford: Oxford University Press.

Erkkilä, J., Punkanen, M., Fachner, J., Ala-Ruona, E., Pöntiö, I., Tervaniemi, M., Vanhala, M., & Gold, C. (2011). Individual music therapy for depression—Randomised Controlled Trial. *British Journal of Psychiatry, 199*(2), 132–139.

Fachner, J. (2011). Time is the key—Music and ASC. In E. Cardenas, M. Winkelmann, C. Tart, & S. Krippner (Eds.), *Altering consciousness: A multidisciplinary perspective* (Vol. 1 History, Culture and the Humanities, pp. 355–376). Santa Barbara: Praeger.

Fachner, J., & Stegemann, T. (2013). Electroencephalography (EEG) and music therapy: On the same wavelength? *Music & Medicine, 5*(4), 217–222. doi:10.1177/1943862113495062

Grocke, D. (1999). Pivotal moments in guided imagery and music. In J. Hibben (Ed.), *Inside music therapy: Client experiences* (pp. 295–305). Gilsum, NH: Barcelona.

Grocke, D. (2009). Guided imagery and music (the Bonny Method) as psychotherapy. *Psychotherapy in Australia, 15*(3), 64–71.

Hanser, S. B. (2009). From ancient to integrative medicine: Models for music therapy. *Music and Medicine, 1*(2), 87–96. doi:10.1177/1943862109345131

Hari, R., Himberg, T., Nummenmaa, L., Hämäläinen, M., & Parkkonen, L. (2013). Synchrony of brains and bodies during implicit interpersonal interaction. *Trends in Cognitive Science, 17*(3), 105–106.

Kern, P., & Aldridge, D. (2006). Using embedded busic therapy tnterventions to support outdoor play of young children with autism in an inclusive community-based child care program. *Journal of Music Therapy, 43*(4), 270–294.

Lindenberger, U., Li, S.-C., Gruber, W., & Muller, V. (2009). Brains swinging in concert: Cortical phase synchronization while playing guitar. *BMC Neuroscience, 10*(1), 22. doi:10.1186/1471-2202-10-22

Magee, W. L. (2014). *Music technology in therapeutic and health settings*. London: Jessica Kingsley Publishers.

Müller, V., Sänger, J., & Lindenberger, U. (2013). Intra- and inter-brain synchronization during musical improvisation on the guitar. *PLoS ONE, 8*(9), e73852. doi:10.1371/journal.pone.0073852

Neugebauer, L., & Aldridge, D. (1998). Communication, heart rate and the musical dialogue. *British Journal of Music Therapy, 12*(2), 46–52.

Nordoff, P., & Robbins, C. (2007). *Creative music therapy: A guide to fostering clinical musicianship* (2nd ed.). Gilsum, NH: Barcelona Publishers.

Ridder, H. M. O., Stige, B., Qvale, L. G., & Gold, C. (2013). Individual music therapy for agitation in dementia: An exploratory randomized controlled trial. *Aging & Mental Health, 17*(6), 667–678. doi:10.1080/13607863.2013.790926

Sänger, J., Müller, V., & Lindenberger, U. (2012). Intra- and interbrain synchronization and network properties when playing guitar in duets. *Frontiers in Human Neuroscience, 6*, 312. doi:10.3389/fnhum.2012.00312

Schall, A., Haberstroh, J., & Pantel, J. (2015). Time series analysis of individual music therapy in dementia: Effects on dommunication behavior and emotional well-being. *GeroPsych: The Journal of Gerontopsychology and Geriatric Psychiatry, 28*(3), 113–122. doi:10.1024/1662–9647/a000123

Smith, E. R., & Semin, G. R. (2004). Socially situated cognition: Cognition in its social context. *Advances in experimental social psychology, 36*, 53–117.

Spintge, M. D., Ralph, & Droh, M. D., Roland (Eds.). (1992). *MusicMedicine Volume II*. Saint Louis, MO: MMB Music.

Street, A. J., Magee, W. L., Odell-Miller, H., Bateman, A., & Fachner, J. (2015). Home-based neurologic music therapy for upper limb rehabilitation with chronic hemiparetic stroke patients—a feasibility study protocol. *Frontiers of Human Neuroscience, 9*, 480. doi:10.3389/fnhum.2015.00480

Trondalen, G. (2005). "Significant moments" in music therapy with young persons suffering from anorexia nervosa. *Music Therapy Today, 6*(3), 396–429.

Trost, W., Frühholz, S., Cochrane, T., Cojan, Y., & Vuilleumier, P. (2015). Temporal dynamics of musical emotions examined through intersubject synchrony of brain activity. *Social Cognitive and Affective Neuroscience, 10*(12), 1705–1721.

WFMT. (2011). What is music therapy? *World Federation of Music Therapy*. Retrieved from http://www.wfmt.info/wfmt-new-home/about-wfmt/

Winnicott, D. (1968). Playing: Its theoretical status in the clinical situation. *The International Journal of Psychoanalysis, 49*, 591–599.

Wosch, T., & Wigram, T. (Eds.). (2007). *Microanalysis in music therapy: Methods, techniques and applications for clinicians, researchers, educators and students.* London: Jessica Kingsley Publishers.

# 9

# MUSIC, PLEASURE, AND SOCIAL AFFILIATION

## Hormones and Neurotransmitters

*Roni Granot*

### Introduction

Of the numerous roles played by music in human society, two stand out as especially ancient and powerful: promotion of social cohesion and physical or emotional healing. The powers of music to improve mood, to treat certain illnesses, and to aid in driving out evil spirits is attested to in healing rituals in numerous traditional cultures (see chapters by Fachner and by Saarikallio, this volume). Music also plays a central role as a vehicle for social cohesion as manifested in rituals and social ceremonies, often also involving dance alongside music. The unique ability of music to entrain bodily movements and to induce motor and emotional synchronization among those participating in its making (Henry & Grahn, this volume) make it especially adept at confering feelings of unity, affiliation, and social bonding. In these contexts the emotional power of music seems to be highly combined with and dependent on social and cultural experiences and beliefs. Yet, even when music is detached from these contexts, becoming a seemingly abstract sonic object (most notably as Western classical instrumental music), it can induce intense feelings and pleasure, often accompanied by physiological changes. These too of course, are imbued with (very different) social and cultural beliefs. This wider perspective on music will accompany us as we describe the emerging findings regarding the brain pathways and underlying neurochemistry supporting some aspects of music's ability to influence us so deeply.

It should be noted at the outset that in contrast to the extensive work on the neural substrates of various aspects of our cognitive and emotional response to music, our understanding of the underlying neurochemistry is in its very infancy. Research has focused on a limited and isolated number of neurotransmitters and neuropeptides in its search to understand the stress-reducing and health-promoting abilities of music (Bernatzky et al., 2011), its ability to induce peaks of pleasure (Zatorre, 2015), and its relation to neuropeptides involved in social behavior. This selection is highly limited by the research methods that can be used in humans, and by the limited ability to cope with the enormous complexities of the neural and chemical interactive systems involved. Nonetheless, these findings are exciting and promising and will surely attract more research in the next upcoming years (for recent reviews see Chanda & Levitin, 2013 and Fancourt, Ockelford, & Belai, 2014; for innovative approaches see Kanduri et al., 2015). In the current chapter we will focus on music's ability to activate the reward system with its underlying dopamine-opioid neurochemistry. We will draw a line from affiliative interactions to the reward system, focusing on affiliative vocalizations. We will show how music activates brain regions and neurochemistry associated with these two aspects of behavior, and we will suggest that music's ability to drive the reward system is not limited to processes of prediction of abstract sequences. Rather, it is related to a sense of agency, and to the fundamental association between prediction of affiliative vocalizations, including motherese and music with its concomitant social reward.

## The Reward System and Dopamine-Opioids

The word "reward" carries with it a number of relevant associations: Reward confers pleasure (hedonic value); we might be willing to invest energies in obtaining it, (motivation); and we might try to figure out and remember what we did to obtain it, in order to maximize our ability to gain it again in the future (incentive learning). All these components are relevant to what we call "reward" in behavioral psychology, where the term is typically used to denote a set of subcortical and cortical processes "engineered" by evolution to ensure motivation to engage in adaptive behaviors such as feeding, social communication, and reproduction ("primary rewards"). Other secondary rewards such as monetary gain, drugs of abuse, humor, and music also engage this same system, though with different involvement of higher cortical areas.

The reward system was first identified by Olds and Milner (1954). They observed that rats would self-stimulate certain brain areas through implanted electrodes, often to the exclusion of all other activities including food intake. The three components of reward—the pleasure or "liking" which ensures initiation of the adaptive behavior, the "wanting" or motivation to obtain the reward, and the reward-related learning—are functionally and anatomically partially independent. They are subserved by different (though overlapping) brain circuits and by different neurotransmitters. The motivational and incentive behavior towards acquisition of reward is mediated by dopamine and, in humans, elicits feelings of desire, urgency, thrill or craving, excitement, elation, enthusiasm, energy, and potency. In contrast, the consummatory stage elicits intense feelings of pleasure, as well as physiological quiescence, rest, and sedation, reinforcing the production and repetition of those behaviors. The consummatory aspects of reward are mediated by endogenous opioids.

*Dopamine* is a monamine neurotransmitter in the same family as epinephrine (adrenaline) and norepinephrine (noradrelanine). It has numerous peripheral and central functions. In the mammalian brain it is expressed widely in four identified groups of pathways; here we focus on the mesolimbic and mesocortical pathways known together as the mesocorticolimbic pathway, which originates in the Ventral Tegmental Area (VTA). In the reward system dopamine seems to regulate motivation and goal directed behavior and is involved in prediction and learning related to future rewards.

The *μ-opioid receptor* (MOR) system is highly involved in analgesic, stress reducing and reward processes involving, among others, μ-opioid receptors in the midbrain VTA (Fields & Margolis, 2015). MORs are involved in pain reduction, either by inhibitng pain transmission substances, or through facilitating a rise in DA levels. Pain avoidance can be conceptualized as the counterpart of pleasure seeking, both being reward behaviors driven by negative and postive reinforcements respectively. In different animals, engaging in affiliative interactions such as social play or grooming is associated with endogenous μ-opioid release. Similarly, in a range of animals from chicks to infants of rhesus monkeys, substances faciltiating MOR, like morphine, reduce distress and social seeking during and following social separation (Loseth, Ellingsen, & Leknes, 2014).

## The Reward System, Complex Vocalizations, and Music in Animal Models

Given the limited methods we can use to study neurochemistry in humans we seek to combine data from human studies on music with relevant data from studies of social animals in which singing or complex vocalizations serve as motivated and directed social signals which involve activity in the reward system (Wöhr & Schwarting, 2013). Here we focus on studies of rats and mice in which the brain circuits mediating affective information are largely similar to those found in humans, mindful that human musical behaviors are different from social vocalizations in animals.

Recent studies in rodents have shown an association between types of vocalizations and affective states. In rats and mice, social situations—such as play and tumble in juveniles and mating in adults—are associated with various types of high 50kHhz Ultrasonic Vocalizations (USVs), coupled with increased activity in the Nacc (nucleus accumbens) and elevated levels of DA. Listening to 50kHz recorded calls, but not to other calls or sounds, induces behaviors of approach to the sound source and increased dopamine release (Willuhn et al., 2014).

Different neural and chemical interventions can be used in these animals to better understand the chemistry underlying these USVs. Psychostimulants such as amphetamine serve as DA faciliators and are very effective in inducing the 50kHz calls (Rippberger et al., 2015). Correspondingly, blocking DA receptors with a substance such as Naloxone reduces these calls. In this context it is fascinating to note that at least two Parkinson's disease (PD) patients developed, in response to increased dosages of DA replacement therapy, compulsive singing associated with a sense of pleasure and relief (Bonvin et al., 2007). This is in line with other compulsive activities related to other rewards such as compulsive eating, hypersexuality, or gambling reported under similar conditions in PD.

Sutoo and Akiyama (2004) suggested a cascade of chemical interactions in which music (like exercise) can reduce blood pressure by increasing levels of DA. In their study, spontaneously hypertensive rats were exposed to two hours of music by Mozart. Blood pressure was measured before and after treatment. The music treated rats showed significantly increased serum calcium, which enhances brain dopamine synthesis, and reduced systolic blood pressure, but this effect was blocked by calcium and dopamine inhibiting chemicals.

In several other studies music served as a modulator of addiction behavior in rats. It is known that cues associated with the drug reward (serving as conditioned stimuli) can lead to craving for the drug, causing relapse in humans and animals. Most animal studies use simple conditioned stimuli such as a tone or a light, Polston et al. (2011) paired music with methamphetamine administration in rats. After seven days of coupling, music was presented alone. Responses to the music mimicked those elicited by the drug: higher locomotion, and higher DA levels in the basolateral amygdala and Nacc. Interestingly, Tavakoli et al., (2012) showed an interaction between the place where the drug is administered (known as condition place preference—CPP) and the type of music presented to mice in conjunction with morphine. While one musical selection increased place preference in comparison to morphine alone, another selection *decreased* preference. Together, these studies demonstrate the feasibility of rodents as models to study some aspects of the relationship between music, social vocalizations, and the reward system.

## Oxytocin, Vasopressin, Social Behavior, and Music

Social affiliation and bonding is one of the strongest rewards affecting dopamine and μ-opioid processes. Affiliative stimuli of potential bonding partners—such as facial features, vocalizations, and gestures—serve as unconditioned incentive stimuli. Within this system vasopressin and oxytocin serve an important role in perceptual and attentional processing of and memory for affiliative stimuli (Depue & Morrone-Strupinsky, 2005).

Oxytocin and vasopressin are genetically and structurally similar neuropeptides studied extensively in animals and more recently in humans. In animals, they are significantly involved in affiliative/aggressive social behaviors, social stress and anxiety, and social memory (Lim & Young, 2006). Parallel findings in humans have been advanced through intranasal administration of these peptides coupled with imaging data, new paradigms taken from neuroeconomics, and genetic mapping (see special issue on "Oxytocin, Vasopressin & Social Behavior" in *Hormones and Behavior*, 2012). These studies reveal associations between oxytocin and/or vasopressin and autism and Williams syndrome; affiliative versus agonistic responses to faces; ability to identify emotions; altruistic behavior, trust and cooperation; social stress; the dance phenotype (Bachner-Melman et al., 2005) and musical memory (Granot et al., 2013).

Oxytocin and vasopressin are synthesized centrally in the hypothalamus, which is strongly implicated in stress responses. The activity of oxytocin is tightly interwoven with that of vasopressin, since these chemicals are able to bind to each other's receptors. In general, pair bonding and parental care seem to be influenced in a similar manner by both peptides. But whereas vasopressin leads to higher arousal, anxiety, stress, and aggression, oxytocin has (beyond its better known role in milk letdown and labour) an anti-anxiety effect and it promotes approach, affiliative behavior, and attachment (Caldwell & Albers, 2015).

Similar to the effects reported in relation to dopamine there is a clear relationship between the two neuropeptides and social vocalizations. Babies' vocalizations elicit increase in oxytocin levels in mothers, and conversely, maternal oxytocin levels are related to the frequency of "motherese" vocalizations, expression of positive affect, and affectionate touch of mothers in relation to their infants (Feldman, 2012). In animals, one can also see the reverse aspect of this association: Changes in oxytocin levels can induce increased affiliative calls and decrease in distress calls (Nagasawa et al., 2012). In humans, singing—which could be a proxy to social vocalizations—elicits affiliative feelings of increased trust and belongingness and has recently been associated with increased oxytocin levels (Keeler et al., 2015).

Another interesting line of research connecting oxytocin and vasopressin to music is found in individuals with Williams Syndrome (WS). WS is a genetic neurodevelopmental disorder characterized, among other things, by increased approach behavior, even to strangers, poor social judgement and peer relationships, extreme emotional reactivity to music, and high general levels of anxiety. Dai and colleagues (2012) examined base levels of oxytocin and vasopressin in WS versus controls, as well as patterns of release of these neuropeptides in response to a positive (music) and negative (cold) experience. Results showed significantly higher base levels of oxytocin in WS as compared to controls. In addition, WS individuals listening to their favorite music elicited exaggerated levels of oxytocin and vasopressin suggesting that music can, under certain conditions, strongly modulate the level of these peptides.

One of the most promising venues for studying the neurochemistry of music in general and in relation to oxytocin and vasopressin in particular is found in genetic studies (for excellent reviews see Gingras et al., 2015; Tan et al., 2014). Explanations of the different approaches to associating genes with behavior is beyond the scope of this chapter (but see Thompson, Mosing, & Ullén, this volume, for further discussion). However, in all of these methods there is an attempt to find out whether polymorphisms (variants of alleles) of genes that regulate activity of neurotranmitters or neuropeptides are over-represented in cohorts of a specific phenotype as compared to the general population or a control group (see for example Balding, 2006).

The *AVPR1a* receptor gene is located on chromosome 12q14–15 and contains three microsatellites (a tract with repeating DNA motives) two of which—*RS1* and *RS3*—are associated with social behavior. In a number of studies it was found that musical memory, musical aptitude and musical creativity (activities of composing, improvising and arranging music) are associated with specific combinations of allelic variants of RS1+RS3. This association can be even stronger when a dependency on genes that regulate the amount of serotonin is taken into consideration (Granot et al., 2007; Ukkola-Vuoti et al., 2011, 2013—although see Morley et al., 2012). Interestingly, a similar pattern was reported for the dance phenotype which shares possible roots with music (Bachner-Melman et al., 2005). In order to examine causal relations, Granot et al. (2013) examined the effects of a single exposure to vasopressin on scores of verbal and musical memory tests. This single dose exerted degrading effects on memory only in the music memory tests, and only in subjects receiving vasopressin in the first session contingent on the state of the subjects in terms of alertness, focused attention and positive valence.

Together these data suggest one pathway through which music—as a social affiliative incentive—can modulate neurochemicals in brain regions associated with social behavior and reward. We will elaborate on this point in this chapter's conclusion.

## Music, Pleasure, and the Reward System

Given what we know about the reward system, it is perhaps not surprising that music experienced as intensely pleasurable engages this system. However, music seems to be different from other primary rewards which ensure survival and well-being, or secondary rewards (such as money) which enable acquisition of primary rewards. In music, as in other aesthetic objects, the reward seems to be intrinsic to the object (Zatorre, 2015). We will return to this question of why is music so pleasurable at the end of the chapter.

One very evident signal of strong engagement and emotional response to music is found in the phenomenon of chills, or *frisson*. This phenomenon as experienced in music listening is characterized by shivers down the spine or goosebumps (piloerection), and is often associated with intense pleasure (Panksepp, 1995).

The interest in chills in response to music was driven by the fact that chills are seemingly easy to define and measure as well as reliable in terms of self-report, and can thus serve as a reliable index of intense emotional and pleasurable responses to music. Many questions can be asked with regard to this phenomenon: Does everyone experience chills in response to music? How is this related to other chill responses in nonmusical contexts? Do chills occur at the extreme point in the continuum of unpleasant–pleasant music, or is it a separate phenomenon? What is it *in* the music that elicits this response, and does everyone experience chills to the same musical pieces? What is it in the person or in her interaction with the music that elicits this response? What other physiological changes does it entail? What happens in our brains when we experience such intense sensations? What happens just before the onset of this response? What about *unpleasant* chills in response to music?

Many of these questions have been at least partially addressed over the years since this phenomenon was first described in relation to music (Goldstein, 1980). Already in that first study, Goldstein noted that the experience of chills is very idiosyncratic, in that a musical selection eliciting chills in one person does not necessarily elicit such a response in another. Not everyone experiences chills, but those who do show it in a consistent manner (Grewe et al., 2005). There are a number of variables which influence the tendency to experience them, though the crucial component seems to be the degree of emotional engagement with the music (Nusbaum & Silvia, 2011)

Consistent with the strong emotional component, chills-inducing excerpts elicit higher activity in the body's sympathetic system, as compared with the same excerpts rated as neutral or low in pleasure. Such responses include higher galvanic skin response, heart rate and respiratory rate, lower blood pulse volume, and lower temperature (Craig, 2005; Grewe, Kopiez, & Altenmüller, 2009). This same pattern of changes was noted in response to excerpts rated as high in pleasure (no chills) and low in pleasure (though to a lesser degree) compared to excerpts rated "neutral" (Salimpoor et al., 2009). Importantly, this indicates that the chills response occurs at one end of the pleasant–unpleasant continuum.

Despite the fact that it is rare to find two people reporting chills to the same piece, it would seem that chills are associated with some unexpected change in the music (hence a salient event). Such changes have been reported to include: a change in dynamics from *p* to *f*, change in texture from solo to orchestra or vice versa, expansion of register, harmonic ambiguity, dissonance, or irregularity (chromaticism, juxtaposition of minor and major, deceptive cadences, unresolved or augmented harmonies, appoggiaturas, etc.), and harmonic or timbre changes of a repeating motive (Huron, 2006; Huron, & Margulis, 2010). This list already points to the role of expectations while listening to, and familiarity with, the selected musical pieces. A number of studies have shown that chills are much more readily elicited in pieces selected by the participants as compared to experimenter-selected music, suggesting that chills could be related to personal memories or associations. Moreover, increased arousal and "craving" may be directed towards the chill response itself rather than the music. However, a number of studies were able to elicit chills in unfamiliar experimenter-selected excerpts albeit in a less consistent manner than self-selected music (e.g. Guhn, Hamm, & Zentner, 2007).

Perhaps the most interesting findings are related to the neural networks underlying the chills phenomenon. In a number of studies, music inducing chills in one subject served as control music for another, thus controlling, at the group level, for effects driven by acoustical information. In a seminal study by Blood and Zatorre (2001), chills were associated with increased pleasure ratings, hightened sympathetic activity, and increased blood flow to a set of brain areas comprising the reward network. These included increased activity in the left ventral striatum (the Nacc) and dorsomedial midbrain (regions rich in opioid receptors) along with decreased activity in the right amygdala, left hippocampus/amygdala and ventro medial prefrontal cortex (VmPFC). Additional paralimbic regions (bilateral insula and OFC), motor related areas (SMA and cerebellum), and arousal related areas (thalamus and AC) also showed association with increased chills intensity. Two following studies by the same group added valuable information. Salimpoor et al. (2011) used a similar paradigm combining fMRI with PET data. This study sought direct measures of DA release in music rated as highly pleasurable and chills-inducing as compared to neutral music. PET data showed increase in DA release in striatal areas. Using the somewhat better temporal resolution of fMRI the researchers could dissociate between two processes: anticipation prior to the chill, associated with increase in DA ("craving") in the right caudate, versus the peak of the experience ("consumption"), associated with increase in DA in the right Nacc.

As mentioned earlier, these elegant results raise the question as to the source of anticipation and reward: Does it lie in one's familiarirty with the music, and already established associations between certain musical events and chills, or is it the music itself interacting with the specific cognitive appraisal attached to it by each listener? Salimpoor et al.(2013) conducted a follow-on study where the degree of pleasure elicited by the piece was measured implicitly, the pieces were unfamiliar to subjects, and no chill response was required. Subjects listened to *new* musical pieces and after each listening offered a bid as to how much they would be willing to pay to hear the piece again (similar to prices on *iTunes*). Bids higher than "0" elicited activity in the reward system. Importantly, this demonstrates that activation of the reward system can be elicited by *schematic* expectations (see also Menon, & Levitin, 2005). Connectivity analyses showed that as the music gained "value" there was an increased connectivity between NAcc and large portions of primary and associative auditory cortices, among other networks. The authors suggest that

> through the temporal dimension, previously neutral cues—tones and other sound sequences that have no inherent reward value—interact with higher-order cognitive brain regions to gain incentive salience, which then influences affective brain regions and impcats behavioral decisions about the value of an abstract stimulus.
>
> *(p. 219)*

## Conclusion: How Musical Sound Becomes Rewarding

The idea that music's "emotion and meaning" stems from ongoing processes of anticipation and expectations, and from delaying, thwarting, or confirming such expectations, was first proposed by Leonard Meyer (1956), and has since received elaboration (e.g., Huron 2006) and experimental support (Koelsch, 2015). Our current review suggests that this process is mediated by the mesolimbic system through dopaminergic activity known to be heavily implicated in learning (Salimpoor et al., 2015). Fluctuations in DA levels serve to signal errors in the prediction of future salient or rewarding stimuli (Schultz, 1998). Through previous learning (or conditioning) we learn to associate sensory cues with forthcoming rewards, and therefore these cues induce predictions about the timing, nature, and magnitude of the reward. Dopaminergic activity is recorded as long as there is some degree of unpredictability, that is some error in any one of these predictions. The highest activity in Dopaminergic areas is recorded when there is a "positive error," in which an actual outcome is even better than predicted.

Such a mechanism can modify even lower level sensory processing, as suggested by Zatorre (2015). In their studies, this pattern was reflected in the changes of connectivity between the striatum and the auditory regions as a function of the reward. That is, processing of the more rewarding music excerpts induced predictions based on stored musical schemata and images (indexed also by the increased activity in frontal regions), which in turn can explain the large variability in subjects' responses to the same piece of music. Furthermore, the complex combination of unfolding "streams" of changes in pitch, timing, texture, harmony, timbre, etc., can induce many layers of predictions, with personal biases driving which of those will become prominent in each listener.

While this explanation shows how the reward system interacts with other brain regions in processing music, it does not explain away the question of why music is so pleasurable. What is the "positive error" or "better than predicted" condition in music? Would *any* type of learning which must include prediction errors and corrections induce—even without a following reward—activation of the reward system? Would it induce subjective pleasure? The answer seems to lead us back to the emotional impact of music, possibly driven by our suggested framework of music as an affiliative social behavior (Tarr, Launay, & Dunbar, 2014; Harrison & Louie, 2014; Sachs et al., 2016). Our first exposures to music (either as such or in the form of motherese), whether after birth or even before, are part of our affiliative relationships with our caretakers. The decoding of these streams of sound sequences entails prediction, anticipation, prediction errors, and a very tangible and strong affiliative reward. Motherese—being slower, repetitive, rhythmic, with prolonged vowels that delineate a clear pitch contour, and combined with other mutltimodal cues—serves as an ideal medium to ensure motivation, reward and incentive learning of these interactions through prediction processes. Later encounters with music in kindergarten, school, family reunions, and parties are all deeply rooted in a socio-emotional context. It may well be that this association between vocalizations and social reward adds an emotional coloring and reward gloss to the ongoing prediction processes, thus providing a crucial layer to the intense pleasure music can provide.

## Core Reading

Blood, A. J., & Zatorre, R. J. (2001). Intensely pleasurable responses to music correlate with activity in brain regions implicated in reward and emotion. *Proceedings of the National Academy of Sciences USA*, 98(20), 11818–11823.

Chanda, M. L., & Levitin, D. J. (2013). The neurochemistry of music. *Trends in Cognitive Science, 17*(4), 179–193. doi:10.1016/j.tics.2013.02.007

Fancourt, D., Ockelford, A., & Belai, A. (2014). The psychoneuroimmunological effects of music: A systematic review and a new model. *Brain, Behavior, and Immunity, 36*, 15–26. doi:10.1016/j.bbi.2013.10.014

Kanduri, C., Kuusi, T., Ahvenainen, M., Philips, A. K., Lahdesmaki, H., & Jarvela, I. (2015). The effect of music performance on the transcriptome of professional musicians. *Scientific Reports*, 5, 9506. doi:10.1038/srep09506

Sachs, E. M., Ellis, R. J., Schalug, G., & Loui, P. (2016). Brain connectivity reflects human aesthetic responses to music. *Social Cognitive and Affective Neuroscience.* doi: 10.1093/scan/nsw009

Salimpoor, V. N., Zald, D. H., Zatorre, R. J., Dagher, A., & McIntosh, A. R. (2015). Predictions and the brain: How musical sounds become rewarding. *Trends in Cognitive Science, 19*(2), 86–91. doi:10.1016/j.tics.2014.12.001

Tan, Y. T., McPherson, G. E., Peretz, I., Berkovic, S. F., & Wilson, S. J. (2014). The genetic basis of music ability. *Frontiers in Psychology, 5*, 658. doi:10.3389/fpsyg.2014.00658

## Further References

Bachner-Melman, R., Dina, C., Zohar, A. H., Constantini, N., Lerer, E., Hoch, S., Sella, S., Nemanov, L., Gritsenko, I., Lichtenberg, P., & Granot, R. (2005). AVPR1a and SLC6A4 gene polymorphisms are associated with creative dance performance. *PLoS Genetics, 1*(3), e42. doi:10.1371/journal.pgen.0010042

Balding, D. J. (2006). A tutorial on statistical methods for population association studies. *Nature Reviews Genetics, 7*(10), 781–791. doi:10.1038/nrg1916

Bernatzky, G., Presch, M., Anderson, M., & Panksepp, J. (2011). Emotional foundations of music as a non-pharmacological pain management tool in modern medicine. *Neuroscience and Biobehavioral Reviews, 35*(9), 1989–1999. doi:10.1016/j.neubiorev.2011.06.005

Bonvin, C., Horvath, J., Christe, B., Landis, T., & Burkhard, P. R. (2007). Compulsive singing: Another aspect of punding in Parkinson's disease. *Annals of Neurology, 62*(5), 525–528. doi:10.1002/ana.21202

Caldwell, H. K., & Albers, H. E. (2015). Oxytocin, vasopressin, and the motivational forces that drive social behaviors. *Current Topics in Behavioral Neuroscience.* doi:10.1007/7854_2015_390

Craig, D. G. (2005). An exploratory study of physiological changes during "chills" induced by music. *Musicae Scientiae, 9*(2), 273–287.

Dai, L., Carter, C. S., Ying, J., Bellugi, U., Pournajafi-Nazarloo, H., & Korenberg, J. R. (2012). Oxytocin and Vasopressin are dysregulated in Williams Syndrome, a genetic disorder affecting social behavior. *PLoS ONE, 7*(6), e38513. http://doi.org/10.1371/journal.pone.0038513

Depue, R. A., & Morrone-Strupinsky, J. V. (2005). A neurobehavioral model of affiliative bonding: Implications for conceptualizing a human trait of affiliation. *Behavioral and Brain Sciences, 28*(3), 313–350; discussion 350–395.

Feldman, R. (2012). Oxytocin and social affiliation in humans. *Hormones and Behavior, 61*(3), 380–391. doi:10.1016/j.yhbeh.2012.01.008

Fields, H. L., & Margolis, E. B. (2015). Understanding opioid reward. *Trends in Neuroscience, 38*(4), 217–225. doi:10.1016/j.tins.2015.01.002

Gingras, B., Honing, H., Peretz, I., Trainor, L. J., & Fisher, S. E. (2015). Defining the biological bases of individual differences in musicality. *Philosophical Transactions of the Royal Society of London B Biological Sciences, 370*(1664), 20140092. doi:10.1098/rstb.2014.0092

Goldstein A. (1980). Thrills in response to music and other stimuli. *Physiological Psychology, 8*(1), 126–129.

Granot, R. Y., Frankel, Y., Gritsenko, V., Lerer, E., Gritsenko, I., Bachner-Melman, R., Israel, S., & Ebstein, R. P. (2007). Provisional evidence that the arginine vasopressin 1a receptor gene is associated with musical memory. *Evolution and Human Behavior, 28*(5), 313–318. doi:10.1016/j.evolhumbehav.2007.05.003

Granot, R. Y., Uzefovsky, F., Bogopolsky, H., & Ebstein, R. P. (2013). Effects of arginine vasopressin on musical working memory. *Frontiers in Psychology, 4*, 712. doi:10.3389/fpsyg.2013.00712

Grewe, O., Nagel, F., Kopiez, R., & Altenmuller, E. (2005). How does music arouse "chills"? Investigating strong emotions, combining psychological, physiological, and psychoacoustical methods. *Annals of the New York Academy of Sciences, 1060*, 446–449.

Grewe, O., Kopiez, R., & Altenmüller, E. (2009). The chill parameter: Goose bumps and shivers as promising measures in emotion research. *Music Perception, 27*(1), 61–74.

Guhn, M., Hamm, A., & Zentner, M. (2007). Physiological and musico-acoustic correlates of the chill response. *Music Perception, 24*(5), 473–483.

Harrison, L., & Louie, P. (2014). Thrills, chills, frissons, and skin orgasms: Toward an integrative model of transcendent psychophysiological experiences in music. *Frontiers in Psychology, 5*, 790. doi:10.3389/fpsyg.2014.00790

Huron, D. (2006). *Sweet anticipation: Music and the psychology of expectation.* Cambridge, MA: MIT Press.

Huron, D., & Margulis, E. H. (2010). Musical expectancy and thrills. In P. N. Juslin & J. A. Sloboda (Eds.), *Handbook of music and emotion: Theory, research, applications* (pp. 575–604). New York, NY: Oxford University Press.

Keeler, J. R., Roth, E. A., Neuser, B. L., Spitsbergen, J. M., Waters, D. J., & Vianney, J. M. (2015). The neurochemistry and social flow of singing: Bonding and oxytocin. *Frontiers in Human Neuroscience, 9*, 518. doi:10.3389/fnhum.2015.00518

Koelsch, S. (2015). Music-evoked emotions: Principles, brain correlates, and implications for therapy. *Annals of the New York Academy of Sciences, 1337*, 193–201. doi:10.1111/nyas.12684

Lim, M. M., & Young, L. J. (2006). Neuropeptidergic regulation of affiliative behavior and social bonding in animals. *Hormones and Behavior 50*(4), 506–517. doi:10.1016/j.yhbeh.2006.06.028

Loseth, G. E., Ellingsen, D. M., & Leknes, S. (2014). State-dependent mu-opioid modulation of social motivation. *Frontiers in Behavioral Neuroscience, 8*, 430. doi:10.3389/fnbeh.2014.00430

Menon, V., & Levitin, D. J. (2005). The rewards of music listening: Response and physiological connectivity of the mesolimbic system. *Neuroimage, 28*(1), 175–184. doi:10.1016/j.neuroimage.2005.05.053

Meyer, L. (1956). *Emotion and meaning in Music.* Chicago, IL: University of Chicago Press.

Morley, A. P., Narayanan, M., Mines, R., Molokhia, A., Baxter, S., Craig, G., . . . Craig, I. (2012). AVPR1A and SLC6A4 polymorphisms in choral singers and non-musicians: A gene association study. *PLoS One, 7*(2), e31763. doi:10.1371/journal.pone.0031763

Nagasawa, M., Okabe, S., Mogi, K., & Kikusui, T. (2012). Oxytocin and mutual communication in mother-infant bonding. *Frontiers in Human Neuroscience, 6*, 31. doi:10.3389/fnhum.2012.00031

Nusbaum, E. C., & Silvia, P. J. (2011). Shivers and timbres: Personality and the experience of chills from music. *Social Psychological and Personality Science, 2*(2), 199–204. doi:10.1177/1948550610386810

Olds, J., & Milner, P. (1954). Positive reinforcement produced by electrical stimulation of septal area and other regions of rat brain. *Journal of Comparative and Physiological Psychology, 47*(6), 419–427.

Panksepp, J. (1995). The emotional sources of "chills" induced by music. *Music Perception, 13*(2), 171–207.

Polston, J. E., Rubbinaccio, H. Y., Morra, J. T., Sell, E. M., & Glick, S. D. (2011). Music and methamphetamine: Conditioned cue-induced increases in locomotor activity and dopamine release in rats. *Pharmacology Biochemistry and Behavior, 98*(1), 54–61. doi:10.1016/j.pbb.2010.11.024

Rippberger, H., van Gaalen, M. M., Schwarting, R. K., & Wohr, M. (2015). Environmental and pharmacological modulation of amphetamine-induced 50-kHz ultrasonic vocalizations in rats. *Current Neuropharmacology, 13*(2), 220–232.

Salimpoor, V. N., Benovoy, M., Longo, G., Cooperstock, J. R., & Zatorre, R. J. (2009). The rewarding aspects of music listening are related to degree of emotional arousal. *PLoS One, 4*(10), e7487. doi:10.1371/journal.pone.0007487

Salimpoor, V. N., Benovoy, M., Larcher, K., Dagher, A., & Zatorre, R. J. (2011). Anatomically distinct dopamine release during anticipation and experience of peak emotion to music. *Nature Neuroscience, 14*(2), 257–262. doi:10.1038/nn.2726

Salimpoor, V. N., van den Bosch, I., Kovacevic, N., McIntosh, A. R., Dagher, A., & Zatorre, R. J. (2013). Interactions between the nucleus accumbens and auditory cortices predict music reward value. *Science, 340*(6129), 216–219. doi:10.1126/science.1231059

Schultz, W. (1998). Predictive reward signal of dopamine neurons. *Journal of Neurophysiology, 80*(1), 1–27.

Sutoo, D., & Akiyama, K. (2004). Music improves dopaminergic neurotransmission: Demonstration based on the effect of music on blood pressure regulation. *Brain Research, 1016*(2), 255–262. doi:10.1016/j.brainres.2004.05.018

Tarr, B., Launay, J., & Dunbar, R. I. (2014). Music and social bonding: "Self-other" merging and neurohormonal mechanisms. *Frontiers in Psychology, 5*, 1096. doi:10.3389/fpsyg.2014.01096

Tavakoli, F., Hoseini, S. E., Mokhtari, M., Vahdati, A., Razmi, N., & Vessal, M. (2012). Role of music in morphine rewarding effects in mice using conditioned place preference method. *Neuroendocrinology Letters, 33*(7), 709–712.

Ukkola-Vuoti, L., Oikkonen, J., Onkamo, P., Karma, K., Raijas, P., & Jarvela, I. (2011). Association of the arginine vasopressin receptor 1A (AVPR1A) haplotypes with listening to music. *Journal of Human Genetics, 56*(4), 324–329. doi:10.1038/jhg.2011.13

Ukkola-Vuoti, L., Kanduri, C., Oikkonen, J., Buck, G., Blancher, C., Raijas, P., . . . Jarvela, I. (2013). Genome-wide copy number variation analysis in extended families and unrelated individuals characterized for musical aptitude and creativity in music. *PLoS One, 8*(2), e56356. doi:10.1371/journal.pone.0056356

Willuhn, I., Tose, A., Wanat, M.J., Hart, A.S., Hollon, N.G., Phillips, P.E., Schwarting, R.K., and Wöhr, M. (2014). Phasic dopamine release in the nucleus accumbens in response to pro-social 50 kHz ultrasonic vocalizations in rats. *Journal of Neuroscience 34*(32), 10616–10623. doi:10.1523/jneurosci.1060–14.2014

Wöhr, M., & Schwarting, R. K. (2013). Affective communication in rodents: ultrasonic vocalizations as a tool for research on emotion and motivation. *Cell and Tissue Research, 354*(1), 81–97. doi:10.1007/s00441–013–1607–9

Young, L., & Flanagan-Cato (Eds.). (2012). Oxytocin, Vasopressin and social behavior [special issue]. *Hormones and Behavior,* 61(3), 227–462.

Zatorre, R. J. (2015). Musical pleasure and reward: Mechanisms and dysfunction. *Annals of the New York Academy of Sciences, 1337,* 202–211. doi:10.1111/nyas.12677

# PART 2

# Hearing and Listening to Music

# 10
# MUSICAL STRUCTURE
## Time and Rhythm

*Peter Martens and Fernando Benadon*

## Introduction

Structure is more familiar to us in things we see than in things we hear. We build structures to inhabit; we observe structures in the natural world such as trees or coral reefs. Musical structure is often visible, too; we can see it in the physical movements that produce musical sounds, in the dance moves drawn from musical rhythms, and in the notation used to represent musical ideas. While any of these visible manifestations of musical structure could serve as a useful place to start our treatment of structured musical time, it is perhaps easiest to begin with the visible traces that are captured in standard music notation.

## A Beginning: Hearing a Beat

Consider the snippet of music below, a simple string of quarter notes, continuing infinitely (Figure 10.1). No pitch, timbral, or tempo information is given, simply unspecified events occurring in a particular sequential relationship.

Though they may look identical on the page, our understanding of these quarter notes morphs as they proceed in time. Our minds are built to predict the future, to extrapolate probabilities for possible future events based on past experience, and we do this unconsciously with all manner of stimuli (Huron, 2006, p. 3). If we've seen three ants emerge from a hole in the ground, we expect more to follow; this is a "what" expectation, and so we would be surprised if an earwig emerged next. Likewise, if we've heard five evenly-spaced drips from a leaky faucet hit the sink bottom, we expect more drips to occur with the same time interval between them. This is both a "what" and "when" expectation; we would be surprised by a large delay before drip number six, but we would also be surprised by a finger snap at the exact time that that sixth drip should occur.

These basic habits have a biological foundation (see Henry & Grahn, this volume). Successfully predicting the timing and type of future events confers significant survival advantage to an organism, and the auditory system—operating as it does in full 360° surround—is one of (if not *the*) most important sensory inputs in terms of this advantage. We bring these habits and reflexive skills to music listening. Returning to Figure 10.1, after we hear only the first two quarter notes we expect a third event to follow the second at the same time interval

*Figure 10.1*   Repeating quarter notes.

that separated the second from the first (Longuet-Higgins & Lee, 1982). More precisely, we expect the beginning, or *onset*, of the third note to correspond to the time span established by the onsets of notes one and two. This span of time from onset to onset, or attack point to attack point, is often referred to as an *interonset interval*, or IOI. A single IOI is bounded by two events, and thus while two events make us expect a third event, just one IOI makes us expect future similar IOIs. In either way of referring to events in our environment, our minds grab hold of a *periodicity*: a sequence of temporally equidistant onsets.

Continuing our thought experiment with Figure 10.1 a step further, if the expectation of a third in-time note (or second equivalent IOI) is met, we have an even stronger expectation of yet another note/IOI with the same spacing in time as the previous, and so on. As the periodic sequence unfolds and our expectations are further validated, our ability to predict the timing of upcoming events is reinforced. This basic ability allows us to synchronize physical movements with other humans (as when playing in a band) or with the sound waves emanating from speakers or headphones (as when moving to a beat). The terms *beat induction* and *entrainment* are commonly used for this phenomenon, which may occur at a cognitive or neural level without physical manifestation (Honing, 2013).

## Beat, Hierarchy, and Meter

Our minds are not content to grasp this single periodicity, however. Once we hear events 1–3, a longer time interval becomes established between events 1 and 3 that leads us to expect event 5 further into the future, while at the same time expecting event 4 immediately next. Event 5 is now expected as a part of two hierarchically organized, or stacked periodicities: the original event string 1,2,3,4,5 and the slower moving event string 1,3,5. Being inextricably linked, these two simultaneous layers of events complement each other's temporal expectations and increase our anticipation of event 5, as shown by the arrows in Figure 10.2.

It is important to note that we form these expectations unconsciously, and that by default we tend to nest layers by aligning each event in the faster layer with every other event in the slower layer, as in Figure 10.2 (Brochard, et al., 2003). Listening to a dripping faucet or undifferentiated metronome clicks, we naturally impose a grouping, often duple, on the acoustically identical events, even from infancy (Bergeson & Trehub, 2005).[1] Any grouping of multiple events into larger time spans is a way to sharpen and heighten our precision as we predict when future events will occur, and these groupings also function to lower the cognitive load by "chunking" a larger number of events in the incoming information stream into fewer discrete units (cf. Zatorre, Chen, & Penhune, 2007).

This nesting of shorter time spans within larger time spans, as conveyed by the brackets and arrows in Figure 10.2, can be applied recursively to include more than just two layers, as long as each event in a slower periodicity is simultaneously a part of all faster

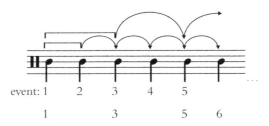

*Figure 10.2* Projection and accrual of temporal expectations.

periodicities. Thus, our expectations develop over longer time spans in an orderly fashion, for instance, expecting a future 9th quarter note as part of three layers: 1,2,3,4,5,6,7,8,9 (original), 1,3,5,7,9 (half as fast), and 1,5,9 (four times slower than the original). As we will see below, this nesting process will not accrue indefinitely, but in this way we invest some moments in the future with greater "expectational weight" than others. We expect the 9th quarter note more strongly than the 8th, for example, because that 9th quarter note would fulfill the expectations of all three levels of periodicity. The 8th quarter note—at least in this musically impoverished abstraction—only serves to continue the original note-to-note periodicity.

The emergent pattern of expectational peaks, foothills, and valleys brought about by layers of nested expectations gives rise to what we experience as *meter* in music (Jones, 1992), and is encoded in music notation via a number of symbolic systems such as time signatures and note durations. When we speak of stronger or weaker beats in music, then, we are projecting the products of our own psychological processing onto a musical sound-scape. It is often fairly easy to recognize these patterns when analyzing music, whether notated or not, and so we can speak of a piece's *metric hierarchy* when referring to the typical strong-weak patterns of common meters. In 4/4 time, for example, we generally experience beat 1 as the "strongest" in each measure, followed by beat 3, and then beats 2 and 4 about equally.

### Beat and Tempo

There are few musical terms used more commonly, yet less precisely, than *beat* and *tempo*. We have just used "beat" in the discussion above to refer to each of the four beats in a measure of 4/4 time. This usage implies that *the* beat in a measure of 4/4 corresponds to the notated quarter note, which is generally true. In terms of cognition, however, we define a beat without recourse to a notated meter, as a periodicity in music onto which we latch perceptually. But already we have two uses of the same term; a beat can refer to a single layer of motion in music (e.g. "this piece has a strong quarter-note beat"), while at the same time we use beat to label each occurrence within that string of events (e.g. "the trumpet enters on beat 4"). To use the term in either sense presupposes a process called *beat-finding*, whereby the listener infers a consistently articulated periodicity from the music, even if not all beats correspond to sounded events. Evidence for beat-finding can be seen in physical movements such as foot tapping or head nodding in synchrony with the music, and appears to be an almost exclusively human trait (cf. Patel et al., 2009).

*Tempo* is another term ubiquitous in music that is used in inconsistent and poorly defined ways. Let's return to Figure 10.1 for a moment. If that rhythm's speed is not too fast or too slow, each quarter note will be perceived as a beat, and that beat will establish the tempo of the music. We often think of tempo as corresponding to a single periodicity, typically expressed by musicians as beats per minute (BPM). However, as we saw earlier, the basic periodicity of our example gives rise to other nested (slower) periodicities. Further, real music is rarely as simple as a bare string of quarter notes. These two points lead to a key question. Of the several periodicities we can perceive as a beat even in a simple string of identical events, which of them would we define as determining a piece's tempo? The simplest notion of beat and tempo revolves around the idea of an optimal range for tempo, centered on 100 BPM (Parncutt, 1994) or 120 BPM (Van Noorden & Moelants, 1999). While this turns out to be a complicated issue in fully musical contexts, we can make some general observations about the main beat in the well-known melody shown in Figure 10.3. If we were to hear that melody performed at ♩ = 120 BPM, most listeners would latch onto the quarter note as their beat, and would likely describe their experience of tempo in the piece as moderate. If the same melody were performed at ♩ = 200 BPM, however, many listeners would instead latch onto the half note at 100 BPM as their beat rate. This brings us to a curious paradox: While our perceived beat would be objectively slower in the second hearing, our judgment of tempo would likely be faster—bouncy or lively (or maybe even too fast!) instead of moderate.

Most commonly, tempo is used by composers, performers, DJs, etc. to refer to the BPM rate of the beat level, often designated as a metronome marking (e.g. mm = 120). Such markings are one way to convey compositional intent in a score or piece of sheet music, or to compare one piece to another as in a BPM table when constructing a set of electronic dance music. Yet BPM rates do not necessarily correspond to a sensation of faster or slower, and this mismatch is the subject of several in-progress research projects. Judgments of tempo are often based on a more general sense of event density (e.g. Bisesi & Vicario, 2015)—how "busy" the musical texture is—and are often encoded by subjective verbal descriptors such as "lively" or "moderate," or by traditional Italian terms such as "largo" or "allegro con brio." But even the composer Beethoven found the imprecision of these terms problematic, leading him to champion the objectivity of BPM rates and the newly invented metronome in the early nineteenth century (Grant, 2014, pp. 254ff.).

## *Foraging for Meter*

Our minds and bodies are constantly searching our environments for periodic information, and when it exists we attempt to synchronize with these periodicities neurally and physiologically (Merchant et al., 2015). Our initial phase of synchronization with complex periodic stimuli such as music begins at an initial beat or *tactus*. London (2012, pp. 30–33) cites several hundred years of historical acknowledgement of the concept of tactus, and Honing

*Figure 10.3*   F. J. Haydn, "Austrian Hymn."

(2012) argues that at least beat-finding (if not meter-finding) is innate, a basic and constant cognitive operation when listening to music.

While we might assume that the tactus in Figure 10.1 is obvious—it's a string of quarter notes, after all—beat-finding is constrained and directed by several salience criteria that serve to mark some musical attacks for attention over others. All such criteria lend accentual weight to these moments, and these accents can come from harmony (the tonic triad feels more stable than other chords), melody (a particularly high or long note stands out), instrumentation (a snare drum attack is prominent in many textures), articulation (a violinist's martelé bow stroke marks notes for attention), and the list could go on. Both Lerdahl and Jackendoff (1983) and Temperley (2001) construct theoretical models for meter perception that attempt to account for these various factors, albeit in more general ways, in the form of metrical preference rules (MPRs). For instance, Temperley's MPR 6 states that we "prefer to align strong beats with changes in harmony" (p. 51), while Lerdahl and Jackendoff's MPR 7 states that we "Strongly prefer a metrical structure in which cadences are metrically stable" (p. 88). In addition to the perceptual cues that accentual markers provide, the particular distribution of accented onsets affects how a listener assigns a specific "internal clock" that most efficiently matches the pattern of the heard rhythm (Povel & Essens, 1985).

Despite the above models' recognition of the importance of a tactus level, what is perhaps the most basic cognitive factor in beat-finding is left under-theorized: tempo. London (2012) summarizes relevant research and creates "Tempo-Metrical Types" that map out the ramifications of tempo for not just tactus but for entire metric structures. Imagine "Flight of the Bumblebee"; now imagine tapping your foot along to each note—impossible! Even though we perceive each note as part of the melody, that periodicity is simply too fast to suggest a beat (defined as beat *perception*) and too fast to match physically (defined as beat *production*). When periodic events are faster than roughly 250 ms (240 BPM), we tend to hear them not as a beat (main or otherwise), but as *divisions* and *subdivisions* (i.e., divisions of divisions) of a slower moving periodicity. If our "Flight of the Bumblebee" melody notes are speeding along at 120 ms (500 BPM), as is typical, we will likely group four attacks per beat and synchronize with the music at the more comfortable rate of 480 ms (125 BPM). On the other end of the tempo spectrum, at rates slower than about two seconds (30 BPM) our production accuracy plummets, and perception suffers as well. Lacking intervening events, we increasingly perceive very slow events as disconnected—still sequential in time, but not periodic.

There is a large and fairly well-defined range of beat interonset values—250 to 2,000 ms, or 30 to 240 BPM—within which beats can emerge. As noted above, some research has pointed to a tempo "sweet spot" in the middle of this tempo window, anywhere from 100 to 140 BPM. These findings, however, were largely extrapolated from empirical studies that elicited physical responses to metronome clicks or other musically impoverished stimuli, an issue of ecology when the behavior under investigation is music listening. In empirical studies using excerpts of real music, beat-finding is often assessed using a similar procedure, asking subjects to tap along with the stimuli; verbal directions in these studies often steer subjects toward the most salient or most comfortable pulse rate in the music. These studies present a more complex picture of meter perception: in addition to the multivalent salience factors present in the music itself, the unique habits and experiences of individual listeners have also been found to be a factor (see Repp & Su, 2013). For example, McKinney and Moelants (2006) found that accent patterns in music from a variety of styles could cause listeners to choose a tapped tactus as slow as 50 BPM and as fast as 220 BPM, and found considerable differences between individual subjects. Martens (2011) theorized a tripartite characterization of individual subjects' beat-finding behaviors based on their preferred beat's degree of nesting within a metric hierarchy, and suggested that the specifics of subjects' musical experience and training (e.g., type of instrument played, years of formal training) might play a role in an individual's beat-finding strategy.

While it is difficult to predict a specific preferred beat percept across individuals and musical situations, there are musical styles in which there may be broad, even uniform agreement about which of the nested periodicities carries the beat. One such musical genre is dance-oriented pop/rock music from about 1950 onward, music that typically contains an alternation of bass drum and snare drum at a moderate tempo of 90–130 BPM. Inherently attractive due to tempo alone, this 4/4 "backbeat" pattern, with bass drum attacks on beats 1 & 3 and snare attacks on beats 2 & 4, clearly defines the tactus in much Western popular music. If the purpose of the music is coordinated group movement like dancing, it only makes sense that the tactus of such music will be strongly felt.[2] Regardless of musical style, once we synchronize to an initial beat can we begin to explore a multi-layered meter by moving to faster or slower beats due to continued metric foraging. Jones and Boltz (1989) propose a model of "dynamic attending" whereby listeners shift their attention and/or movements from a tactus to faster or slower beats, whether in response to subtle changes in the music or the physical, mental, or emotional needs of the moment.

If we explore a piece's metric hierarchy from the anchoring periodicity of our initial beat, the most obvious choices from a perceptual perspective are the periodicities immediately faster and slower than that beat rate—divisions and groupings, respectively. This basic multi-layered conception of meter cognition is built into Western notation. See Table 10.1. In this outlay of typical *meter* or *time signatures*, the existence of a main beat or tactus is assumed. The three columns reflect possible groupings of that beat in twos, threes, and fours, while the two rows reflect divisions of that beat into two (simple) or three (compound).[3] Different meters of the same general type (i.e., having the same division and grouping) have been used historically for different stylistic or genre-based reasons, but they share basic perceptual characteristics.

## Timing in Music Performance

A central assumption of the metric framework explored above is that it conforms to an isochronous grid. This assumption stipulates that all note values bearing the same name also have the same duration: for example, all sixteenth notes are equal. Despite its explanatory power, the metric model appears to be at odds with the fact that music is often played with little regard to

*Table 10.1* Common meter signatures arranged by type.

|  | duple beat grouping | triple beat grouping | quadruple beat grouping |
|---|---|---|---|
| simple beat division | 2 2<br>4 2 | 3 3<br>8 4 2 | 4 4 4<br>8 4 2 |
| compound beat division | 6 6<br>8 4 | 9<br>8 | 12<br>8 |

strict isochrony (Seashore, 1938). In contrast to the rigid evenness of the metric grid, analysis of performance timing—also known as microtiming, expressive timing, or rubato—reveals widespread non-isochrony in a wide range of repertoires, including Western classical music (Povel, 1977), Mozambiquean xylophone duos (Kubik, 1965), Cuban drumming (Alén, 1995), Swedish folk music (Bengtsson & Gabrielsson, 1983), and American jazz (Ashley, 2002).

Timing inflections are often a function of a performer's individual preferences (Repp, 1992a). Figure 10.4 shows timing information for two different recordings of the same excerpt; interonset intervals for each violinist are plotted on the y-axis. Whereas the graph of an isochronous performance would look like a flat horizontal line, these renditions contain some temporal variance, each outlining a distinct contour. In contour A, there is a durational peak occurring on the fifth note, highlighting the perceptual importance of the measure downbeat (and its associated $V^7$-I harmonic resolution). Timing can therefore interact with meter irrespective of isochrony. A different kind of timing-meter interaction can be seen in contour B, where the start of each four-note group is emphasized with a mild elongation. Both cases underscore the notion that timing is often closely linked to grouping structure, as exemplified by the characteristic deceleration known as phrase-final lengthening (Todd, 1985).

The link between timing and grouping structure is not confined to production, but involves perception as well. Repp (1992b) presented listeners with classical piano excerpts that had been altered to lengthen certain notes within an otherwise isochronous texture. Participants had more difficulty detecting the note elongations when they occurred at structurally salient moments. Since the expectation was that a performer would normally apply some degree of local deceleration at precisely those moments, the magnitude of the artificial alteration in the stimuli's corresponding notes had to be particularly prominent in order for participants to detect it. Structure "warped" the listener's mental timekeeper. Interestingly, detection accuracy scores were not strongly correlated with musical training or familiarity with the repertoire. In a later replication, Repp (1999) suggested that the ability of musically untrained participants to perform the detection task comparably to trained musicians could be attributed to innate perceptual skills. What is certain is that the cognitive implications

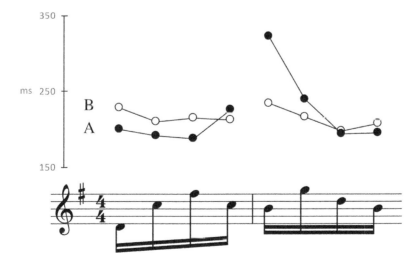

*Figure 10.4* Timing contours for two different violinists, from Haydn Op. 76/3, Mvt. 2. A = Erich Höbarth (Quatuor Mosaïques), B = Norbert Brainin (Amadeus Quartet).

of performance timing depend in large part on the magnitude of the effect. While most listeners can likely detect the spike in Figure 10.4's contour A, the fluctuations in B are more understated—perhaps more felt than heard, such that their absence would rob the performance of some of its underlying expressivity. Honing (2006) has shown that experienced listeners are sensitive to the subtle expressive timing changes that result from altering a recording's tempo. Presented with pairs of recordings of the same composition (one of which had been digitally transformed to match the tempo of the other rendition), participants correctly identified the recording that had been left intact. This ability to pick up on relative and presumably subliminal timing cues was later shown by Honing and Ladinig (2009) to be enhanced by prior exposure to the genre of the presented recordings. Timing perception is shaped by both biology and enculturation.

To understand why metric structure does not break down in the face of non-isochrony, it helps to think of note durations as determined categorically rather than by fixed absolute values. In a study by Desain & Honing (2003), expert musicians used music notation to transcribe a variety of aurally presented three-note rhythms. Even though most of the rhythms featured complex interonset ratios, these tended to be consistently "clumped" by transcribers into a small number of simpler rhythmic categories. For instance, almost all participants notated the rhythm 1.8:1:1 as a quarter-note followed by two eighth-notes, the equivalent of 2:1:1. The study's second experiment repeated the same procedure, but now the rhythms were immediately preceded by two measures divided into either two or three isochronous notes, thus suggesting either duple or triple meter. The metric priming affected the category boundaries, leading participants to use duple-meter transcriptions 99% of the time when the prime was duple but only rarely when the prime was triple.

Context is therefore a key factor in how timing patterns are processed. In Figure 10.4, violinist A's notes are heard as categorically equivalent—as sixteenth notes—even though the fifth note is drastically longer than the rest. By this point in the passage, the listener has inferred a metric scaffold whereby four sixteenth notes group into beats, which in turn group into 4/4 measures. It would be unwise in terms of cognitive efficiency to topple this perceptual tower by interpreting the lengthened note as anything but a sixteenth note.

While categorical perception helps us reconcile the abstract isochrony of meter with the realized non-isochrony of performance, in some instances this reconciliation is more elusive. In an isochronous setting, the second of a beat's two eighth notes lies halfway along the beat – both eighths have the same duration, represented as a binary 1:1 ratio. If the same beat is instead subdivided so that the first note is twice as long as the first, the result is a ternary 2:1 ratio (a triplet quarter note followed by a triplet eighth note). These ratios need not be exact in order for either category—binary or ternary—to emerge, so that, for example, 1.9:1 still sounds ternary (Clarke, 1987). However, the category boundary is fuzzy enough that a slightly longer first eighth note (roughly between 1.2:1 and 1.5:1) creates a particular rhythmic "feel" that is neither clearly binary or clearly ternary. This kind of categorical ambiguity is prevalent across multiple musical traditions and has been extensively documented in jazz (Benadon, 2006) and African drumming (Polak & London, 2014).

## Rhythm and Meter in Fully Musical Material

If rhythms are patterns of events in sounded music that can be imprecise, expressive, and messy, while meter is a quantized mental construct of regular nested periodicities, how do the two interact during a music listening experience? As we listen over longer spans of time,

Lerdahl and Jackendoff (1983, p. 36) point out that we automatically segment or chunk music into informal structural units of varying sizes (e.g. phrases, themes, or motives) in the same way that we group events or items of any kind (e.g. the things in my pocket, or people I've seen today) (cf. Temperley, 2001, p. 55ff. for a more thorough discussion). These segments, or rhythmic *groups*, are independent of metric groups (e.g. measures), although the two are frequently coterminous.

Both types of groups are grasped in time, as they develop. The steady quarter notes of Figure 10.1 represent a rhythmic group, albeit a rather boring one, that causes us to perceive an analogous steady beat that accrues into metric groups. The rhythms in the Haydn and Beethoven melodies shown in Figures 10.3 and 10.5, respectively, give rise to metrical percepts very similar to those formed by Figure 10.1, even though the rhythms of both melodies are less regular and more complex. What accounts for the different rhythmic feel of musical melodies versus repeated quarter notes? Lacking any additional information, the first event of a rhythmic group will be invested with the weight of a strong metrical beat (cf. Temperley, 2001, MPR 4, p. 32; Lerdahl & Jackendoff, 1983, MPR 2, p. 76). In the quarter notes of Figure 10.1 and the Haydn melody, the rhythmic group begins with the first quarter note, as does our perceived meter. In Beethoven's melody, by contrast, the bracketed rhythmic groups are offset from groups of metrical events (i.e., measures), as indicated by brackets in Figure 10.5. Our judgments about that melody's pitch relationships, melodic contour, and relative note durations combine to suggest that the beginning of this rhythmic group does not initiate a metrical group, and instead forms a series of pickup notes. When listening to the Beethoven melody, then, our basic procedure of grouping produces segments that are offset from the segments of meter.

In both simple and complex musical contexts, sounding rhythms give rise to a perception of meter. Even though meter is in this way dependent upon rhythm, the periodic expectations of meter can and will persist for a while if rhythmic support disappears, or in the face of rhythmic input that conflicts with an established meter. This relationship accounts for the phenomenon of "loud rests" (London, 2012, p. 107) and other silent moments in music at time points when we were expecting something to occur. Snyder and Large (2005) collected electroencephalography (EEG) data that showed undiminished neural activity in response to repeated loud-soft tone sequences when either a single loud or soft tone was occasionally omitted; in this way metrical patterns are literally mimicked by the brain, which will continue them (if only briefly) on its own. The interplay between events in the sounding music (i.e., rhythms) and an established set of metric expectations provides one basis for the basic psychological effects of music, first theorized by Meyer (1956) and notably refined and expanded by Huron (2006). Yet in terms of musical time, there is a paradox; as described above, sounding rhythms created those metric expectations in the first place.

*Figure 10.5*   L. van Beethoven, theme from Piano Sonata Op. 13, Mvt. 3 with brackets showing rhythmic groups offset from metrical units (barlines).

The perceptual balance between rhythm and meter is a delicate one. Two possible rhythm-meter cycles are shown in Figure 10.6. Figure 10.6A depicts the perceptual loop experienced in music that is consistently metric: there are few or no cross-accents, and thus our metric expectations are not only explicitly confirmed but also renewed. Now imagine that the music begins to bombard us with rhythms that emphasize weak time points in the established meter (such as offbeats or syncopations), or even rhythms that simply emphasize a different beat rate in the existing meter. Figure 10.6B conveys how a metric percept might change during a piece of music in response to conflicting rhythmic information. In these situations, the acoustic stimulus of rhythm reshapes the mental percept of meter (cf. London, 2012, p. 100ff. for an analytical example of this process occurring during music listening).

In highly complex rhythmic contexts, it is not uncommon for listeners—sometimes even the players themselves—to "lose their place" by mistaking beats for upbeats (and vice-versa) or by assigning the measure's downbeat to the wrong beat.

In much of the music performed around the world, we would expect to experience a continuum of relationships between rhythm and meter, with the perceptual options captured

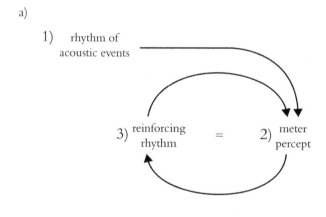

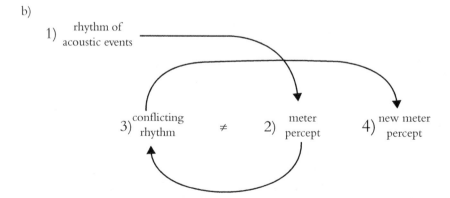

*Figure 10.6* Rhythm/Meter cycles: (A) Rhythm establishing meter, meter reinforced by subsequent rhythm. (B) Rhythm establishing meter, meter contradicted by subsequent rhythm, new meter established.

in Figure 10.6 functioning as endpoints. We often hear rhythms that briefly suggest or point to a meter other than the one we are currently experiencing, but these rhythms are not sufficiently strong or long-lasting to induce a new metric percept. Indeed, the interplay between rhythm and meter, the gray perceptual area between Figure 10.6A and B, is an essential spice of musical time. If our expectations are consistently met by highly predictable rhythms, we can lose interest and push the music to the background of our attention—this can actually be an intentional compositional strategy in music intended as "acoustic wallpaper." Conversely, if a string of musical rhythms gives us no periodic information from which to predict future events, we may also lose interest, unconsciously deeming the music biologically unhelpful, and turn our attention elsewhere. These aesthetic responses are a musical manifestation of "subjective complexity," one dimension of an individual's musical taste (cf. Lamont & Greasley, 2009).

## Conclusion

The boundary between these processes, and indeed the process itself shown in Figure 10.6B, has received little empirical attention. While the amount of literature on the perception and cognition of rhythm and meter has exploded during the past 40 years, it should perhaps not be surprising that, given such a complex set of relevant physiological and psychological processes, matched by an equally complex set of musical possibilities, this area of study is only approaching adolescence. Further, identifying and describing the procedures by which we apprehend time in music is only a first step in coming to understand what, and how, music means to us—the reason so many of us are drawn to music in the first place. As our cognitive faculties continually assess incoming temporal information for regularities, the manipulation of time in the structure or performance of musical rhythms is a potent means to musical meaning, a significant tool in the kit of composers and performers across musical styles, cultures, and epochs.

## Notes

1. Of course, our preference for duple grouping does not preclude other groupings, with triple groupings certainly being common in some musical contexts. The propensity for one or another grouping is possibly affected by enculturation (cf. Hannon & Trehub, 2005).
2. This is not the same, however, as saying that the tactus must be strongly *articulated*; cf. Butler (2006) for the idea that omitting attacks from the tactus level actually invites dancers to supply the "missing" tactus level with their physical movements.
3. Diverse musical traditions may have less regular patterns of beat grouping or division, and these also exist in the Western tradition as "mixed" or "asymmetrical" meters.

## Core Reading

Desain, P., & Honing, H. (2003). The formation of rhythmic categories and metric priming. *Perception, 32*, 341–365.

Honing, H. (2013). Structure and interpretation of rhythm in music. In D. Deutsch. (Ed.) *The psychology of music* (3rd ed.) (pp. 369–404). London: Academic Press.

Jones, M. R. (2009). Musical time. In S. Hallam, I. Cross, & M. Thaut (Eds.) *The Oxford handbook of music psychology* (pp. 81–92). Oxford: Oxford University Press.

Lerdahl, F., & Jackendoff, R. (1983). *A generative theory of tonal music.* Cambridge, MA: MIT Press.

London, J. (2012). *Hearing in time.* Oxford and New York, NY: Oxford University Press.

Repp, B., & Su, Y. (2013). Sensorimotor synchronization: a review of recent research (2006–2012). *Psychonomic Bulletin Review, 20*(3), 403–452.

Temperley, D. (2001). *The cognition of basic musical structures*. Cambridge, MA: MIT Press.

# Further References

Alén, O. (1995). Rhythm as duration of sounds in Tumba Francesa. *Ethnomusicology, 39*(1), 55–71.

Ashley, R. (2002). Do[n't] change a hair for me: The art of jazz rubato. *Music Perception, 19*(3), 311–332.

Benadon, F. (2006). Slicing the beat: Jazz eighth-notes as expressive microrhythm. *Ethnomusicology, 50*(1), 73–98.

Bengtsson, I., & Gabrielsson, A. (1983). Analysis and synthesis of musical rhythm. In J. Sundberg (Ed.), *Studies of Music Performance*. (No. 39) (pp. 27–60). Stockholm: Royal Swedish Academy of Music.

Bergeson, T., & Trehub, S. (2005). Infants' perception of rhythmic patterns. *Music Perception, 23*(4), 345–360.

Bisesi, E., & Vicario, G. B. (2015). The perception of an optimal tempo: The role of melodic event density, in A. Galmonte & R. Actis-Grosso. (Eds.), *Different psychological perspectives on cognitive processes: Current research trends in Alps-Adria region*, (pp. 25–43). Cambridge: Cambridge Scholars Publishing.

Brochard, R., Abecasis, D., Potter, D., Ragot, R., & Drake, C. (2003). The "ticktock" of our internal clock direct brain evidence of subjective accents in isochronous sequences. *Psychological Science, 14*(4), 362–366.

Butler, M. (2006). *Unlocking the groove: Rhythm, meter, and musical design in electronic dance music*. Bloomington, IN: Indiana University Press.

Clarke, E. (1987). Categorical rhythm perception: An ecological perspective. In A. Gabrielsson (Ed.), *Action and Perception in Rhythm and Music* (No. 55) (pp. 19–33). Stockholm: Royal Swedish Academy of Music.

Grant, R. M. (2014). *Beating time and measuring music in the early modern era*. Oxford: Oxford University Press.

Hannon, E., & Trehub, S. (2005). Tuning in to musical rhythms: Infants learn more readily than adults. *Proceedings of the National Academy of Sciences, 102*(35), 12639–12643.

Honing, H. (2006). Evidence of tempo-specific timing in music using a web-based experimental setup. *Journal of Experimental Psychology: Human Perception and Performance, 32*(3), 780–786.

Honing, H. (2012). Without it no music: Beat induction as a fundamental musical trait. *Annals of the New York Academy of Sciences, 1252, The Neurosciences and Music IV – Learning and Memory*, 85–91.

Honing, H., & Ladinig, O. (2009). Exposure influences expressive timing judgments in music. *Journal of Experimental Psychology: Human Perception and Performance, 35*(1), 281–288.

Huron, D. (2006). *Sweet anticipation: Music and the psychology of anticipation*. Cambridge, MA: MIT Press.

Jones, M. R. (1992). Attending to musical events. In M. R. Jones and S. Holleran (Eds.), *Cognitive bases of musical communication* (pp. 91–110). Washington, DC: American Psychological Association.

Jones, M. R., & Boltz, M. (1989). Dynamic attending and responses to time. *Psychological Review, 96*(3), 459–491.

Kraemer, D. J. M., Macrae, C. N., Green, A. E., & Kelley, W. M. (2005). Musical imagery: Sound of silence activates auditory cortex. *Nature, 434*(7030), 158.

Kubik, G. (1965). Transcription of Mangwilo xylophone music from film strips. *African Music, 3*(4), 35–51.

Lamont A., & Greasley, A. E. (2009). Musical preferences. In Hallam, S., Cross, I., Thaut, M. (Eds.) *Oxford handbook of music psychology*. (pp. 160–168). New York, NY: Oxford University Press.

Longuet-Higgins, H. C., & Lee, C. S. (1982). The perception of musical rhythm. *Perception, 11*, 115–128.

Martens, P. (2011). The ambiguous tactus: Tempo, subdivision benefit, and three listener strategies. *Music Perception, 28*, 433–448.

McKinney, M. F., & Moelants, D. (2006) Ambiguity in tempo perception: What draws listeners to different metrical levels? *Music Perception, 24*, 155–166.

Merchant, H., Grahn, J., Trainor, L., Rohrmeier, M., & Fitch, W.T. (2015). Finding the beat: A neural perspective across humans and non-human primates. *Philosophical Transactions of the Royal Society B, 370*, 20140093.

Meyer, L. (1956). *Emotion and meaning in music*. Chicago, IL: University of Chicago Press.

Parncutt, R. (1994). A perceptual model of pulse salience and metrical accent in musical rhythms. *Music Perception, 11*(4), 409–464.

Patel, A., Iversen, R., Bregman, M., & Schulz, I. (2009). Experimental evidence for aynchronization to a musical beat in a nonhuman animal. *Current Biology, 19*, 827–830.

Polak, R., & London, J. (2014). Timing and meter in Mande drumming from Mali. *Music Theory Online 20*(1). http://mtosmt.org/issues/mto.14.20.1/mto.14.20.1.polak-london.html

Povel, D. J. (1977). Temporal structure of performed music: Some preliminary observations. *Acta Psychologica, 41*, 309–320.

Povel, D. J., & Essens, P. (1985). Perception of temporal patterns. *Music Perception, 2*(4), 411–440.

Repp, B. (1992a). Diversity and commonality in music performance: An analysis of timing microstructure in Schumann's "Träumerei." *Journal of the Acoustical Society of America, 92*(5), 2546–2568.

Repp, B. (1992b). Probing the cognitive representation of musical time: Structural constraints on the perception of timing perturbations. *Cognition, 44*, 241–281.

Repp, B. (1999). Detecting deviations from metronomic timing in music: Effects of perceptual structure on the mental timekeeper. *Perception and Psychophysics, 61*(3), 529–548.

Seashore, C. (1938). *Psychology of music*. New York, NY: McGraw Hill.

Snyder, J. S., & Large, E. W. (2005). Gamma-band activity reflects the metric structure of rhythmic tone sequences. *Cognitive Brain Research, 24*(1), 117–126.

Todd, N. (1985). A model of expressive timing in tonal music. *Music Perception, 3*, 33–58.

Van Noorden, L., and Moelants, D. (1999). Resonance in the perception of musical pulse. *Journal of New Music Research, 28*(1), 43–66.

Zatorre, R., Chen, J., & Penhune, V. (2007). When the brain plays music: Auditory-motor interactions in music perception and production. *Nature Reviews Neuroscience, 8*, 547–558.

# 11

# MUSICAL STRUCTURE
## Sound and Timbre

*Stephen McAdams and Meghan Goodchild*

## Introduction

We define timbre as a set of auditory attributes—in addition to those of pitch, loudness, duration, and spatial position—that both carry musical qualities, and collectively contribute to sound source recognition and identification. Timbral properties can arise from an event produced by a single sound source, whether acoustic or electroacoustic, but they can also arise from events produced by several sound sources that are perceptually fused or blended into a single auditory image. Timbre is thus a perceptual property of a specific fused auditory event.

It is important at the outset to pinpoint a major misuse of this word, that is, referring to the "timbre" of a given instrument: the timbre of the clarinet, for instance. This formulation confuses source identification with the kinds of perceptual information that give rise to that identification. Indeed, a specific clarinet played with a given fingering (pitch) at a given playing effort (dynamic) with a particular articulation and embouchure configuration produces a note that has a distinct timbre. Change any of these parameters and the timbre will change. Therefore, in our conception of timbre, an instrument such as a clarinet does not have "a timbre," but rather it has a constrained universe of timbres that co-vary with the musical parameters listed above to a greater or lesser extent depending on the instrument and the parameter(s) being varied. For example, a French horn player can make the sound darker by playing a bit softer, and the timbre of clarinet sounds is vastly different in the lower chalumeau register than in the higher clarion register. That being said, as we will see below, there may be certain acoustic invariants that are common across all of the events producible by an instrument that signal its identity. Timbre is thus a rather vague word that implies a multiplicity of perceptual qualities. It is associated with a plethora of psychological and musical issues concerning its role as a form-bearing element in music (McAdams, 1989). The issues that will be addressed in this chapter include the perceptual and acoustic characterization of timbre, its role in the identification of sound sources and events, the perception of sequential timbral relations, timbre's dependence on concurrent grouping, its role in sequential and segmental grouping, and its contribution to musical structuring.

## Acoustic and Psychophysical Characterization of Musical Sounds

Timbre perception depends on acoustic properties of sounds and how these properties are represented in the auditory system. These acoustic properties, in turn, depend on the mechanical properties of vibrating objects in the case of acoustic instruments, or the properties of electronic circuits, digital algorithms, amplifiers, and sound reproduction systems in the case of electroacoustic sounds. It thus behooves us to understand the perceptual structure of timbre and its acoustic and mechanical underpinnings.

The notion of timbre encompasses many properties such as auditory brightness, roughness, attack quality, richness, hollowness, inharmonicity and so on. One primary approach to revealing and modeling the complex perceptual representation of timbre is through multidimensional scaling (MDS) analyses of subjective ratings of how dissimilar sounds are from one another. All pairs of sounds in a set are compared, giving rise to a matrix of dissimilarities, which are then analyzed by an algorithm that fits the dissimilarities to a distance model with a certain number of dimensions (see McAdams, 1993, for more details). Studies with synthesized sounds (Grey, 1977; Krumhansl, 1989; McAdams et al., 1995; Wessel, 1979) and recorded sounds (Iverson & Krumhansl, 1993; Lakatos, 2000) generally find "timbre spaces" with two or three dimensions. This low dimensionality, compared with all of the ways the timbre could vary between sounds in a given set, suggests limits either in listeners' abilities to form ratings based on a large number of dimensions, or in the algorithms' abilities to reliably distinguish high-dimensional structures given the inter-individual variability in the data. Some algorithms also allow for specific dimensions or discrete features on individual sounds (called "specificities") and for different weights on the various dimensions and specificities for individual listeners or groups of listeners (McAdams et al., 1995). Specificities capture unique qualities of a sound that are not shared with other sounds and that make it dissimilar with respect to them. The weights on the dimensions reflect listeners' differing sensitivities to the individual dimensions and specificities. The perceptual dimensions correlate most often with acoustic descriptors that are temporal (e.g., attack qualities), spectral (e.g., timbral brightness) or spectrotemporal (e.g., timbral variation over the duration of a tone); but, the acoustic nature of the perceptual dimensions of a given space depends on the stimulus set: different properties emerge for a set of wind and string tones than for percussive sounds, for example (Lakatos, 2000).

The interpretive challenge of timbre spaces is to determine whether they have an underlying acoustic basis. This approach presumes that individual perceptual dimensions would have independent (orthogonal) acoustic correlates. A profusion of quantitative acoustic descriptors derived directly from the acoustic signal or from models of its processing by peripheral auditory mechanisms has been developed and integrated into MATLAB toolboxes such as the MIR Toolbox (Lartillot & Toiviainen, 2007) and the Timbre Toolbox (Peeters et al., 2011). Authors often pick and choose the descriptors that seem most relevant, such as spectral centroid (related to timbral brightness or nasality), attack time of the energy envelope, spectral flux (degree of variation of the spectral envelope over time), and spectral deviation (jaggedness of the spectral fine structure). However, Peeters et al. (2011) computed measures of central tendency and variability over time of the acoustic descriptors in the Timbre Toolbox on a set of over 6,000 musical instrument sounds with different pitches, dynamics, articulations, and playing techniques. They found that many of the descriptors co-vary quite strongly within even such a varied sound set and concluded that there were only about ten classes of independent descriptors. This can make the choice among similar descriptors somewhat arbitrary. Techniques such as partial least-squares regression allow for an agnostic approach, reducing similar descriptors to a single variable (principal component) that represents the common variation among them.

What has yet to be established is whether these descriptors actually have status as perceptual dimensions: are they organized along ordinal, interval or ratio scales? Another question is whether the descriptors can actually be perceived independently as is suggested by the MDS approach. It is also unclear whether combinations of descriptors may actually form perceptual dimensions through the long-term auditory experience of them as strongly co-varying parameters. One confirmatory study on synthetic sounds has shown that spectral centroid, attack time and spectral deviation do maintain perceptual independence, but that spectral flux collapses in the presence of variation in spectral centroid and attack time (Caclin et al., 2005).

A very different approach is to treat the neural representation of timbre as a monolithic high-dimensional structure rather than as a set of orthogonal dimensions. In a new class of *modulation representations*, sound signals are described not only according to their frequency (tonotopic, arranged by frequency or placement in a collection of neurons) and amplitude variation over time, but include a higher-dimensional topography of the evolution of frequency-specific temporal-envelope profiles. This approach uses modulation power spectra (Elliott et al., 2013) or simulations of cortical spectrotemporal receptive fields (STRF; Shamma, 2000). Sounds are thus described according to the dimensions of time, tonotopy, and modulation rate and scale. The latter two represent temporal modulations derived from the cochlear filter envelopes (rate dimension) and modulations present in the spectral shape derived from the spectral envelope (scale dimension), respectively. These representations have been proposed as possible models for timbre (Elliott et al., 2013; Patil et al., 2012). However, the predictions of timbre dissimilarity ratings have relied heavily on dimensionality reduction techniques driven by machine learning algorithms (e.g., projecting a 3,840D representation with 64 frequency, 10 rate and 6 scale filters into a 420D space in Patil et al., 2012), essentially yielding difficult-to-interpret black-box approaches, at least from a psychological standpoint. Indeed, in using high-dimensional modulation spectra as predictors of positions of timbres in low-dimensional MDS spaces, the more parsimonious acoustic descriptor approach has similar predictive power to the modulation spectrum approach (Elliott et al., 2013). This leads to the question of whether timbre is indeed an emergent, high-dimensional spectrotemporal "footprint" or whether it relies on a limited bundle of orthogonal perceptual dimensions.

Most studies have equalized stimuli as much as is feasible in terms of pitch, duration, and loudness in order to focus listeners on timbral differences. However, some studies have included sounds from different instruments at several pitches. They have found that relations among the instruments in the timbre spaces are similar at pitches differing by as much as a major seventh, but that interactions between pitch and timbre appear with sounds differing by more than an octave (Marozeau & de Cheveigné, 2007). Therefore, pitch appears as an orthogonal dimension independent of timbre, and pitch differences systematically affect the timbre dimension that is related to the spectral centroid (auditory brightness)—the center of mass of the frequency spectrum. This result suggests that changes in both pitch height and timbral brightness shift the spectral distribution along the tonotopic axis in the auditory nervous system. That being said, Demany and Semal (1993) found with three highly trained listeners that detection of a change in pitch and timbral brightness was independent, even when these parameters co-varied, suggesting that the degree of independence may depend on stimulus, task, and training.

## Timbre's Contribution to the Identity of Sound Sources and Events

The sensory dimensions making up timbre constitute indicators that collectively contribute to the categorization, recognition, and identification of sound events and sound sources (McAdams, 1993). Studies on musical instrument identification show that important information is present in the attack portion of the sound, but also in the sustain portion, particularly when vibrato is present (Saldanha & Corso, 1964); in fact, the vibrato may better define the resonant structure of the instrument (McAdams & Rodet, 1988). In a meta-analysis on published data derived from instrument identification and dissimilarity rating studies, Giordano and McAdams (2010) found that listeners more often confuse tones generated by musical instruments with a similar mechanical structure (confusing oboe with English horn, both with double reeds) than with sounds generated by very different structures. In a like manner for dissimilarity ratings, sounds resulting from similar resonating structures and/or from similar excitation mechanisms (two struck strings—guitar and harp) occupied the same region in timbre space, whereas those with large differences (a struck bar and a sustained air jet—xylophone and flute) occupied distinct regions. Listeners thus seem able to identify differences in the mechanisms of tone production by using the timbral properties that reliably carry that information. Furthermore, dissimilarity ratings on recorded acoustic instrument sounds and their digital transformations, which maintain a similar acoustic complexity but reduce familiarity, are affected by long-term memory for the familiar acoustic sounds (Siedenburg et al., 2016). A model that includes both acoustic factors and categorical factors such as instrument family best explains the results.

A fascinating problem that has been little studied is how one builds up a model of a sound source whose timbral properties vary significantly with dynamics and pitch. Some evidence indicates that musically untrained listeners can recognize sounds at different pitches as coming from the same instrument only within the range of about an octave (Handel & Erickson, 2001), although musically trained listeners can perform this task fairly well even at differences of about 2.5 octaves (Steele & Williams, 2006). Instrument identification across pitches thus depends on musical training, and it seems that the mental model that represents the timbral covariation with pitch needs to be acquired through experience. An important question concerns how recognition and identification are achieved by information accumulation strategies with such acoustically variable sources. The STRF representation is claimed both to capture source properties of musical instruments that are invariant over pitch and sound level (Shamma, 2000) and to provide a sound source signature that allows very rapid and robust musical source categorization (Agus, et al., 2012). One proposal that emerges from this view is that extracting and attending separately to the individual features or dimensions may require additional processing. These possibilities need further study and could elucidate the confusion in the field between timbre as a vehicle for source identity and timbre as an abstract musical quality.

## Perception of Timbral Relations

Timbre space provides a model for relations among timbres. Based on this representation, we can consider theoretically the extension of certain properties of pitch relations and many of the operations traditionally used on pitch sequences to the realm of timbre. A timbre interval can be considered as a vector in timbre space, and transposing that interval maintains the same amount of change along each perceptual dimension of timbre. One question concerns whether listeners can perceive timbral intervals and recognize transpositions of those intervals to other points in the timbre space as one can perceive pitch intervals and their transpositions in pitch space. McAdams and Cunibile (1992) selected reference pairs of timbres from the space used by Krumhansl (1989), as well as comparison pairs that either respected the interval relation or violated it in terms of the orientation or length of the vector. Listeners were generally better than chance at choosing the correct interval, although electroacoustic composers outperformed nonmusicians. Not all pairs of timbre intervals were as successfully perceived as related, suggesting that factors such as specificities of individual timbres may have distorted the intervals. It may well be difficult to use timbre intervals as an element of musical discourse in a general way in instrumental music given that timbre spaces of acoustic instruments tend both to be unevenly distributed and to possess specificities, unlike the equal spacing of pitches in equal-temperament. However, one should not rule out the possibility in the case of synthesized sounds or blended sounds created through the combination of several instruments. At any rate, whether or not specific intervals are precisely perceived and memorized, work in progress shows that perception of the *direction of change* along the various dimensions is fairly robust, allowing for the perception of similar contours in trajectories through timbre space.

## Timbre and Auditory Grouping

Timbre emerges from the perceptual fusion of acoustic components into a single auditory event, including the blending of sounds produced by separate instruments. According to Sandell (1995), the possible perceptual results of instrument combinations include timbral heterogeneity (sounds are segregated and identified), augmentation (subservient sounds are blended into a dominant, identifiable sound), and emergence (all sounds are blended and unidentifiable). There is an inverse relation between degree of blend and identification of the constituent sounds (Kendall & Carterette, 1993). Fusion depends on concurrent grouping cues, such as onset synchrony and harmonicity (McAdams & Bregman, 1979); that is, instruments that play with synchronous onsets and in consonant harmonic relations are more likely to blend. However, the degree of fusion also depends on spectrotemporal relations among the concurrent sounds: Some instrument pairs can still be distinguished in dyads with identical pitches and synchronous onsets because their spectra do not overlap significantly. Generally, sounds blend better when they have similar attacks and spectral centroids, as well as when their composite spectral centroid is lower (Sandell, 1995). When impulsive and sustained sounds are combined, blend is greater for lower spectral centroids and slower attacks, and the timbre resulting from the blend is primarily determined by the attack of the impulsive sound and the spectral envelope of the sustained sound (Tardieu & McAdams, 2012). More work is needed on how to predict blend from the underlying perceptual representation, on the resulting timbral qualia of blended sounds, and on which timbres will remain identifiable in a blend.

Timbre also plays a strong role in determining whether successive sounds are integrated into an auditory stream or segregated into separate streams on the basis of timbral differences that potentially signal the presence of multiple sound sources (McAdams & Bregman, 1979). Larger differences in timbre create stream segregation, and thus timbre strongly affects what is heard as melody and rhythm, because these perceptual properties of sequences are computed within auditory streams. In sequences with two alternating timbres, the more the timbres are dissimilar, the greater is the resulting degree of segregation into two streams (Iverson, 1995; Bey & McAdams, 2003). The exact representation underlying this sequential organization principle and how it interacts with attentional processes is not yet understood, but it seems to include both spectral and temporal factors that contribute to timbre. Timbral difference is also an important cue for following a voice that crosses other voices in pitch or for hearing out a given voice in a polyphonic texture (McAdams & Bregman, 1979). If a composer seeks to create melodies that change in instrumental timbre from note to note (called *Klangfarbenmelodien* or sound-color melodies by Schoenberg, 1911/1978), timbre-based streaming may prevent the listener from integrating the separate sound sources into a single melody if the changes are too drastic. We have a predisposition to identify a sound source and follow it through time on the basis of continuity in pitch, timbre, loudness, and spatial position. Cases in which such timbral compositions work have successfully used smaller changes in timbre from instrument to instrument, unless pointillistic fragmentation is the desired aim, in which case significant timbre change is effective in inducing perceptual discontinuity.

We propose two other kinds of grouping that are often mentioned in orchestration treatises: textural integration and stratification or layering. Textural integration occurs when two or more instruments featuring contrasting rhythmic figures and pitch material coalesce into a single textural layer. This is perceived as being more than a single instrument, but less than two or more clearly segregated melodic lines. Stratification creates two or more different layers of orchestral material, separated into more and less prominent strands (foreground and background), with one or more instruments in each layer. Integrated textures often occupy an orchestral layer in a middleground or background position. Future research will need to test the hypothesis that it is the timbral similarity within layers, and timbral differences between layers, that allow for the separation of layers and also whether timbral characteristics determine the prominence of a given layer (i.e., more salient timbres or timbral combinations occur more frequently in foreground layers).

## Role of Timbre in Musical Structuring

In addition to timbre's involvement in concurrent and sequential grouping processes, timbral discontinuities also promote segmental grouping, a process by which listeners "chunk" musical streams into units such as phrases and themes. Specific evaluation of the role that timbre plays in segmental structuring in real pieces of music is limited in the literature. Repeating timbral patterns and transition probabilities that are learned over sufficient periods of time can also create segmentation of sequences into smaller-scale timbral patterns (Tillmann & McAdams, 2004). Discontinuities in timbre (contrasting instrument changes) can provoke segmentation of longer sequences of notes into smaller groups or of larger-scale sections delimited by significant changes in instrumentation and texture (Deliège, 1989).

We are developing a taxonomy of timbral contrasts that occur frequently in the orchestral repertoire. These contrast types include: 1) antiphonal alternation of instrumental groups in call-and-response phrase structure, 2) timbral echoing in which a repeated musical phrase or idea appears with different orchestrations, with one seeming more distant than the other due to the change in timbre and dynamics, and 3) timbral shifts in which musical materials are reiterated with varying orchestrations, being passed around the orchestra and often accompanied by motivic elaboration or fragmentation. The perceptual strengths of these different contrasts, as well as the call-response or echo-like relations, depend on the timbral changes used.

Formal functions (e.g., exposition, recapitulation), processes (e.g., repetition, fragmentation) and types (e.g., motives, ideas, sentences, periods, sonata, rondo) have been theorized in Classical music, and there has been some discussion of how they are articulated through orchestration. Cannon (2015) demonstrates that contrasts in dynamics and orchestration (instrument density) are key determinants that influence whether the onset of a recapitulation serves as a resolution, climax, or arrival, on the one hand, or as a new beginning or relaunch, on the other. Dolan (2013) examines Haydn's structural and dramatic use of orchestration, including the process of developing variation. Future work should address how orchestral variations are used to reinforce, vary or even contradict these pitch- and rhythm-based structures and their resulting effect on the listening experience.

There is very little music-theoretical or perceptual research on the topic of large-scale orchestral shaping. However, these orchestral gestures, such as the sudden contrast between the orchestra and a soloist, have been shown to contribute to peak emotional experiences in orchestral music (Guhn et al., 2007). While some orchestration treatises mention certain of these gestures, a major concern is the lack of a clear taxonomy of techniques and of a conceptual framework related to their musical function. Goodchild (2016) developed a typology of orchestral gestures defined by changes in instrumentation based on the time course (gradual or sudden) and direction (additive or reductive) of change. She hypothesized that extended patterns of textural and timbral evolution create orchestral gestures, which possess a certain cohesiveness as auditory images and have a goal-directed sense of motion. These gestures often give rise to strong emotional experiences due to a confluence of change along many timbral dimensions, but also in loudness, tempo, and registral extent, giving them expressive agency. Listeners' continuous ratings of emotional intensity while listening to orchestral excerpts reveal different response profiles for each gestural type, in particular a lingering effect of high emotional intensity for the reductive gestures (Fig. 11.1). Using re-orchestration and digital orchestral rendering as tools for testing hypotheses concerning the role of timbral brightness in emotional valence, Goodchild showed with psychophysiological measures that the brightness of the orchestration (measured as spectral centroid) leading up to an expressive event dramatically shapes the resulting experience.

Another way that timbre contributes to larger-scale musical form by way of orchestration is through the sense of movement between tension and relaxation. Timbre may affect the perception of harmonic tension by influencing the perception of voice leading through sequential integration of notes with similar timbres and segregation of those with different timbres. The competition between fusion and sequential streaming has been argued to affect the perception of dissonance (Wright & Bregman, 1987). Paraskeva & McAdams (1997) asked listeners to make ratings of perceived degree of completion (the inverse of tension) at several points in piano and orchestral versions for both tonal and nontonal works (Bach's *Ricercar* from the *Musical Offering* orchestrated by Webern and the first of Webern's *Six Pieces for Orchestra*, Op. 6). When differences were found in the completion profiles, the orchestral version was consistently less tense than the piano version. This effect may have been due to the processes involved in auditory stream formation, especially the perception of timbral roughness. Roughness is a timbral attribute that results from the beating of proximal frequency components within auditory filters. Roughness largely determines sensory dissonance. As a timbral attribute, it depends on what gets grouped concurrently: If several notes

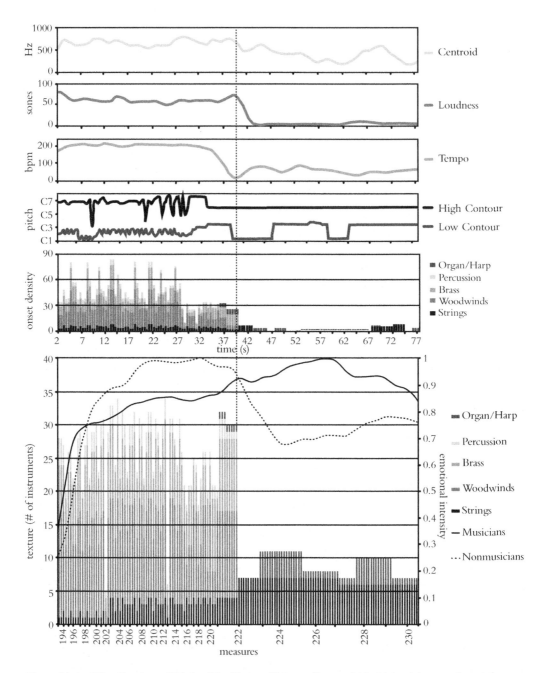

*Figure 11.1*  Visualization of Holst, *The Planets*, "Uranus," mm. 193–236, with score-based features (instrumental texture, onset density, and melodic contour), performance-based features (loudness, spectral centroid, and tempo), and average emotional intensity ratings for musician and non-musician listeners. See insert for color figure.

From Goodchild (2016), Fig. A.10.

with the impulsive attack of a piano sound occur simultaneously in a vertical sonority with dissonant intervals, they would be synchronous and of similar timbre, leading to greater concurrent grouping and resulting sensory dissonance. Due to timbral differentiation and attack differences in the orchestral version, individual voices played by different instruments would have a greater tendency to segregate, thus decreasing the fusion of vertical sonorities and the dissonance that derives from that fusion, thereby reducing the perception of musical tension.

## Conclusion

Timbre depends on concurrent auditory grouping processes. Its qualities are based on emergent acoustic properties that arise from perceptual fusion. Timbre can distinguish voices in polyphonic textures and among orchestral layers. It can underscore contrastive structures and define sectional structure. It also contributes to the building of large-scale orchestral gestures. Future possibilities for timbre research in music theory, orchestration theory, and music psychology include: determining how to predict blend from the underlying perceptual representation, the resulting timbral qualia of blended sounds, and which timbres will remain identifiable in a blend; the way timbre affects the interaction of concurrent and sequential grouping processes in the perception of dissonance and harmonic tension; and the contributions of timbre to the perception and cognition of formal processes and harmonic schemas.

## Acknowledgments

Portions of the research reported in this chapter were supported by funding from the Fonds de recherche Québec—Société et culture (2014-SE-171434) and the Social Sciences and Humanities Research Council of Canada (890–2014–0008).

## Core Reading

Grey, J. M. (1977). Multidimensional perceptual scaling of musical timbres. *Journal of the Acoustical Society of America, 61*, 1270–1277.

Krumhansl, C. L. (1989). Why is musical timbre so hard to understand? In S. Nielzén & O. Olsson (Eds.), *Structure and perception of electroacoustic sound and music* (pp. 43–53). Amsterdam: Excerpta Medica.

McAdams, S. (1989). Psychological constraints on form-bearing dimensions in music. *Contemporary Music Review, 4*(1), 18–98.

McAdams, S. (1993). Recognition of sound sources and events. In S. McAdams, & E. Bigand (Eds.), *Thinking in sound: The cognitive psychology of human audition* (pp. 146–198). Oxford: Oxford University Press.

McAdams, S., & Bregman, A. S. (1979). Hearing musical streams. *Computer Music Journal, 3*(4), 26–43.

McAdams, S., Winsberg, S., Donnadieu, S., De Soete, G., & Krimphoff, J. (1995). Perceptual scaling of synthesized musical timbres: Common dimensions, specificities, and latent subject classes. *Psychological Research, 58*, 177–192.

Sandell, G. J. (1995). Roles for spectral centroid and other factors in determining "blended" instrument pairings in orchestration. *Music Perception, 13*, 209–246.

Wessel, D. L. (1979). Timbre space as a musical control structure. *Computer Music Journal, 3*(2), 45–52.

## Further References

Agus, T., Suied, C., Thorpe, S., & Pressnitzer, D. (2012). Fast recognition of musical sounds based on timbre. *Journal of the Acoustical Society of America, 131*, 4124–4133.

Bey, C., & McAdams, S. (2003). Post-recognition of interleaved melodies as an indirect measure of auditory stream formation. *Journal of Experimental Psychology: Human Perception and Performance, 29,* 267–279.

Caclin, A., McAdams, S., Smith, B. K., & Winsberg, S. (2005). Acoustic correlates of timbre space dimensions: A confirmatory study using synthetic tones. *Journal of the Acoustical Society of America, 118,* 471–482.

Cannon, S. (2015). Arrival or relaunch? Dynamics, orchestration, and the function of recapitulation in the nineteenth-century symphony. Poster presented at the 2015 meeting of the Society for Music Theory, Saint Louis, MO.

Deliège, I. (1989). A perceptual approach to contemporary musical forms. *Contemporary Music Review, 4,* 213–230.

Demany, L., & Semal, C. (1993). Pitch versus brightness of timbre: Detecting combined shifts in fundamental and formant frequency. *Music Perception, 11,* 1–14.

Dolan, E. (2013). *The orchestral revolution: Haydn and the technologies of timbre.* Cambridge: Cambridge University Press.

Elliott, T., Hamilton, L., & Theunissen, F. (2013). Acoustic structure of the five perceptual dimensions of timbre in orchestral instrument tones. *Journal of the Acoustical Society of America, 133,* 389–404.

Giordano, B. L., & McAdams, S (2010). Sound source mechanics and musical timbre perception: Evidence from previous studies. *Music Perception, 28,* 155–168.

Goodchild, M. (2016). *Orchestral gestures: Music-theoretical perspectives and emotional responses.* PhD Dissertation, McGill University, Montreal, Canada.

Guhn, M., Hamm, A., & Zentner, M. (2007). Physiological and music-acoustic correlates of the chill response, *Music Perception, 24,* 473–483.

Handel, S., & Erickson, M. (2001). A rule of thumb: The bandwidth for timbre invariance is one octave. *Music Perception, 19,* 121–126.

Iverson, P. (1995). Auditory stream segregation by musical timbre: Effects of static and dynamic acoustic attributes. *Journal of Experimental Psychology: Human Perception and Performance, 21,* 751–763.

Iverson, P., & Krumhansl, C. L. (1993). Isolating the dynamic attributes of musical timbre. *Journal of the Acoustical Society of America, 94,* 2595–2603.

Kendall, R. A., & Carterette, E. C. (1993). Identification and blend of timbres as a basis for orchestration. *Contemporary Music Review, 9,* 51–67.

Lakatos, S. (2000). A common perceptual space for harmonic and percussive timbres. *Perception & Psychophysics, 62,* 1426–1439.

Lartillot, O., & Toiviainen, P. (2007). A Matlab toolbox for musical feature extraction from audio. In *Proceedings of the 10th International Conference on Digital Audio Effects (DAFx-07),* Bordeaux, France.

Marozeau, J., & de Cheveigné, A. (2007). The effect of fundamental frequency on the brightness dimension of timbre. *Journal of the Acoustical Society of America, 121,* 383–387.

McAdams, S., & Cunibile, J.-C. (1992). Perception of timbral analogies. *Philosophical Transactions of the Royal Society, London,* series B, *336,* 383–389.

McAdams, S., & Rodet, X. (1988). The role of FM-induced AM in dynamic spectral profile analysis. In H. Duifhuis, J. W. Horst, & H. P. Wit (Eds.), *Basic Issues in Hearing* (pp. 359–369). London: Academic Press.

Moore, B. C. J., & Gockel, H. (2002). Factors influencing sequential stream segregation. *Acustica united with Acta Acustica, 88,* 320–332.

Paraskeva, S., & McAdams, S. (1997). Influence of timbre, presence/absence of tonal hierarchy and musical training on the perception of tension/relaxation schemas of musical phrases. *Proceedings of the 1997 International Computer Music Conference, Thessaloniki* (pp. 438–441).

Patil, K., Pressnitzer, D., Shamma, S., & Elhilali, M. (2012). Music in our ears: The biological basis of musical timbre perception. *PLoS Computational Biology, 8,* e1002759. doi:10.1371/journal.pcbi.1002759

Peeters, G., Giordano, B. L., Susini, P., Misdariis, N., & McAdams, S. (2011). The Timbre Toolbox: Extracting audio descriptors from musical signals. *Journal of the Acoustical Society of America, 130,* 2902–2916.

Saldanha, E. L., & Corso, J. F. (1964). Timbre cues and the identification of musical instruments. *Journal of the Acoustical Society of America, 36*, 2021–2126.

Schoenberg, A. (1978). *Theory of harmony.* R. E. Carter, Trans. Berkeley, CA: University of California Press. (Original German publication, 1911)

Shamma, S. (2000). The physiological basis of timbre perception. In M. Gazzaniga (Ed.), *The new cognitive neurosciences* (pp. 411–423), Cambridge, MA: MIT Press.

Siedenburg, K., Jones-Mollerup, K., & McAdams, S. (2016). Acoustic and categorical dissimilarity of musical timbre: Evidence from asymmetries between acoustic and chimeric sounds. *Frontiers in Psychology, 6*, 1977. doi: 10.3389/fpsyg.2015.01977

Steele, K., & Williams, A. (2006). Is the bandwidth for timbre invariance only one octave? *Music Perception, 23*, 215–220.

Tardieu, D., & McAdams, S. (2012). Perception of dyads of impulsive and sustained instrument sounds. *Music Perception, 30*, 17–128.

Tillmann, B., & McAdams, S. (2004). Implicit learning of musical timbre sequences: Statistical regularities confronted with acoustical (dis)similarities. *Journal of Experimental Psychology: Learning, Memory and Cognition, 30*, 1131–1142.

Wright, J. K., & Bregman, A. S. (1987). Auditory stream segregation and the control of dissonance in polyphonic music. *Contemporary Music Review, 2*(1), 63–92.

# 12

# MUSICAL STRUCTURE

## Tonality, Melody, Harmonicity, and Counterpoint

*Daniel Shanahan*

When the melody in Figure 12.1 rings on my mobile phone, I'm able to infer a sense of stability and repose when it has reached its conclusion, and the final note, C-natural, sounds like a resting point: a tonic. Yet, from looking at the melody, it's not really clear why that would be the case. The melody doesn't begin on C, and the note that it does begin with (G) occurs more frequently than C. In fact, the only time C occurs before the final measure is in a position not emphasized rhythmically, as a part of descending motive that I've already heard twice before. For some reason, however, I'm able to hear closure and rest on the C at the end of the phrase, as if the melody has "arrived home." Thus, our perception of tonality is a complex network of relationships that are often not apparent upon first glance.

We are able to infer a tonal center from the melody in Figure 12.1 in large part because we've learned the organizing principles that govern the Western tonal system in which that melody is composed. Of course, such organizing principles vary across time and cultures, but there are many that remain consistent. For example, most cultures employ scales that contain between 5 and 7 tones in an octave, even in cultures that employ microtonal tuning systems; there is a ubiquity of five-note scales across cultures (Van Khe, 1977). Additionally, intervals between adjacent notes of these scales rarely extend beyond the range of 1–3 semitones, and most scales employ some sort of asymmetry in interval size (Nettl, 2000); scales containing only one interval (such as the "whole tone" scale) are quite rare, as they prevent the listener from hearing a "perceptual anchor" (for reasons to be discussed below).

Tonality (in any culture or epoch), defined here as a series of relationships between notes or pitches that creates a "pull" toward a musical "center," provides the listener with a set

*Figure 12.1* Excerpt from Francisco Tarrega's "Grand Valse" (1902), commonly known as the Nokia ringtone.

of organizational principles which they might latch onto. This chapter discusses the factors that contribute to our understanding these relationships governing a musical idea in a tonal idiom. Such factors include how physical and linguistic constraints can influence melodic features, how listeners learn to understand these features, relationships, and grammars, the role of hierarchical relationships within a tonal framework, the comprehension of co-occurrent sounds (harmonicity), and finally a listener's ability to disentangle multiple melodies performed at once (counterpoint).

## Melodic Structure

The fact that certain principles of musical organization seem to be consistent across cultures might lead us to conclude that music typically contains a number of inherent elements that allow for a listener to more readily perceive and organize it. The construction of melody provides us with an interesting case study on how certain organizational aspects of music exist not as the result of something outside of human actions and experience, but rather as related to phenomena found in physiological and linguistic domains. Melodic contour and trajectory, for example, display a number of features paralleling those seen in linguistic prosody and phonology: Notably, just as vocal utterances tend to decline in pitch—the result of a decrease in air pressure as air is let out of the lungs (t'Hart & Cohen, 1973)—melodies decline in pitch. Shanahan and Huron (2011) similarly found that, in European folksongs, the size of intervals in a melody also decreased over the melody's course, similar to the intervallic compression that occurs over the course of a vocal utterance. Melodic rhythm has also been linked to linguistic factors. Patel and Daniele (2003) found a correlation between the rhythmic variability—the note-to-note differences in duration—of instrumental themes drawn from Western "classical" music and the variability of the spoken language of the theme's composer. Such connections, however, are not absolute. For example, musical melodies incorporate fixed interval sizes, whereas speech uses variable interval sizes (Patel, 2008, p. 205). The many connections between the sound patterns of language and music, however, suggest that musical practices don't exist in a vacuum, and are shaped by the sounds that already surround us in our daily environment. Melodic ideas are, at least in part, more understandable to a listener because they can be related to non-musical aspects of the listener's life, such as speech.

Much of the research on the perception of melodies within a tonal framework revolves around a listener's expectations while hearing music. Meyer (1956) argued that emotion in music was conveyed when an expectation—a listener's sense or prediction about how the music would proceed—was either fulfilled or inhibited. Meyer's student and colleague Narmour (1990) expanded upon this theory, arguing that the repetition of a melodic idea implies that it will continue, while a changing melodic idea implies that further change will occur (for example, A+B→C, but A+A→A). This might be thought of as a "bottom-up" approach to melodic structure and comprehension, in that it argues that a listener's expectation is provided by a melody's note-to-note relationships, rather than beginning with its larger-scale contour or shape. In a contrasting vein, Dowling (1978) proposes a "top-down" approach to melodic learning, proposing that listeners grasp melodic contours first, and specific notes and intervals later as the melodies became more familiar. These approaches are hardly mutually exclusive, and are in fact quite complementary—Narmour provides a prospective approach whereas Dowling's is retrospective. Examining both approaches, however, illustrates the points that melodic structure is comprised of both the note-to-note interactions, and a broader, more "structural" set of interactions.

Many theorists have discussed the role of "structural" as opposed to "ornamental" notes in melodies (Schenker, 1905/1980) and there is experimental support for this distinction: listeners are able to accurately recognize a melody when ornamental tones are removed, but are unable to do so when structural tones are removed (Dibben, 1994). Structural tones serve as anchors for pitches of lesser importance, and tones that are understood to be stable (such as the first, fifth, or third scale degrees) can serve as cognitive reference points for the composition as a whole (Bharucha & Krumhansl, 1983). It's quite likely that this anchoring is facilitated by small pitch movements (such as $\hat{2} \rightarrow \hat{1}$ or $\hat{7} \rightarrow \hat{1}$; the caret above the number is a common way of denoting scale degree): Deutsch (1978) found that participants were better able to discriminate between pitches if they were interrupted by pitches that were separated by only a small number of steps (rather than skips or leaps), concluding that participants were able to perform better if they heard the tones as anchoring pitches that were separated by smaller intervals. In Figure 12.1, for example, it would be a fair assumption to say that most people might hear the G, E, D, and C on the downbeat of each bar to be the structural tones, because of the emphasis heard on a downbeat—what music theorists call a "metric accent"—as well as the motivic repetition.

## Tonality and Key

### *Hierarchy and Centricity*

To hear a hierarchy of pitches within a key is to hear that some pitches are more important in, central to, or prototypical of that key than others. For example, $\hat{1}$, $\hat{3}$, and $\hat{5}$ in the key of C (C, E, and G) are more easily identified with the key of C than they are with F major, where they also occur (as $\hat{5}$, $\hat{7}$, and $\hat{2}$). Krumhansl's work on key profiles (perhaps best summarized in Krumhansl, 1990) might be thought of as a musical analogue to Rosch's notions of prototypes (Rosch, 1975), which argued that prototypes or "cognitive reference points" have an elevated status within a category of objects or events. In this framework, less prototypical members of a category are judged as being more similar to a more prototypical member than a prototypical member is judged to be similar to a less typical one; in other words, these similarity relationships are asymmetrical. To study relationships between musical events in a tonal framework, Krumhansl and Kessler (1982) focused on using chord progressions in both major and minor keys, and asked participants how well certain tones (called "probe tones") "fit" within the context. Their results demonstrated what might be expected: The tonic of a key was perceived as the best fitting tone, followed by the other notes in the tonic triad, followed by the four remaining diatonic pitches, and finally the five chromatic pitches (in decreasing order of "goodness of fit").

While these probe-tone results are widely accepted, a number of points have been made regarding the analysis of pitch-class distributions as an indicator of key. Firstly, a listener's ability to understand what key a piece of music is in is strongly dependent on the order in which they experience pitches. Deutsch (1984) found that listeners could confidently hear a melody as being in either C major or E minor, depending on whether it was played forward or backward, and West and Fryer (1990) found that when the diatonic scale was presented in a random order, the tonic of the key was judged as the tonal center just as often as scale degrees $\hat{3}$, $\hat{4}$, and $\hat{5}$. Brown (1988) found that 86% of listeners were able to correctly identify the key of Schubert's Sonata in D major, D.644, but only 41% could do the same task when the pitches were re-ordered, indicating again that the order of pitches is important in establishing their tonal relationships.

An alternative to the pitch-class distribution approach focused not on the statistical distribution of pitches in a key, but on the relationship between a perceived tonic and the intervals that occur least frequently in a piece. Butler's "theory of intervallic rivalry" argued that the perception of tonality was not the result of a hierarchy of tones, but rather a pull toward a tonic provided by rare intervals (such as a minor second or a tritone), stating that "any tone will suffice as a perceptual anchor—a tonal center—until a better candidate defeats it" (Butler, 1989, p. 238). This theory allows for a temporally ongoing aspect to key-finding, drawn upon the notion of "tendency tones." Whether we determine key based on presence of common pitches or the salience of rare intervals, it's clear that the statistical distribution of a piece plays a part in our perception of the key, although our perception of tonal centricity requires a contextual understanding, as well as the input of several other musical factors including how tones are likely to resolve, and overall sense of stability (or lack thereof) that certain intervals might provide.

## *Focus Point: Key-Finding Algorithms*

What seems like an inherently straightforward, fundamental question ("what key is this excerpt in?") proves, on further investigation, to be multi-faceted and replete with complexities that listeners never need to consider when hearing a piece of music. Any musician would tell you that the answer to this question cannot be answered by simply providing the pitch that appears the most frequently, nor can it be addressed by providing the pitches that come first or last (pieces begin away from the tonic quite a bit, whether the piece is a Brahms *Intermezzo* or the excerpt in Figure 12.1). Therefore, the computational exercise of key-finding has frequently served as a means of modeling the complexities of the perception of tonality. In a way, this is not unlike what computer programmers refer to when they speak of "rubber duck debugging," in which (as legend has it) one would talk through lines of code to a (literal) rubber duck—a hearer who understands nothing of the situation, and to whom everything must be explained completely and in detail. In doing so, the programmer would find any errors as the difference between what the program was supposed to do and what it actually does as written come to light. In a sense, a computational approach to key-finding, whether used as a stand-alone computer program or taken as a model for human key finding processes, is akin to the rubber duck debugging of tonal perception.

Perhaps the first key-finding algorithm (a process or program for finding a definitive solution to a problem) was Longuet-Higgins & Steedman's *shape-matching algorithm* (Longuet-Higgins, & Steedman, 1971), which used an exclusionary approach, eliminating key possibilities as pitch classes were introduced over the course of a musical passage. For example, in Figure 12.1, the opening G would fit into seven major keys (G, C, D, F, B♭, A♭, E♭); six of those keys would include the opening two notes; and three of those six would still be possible when presented with the first three notes. By the end of the first measure, however, the only major key that would encompass all four melody notes would be C major. If more than one key was still available, however, the algorithm would place more weight on the pitches present at the start of the piece. This worked quite well on pieces that were overtly tonal, but it was less effective for pieces that contained non-diatonic pitches.

Krumhansl and Schmuckler (Krumhansl, 1990) later devised an algorithm that tallied up the pitch classes of an excerpt and compared the distribution of these pitch classes to ratings from earlier probe-tone research (Krumhansl & Kessler, 1982; see above). Other key-finding algorithms have taken a similar approach, but have generated the original distribution of pitches from large sets of musical works, rather than from experimental data. For example, Aarden (2003) generated key-profiles from the Essen Folksong collection, whereas Bellman (2005, discussed in Sapp, 2011) employed distributions generated from compositions of the 18th and 19th centuries. Albrecht and Shanahan (2013) trained a key-finding algorithm on nearly 500 classical music scores, used a Euclidean distance measure in which pitches were mapped onto coordinates in space, and the distance between the distribution of a certain piece and the distributions of each of the 24 major and minor keys was calculated. This algorithm performed more accurately on pieces with greater variation in pitches.

Although the goal of key-finding algorithms was originally to model the perception of a listener, they often stray from this purpose, instead striving for the highest accuracy possible. Albrecht and Shanahan (2013), for instance, tried to obtain the highest possible accuracy for pieces in both major and minor keys, for the purpose of adding key signatures to large collections of pieces, but it's likely that listeners do not perform as well in minor-key identification as they do with major keys, in general (see Temperley & Marvin, 2008, p. 207). A modeling algorithm would not strive to have an equal level of accuracy between major and minor, due to this difference seen in human listeners. The goals of an algorithm can therefore be seen as ranging from the practical (such as ascribing a key-signature to pieces without notated key signatures) to the more theoretical (e.g., a modeling of perception). It can be argued that key-finding algorithms present a solution that is, in many cases, too unidimensional and simplistic. Listeners hear dynamically, and pieces contain tonicizations or modulations (a temporary emphasis on another key area, or a change to another key, respectively) that are often not reflected by a single algorithm. A windowed approach, such as Temperley's Bayesian model (2007), which infers a key from a musical surface's pitch classes within a given timeframe, might be a more accurate representation of the dynamic nature of musical listening.

## Multiple Voices: Harmony and Counterpoint

The study of harmonics, vibrations, and consonance/dissonance predates Western tonality by centuries, going far beyond the study of music and reflecting changing attitudes in scientific and empirical thought, while also informing the sciences outside of music (see Lee, this volume). In an example of an early, empirically derived theory of consonance, Mersenne argued that the pleasant nature of musical consonance was the result of the frequency of the vibrations produced by strings as they hit the ear. The perception of a pleasant interval, Mersenne wrote, was the result of the coinciding of vibrations, generally referred to as the "coincidence theory of consonance" (Mersenne, 1636/1975; quoted in Gouk, 2002).

Two centuries later, Helmholtz (1863) would provide both scientists and theorists with an explanation for consonance and dissonance that could be extended to tonal harmony, and was published at a time when it could influence many music theorists looking for a science of harmony. Helmholtz's theory was based on the physiology of the ear, comparing the hairs of the basilar membrane to a series of tuning forks, each tuned to its own frequency, which corresponded to the vibrations of sound, and argued that sensory dissonance was the result of beats that occurred when two frequencies generated an out-of-phase relationship between themselves. Georg von Békésy would later win the Nobel Prize for expanding on this physiological approach to consonance and dissonance, providing a cochlear mapping of the interaction of the hairs in the basilar membrane ("a *tonotopic map*") (1960). Greenwood (1961) would expand on these theories, providing a frequency mapping of the cochlea, and positing that when two tones were close in frequency, the perceived roughness of their combination was the result of pitches co-occurring within a *critical band,* where the distance between the hairs of the basilar membrane is short enough so that there might be some interaction between them. Plomp and Levelt (1965) found that composers arranged chordal voicings in correlation with the tonotopic map of sensory consonance and dissonance, leading them to conclude that critical bandwidth was directly related to chordal spacing.

Unlike the theories above, which suppose that scale construction is the result of perceived consonance and dissonance, other theories have argued that perceived consonance and dissonance are the effect of harmony and tonal elements. Terhardt (1974) argued that consonance was the product of "harmonicity," in which the perceived consonance might be associated with how similarly the frequencies of a sonority reflect a harmonic series. Parncutt's theory of harmony (1989) extends Terhardt's work, arguing that chordal perception is the result of "tonalness" (how much a sonority is able to sound as a single tone), multiplicity (the number of perceptible tones in a sonority), and salience (the perceptual noticeability of a pitch within a sonority). Parncutt also looks at harmonic progressions, which he discusses in terms of pitch commonality and pitch distance (similarly to how parsimonious voice-leading is taught in music theory class, in which students are encouraged the find the "smoothest" possible options that require voices to leap and skip as little as possible). Progressions are analyzed depending on the consonance of the individual chords in a progression, how well two successive chords work together (the consonance between them), the melodic streaming, and the strength of the tonal structure (Parncutt, 1989, p. 75). Experimental work has further investigated the relationship of consonance, dissonance, and chordal progressions. Tillman, Bigand, and Pineau (1998) found that participants were more accurate and quicker to identify consonance in a final chord when that chord was of great "structural" importance (for example, a tonic chord). This is also the case with untrained listeners and children (Bigand, & Poulin-Charronnat, 2006). These studies provide a way with which we may discuss the logical extension of consonance and dissonance to the perception of chords, and finally to the perception of chordal progressions.

### *Harmonic Progressions*

The order in which harmonies occur—their harmonic progression—is often considered to be guided by the foundational grammar of tonal music (but for an alternate viewpoint, see Gjerdingen, this volume). For example, many theory textbooks use as their foundation a flow chart that indicates which chords may follow each other (see Kostka & Payne, 1995; Piston, 1987). To some extent, this makes sense, as the harmonic progression of a piece is nearly impossible to ignore. In fact, even melodies with no accompaniment are analyzed and heard as containing *implied* harmonic progressions. Returning to Figure 12.1, we see that, in addition to the duration of the final note, the perception of C being the tonic hinges upon a certain implied harmony: $\hat{5}$ going to $\hat{1}$ on the downbeat of the final measure allows for us to infer a dominant harmony (V) moving to a tonic harmony (I), creating a cadence. Although this seems as though it might be difficult for a listener to process, children are able to manage this apparently complex task of understanding implied harmony by the age of seven (Trainor & Trehub, 1994). This task is quite a bit simpler when chords are present, but whether in melodic or chordal contexts, the governing principles are present.

A listener's processing of harmonic progressions seems to overlap somewhat with a hearer's processing of linguistic syntax (Patel, 2008). For example, Patel et al. (2008) found that patients afflicted with Broca's aphasia (in which the processing of linguistic syntax is impaired) also struggle with the processing of harmonic progressions and identifying out-of-key chords. Drawing another linguistic comparison, listeners are able to learn (and prefer) completely unfamiliar harmonic grammars after relatively little exposure, even when hearing harmonic structures in an unfamiliar tuning and scale, much like listeners are able to do with language (Loui, Wessel, & Kam, 2010; Saffran, Aslin, & Newport, 1996).

Methods of musical analysis that are informed by methods from linguistics, such as in Lerdahl and Jackendoff (1983), provide a framework for the analysis of harmonic progressions that analyzes harmonic structure, as well as the analysis of harmonic tension and relaxation. Dichotomies such as tense/resolved, stable/unstable, and the like are crucial to understanding harmonic progressions in Western art music—to understanding harmonic motion, expectation, and closure. The harmonic distance between two keys (that is, how far one key is from another, for example on the circle of fifths) corresponds with the amount of tension perceived by a listener in a harmonic progression (Bharucha & Stoeckig, 1986; Bigand, et al., 1999), and both the interruption of a harmonic progression and a key change can generate the sense of increased tension in a progression (Krumhansl, 1996). The harmonic quality of a chord, such as major, minor, or dominant, is style-dependent (see Temperley & de Clerq this volume). For example, a dominant seventh chord sounds like an unresolved sonority in Western art music, but may sound as if it's at rest in a twelve-bar blues or in Jimi Hendrix's "Purple Haze." Tension, relaxation, and a general motion from stable to unstable, and back to stable, are dependent upon context, and the heuristics of how chords follow one another—of harmonic progressions—provide an important part of that context.

## Counterpoint

As we've seen, the perception of tonality depends on the understanding of sequential (melodic) as well as concurrent (harmonic) relationships. These two dimensions, however, don't exist in isolation. Listeners must discern the melodic alongside the harmonic, and musical ideas must "work" both sequentially and concurrently. A final case-study might therefore be one with which musicians are likely to be most familiar: Western counterpoint and part-writing, where the goal of the composer is to create an independence of voices, despite a co-occurrence of tones (for more on this, see Gjerdingen, this volume). Huron (2001) argued that many of the rules of counterpoint and voice-leading—including the avoidance of unisons, parallel fifths and octaves, movement to the closest available pitch (often called parsimonious voice-leading), the avoidance of leaps, part-crossing, and the even spacing of voices—are not an historical accident. They achieve the goal of independent voices by reinforcing certain perceptual principles, namely *toneness, temporal continuity, minimum masking, tonal fusion, pitch proximity*, and *pitch co-modulation. Toneness* simply refers to a listener's ability to perceive pitches clearly, but it also explores one of the first aspects of any harmony or counterpoint class: the range in which melodies may be written. The perceived clarity of a tone can be measured in terms of a "pitch weight," which is greatest from about 80 to 800Hz, or roughly E2 to G5 (this actually corresponds with the range of the bass and treble clef range in Western music notation). In both Western and non-Western music, the average pitches used fall very near the center of this spectrum, leading Huron to state "'middle C' truly is near the middle of something" (Huron, 2001, p. 9).

In order to allow for a melodic line to be perceived as a single entity, there should be an element of *temporal continuity*, in which there is rarely a gap in time between notes (see Bregman & Campbell, 1971). Additionally, in order to maximize the perceptual independence of voices, composers are urged to minimize *masking*, which occurs when the perception of one sound affects the perception of another (see Von Békésy, 1960). Because auditory masking is reduced when partials—the components that make up complex sounds—are evenly spaced, it would make sense that chord tones should be spaced evenly but with wider intervals occurring between the lower voices (Huron, 2001, p. 33). Similarly, one would want to minimize tonal *fusion* (e.g. the coherence of multiple tones into a single entity), which occurs most frequently at the unison, followed by the octave, and the perfect fifth (see Greenwood, 1961; Plomp & Levelt, 1965). Therefore, effective counterpoint should minimize such intervals, demonstrating a nice conflation of perceptual principles and music-theoretic rules (Huron, 2001, p. 19).

A great deal of work has been carried out that investigates the role of *pitch proximity* in the perception of melodic ideas. Dowling (1973) found that, when given melodies of randomly distributed tones, listeners prefer those that employ smaller interval sizes. Additionally, it seems that the proximity of pitches is more important to the perception of auditory streaming—the perceptual grouping of tones in a complex auditory signal into different "melodic lines"—than direction and trajectory of a melody (see Bregman, 1994, pp. 417–422). Deutsch (1975) and Van Noorden (1975) found that listeners tend to hear a "bouncing" of melodies whose trajectories cross. That is, listeners seem to infer melodic separation, rather than a crossing of two melodic lines, when possible. Therefore, effective counterpoint would strive to minimize voice crossing when possible. Lastly, the principle of *pitch co-modulation* argues that listeners perceive tones as a single unit if they change to a similar frequency, as for example when simultaneous melodies move in similar or parallel motion. Avoiding such parallel and similar motion, therefore, creates a sense of independence between voices (and minimizes the effect of tonal fusion), which is also in keeping with compositional rules favoring contrary motion (where voices move in opposite directions) and forbidding parallel perfect intervals (see Huron, 2001, p. 30).

## Conclusion

This chapter has focused on what we mean when we speak of tonality, how we perceive and understand tonal structures, and how such structures influence the organization of music. In Western music, this involves the interaction of vertical (concurrent) and horizontal (sequential) tones, in conjunction with a hierarchical structuring for these tones and their employment in a goal-directed framework. These organizing principles are learned early on by children, but can also, when necessary, be learned quickly, and influence a listener's sense of tonal organization. In this sense, the "why" of tonality is understood as enabling a listener to navigate through a complex network of tones, understanding hierarchies and relationships as she goes, and is just as interesting as the "how" of tonality. Listeners to the Blues music of the Mississippi Delta will be able to infer structural principles that differ from those in a Mozart sonata or a pop song. The fact that a single listener can infer these principles from disparate styles demonstrates that most of music's organizing principles are cognitively malleable and are learned through experience with specific musical styles and cultures, but many are consistent cross-culturally. Tonality (defined informally here) provides listeners with a way of parsing the musical environments they encounter, using processes derived from physiological, linguistic, cognitive, and cultural constraints and facilitating a perception of centricity, hierarchy, and goal-directedness.

## Core Reading

Bharucha, J., & Krumhansl, C. L. (1983). The representation of harmonic structure in music: Hierarchies of stability as a function of context. *Cognition, 13*(1), 63–102.

Bregman, A. S. (1994). *Auditory scene analysis: The perceptual organization of sound.* Cambridge, MA: MIT Press.

Huron, D. (2001). Tone and voice: A derivation of the rules of voice-leading from perceptual principles. *Music Perception, 19*, 1–64.

Krumhansl, C. L. (1990). *Cognitive foundations of musical pitch.* New York, NY: Oxford University Press.

Meyer, L. B. (1956). *Emotion and meaning in music.* Chicago, IL: University of Chicago Press.

## Further References

Aarden, B. J. (2003). *Dynamic melodic expectancy.* Doctoral dissertation, The Ohio State University.

Albrecht, J., & Shanahan, D. (2013). The use of large corpora to train a new type of key-finding algorithm: An improved treatment of the minor mode. *Music Perception, 31*, 59–67.

Bellman, H. (2005). About the determination of key of a musical excerpt. In *Proceedings of Computer Music Modeling and Retrieval (CMMR)* (pp. 187–203). Pisa, Italy.

Bharucha, J. J., & Stoeckig, K. (1986). Reaction time and musical expectancy: Priming of chords. *Journal of Experimental Psychology: Human Perception and Performance, 12*(4), 403–410.

Bigand, E., Madurell, F., Tillmann, B., & Pineau, M. (1999). Effect of global structure and temporal organization on chord processing. *Journal of Experimental Psychology: Human Perception and Performance, 25*(1), 184–197.

Bigand, E., & Poulin-Charronnat, B. (2006). Are we "experienced listeners"? A review of the musical capacities that do not depend on formal musical training. *Cognition, 100*(1), 100–130.

Bregman, A. S., & Campbell, J. (1971). Primary auditory stream segregation and perception of order in rapid sequences of tones. *Journal of Experimental Psychology, 89*(2), 244.

Brown, H. (1988). The interplay of set content and temporal context in a functional theory of tonality perception. *Music Perception, 5*(3), 219–249.

Butler, D. (1989). Describing the perception of tonality in music: A critique of the tonal hierarchy theory and a proposal for a theory of intervallic rivalry. *Music Perception, 6*, 219–241.

Deutsch, D. (1975). Two-channel listening to musical scales. *Journal of the Acoustical Society of America, 57*, 1156–1160.

Deutsch, D. (1978). Delayed pitch comparisons and the principle of proximity. *Perception & Psychophysics, 23*, 227–230.

Deutsch, D. (1984). Two issues concerning tonal hierarchies: Comment on Castellano, Bharucha, and Krumhansl. *Journal of Experimental Psychology: General, 113*(3), 413–416.

Dibben, N. (1994). The cognitive reality of hierarchic structure in tonal and atonal music. *Music Perception, 12*, 1–25.

Dowling, W. J. (1973). The perception of interleaved melodies. *Cognitive Psychology, 5*(3), 322–337.

Dowling, W. J. (1978). Scale and contour: Two components of a theory of memory for melodies. *Psychological Review, 85*(4), 341–354.

Gouk, P. (2002). The role of harmonics in the scientific revolution. In T. Christensen (Ed.) *The Cambridge history of Western music theory* (pp. 223–45). Cambridge: Cambridge University Press.

Greenwood, D. D. (1961). Critical bandwidth and the frequency coordinates of the basilar membrane. *The Journal of the Acoustical Society of America, 33*(10), 1344–1356.

Helmholtz, H. V. (1885). On the sensations of tone (1863). English translation by AJ Ellis. London: Longman, Green, & Co.

Huron, D. (2001). Tone and voice: A derivation of the rules of voice-leading from perceptual principles. *Music Perception, 19*, 1–64.

Kostka, S., & Payne, D. (1984). *Tonal harmony: With an introduction to twentieth-century music.* New York, NY: Knopf.

Krumhansl, C. L., & Kessler, E. J. (1982). Tracing the dynamic changes in perceived tonal organization in a spatial representation of musical keys. *Psychological Review, 89*(4), 334.

Krumhansl, C. L. (1996). A perceptual analysis of Mozart's Piano Sonata K. 282: Segmentation, tension, and musical ideas. *Music Perception, 13*, 401–432.

Lerdahl, F., & Jackendoff, R. (1983). *A generative theory of tonal music.* Cambridge, MA: MIT Press.

Longuet-Higgins, H. C., & Steedman, M. J. (1971). On interpreting Bach. *Machine Intelligence, 6*, 221–241.

Loui, P., Wessel, D. L., & Kam, C. L. H. (2010). Humans rapidly learn grammatical structure in a new musical scale. *Music Perception, 27*, 377.

Mersenne, M. (1636/1975). *Harmonie universelle, contenant la théorie et la pratique de la musique* (Vol. 2). Paris: Editions du centre national de la recherche scientifique.

Narmour, E. (1990). *The analysis and cognition of basic musical structures.* Chicago, IL: University of Chicago Press.

Nettl, B. (2000). An ethnomusicologist contemplates universals in musical sound and musical culture. In N. L. Wallin, B. Merker, & S. Brown (Eds.), *The Origins of Music* (pp. 463–472). Cambridge, MA: MIT Press.

Parncutt, R. (1989). *Harmony: A psychoacoustical approach.* Berlin: Springer Verlag.

Patel, A. D. (2008). *Music, language, and the brain.* New York, NY: Oxford University Press.

Patel, A. D., & Daniele, J. R. (2003). An empirical comparison of rhythm in language and music. *Cognition, 87*(1), B35–B45.

Patel, A. D., Iversen, J. R., Wassenaar, M., & Hagoort, P. (2008). Musical syntactic processing in agrammatic Broca's aphasia. *Aphasiology, 22*(7–8), 776–789.

Piston, W. (1987). *Harmony.* (M. DeVoto, Ed.). New York, NY: W.W. Norton.

Plomp, R., & Levelt, W. J. (1965). Tonal consonance and critical bandwidth. *The Journal of the Acoustical Society of America, 38*(4), 548–560.

Rosch, E. (1975). Cognitive reference points. *Cognitive Psychology, 7*(4), 532–547.

Saffran, J. R., Aslin, R. N., & Newport, E. L. (1996). Statistical learning by 8-month-old infants. *Science, 274*(5294), 1926–1928.

Sapp, C. S. (2011). *Computational methods for the analysis of musical structure.* Doctoral Dissertation, Stanford University.

Schenker, H. (1905/1980). *Harmony*, O. Jonas, trans. (Vol. 1). Chicago, IL: University of Chicago Press. Originally published in 1905.

Shanahan, D., & Huron, D. (2011). Interval size and phrase position: A comparison between german and chinese folksongs. *Empirical Musicology Review, 6*(4), 187–197

Temperley, D. (2007). *Music and probability.* Cambridge, MA: The MIT Press.

Temperley, D., & Marvin, E. W. (2008). Pitch-class distribution and the identification of key. *Music Perception, 25*(3), 193–212.

Terhardt, E. (1974). Pitch, consonance, and harmony. *The Journal of the Acoustical Society of America*, *55*(5), 1061–1069.

'tHart, J., & Cohen, A. (1973). Intonation by rule: A perceptual quest. *Journal of Phonetics, 1*, 309–321.

Tillmann, B., Bigand, E., & Pineau, M. (1998). Effects of global and local contexts on harmonic expectancy. *Music Perception, 16*, 99–117.

Trainor, L. J., & Trehub, S. E. (1994). Key membership and implied harmony in Western tonal music: Developmental perspectives. *Perception & Psychophysics, 56*(2), 125–132.

Van Khe, T. (1977). Is the pentatonic universal? A few reflections on pentatonism. *The World of Music, 19*(1/2), 76–84.

van Noorden, L. P. A. S. (1975). *Temporal coherence in the perception of tone sequences*. Eindhoven: Eindhoven University of Technology.

Von Békésy, G. (1960). *Experiments in hearing* (Vol. 8). E. G. Wever (Ed.). New York, NY: McGraw-Hill.

West, R. J., & Fryer, R. (1990). Ratings of suitability of probe tones as tonics after random orderings of notes of the diatonic scale. *Music Perception, 7*, 253–258.

# 13

# MUSICAL STRUCTURE

## Melody, Texture, and Harmony
## in the Classical Tradition

*Robert Gjerdingen*

## Introduction

Tremendous strides have been made in recent decades in our understanding of how composers in the European classical tradition learned their craft. That new understanding bears little resemblance to the ahistorical chord-centered simplifications taught in collegiate harmony classes. Because a significant gap exists between the complex mental representations learned by European composers and the simplistic harmony-class assumptions often underlying experiments in music cognition, this chapter seeks to bridge that gap by sketching a historically defensible outline of musical structure as it was understood by its "native speakers." Aside from a tantalizing study by Meyer and Rosner (1982), hardly any investigations of "historically informed" listening have been undertaken. This chapter presents a number of ideas to stimulate such studies in the future.

## From Melodies to Counterpoint

From the time of Charlemagne (ca. 800 CE), the liturgical chants now known as Gregorian Chant (after Pope Gregory I) formed a bedrock of organized religious expression in both churches and monasteries (Hiley, 1993, p. 479). As a sacred heritage, the melodies of these chants could not, in general, be altered. One could, however, embellish them in a process called "troping." Troping was a general Medieval practice. Verbally, a phrase like "Ave Maria, gratia plena" (Hail Mary, full of grace) might be troped as "Ave Maria celi regina, gratia plena" (Hail Mary, Queen of heaven, full of grace). The original text remains, but an extra thought amplifies and decorates it. Musically, one could trope a chant by adding a second voice to it. Polyphony (music with more than one voice or instrument) and counterpoint (the art of placing one note or "point" against another in stylistically appropriate ways— *punctus contra punctum*) thus have their origins in the desire of musicians to exalt and amplify an important chant (Burkholder, et al., 2010, p. 84).

In polyphony, chant served as a reference or cognitive anchor from which the cantor who improvised the embellishing voice took his bearings. The beginnings and endings of phrases in the reference chant would be aurally marked by "perfect intervals," the word *perfect* meaning complete and stable (Lat.: *perfecta* (Fuller, 1992). By contrast, the internal tones of phrases could have "imperfect intervals." The perfect intervals had perceptually simpler frequency ratios (1:1, 1:2, 2:3, or in musicians' language "unisons, octaves, and fifths") and the imperfect intervals had more complex ratios (musical "thirds and sixths"). Thus the closure of phrase boundaries correlated with increased consonance, while the sense of instability and the need to move forward correlated with decreased consonance or even dissonance. A listener's ability to anticipate a satisfying close on a perfect interval was aided by the compositional use of stereotyped and coordinated melodic formulas in both voices, formulas that habitually terminated on the final tone of a phrase.

In the late 1200s a system of "mensural" (measured) music evolved, where differently shaped notes represented tones of different durations. In many respects that same system has been retained until the present day in standard music notation. The new ability provided by this system of notation—to coordinate time within and between voices—allowed for the construction, manipulation, and transmission of a perceptually active metrical grid, with pulses or beats that could alternate as perceptually "strong" and "weak." Traditional and improvised musics have had musical meters for thousands of years, but mensural notation allowed for a higher degree of advance planning and the control of voice-to-voice interactions. In about the year 1280, a monk named Franco of Cologne (fl. mid-13th cent.) set forth the "Franconian Rule" whereby, expressed in modern terms, he stated that consonance should be correlated with metrical strength. Metrically strong and salient moments required stability and consonance, while metrically weak and inconspicuous moments could feature imperfect consonances and fleeting dissonances: In his words, "Let it be understood that in all rhythmic modes one must employ consonances at the beginning of each perfection" (quoted in Gerbert, 1784, p. 13).

## A Sixteenth-Century Example

For an illustration of these principles in the late Renaissance, let us examine the opening phrase of a sacred motet ("Sicut cervus," 1584) by the Pope's head musician: Palestrina (ca. 1525–1594) (see Figure 13.1).

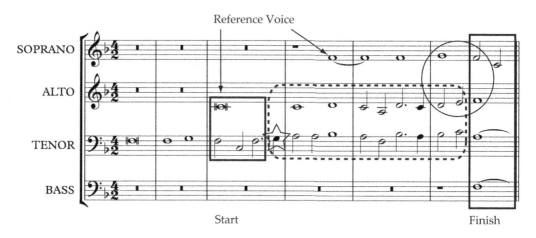

*Figure 13.1* Giovanni di Palestrina, "Sicut cervus," mm. 1–7.

Counterpoint begins between the alto and tenor voices in measure 3. As shown by the rectangles overlaid on the notation, those two voices start with perfect consonances (fifths and an octave), and three of the four voices finish the phrase with perfect consonances. In between, the dashed line encloses a series of imperfect consonances (major and minor thirds). In this style of music, no single voice serves as a fixed reference voice. The role of reference voice shifts among the four voices, being defined by relative stability. Practically speaking, that meant that the tone with the longest duration within a given passage tended to take on the role of stable anchor and reference. The star over the tone G3 indicates a dissonance that, following the Franconian Rule, is placed at a very weak location in the metrical grid. By measure 5, the soprano voice takes on the role of reference voice due to its relative stability compared to the more mobile tenor and alto. Those two voices perform in tandem what was once called "gymel" ("twins") (cf. Bukofzer, 1935); the term indicates how performers and listeners were influenced by the effects of auditory streaming to think of two such voices as being closely related, sharing, in Gestalt terms, a "common fate" (see Lee, this volume). The circle around the soprano and alto at the end of the passage indicates a stereotyped closing gesture or "cadence" (Janin, 2012).

Note that Palestrina was able to satisfy and artistically exploit all these constraints while simultaneously beginning each voice with nearly the same melody in the manner of a round or fugue. Such an esoteric art required many years of training, beginning at around seven years of age in service as a choirboy. The choirboy's daily experience of chant and polyphony, along with training in how to improvise a counterpoint to a "fixed song" (*cantus firmus*, meaning an isochronous reference voice), helped prepare future composers and improvisers. The melodic style absorbed from this training favored easily sung intervals in predominantly stepwise motion (see Shanahan, this volume). A number of traits in Palestrina's melodic contours can be traced to an avoidance of patterns that were difficult to sing accurately and securely (Cohen, 1971).

## Managing Musical Complexity

The texture of sacred polyphony in the late 1500s was complex, with from three to twelve notated voices moving in a number of perceived auditory streams. The gymel in Figure 13.1 (tenor and alto "twins") indicates how correlated or "parallel" motion between voices could reduce the number of perceived streams. If one thinks of melodic motion as taking place in a two-dimensional space of time and pitch, there are only three basic directions possible: Up, down, or "sideways" (meaning repetition of the same pitch). In a four-voice motet like that shown in Figure 13.1, three voices can move in three different directions but a fourth voice will need to duplicate one of those directions. In a six-voice motet there are fifteen nominal voice pairs, but a listener cannot perceive that many contrapuntal relationships (Huron, 1989).

As the number of voices increased there were offsetting simplifications that kept a listener's processing load within a reasonable range. In one reduction, multi-voice sonorities, which could appear in hundreds of unique configurations, came to be treated categorically. Accompanists in the early 1600s developed a numerical shorthand to help them recognize the global nature of collective sonorities. Given the requirements for voice-pair consonances, there emerged only two consonant multi-voice sonorities: A 1/3/5 "chord" (meaning a sonority comprising a bass tone and the intervals of a third and fifth above it, e.g., the tones C4–E4–G4 or their octave duplications) and a 1/3/6 chord (e.g., C4–E4–A4).

A bass with numerical figures above or below it was called a "figured bass." The default sonority was 1/3/5, which received no figure. The other sonority, 1/3/6, was marked by a "6," which highlighted the difference from the default case. Any important dissonance was indicated by its particular interval above the bass (Arnold, 1931). The result was that the three old categories of two-note intervals—perfect, imperfect, and dissonant—transformed into three categories of multi-note sonorities—plain triads (1–3–5), "sixth" chords (1–3–6), and all dissonant combinations.

A second simplification involved the coordination of larger contrapuntal patterns with longer and more hierarchically differentiated musical meters (McClary, 2012, 241ff.). In the sacred style of Palestrina, meter was perceptually present largely as a simple alternation of strong and weak beats. Most instantiations of the Franconian Rule, for instance, only concerned one or two adjacent beats. A listener was thus rarely able to predict the course of musical events beyond the next beat or two. Even the longest stereotyped cadence formulas extended to only four or five adjacent beats. By contrast, musical patterns of much longer temporal spans developed during the course of the 1600s, supported and made salient by more complex meters. An important characteristic of these extended patterns was the listener's ability to connect and associate nonadjacent events (Gjerdingen, 2014). Figure 13.2 shows measures 6–11 of the first movement of Antonio Vivaldi's Concerto in C Major for Recorder (RV444).

Note how a model pattern ("Model" in Figure 13.2) of twenty-four tones in the melody recurs three more times in copies, each of which is transposed downward one step of the scale. The most salient tones, annotated on the score with Arabic numerals in circles, coincide with the strongest moments in the meter, i.e., the downbeats of each measure. Those

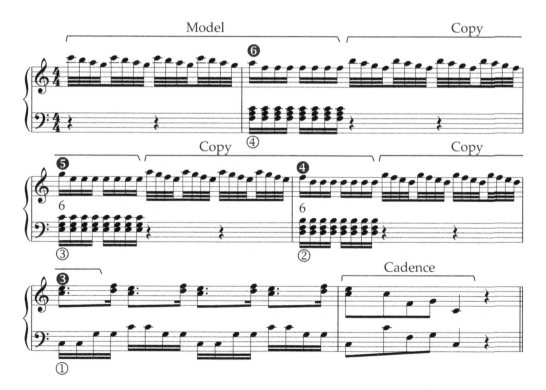

*Figure 13.2* Antonio Vivaldi, Concerto in C Major for Recorder (RV444), Mvt. 1, mm. 6–11.

Arabic numerals indicate the position of the salient tones in terms of a governing scale. The idea of a governing scale with perceptually recognizable locations (musicians say "steps" or "degrees") indicates a hierarchy of pitch relationships in tandem with the hierarchy of metrical relationships. This is what is meant by "key" in musicians' parlance, and contrasts to the more localized tonal and metrical patterns in the music of Palestrina and many other early composers.

Focusing on the remarkably large and innovative hierarchies of tones and moments in Vivaldi's score may cause observers to overlook how many of the prior traditions had nevertheless been retained. Take for instance the tones marked by numbers in circles. Scale degrees **❻**–**❺**–**❹**–**❸** in the melody are matched with ④–③–②–① in the bass. In other words, the core tones of the melody and bass are performing gymel, the centuries-old tradition of counterpoints that were improvised in parallel imperfect consonances (here thirds, separated by additional octaves). This is true even though the tones are no longer adjacent in their voices' time series. These core tones have perceived similarity from their similar positions in the meter and can thus perceptually "pop out" from the background in accordance with Gestalt principles of pattern recognition.

The figured bass indicates a syntax of sonorities that also has many features in common with the phraseology of much older two-voice counterpoint. The first core event (**❻** in the melody, ④ in the bass) has the default 1/3/5 sonority (F4–A4–C5) and thus receives no figure. At the next two core events the figure "6" indicates less stability, suggesting a continuation to the final 1/3/5 event (**❸** in the melody, ① in the bass). Plain 1/3/5 "triads" thus took over some of the syntactical meanings of perfect consonances, while "6-chords" (e.g., 1/3/6 sonorities) became the analogues of imperfect consonances—"6," after all, *is* an imperfect consonance (Holtmeier, 2007).

### Practice and Its Codification

In Vivaldi's era this ancient syntax of stable perfection and unstable imperfection became tied explicitly to scale steps through what was known as the "Rule of the Octave" (Christensen, 1992). As taught to young musicians, the Rule encapsulated a quite specific linkage of four factors: Scale step, contour in the bass, perfection/imperfection, and dissonance. In a fascinating cross- domain mapping, the correlation of intervallic perfection with beginning and ending points in time was transferred to a correlation of chordal perfection with the tonic (①) and dominant (⑤) notes of the scale. Something of this idea is retained in current French terminology, where a 1/3/5 triad is still termed an *accord parfait* (perfect). All the other degrees of the scale should have "6" chords. The diagram in Figure 13.3 presents an illustrative outline of the Rule of the Octave.

Circled numbers indicate degrees or steps of the governing scale or key. The boldface "5"s indicate 1/3/5 triads on the important tonic and dominant tones of the scale (unchanging for both major and minor modes). The "6"s show how sixth-chords fill in the space between those framework tones. Some of those "6" degrees will be flatter in the minor mode, again emphasizing the labile nature of "imperfection." The curved arrows indicate where specific dissonances begin and then resolve to a more stable chord. These resolutions conclude on degrees ①, ③, or ⑤. Note that the pattern of dissonances (and the exact type of dissonant chord, though unspecified in the diagram) is different when the bass rises or falls. So the up-or-down contour of the bass, the particular scale degrees of the bass, the resolution of dissonance, and the perfect/imperfect distinction between "5" and "6" chords

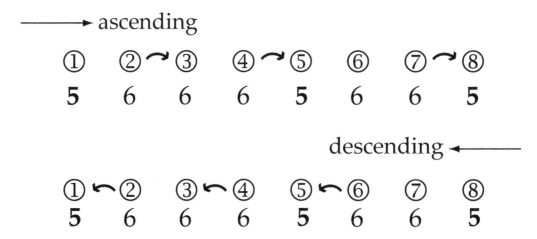

*Figure 13.3*  Rule of the Octave.

are all connected by the Rule of the Octave. An adult composer's knowledge of eighteenth-century composition would have involved more than the Rule of the Octave, but as a summary of the default harmonizations of stepwise basses it comes very close to capturing the norms of that musical repertory. The Rule of the Octave demonstrates that most chords do not have essential meanings. That is, abstractions like "IV" or "Subdominant" suppose an essential meaning to a triad on the fourth scale degree, when the historical fact was that the default sonorities on the fourth scale degree were not triads and depended on the direction of motion in the bass.

## Music and Language: A Comparison

In the European classical tradition, the status of music as a language has long been a subject of debate. On the negative side, music rarely involves denotation, so music lacks truth values and a secure communication of agent, topic, or aspect. One might conceivably say, "Oh, that trill in the flute is about birdsong," but saying that a Bach fugue in D major is about the Lutheran concept of grace would be extremely difficult to substantiate. Similarly, Umberto Eco once quipped that the *sine qua non* of a semiotic system is the ability to tell a lie (Eco, 1976, p. 7). Whatever sonatas may do, they do not lie. One might point to a "deceptive" cadence, but the substitution of an unexpected chord for an expected one is no more a lie than would be slipping on a banana peel.

On the positive side, music does share a number of other features of language. The linguist Talmy Givón (2001, pp. 7–13) has described the structure of human language as a three-level, non-uniform hierarchy. At the lower level words code semantic content; at the middle level clauses code propositional information; and at the upper level multi-propositional structures code discourse coherence. Givón describes this hierarchy as non-uniform because each level depends on different types of entities and relationships. Supporting this idea of hierarchy are the brain's three functionally different types of memory: (1) a sensory store, (2) short-term or working memory, and (3) long-term memory (Baddeley, 2007).

The musical analogues of Givón's three levels are (1) tones, brief melodic motives, chords, and timbres, (2) musical phrases, sequences, and cadences, and (3) musical form, with the associated concepts of repetition, return, variation, digression, and so forth. Young musicians in the classical tradition learned all these many patterns and relationships through exercises intended to provide them with ready exemplars and practice in employing them in different musical contexts. In the 1600s such training began to move from apprenticeship in the home of a master musician to apprenticeship in special institutions called conservatories. In conservatories, the focus on exemplar-based learning and improvisation continued throughout the eighteenth and nineteenth centuries.

### The Tradition vs. the Rise of Harmonic Theory

Paralleling the development of an exemplar-based pedagogy were various attempts to provide scientific or scientistic explanations for how music works. The great French composer Jean-Philippe Rameau (1683–1764), for example, attempted to describe music as Isaac Newton had described physics. Musical atoms, in the guise of 1/3/5 triads, were subject to laws of "motion" determined by consonance. The actual bass of a composition was held to be the variable appearance of a more "fundamental bass," which represented the lowest tones or "roots" of the proposed triads. "Roman numeral analysis" (i.e., marking the scale degrees of the fundamental bass with Roman numerals) in the modern music classroom is a descendant of Rameau's approach. That approach, however ingenious, could never be fully reconciled with the actual behaviors of musicians. In several of his publications Rameau attempted unsuccessfully to show how his theories could fully explain the Rule of the Octave (Christensen, 2010, pp. 27–28).

When he learned about overtones (late 1722), Rameau began to modify his theories, switching the presumed underlying cause of musical relationships from mathematics to physics, from numerical ratios of string lengths to overtones. This idea of a microcosm of tones within each musical note had a lasting effect on music theory, especially as developed by nineteenth-century writers with notions of the organic growth of acorns into oak trees, of single tones into great symphonies (Neff, 1993). As attractive as the science of physics and biology might be as a fund of analogies, music is a product of human culture, not nature. Given the similarities of music and language mentioned above, the proposition that the physics of tones determines musical relationships makes no more sense than the proposition that the same physics determines language. Physics, or more aptly psychophysics, does constrain the transmission of musical and linguistic communications, but psychophysics has little to do with their contents.

### Historically Informed Understandings of Music and Their Challenge to Researchers

The theories just alluded to, Rameau's included, are usually described as theories of harmony. The importance of harmony as a central concept of Romantic music-theoretical thought can hardly be overstated. Textbooks in harmony (Ger.: *Harmonielehren*) were written to serve the same roles in colleges and universities as textbooks in geology or astronomy. A student took the course, read the text, passed the examination, and then moved on to the next subject. For this to work with a cultural product like music, one needed to ignore the diversity and historically contingent nature of musical artworks and focus instead on a single attribute or essence. Patterns of adjacent chords served that purpose.

Given the historical sketch of compositional training and practice presented here, a careful reader may note that there was little mention of patterns of adjacent triads. In fact "chords" and "harmony" were not even central concepts in music theory until the time of Rameau. Throughout the eighteenth and nineteenth centuries young professional musicians continued to study two-voice counterpoint, the construction of two-voice frameworks, and the handling of sonorities in contexts like the Rule of the Octave. The schism between the exemplar-based training of professional musical artisans and the textbook caricatures of college courses in harmony might seem like a harmless detail of pedagogical history. But the fact that most experimental work in the area of harmony mistakes the latter for the former means that the well-documented musical conceptualizations held by the creators and performers of the European classical tradition are generally not being considered in empirical studies of their music.

To give some specificity to this distinction, let us examine three cases, one simple, one more complex, and one very complex. For the simple case, consider Pachelbel's Canon in D, which is readily available online. In terms of Roman numerals, Pachelbel's first three chords are I–V–vi (triads of D major, A major, and B minor). To some, "harmonic theory" defines this sequence as a deceptive cadence, meaning that the third chord is unexpected. But in the historical tradition of music apprentices, this pattern and its continuation were explicitly taught, meaning that the third chord was fully expected. For a more complex case, refer back to Figure 13.2, the excerpt from Vivaldi. What is the nature of the musical relationships in that excerpt? Clearly a literal concept of temporal adjacency would not be adequate. There are more than 100 adjacent events in this passage, even through syntactically the passage presents only four core events followed by a cadence. The particular sonorities used by Vivaldi could have been replaced by other sonorities, but how would one determine whether a replacement was or was not "correct"? In Vivaldi's style, acceptable substitute sonorities would avoid disturbing the two-voice framework in the melody and bass. Yet if the two-voice framework determines categories of chords, chord successions are more a byproduct of counterpoint than the origin of musical coherence. The same question, expressed differently, would ask: Why are Vivaldi's melody and bass exactly as presented and not a random selection from different notes of those same chords? That single excerpt cannot answer the question, but a study of a large corpus of Vivaldi's concertos (he wrote several hundred of them) would reveal that the two-voice framework of Figure 13.2 is an extremely common element of Vivaldi's usage.

If a harmony textbook says that the subdominant chord (IV, the F-major chord at the beginning of the Vivaldi excerpt) "goes to" the dominant chord (V), why does Vivaldi not do that, and is the failure to do so an artistic statement or license? If we eschew imagined physical explanations, we are left with explanations based on human behavior and usage. Imagine a situation in language where we have an idiomatic phrase like "It cost an arm and a leg," meaning "It was very expensive." Is the idiom wrong? No, because it is sanctioned by usage. Similarly in Vivaldi, ideas about what chord "goes to" what chord are of little use when the idiom in question reflects a different high-frequency usage. Classical composers did not pick chords from a pile on their desks and then arrange them in pleasing sequences. They learned and then reproduced specific idioms with origins in two-voiced counterpoint, idioms that have been termed musical schemata (Gjerdingen, 1988). In Vivaldi's case he was employing an idiomatic riposte to the previous passage. That riposte, recently named a Prinner (Gjerdingen, 2007, ch. 2), is one of the most common patterns in all of eighteenth-century music. A statistical study (Symons, 2012) on a corpus of 300 compositions from the conservatories in Naples has confirmed the prevalence of the Prinner schema; it was the second most common four-event pattern out of thousands of such patterns. Following the practice of some corpus grammarians in linguistics (Stefanowitsch & Gries, 2003), one can say "In the context of a Prinner, an initial IV goes to I⁶" because usage is determined idiom by idiom. So-called construction grammarians in linguistics would go further and say that language is nothing *but* idioms or constructions (Goldberg, 2013). The same may be true of classical music.

### *A Nineteenth-Century Example*

For the most complex case of how "chord grammar" and the older traditions of musical understanding diverge, let us turn to the Romantic repertory. The extent to which schematic contrapuntal frameworks served as scaffoldings for highly complex musical expressions can be observed in a dramatic and emotionally charged passage from the G-Minor Ballade of Frédéric Chopin (1810–1849), his Op. 23. Figure 13.4 illustrates how, in the local key of E-flat major, one could construct Chopin's amazing design from common schematic constituents.

*Figure 13.4*  Frédéric Chopin, G-Minor Ballade Op. 23, mm. 167–170 with analysis.

In the terminology of construction grammar, the Prinner schema seen in the Vivaldi excerpt (Fig. 13.2) is the main and governing construction. Most obvious are the scale degrees **❻**–**❺**–**❹**–**❸** in the melody, presented on the downbeats of successive measures just as with Vivaldi. The collocated bass, with scale degrees ④–③–②–①, has a weaker presence in Chopin's actual passage, occurring in the lower tones of the right-hand part on the treble clef. It is contrapuntally shifted forward in time through the incorporation, at each of the four stages of the Prinner, of a smaller but historically important schema: a "1/3/5/6" chord moving to a 1/3/5 chord, as imperfection and dissonance resolving to perfection or as the ascent from ⑦ to ⑧ in the Rule of the Octave (e.g., in the upper tones of measure 167, E♮–G–B♭–C moving to F–A♭–C). That sense of instability resolving to stability is inherited by each stage of the governing schema. To this considerable level of complexity four further patterns are added. First, a low B♭ is placed in the bass as ⑤, a so-called "dominant pedal point" after the practice of organists holding an extended note on their pedalboard. Second, the expected concluding tone in the bass, E♭, is replaced by C, creating the well-known Deceptive Cadence. Third, a five-note melodic turn (e.g., C–D♭–C–B♮–D) is added to decorate each of the first three stages of the Prinner (note the turn's B♮ clashing with the 1/3/5/6 chord's B♭ in measure 161). The upper tone of each turn is determined by the local key of that stage of the Prinner. So, the turn of measure 167 is oriented to F minor while the turn of measure 168 is oriented to E♭ major. Finally, as a fourth complication, the descending melodic leap from the high F6 in measure 167 to the A♭5 and then in measure 168 to G5–a small schema known as a High-2 Drop (Gjerdingen, 2007, ch. 5) is added to the first three stages of the Prinner (i.e., to the model and its copies).

While Chopin's passage represents breathtaking compositional skill coupled with pianistic virtuosity and artistic passion, it was not a wholly original combination. The linkage of several component patterns in the context of a large Prinner schema played over a dominant pedal was itself a traditional construction used for impressive moments in large compositions. Mozart frequently used it to set up the return of an opening theme (Ivanovitch, 2011), and it can be traced all the way back to the closing section of Pergolesi's *Stabat Mater* (1736; see Gjerdingen, 2007, ch. 30). The student of harmony who might try to label the chords in this construction would most likely find the passage thoroughly baffling. Yet listeners familiar with the classical tradition find the passage quite lucid and moving because, due to frequent exposure, they have become familiar with all its component constructions and their typical musical meanings, all of which Chopin respects and exploits.

## Conclusion

To sum up, the structure of European music in the classical tradition is based on the counterpoint of two-voice frameworks. In earlier centuries dense textures of many voices were woven together, with two-voice frameworks moving freely among the many voice pairs. From the eighteenth century onward, it became a norm for the melody and bass, the perceptually most salient voices, to present the two-voice framework while the inner voices took on subsidiary roles. Today the roles of "lead, rhythm, and bass" in popular ensembles are descendants of that classical division of labor. Melodies were fashioned by a technique called "diminution," where the slower moving tones of a two-voice framework were replaced by faster moving decorative patterns. In over-learned schemata like cadences, the succession of sonorities could themselves become schematized, and it was this schematization of chordal successions that prompted several attempts to establish a syntax of harmony.

To essentialize harmony, however, is to mistake the moment-to-moment coloration of sonorities for the contrapuntally determined two-voice frameworks that defined the underlying musical syntax. How do we know such frameworks existed? We know because the pedagogical lessons and exercises used to teach the children apprenticed in conservatories have been recovered and republished (Gjerdingen, 2004, 2008). These lessons were arranged framework by framework. Some lessons tested the young apprentice's ability to produce a given framework in different keys and meters. Others tested the apprentice's ability to complete a series of frameworks when provided with only an upper or a lower voice.

Because these lessons forced the children (some of whom would later become great composers like Debussy and Ravel) to internalize these frameworks in both working and long-term memory, and because these frameworks have left obvious traces in the classical repertory of compositions, it is a fascinating yet empirically unanswered question if these regularities of pattern have also been internalized in twenty-first-century listeners with significant exposure to the classical repertory. In line with the many psycholinguistic studies of bilingualism in speech, a better understanding of the cognitive underpinnings of the classical tradition may provide a means of teasing out the effects of the other styles of music known to modern listeners. And finally, understanding the schematic nature of two-voice frameworks may provide a new way to study counterpoint, one of the least understood domains and most difficult areas to study in all of music cognition.

## Core Reading

Givón, T. (2001). *Syntax: An introduction* (Vols. 1 & 2). Philadelphia, PA: John Benjamins Publishing Co.

Gjerdingen, R. O. (2007). *Music in the galant style.* New York, NY: Oxford University Press.

Huron, D. (1989). Voice denumerability in polyphonic music of homogeneous timbres. *Music Perception, 6,* 361–382.

Meyer, L., & Rosner, B. (1982). Melodic processes and the perception of music. In D. Deutsch (Ed.), *The psychology of music* (pp. 317–341). New York, NY: Academic Press.

## Further References

Arnold, F. T. (1931). *The art of accompaniment from a thorough-bass.* Oxford: Oxford University Press.

Baddeley, A. D. (2007). *Working memory, thought, and action.* Oxford: Oxford University Press.

Bukofzer, M. (1935). The gymel, the earliest form of English polypony. *Music and Letters, 16* (1), 77–84.

Burkholder, P. J., Grout, D. J., & Palisca, C. V. (2010). *A history of Western music* (8th ed.). New York, NY: Norton.

Christensen, T. (1992). The "règle de l'octave" in thorough-bass theory and practice. *Acta Musicologica, 64* (2), 91–117.

Christensen, T. (2010). Thoroughbass as music theory. In D. Moelants (Ed.), *Partimento and continuo playing in theory and practice* (pp. 9–42). Leuven: Leuven University Press.

Cohen, D. (1971). Palestrina counterpoint—A musical expression of unexcited speech. *Journal of Music Theory, 15,* 84–111.

Eco, U. (1976). *A theory of semiotics.* Bloomington, IN: Indiana University Press.

Fuller, S. (1992). Tendencies and resolutions: The directed progression in "Ars Nova" music. *Journal of Music Theory, 36,* 229–258.

Gerbert, M. (Ed.). (1784). *Scriptores ecclesiastici de musica sacra potissimum.* St. Blasien.

Gjerdingen, R. O. (1988). *A classic turn of phrase: Music and the psychology of convention.* Philadelphia, PA: University of Pennsylvania Press.

Gjerdingen, R. O. (2004). *Monuments of partimenti: A series presenting the great collections of instructional music intended for the training of European court musicians*. Retrieved from: http://faculty-web. at.northwestern.edu/music/gjerdingen/partimenti/index.htm (last accessed 17 January 2017).

Gjerdingen, R. O. (2008). *Monuments of solfeggi: A series presenting the great collections of instructional music intended for the training of European court musicians*. Retrieved from: http://faculty-web. at.northwestern.edu/music/gjerdingen/solfeggi/index.htm (last accessed 18 January 2017).

Gjerdingen, R. O. (2014). "Historically informed" corpus studies. *Music Perception, 31*, 192–204.

Goldberg, A. (2013). Constructionist approaches. In T. Hoffman & G. Trousdale (Eds.), *Oxford handbook of construction grammar* (pp. 15–31). New York, NY: Oxford University Press.

Hiley, D. (1993). *Western plainchant: A handbook*. Oxford: Clarendon Press.

Holtmeier, L. (2007). Heinichen, Rameau, and the Italian thoroughbass tradition: Concepts of tonality and chord in the rule of the octave. *Journal of Music Theory, 51*, 5–49.

Ivanovitch, R. (2011). Mozart's art of retransition. *Music Analysis, 30*(1), 1–36.

Janin, B. (2012). *Chanter sur le livre, Manuel pratique d'improvisation polyphonique de la Renaissance*. Langres: Dominique Guéniot.

McClary, S. (2012). *Desire and pleasure in seventeenth-century music*. Los Angeles, CA: University of California Press.

Neff, S. (1993). Schoenberg and Goethe: Organicism and analysis. In C. Hatch and D. W. Bernstein (Eds.), *Music theory and the exploration of the past* (pp. 409–433). Chicago, IL: University of Chicago Press.

Stephanowitsch, A., & Gries, S. (2003). Collostructions: Investigating the interaction between words and constructions. *International Journal of Corpus Linguistics, 8*, 209–243.

Symons, J. (2012). Temporal regularity as a key to uncovering statistically significant schemas in an eighteenth-century corpus. Paper presented at the Society for Music Theory National Conference, New Orleans, LA.

# 14

# HARMONY AND MELODY IN POPULAR MUSIC

*David Temperley and Trevor de Clercq*

## Introduction

Much of the research in music psychology has assumed the conceptual framework of "common-practice" music: Western art music of the 18th and 19th centuries. The questions asked often pertain most directly to the common-practice style—for example, questions about the perception of major and minor keys, classical harmonic progressions, and classical formal conventions—and stimuli are often drawn from this repertoire, or designed to imitate it. But in modern Western society, classical music is a relatively small part of the experience of most listeners. (This is especially true for younger listeners—e.g. college students—who provide the subject population for many music psychology experiments.) While it is certainly valid to study the perception and cognition of common-practice music, it also makes sense to explore other styles with which modern listeners may have greater familiarity.

In this chapter, we focus on melody and harmony in popular music, particularly rock. Recent work by a number of musicologists has contributed greatly to our understanding of harmony and melody in rock; in what follows, we survey this work. Nonetheless, there is to date no well-developed, widely accepted music-theoretical framework for rock as there is for common-practice music. Perhaps partly for this reason, the perception and cognition of rock music has also received little attention; psychological work on popular music has focused more on sociological issues, such as social identity (North & Hargreaves, 1999) and functions of music in everyday life (Sloboda, O'Neill, & Ivaldi, 2001). An important development has been the rise of corpus approaches to popular music (Bertin-Mahieux, Ellis, Whitman, & Lamere, 2011; Burgoyne, Wild, & Fujinaga, 2011), which can shed interesting light on issues of perception and cognition. In this chapter, we discuss our own statistical, corpus-based work on rock music, alongside other theoretical and empirical work as applicable.

Like many stylistic labels, "rock" resists precise definition. A sense of the common understanding of the term is provided by a recent survey by *Rolling Stone* magazine (2004), in which "rock musicians and other industry professionals" were asked to name the greatest songs of the "rock and roll era"; the results were compiled into a list of 500 songs. The top 10 songs of the list are shown in Table 14.1. It can be seen that the list includes a variety

165

*Table 14.1* The top 10 songs from *Rolling Stone* magazine's list of the "500 Greatest Songs of All Time" (2004).

| RANK | TITLE | YEAR | ARTIST |
|------|-------|------|--------|
| 1 | Like a Rolling Stone | 1965 | Bob Dylan |
| 2 | Satisfaction | 1965 | The Rolling Stones |
| 3 | Imagine | 1971 | John Lennon |
| 4 | What's Going On | 1971 | Marvin Gaye |
| 5 | Respect | 1967 | Aretha Franklin |
| 6 | Good Vibrations | 1966 | The Beach Boys |
| 7 | Johnny B. Goode | 1958 | Chuck Berry |
| 8 | Hey Jude | 1968 | The Beatles |
| 9 | Smells Like Teen Spirit | 1991 | Nirvana |
| 10 | What'd I Say | 1959 | Ray Charles |

of sub-genres: 1950s rock and roll, "British Invasion" bands such as The Beatles and The Rolling Stones, soul and Motown, and 1990s alternative rock. A selection of 200 songs from the list provides the basis for the statistical corpus analysis that we discuss below. (Many of the details provided below are drawn from our earlier publications—de Clercq & Temperley, 2011, Temperley & de Clercq, 2013—although a significant portion of what follows also presents new findings.)

## Tonality and Scale

It is generally agreed that rock is "tonal" in the broad sense that every song has a *tonal center*—a pitch class that serves as a point of focus and stability (see Shanahan, this volume). Beyond this, however, there is little agreement as to the nature of tonality in rock. One controversial issue is the distinction between major and minor keys: while some scholars of rock label keys as major or minor, others have questioned the validity of this distinction (Stephenson, 2002; Covach, 1997), since some traditional markers of a "key"—such as the leading tone in minor—are not commonly found in rock. Another, related issue is the kinds of scales that are used in rock. Moore (1992, 1995, 2001) has emphasized the importance of diatonic modes in rock, citing Ionian (major), Mixolydian, Dorian, and Aeolian as especially common (see Figure 14.1). Pentatonic scales have also been widely discussed. Many rock melodies and chord progressions do not fit neatly into any conventional scale, however. For example, some songs, such as The Beatles' "Can't Buy Me Love," combine $\flat\hat{3}$ in the melody with $\hat{3}$ in the accompaniment. Wagner (2003) argues that this usage results from a combination of the minor pentatonic scale—widely used in the blues—with major-mode chords in the accompaniment.

In our own research, we have explored scales in rock from a statistical perspective, using the *Rolling Stone* corpus discussed above. We transcribed the melodies of the 200 songs, and analyzed their harmony in Roman numeral notation (de Clercq & Temperley,

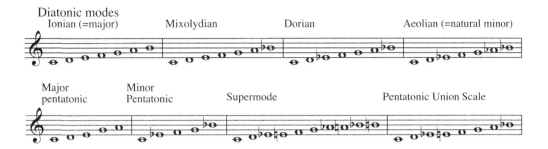

*Figure 14.1*   Common scales used in rock (always assuming a tonal center of C).

2011; Temperley & de Clercq, 2013). We then examined the distribution of scale-degrees (pitch-classes relative to the tonic) in both the melodies and the harmonic progressions. In examining the harmonic progressions, we took each chord to imply one instance of each scale-degree that it contained: for example, a I chord contains a $\hat{1}$, a $\hat{3}$, and a $\hat{5}$. In both the melodic and harmonic distributions, we found that the two least common scale-degrees were $\flat\hat{2}$ and $\sharp\hat{4}$, well below the other ten degrees in frequency; in the melodies, the value for $\flat\hat{6}$ was also quite low. This suggests that there is a "global" or "master" scale in rock, consisting of all the pitch-classes except $\flat\hat{2}$ and $\sharp\hat{4}$, from which the scales of individual songs are drawn; elsewhere one of us has called this the "supermode" (Temperley, 2001). This does not mean that $\flat\hat{2}$ and $\sharp\hat{4}$ are *never* used, but when they occur, they tend to have a surprising or destabilizing effect. Consider, for example, the striking $\flat$II chord at the end of the bridge in the Beatles' "Things We Said Today" (supporting the lyric "Love is here to *stay and that's enough*"). Instead of the V chord that ended the previous phrase ("say that love is luck"), the $\flat$II facilitates a dramatic shift from the A major tonality of the bridge back to the A minor tonality of the verses.

To explore the scales used in individual songs, we used the method of statistical clustering. In this method, each song is represented by a scale-degree distribution; the distributions are then sorted into two categories or "clusters," such that songs with similar distributions are placed in the same category. We performed this process for both the melodic and harmonic datasets. For the melodies, the average distributions of the two clusters are shown in Figure 14.2. One cluster (C1) clearly represents the major scale: the seven major degrees have much higher values than the remaining five. Within the major scale, the five major pentatonic degrees ($\hat{1}$, $\hat{2}$, $\hat{3}$, $\hat{5}$, and $\hat{6}$) have the highest values. The other cluster (C2) could roughly be described as "minor", in that $\flat\hat{3}$ has a higher value than $\hat{3}$. In "classical" music in the minor mode, $\hat{7}$ is more common than $\flat\hat{7}$, and $\flat\hat{6}$ is more common than $\hat{6}$ (Temperley, 2007b); in the rock "minor" distribution, however, the reverse is true in both cases. One could say the minor cluster implies Dorian mode ($\hat{1}$–$\hat{2}$–$\flat\hat{3}$–$\hat{4}$–$\hat{5}$–$\hat{6}$–$\flat\hat{7}$). Note also that $\hat{3}$ has a fairly high value in the rock minor distribution: adding $\hat{3}$ to the Dorian scale creates an eight-note scale, $\hat{1}$–$\hat{2}$–$\flat\hat{3}$–$\hat{3}$–$\hat{4}$–$\hat{5}$–$\hat{6}$–$\flat\hat{7}$. We call this the "pentatonic union" scale, since it can be formed from the union of the major and minor pentatonic scales (see Figure 14.1). In almost 20% of melodies in the corpus, the eight degrees of this scale are more frequent than the remaining four.

The same clustering process was applied to the harmonic distributions, and the results were similar, yielding "major" and "minor" clusters much like the ones generated from the

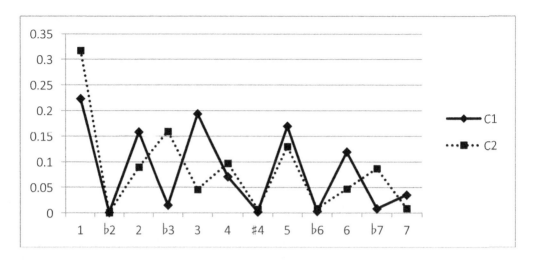

*Figure 14.2* Scale-degree distributions from cluster analysis of melodies in the *Rolling Stone* corpus.

melodic data. Interestingly, however, a substantial number of songs (over 20%) were in the minor *melodic* cluster but the major *harmonic* cluster. This captures the fact—noted earlier—that many rock songs employ $\flat\hat{3}$ in the melody but $\hat{3}$ in the harmony. Altogether, then, our results give support for some kind of major/minor distinction in rock, but one which is rather different from the classical major/minor system. In particular, the rock minor system privileges $\hat{6}$ and $\flat\hat{7}$ over $\flat\hat{6}$ and $\hat{7}$, and there is a high degree of "mixture" of $\hat{3}$ and $\flat\hat{3}$, both in rock melodies and between melodies and the accompanying harmonies. This suggests that the major-minor dichotomy in rock is more of a continuum than a hard-and-fast distinction; in many cases, such as "Can't Buy Me Love," it is difficult to know which label to apply.

Have these patterns of scale-degree distributions in rock changed over time? Analysis of our corpus data suggests that, by and large, they have not. There is, however, one striking and curious exception: the use of $\hat{6}$ and $\flat\hat{6}$ in "minor" melodies, which we define here as those in which $\flat\hat{3}$ is more common than $\hat{3}$. The $\hat{6}$ degree was more frequent than $\flat\hat{6}$ in more than 90% of minor melodies before 1980, but in less than half of minor melodies after that date. Our analyses of some songs since 2000, using another *Rolling Stone* list, suggests that the predominance of $\flat\hat{6}$ in minor songs has become even more pronounced in recent years (Temperley, Waller, & de Clercq, 2015). It appears that the Dorian or "pentatonic union" orientation of early "minor" rock has evolved toward something more like an Aeolian (natural minor) orientation.

Scales can have strong emotional connotations; in common-practice music, the positive and negative associations of major and minor, respectively, are well-known. One might wonder about the expressive implications of the various scales used in rock. Temperley and Tan (2013) undertook a partial exploration of this issue by examining the emotional connotations of diatonic modes: listeners heard melodies in different modes and judged how "happy" they were. A strong pattern emerged, in which modes seemed less happy as scale-degrees were lowered: Ionian > Mixolydian > Dorian > Aeolian > Phrygian. (The exception was Lydian, which was less happy than Ionian, though it has a raised scale-degree—$\sharp\hat{4}$.) If one arranges the modes on the "line of fifths," the circle of fifths stretched out into a line (assuming a constant tonic), it appears that scales get less happy as they move in the flat direction. This principle plays an important role in the emotional connotations of rock songs, and shifts of scale within songs (Temperley, 2013). It may also account for the practice of heavy metal, in which Phrygian mode is widely used, often coupled with extremely negatively charged lyrics (Walser, 1993; Biamonte, 2010).

## Key Identification and Modulation

Related to scales is the issue of key identification in rock; here we define the "key" of a song as its tonal center, without specifying major or minor. Research on key-finding in common-practice music suggests that it depends largely on the distribution of pitch-classes in the piece; this is matched to an ideal distribution or "key-profile" for each key and the key is chosen that yields the best match (Krumhansl, 1990). We experimented with this and other approaches to key-finding in rock, using the *Rolling Stone* corpus. We found that, indeed, scale-degree distribution is a valuable indicator of key in this repertoire. The role of scale-degree distribution in key-finding can be reduced to three factors. First, there is a preference for an interpretation that remains within the "supermode"—avoiding $\sharp\hat{4}$ and $\flat\hat{2}$. For example, if a song contains a repeated chord progression F major–G major, we will tend not to hear it as being in F, since the G major chord contains a B which is $\sharp\hat{4}$ of F. Second, within the supermode, we tend to favor major mode: that is, if a song uses the C major scale, we will prefer a tonal center of C, though other tonics such as G, D, and A are possible. And, third, we favor an interpretation such that the most emphasized tones in the melody are tonic-triad degrees ($\hat{1}$, $\flat\hat{3}$, $\hat{3}$, and $\hat{5}$).

While scale-degree distribution is important in key-finding, it proves not to be the only factor. Consider these two harmonic progressions (all major triads; vertical bars represent barlines):

F Bb | F C        C F | Bb F

The first appears in Bruce Springsteen's "Rosalita," the second in the Romantics' "That's What I Like About You" (transposed here for ease of comparison). The two patterns use exactly the same harmonies in the same sequence (imagine them repeating many times); yet, the tonal center seems to be F in the first case, but C in the second. We propose that this is due to the interaction of meter with the chords, specifically the placement of the chord progression relative to the two-bar "hypermeasures." The change in tonal emphasis is a result of the hypermetrical placement of the harmonies: we prefer a tonal interpretation that locates the tonic harmony in a metrically strong position. Combining this rhythmic factor with melodic scale-degree distribution, we created a key-finding algorithm that matched human judgments of key in 97% of songs.

A large proportion of rock songs (83% in our corpus) remain in one key all the way through. With regard to modulating songs, a few general patterns can be noted. Many songs establish one tonal center in the verse and another in the chorus (de Clercq, 2012). A particularly common pattern is for a song to establish a minor orientation in the verse and then a major one in the chorus, maintaining the same diatonic scale but shifting tonal center (as in Neil Young's "Keep on Rockin' in the Free World"). Other songs, such as Duran Duran's "Rio," perform a similar minor-to-major shift by maintaining the same tonal center but altering the scale. While some tonal moves (such as minor to relative major) are especially common, instances of almost every possible modulation can be found; see Doll (2011) for examples. Frequently, modulations in rock seem to have an expressive motivation; an example is The Beatles' "Penny Lane." In this song, the verse, a nostalgic flashback to the narrator's old neighborhood, contrasts with the chorus, depicting his current situation under "blue suburban skies"; the song mirrors this contrast tonally, modulating down a whole step for the chorus (from B to A).

## Harmony

Harmony in rock has been the subject of considerable discussion. Two influential and contrasting viewpoints are those of Everett (2008) and Stephenson (2002). Everett sees rock harmony as grounded in the norms of classical tonality. He argues that the basic I–V–I progression of common-practice music is often implied in rock even when it is not literally present. Progressions that violate classical harmonic norms, such as ♭VII–IV–I, are usually viewed as being not truly harmonic, but rather contrapuntal in origin. By contrast, Stephenson sees the logic of rock harmony as being fundamentally different from that of classical music. The normative root motions of rock music, in his view, are opposite to those of classical music: that is, ascending fifths and thirds, rather than descending fifths and thirds. While both authors recognize the diversity of rock harmony—Everett notes songs that deviate from classical norms, and Stephenson notes songs that adhere to them—there is clearly a marked difference in perspective here.

We examined rock harmony from a statistical viewpoint, using our harmonic analyses of the *Rolling Stone* corpus. We again began by examining the overall distribution of roots—the primary note of a chord, which determines its function—in the corpus. Not surprisingly, I was the most common root (33% of all chord tokens in the corpus), followed by IV (23%), V (17%), ♭VII (7%), and VI (6%). This already indicates a contrast with classical music, in which V is much more common than IV (for data on common-practice harmony, see Temperley, 2009). We also examined the frequencies of transitions from one chord to another. IV is the most common chord to precede I, and also the most common chord to follow it; V is second-most common in both cases. It is instructive to examine the motions between these three chords; see Figure 14.3. Whereas in classical harmony, moves from IV to V are far

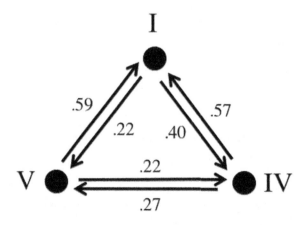

*Figure 14.3*   Harmonic motions between I, IV, and V in the *Rolling Stone* corpus.

more common than the reverse, in rock, V is almost as likely to move to IV as IV is to move to V. (The popularity of the first of these motions, V to IV, may stem from its occurrence in the standard 12-bar blues progression: I–I–I–I–IV–IV–I–I–V–IV–I.) Note also that IV and V are about equally likely to move to I; however, I is much more likely to move to IV than to V. In general, it seems that the directional asymmetries of classical harmony—where a move between two chords may be much more common than the reverse move—are largely absent in rock.

We also examined the frequency of different root motions categorized by interval; the results are shown in Table 14.2. Classical theory privileges root motion by descending fifth (-P5), descending third (-m3/-M3), and ascending second (+m2/+M2); if Stephenson is correct that rock norms are "opposite" to classical ones, we would expect the opposite motions (ascending fifth, ascending third, descending second). Our data suggests that the "classical" moves are more common than the "opposite" ones, but only slightly; ascending and descending forms of each interval are roughly equally common. The root motions in Table 14.2 are arranged on the "line of fifths": a major second is two fifths (e.g. C–G–D), and so on. This reveals a very consistent pattern: root motions decline in frequency as line-of-fifths distance increases. In short, rock harmony shows no strong tendency either to adhere to classical harmonic norms or to go against them, but it does show a strong preference for motion by fifths, and more generally, motions that are "close" on the line of fifths.

At a larger scale, too, the norms of common-practice harmony seem to have little relevance to rock. In particular, there is no obligatory closing gesture—or "cadence"—analogous to the V–I cadence in classical music. However, a significant number of the songs in our corpus do have harmonic patterns that could be considered cadential. Temperley (2011) has suggested that a useful definition of "cadence" in a rock context is a harmonic gesture that moves to I at the end of the chorus, coinciding with the end of the vocal line (compare with Gjerdingen, this volume). Choruses ending with cadences create a sense of arrival and closure; those that do not project instability and motion (or, perhaps, stasis) into the following verse. By this definition, slightly more than half of songs in the *Rolling Stone* corpus (59%) have cadences; by far the most common chords preceding the tonic in these cadential gestures are V and IV. Among the songs that do not have cadences, the chorus either does not end on tonic harmony (AC/DC's "Back in Black" is an example), or else settles on tonic harmony well before the end of the vocal line (as in Creedence Clearwater Revival's "Proud Mary"). 

Certain harmonic patterns in rock occur with particular frequency. In the early years of rock, the 12-bar blues progression (presented above) was predominant; many songs from the 1950s consist entirely of repetitions of this pattern, such as Elvis Presley's "Hound Dog." The popularity of the blues progression declined in later decades, but variants of it can still be seen: Bruce Springsteen's "Cover Me" could be regarded as a (minor) blues pattern, except using ♭VI– ♭VII–i instead of the V–IV–I progression. The late 1950s and early 1960s saw the rise of the "doo-wop" progression, I–vi–IV–V; innumerable songs of the period were built on this pattern (for some data, see Everett, 2009, p. 220). Over the

*Table 14.2* Root motions in the *Rolling Stone* corpus as proportions of the total, shown on the "line of fifths."

| Interval | -m2 | +M3 | -m3 | +M2 | +P5 | – | -P5 | -M2 | +m3 | -M3 | +m2 | TT |
|---|---|---|---|---|---|---|---|---|---|---|---|---|
| Instances | .01 | .03 | .05 | .15 | .24 | – | .29 | .13 | .04 | .04 | .01 | .00 |

next three decades, no single progression seems to have enjoyed such a central role. In recent years, however (since 2000), the progression I–V–vi–IV has become extremely widespread; an interesting feature of this pattern is that it occurs frequently in different rotations, often starting on vi and sometimes even on IV or V.

A controversial issue in the analysis of rock harmony is the validity of a reductive or "Schenkerian" approach, in which events (notes and chords) elaborate other events in a hierarchical manner. Such an approach entails a distinction between chords that are truly harmonic and those that are merely contrapuntal (linear) elaborations of other chords. While a number of scholars have applied the Schenkerian approach to rock (Wagner, 2003; Burns, 2005; Everett, 2008), others have expressed skepticism about its applicability (Middleton, 1990; Moore, 1995). It is difficult to resolve this issue using experimental or corpus methods. There is general agreement that at least some harmonic progressions in rock are best explained linearly, emerging as the result of melodic or bass lines: an example is the verse progression of the Eagles' "Hotel California," i–V– ♭VII–IV– ♭VI– ♭III–iv–V, in which the first six chords are clearly based on a descending chromatic line, $\hat{1}$–$\hat{7}$–♭$\hat{7}$–$\hat{6}$–♭$\hat{6}$–$\hat{5}$. In other cases, the validity of a linear/hierarchical approach is less obvious, and even advocates of such analytic approaches often disagree as to how some progressions should be analyzed. A case in point is the common progression V–IV–I: Everett (2004) analyzes the IV in this progression as an interpolation between V and I, while Spicer (2005) argues that the V chord elaborates IV. Another example is the progression ♭VII–IV–I; in this case, Everett (2008) analyzes the ♭VII as a contrapuntal elaboration of IV, while Doll (2009) suggests that IV is elaborative. Again, such judgments are subjective and it is hard to see how they can be resolved empirically.

There has been very little experimental work focusing directly on rock harmony (or indeed rock music in general). One relevant study by Craton et al. (2016) examined nonmusician listeners' judgments of liking and surprise for major, minor, and dominant chords, given a major-mode context. They found that the chords eliciting high liking ratings included some that are uncommon in (major-mode) classical music but common in rock, such as ♭VII and ♭III. This suggests—not too surprisingly—that listeners' perception of harmony may be affected by rock music—or, possibly, that rock music takes more advantage than does classical music of innate perceptual preferences for certain harmonic relationships. Clearly, there is much room for further research in this area.

## Melody: Pitch Organization

We now turn our attention to melody. One issue—the set of scale-degrees from which a melody is drawn—has already been addressed. In this section we consider several other topics relating to the pitch organization of melody.

An interesting aspect of rock melody is its relationship with harmonic structure. In classical music, melodies are generally strongly constrained by the underlying harmony: melodic notes are either part of the underlying chord, or else are non-chord-tones that almost always "resolve" by step to another pitch (cf. Shanahan, this volume, on "anchoring"). In rock, however, Moore (1995) has argued that there is a kind of melodic–harmonic "divorce" that frees rock melody from its dependence on the accompanying harmony. Examining this situation more closely, Temperley (2007a) finds that, indeed, there are many cases in which the notes of a melody are neither chord-tones nor stepwise-resolving non-chord-tones. Temperley argues that this situation is especially common when the melody is pentatonic, and occurs more in verses than in choruses: In many songs, melody and harmony seem only loosely connected in the verse, but come together more tightly in the chorus. Nobile (2015) explores this phenomenon further, finding that it occurs in several different types of situations. In some cases of melodic–harmonic divorce, both the melody and harmony essentially prolong the same underlying harmony (usually tonic), but the accompaniment contains elaborating chords that momentarily clash with the melody. In other cases, the accompaniment "loops" over a simple repeated progression that may be truly independent of the melody.

Another distinctive feature of rock melody is the mixing of $\hat{3}$ and $\flat\hat{3}$ within a melodic line. This is of interest since, as noted earlier, $\hat{3}$ and $\flat\hat{3}$ are not combined within any conventional scale. In such situations, the factors governing the choice between $\hat{3}$ and $\flat\hat{3}$ at particular moments prove quite complex. Sometimes the choice of pitch is guided by the harmony: In the verse of the Who's "I Can See For Miles," $\hat{3}$ is used over a major I triad followed by $\flat\hat{3}$ over a $\flat$III triad, hewing to the harmony in both cases. Harmony is not the only influential factor, however. Consider the first phrase of the Jackson Five's "ABC"— "You went to school to learn, girl / things you never, never knew before": The melody features $\hat{3}$ at "went" but $\flat\hat{3}$ at "never never." The determining factor here seems to be the fact that the first half of the line gravitates around $\hat{5}$, and the second half around $\hat{1}$; in general, $\hat{3}$ tends to be used in proximity to $\hat{5}$, and $\flat\hat{3}$ in proximity to $\hat{1}$. There is also a tendency to use $\hat{3}$ rather than $\flat\hat{3}$ at cadential points. In the chorus of Crosby, Stills, Nash, and Young's "Woodstock", $\flat\hat{3}$ is used throughout the chorus but shifts to $\hat{3}$ on the final word, coinciding with the cadential move to tonic: "And we've got to get ourselves back to the *gar*-den." Choices between $\hat{3}$ and $\flat\hat{3}$ may also be influenced by expressive considerations; in "Woodstock," the shift to $\hat{3}$ at the end of the chorus perhaps represents the triumphant return to the "garden."

Most rock melodies contain a large amount of melodic repetition. This repetition may be exact, but more often it involves variation and elaboration. For example, in the first verse of Marvin Gaye's "I Heard it through the Grapevine," the first and third phrases ("I bet you wonder how I knew / With some other guy you knew before") are clearly related, but neither the pitches nor the rhythms are identical—the same with the second and fourth phrases. Many successful songs feature repetition at different temporal levels. In Avril Lavigne's "Complicated," we find a repeated one-measure pattern in the verse, a half-measure pattern in the pre-chorus, and a two-measure pattern in the chorus. This complex repetition structure helps to maintain the listener's interest. There is also, of course, larger-scale repetition of entire sections; this gets into the topic of form, which is beyond our scope here (see Covach, 2005; de Clercq, 2012).

## Melody: Rhythmic Organization

The rhythmic aspects of a rock song must be understood in relation to its meter. Rock employs conventional metrical frameworks similar to those in common-practice music and many other Western styles; the vast majority of songs are in 4/4. Whereas the inference of meter in common-practice music is a complex process, in rock the meter is usually conveyed quite unambiguously by the drum pattern, which typically marks stronger beats of the measure (normally beats 1 and 3) with the kick drum and weaker beats (beats 2 and 4) with the snare.

Because the meter is expressed so clearly by the drums, the vocals—and to some extent the other instruments as well—need not constantly reinforce it and may indeed play against it with considerable freedom. This is clearly reflected in our corpus. Figure 14.4

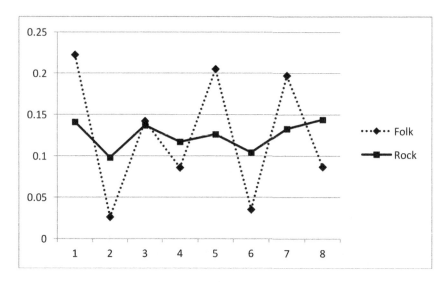

*Figure 14.4* Distribution of events across positions of the 4/4 measure in European folk songs (the Essen Folksong Collection; Schaffrath, 1995), and rock songs (the *Rolling Stone* corpus).

shows the distribution of note-onsets across positions in the measure, for a corpus of European folk melodies (Schaffrath, 1995) and also for the melodies in the *Rolling Stone* corpus. (In both cases, we included only melodies in 4/4 that contain some notes on weak eighth-note beats but no notes on lower-level beats.) The folk melodies align strongly with the metrical framework, with the most notes occurring on strong quarter-note beats (positions 1 and 5), somewhat fewer notes on weak quarter-note beats (3 and 7), and still fewer on weak eighth-note beats. By contrast, in the rock corpus, the frequency of onsets is roughly uniform across the eight positions. With regard to the distribution of onsets, then, rock melodies would appear to conflict with the underlying meter almost as much as they support it.

This is not to say, however, that rock melodies are completely unconstrained by the meter. An important phenomenon here is *anticipatory syncopation*: accented events, such as stressed syllables, long notes, and changes of harmony, often occur on a beat just before a metrically strong beat. In such cases, they are understood as "belonging" on the following strong beat. Sometimes, unstressed syllables next to stressed ones are also understood as anticipatory. Michael Jackson's "Billie Jean" is illustrative (see Figure 14.5A). The phrase "beauty queen" seems on the surface to conflict with the meter, since the unstressed syllable "-ty" falls on the downbeat. But if the phrase is shifted to the right by one eighth-note, as shown in the figure, the text and the meter line up perfectly: the main stress of the phrase "beau-" falls on the downbeat, the secondary stress "queen" on a weak quarter-note beat, and the unstressed "-ty" on an weak eighth-note beat. (It is perhaps significant that the metrical position with the most onsets in the rock data in Figure 14.4 is the *last* eighth-note beat of the measure; this may partly reflect syncopated events anticipating the following downbeat.) Later in the song, the phrase "people always told me" (Figure 14.5B) reflects a more complex pattern of syncopation. One could understand it as implying the underlying rhythm shown in the

A.

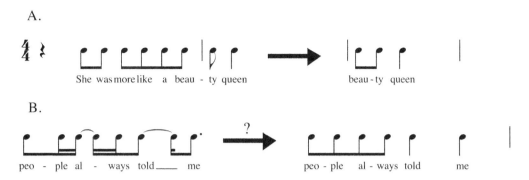

B.

*Figure 14.5* Two phrases from Michael Jackson's "Billie Jean," showing anticipatory syncopations.

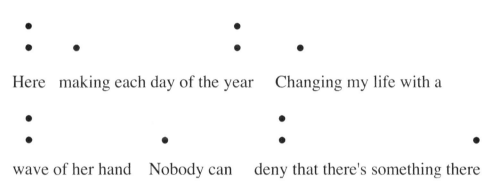

*Figure 14.6* The Beatles, "Here, There, and Everywhere," showing phrases and hypermeter. (Double dots indicate strong measures; single dots indicate weak measures.)

figure (in which "al-" is syncopated by a sixteenth-note, "told" by an eighth-note, and "me" by a dotted eighth). At the same time, the surface rhythm also creates a cross-rhythm, with dotted-eighth intervals between the stressed syllables "peo-," "al-," "told," and "me"; such cross-rhythms are common in rock (Traut, 2005).

Also important is the alignment between melodic phrases and hypermeter (meter at a higher level). We may distinguish between beginning-accented phrases, in which the strongest beat in the phrase occurs near the beginning, and end-accented phrases, in which the strongest beat occurs at or near the end. Some songs maintain one kind of structure or another throughout, while others mix the two. The Beatles' "Here, There, and Everywhere" is a case of the latter kind (Figure 14.6). After the first, very short phrase—just a single syllable—the next phrase is end-accented, ending on (or just before) the third downbeat. (In general, odd-numbered measures are assumed to be stronger than even-numbered ones.) The third phrase is rhythmically parallel to the second, but is extended past the fifth down-beat, so that its strongest beat falls in the middle of the phrase. The next short phrase is beginning-accented, and a longer beginning-accented phrase follows. The variety of phrase accentuation, and also of phrase length, is partly what makes this melody engaging and satisfying.

# Conclusions

A central concern of music psychology has been the exploration of tacit musical knowledge that listeners have acquired simply through exposure to music. While some of this knowledge may relate to musical phenomena that are universal or nearly so—for example, the preponderance of small melodic intervals (Huron, 2006)—much of it is style-specific. To date, little research in music psychology—at least, research using non-musician subjects—has focused on the styles of music with which such listeners are most familiar. In this chapter, we have put forth a number of concepts that we believe are important in rock melody and harmony, based on our own experience and intuitions, other authors' views, and corpus data. These include concepts of scale and key (such as the "supermode"), harmony (the prevalence of fifth motions and other "close" moves on the circle of fifths), melody (the complex interplay between $\hat{3}$ and $\flat\hat{3}$), and rhythm (anticipatory syncopation). At present, we know very little about listeners' grasp of these concepts; this would seem to be a ripe area for exploration in experimental psychology. In addition, we hope this chapter has helped to demonstrate the great value of statistical corpus data in music research, both as a way of helping untangle disputed issues (such as the validity of the major/minor distinction) and as a source of new insights.

# Core Reading

de Clercq, T., & Temperley, D. (2011). A corpus analysis of rock harmony. *Popular Music, 30,* 47–70.

Everett, W. (2009). *Foundations of rock.* New York, NY: Oxford University Press.

Moore, A. (2001). *Rock: The primary text.* Aldershot, UK: Ashgate.

Stephenson, K. (2002). *What to listen for in rock.* New Haven, CT: Yale University Press.

Temperley, D., & de Clercq, T. (2013.) Statistical analysis of harmony and melody in rock music. *Journal of New Music Research, 42,* 187–204.

# Further References

Bertin-Mahieux, T., Ellis, D., Whitman, B., & Lamere, P. (2011). The million song dataset. In A. Klapuri & C. Leider (Eds.), *Proceedings of the 12th International Society for Music Information Retrieval Conference,* Utrecht, Netherlands.

Biamonte, N. (2010). Modal and pentatonic patterns in rock music. *Music Theory Spectrum, 32,* 95–110.

Burgoyne, J., Wild, J., & Fujinaga, I. (2011). An expert ground truth set for audio chord recognition and music analysis. In A. Klapuri, & C. Leider (Eds.), *Proceedings of the 12th International Society for Music Information Retrieval Conference, Miami, Florida.*

Burns, L. (2005). Meaning in a popular song: The representation of masochistic desire in Sarah McLachlan's "Ice." In D. Stein (Ed.), *Engaging music: Essays in musical analysis* (pp. 136–148). New York, NY: Oxford University Press.

Covach, J. (1997). Progressive rock, "Close to the Edge", and the boundaries of style. In J. Covach & G. M. Boone (Eds.), *Understanding rock: Essays in musical analysis* (pp. 3–31). New York, NY: Oxford University Press.

Covach, J. (2005). Form in rock music: A primer. In D. Stein (Ed.), *Engaging Music* (pp. 65–76). New York, NY: Oxford University Press.

Craton, L., Juergens, D., Michalak, H., & Poireier, C. (2016). Roll over Beethoven? An initial investigation of listeners' perception of chords used in rock music. *Music Perception, 33,* 332–343.

de Clercq, T. (2012). Sections and successions in successful songs: A prototype approach to form in rock music. PhD dissertation, Eastman School of Music.

Doll, C. (2009). Transformation in rock harmony: An explanatory strategy. *Gamut, 2*(1), 1–44. doi:10.7282/T31J9CD8

Doll, C. (2011). Rockin' out: Expressive modulation in verse-chorus form. *Music Theory Online, 17*(3). www.mtosmt.org/issues/mto.11.17.3/mto.11.17.3.doll.html

Everett, W, (2004). Making sense of rock's tonal systems. *Music Theory Online, 10*(4). www.mtosmt.org/issues/mto.04.10.4/mto.04.10.4.w_everett.html

Everett, W. (2008). Pitch down the middle. In W. Everett (Ed.), *Expression in pop-rock music* (2nd ed.) (pp. 111–74). New York, NY: Routledge.

Hansen, C., & Hansen, R. (1988). How rock music videos can change what is seen when boy meets girl. *Sex Roles, 19*, 287–316.

Huron, D. (2006). *Sweet anticipation: Music and the psychology of expectation*. Cambridge, MA: MIT Press.

Krumhansl, C. (1990). *Cognitive foundations of musical pitch*. New York, NY: Oxford University Press.

Middleton, R. (1990). *Studying popular music*. Buckingham, UK: Open University Press.

Moore, A. (1992). Patterns of harmony. *Popular Music, 11*, 73–106.

Moore, A. (1995). The so-called "flattened seventh" in rock. *Popular Music, 14*, 185–201.

Nobile, D. (2015). Counterpoint in rock music: Unpacking the melodic-harmonic divorce. *Music Theory Spectrum, 37*, 189–203.

North, A., & Hargreaves, D. (1999). Music and adolescent identity. *Music Education Research, 1*, 75–92.

*Rolling Stone*. (2004). The 500 greatest songs of all time. *Rolling Stone, 963*, 65–165.

Schaffrath, H. (1995). *The Essen Folksong Collection in the Humdrum kern format*. D. Huron (Ed.). Menlo Park, CA: Center for Computer Assisted Research in the Humanities.

Sloboda, J., O'Neill, S., & Ivaldi, A. (2001). Functions of music in everyday life: An exploratory study using the experience sampling method. *Musicae Scientiae, 5*, 9–32.

Spicer, M. (2005). Review of Everett, *The Beatles as musicians: The Quarry Men through Rubber Soul*. *Music Theory Online, 11*(4). http://www.mtosmt.org/issues/mto.05.11.4/mto.05.11.4.spicer.html

Temperley, D. (2001). *The cognition of basic musical structures*. Cambridge, MA: MIT Press.

Temperley, D. (2007a). The melodic-harmonic "divorce" in rock. *Popular Music, 26*, 323–342.

Temperley, D. (2007b). *Music and probability*. Cambridge, MA: MIT Press.

Temperley, D. (2011). The cadential IV in rock. *Music Theory Online, 17*(1). http://www.mtosmt.org/issues/mto.11.17.1/mto.11.17.1.temperley.html

Temperley, D. (2012). Scalar shift in popular music. *Music Theory Online, 17*(4). www.mtosmt.org/issues/mto.11.17.4/mto.11.17.4.temperley.html

Temperley, D. (2009). *A statistical analysis of tonal harmony*. www.theory.esm.rochester.edu/temperley/kp-stats

Temperley., D., & Tan, D. (2013). Emotional connotations of diatonic modes. *Music Perception, 30*, 237–57.

Temperley, D., Waller, A., & de Clercq, T. (2015). Changes in rock melody, 1954–2009. Paper presented at the Society for Music Perception and Cognition Annual Meeting, Nashville, TN.

Traut, D. (2005). "Simply Irresistible": Recurring accent patterns as hooks in mainstream 1980s music. *Popular Music, 24*, 57–77.

Wagner, N. (2003). "Domestication" of blue notes in the Beatles' songs. *Music Theory Spectrum, 25*, 353–365.

Walser, R. (1993). *Running with the devil: Power, gender, and madness in heavy metal music*. Hanover, NH: University Press of New England.

# 15

# MUSICAL STRUCTURE
## Form

*Richard Ashley*

## Introduction

When musicians speak of the "form" of a piece of music they are referring to its overall design, plan, pattern, or structure. The nature of musical form is a central concern in Western musical scholarship; systematic writings on form date from the 18th century (Burnham, 2002). This chapter introduces some basic concepts of form in Western tonal music, relates these theoretical constructs to empirical research into the perception and comprehension of larger-scale musical structure, evaluates such research, and offers some directions for future investigation. We will deal only with tonal music, primarily from the Western classical tradition as consideration of nontonal music would require another chapter-length treatment.

## Musical Form and Its Description

Musical works, composed or improvised, are rarely so brief as to be contained within the perceptual present (a duration of a few seconds). Folk songs, nursery rhymes, music for dancing, concert works, and popular songs exhibit global as well as local musical structure. What might serve as the foundation for perceiving and comprehending formal structures in music? The basis of perceptual patterning, in music as elsewhere, begins with detection of similarities and dissimilarities among the features, dimensions, or attributes of the perceptual signal (Francès, 1988; Deliège, 2001). Music, like speech, is built on contrastive aspects of acoustic units. To create patterns, percepts—in our case, musical events—must be discriminable from one another, allowing us to perceive them as individual acoustic events, whether notes and motives or phonemes and words. In Western music theory, analysis involves the *segmentation* of the musical work into smaller units and the *description of relationships* between these segments (Hanninen, 2012). Many kinds of musical events can be taken as segments out of which form may be built: individual notes; "ideas," "motives," or "gestures"; "phrases," "periods," and "sections"; and, in some compositions, "movements." Such units' combinations and relationships are the domain of formal analysis (e.g. Berry, 1966; Caplin, 1998).

Two aspects of musical structure are typically seen as fundamental in analysis of musical form: the pattern, plan, or design of the piece's divisions and subdivisions, and the tonal relationships across the work. The first typically focuses on segments, which are identified and distinguished from others primarily by some kind of motivic or melodic content, whereas the second relates segments to one another by their tonal, harmonic functions. The first approach investigates, for example, a first or "principal" theme as opposed to a "secondary" theme in the opening movement of a Beethoven piano sonata, or the verse and chorus distinctions of pop songs. The second approach views sonata form not primarily as a sequence of contrasting melodies or themes, but as harmonic contrasts over time. Most current music-theoretic approaches to musical form integrate the two and recognize the simultaneous, interacting operations of musical parameters in both the frequency and time domains. First and second themes in sonatas may contrast not only harmonically, but also melodically and texturally (Berry, 1966; Caplin, 1998; Hepokoski & Darcy, 2006), or may be understood as a work's "deep structure" elaborated at different levels or time-scales. Such elaborations are often conceived of hierarchically, using basic melodic, harmonic, and contrapuntal patterns such as harmonic motion from tonic to dominant and back to tonic (I–V–I), or ascending melodic arpeggios, such as an upward gesture of the scale degrees $\hat{1}$–$\hat{3}$–$\hat{5}$, which is then filled in with descending stepwise motion before coming to rest on the tonic. These patterns will be found simultaneously occurring at two or more different levels, with some unfolding more quickly near the musical surface, and others more slowly, at higher, more basic levels of musical structure (Schenker, 1979).

According to one current family of music theories, the fundamental building blocks of musical works are contrapuntal patterns which serve as "schemata," which composers thread together skillfully, based on a deep, practiced understanding of their properties, relationships, and typical deployment (Gjerdingen, 2007, this volume). Timbre and texture may motivate form, as in popular music, where segmentation is often clearly marked by these parameters, or musical form may be seen as the result of processes of the ongoing transformation of groups of pitches over time, through processes such as inversion or reordering (Lewin, 1993). Other approaches to form are based in musical rhythm, arising from hierarchic patterns of upbeats and downbeats (Cone, 1968), or present approaches to repertoires outside the Western art music canon (Covach, 2005).

Common to most analytic approaches to musical form is a notion of *coherence* or *unity* in the musical work. An analyst is motivated to reveal not only a work's constituent elements, but how the relationships between these elements cause the work to be unified and coherent in an organic or logical manner, thereby demonstrating a composer's skill and adherence to fundamental principles of good musical organization (Schenker, 1979). As we will see, numerous studies have investigated compositional coherence and unity empirically.

## Structuring Tonal Musical Works: A Cognitively Oriented Theory

Traditional music theory sees compositions as hierarchically structured, with smaller units combining into larger ones. An influential cognitively oriented theory of music's hierarchical structure is Lerdahl and Jackendoff's Generative Theory of Tonal Music, or GTTM (Lerdahl & Jackendoff, 1983). GTTM aims to explicate how a listener familiar with a tonal idiom understands works in that idiom; it is not a theory of the listening process, but of final-state understanding. GTTM proposes that a listener transforms the "musical surface"—the piece in sounding form, although conceived of as an aggregation of discrete events rather than as continuously varying amplitudes and spectra—through four interacting musical parameters which we now consider briefly.

Rhythmic analysis in GTTM begins with *grouping structure,* which segments the musical surface into contiguous events, or groups; lower-level segments combine into larger ones hierarchically. Grouping structure has parallels with traditional theories of phrase-structure and related hierarchical formal analyses. Grouping structure is produced through the application of analytic rules. As with Gestalt principles of perceptual organization (Lee, this volume), similar events are grouped together, and difference produces segmentation; likewise, events proximate in pitch or in time are grouped together, and grouping boundaries occur when distances of time or pitch are larger. GTTM also describes *metric structure,* based on previous hierarchic theories of musical rhythm (e.g. Cooper & Meyer, 1960; Cone 1968). In place of simpler accented/unaccented or upbeat/downbeat categorizations of musical events, and their hierarchical organization, GTTM begins with the beat—a durationless point in time—employed in a recurring, isochronous *tactus* or reference level pulse. The tactus may be divided and subdivided into faster levels, and also subsumed by hierarchically slower beat trains. These faster and slower sequences occur in phase with each other, creating emphases on higher-level beats and thus the structures of musical meter (see Martens & Benadon, this volume).

The third and fourth parameters in GTTM are pitch-based and are derived from prior music-theoretic notions (such as those of Schoenberg, 1969, and Schenker, 1979); they focus on harmony rather than melody or theme. *Time-span reduction* identifies a tone, or a chord, as being the most important in any event in grouping structure and can be thought of as a harmonic "reduction," an underlying tonal structure for the composition. *Prolongational structure* addresses the phenomenological sense that pieces based on the harmonic principles of Western "classical" music change in their musical "tension" over time: ". . . the kind of tension we wish to address here is the . . . sort whose opposite is relaxation—the incessant breathing in and out of music in response to the juxtaposition of pitch and rhythmic factors" (Lerdahl & Jackendoff, 1983, p. 179). GTTM's view of musical structure, especially hierarchical grouping and harmonic structure, has provided fertile ground for empirical researchers. We begin our survey of empirical research into musical form with segmentation and grouping structure.

## Dividing Up Musical Structure: Segmentation and Grouping

GTTM's grouping rules have been used as the basis for a number of experimental studies. In an early example, Deliège (1987) investigated listeners' segmentations of musical works. Her participants' judgments were generally found to be in agreement with the segmentations produced by the GTTM rules, although additional parameters (such as timbre and texture) were implicated, and segmentations were not always placed at the precise rhythmic positions proposed by GTTM. Additionally, some complexities related to multiple rules' simultaneous application were noted. Clarke and Krumhansl (1990), using music by Mozart and Stockhausen, and Krumhansl (1996), focusing on Mozart's Sonata K. 282, Mvt. 1, also provided support for GTTM's segmentation rules; the sonata movement was segmented into three main parts as expected. Throughout these studies, participants were in greater agreement at primary divisions of the compositions' forms than at intermediate or lower level divisions; thus higher levels of hierarchic grouping structure were more strongly attested. The variability seen in listeners' segmentations of the music, as when some listeners hear a segment boundary at a particular location and others do not, are in line with the spirit of GTTM's preference rules, which indicate possible but not obligatory interpretations of musical structure. We will discuss processing of musical themes in more detail shortly.

## Formal Design and Thematic Content

A musical work's form is typically analyzed not only in terms of segmentation or grouping structure but also with regard to the content of these groups and their relationships to one another. The presence of different, contrasting melodic or thematic materials is integral to sectional design, with sections often clearly distinguished by these means. Describing designs as ABA' (e.g. rounded binary), ABACABA (as in a rondo), or Intro-Verse-Verse-Chorus-Bridge-Chorus (in a pop song), illustrates this approach. More complicated structures, including sonata-allegro form, can also be understood thematically (Hepokoski & Darcy, 2006).

A refinement of these approaches considers musical segments or groups in terms of their *formal functions,* such as *beginning, middle, end, before-the-beginning,* and *after-the-end* (Caplin, 1998); parallels may be seen in popular music, where such functions as *introduction* and *bridge* are common (Covach, 2005). GTTM considers the beginnings and ends of groups to be important, but gives little attention to thematic design; however, these matters have engaged empirical researchers. These studies often focus on listeners' abilities to recognize different musical ideas or themes in a composition and to use these in comprehending the work's structure.

## Perception and Cognition of Musical Themes

Melodies and themes are of analytic and cognitive importance and researchers have sought to understand how they are represented and processed. However, it is common for musical ideas to undergo transformations during a composition, and thus thematic comprehension must involve abstraction from the musical surface. Listeners' capacities to identify themes and melodies, including transformed versions, is thus an important topic.

It has long been known that listeners' perception of and memory for melodies is imperfect and schematic in nature, even in studies using simplified stimuli (Dowling, 1978). Given the limitations of real-time perception and of working memory seen in such studies, the question arises: how do listeners deal with these constraints and come to grips with the rich, detailed and evanescent musical surfaces of "real" musical works? Addressing this question, Pollard-Gott (1983) investigated listeners' abilities to recognize relationships between varied versions of musical themes in a complex nineteenth-century piano work, the Sonata in B minor by Liszt. Pollard-Gott focused on versions of the first (A) and second (B) main themes from the sonata. For each theme, four variants were excerpted which differed in their surface attributes (register, dynamics, etc.). Participants heard the first 12 minutes of the work, then the excerpts, taking notes on each of them. The excerpts were then presented in pairs and participants judged the similarity of each pair. Thereafter, the A and B themes were presented as examples of melodic categories in the work and participants assigned each of a new set of excerpts to one of these two categories.

Crucially, one group of participants made these categorical judgments after carrying out the listening, notetaking, and similarity judgments only once, but another group followed this procedure three times before categorizing the novel themes. A multidimensional scaling analysis indicated that the single-listening group's similarity judgments were based largely on surface features such as loud-soft and smooth-jumpy; the repeated-listening group used such features as well, but by the final iteration, theme identity had emerged as one significant dimension, with A and B themes spaced well apart, rather than interspersed as in the other dimensions. Thus, listeners were able to infer—develop—categories, given more exposure to the music and the "depth of processing" facilitated by the notetaking procedure. Using an approach related to Pollard-Gott's, Lamont and Dibben (2001) asked listeners to rate similarities of excerpt pairs from compositions by Beethoven and Schoenberg. As in Pollard-Gott's single-listening condition, parameters such as register and features such as melodic contour were found to be more important than motivic content in explaining listeners' judgments, although the authors note that a clean disjunction between thematic content and such "surface" features is not always possible to obtain.

What processes of thematic abstraction in music listening might explain such findings? GTTM provides one approach, through its time-span and prolongational reductions, which provide an underlying musical structure which listeners infer from the musical surface. Dibben (1994) investigated perceptual relationships between such reductions and their original sources. For brief musical excerpts (1 to 16 measures) from compositions by Handel and Brahms, Dibben produced two different reductions, one a "correct" or appropriate structural reduction and another "incorrect" one. Participants heard the original excerpt and then the reductions, indicating which of these best matched the original; they chose the correct version over its incorrect counterpart in a statistically reliable manner. Dibben concluded that her results supported listeners' use of a hierarchical representation of the music. Aware that her "incorrect" reductions may have been less tonally coherent than their "correct" counterparts, Dibben conducted a second experiment that did not support lack of coherence as a factor in such judgments.

However, GTTM's reductions are primarily harmonic in nature, and other approaches have been explored to deal with melodic and other significant musical features. In an extended research program, Deliège proposed and investigated a "cue abstraction" model (Deliège, & Mélen 1997; Deliège 2001), in which a listener first segments the musical surface, and then extracts salient cues from each group. These cues are then used as the basis for processes of categorization, recall, and comparison of groups and events. In one study, Deliège (1996) investigated listeners' categorical perception of musical motifs in the Finale of Bach's Sonata for unaccompanied violin, BWV 1005. Like Pollard-Gott, Deliège found that repeated listenings clarified categorical memberships of individual events, and that surface features as well as music-structural relationships were important in these processes; participants with less musical background benefitted the most from repeated exposure to the music. In this study, participants were presented with pre-identified thematic categories. To address these matters in a more naturalistic listening situation, Deliège, Mélen, Stammers, & Cross (1996) used a short but complete composition (Schubert's *Valse Sentimentale*, D. 779) as the musical material for a set of three experiments. In the first of these, participants without musical training identified musically salient events—cues—while listening to the piece. Their choices, mostly consistent between a first and second listening, were based primarily on surface features, with harmonic structures being less rarely invoked. Subsequent experiments had participants place the piece's segments on a timeline or attempt to reconstruct the piece from its segments; results showed considerable divergence from the original's structure. Nonmusicians oriented toward surface features as the basis for their decisions whereas musically trained participants showed some sensitivity to formal function and larger patterns of tension/release.

## Musical Form and Tonal Structure

Many music analysts consider the tonal plan of a work—the key areas set out and traversed over time—to be its most important structural factor. From a cognitive standpoint, this implies that listeners need to be able to, in some probably tacit manner, find keys and track their changes over moderate to extended time spans. Different approaches to investigating the influence of tonal structure and design on the perception of musical form have been used in the literature, including probing memory for tonal centers and relating tonal change to musical tension; we address these next.

## Memory for Long-Range Tonal Relationships

Tonal structure in much Western art music follows certain statistically regulated patterns of chord progression (see Shanahan, this volume), although other tonal idioms, such as those used in popular music, may behave differently (Temperley and de Clerq, this volume). Some progressions, such as tonic to dominant and back, are found at multiple hierarchic levels in tonal music. A C chord may move directly to a G chord and back; a symphony movement in sonata-allegro may begin in the key of C major, modulate to G major after some time (all in the exposition), and after changing keys for some time in the development, move fixedly to C (recapitulation). The assumption is that return to the original key is perceived by listeners and provides perceptual coherence to the musical piece. Here we outline some findings regarding perception of larger (higher) levels of structure.

Cook (1987) addressed memory for tonal centers in two experiments. In Experiment 1, Cook's participants listened to six excerpts from the Western art music repertoire in their original versions, in which establishing and returning to a central key is presumed to be crucial to structural unity and aesthetic value; each excerpt was also presented in a version where such tonal unity was disrupted by ending in a different key. Care was taken to make surface transitions in the modified excerpts unobtrusive. Listeners compared the two versions of each piece, rating them for pleasure, expressiveness, coherence, and sense of completion. Only two of the six stimuli—the shortest ones—showed any significant results in the ratings, suggesting that tonal closure had at best a limited role in listeners' assessments of the works. A follow-up experiment produced similar results: tonal closure seemed to affect judgments only for very short pieces (ca. one minute).

Marvin and Brinkman (1999) revisited the question of tonal memory. In a first experiment, they presented musical excerpts (1.5–3 minutes) to participants with substantial musical experience. Excerpts remained in one key, modulated to the dominant, or modulated to a less-closely-related key. Participants answered various questions about each excerpt, including its historical style/period, meter, and texture; the crucial question was whether or not the excerpt began and ended in the same key, testing memory for tonality explicitly. Performance was significantly above chance regarding tonal change or not, indicating that skilled musicians were sensitive to longer-range tonal movement. A second experiment used short pieces (primarily Baroque dance movements) in two versions: originals, with idiomatic tonal relationships including the establishment of, departure from, and return to a central tonality, and alterations, where tonal plans of the works were disrupted by reordering the works' segments so as to not begin and end in the originals' tonic. Participants were unable to determine if the works began and ended in the same key, although they were able to distinguish between works that ended in the tonic from those that did not.

Research into memory for tonality and tonal structure continues to this writing. In a recent study, Farbood (2016) sought to determine for how long tonal centers were held in memory by listeners. Using tension judgments, and in particular the ways in which their slopes change as harmonic progressions unfold, Farbood's two experiments found that some memory trace for a tonal center could persist for up to 20 seconds, but there was no evidence for times longer than this. We are thus unable to directly evaluate listeners' comprehension or use of tonal structure over longer time spans.

## Tonal Structure and Musical Tension

Some researchers have related tonal progressions to a felt sense of musical tension. The empirical literature based on this notion stems from a variety of theoretical sources (Schoenberg, 1969; Parncutt, 1989; Lerdahl & Jackendoff, 1983; Lerdahl, 2001). Theories of tonal tension connect dynamic internal or phenomenological states (tension and relaxation) to the establishment of, departure from, and return to tonal points of repose (cf. Shanahan, this volume). Moving away from a tonal resting place increases tension: the further the distance, the greater the tension.

Krumhansl (1996) investigated listeners' responses to the first movement of Mozart's piano sonata K. 282. This movement is either a binary, two–part form, or a sonata–allegro form (Hepokoski & Darcy 2006) with three main divisions (exposition, development, and recapitulation); it presents a typical harmonic plan of tonic moving to dominant (exposition), working through other key areas more briefly (development), and returning to and remaining in the tonic (recapitulation). Krumhansl's participants provided segmentations of the movement, continuous ratings of musical tension using a slider, and identifications of new ideas in the music as they arose. Musical tension responses seemed to be based on a variety of musical features including harmonic tension as well as melodic contour, dynamics, structural and stylistic details, and fluctuations in tempo. When tempo and dynamics were controlled for, tension ratings remained much the same, indicating that performance parameters may contribute to, but do not define, the ebb and flow of musical tension.

Bigand and Parncutt (1999) investigated musical tension in chord sequences longer than in most experiments but briefer than full compositions; one sequence was a simplification of most of the Prelude Op. 28/9 by Chopin. They tested predictions from Parncutt (1989) and Lerdahl (Lerdahl & Jackendoff, 1983; Lerdahl, 1988): Pitch commonality between successive chords versus hierarchic "distances" between harmonic events as sources of perceived tension. Their findings supported an important role for harmony in such judgments, but not necessarily as predicted: Local phenomena, such as cadence formulas, were more influential than higher-level hierarchic structures. Further, a return to tonic after a modulation was heard as *increasing* tension, rather than decreasing it. These results indicated that listeners were able to use harmonic information at local levels but not as part of an integrated hierarchic view of the excerpts, in line with findings of Tillmann, Bigand, and Madurell (1998) and Cook (1987).

Building on these earlier studies, Lerdahl and Krumhansl (2007) present a quantitative model of tonal tension with four components: hierarchical (prolongational) event structure, tonal pitch space distance, surface (psychoacoustic) dissonance, and voice-leading attraction (the sense that some tones tend more or less strongly toward others, e.g. "ti" → "do"). Excerpts included all of Chopin Op. 28/9 (ca. 90 seconds), as well as excerpts by Bach and Wagner. Participants heard the first event and made a judgment, then the first two events, and so on until the entire excerpt had been heard. Judged and predicted tension matched well after the addition of a fifth parameter, melodic contour. The authors conclude that their model is suitable for understanding perception of hierarchical tonal structure, although some tension will be situational rather than algorithmic.

## Formal Functions and Signposts

An alternative to tonal hierarchy models suggests that idiom-specific categories of musical events act as "signposts" in a composition's rhetorical flow to help a listener track long-range structure. Granot and Jacoby (2011a, 2011b) used a version of the puzzle-unscrambling task, with the first movement of sonatas by Mozart (first study) or Haydn (second study) as stimuli. The segments of a movement were presented in a random order, to be reassembled into a musically logical and coherent order. Few participants replicated the original composition, but their responses showed sensitivity to the placement of the opening and ending segments, with their conventional rhetorical features; the overall ABA' design of a movement based on exposition, development, and recapitulation; and the function within the movements of the less stable segments (bridge and development). Their responses also indicated sensitivity to relationships between motivic/thematic materials, but as in other studies harmonic structure was important only at local, not global, levels. Participants' decisions seemed to be guided by their knowledge of musical symmetry, tension, and repose; the uses of typical opening and closing gestures; and thematic, but not harmonic, organization.

On a musically smaller scale (ca. 10 seconds), Neuhaus (2013) provides evidence from both behavioral tasks and EEG (focusing on the N300 ERP) that participants were sensitive to formal units and their combinations, such as grouping AABB hierarchically into two chunks of AA and BB, or ABAB into two chunks, AB AB, as opposed to hearing these purely as linear sequences. Behavioral results indicated that contrasts between adjacent segments, for example in melodic content (A vs B) or contour, facilitated hierarchic interpretations. Contrastingly, the brain responses shown in the ERPs indicated participants' recognition of recurring patterns in the music, particularly rhythmic patterns, irrespective of whether the same pattern occurred in adjacent or nonadjacent segments (e.g. **AA**BB or **A**BA**B**). Neither of these results support a strict concatenationist account of music listening.

Vallières, Tan, Caplin, and McAdams (2009) investigated formal functions (Caplin, 1998) directly, using excerpts from compositions by Mozart with functions of beginning, middle, or end, and asking participants to categorize each with one of these labels, as well as assessing how strongly the function was conveyed. Excerpts were correctly labeled at levels significantly above chance; endings were the most successfully identified, followed by middles and beginnings. Musical experience also impacted performance, with musically trained participants performing better, due to their greater experience with the musical style and its characteristic gestures (see Gjerdingen, this volume). These results echo the findings of Granot and Jacoby (2011a, 2011b), showing listeners are sensitive to such formal functions both in and out of whole-composition contexts.

Finally, Sears, Caplin, and McAdams (2012), focusing on stereotyped ending formulae, found that listeners distinguished between different types of cadential formulae (perfect, imperfect, and half) in their ratings of how complete a sense of closure these types communicated. Unlike some other studies of cadences, this study used repertoire excerpts (rather than more abstract chord progressions). Listeners did not have to rely solely on harmonic progression, but could make use of the rich variety of musical details available in understanding the excerpts they heard (cf. Gjerdingen, this volume).

## Form, Coherence, and Aesthetics

We have seen that listeners' ability to remember several larger-scale aspects of musical works seems to be quite limited, calling into question the status of music-analytic theories as psychological theories. But what if the goal of musical structures, and the listenings they enable, is not *comprehension* of musical events, but is instead *aesthetic* experience—to find the work pleasing, moving, or expressive (Margulis, this volume)? Remembering events and their interrelationships would then not be as important as aesthetic response.

This question has been investigated extensively by Bigand and Tillmann and their various collaborators; for a broad and thoughtful review, see Tillmann and Bigand (2004). A basic method used in their collaborations (Tillmann & Bigand, 1996, 1998; Tillmann, Bigand, & Madurell, 1998; Bigand, Madurell, Tillmann, & Pineau, 1999) was the manipulation of relatively short musical compositions (up to about three minutes in duration) so as to potentially impact their structural cohesiveness or musical expressiveness.

Tillmann and Bigand (1996) presented participants with three short compositions (by Bach, Mozart, and Schoenberg) in their normal form and with each piece divided into brief "chunks" and played with these segments in reverse order. Participants without significant musical expertise found the original and retrograded versions equivalent when rated on various scales related to expressiveness; the retrograding did affect ratings for the Schoenberg composition somewhat. The experimenters conclude that musical structure is not necessarily important at the global level for a piece to be heard as expressive. In a subsequent study (Tillmann & Bigand, 1998), short minuets were segmented into "chunks" of 4, 2, or 1 measures, and the coherence of the composition disrupted, for example by scrambling the order of the segments or by transposing the pitch level of the segments by 1 or 2 semitones. Transformations had little impact on listeners' abilities to comprehend the music, as measured by their performance in identifying a "target" passage while listening; disturbing a piece's tonal coherence by transposition had no significant effect, and the reordering manipulation's impact was limited to the most extreme version, in which 15 of 16 measures were reordered. The overall conclusion was that musical coherence was a local phenomenon, not one related to a piece's overall structure. Tillmann and Bigand read these results as support for the moment-to-moment "concatenationist" listening framework of Levinson (1997), in which musical comprehension is strongly constrained to the perceptual present.

However, claims for a purely concatenationist view of musical perception need some moderating. Lalitte and Bigand (2006) presented listeners with 3-minute excerpts from six pieces, original and segmented-(into 29 chunks)-and-scrambled. Participants found the original versions more musical (as assessed by their judgment of the musical skill of the producer assembling the segments into a whole), indicating that the lack of coherence in large-scale structure was perceptible.

Mindful of the violence being done to musical structure by such scrambling methods, Eitan and Granot (2008) took another approach. Their participants heard either intact compositions by Mozart (K. 332 Mvt. 1, or K. 280, Mvt. 1) or hybrids, where analogous sections from the two movements were interchanged, preserving the structural plan but changing content and disrupting any compositionally-ordained coherence and unity. Participants heard one intact and one hybrid version with a cover story: Mozart composed both of these but chose to publish only one—which one? Responses included ratings for coherence, interest, and other musical and aesthetic aspects, as well as indicating the preferred version. Listeners did not significantly prefer original versions to hybrids, sometimes preferring the hybrids. The authors conclude that these results provide evidence against organic coherence and inner unity as the basis for listeners' assessment of musical works.

## Conclusions: Nothing but Music in the Moment?

Empirical research into the perception of form in tonal music indicates that traditional theories of musical structure can provide motivation and hypotheses but are not satisfactory as theories of perception. In particular, limitations on real-time processing and on memory constrain listeners' performance on many experimental measures of formal perception—but seemingly without fatally damaging the hedonic and aesthetic dimensions of music listening. Nevertheless, we are beginning to understand how listeners make sense of larger musical structures—of what matters and how. Cognitively-based theories of rhythmic and pitch structures have arisen in part as the result of such insights and have been useful in understanding hierarchical structure and the ebb and flow of musical tension; listeners understand the typical and schematic aspects of musical idioms, including formal functions and important semiotic and rhetorical signposts related to beginnings, middles, and ends of musical groups.

Taken together, such results reinforce findings from other studies which show that participants' familiarity with the music they are hearing—for example in repeated and focused listening—facilitates the kind of categorization and associative thought which is crucial for grasping musical structure involving nonlocal relationships and nonadjacent events (Zbikowski, this volume). Passive listening, especially to less preferred or unfamiliar musical idioms, should not be expected to particularly facilitate musical comprehension, compared to the enriched results to be obtained with more active involvement with the music (Godhino, 2016). Listeners' existing knowledge of music, stored in long-term memory, is the basis on which their comprehension of any new musical work is predicated, and to the degree their knowledge does not match new percepts, comprehension of these will be difficult and incomplete (cf. Danielssen & Brøvig-Hanssen, and Gjerdingen, this volume). Results from my own research group (Ashley, 2015, submitted) indicate that testing college-aged participants on their memory for and perception of form in pop songs—the kind of music with which all of them are most familiar—yields quite high levels of performance. We should not be surprised that listeners for whom "classical" music is a foreign or acquired musical language do not experience it as might be expected; we should, rather, seek to understand the ways they use their everyday musical experiences to understand new works, and to better understand how they comprehend musical works in their "mother tongues."

## Core Reading

Burnham, S. (2002). Form. In T. Christensen (Ed.), *The Cambridge history of Western music theory* (pp. 880–906). Cambridge: Cambridge University Press.

Deliège, I., & Mélen, M. (1997). Cue abstraction in the representation of musical form. In I. Deliège & J. A. Sloboda (Eds.), *Perception and cognition of music* (pp. 387–412). Hove, UK: Psychology Press.

Dibben, N. (1994) The cognitive reality of hierarchic structure in tonal and atonal music. *Music Perception, 12*, 1–25.

Krumhansl, C. (1996). A perceptual analysis of Mozart's Piano Sonata K. 282: Segmentation, tension, and musical ideas. *Music Perception, 13*, 401–432.

Lerdahl, F., & Jackendoff, R. (1983). *A generative theory of tonal music.* Cambridge, MA: MIT Press.

Marvin, E. W., & Brinkman, A. (1999). The effect of modulation and formal manipulation on perception of tonic closure by expert listeners. *Music Perception 16*, 389–407.

Pollard-Gott, L. (1983). Emergence of thematic concepts in repeated listening to music. *Cognitive Psychology, 15*, 66–94.

Tillmann, B., & Bigand, E. (2004). The relative importance of local and global structures in music perception. *The Journal of Aesthetics and Art Criticism, 62*, 211–222.

## Further References

Ashley, R. (2015). Grammaticality in popular music form: Perceptual and structural aspects. Presentation at the Society for Music Perception and Cognition, Nashville, Tennessee.

Ashley, R. (submitted). Comprehension of musical form in popular songs: Structure, perception, and memory.

Berry, W. (1986). *Form in music* 2nd ed. Englewood Cliffs, NJ: Prentice-Hall.

Bigand, E., Madurell, F., Tillmann, B., & Pineau, M. (1999). Effect of global structure and temporal organization on chord processing. *Journal of Experimental Psychology: Human Perception and Performance, 25*(1), 184–197.

Bigand, E., & Parncutt, R. (1999). Perceiving musical tension in long chord sequences. *Psychological Research, 62*(4), 237–254.

Caplin, W. E. (1998). *Classical form: A theory of formal functions for the instrumental music of Haydn, Mozart, and Beethoven.* New York, NY: Oxford University Press.

Clarke, E. F., & Krumhansl, C. L. (1990). Perceiving musical time. *Music Perception, 7*, 213–251.

Cone, E. T. (1968). *Musical form and musical performance.* New York, NY: W.W, Norton.

Cook, N. (1987). The perception of large-scale tonal closure. *Music Perception, 5*, 197–205.

Cooper, G., & Meyer, L. (1960) *The rhythmic structure of music.* Chicago, IL: University of Chicago Press.

Covach, J. (2005). Form in rock music. In D. Stein (Ed.,) *Engaging music: Essays in music analysis* (pp. 65–76). New York, NY: Oxford University Press.

Deliège, I. (1987). Grouping conditions in listening to music: An approach to Lerdahl & Jackendoff's grouping preference rules. *Music Perception, 4*, 325–360.

Deliège, I. (1996). Cue abstraction as a component of categorisation processes in music listening. *Psychology of Music, 24*, 131–156.

Deliège, I. (2001). Introduction: Similarity perception ↔ Categorization ↔ Cue abstraction. *Music Perception, 18*, 233–243.

Deliège, I., Mélen, M., Stammers, D., & Cross, I. (1996). Musical schemata in real-time listening to a piece of music. *Music Perception, 14*, 117–160.

Dowling, W. J. (1978) Scale and contour: Two components of a theory of memory for melodies. *Psychological Review 85*, 341–354.

Eitan, Z., & Granot, R. Y. (2008). Growing oranges on Mozart's apple tree: "Inner form" and aesthetic judgment. *Music Perception 25*, 397–418.

Farbood, M. (2016). Memory of a tonal center after modulation. *Music Perception 34,* 71–93.

Francès, R. (1988). *The perception of music.* (W.J. Dowling, trans.). New York, NY: Psychology Press. (Originally published in 1958)

Gjerdingen, R. (2007). *Music in the galant style.* New York, NY: Oxford University Press.

Godinho, J. C. (2016). Miming to recorded music: Multimodality and education. *Psychomusicology: Music, Mind, and Brain, 26*, 189–195.

Granot, R., & Jacoby, N. (2011a). Musically puzzling I: Sensitivity to overall structure in the sonata form? *Musicae Scientiae, 15*, 365–386.

Granot, R., & Jacoby, N. (2011b). Musically puzzling II: Sensitivity to overall structure in a Haydn E-minor sonata, *Musicae Scientiae, 16*, 67–80.

Hanninen, D. (2012). *A theory of music analysis: On segmentation and associative organization.* Rochester, NY: University of Rochester Press.

Hepokoski, J. A., & Darcy, W. (2006). *Elements of sonata theory: Norms, types, and deformations in the late-eighteenth-century sonata.* New York, NY: Oxford University Press.

Lalitte, P., & Bigand, E. (2006). Music in the moment? Revisiting the effect of large scale structures 1, 2. *Perceptual and Motor Skills, 103,* 811–828.

Lamont, A., & Dibben, N. (2001) Motivic structure and the perception of similarity. *Music Perception, 18,* 245–274.

Lerdahl, F. (1988). Tonal pitch space. *Music Perception 5,* 315–345.

Lerdahl, F. (2001). *Tonal pitch space.* New York, NY: Oxford University Press.

Lerdahl & Krumhansl (2007). Modeling tonal tension. *Music Perception, 24,* 329–366.

Lewin, D. (1993). *Musical form and transformation: Four analytic essays.* New Haven, CT: Yale University Press.

Levinson, J. (1997). *Music in the moment.* Ithaca, NY: Cornell University Press.

Neuhaus, C. (2013). Processing musical form: Behavioural and neurocognitive approaches. *Musicae Scientiae, 17,* 109–127.

Parncutt, R. (1989). *Harmony: A psychoacoustical approach.* Berlin: Springer-Verlag.

Schenker, H. (1979). *Free composition: Volume III of new musical theories and fantasies.* (E. Oster, trans.) New York, NY: Pendragon Press. (Original work published 1935)

Schoenberg, A. (1969). *Structural functions of harmony.* New York, NY: W.W. Norton.

Sears, D., Caplin, W., & McAdams, S. (2012). Perceiving the classical cadence. *Music Perception, 31,* 397–417.

Tillmann, B., & Bigand, E. (1996). Does formal musical structure affect perception of musical expressiveness? *Psychology of Music, 24,* 3–17.

Tillmann, B., & Bigand, E. (1998). Influence of global structure on musical target detection and recognition. *International Journal of Psychology, 33,* 107–122.

Tillmann, B., Bigand, E., & Madurell, F. (1998). Local versus global processing of harmonic cadences in the solution of musical puzzles. *Psychological Research, 61,* 157–174.

Vallières, M., Tan, D., Caplin, W. E., & McAdams, S. (2009). Perception of intrinsic formal functionality: An empirical investigation of Mozart's materials. *Journal of Interdisciplinary Music Studies, 3,* 17–43.

# 16

# MUSIC PRODUCTION

## Recording Technologies and Acousmatic Listening

*Ragnhild Brøvig-Hanssen and Anne Danielsen*

### Introduction

For centuries, all forms of music were realized by musicians at a specific place and unfolded organically in time. Accordingly, music was, without exception, only accessible to those who were there when it was performed, and that the audience was always able to link the sound they heard to a visible and present source. These specific and defining qualities of music did not change until the invention of the phonograph in 1877, which occasioned the cultural shift to an era of what Canadian composer and writer R. Murray Schafer (1969) has labeled *schizophonia*, to draw attention to the newfound ability to separate (*schizo* is "split" in Greek) the sound (*phōnē* in Greek) from its source and, importantly, from the performative moment.

In this chapter, we will start by reviewing research into the relationship between live and recorded music, as well as discussing the constraints that pertain to *acousmatic* listening—that is, listening to sound without a visible source (Schaeffer, 2004, pp. 76–77). Then we will focus on two perceptual mechanisms that are at work when one experiences recorded or *acousmatic* sound. The first of these mechanisms concerns the perceptual disconnect that can arise when people compare music to a historically and culturally deep-rooted notion of music as *source bonded* (coming from a specific source) and *spatiotemporally coherent* (emerging at one specific place and time). Here, we will also address the surreal effects that can accompany discrepancies between recorded sound and people's expectations, whether driven by ecological constraints, that is, the relation of living organisms to their physical sonic surroundings as regulated by acoustic laws, or previous experiences with live and recorded sound. The second mechanism concerns processes of naturalization, or the continuous "tuning of the ear." What we mean by this is that new musical expressions, made possible by recording technology, eventually become naturalized, transforming one's reference and starting point for new listening experiences. Ultimately, we will point to some directions for future research related to this discussion.

### The Recording Becomes the Primary Text

While Schafer characterized schizophonia as a permanent and uniform condition after the splitting of sounds from their sources by recordings, Ragnhild Brøvig-Hanssen (2013) distinguishes between three different phases within this condition: the mechanical, the magnetic, and the digital. The mechanical era is related to the invention of the phonograph, which challenged our traditional understanding of sounds as emerging directly from a live source. When Edison demonstrated his speaking phonograph in 1888 members of the audience fainted and this disembodied sound must, in Dave Laing's words, have been "a vital shift in the experience of listening to music" (1991, p. 7). However, although the sounds of a musical performance were liberated from their origins in time and space, these sounds remained a unit on recordings for a long time—what one heard there was the sound of a spatiotemporally coherent event that had been recorded in one "take" (the rare exceptions to this fact were recordings that resulted from very early applications of the technique of overdubbing). Despite the degraded sound quality of the recorded sounds, the musical reproduction presented by the mechanical recording medium remained "trustworthy," in that the sounds were legitimate signs of a previous performance, with an actual and causal connection to what they represented (see note 3). As such, in the earliest phase of schizophonia, the original and reproduced musical events were connected by similarity and affinity, but, in addition, the recorded sounds were *indexical* signs of the preexisting event, to use the vocabulary of Charles S. Peirce.[1]

Whereas music was still generally heard as a spatiotemporally coherent event even after the invention of the phonograph, the invention of the magnetic tape recorder would revolutionize people's conception of music, and of musical recordings. This magnetic era meant dramatic new possibilities for spatial and temporal designs, embracing the disjuncture between sound and its source(s). The tape recorder offered sound engineers the ability to literally cut tracks apart and paste them together again, and this spatiotemporal disjuncture of sound was even further ushered along by the magnetic multitrack recorder. Musical parts could now be recorded separately, at different times, and, if desired, in different locations. The multitrack recorder also solved the problem of degradation of sound quality that took place after each subsequent overdub. Moreover, because sounds could be recorded through several channels without being automatically merged into a single track afterward, the individual tracks could be altered separately even *after* they had been recorded. This new capacity for manipulation altered the ways in which many musicians, producers, and sound engineers worked in the studio while recording and mixing sound. While some engineers simply applied the multitrack recorder according to the longstanding conception of music as, at heart, spatiotemporally coherent, others saw new possibilities for "improving" upon reality. Still others experimented with these new recording and editing abilities in entirely unanticipated ways—for example, molding virtual spaces that appeared contrary to natural acoustic laws or exposing the music's fragmented construction. Such experiments often resulted in a sonic collage of sounds representing different times and spaces.

As emphasized in Brøvig-Hanssen and Danielsen (2016), digital technology did not split these sounds any further from their sources than the magnetic tape recorder had, but the digital conversion of sounds into binary numbers made the practice of splitting them from their sources much easier. The ease with which such "splitting" could be accomplished caused changes in the musicians' and engineers' practice and, in turn, in the resulting music, constituting a third *digital* era of schizophonia, examples of which are given below.

After the multitrack magnetic tape recorder entered the market, the relationship between reproduced performance and original musical performance was no longer causal. The recording studio changed from an archiving center to a laboratory for "sculpting" patchwork performances out of multiple takes. Already in the mid-1980s Jacques Attali (1985) noticed that the relationship between a live performance and a musical recording had, for all intents and purposes, reversed: "What irony: people originally intended to use the record to preserve the performance, and today the performance is only successful as a simulacrum of the record" (p. 85). Drawing upon Jean Baudrillard's concept of simulation, Philip Auslander (2008) argues that the distinction between live performances and musical recordings has in fact vanished, due to the ever-increasing two-way interaction between these respective musical settings (p. 35). By this he alludes to the fact that live performances often include prerecorded musical material as well as an extensive use of studio production tools, while recordings, on the other hand, often imply a performance behind the given recording either in terms of their sound or promotion. Whereas there are still important differences between these two formats in terms of their different settings (performance vs. recording), distinguishing between live and recorded music does not always make sense because the musical expressions can, in fact, be identical. Today, the recording seldom only mediates a preexisting performance but has instead become, to borrow Theodore Gracyk's (1996) characterization, the *primary text* in and of itself (p. 21). In line with this Evan Eisenberg (2005) questions (as does Sterne, 2003, p. 218) whether "recording" is an appropriate term for this format:

> Only live recordings record an event; studio recordings, which are the great majority, record nothing. Pieced together from bits of actual events, they construct an ideal event. They are like the composite photograph of a minotaur. Yet Edison chose the word deliberately. He meant his invention to record grandparents' voices, business transactions and, as a last resort, musical performances. The use we put it to now might strike him as fraudulent, like doctoring the records.
>
> *(p. 89)*

This artistic aspect of the development of recording technologies was first acknowledged within the fields of film, electroacoustic, and popular music. Pierre Schaeffer and his Groupe de Recherches Musicales (GRM) were among the pioneers experimenting with "reduced" or acousmatic listening, which Schaeffer (2004) defined as the act of listening to sound for its own sake, and blotting out the listener's associations with the sound's source. Continuing the tradition of Schaeffer, Francois Bayle experimented with an acousmatic orchestra (the Acousmonium, created in 1974) that consisted of loudspeakers of different sizes that were positioned like musicians in a traditional orchestra (Battier, 2007, p. 200).[2] In classical music, on the other hand, the idea of recording as documentation—that is, as a particular manifestation of an idealized work—persisted rather longer. However, as Arved Ashby (2010) points out, the recording has now become primary in classical music as well: "While the musical work played an originative role in the past—acting as the source and origin of the musical experience—it now serves primarily an aesthetic function, as a point of orientation and demarcation while the listener grapples with the departing landscape of the heard music" (p. 10). Classical music is now *less* likely to be heard in a concert hall than in its recorded form, meaning that people are now, according to Ashby, at a point in history where "recorded simulacra or performances of musical works are [. . .] more relevant, accessible and real than any lingering notion of the pieces themselves" (ibid.).

Since the function of the recording medium is no longer merely to *document* performances,[3] recordings have, in a way, developed their own set of acoustical and perceptual rules, creating a sonic environment that serves not only to replicate "real life" but also to expand it and subvert it. Sounds have been liberated from their dependence upon "live" acoustical laws, and between the speakers, anything goes, thanks to technological editing tools and human creativity.

## Sound as Virtual Space-Form

Experimental research has shown that a very brief sonic experience often sums up the sound of a whole in a way that makes listeners able to, for example, differentiate between spoken voices, instrumental music and environmental sounds based on 50 milliseconds of sound (Bigand et al., 2011), decide upon the style of the music (Gjerdingen and Perrott, 2008), or identify an actual tune (Schellenberg, Iverson, & Mckinnon, 1999) after only 200 ms. Accordingly, a given musical recording's overall "sound" has been defined as the fundamental character of the particular musical elements that can be identified and described in a relatively short time sample but are nevertheless characteristic of a significant portion of the work (Brolinson and Larsen, 1981, pp. 181–82). This definition rightfully emphasizes that a very brief sonic experience often sums up the sound of the whole, evoking Smalley's concept of "space-form" (the aesthetically created spatial environment) in his discussions of acousmatic music. This means that when people perceive and remember sound, they sometimes set aside time's formative role in the music: "although gathered in time, [the space-form] can be contemplated outside the time of listening" (Smalley, 2007, p. 40). The whole experience collapses into a single present moment and resides in the memory as a space-form (ibid., pp. 37–38).

Scholars have proposed various analytical models for conceptualizing acousmatic sound as such virtual space-forms. For example, Allan F. Moore (Moore, Schmidt, & Dockwray, 2009) introduces a "sound box" model, in which the vertical dimension of the sound box represents the sounds' frequency register; the horizontal dimension represents the sounds' placement within the stereo image; and the depth axis represents the perceived distance from the listener on the saggital (front/back) axis. While Moore's sound box denotes an *abstract* space, other scholars have introduced analytical models or metaphors in which the sound of a recording is directly compared to *actual* spatial environments (see Brøvig-Hanssen & Danielsen, 2013; Danielsen, 1998; Doyle, 2005; Lacasse, 2000; and Moylan, 2002). The latter approaches demonstrate an awareness of the fact that listeners often conceptualize acousmatic sound by comparing it to previous experiences with sound.

## Ecological Constraints?

According to James J. Gibson's theory of ecological perception, first published in 1979, people (and animals) always approach and understand new environments according to their previous interactions with similar environments. Eric Clarke (2005) introduced Gibson's work in the visual domain to music psychology, including, in particular, Gibson's assumption that perception is a two-way interaction between a person or animal and the environment. In line with phenomenology, this also means that perception is always-already intentional— those who "perceive and behave" (Gibson, 1986, p. 7) are not processing masses of undifferentiated information but rather engaging with the environment to gather only that information that is meaningful given their purposes and context. Gibson's notion of *affordance* also acknowledges that the same environment can afford different things to different people. Mechanical noise, for example, might be perceived as unbearable repetitive noise for one listener, whereas it is heard as a compelling musical rhythm by another. Applying one of Gibson's key terms, then, people perceive what the environment *affords* according to their needs. Clarke, in fact, remarks that Gibson developed the whole notion of affordance to describe the *variousness* of the dialectic between the properties of a given environment and the needs and capacities of its perceiver. Regarding a new sonic "environment" on a musical recording, this means that people first of all engage with those aspects of it that are most meaningful to them, given their range of experience; an experience with one sound environment becomes an instant resource for the structuring and comprehension of a similar environment. Similarly, engaging with and making sense of a recorded sound will probably follow paths established by one's previous engagements with sounds. The importance of previous experience is emphasized by scholars such as Marc Leman and Albert S. Bregman. Leman (2008) is principally concerned with people's attribution of meaning to sound through habits or conventions—what he calls their "cultural constraints" (p. 56). Bregman (2001) is also interested in the ways in which experiential regularities form mental "schemas" that affect the perceptual organization of sound (p. 43).

The fact that people often compare the acousmatic sound of a recording to previous experiences with sound does not mean that they compare it to an imagined *live performance*. Although people often associate "live performance" with certain qualities rooted in music that existed before the recording medium was introduced, live performances are today as diverse as musical recordings and often involve prerecorded musical material, as well as the extensive use of manipulating tools and signal-processing effects. The live music scene has become a hybrid and pliant environment that falls somewhere between the traditional, spatiotemporally coherent and source-specific musical performance (with its strict acoustical laws) and the virtual spatial environment between the sound speakers (where anything and everything goes). The musicians' degree of involvement in the musical output can vary (from producing the music on the spot to merely imitating an accompanying pre-recorded music, for example), the music will not necessarily emerge from a visible source, and it might not sound especially spatiotemporally coherent. A pertinent question is, however, whether the long history of musical performance that preceded the phonographic era constrains music perception even today by providing a source for perceptual comparison to what one hears. This hypothesis, which follows from the theory of ecological perception, remains to be empirically studied.

## Perceptual Friction and the Tuning of the Ear

According to the theory of ecological perception people will immediately look for, or start to imagine, the sources of the music, compare the virtual space-forms projected by the music to existing acoustical models, and perceptually "integrate" sounds that stem from different times and spaces into a spatiotemporal whole, despite their fragmented character. This presumed tendency to compare acousmatic music to a pre-phonographic state of the art can create in the listener an "experiential friction," which might result in the sound being experienced by the listener as surreal, hyperreal, or defamiliarized. Recording technologies are used artistically to generate such perceptual discrepancies between what the listeners are likely to expect and what they hear. In what follows, we will present three forms of such perceptual friction that can emerge when one listens to recorded sound, namely those linked to the bonding of sound to a *source*, the bonding of sound to an existing *acoustic space*, and the bonding of sound to a *temporally coherent performance*, respectively.

## *Identifying the Sound Source*

When one hears a sound, one naturally thinks first of the sound source: Who or what is producing the sounds one hears? As Clarke makes clear, "The primary function of auditory perception is to discover what sounds are the sound *of*, and what to do about them" (ibid., p. 3). This is a very fundamental mechanism that also constrains the way one hears music. Even though it is now no longer a given that, for example, a live concert (including electronics and electronic amplification) will present either a temporal or a physical correspondence between the sound that is heard and its production (see, for example, Danielsen & Helseth, 2016), people still search for meaningful relationships between what they see and what they hear, or imagine possible sound sources for the sounds they perceive. In principle, however, acousmatic sound leaves the question of possible sound sources open (due to a lack of visual confirmation). Sounds from electronic and digital instruments are particularly difficult to map to sources because the action-sound *relationships* in such instruments are arbitrary (Jensenius, 2013, p. 181). In acoustic instruments, on the other hand, perceptual action-sound couplings are strong, both because they have a long history and because they are based on mechanical laws.

When dealing with complex auditory environments such as music, listeners tend to group sounds with similar timbres together and hear them as one "auditory stream" coming from a distinct environmental source (Bregman, 2001, ch. 2; McAdams & Goodchild, this volume). Regarding musical instruments, the attack portion has been proved to be crucial for the timbre of the sound, and thus for identifying the sound's source, followed by information about the spectral envelope and its evolution through time (for example, in the form of a vibrato) in the sustain phase (Handel, 1995, pp. 430–431; McAdams, 1993; McAdams & Goodchild, this volume). One way to detach the listener from the sound source, thus, is to conceal the source by manipulating or eliminating the early and transient-rich part of the sound. An early example of this is Schaeffer and GRM's experimentation, starting in the 1940s, with removing the attack or transient-phase part of the sound from the sustain-phase part (Schaeffer, 2004). A more contemporary example of distorting the relationship between the sound and its source is the use of digital pitch manipulation in popular music production, which affects the attack as well as the sustain phase of the sound. In this case, one recognizes the sound source but in a defamiliarized form (see Brøvig-Hanssen & Danielsen, 2016, ch. 8). One of the first and most famous examples of digital pitch manipulation (Auto-Tune) used as a vocal effect is Cher's "Believe" from 1998.

Another potentially uncanny or surreal experience arises when one sees the sound source producing sounds, such as in a live performance, but no sound is heard. If the time from the sound's origination (excitation) to when one hears the sound exceeds what is expected for a particular sound source and space, the engagement might be experienced as unnatural or strange. This might happen, for example, when the sound of a voice is being sampled and processed for later use, or when a performance displayed at a Jumbotron at a large venue is out of sync with the sounds coming from the loudspeakers. The latter examples of a discrepancy between what one hears and what one expects (from what one sees) also demonstrate that the type of sound source, the features of the acoustical space of the sound source, and the temporal unfolding of the sound depend on each other.

Although the experience of a sound from a non-recognizable source or a source that comes forward as audibly and radically transformed may come across as uncanny, such effects generally become more or less naturalized. For example, when the microphone was introduced in the mid-1920s, the close-up microphone singing pioneered by so-called "crooners," such as Bing Crosby and Frank Sinatra, was at first regarded as uncanny: the intimate voice had never before been able to penetrate in a concert hall (for a discussion of the reception of "crooning," see Frith, 1986). As listeners grew accustomed to this familiar-made-unfamiliar vocal sound, however, the microphone-staged voice gradually came to stand for the musical voice itself. Likewise, a distorted guitar sound is today commonly heard as a "natural" sound source even though the source (the guitar) has in fact been manipulated by processing effect(s). Generally, what can be regarded as a "normal" sound source in a musical context seems highly malleable.

## *The Virtual Acoustical Space*

Physical spaces operate according to strict acoustical laws, and in an enclosed space, such as a room, sound travels until it meets a surface, (mostly) bounces off of that surface, and then travels until it meets another surface. It gradually weakens as the air and surfaces absorb it, until it dies out entirely. Sounds situated within open spaces do not contain reverberation (but might nevertheless produce an echo, if, for instance, the sounds hit neighboring mountains, tall concrete fences, canyon walls, or cliffs facing water; see, for example, Rossing et al., 2002, p. 528). The architectural design and size of the given space—enclosed or open—as well as the texture of its surfaces determine the character of a reverb or echo. When people engage with acousmatic musical sound, which has no visible source, their experiences with these sorts of different acoustical reflection patterns allow them to imagine specific actual spaces. As Denis Smalley (2007) points out, this process is automatic and unconscious, as sounds always will be perceived as bearers "of space in nature and culture" (p. 54). One possible consequence of such a perceptual equation process is that, when a virtual sonic environment is displaying sonic features that could never occur in real physical environments, the virtual space can be experienced as utterly surreal, hyperreal or defamiliarized.

In Prince's 1986 song "Kiss" (*Parade*, Paisley Park/Warner Bros.), a surrealistic effect arises when two of the axes of the virtual acoustical space (the horizontal and the vertical) display the characteristics of a large hall, while the third axis (the depth) reflects a small "dry" or dampened environment. Another example that is likely experienced as unnatural is Suede's "Filmstar" (*Coming Up*, Nude Records) from 1996. While a recording sometimes aims at simulating an *in situ* performance space in order to assert the recording's faithfulness to a pre-existing performance, there is in this song a profound contrast between the simulated *in situ* performance spaces of the verse of the song, which suggests a small, narrow space, and the chorus, which suggests a much larger, broader spatial environment. The sonic result of this radical contrast in spatial settings conforms to what Smalley (1997) calls "multiple spatial settings," where "throughout the work, the listener is aware of different types of space which cannot be resolved into a single setting" (p. 124).

A third example of discrepancy between the virtual space projected by a recording and the acoustics of physical spaces is "Half Day Closing" by Portishead (*Portishead*, GO! Beat Records), from 1997. Here, several very distinctly different-sounding spaces (a relatively dry small room for a bass guitar, atmospheric sounds that evoke a long, narrow, cylindrical, enclosed environment, like a shaft or a tunnel, and a singer that sounds as though she is performing through a megaphone) are combined, thus forming a surreal space. This conforms to what Smalley calls "spatial simultaneity" (ibid.). At the same time, the surrealistic effect of what is at one point in time a radical juxtaposition of virtual spaces tends to vanish with the passage of time due to the naturalization processes related to acousmatic sound. The spatial simultaneity produced by multitracking in the 1970s and sampling in the 1980s is most likely no longer heard as such but rather as a new type of virtual space against which new spatial montages gain their perceptual effect.

### *Temporal Coherence vs. Temporal Fragmentation*

As already suggested, it is likely that people perceive the new music they hear in relation to the historically and culturally deep-rooted notion of music as caused by spatiotemporally-coherent sources. In fact, it is only against such a backdrop that people are able to hear sounds as, for example, a montage. If one experiences a sound as fragmented, it means that one actually hears it as a collage of different temporally (and spatially) coherent performances. Previous research has shown that whether this happens or not, that is, the sensitivity to musical incoherence, varies with both musical context and learning (Tillmann, & Bigand, 1996; Lalitte & Bigand, 2006; Ashley [Form], this volume).

The ability to cut and paste recorded material with scissors accompanied the development of the magnetic tape recorder and was soon used to fragment the music's temporal structure (listen, for example, to the tape experimentation by participants in the early-1950s electroacoustic music scene, such as John Cage, Pierre Schaeffer, and Karlheinz Stockhausen). Digital sequencer programs eliminated the extremely time-consuming processes of physically splicing tapes, and the sonic traces of cut-ups are now to be found in more mainstream contemporary popular music as well. An example of this is Squarepusher's "My Red Hot Car" (2001), in which the vocals are "all chopped up" and the sound pieces are often repeated as a stutter or separated by sound signal dropouts, which in turn overlay a more staccato rhythm upon the performance (see analysis in Brøvig-Hanssen & Danielsen, 2016, ch. 5). Of course, hearing sound as being "cut up" presupposes that one has the capacity to imagine (an) "uncut" version(s) "underlying" the fragmented result—even though one knows that this version might never have existed. When the music is heard as fragmented in this way, it challenges people's inclinations toward bonding the different sounds in a musical soundscape to a temporally coherent performance, and the music might thus be perceived as containing a surrealistic dimension to its sound. However, cut-and-paste techniques have today become so common in the fields of popular and electroacoustic music, that they probably no longer generate a "shock effect." As Caleb Kelly points out, stuttering and skipping sounds "are now simply another part of the sound palette of the digital producer" (Kelly, 2009, p. 10). As we become more familiar with this palette, the fragmented musical event becomes naturalized. In fact, any given experience with a musical environment promptly becomes a reference point as people structure and comprehend the next environment (Loui, Wessel, & Kam, 2010). Thanks to this tuning of the ear the elasticity as to what is regarded as "natural" is most likely enormous.

### Conclusion and Future Research

The reason why people might conceptualize musical environments as surreal is because they understand the music as a representation of something else and expect this "something else" to comply with their listening experiences. That is, when people listen to recorded sound, they apply their previous experiences with the acoustical conditions of sounds to the new experience. Divergence from these expectations results in an experience of the music as unnatural, uncanny, hyperreal or surreal—that is, as an expansion of the world as one knows it. However, another force also affects auditory perception: the tuning of people's ears, or the mind's ability to adjust to new sonic environments with dispatch.

On the one hand, then, music that evokes a sense of surreality generally becomes naturalized over the course of time. On the other hand, the human mind persists in meeting music not *only* on its own terms—as a musical environment in which anything goes—but also in the context of the real world in which people live and accumulate experience. As Smalley (2007) points out, "The idea of source-bonded space is never entirely absent" (p. 38). And, we might add, neither is the idea of a spatiotemporally coherent performance. This relationship between the ecological constraints of listening and the liberating processes of naturalization generates a perceptual friction that remains a perceptual conundrum.

Further investigation of this friction is needed in order to understand more of the richness of people's experience with acousmatic music. What are the role(s) of and interaction between these two perceptual forces, which are constantly competing for the listener's attention? Another interesting topic for future research is to study the various significations that music which deconstructs our normal assumptions of sounds and sonic environments have, such as, for example, whether they open up for new representations and understandings of gender, sexuality, ethnicity, human abilities, authenticity, etc. To summarize, deeper insight is needed into the ways in which acousmatic music continues to flout the consequences of evoking people's familiarity with spatiotemporally coherent and source-bonded performances even as it subverts it.

## Notes

1. An index is, according to Peirce, "a sign which refers to the Object that it denotes by virtue of being really affected by that Object" (Peirce, 1960, p. 143).
2. Michel Chion, also a member of GRM, used Schaeffer's concept of acousmatic listening to describe off-screen music in film, introducing the distinction between diegetic and non-diegetic music. The latter term denotes "sound whose supposed source is not only absent from the image but is also external to the story world" (Chion, 1994, p. 73).
3. Although the recording medium once had a documentary function, it has, as Alan Williams emphasizes, never been a neutral tool: "It is never the literal, original 'sound' that is reproduced in recording, but one perspective on it" (Williams, 1980, p. 53). For a similar point, see Sterne, 2003, pp. 219, 235.

## Core Reading

Ashby, A. (2010). *Absolute music, mechanical reproduction*. Berkeley, CA: University of California Press.

Brøvig-Hanssen, R., & Danielsen, A. (2016). *Digital signatures: The impact of digitization on popular music sound*. Cambridge, MA: MIT Press.

Clarke, E. F. (2005). *Ways of listening: An ecological approach to the perception of musical meaning*. New York, NY: Oxford University Press.

Frith, S. (1986). Art versus technology: The strange case of popular music. *Media, Culture and Society, 8*, 263–279.

Gibson, J. J. (1986). *The ecological approach to visual perception*. Hillsdale, NJ: Lawrence Erlbaum Associates. (Original work published in 1979.)

Moore, A. F., Schmidt, P., & Dockwray, R. (2009). A hermeneutics of spatialization for recorded song. *Twentieth-Century Music, 6*(1), 83–114. http://doi.org/10.1017/S1478572210000071

Schaeffer, P. (2004). Acousmatics. In C. Cox, & D. Warner (Eds.), *Audio culture: Readings in modern music* (pp. 76–81). New York, NY: Continuum. (Original work published in 1966.)

Smalley, D. (2007). Space-form and the acousmatic image. *Organised Sound, 2*(2), 107–126.

## Further References

Attali, J. (1985). *Noise: The political economy of music.* Minneapolis, MN: University of Minneapolis Press.

Auslander, P. (2008). *Liveness: Performance in a mediatized culture.* London/New York, NY: Routledge.

Battier, M. (2007). What the GRM brought to music: From musique concrete to acousmatic music. *Organised Sound, 12*(3), 189–202.

Bigand, E., Delbé, C., Gérard, Y., & Tillmann, B. (2011). Categorization of extremely brief auditory stimuli: Domain-specific or domain-general processes?. *PloS ONE, 6*(10), e27024. doi:10.1371/journal.pone.0027024

Bregman, A. S. (2001). *Auditory scene analysis: The perceptual organization of sound.* Cambridge, MA: MIT Press.

Brolinson, P. E., & Larsen, H. (1981). *Rock . . .: Aspekter på industri, elektronik og sound.* Falköping: Gummerssons Tryckeri AB.

Brøvig-Hanssen, R. (2013). The magnetic tape recorder: Recording aesthetics in the new era of schizophonia. In F. Weium & T. Boon (Eds.), *Material culture and electronic sound* (pp. 131–157). Washington, D.C.: Smithsonian Institution Scholarly Press/Rowman and Littlefield Publishers.

Brøvig-Hanssen, R., & Danielsen, A. (2013). The naturalised and the surreal: Changes in the perception of popular music sound. *Organised Sound, 18*(1), 72–81.

Chion, M. (1994). *Audio-vision: Sound on screen.* (C. Gorbman, Trans.) New York, NY: Columbia University Press. (Original work published 1991.)

Danielsen, A. (1998). His name was Prince: A study of "Diamonds and Pearls". *Popular Music, 16*(3), 275–291.

Danielsen, A., & Helseth, I. (2016). Mediated immediacy: The relationship between auditory and visual dimensions of live performance in contemporary technology-based popular music. *Rock Music Studies, 3*(1), 1–17.

Doyle, P. (2005). *Echo and reverb: Fabricating space in popular music recording, 1900–1960.* Middletown, CT: Wesleyan University Press.

Eisenberg, E. (2005). *The recording angel: Music, records and culture from Aristotle to Zappa.* New Haven, CT: Yale University Press.

Gjerdingen, R. O., & Perrott, D. (2008). Scanning the dial: The rapid recognition of music genres. *Journal of New Music Research, 37*(2), 93–100.

Gracyk, T. (1996). *Rhythm and noise: An aesthetics of rock.* Durham, NC: Duke University Press.

Handel, S. (1995). Timbre perception and auditory object identification. In B. Moore (Ed.). *Hearing* (pp. 425–460). Cambridge, MA: Academic Press.

Jensenius, A. R. (2013). An action-sound approach to teaching interactive music. *Organised Sound, 18*(2), 178–189.

Kelly, C. (2009). *Cracked media: The sound of malfunction.* Cambridge, MA: MIT Press.

Lacasse, S. (2000). *"Listen to my voice": The evocative power of vocal staging in recorded rock music and other forms of vocal expression.* Doctoral dissertation, University of Liverpool, Liverpool. Retrieved from http://www.mus.ulaval.ca/lacasse/texts/THESIS.pdf [29.06.16].

Laing, Dave, 1991. A voice without a face: Popular music and the phonograph in the 1890s. *Popular Music, 10*(1), 1–9.

Lalitte, P., & Bigand, E. (2006). Music in the moment? Revisiting the effect of large scale structures. *Perceptual and Motor Skills, 103*(3), 811–828.

Leman, M. (2008). *Embodied music cognition and mediation technology.* Cambridge, MA: MIT Press.

Loui, P., Wessel, D. L., & Kam, C. L. H. (2010). Humans rapidly learn grammatical structure in a new musical scale. *Music Perception 27*, 377–388.

McAdams, S. (1993) Recognition of sound sources and events. In E. Bigand and S. McAdams (Eds.), *Thinking in sound: The cognitive psychology of human audition* (pp. 10–36). Oxford: Clarendon Press/ Oxford University Press.

Moylan, W. (2002). *The art of recording: Understanding and crafting the mix*. Boston, MA: Focal Press.

Peirce, Charles Sanders. (1960) *Collected papers of Charles Sanders Peirce*. Volumes I and II. Cambridge, MA: Harvard University Press.

Rossing, T. D., Moore, F. R., and Wheeler, P. A. (2002). *The science of sound*. San Francisco, CA: Addison Wesley.

Schafer, R. M. (1969). *The new soundscape: A handbook for the modern music teacher*. Toronto: Berandol.

Schellenberg, E. G., Iverson, P., & Mckinnon, M. C. (1999). Name that tune: Identifying popular recordings from brief excerpts. *Psychonomic Bulletin & Review, 6*(4), 641–646.

Smalley, D. (1997). Spectromorphology: Explaining sound-shapes. *Organised Sound 12*(1), 35–58.

Sterne, J. (2003). *The audible past: Cultural origins of sound reproduction*. Durham, NC: Duke University Press.

Tillmann, B., & Bigand, E. (1996). Does formal musical structure affect perception of musical expressiveness? *Psychology of Music, 24*(1), 3–17.

Williams, A. (1980). Is sound recording like a language? *Yale French Studies, 60*, 51–66.

# 17

# MUSICAL CONNECTIONS
## Absolute Pitch

*Elizabeth West Marvin*

Absolute pitch (AP), sometimes called "perfect pitch," is typically defined as the ability to label or produce a pitch (e.g., F♯) without reference to an external standard. Such labeling is typically effortless and rapid. Although AP is rare in the general population—its incidence is often cited as 1 in 10,000 (Deutsch, 2013; Levitin & Rogers, 2005; Takeuchi & Hulse, 1993)—subgroups of musicians trained in Western classical music have a much higher incidence. For example, in a survey of professional music schools in the United States, researchers found that roughly 12% of entering students self-identified as having AP (Gregersen, Kowalsky, Kohn, & Marvin, 2000); among Asian music students in their sample, 47% reported AP. In another specialized population, the early blind, researchers found that 57% of participants with musical training had AP (Hamilton, Pascual-Leone, & Schlaug, 2004). Clearly AP is not so rare among those with musical training. Yet it is unclear whether AP is the result of that training or whether it is an inborn trait in some individuals, who later go on to study music.

The question of how and when AP is acquired interests both cognitive scientists and musicians. For the scientist, AP represents a discrete, testable ability possessed by a small proportion of the population; thus its study can shed light on the influence and interaction of innateness, learning, maturation, and genetics. Comparing pitch processing with other types of auditory processing, such as language, can reveal areas of overlap and the special cognitive properties of each domain. For example, both language and AP are thought to require learning during a critical period in childhood (Deutsch, 2013; Levitin, & Rogers, 2005). Of interest to musicians, on the other hand, are potential practical advantages of AP, such as ease of musical transcription, score reading, memorization, and tuning of voices and instruments. Musicians and nonmusicians alike often associate AP with exceptional talent and with prodigies like Mozart (though a causal relationship between AP and high musical achievement has not been scientifically demonstrated). Some musical pedagogues argue that relative-pitch processing—understanding hierarchical relationships between pitches or chords in a key- or scale-context (like *sol* to *do,* or scale-degrees 5 to 1)—rather than their absolute identity in frequency, is as important as AP for strong musicianship (Marvin, 2007; Miyazaki, 1993). Nevertheless, the perception that absolute pitch connotes strong musical ability persists. Because AP possessors typically began musical training at a younger age, their perceived virtuosity may be due instead to more years of practice and performance.

## Absolute Pitch Acquisition

The question of why some individuals can identify pitches absolutely and others cannot is an active area of research with multiple, sometimes conflicting, hypotheses (for other surveys of acquisition theories, see Deutsch, 2013; Levitin & Rogers, 2005; Parncutt & Levitin, 2001; and Ross, Gore, & Marks, 2005). These hypotheses may be divided into two broad categories, roughly corresponding to a nature vs. nurture dichotomy. The nature hypothesis holds either that AP is an innate processing strategy that is usually replaced with relational processing as children mature, or alternatively that AP is innate only in those few who possess specific genetic markers. The nurture hypothesis holds that AP is a learned phenomenon.

### *Innate Hypotheses*

Saffran and Griepentrog (2001) demonstrated absolute processing of pitches by infants, based on an auditory learning task given to eight-month-old children. In a design analogous to artificial language-learning studies, the authors familiarized infants with a three-minute melody of isochronous tones, constructed of randomly ordered repetitions of four unvarying three-note patterns; these patterns, when combined, contained one each of the 12 possible notes in an octave (C, C♯, D, etc.). The resulting melody had predictable transitional probabilities from note to note that infants learned through exposure: the transitional probability within the unvarying three-note patterns was high (1.0), but between three-note patterns was low (.33). At test, infants successfully discriminated between three-note patterns that occurred with high probability in familiarization versus those that occurred with low probability. Discrimination was measured by the amount of looking time spent gazing toward the loudspeaker where the sound originated (each three-tone pattern was repeated as long as the infant looked).

Crucial to this design was the fact that the low-probability patterns at test contained the same intervals (the relative distances between pitches) as the high-probability ones—that is, they were transpositions of the familiarized patterns. In order to discriminate between the high- and low-probability patterns, infants had to remember the pitches absolutely. A relative-pitch processing strategy would likely confuse the two types of pitch patterns, based on their identical intervals. However, infants showed differential looking times, suggesting discrimination by an absolute-pitch strategy. Comparison of results with adult listeners led the authors to hypothesize that infants begin life with an absolute-pitch processing strategy, which is gradually replaced through maturation and learning by a relative-pitch strategy. Relative pitch is understood here as computationally more complex, since listeners must hold two pitches in memory and calculate the intervallic distance between them.

Saffran and Griepentrog's result contrasts with other studies showing strong evidence of relative-pitch strategies in infants, especially when the experimenters use more music-like stimuli, such as folk songs, that encourage relative-pitch processing (Trehub, 2001). It may be, as Saffran noted in a subsequent article, that infants have both strategies available to them, and that the nature of the stimulus and task determines the processing strategy used. The two-strategy explanation has been found in animal cognition as well (MacDougall-Shackleton & Hulse, 1996). European starlings were trained to discriminate between pitch sequences that began low and ascended vs. those that began high and descended, with all sequences spanning the same frequency range. The starlings were then tested for generalization outside of the training range, with test items beginning at the same frequency as the trained stimuli, but reversed in contour (e.g., they began low and descended, or began high and ascended). Birds initially responded based on the frequency of the first pitch, an absolute-pitch strategy, but with reinforcement they learned to use relative pitch—that is, to treat the ascending sequences at test like the ascending sequences during training, regardless of the starting pitch and range. This and other research suggests that starlings are biased toward absolute-pitch perception. Recent work by Bregman, Patel, and Gentner (2016) challenges this finding, however, by testing starlings with acoustically more complex tones and varying either pitch or timbre independently. They find that starlings can generalize based on acoustic and timbral cues, even in sequences where the pitch does not vary.

An alternative hypothesis on the "innate" side of the AP acquisition question is that this trait is inherited in some, but not all, people. Evidence for this hypothesis is found both by tracking the incidence of AP running in families and by genetic testing. Zatorre (2003) and Gingras, Honing, Peretz, Trainor, and Fisher (2015) provide thorough overviews of this research in the context of discussing possible biological bases for various individual differences in musical abilities, including AP. Gingras et al. summarized these results in tabular form; a study of twins, identical and non-identical, cited there showed the concordance of AP between pairs of identical twins at 78.6%, but only 45.2% in non-identical twins (Theusch & Gitschier, 2011). Gingras et al. identify several research groups who demonstrate familial aggregation of AP and linkage to particular chromosomal regions for AP. Gregersen, et al. (2013) found a co-occurrence of AP and synesthesia (typically color-pitch association) in 20% of their AP possessors and identified joint linkage of these traits on particular chromosomes. Other data supporting a genetic explanation for AP come from neuroimaging studies, which find differences in the brains of AP musicians, such as a leftward asymmetry in the planum temporale and differences in cortical thickness in particular areas of the brain (Dohn et al., 2013; Schlaug, 2001; Zatorre, 2003). It is not easy to untangle whether these differences are the cause or the result of AP, but genetics may be a factor.

### Learning Hypotheses

The nurture side of the nature–nurture divide holds that AP is learned, possibly during a critical period in childhood. Numerous studies have reported significant differences in the age at which AP possessors and non-possessors began instrumental music study, with AP musicians typically beginning at age 6 or younger (for summaries and citations, see Deutsch, 2013; Takeuchi & Hulse, 1993; and Sakakibara, 2014). It may be that the association of a verbal label with a particular pitch is only retained when introduced early in childhood, before a general processing shift from retaining absolute features to relational ones occurs. Support for this hypothesis comes from musicians' direct reporting of their age of onset for musical training, and also from indirect evidence. For example, AP possessors are both faster and more accurate at identifying pitches that correspond with the white notes of the piano than black notes (Bermudez & Zatorre, 2009; Takeuchi & Hulse, 1993). Deutsch (2013) discusses a number of possible explanations reported in the literature for this finding. Among them is the possibility that children acquire the names for only the white-key pitches in early childhood—before the critical period's window of opportunity has closed—because the repertoire for beginning piano students typically consists of simple "five-finger" pieces played on the white keys. According to this argument, identification of black-key pitches would be judged as displacements from the more familiar white-key notes, resulting in slower labeling that is more prone to error. However, this pattern of differential white- and black-key identification is found in AP musicians who are not pianists and also in non-AP musicians (when naming pitches from a given reference tone). A likely explanation is that the speed of AP identification is correlated with frequency of occurrence in the corpus of Western tonal music to which listeners are exposed: because white-key pitches are more common in the corpus, they are identified more quickly. Another possible factor is a cognitive bias toward a simpler label that has one element rather than two (C rather than C♯, for example).

It would seem that the early-learning hypothesis might be tested directly by taking a group of young children, unselected for musical ability, and training them explicitly in pitch identification. Several researchers have engaged in longitudinal studies of this type. Sakakibara (2014) begins by surveying previous literature in support of the early-learning hypothesis, beginning with two points already discussed: the hypothesized critical period before age 6 for learning AP, and the developmental shift from absolute to relational processing in domains other than music. Her third point follows from Gregersen, et al. (2000), regarding the higher incidence of AP in Asian music students. She discusses two early-learning explanations. The first, originating with Diana Deutsch's research (see Deutsch, 2013), is that infants whose first language is a tone language are sensitized to pitch in a way that facilitates the learning of pitch labels when the child studies an instrument. The second explanation has to do with music pedagogy in Asian cultures, which is more likely to employ fixed-do labels for each pitch (*do* = C, *re* = D, *mi* = E, etc. always, no matter the musical key) rather than moveable-do labels (a relative-pitch system that labels pitches in relation to their function in a key). Finally, she reviews several studies that attempted to train adults in AP, which yielded some improvement but no true AP acquisition.

Sakakibara (2014) trained her participants—24 children, ages 2 to 6, with 0 to 9 months of prior music study—with the Eguchi Chord Identification Method. This method requires at least two years of training, with 4–5 daily sessions of 2–5 minutes each. Children continue training until they attain 100% accuracy on an AP test of 30 isolated piano tones. Training begins by teaching children to associate individual white-key chords, played on a piano, with colored flags. The trainer (usually a parent) plays the set of learned chords repeatedly until the child raises the appropriate flags with 100% accuracy. One new chord is added to the training set no sooner than two weeks later, depending upon the child's success to that point. Once the white-key chords are mastered (typically after one year), children begin black-key chords and learn the pitch names in each chord. Of the 24 children enrolled in Sakakibara's study, 22 completed the training with 100% accuracy on the AP post-test, but the length of training varied widely to reach this goal (for white-key chords, 22 to 76 weeks; for black-key chords, 34 to 94 weeks). This study provides strong evidence for the early-learning hypothesis.

## "Perfect" Pitch and Quasi-AP

Musicians tend to think that AP is a dichotomous trait—either you have it, or you don't—but numerous studies have shown that this is not the case. For some AP listeners, identification accuracy may vary when pitches differ in timbre, tuning standard, or octave. Some make octave-identification errors, even when they correctly identify the letter name of pitches. Others have accurate long-term memory for some pitches and not others, and quickly calculate the remaining pitches from these standards; this ability is sometimes known as "quasi-AP." Those with any such limitation tend to be uncomfortable with the label "perfect" pitch, since their pitch identification is not always perfect.

Bermudez and Zatorre (2009) provided a robust demonstration that AP in musicians is not a dichotomous trait. They tested 51 university music students, roughly half self-identified as AP and half as non-AP, in a computerized note-naming task. Participants identified over 100 synthesized complex tones (a timbre chosen because it would be unfamiliar to all participants), in three different intensities. The tones spanned three octaves and were tuned in an equal-tempered tuning with A = 440 Hz as the standard. The researchers reported identification accuracy, as well as mean deviation from accuracy measured in semitones (a deviation of 0 was a correct response, +1 was a response one semitone above and −1 was one semitone below, etc.). When overall accuracy was plotted against mean deviation, the plot revealed a high-accuracy AP group with mean deviation close to 0, and a low-accuracy non-AP group with deviations that varied widely; however, a large number of participants scored somewhere between these two extremes, showing a continuum of note-naming ability. Bermudez and Zatorre's results also replicated previously discussed white- and black-key differences for AP listeners, with higher accuracy and quicker reaction times for white-key pitches.

Ross, Gore, and Marks (2005) suggest that the term "absolute pitch" is also an imperfect one, because it lumps together what they suggest are two distinct types of AP: HTM ("heightened tonal memory") and APE ("ability to perceptually encode"). According to this theory, those with HTM have stored a template for pitches in long-term memory, learned through exposure to particular instruments and tuning. An HTM possessor will (unconsciously) compare each test tone with this memorized template in order to name it. Labeling accuracy for these listeners may be impaired when the tuning or timbre of test tones differ from the learned template. (HTM also accounts for anecdotal stories of AP possessors who initially studied music on an out-of-tune piano or B♭ instrument, and thus learned every note offset from the Western A440 standard.) Ross et al. hypothesize that APE possessors encode frequencies in a physiologically different way from other people. This ability is not learned; it is innate and automatic. APE encoding occurs at a precategorical stage of processing—that is, it takes place before labeling—and it encodes all frequencies, not just those within a particular tuning norm. For this reason, APE listeners are equally able to identify both equally-tempered pitches with an A440 standard and pitches mistuned from this standard. Likewise, because they are not comparing to a memorized template with familiar timbre, APE listeners are equally able to identify pitches heard in different timbres and ranges. This distinction would explain why some AP musicians are distinctly bothered when singing in a choir that goes flat or when playing in a Baroque ensemble (where the pitch standard is lower, ca. A = 415Hz), but others quickly adjust.

## Implicit Learning of AP

Our auditory environment contains rich information from which to learn. Even without conscious effort, listeners' brains track the statistical probabilities that one syllable will follow another in language, or that one pitch will follow another in music (Creel, Newport, & Aslin, 2004). These probabilities shape our expectations of what will come next; they help us to segment words and parse grammars, and to understand pitch hierarchies within a tonal system. This type of learning, which takes place without conscious effort, is implicit learning.

Hedger, Heald, and Nusbaum (2013) provide evidence that AP listeners continuously update their pitch label categories through implicit learning from music around them. The prevalence of an A440 tuning norm in Western classical music means that each day as musicians engage in music performance and listening, they reinforce these culturally assigned pitch labels through implicit learning. Hedger et al. asked whether AP listeners who were exposed to music that was gradually shifted lower than this cultural norm would adjust their pitch labels to a new standard. They began by asking participants to name and rate the tuning accuracy of a series of tones; some of these were in tune, some were 33 cents flat, and others 33 cents sharp. Next, participants heard a Brahms symphony in which the first movement was gradually lowered in pitch by just 2 cents per minute (a pitch difference that is too small to be detected), until it reached a level that was 33 cents flat. The rest of the movement and the remaining three movements, about 15 minutes of music, were heard in the new detuned key. Afterwards, listeners repeated the first pitch identification and tuning task. This time, however, participants rated the flat notes (by an A440 standard) as more in tune than they had rated them in the pre-Brahms test. The in-tune notes were now judged as out of tune, suggesting that listeners had shifted their pitch categories by listening to the detuned Brahms symphony. The authors conclude that AP listeners may learn to label pitches through early experience with music; however, these pitch levels are not linked absolutely to particular frequencies, but are malleable depending on the music and tuning systems listeners are exposed to. Hedger et al. suggest that AP abilities may require constant updating through implicit learning from music exposure to keep these pitch categories in place. This finding may help explain why AP is well documented in Western musical cultures, but is less so in non-Western cultures, where tunings may be less rigidly fixed and may vary from instrument to instrument, or from village to village; see, for example, the descriptions of tunings for the Zimbabwean mbira in Berliner (1993), or for the Balinese gamelan in Tenzer (1998). Variable tuning discourages implicit learning of a fixed pitch with a pitch label.

If implicit learning informs and reinforces the pitch memory of AP possessors, we might ask whether it has any effect on people without AP. Does repeated exposure to music in a canonical key—such as recorded popular music, or TV and film music—result in absolute representation of those keys in long-term memory, or is encoding in memory effected solely by relative-pitch means? To investigate this question, Levitin (1994) instructed college students, not selected for musical background, to choose their two favorite pop songs from a shelf of CDs, imagine the songs, and sing them (see also Frieler, et al., 2013 for a replication study). Levitin then compared the sung responses to the key of the recordings and discovered that 40% of participants sang the correct pitches on at least one of the two songs. This result led him to posit a "two-component" theory of absolute pitch, consisting of pitch memory (which many listeners have) and pitch labeling (which is rare).

In a subsequent study that removed the production aspect of Levitin's experiment, Schellenberg and Trehub (2003) played participants two versions of theme songs from popular TV shows, and asked them to choose the one they believed was in the correct key. In this two-alternative forced-choice design, one alternative was played in the correct key and the other was digitally shifted up or down by 1 or 2 semitones. Participants were 58% correct on the 1-semitone transpositions and 70% correct on 2-semitone transpositions (where 50% is chance). The researchers concluded that the ability to remember the absolute pitches of familiar music is widespread and normally distributed, as long as the requirements for production and labeling are not required. Deutsch (2013) calls this type of pitch memory without labeling "implicit AP."

If implicit AP is a component of musical memory in many listeners, then we should see a processing advantage for pitches and keys that occur more frequently in our musical environment, when compared with those that are more rare. This is the premise that underlies an experiment by Ben-Haim, Eitan, and Chajut (2014). The researchers first determined the distribution of keys in top international popular music hits on a local radio station (D, G, and C are the most frequent major keys; Am and Em are the most frequent minor keys). Each participant in the experiment was assigned four pitches in a single key, and trained to depress number keys 1–4 on a computer keyboard to four corresponding pitches. At test, participants heard the four tones in random order, and were asked to press the appropriate number when they heard the piano tone that corresponded with that number. Results showed quicker reaction times for stimuli heard in frequent keys vs. infrequent keys; further, over the course of the trials, the rate of improvement was superior for responses to frequent vs. infrequent keys. If we assume that most listeners use a relative-pitch processing strategy, then the key of the stimulus should not matter at all: listeners would respond based on the relationships among the tones, no matter what the key. The fact that participants responded differently to frequent keys suggests a long-term representation for key in memory, acquired presumably through implicit learning.

Other tests of AP without labeling have shown that some listeners—even without musical training—can demonstrate accuracy comparable to AP musicians in some pitch memory tasks. For example, Ross, Olsen, and Gore (2003) asked participants to remember sine tones through varying periods of silence or interference tones, and then to tune a sine wave generator to the remember pitch. Crucial to this design is the fact that listeners were not required to label pitches with letter names. Participant responses were graphed in terms of semitone deviations from the correct response; highly accurate responses yielded a normal distribution that peaks at 0, and low accuracy yielded a flat distribution with no peak. This testing method discriminated well between AP and non-AP groups: in the silence conditions, histograms of AP listeners peaked at 0 with a narrow distribution of a few semitone errors on either side, while non-AP responses showed the same peak, but a wider distribution of errors (up to 6 semitones above or below the correct response). In the longer interference-tone conditions, AP responses still peaked at 0, but non-AP responses yielded no peak and a flat distribution, showing low accuracy and high variability. Interestingly, Ross et al. identified one participant without musical training who was unable to name pitches, but whose histogram in the interference-tone condition did not differ significantly from participants with AP.

Marvin and Newport (2011) likewise identified a small group of high-performing adults with implicit AP, using an implicit-learning paradigm similar to Saffran and Griepentrog (2001), discussed previously. Like the earlier study, Marvin and Newport designed a melody with predictable transitional probabilities between adjacent notes that the adults learned implicitly during a familiarization phase. After familiarization, they were asked to discriminate between pairs of three-note patterns based on their memory of the familiarization melody. The discrimination pairs were of two types: (1) a three-note pattern that had occurred in the familiarization melody with high probability vs. one that occurred with low probability; or (2) a high-probability pattern from the familiarization melody vs. a high-probability pattern transposed up or down three semitones. The transposition condition was the discrimination of interest: here, the absolute pitches of the transposed patterns had never been heard together during familiarization, but the interval succession of these patterns (a relative-pitch processing strategy) had been. Participants were classified as AP or non-AP by a traditional note-labeling task, and their results compared. For the transposition trials, AP musicians' scores differed significantly from non-AP musicians; the former were normally distributed around .82 and the latter around .67 (where .50 is chance). Thus even those without AP showed some degree of implicit AP. The experiment was repeated on 24 college students with little or no music training and yielded similar results to those for non-AP musicians; however three nonmusicians were identified in this group who scored above 80% in the transposition discrimination task, in the same range as the AP musicians.

These studies and others demonstrate a possible role for implicit learning both in AP acquisition and retention, as well as in pitch memory for those without AP (as traditionally defined). Although research has "demystified" a number of aspects of AP, many avenues for exploration remain. In particular, the biological and physiological results reported here raise intriguing chicken-and-egg questions about genetic markers for AP and differences in the brains of AP musicians. Genetics might also explain the hypothesized distinction between HTM and APE listeners (Ross, Gore, & Marks, 2005). How exactly APE possessors differ from HTM in how the auditory system transmits frequency information to the brain remains to be explored. The longitudinal studies of children undergoing intensive AP training need to be replicated in different populations. Researchers might explore whether such training methods are successful in most children, or only in those with a genetic predisposition for AP. Longitudinal studies of AP possessors as they age could be conducted to provide hypotheses that explain why AP often becomes less reliable in middle and old age. The higher incidence of AP among Asian musicians deserves further study—is it culture and pedagogy, language differences, genetic factors? Researchers have left relatively unexplored the question of AP possession in non-Western musical cultures. Ethnographic studies of exposure to music and tuning systems in early childhood and of transmission of musical knowledge could be conducted, as could corpus analyses of music with behavioral tests of implicit learning; finally, direct testing of pitch memory could be employed using methods described above that do not require labeling.

Research on absolute pitch provides a focal point for the interaction of those who study the auditory system and brain, cognition and memory, auditory learning, corpus analysis, and music pedagogy. It invites a collaborative space for musicians and scientists to work together to seek answers to important questions about human cognition.

## Core Reading

Deutsch, D. (2013). Absolute pitch. In D. Deutsch (Ed.), *Psychology of music* (3rd ed) (pp. 141–182). London: Academic Press.

Levitin, D. J., & Rogers, S. E. (2005). Absolute pitch: Perception, coding, and controversies. *Trends in Cognitive Sciences, 9*(1), 26–33.

Parncutt, R., & Levitin, D. J. (n.d). Absolute pitch. In *Grove music online*. Retrieved from www.oxford musiconline.com/subscriber/article/grove/music/00070

Ross, D. A., Gore, J. C., & Marks, L. E. (2005). Absolute pitch: Music and beyond. *Epilepsy & Behavior, 7*, 578–601.

Takeuchi, A. H., & Hulse, S. H. (1993). Absolute pitch. *Psychological Bulletin, 113*(2), 345–361.

## Further References

Ben-Haim, M. S., Eitan, Z., & Chajut, E. (2014). Pitch memory and exposure effects. *Journal of Experimental Psychology: Human Perception and Performance, 40*(1), 24.

Berliner, P. F. (1993). *The soul of mbira: Music and traditions of the Shona people of Zimbabwe*. Chicago, IL: University of Chicago Press.

Bermudez, P., & Zatorre, R. J. (2009). A distribution of absolute pitch ability as revealed by computerized testing. *Music Perception, 27*, 89–101.

Bregman, M. R., Patel, A.D., & Gentner, T. Q. (2016). Songbirds use spectral shape, not pitch, for sound pattern recognition. *Proceedings of the National Academy of Sciences, 113*(6), 1666–1671.

Creel, S. C., Newport, E. L, & Aslin, R. N. (2004). Distant melodies: Statistical learning of nonadjacent dependencies in tone sequences. *Journal of Experimental Psychology: Learning, Memory, and Cognition, 30*(5), 1119–1130.

Dohn, A., Garza-Villarreal, E. A., Chakravarty, M. M., Hansen, M., Lerch, J. P., & Vuust, P. (2013). Gray-and white-matter anatomy of absolute pitch possessors. *Cerebral cortex, 25*(5), 1379–1388.

Frieler, K., Fischinger, T., Schlemmer, K., Lothwesen, K., Jakubowski, K., & Müllensiefen, D. (2013). Absolute memory for pitch: A comparative replication of Levitin's 1994 study in six European labs. *Musicae Scientiae, 17*(3), 334–349.

Gingras, B., Honing, H., Peretz, I., Trainor, L. J., & Fisher, S. E. (2015). Defining the biological bases of individual differences in musicality. *Philosophical Transactions of the Royal Society of London B: Biological Sciences, 370*(1664), 20140092. Retrieved from http://dx.doi.org/10.1098/rstb.2014.0092

Gregersen, P. K., Kowalsky, E., Kohn, N., & Marvin, E. W. (2000). Early childhood music education and predisposition to absolute pitch: Teasing apart genes and environment. *American Journal of Medical Genetics, 98*, 280–282.

Gregersen, P. K., Kowalsky, E., Lee, A., Baron-Cohen, S., Fisher, S. E., Asher, J. E., Ballard, D., Freudenberg, J. & Li, W. (2013). Absolute pitch exhibits phenotypic and genetic overlap with synesthesia. *Human Molecular Genetics, 22*(10), 2097–2104.

Hamilton, R. H., Pascual-Leone, A., & Schlaug, G. (2004). Absolute pitch in blind musicians. *NeuroReport, 15*(5), 803–806.

Hedger, S. C., Heald, S. L. M., and Nusbaum, H. C. (2013). Absolute pitch may not be so absolute. *Psychological Science, 24*(8), 1496–1502.

Levitin, D. J. (1994). Absolute memory for musical pitch: Evidence from the production of learned melodies. *Perception & Psychophysics, 56*(4), 414–423.

MacDougall-Shackleton, S. A., & Hulse, S. H. (1996). Concurrent absolute and relative pitch processing by European starlings (*Sturnus vularis*). *Journal of Comparative Psychology, 110*(2), 139–146.

Marvin, E. W. (2007). Absolute-pitch perception and the pedagogy of relative pitch. *Journal of Music Theory Pedagogy, 21*, 1–34.

Marvin, E. W., & Newport, E. L. (2011). The absolute pitch continuum: Evidence of incipient AP in musical amateurs. Paper presented at the *Conference of the Society for Music Perception and Cognition*, Rochester, NY.

Miyazaki, K. (1993). Absolute pitch as an inability: Identification of musical intervals in a tonal context. *Music Perception, 11*, 55–71.

Parncutt, R., & Levitin, D. J. (2001). Absolute pitch. In Sadie, S. & Tyrrell, J. (Eds.), *New Grove dictionary of music and musicians* (pp. 37–38). New York, NY: St Martin's Press.

Ross, D. A., Olson, I. R., & Gore, J. C. (2003). Absolute pitch does not depend on early musical training. *Annals of the New York Academy of Sciences, 999*(1), 522–526.

Saffran, J. R., & Griepentrog, G. J. (2001). Absolute pitch in infant auditory learning: Evidence for developmental reorganization. *Developmental Psychology, 37*(1), 74–85.

Sakakibara, A. (2014). A longitudinal study of the process of acquiring absolute pitch: A practical report of training with the "chord identification method." *Psychology of Music, 42*(1), 86–111.

Schellenberg, E. G., & Trehub, S. E. (2003). Good pitch memory is widespread. *Psychological Science, 14*(3), 262–266.

Schlaug, G. (2001). The brain of musicians. *Annals of the New York Academy of Sciences, 930*(1), 281–299.

Tenzer, M. (1998). *Balinese music*. Hong Kong: Periplus Editions.

Theusch, E., & Gitschier, J. (2011). Absolute pitch twin study and segregation analysis. *Twin research and human genetics, 14*(2), 173–178.

Trehub, S. E. (2001). Musical predispositions in infancy. *Annals of the New York Academy of Sciences, 930*(1), 1–16.

Zatorre, R. J. (2003). Absolute pitch: A model for understanding the influence of genes and development on neural and cognitive function. *Nature Neuroscience, 6*(7), 692–695.

# 18

# MUSICAL CONNECTIONS
## Cross-modal Correspondences

*Zohar Eitan*

Like the mercilessly overcited Monsieur Jourdain, music practitioners and scholars have been engaged with *cross-modal correspondences* for centuries without knowing it.[1] Musicians use cross-modal correspondences (CMC)—"systematic associations found across seemingly unrelated features from different sensory modalities" (Parise, 2016)—when employing Western music notation, where "higher" pitch is located higher on the page, and changes in loudness are depicted by changes in spatial width (i.e., *crescendo* and *diminuendo* wedges); when, as composers or improvisers, they apply slow, *pianissimo*, muted or low-register sound to depict a dark night; or when (as conductors) they use rising or expanding hand gestures to enhance an orchestral or choral *crescendo*. Such commonplace musical activities—as well as the most basic terms of music-related vocabulary, like "high" or "low" tones (associating musical pitch and spatial location), "bright" sound (associating musical timbre with visual luminosity), or "soft" sound "volume" (associating loudness with both touch and size)—all indeed employ systematic associations between musical features and "seemingly unrelated" features of non-auditory modalities.

Numerous empirical studies in human perception and cognition, using converging experimental methodologies, have investigated CMC. Several excellent surveys of that research have been published (Marks, 2004, 2014; Parise & Spence, 2013; Spence, 2011; Walker, 2016), and this chapter will not attempt to replicate them. Rather, the chapter primarily aims to suggest how current CMC research—though performed mainly in non-musical contexts, using simple auditory stimuli—may inform musical thought and practice, and how studies of CMC utilizing music-specific features and contexts may in turn enhance CMC research, associating it with complex, culturally significant contexts.

CMC do not seem to present a single, unified phenomenon. Rather, the term has been applied to diverse mappings, which utilize a variety of psychological mechanisms, have different origins, and accomplish a gamut of psychological roles, ranging from basic perceptual and motor functions to the shaping of language metaphors and cultural practices. Below, I briefly survey some of the mappings, psychological functions and sources constituting CMC. Discussing the ramifications of that diversity for music, I highlight gaps remaining to be filled in music-related CMC research.

## Mappings

What musical features partake in CMC, and with what features of non-auditory modalities are they associated? CMC Research involving auditory dimensions has mainly focused on pitch height and loudness, possibly since both are bipolar dimensions, structured along a more-or-less axis (higher/lower, louder/softer), and are thus readily comparable with bipolar dimensions such as visual brightness (bright/dark), physical size (large/small; e.g., Gallace & Spence, 2006), or spatial elevation (high/low). Fewer studies have examined CMC involving other auditory domains, such as tempo (Küssner, Tidhar, Prior, & Leech-Wilkinson, 2014) or dimensions of acoustic timbre (e.g., Pitteri, Marchetti, Priftis, & Grassi, 2015). Importantly, hardly any empirical CMC research has examined whether and how musically specific features and structures (e.g., tonal stability or metric hierarchy) systematically associate with non-auditory features. Rather, even when applying musical stimuli, CMC research typically focuses on their basic auditory features, ignoring possible cross-modal associations of music-specific, higher-level configurations.

For basic auditory dimensions, however (particularly pitch and loudness), research has established a variety of CMC, involving multiple visual, kinesthetic, tactile, and even gustatory and olfactory features. For instance, high-pitched sounds, in addition to their established association with higher spatial position, are (compared to lower pitch) bright, visually light, fast, small, thin, lightweight, sharp, hard, dry, and cold. They also associate perceptually with faster vibrotactile frequencies, are either sweet or sour (while low pitches are bitter or salty), and consistently match specific odors (for research surveys, see Marks, 2004; Spence, 2011; Walker, 2016).

Similarities and differences between cross-modal mappings of auditory dimensions may elucidate their connotative relationships in surprising ways. Consider, for instance, the CMC of pitch and loudness. Loud sound and high pitch match in many of their mappings: both are associated with spatially higher position (Evans & Treisman, 2010; Eitan, Schupak, & Marks, 2008), brighter light (e.g., Marks, 1987), and also sharper shapes and harder surfaces (Eitan & Rothschild, 2010). Furthermore, loudness and pitch were themselves shown to be congruent dimensions, such that higher pitch is perceptually associated with louder sound (Melara & Marks, 1990), and rising pitch with crescendi (Neuhoff & McBeath, 1996). Yet, despite their congruence, loudness and pitch *contrast* with regard to mappings related to size and mass: high pitch is small, thin, and lightweight, while loud sound "volume" is associated with large (voluminous), thick, and heavy physical objects.

The proliferation of CMC research of basic auditory dimensions notwithstanding, substantial lacunas concerning music-specific cross-modal correspondences are awaiting investigation. As noted above, even when actual musical stimuli are used (rather than rarified stimuli like single sine tones), CMC research mainly examines music as sound, focusing on basic features shared by most auditory domains, like pitch and loudness. Little CMC research examines intrinsically musical features, such as harmonic and melodic intervals, chord structure, or modality, and CMC involving higher-level musical structures, such as tonality, metric hierarchy, or rhythmic and melodic configuration, are almost completely ignored.

One reason such investigation may be worthwhile is the abundance and importance of cross-modal metaphor in historical and contemporary discourse involving musical structures such as Western tonality (Rothfarb, 2001). Lakoff and Johnson (1980) showed how abstract concepts are constructed in terms of physical metaphors, a perspective adapted to investigate metaphors for musical structure (Zbikowski, 2008, this volume). Tonal relationships were mapped, for instance, onto motion and its underlying forces, (e.g., gravity; Rameau, 1722), spatial image schemas like center/periphery, top/bottom, or front/back (see Spitzer, 2004), or visual brightness ("dark" chromaticism vs. "bright" diatonicism; e.g., Boulez, 1986).

Studying musically-specific CMC may be particularly intriguing since CMC may implicitly and subconsciously affect perception and behaviour. Are musically-specific CMC also associated implicitly with musical meanings and behaviours? Do non-musicians, for instance, perceive chromatic tones as "darker" than stable diatonic tones (See Maimon, 2016, for an exploratory study)? For a fuller understanding of CMC in musical contexts, one would need to elucidate such issues empirically.

A second musically-relevant lacuna in CMC research concerns the interaction of dynamic (time-varying) auditory parameters. Music usually involves simultaneous changes in multiple parameters. Few studies, however, have systematically examined how such interactions affect the listener's cross-modal mappings, and these studies (Eitan & Granot, 2011; Küssner et al., 2014) present surprising interactions. For instance, when combined with a diminuendo, an accelerando may lose its association with accelerated physical motion, and pitch direction disassociated from vertical spatial motion (e.g., a rising pitch in diminuendo would no longer be associated with spatial rise). Such findings indicate that CMC derived from experiments involving a single pair of dimensions (e.g., pitch direction and vertical motion) do not necessarily predict mappings resulting from the complex interaction of multiple dimensions, characteristic of musical contexts. Further examination of multi-parametric interactions in musical contexts is thus called for.

## Functions

One reason CMC may be particularly intriguing to music research is their role in both high-level and low-level mental processes. While often involved with activities and cultural products requiring conscious awareness, contemplation, and conceptualization (such as the application of synesthetic metaphors to music, or the use of "tone painting"; Zbikowski, 2008, this volume), CMC have also been shown to affect basic perceptual and cognitive domains automatically and subconsciously.

CMC effects cover a range of basic perceptual and information-processing domains. CMC may affect the perception of elementary *perceptual attributes*, such as spatial location or movement direction: we actually perceive "higher" pitches as stemming from spatially higher locations (Pratt, 1930), and pitch direction may affect the perceived spatial direction of concurrent visual motion (Maeda, Kanai, & Shimojo, 2004). CMC also enhance *cross-modal binding*—the vital capacity to associate stimuli from different sensory modalities with the same source object—affecting our ability to associate visual and auditory stimuli to each other in time and space (Parise & Spence, 2009). Likewise, CMC affect *perceptual learning* of cross-modal pairings, facilitating implicit learning of congruent cross-modal pairings such as low pitch and dark visual stimuli, as compared to incongruent pairings (Brunel, Carvalho, & Goldstone, 2015). CMC also affect *selective attention*—the ability to focus on a specific stimulus or feature in our environment, while ignoring others – as demonstrated in numerous speeded classification and speeded detection tasks (Marks, 2004); and CMC may influence *motor responses* as well: for instance, responses to a high pitch via a spatially high key are faster and more accurate than responses via a low key (Rusconi et al., 2006).

Importantly, such CMC effects do not require conscious awareness or conceptualization. Rather, they mostly influence mental processes and their outcomes implicitly, automatically, and subconsciously. This suggests that CMC may also operate under the surface of music processing, implicitly shaping musical structures, emotions, and meanings.

However, the implicit and automatic qualities of CMC highlight a lacuna in our understanding of their musical roles. Cross-modal mappings and metaphors significantly partake in the conceptual processing of music, from its basic vocabulary to seemingly abstract systems of music theory and analysis (Zbikowski, 2008, this volume). The gap between such rarified cultural products and the elementary perceptual functions of CMC, as studied by experimental psychologists, may seem insurmountable. Bridging that challenging gap, however, may be highly rewarding for music researchers of diverse orientations – cognitive, historical, and theoretical.

## Origins

As their involvement in basic perceptual functions may suggest, some CMC featured prominently in musical contexts—for instance, the associations of higher pitch with higher elevation or small physical size, or of increased loudness with increased visual brightness—apply cross-culturally and pre-linguistically. Indeed, increasing evidence suggests that these cross-modal mappings are not solely based on culture-specific conventions or on language idioms, though both sources may partake in shaping their applications in specific cultural contexts. Rather, they reflect cross-cultural, possibly universal dispositions to associate dimensions in different sense modalities.

Spence (2011) proposes two possible sources for such cross-cultural dispositions. "Statistical" CMC stem from natural correlations of stimulus dimensions, experienced since infancy and internalized through processes of statistical learning. Such, for instance, are the associations of pitch and physical size, loudness and distance, and even pitch and elevation (Parise, Knorre, & Ernst, 2014). "Structural" CMC stem from inborn neural connections, or analogies in neural processing. For instance, increases in stimulus intensity (e.g., louder sound, brighter light) are often associated with increased neural firing rate (Stevens, 1957).

Several lines of research suggest that some CMC may indeed be based on such universal (though not necessarily innate) origins: studies of pre-linguistic infants; comparative cross-cultural and cross-linguistic research; and ethological studies, examining CMC as reflected in the behavior of non-human species (e.g., Morton, 1994; Ludwig, Adachi, & Matsuzawa, 2011). Yet, CMC may also stem from culture- or language-specific origins; for instance, they may occur when identical or similar terms are used to describe dimensions in different modalities—for instance, when "high" and "low" are used to denote both pitch and spatial elevation ("semantically" mediated CMC; Spence, 2011). To illustrate the interactions between apparent universal tendencies and the effects of specific language and culture, I briefly describe findings of infant and cross-cultural studies, and then survey recent research demonstrating the complexity of such interactions.

### *Infant Studies*

As repeatedly demonstrated by studies utilizing the preferential looking paradigm, infants (<6 months old) associate rising and falling pitch, respectively, with rising and falling visual stimuli (Dolscheid, Hunnius, Casasanto, & Majid, 2014; Wagner, Winner, Cicchetti, &

Gardner, 1981; Walker et al., 2010), as well as higher pitch with sharper (Walker et al., 2010), thinner (Dolscheid et al., 2014), and smaller (Fernández-Prieto, Navarra, & Pons, 2015) visual stimuli. Infants as young as 10 months associate higher pitch with brighter colour (Haryu & Kajikawa, 2012). A physiologically-based CMC involving loudness and visual brightness was found for 3-weeks olds, who transferred a cardiac attenuation response generated by exposure to light onto sound of comparable intensity (Lewkowicz & Turkewitz, 1980). These studies suggest that several types of CMC, all commonly used in music and musical discourse, are either inborn or learned through very early experience, and in any case are not dependent on language or acculturation.

### *Cross-Cultural Studies*

Several lines of cross-cultural research suggest that CMC involving auditory features are not solely bound by language or cultural convention. One line of this research involves sound symbolism—the systematic association of sound and meaning in speech. Sound symbolism studies indicate cross-cultural consistency in associating specific features of speech or vocal sound with non-auditory features, such as shape, height, or size (see Hinton, Nichols, & Ohala, 2006, for research survey). For instance, Köhler's well-known demonstration of sound-shape association (1929), in which the nonsense words "maluma" and "takete" were almost unanimously associated by Westerners with rounded and spiky visual shapes, respectively, was as strongly exhibited by the Himba of Northern Namibia, a remote population with hardly any contact with Western culture (Bremner et al., 2013).

Analogies of sound and movement features may provide another source for cross-cultural analogies. Sievers, Polansky, Casey, and Wheatley (2013) investigated such analogies by examining analogous depiction of basic emotions by Western and non-Western participants. Sievers and associates applied a model representing corresponding features of music and movement (tempo/movement rate, jitter, interval/step size, pitch direction/vertical movement direction, consonance/surface smoothness) analogously. A computer program utilizing the model generated both movement patterns (animations of a moving ball) and musical sequences (monophonic melodies). Participants were asked to create movement animations or musical sequences subjectively representing five basic emotions (angry, happy, peaceful, sad and scared). Results revealed that each emotion was represented by a unique combination of features, features similarly represented through movement or music. Importantly to the present concern, these cross-modal representations were shared by participants of both cultures.

Cross-cultural studies have also examined specific audio-visual CMC directly. Parkinson, Kohler, Sievers, and Wheatley (2012) using a speeded classification paradigm (a paradigm often applied to investigate audio-visual CMC; Marks, 2004), established that members of an isolated community in Northeastern Cambodia, whose language does not use spatial terminology for pitch, implicitly associate pitch direction with vertical visuo-spatial direction. Correspondingly, Westerners applied non-Western metaphors for high and low pitch in accordance with their original use, of which they had no prior information, suggesting that these metaphors may be grounded in basic, cross-cultural CMC (Eitan & Timmers, 2010).

### *Cross-modal Tendencies and Their Cultural Realizations*

While tendencies for certain cross-modal associations may be universal, these tendencies are not necessarily realized universally in the same ways. For instance, though the pitch/elevation mapping is prevalent across cultures and languages, languages use many other mappings to denote auditory pitch (Eitan & Timmers, 2010), and at least in one language (the Austronesian language 'Are'are), our "high" pitch is denoted as "low" (Zemp & Malkus, 1979). A key question is, then: how do "natural" cross-modal predispositions (innate or acquired through statistical learning prior to the acquisition of language or enculturation) interact with cross-modal mappings suggested by language or cultural convention?

A series of studies by Dolschied and associates (Dolscheid, Shayan, Majid, & Casasanto, 2013; Dolscheid et al., 2014) demonstrate how complex such interactions may be. In Dolscheid et al. (2013), Dutch speakers (whose language maps pitch onto spatial elevation) and speakers of Farsi (which maps pitch onto thickness—"lower" pitch is thicker—rather than elevation) were asked to sing back a tone while viewing lines that varied in elevation or thickness. Elevation, but not thickness, affected Dutch speakers' pitch reproduction; Farsi speakers' performance, in contrast, was affected by thickness, but not by elevation.

These results could suggest that even when non-linguistic tasks are involved, language and acculturation (rather than presumed "natural" tendencies), shape adults' CMC. Implicit associations of pitch with both elevation and thickness, however, were found in 4 months old infants (Dolscheid et al., 2014; Walker et al., 2010). Are such early CMC simply extinguished later in development by language and cultural practice? Several studies suggest a more complex interaction. In Dolscheid et al. (2013), pitch reproduction of Dutch speakers trained to use the thickness metaphor was affected, as in Farsi speakers, by the thickness of irrelevant visual stimuli. However, training for a "reversed-thickness" mapping, in which higher pitch is associated with thicker lines, did not produce any effects. This suggests that linguistic metaphors and other cultural practices do not create CMC, but modify the expression of preexisting tendencies, such as those revealed in infant studies.

Indeed, the transition from early non-linguistic correspondences to mappings codified in language may create complex interactions even when the two kinds of mappings are expected to support each other. For instance, young Hebrew-speaking children were unable to consistently apply pitch-elevation mappings in music-induced movement or in motion imagery tasks, though Hebrew uses elevation terms for pitch (Eitan & Tubul, 2011; Kohn & Eitan, 2016). Rather, they often applied other CMC, such as loudness-elevation, better. Thus, while language metaphors (and other cultural symbols and practices) may ultimately strengthen corresponding pre-linguistic mappings, such metaphors may initially hinder their early equivalents. This apparently counterintuitive conclusion suggests that there are still considerable gaps to fill in our understanding of how the interaction of "nature" and "nurture" shapes CMC—gaps which are of particular importance for the historically and culturally-laden realm of music.

## A Note about CMC and Synesthesia

At this point, a reader may wonder whether and how CMC are related to synesthesia—that intriguing condition in which an experience in one perceptual domain vividly arouses an experience of a different, unrelated domain. How, for instance, is pitch-color synesthesia—in which specific auditory pitches vividly evoke specific color hues—distinguished from (and related to) the widespread association of pitch and visual lightness (Marks, 1987)? And what roles may each phenomenon have in music processing?

Synesthesia and CMC may use similar mechanisms. Thus, the association of lighter color with higher pitch guides both "genuine" pitch-color synesthetes and the rest of us, experiencing pitch-lightness CMC. Indeed, researchers debate whether synesthesia and CMC are distinct phenomena, or different points along the same continuum (Marks & Mulvenna, 2013; Parise & Spence, 2013). This debate notwithstanding, one may point out some distinctions between the two phenomena.

First, CMC lack the vivid, conscious perceptual experience of the induced dimension characteristic of synesthesia. Pitch-lightness correspondence, for instance, does not involve actually seeing lighter colors when hearing higher pitches. Nevertheless, as discussed above (under the heading "Functions"), CMC does affect perception in important ways, both consciously and subconsciously.

Second, synesthesia is involuntary: the induced synesthetic sensation is activated automatically, does not require any conscious effort, and cannot be inhibited at will. While CMC also involve automatic perceptual processes, its manifestations are amenable to voluntary control, and may be affected by training (e.g., Dolscheid et al., 2013).

Third, synesthetic mappings tend to be absolute (context-independent) for each synesthete, and are consistent over time. Thus, sound–color synesthetes associate the same tones and color hues in repeated tests, conducted months apart (Ward, Huckstep & Tsakanikos, 2006). In contrast, CMC is mostly contextual and variable over time: thus, we systematically associate higher pitch with lighter color, but do not consistently match a particular pitch with a specific degree of lightness when presented in isolation or in different contexts (e.g., when the range of compared pitch- or lightness values changes).

However, though synesthetic mappings may be remarkably consistent for individual synesthetes, they considerably vary among synesthetes. For instance, the pitch-color mappings of composers reputed to be synesthetes (e.g., Scriabin, Rimsky-Korsakov, Messiaen) vary widely (Shaw-Miller, 2013).

Finally, while CMC are widespread, and some may be universal (see "origins" above), vivid synesthesias are rare; surprisingly, sound–color synesthesias, their cultural prominence notwithstanding, are among the rarest (Simner et al., 2006).

Synesthesia is fascinating, and may serve as an important tool in studying perceptual and cognitive processing, both behaviorally and neurophysiologically. Yet music-color synesthesias, being rare and idiosyncratic conditions, cannot easily serve to explain how the rest of us assign connotative meanings to music. Cross-modal correspondences, though less exotic than hearing colors or tasting shapes, affect a range of perceptual and cognitive functions deeply, widely and consistently, and are thus highly relevant to understanding how listeners, performers and composers apply and process musical meanings.

## Emotional Mediation?

The auditory features partaking in CMC often associate with emotional features as well. For instance, low pitch, associated with features such as dark colour or low elevation, also suggests negative emotional valence, particularly sadness (Collier & Hubbard, 2001). Correspondingly, non-auditory sensory dimensions that often map onto features of sound, such as brightness or spatial height, are strongly associated with emotion. Such relationships are evident not only through language metaphors and idioms (e.g. "dark" and "bright" moods; "high" and "low" spirits), but also in non-verbal measures of emotion, often expressed implicitly. For instance, positively-valenced words are processed faster when printed in lighter shades of grey, and negative words—when printed in darker shades (Meier, Robinson, & Clore, 2004);

complementarily, valence of evaluation words affects brightness perception—"good" words are perceived as brighter (Meier & Robinson, 2005). Similarly, a word's valence affects spatial-visual attention: positive words shift attention upward, and negative words downward (Meier & Robinson, 2004); comparably, moving objects up or down enhances recall of positive and negative episodic memories, respectively (Casasanto & Dijkstra, 2010).

In interpreting CMC in music, then, one may consider an interconnected threesome: mappings of sound and non-auditory perceptual dimensions, mappings of sound and emotion, and mappings of non-auditory dimensions and emotion (e.g. low pitch—dark colour, low pitch—sadness, dark colour—sadness). An intriguing hypothesis concerning this triadic complex of mappings suggests that some cross-modal mappings are mediated, at least in musical contexts, by emotion. That is, musical features may correspond with non-auditory features since both associate with emotion in a similar way. For instance, the association between low pitch and dark color may be activated by the shared association of these dimensions with negative valence. Thus, the apparent synesthetic correspondence would actually be a second-order reflection of the emotional associations of sound and vision.

The emotional mediation hypothesis has been recently corroborated for several dimensions. Palmer, Schloss, Xu, and Prado-León (2013) show, in a cross-cultural study, that listeners' colour and emotional associations of musical pieces are strongly correlated (see also Lindborg & Friberg, 2015), while Levitan, Charney, Schloss, and Palmer (2015) found that emotion mediates correspondences between music and smell. Bhattacharya and Lindsen (2016) show that perceived emotional valence of music biases judgements of visual brightness: stimuli were rated as brighter after listening to positively-valenced music, compared to negatively-valenced music.

Support for the role of emotion in mediating CMC in music is also provided by studies indicating that the emotions associated with specific visual stimuli influence the perception of music presented concurrently with these stimuli (Boltz, 2013; Timmers & Crook, 2014). Likewise, the positive or negative valence of words enhances the perception of simultaneously presented high and low pitches, respectively (Weger, Meier, Robinson, & Inhoff, 2007). Evidence supporting the role of emotion in CMC—particularly the correspondences of musical and movement features—is provided by Sievers et al. (2013), discussed above, revealing that basic emotions are characterized across cultures by a unique combination of analogous musical and movement features.

This intriguing research notwithstanding, the interrelations of emotional and cross-modal mappings in complex musical contexts, and particularly the ways listeners perceive and respond to such interrelationships, have hardly been explored empirically. As Eitan, Timmers, and Adler (in press) demonstrate, conflicts between the emotional and cross-modal connotations of musical features (such as rising pitch) may often underlie complex connotative contexts, particularly when text or visual imagery are also involved. The investigation of such interactions is, then, a challenge for both music analysis and music psychology.

## Conclusion: Music as a CMC Laboratory

Music is uniquely positioned to serve as a real-world laboratory for the examination of cross-modal correspondences in complex settings. As noted at the beginning of this chapter, cross-modal mappings pervade music and its related activities and artifacts. Across historical and cultural domains, mappings of musical features onto visual, spatial or kinesthetic features (directly or through verbal mediation) are presented through text-settings, "programme" and descriptive music, music aimed to induce movement (e.g., dances, marches, work-songs), and diverse audio-visual musical multimedia, including opera, film music, and music for computer and video games (Tan, Cohen, Lipscomb, & Kendall, 2013). CMC are also ubiquitous in music-induced movement, both spontaneous and pre-organized (Godøy & Leman, 2010; Kohn & Eitan, 2016), in aspects of musical notation, and in music-related vocabulary and metaphor (Zbikowski, 2008), including the conceptual metaphors underlying music theories (Zbikowski, 2005).

While research on cross-domain mappings in these diverse musical contexts is not scant (see also chapters by Clarke and Zbikowski, this volume), several general directions for further research may be pointed out. First, as noted above, empirical CMC research needs to explore facets of the inherent complexity of music: how music-specific features and structures affect CMC; how dynamic interactions of multiple musical parameters are reflected in music's cross-modal mappings, and how emotional and cross-modal mappings of auditory features interact in musical contexts. Second, perception and performance studies of CMC may be complemented by computer-assisted musical corpus studies. For instance, quantitative studies of musical text settings may systematically explore the association of musical features (extracted from musical scores and recordings) with specific visual, spatial, kinesthetic or tactile references or connotations in the text. Such studies may allow for systematic comparisons of musical CMC across musical styles and genres, highlighting composers' idiosyncrasies, style-specific idioms, and perhaps universals. Correspondences of musical or auditory features with visuo-kinetic dimensions in film and other audiovisual media could also be investigated quantitatively, applying some of the rich apparatus developed for multimedia information retrieval (see Rüger, 2009, for a survey). Combined with current CMC research methods, such largely unexplored avenues for investigation may produce valuable, perhaps unexpected revenues for both music research and cognitive science.

## Note

1. Monsieur Jourdain, Molière's Bourgeois gentilhomme, was surprised to learn that he has been speaking prose throughout his life.

## Core Reading

Marks, L. E. (2014). *The unity of the senses: Interrelations among the modalities.* Cambridge, MA: Academic Press.

Spence, C. (2011). Cross-modal correspondences: A tutorial review. *Attention, Perception & Psychophysics, 73*, 971–995.

Tan, S. L., Cohen, A., Lipscomb, S., & Kendall, R. (Eds.) (2013). *The psychology of music in multimedia.* Oxford: Oxford University Press.

Walker, P. (2016). Cross-sensory correspondences: A theoretical framework and their relevance to music. *Psychomusicology: Music, Mind, & Brain, 26*, 103–116.

## Further References

Bhattacharya, J., & Lindsen, J. P. (2016). Music for a brighter world: Brightness judgment bias by musical emotion. *PloS ONE, 11*, 0148959. doi:10.1371/journal.pone.0148959

Boltz, M. (2013). Music videos and visual influences on music perception and appreciation: Should you want your MTV? In S. L. Tan, A. Cohen, S. Lipscomb, & R. Kendall (Eds.), *The psychology of music in multimedia* (pp. 217–235). Oxford: Oxford University Press.

Boulez, P. (1986). *Orientations.* J-J Nattiez (Ed.), M. Cooper (Trans.). London: Faber.

Bremner, A. J., Caparos, S., Davidoff, J., de Fockert, J., Linnell, K. J., & Spence, C. (2013). "Bouba" and "Kiki" in Namibia? A remote culture makes similar shape–sound matches, but different shape–taste matches to Westerners. *Cognition, 126,* 165–172.

Brunel, L., Carvalho, P. F., & Goldstone, R. L. (2015). It does belong together: Cross-modal correspondences influence cross-modal integration during perceptual learning. *Frontiers in Psychology, 6,* 358. doi:10.3389/fpsyg.2015.00358

Casasanto, D., & Dijkstra, K. (2010). Motor action and emotional memory. *Cognition, 115,* 179–185.

Collier, W. G., & Hubbard, T. L. (2001). Judgments of happiness, brightness, speed and tempo change of auditory stimuli varying in pitch and tempo. *Psychomusicology, 17,* 36–55.

Dolscheid, S., Hunnius, S., Casasanto, D., & Majid, A. (2014). Prelinguistic infants are sensitive to space-pitch associations found across cultures. *Psychological Science, 25,* 1256–1261.

Dolscheid, S., Shayan, S., Majid, A., & Casasanto, D. (2013). The thickness of musical pitch: Psychophysical evidence for linguistic relativity. *Psychological Science, 24b,* 613–621.

Eitan, Z., & Granot, R. Y. (2011). Listeners' images of motion and the interaction of musical parameters. Paper presented at the *10th Conference of the Society for Music Perception and Cognition (SMPC).* Rochester, NY.

Eitan, Z., & Rothschild, I. (2010). How music touches: Musical parameters and listeners' audiotactile metaphorical mappings. *Psychology of Music, 39,* 449–467.

Eitan, Z., Schupak, A., & Marks, L. E. (2008). Louder is higher: Cross-modal interaction of loudness change and vertical motion in speeded classification. In K. Miyazaki, Y. Hiraga, M. Adachi, Y. Nakajima, & M. Tsuzaki (Eds.), *Proceedings of the 10th international conference on music perception & Cognition (ICMPC10).* Adelaide, Australia: Causal Productions.

Eitan, Z. & Timmers, R. (2010). Beethoven's last piano sonata and those who follow crocodiles: Cross-domain mappings of auditory pitch in a musical context. *Cognition, 114,* 405–422.

Eitan, Z., Timmers, R., & Adler, M. (In press). Cross-modal correspondences in a Schubert song. In D. Leech-Wilkinson and H. Prior (Eds.), *Music and shape.* Oxford and New York: Oxford University Press.

Eitan, Z., & Tubul, N. (2010). Musical parameters and children's images of motion. *Musicae Scientiae, 14,* 89–111.

Evans, K. K., & Treisman, A. (2010). Natural cross-modal mappings between visual and auditory features. *Journal of Vision, 10,* 1–12.

Fernández-Prieto, I., Navarra, J., & Pons, F. (2015). How big is this sound? Cross-modal association between pitch and size in infants. *Infant Behavior and Development, 38,* 77–81.

Gallace, A., & Spence, C. (2006). Multisensory synesthetic interactions in the speeded classification of visual size. *Perception & Psychophysics, 68,* 1191–1203.

Godøy, R. I., & Leman, M. (Eds.). (2010). *Musical gestures: Sound, movement, and meaning.* New York, NY: Routledge.

Haryu, E., & Kajikawa, S. (2012). Are higher-frequency sounds brighter in colour and smaller in size? Auditory-visual correspondences in 10-month-old infants. *Infant Behavior and Development 35,* 727–732.

Hinton, L., Nichols, J., & Ohala, J. J. (2006). *Sound symbolism.* Cambridge: Cambridge University Press.

Köhler, W. (1929). *Gestalt psychology.* New York, NY: Liveright.

Kohn, D., & Eitan, Z. (2016). Moving music: Correspondences of musical parameters and movement dimensions in children's motion and verbal responses. *Music Perception, 34,* 40–55.

Küssner, M. B., Tidhar, D., Prior, H. M., & Leech-Wilkinson, D. (2014). Musicians are more consistent: Gestural cross-modal mappings of pitch, loudness and tempo in real-time. *Frontiers in Psychology, 5,* 789. doi:10.3389/fpsyg.2014.00789

Lakoff, G., & Johnson, M. (1980). *Metaphors we live by.* Chicago, IL: University of Chicago Press.

Levitan, C. A., Charney, S. A., Schloss, K. B., & Palmer, S. E. (2015). The smell of jazz: Cross-modal correspondences between music, odor, and emotion. In Noelle, D.C., Dale, R., Warlaumont, A. S., Yoshimi, J., Matlock, T., Jennings, C. D., & Maglio, P. P. (Eds.), *Proceedings of the 37th Annual Meeting of the Cognitive Science Society* (pp. 1326–1331). Austin, TX: Cognitive Science Society.

Lewkowicz, D. J., & Turkewitz, G. (1980). Cross-modal equivalence in early infancy: Auditory–visual intensity matching. *Developmental Psychology, 16*, 597–607.

Lindborg, P., & Friberg, A. K. (2015). Colour association with music is mediated by emotion: Evidence from an experiment using a CIE lab interface and interviews. *PloS ONE, 10*(12), e0144013.

Ludwig, V. U., Adachi, I., & Matsuzawa, T. (2011). Visuoauditory mappings between high luminance and high pitch are shared by chimpanzees (Pan Troglodytes) and humans. *Proceedings of the National Academy of Sciences, 108*, 20661–20665.

Maeda, F., Kanai, R., & Shimojo, S. (2004). Changing pitch induced visual motion illusion. *Current Biology, 14*, R990–R991.

Maimon, N. (2016). *Bright tonic, grey subdominant? Cross-modal correspondence between tonal stability and visual brightness.* M.A. Thesis (Cognitive Psychology), Tel Aviv University.

Marks, L. E. (1987). On cross-modal similarity: Auditory-visual interactions in speeded discrimination. *Journal of Experimental Psychology: Human Perception and Performance, 13*, 384–394.

Marks, L. E. (2004). Cross-modal interactions in speeded classification. In G. Calvert, C. Spence, and B. E. Stein (Eds.), *Handbook of multisensory processes* (pp. 85–106). Cambridge, MA: MIT Press.

Marks, L. E., & Mulvenna, C. M. (2013). Synesthesia, at and near its borders. *Frontiers in Psychology, 4*, 651. doi:10.3389/fpsyg.2013.00651

Meier, B. P., Robinson, M. D., & Clore, G. L. (2004). Why good guys wear white: Automatic inferences about stimulus valence based on brightness. *Psychological Science, 15*, 82–87.

Meier, B. P., & Robinson, M. D. (2004). Why the sunny side is up: Associations between affect and vertical position. *Psychological Science, 15*, 243–247.

Meier, B. P., & Robinson, M. D. (2005). The metaphorical representation of affect. *Metaphor and Symbol, 20*, 239–257.

Melara, R. D., & Marks, L. E. (1990). Interaction among auditory dimensions: Timbre, pitch, and loudness. *Perception & Psychophysics, 48*, 169–178.

Morton, E. (1994). Sound symbolism and its role in non-human vertebrate communication. In L. Hinton, J. Nichols, and J. Ohala (Eds.), *Sound symbolism* (pp. 348–365). Cambridge: Cambridge University Press.

Neuhoff, J. G., & McBeath, M. K. (1996). The Doppler illusion: The influence of dynamic intensity change on perceived pitch. *Journal of Experimental Psychology: Human Perception and Performance, 22*, 970.

Palmer, S. E., Schloss, K. B., Xu, Z., & Prado-León, L. R. (2013). Music–colour associations are mediated by emotion. *Proceedings of the National Academy of Sciences, 110*, 8836–8841.

Parise, C. V. (2016). Cross-modal correspondences: Standing issues and experimental guidelines. *Multisensory Research, 29*, 7–28.

Parise, C. V., Knorre, K., & Ernst, M. O. (2014). Natural auditory scene statistics shapes human spatial hearing. *Proceedings of the National Academy of Sciences, 111*, 6104–6108.

Parise, C. V., & Spence, C. (2009). 'When birds of a feather flock together': Synesthetic correspondences modulate audiovisual integration in non-synesthetes. PLoS ONE, 4, e5664. doi:10.1371/journal.pone.0005664

Parise, C., & Spence, C. (2013). Audiovisual cross-modal correspondences in the general population. In J. Simner, & E. M. Hubbard (Eds.), *The Oxford handbook of synaesthesia* (pp. 790–815). Oxford: Oxford University Press.

Parkinson, C., Kohler, P. J., Sievers, B., & Wheatley, T. (2012). Associations between auditory pitch and visual elevation do not depend on language: Evidence from a remote population. *Perception, 41*, 854–861.

Pitteri, M., Marchetti, M., Priftis, K., & Grassi, M. (2015). Naturally together: Pitch-height and brightness as coupled factors for eliciting the SMARC effect in non-musicians. *Psychological Research, 15*, 1–12.

Pratt, C. C. (1930). The spatial character of high and low tones. *Journal of Experimental Psychology, 13*, 278–285.

Rameau, J.-P. (1722). *Traité de l'harmonie réduite à ses principes naturels.* Paris: Ballard.

Rusconi, E., Kwan, B., Giordano, B. L., Umilta, C., & Butterworth, B. (2006). Spatial representation of pitch height: The SMARC effect. *Cognition, 20,* 1–17.

Rothfarb, L. (2001). Energetics. In T. Christensen (Ed.), *The Cambridge history of Western music theory* (pp. 927–955). Cambridge: Cambridge University Press.

Shaw-Miller, S. (2013). Synesthesia. In T. Shephard, & A. Leonard (Eds.), *The Routledge companion to music and visual culture*. New York, NY: Routledge.

Sievers, B., Polansky, L., Casey, M., & Wheatley, T. (2013). Music and movement share a dynamic structure that supports universal expressions of emotion. *Proceedings of the National Academy of Sciences, 110,* 70–75.

Simner, J., Mulvenna, C., Sagiv, N., Tsakanikos, E., Witherby, S. A., Fraser, C., & Ward, J. (2006). Synesthesia: The prevalence of atypical cross-modal experiences. *Perception, 35,* 1024–1033.

Spitzer, M. (2004). *Metaphor and musical thought.* Chicago, IL: University of Chicago Press.

Stevens, S. S. (1957). On the psychophysical law. *Psychological Review, 64,* 153–181.

Timmers, R., & Crook, H. (2014). Affective priming in music listening: Emotions as a source of musical expectation. *Music Perception, 31,* 470–484.

Wagner, Y. S., Winner, E., Cicchetti, D., & Gardner, H. (1981). "Metaphorical" mapping in human infants. *Child Development, 52,* 728–731.

Walker, P., Bremner, J. G., Mason, U., Spring, J., Mattock, K., Slater, A., & Johnson, S. P. (2010). Preverbal infants' sensitivity to synaesthetic cross-modality correspondences. *Psychological Science, 21,* 21–25.

Ward, J., Huckstep, B., & Tsakanikos, E. (2006). Sound-colour synaesthesia: To what extent does it use cross-modal mechanisms common to us all? *Cortex, 42,* 264–280.

Weger, U. W., Meier, B. P., Robinson, M. D., & Inhoff, A. W. (2007). Things are sounding up: Affective influences on auditory tone perception. *Psychonomic Bulletin & Review, 14,* 517–521.

Zbikowski, L. M. (2005). *Conceptualizing music: Cognitive structure, theory, and analysis.* New York, NY: Oxford University Press.

Zbikowski, L. (2008). Metaphor and music. In R. Gibbs, Jr. (Ed.), *The Cambridge handbook on metaphor* (pp. 502–24). Cambridge: Cambridge University Press.

Zemp, H., & Malkus, V. (1979). Aspects of 'Are'are musical theory. *Ethnomusicology, 23,* 5–48.

# 19

# MUSICAL CONNECTIONS
## Music Perception and Neurological Deficits

*Barbara Tillmann, Catherine Hirel, Yohana Lévêque, and Anne Caclin*

Studying music perception in normal and patient populations provides insights into neural networks of music processing and also into how far these are domain-specific or shared with other materials (e.g., language). Studying impairments and malfunctioning is complementary to studying the healthy system with its musical networks and connections. It also provides perspectives on how music may be used to stimulate impaired perceptual, cognitive and motor functions (Bigand et al., 2015).

This chapter reviews impairments of different aspects of music perception and cognition in various pathologies or disorders. Studying acquired amusia following brain lesions has been the classical approach in neuropsychology, which continues to be developed today. More recently, the phenomenon of congenital amusia has attracted numerous researchers, in part due to the Montreal Battery of Evaluation of Amusia (MBEA) (Peretz, Champod, & Hyde, 2003) that led to a common definition of this phenomenon, as previously proposed for acquired amusia. In addition, music perception has been studied in other pathologies, and we present some conditions for which altered music processing has been reported, furthering our understanding of shared networks with language processing.

## Acquired Amusia

The study of musical impairments in brain-damaged patients has been a cornerstone of the neurosciences of music. The description of patients with selective musical deficits, with other auditory and cognitive domains (including language) being preserved, has been taken as strong evidence for (at least partly) separate neural resources for music and language processing, and contributing to the interest in characterizing music networks. Neurological reports of musical symptoms have been accumulating over more than a century, with a first symposium on the "neurology of music" in 1972, covering normal music perception, musical dysfunctions and disorders provoked by music (Critchley & Henson, 1977). These neurological reports are symptom-led reports, describing case studies with prominent musical deficits about which the patient is generally complaining (with striking cases of professional musicians) or lesion-led reports, where music abilities are assessed in patient groups with rather homogeneous lesions, in particular temporal cortectomies in epileptic patients (i.e., removal of cortical tissue creating epileptic seizures; see Stewart, von

Kriegstein, Warren, & Griffiths, 2006, for a review). Various models of music processing have been proposed, partly based on patient studies (e.g., Clark, Golden, & Warren, 2015; Peretz & Coltheart, 2003). Our review does not present deficits of music production or score reading as they refer to the loss of specialized expert skills, but we focus on more general processes underlying music perception and cognition.

## Deficits Along Music-Relevant Perceptual Dimensions: Pitch, Timbre, Time

The majority of reports on music abilities in brain-damaged patients focus on deficits in processing basic perceptual attributes of musical sounds: pitch, timbre, and temporal characteristics. Some of these deficits can occur in isolation, with for example double dissociations between pitch and temporal processing deficits (Ayotte et al., 2000): one patient shows impaired pitch processing, but intact temporal processing, while another patient shows the reverse pattern.

Regarding deficits on the pitch dimension, processing of pitch interval (a local feature), pitch patterns or contour (a more global feature) or melodic and tonal structure processing has been distinguished (review in Clark et al., 2015). Some reports revealed dissociations, with, for example, intact pitch interval processing, but impaired tonality processing (Peretz et al., 1994). Pitch short-term memory is altered after right anterior temporal lobectomy sparing the primary auditory cortex (Liégeois-Chauvel, Peretz, Babaï, Laguitton, & Chauvel, 1998). Timbre perception can also be affected after brain damage (e.g., Mazzucchi, Marchini, Budai, & Parma, 1982), and studies investigating epileptic patients before/after cortectomy suggest a role of the right anterior temporal lobe in the perception of spectral and temporal dimensions of timbre (Samson, Zatorre, & Ramsay, 2002). Comparable to neuropsychological cases in other domains (e.g., aphasia, prosopagnosia), implicit processing of tonal features (i.e., processing that does not require explicit verbalization or conscious analysis) can remain spared in acquired amusia even though explicit processing is impaired (e.g., Tillmann, Peretz, Bigand, & Gosselin, 2007).

Regarding deficits on the time dimension, different levels of the hierarchical organization of temporal structures in music (i.e., note duration, rhythm, meter) can be altered after brain damage, and some deficits at these levels can occur in isolation (Clark et al., 2015).

Although numerous studies have suggested some degree of modularity in music processing, our understanding of the critical neural substrates of the various components of music perception remains incomplete (see also Loui & Przysinda, this volume; Henry & Grahn, this volume). The meta-analysis of musical symptoms in brain damage by Stewart et al. (2006) suggests the involvement of bilateral areas in temporal, frontal, parietal and insular cortex in pitch, timbre, and time perception, with a right-hemispheric asymmetry and substantial overlap, in keeping with functional neuroimaging results in healthy participants (see also Clark et al., 2015).

## Musical Memory

Even non-musician listeners develop long-term memories of familiar tunes, also referred to as a "musical lexicon." These memories are powerful inducers of emotion and are strongly engraved, as attested for example by their long sparing in neurodegenerative disorders (e.g., Cuddy, Sikka, & Vanstone, 2015). The loss of the ability to recognize familiar tunes (also referred to as "associative agnosia") has been reported for brain-damaged patients, often accompanied by impaired pitch pattern perception (e.g., Peretz et al., 1994), but sometimes occurring in isolation (Eustache, Lechevalie, Viader, & Lambert, 1990). A distributed bilateral network of cortical areas (frontal, temporal, parietal, insula) has been implicated in such deficits, with lesion-led studies suggesting a left-hemispheric bias (see Clark et al., 2015).

## Musical Emotions

The most consistent association of altered emotional responses to music across studies is damage involving the right posterior temporal lobe and insula (Stewart et al., 2006). A patient with an isolated lesion of the amygdala showed impaired recognition of fearful and sad music (Gosselin, Peretz, Johnsen, & Adolphs, 2007). A group of patients with medial temporal lobectomy were impaired in the recognition of fearful faces and music (Gosselin et al., 2011). Musical emotions and perception seem relatively dissociated: cases of brain-damaged patients with musical anhedonia without perceptual deficits have been reported (Satoh, Nakase, Nagata, & Tomimoto, 2011), as well as cases of acquired amusia with preserved emotion recognition (Peretz, Gagnon, & Bouchard, 1998). However, perceptual (amusia) and emotional (anhedonia) symptoms can also co-occur (Hirel et al., 2014).

## Music, Language, and Environmental Sounds

The selectivity of music disorders with respect to other auditory cognitive abilities (language, environmental sounds) has been investigated in brain-damaged patients. Cases of fairly generalized auditory agnosias are not rare, but double dissociations between domains can be observed (review in Griffiths, 1999). Some examples of amusia without aphasia can be found in Griffiths et al. (1997) and Peretz et al. (1994, 1997). For a review of disorders in the processing of environmental sounds (e.g., sounds created by animals, objects, machines, vocalizations) and their relation to music processing, see Vignolo (2003).

Overall, research on brain-damaged patients reveals a large array of musical disorders. Selective deficits can occur, both between musical abilities and with respect to other auditory domains. Comparing lesion sites across patients suggests the involvement of distributed neural networks, with major nodes in temporal, frontal, parietal and limbic structures. A right-hemispheric predominance of musical deficits can be evidenced, but this is tempered by several factors: first, patients with left-hemisphere lesions are more prone to aphasia, and a sampling bias might result as assessing musical abilities in aphasic patients might be complicated; second, in lesion-led studies this rightward bias is limited, if present at all (e.g., Särkämö et al., 2009; Schuppert, Münte, Wieringa, & Altenmüller, 2000). Musical deficits are not rare after brain damage: In Särkämö et al. (2009), 60% of the stroke patients had acquired amusia (as diagnosed with the MBEA) one week after stroke in the territory of the middle cerebral artery, and 42% remained amusic three months later. In Schuppert et al. (2000), 69% of the stroke patients had deficits in perceptual musical functions, whatever the lateralization of the lesions in frontal, temporal, and parietal areas.

## Congenital Amusia

Music-related deficits can also arise as neurodevelopmental disorders, such as congenital amusia (Peretz et al., 2002; see Tillmann, Albouy, & Caclin, 2015, for a review). Congenital amusics tend to fail recognizing out-of-key or out-of-tune notes, have trouble recognizing familiar tunes without lyrics, and memorizing even short melodies. Congenital amusia arises without brain lesions, peripheral auditory disorders or more general cognitive disorders, and is estimated to afflict about 2–4% of the population (Peretz, 2013).

### Pitch Perception and Memory Deficits

Congenital amusia is currently understood as a pitch-based deficit (Figure 19.1A). Amusics are impaired in pitch discrimination tasks, including pitch direction (i.e., up, down) and pitch change detection (e.g., Foxton et al., 2004; Hyde & Peretz, 2004; Peretz et al., 2002), including difficulties to detect pitch changes of a semi-tone (or more), the smallest musical interval in Western tonal music. Impaired music processing might be a consequence of

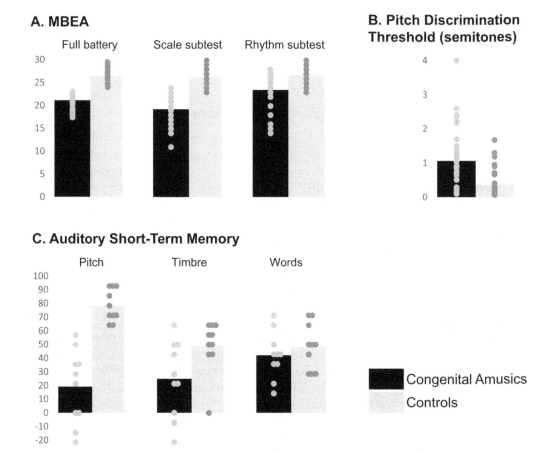

*Figure 19.1*   Group data for congenital amusic and control participants presented together with individual data points (black: amusics, grey: controls) for the following tests: **A.** MBEA (Peretz et al., 2003), expressed as numbers of correct responses (maximum score = 30). Scores are presented for the entire battery (cut-off for amusia diagnosis = 23/30) and two of the six subtests (scale and rhythm, maximum score = 30 in each case). **B.** Pitch Discrimination Thresholds (as measured in Tillmann et al., 2009) in semitones (for the same participants as in Figure 19.1A, N_amusics=34, N_controls=34). **C.** Performance (presented in terms of percentage of Hits-False Alarms) in auditory short-term memory tasks for pitch (melodies), musical timbre, and word materials (data from Tillmann et al., 2009, N_amusics=10, N_controls=10). See insert for color figure.

this fine-grained pitch deficit, impacting on tonal knowledge acquisition. However, as some amusic individuals exhibit normal pitch discrimination thresholds (Figure 19.1B), impaired pitch short-term memory seems to also have a central role in this condition (see Tillmann, Lévêque, Fornoni, Albouy, & Caclin, 2016, for a review, Figure 19.1C). Amusic participants' performance in delayed-matching-to-sample tasks is particularly affected by the presence of interfering tones (Gosselin, Jolicoeur, & Peretz, 2009) or increased retention delay (Williamson, McDonald, Deutsch, Griffiths, & Stewart, 2010). As psychoacoustic tasks measuring pitch discrimination thresholds require the comparison of stimuli over time, deficits in pitch short-term memory might explain increased pitch discrimination thresholds. A recent study suggests that amusics benefit from increased tone duration (i.e., giving more time for pitch encoding in memory), reaching controls' performance in pitch discrimination and memory tasks for Stimulus-Onset-Asynchronies over 350ms (Albouy et al., 2016).

## Functional and Anatomical Anomalies in the Amusic Brain

Anatomical and functional brain imaging studies in congenital amusia have revealed anomalies in a fronto-temporal network, with a right-sided predominance, in agreement with its role reported for pitch-based tasks in controls (e.g., Zatorre, Evans, & Meyer, 1994). Subtle anatomical abnormalities in the inferior frontal gyrus and supra-temporal auditory areas have been reported using voxel-based morphometry (Albouy et al., 2013; Hyde, Zatorre, Griffiths, Lerch, & Peretz, 2006) and cortical thickness measures (Hyde et al., 2007). Tractography from diffusion tensor imaging (i.e., representations of neural fiber tracks based on a methodology using magnetic resonance imaging) suggests a disconnection between auditory and frontal areas (Loui, Alsop, & Schlaug, 2009, but see Chen et al., 2015).

Functional MRI studies have revealed decreased activity in frontal areas in amusic individuals, but failed to evidence abnormalities in auditory cortex (Hyde, Zatorre, & Peretz, 2011; Norman-Haignere et al., 2016). However, with the greater temporal precision offered by MEG, abnormalities were shown in amusics' auditory cortex responses as early as 100 ms post-stimulus onset during the encoding of tones in short-term memory (Albouy et al., 2013). Abnormal activity in auditory and inferior frontal areas is accompanied by abnormal functional connectivity between these areas (e.g., Albouy et al., 2013; Hyde et al., 2011).

## How Specific are the Musical Deficits in Congenital Amusia?

While the most affected dimension is pitch, a subset of congenital amusics also shows impaired processing of the time dimension. While they do not show deficits in detecting subtle anisochronies (i.e., deviations from isochrony) in tone sequences using only one tone repeatedly (Hyde & Peretz, 2004), temporal processing was impaired when the material incorporates pitch variations (Foxton et al., 2004). Timbre-related deficits, although somewhat more limited than pitch deficits, have also been reported (Tillmann, Schulze, & Foxton, 2009; Figure 19.1C). In accordance with their pitch (and sometimes temporal) processing deficits, singing is impaired in amusic individuals, with major impairments in pitch contour and intervals, but also some temporal errors (Dalla Bella, Giguère, & Peretz, 2009). However, singing can be relatively preserved in some amusics, supporting a dual-route model of pitch processing (Loui, Guenther, Mathys, & Schlaug, 2008).

Despite the pitch (and to some extent temporal, timbre, and production) deficits observed with explicit paradigms, behavioral and electrophysiological data have revealed spared implicit pitch and music abilities in congenital amusia (e.g., Peretz et al., 2009; Tillmann et al., 2012), suggesting a deficit in pitch awareness. Perhaps related to these findings, musical emotions seem relatively preserved (Gosselin, Paquette, & Peretz, 2015), as well as a musical lexicon allowing at least feelings of familiarity to be evoked (Tillmann, Albouy, Caclin, & Bigand, 2014).

Arguments for a music specificity of the disorder can be found in early studies showing intact recognition of speech prosody (Ayotte et al., 2002), and intact auditory verbal short-term memory (Tillmann et al., 2009, Figure 19.1B). However, it has been shown that the pitch deficits also impact speech processing (e.g., emotional prosody, intentional prosody, tone language material), even though when comparing F0-matched speech and musical analogs, deficits are more pronounced for non-speech sounds, suggesting that speech features or representations might temper the deficits (see Tillmann et al., 2015, for a review). Additionally, after an initial report suggesting that the pitch processing deficit was linked to altered processing of spatial visual information (Douglas & Bilkey, 2007), this hypothesis has been dismissed (Tillmann et al., 2010; Williamson, Cocchini, & Stewart, 2011).

## Other Congenital Disorders of Music Perception and Production

Various profiles of developmental disorders of music processing have been described without pitch-processing deficits as central elements. Specific rhythm processing deficits have been documented (Phillips-Silver et al., 2011), with poor abilities to synchronize to the beat as the main behavioral deficit. Music production capacities can also be affected without co-occuring perceptual deficits, such as poor pitch singing (Dalla Bella & Berkowska, 2009). In other cases, despite normal perceptual abilities, listeners do not feel musical emotions, thus exhibiting musical anhedonia (Mas-Herrero et al., 2014).

## Altered Music Processing in Pathological Populations

Altered music processing has been reported in various pathologies, and here we focus on developmental disorders. Not being part of the primary description for diagnosis, the musical deficits could be referred to as secondary or minor characteristics of the pathological condition, but in some cases, they are linked to the main deficits of the condition.

### Developmental Language Disorders

Research investigating children with developmental language disorders (i.e., dyslexia, SLI) has revealed deficits in pitch processing (e.g., Ziegler et al., 2012) and temporal processing (rhythm, beat, meter) in tone and music materials (e.g., Muneaux et al., 2004). For example, dyslexics' performance in beat perception predicted word/non-word reading and phonological awareness (Muneaux et al., 2004), and musical training programs (focusing on temporal processing) improved reading skills and phonological awareness (Flaugnacco et al., 2015).

### Neurodevelopmental Disorders: Autism and Williams Syndrome

In autism spectrum disorders, enhanced pitch perception and memory has been reported, with better pitch discrimination and melodic short-term memory in comparison to control participants (see Ouimet et al., 2012, for a review). Regarding musical emotion, some reports indicated intact performance (e.g., Gebauer et al., 2014), while Bhatara et al. (2010), using finely manipulated material, revealed some impairments in adolescents with autism spectrum disorders when compared to typically developing controls and patients with Williams syndrome (a neurogenetic developmental disorder associated with, for example, developmental delay, hypersociability and strong language skills). Individuals with autism spectrum disorders also exhibited deficits for meter processing (De Pape, Hall, Tillmann, & Trainor, 2012). Nevertheless, the relatively intact music processing found in autistic children allows for considering music as a tool for language and motor rehabilitation with them (e.g., Wan et al., 2011).

Individuals with Williams syndrome seem to be more engaged in musical activities than typically developing children, show heightened emotional responsiveness to music and present particular attraction to some sound types in general (see Levitin, 2005, for a review). However, recent findings suggest that children with Williams syndrome do not perform better in absolute pitch tasks than controls, do not show a benefit in melody perception tasks, when contour cues were available, compared to typically developing control children (e.g., Elsabbagh, Cohen, & Karmiloff-Smith, 2010).

### *Landau–Kleffner Syndrome: A Rare Childhood Epileptic Encephalopathy*

In Landau–Kleffner syndrome (LKS), the clinical hallmark is verbal auditory agnosia, starting between 3 and 7 years, generally followed by a deterioration of expressive language. The severity of language disorders in this condition is related to early symptom onset and duration of abnormal epileptic spikes (Cockerell, Bølling, & Nakken, 2011). Some reports suggest that general auditory processing may also be altered (Bishop, 1985), including environmental sound recognition (Cockerell et al., 2011).

We have tested musical performance in four adults having presented LKS during childhood (Lévêque et al., in preparation), with severity levels from mild (onset age: 6, active phase: 1 year), through moderate (onset age: 3, active phase: 2 years) to severe (onset age: 3, active phase: 7 years, 2 patients). According to the MBEA, amusia was strong in the two patients with severe LKS, and moderate in the patient with moderate LKS. These three patients had abnormally high pitch discrimination thresholds (4.79 and 3.6 semi-tones for patients with severe LKS, 0.92 semi-tones for the patient with moderate LKS, *versus* controls' mean threshold: 0.27±0.18 semi-tones). The patient with mild LKS did not show any musical impairment. These findings confirm the hypothesis that LKS is not a language-specific syndrome. The inverse relation between syndrome severity and musical performance suggests temporal epileptic discharges as a source of auditory processing disorders altering music and language perception. Musical impairment remained in adulthood even though the patients did not complain about music and had a positive relationship with music listening.

### Concluding Comments

Research on musical deficits provides information about the underlying neural correlates of music processing and their potential overlap with the processing of other materials, thus contributing to the debate surrounding the domain-generality and domain-specificity of musical processing. Some results provide converging evidence for the involvement of temporo-frontal areas in music processing, with an asymmetry to the right hemisphere, even though both hemispheres are involved.

Beyond the analyses of the effect of focal lesions or local anomalies in specific brain structures, the time is ripe to investigate underlying networks and connectivity patterns in music processing also for the impaired brain. Brain imaging methods allow for investigating anatomical and functional connectivity. Even though these methods are used to investigate congenital amusia, future studies should exploit these techniques for acquired amusia. Investigations of musical connections and disconnections allow for developing more sophisticated models of music processing, including neural correlates specific to music or shared with other domains. Musical processing seems to be related to multiple neural networks, not only related to language processing, but also to emotion processing, memory and movement. More generally, music processing relates to both external, executive networks (situated in lateral parts of frontal, temporal and parietal lobes) and internal, self-related networks (situated along the midline, Janata, 2009). This central interconnected position gives music a potentially powerful role for perceptual, cognitive and motor stimulation and rehabilitation (Bigand, et al., 2015; see also chapters by Henry & Grahn and Fachner, this volume).

## Acknowledgments

This work was supported by grants from "Agence Nationale de la Recherche" (ANR) of the French Ministry of Research ANR-11-BSH2-001-01 to BT and AC, and ANR-14-CE30-0001-01 to AC. CH was funded by an "Année Recherche" grant from "ARS (Agence Régionale de Santé) Rhône-Alpes". This work was conducted in the framework of the LabEx CeLyA ("Centre Lyonnais d'Acoustique," ANR-10-LABX-0060) and of the LabEx Cortex ("Construction, Function and Cognitive Function and Rehabilitation of the Cortex", ANR-11-LABX-0042) of Université de Lyon, within the program "Investissements d'avenir" (ANR-11-IDEX-0007) operated by the French National Research Agency (ANR). The authors thank Lesly Fornoni for her continuous help with the amusia project in Lyon, and Dr. Thierry Deonna and his team (CHUV, Lausanne, Switzerland) for the collaboration on music in LKS patients.

## Core Reading

Clark, C. N., Golden, H. L., & Warren, J. D. (2015). Acquired amusia. *Handbook of Clinical Neurology, 129,* 607–631.

Peretz, I. (2013). The biological foundations of music: Insights from congenital amusia. In D. Deutsch (Ed.) *The Psychology of Music* (pp. 551–564). San Diego, CA: Elsevier.

Peretz, I., & Coltheart, M. (2003). Modularity of music processing. *Nature Neuroscience, 6*(7), 688–691.

Stewart, L., von Kriegstein, K., Warren, J. D., & Griffiths, T. D. (2006). Music and the brain: Disorders of musical listening. *Brain: A Journal of Neurology, 129*(Pt 10), 2533–2553.

Tillmann, B., Albouy, P., & Caclin, A. (2015). Congenital amusias. *Handbook of Clinical Neurology, 129,* 589–605.

## Further References

Albouy, P., Cousineau, M., Caclin, A., Tillmann, B., & Peretz, I. (2016). Impaired encoding of rapid pitch information underlies perception and memory deficits in congenital amusia. *Scientific Reports, 6,* 18861. http://doi.org/10.1038/srep18861

Albouy, P., Mattout, J., Bouet, R., Maby, E., Sanchez, G., Aguera, P-E., S. Daligault, S., Delpuech, C., Bertrand, O, Caclin, A, & Tillmann, B. (2013). Impaired pitch perception and memory in congenital amusia: The deficit starts in the auditory cortex. *Brain: A Journal of Neurology, 136* (Pt 5), 1639–1661.

Ayotte, J., Peretz, I., & Hyde, K. (2002). Congenital amusia: A group study of adults afflicted with a music-specific disorder. *Brain: A Journal of Neurology, 125*(Pt 2), 238–251.

Ayotte, J., Peretz, I., Rousseau, I., Bard, C., & Bojanowski, M. (2000). Patterns of music agnosia has-sociated with middle cerebral artery infarcts. *Brain: A Journal of Neurology, 123* (Pt 9), 1926–1938.

Bhatara, A., Quintin, E.-M., Levy, B., Bellugi, U., Fombonne, E., & Levitin, D. J. (2010). Perception of emotion in musical performance in adolescents with autism spectrum disorders. *Autism Research: Official Journal of the International Society for Autism Research, 3*(5), 214–225.

Bigand, E., Tillmann, B., Peretz, I., Zatorre, R. J., Lopez, L., & Majno, M. (Eds.). (2015). *The neurosci-ences and music V: Cognitive stimulation and rehabilitation. Annals of the New York Academy of Sciences, 1337.*

Bishop, D. V. (1985). Age of onset and outcome in "acquired aphasia with convulsive disorder" (Landau-Kleffner syndrome). *Developmental Medicine and Child Neurology, 27*(6), 705–712.

Chen, J. L., Kumar, S., Williamson, V. J., Scholz, J., Griffiths, T. D., & Stewart, L. (2015). Detection of the arcuate fasciculus in congenital amusia depends on the tractography algorithm. *Frontiers in Psychology, 6*, 9. http://doi.org/10.3389/fpsyg.2015.00009

Cockerell, I., Bølling, G., & Nakken, K. O. (2011). Landau-Kleffner syndrome in Norway: Long-term prognosis and experiences with the health services and educational systems. *Epilepsy & Behavior: E&B, 21*(2), 153–159.

Critchley, M., & Henson, R. A. (Eds.). (1977). *Music and the brain: Studies in the neurology of music.* London: Heinemann Medical.

Cuddy, L. L., Sikka, R., & Vanstone, A. (2015). Preservation of musical memory and engagement in healthy aging and Alzheimer's disease. *Annals of the New York Academy of Sciences, 1337*, 223–231.

Dalla Bella, S., & Berkowska, M. (2009). Singing proficiency in the majority: Normality and "phe-notypes" of poor singing. *Annals of the New York Academy of Sciences, 1169*, 99–107.

Dalla Bella, S., Giguère, J.-F., & Peretz, I. (2009). Singing in congenital amusia. *The Journal of the Acoustical Society of America, 126*(1), 414–424.

De Pape, A.-M. R., Hall, G. B. C., Tillmann, B., & Trainor, L. J. (2012). Auditory processing in high-functioning adolescents with Autism Spectrum Disorder. *PloS One, 7*(9), e44084. http://doi.org/10.1371/journal.pone.0044084

Douglas, K. M., & Bilkey, D. K. (2007). Amusia is associated with deficits in spatial processing. *Nature Neuroscience, 10*(7), 915–921.

Elsabbagh, M., Cohen, H., & Karmiloff-Smith, A. (2010). Discovering structure in auditory input: Evidence from Williams syndrome. *American Journal on Intellectual and Developmental Disabilities, 115*(2), 128–139.

Eustache, F., Lechevalier, B., Viader, F., & Lambert, J. (1990). Identification and discrimination disor-ders in auditory perception: A report on two cases. *Neuropsychologia, 28*(3), 257–270.

Flaugnacco, E., Lopez, L., Terribili, C., Montico, M., Zoia, S., & Schön, D. (2015). Music training increases phonological awareness and reading skills in developmental dyslexia: A randomized con-trol trial. *PloS One, 10*(9), e0138715. http://doi.org/10.1371/journal.pone.0138715

Foxton, J. M., Dean, J. L., Gee, R., Peretz, I., & Griffiths, T. D. (2004). Characterization of deficits in pitch perception underlying "tone deafness." *Brain: A Journal of Neurology, 127*(Pt 4), 801 810.

Gebauer, L., Skewes, J., Westphael, G., Heaton, P., & Vuust, P. (2014). Intact brain processing of musi-cal emotions in autism spectrum disorder, but more cognitive load and arousal in happy vs. sad music. *Frontiers in Neuroscience, 8*, 192. http://doi.org/10.3389/fnins.2014.00192

Gosselin, N., Jolicoeur, P., & Peretz, I. (2009). Impaired memory for pitch in congenital amusia. *Annals of the New York Academy of Sciences, 1169*, 270–272.

Gosselin, N., Paquette, S., & Peretz, I. (2015). Sensitivity to musical emotions in congenital amusia. *Cortex, 71*, 171–182.

Gosselin, N., Peretz, I., Hasboun, D., Baulac, M., & Samson, S. (2011). Impaired recognition of musical emotions and facial expressions following anteromedial temporal lobe excision. *Cortex; A Journal Devoted to the Study of the Nervous System and Behavior, 47*(9), 1116–1125.

Gosselin, N., Peretz, I., Johnsen, E., & Adolphs, R. (2007). Amygdala damage impairs emotion recog-nition from music. *Neuropsychologia, 45*(2), 236–244.

Griffiths, T. D. (1999). Human complex sound analysis. *Clinical Science, 96*(3), 231–234.

Griffiths, T. D., Rees, A., Witton, C., Cross, P.M., Shakir, R. A., & Green, G. G. (1997). Spatial and temporal auditory processing deficits following right hemisphere infarction. A psychophysical study. *Brain: A Journal of Neurology, 120* (Pt 5), 785–794.

Hirel, C., Lévêque, Y., Deiana, G., Richard, N., Cho, T.-H., Mechtouff, L., Derex, L., Tillman, A., Caclin, A., & Nighoghossian, N. (2014). [Acquired amusia and musical anhedonia]. *Revue Neurologique, 170*(8–9), 536–540.

Hyde, K. L., Lerch, J. P., Zatorre, R. J., Griffiths, T. D., Evans, A. C., & Peretz, I. (2007). Cortical thickness in congenital amusia: When less is better than more. *The Journal of Neuroscience: The Official Journal of the Society for Neuroscience, 27*(47), 13028–13032.

Hyde, K. L., & Peretz, I. (2004). Brains that are out of tune but in time. *Psychological Science, 15*(5), 356–360.

Hyde, K. L., Zatorre, R. J., Griffiths, T. D., Lerch, J. P., & Peretz, I. (2006). Morphometry of the amusic brain: A two-site study. *Brain: A Journal of Neurology, 129*(Pt 10), 2562–2570.

Hyde, K. L., Zatorre, R. J., & Peretz, I. (2011). Functional MRI evidence of an abnormal neural network for pitch processing in congenital amusia. *Cerebral Cortex, 21*(2), 292–299.

Janata, P. (2009). The neural architecture of music-evoked autobiographical memories. *Cerebral Cortex, 19*(11), 2579–2594. http://doi.org/10.1093/cercor/bhp008

Levitin, D. J. (2005). Musical behavior in a neurogenetic developmental disorder: Evidence from Williams Syndrome. *Annals of the New York Academy of Sciences, 1060*, 325–334.

Liégeois-Chauvel, C., Peretz, I., Babaï, M., Laguitton, V., & Chauvel, P. (1998). Contribution of different cortical areas in the temporal lobes to music processing. *Brain: A Journal of Neurology, 121* (Pt 10), 1853–1867.

Loui, P., Alsop, D., & Schlaug, G. (2009). Tone deafness: A new disconnection syndrome? *The Journal of Neuroscience: The Official Journal of the Society for Neuroscience, 29*(33), 10215–10220.

Loui, P., Guenther, F. H., Mathys, C., & Schlaug, G. (2008). Action-perception mismatch in tone-deafness. *Current Biology: CB, 18*(8), R331–332.

Mas-Herrero, E., Zatorre, R. J., Rodriguez-Fornells, A., & Marco-Pallarés, J. (2014). Dissociation between musical and monetary reward responses in specific musical anhedonia. *Current Biology: CB, 24*(6), 699–704.

Mazzucchi, A., Marchini, C., Budai, R., & Parma, M. (1982). A case of receptive amusia with prominent timbre perception defect. *Journal of Neurology, Neurosurgery, and Psychiatry, 45*(7), 644–647.

Muneaux, M., Ziegler, J. C., Truc, C., Thomson, J., & Goswami, U. (2004). Deficits in beat perception and dyslexia: Evidence from French. *Neuroreport, 15*(8), 1255–1259.

Norman-Haignere, S. V., Albouy, P., Caclin, A., McDermott, J. H., Kanwisher, N. G., & Tillmann, B. (2016). Pitch-responsive cortical regions in congenital amusia. *The Journal of Neuroscience, 36*(10), 2986–2994.

Ouimet, T., Foster, N. E. V., Tryfon, A., & Hyde, K. L. (2012). Auditory-musical processing in autism spectrum disorders: A review of behavioral and brain imaging studies. *Annals of the New York Academy of Sciences, 1252*, 325–331.

Peretz, I., Ayotte, J., Zatorre, R. J., Mehler, J., Ahad, P., Penhune, V. B., & Jutras, B. (2002). Congenital amusia: A disorder of fine-grained pitch discrimination. *Neuron, 33*(2), 185–191.

Peretz, I., Belleville, S., & Fontaine, S. (1997). [Dissociations between music and language functions after cerebral resection: A new case of amusia without aphasia]. *Canadian Journal of Experimental Psychology = Revue Canadienne De Psychologie Expérimentale, 51*(4), 354–368.

Peretz, I., Brattico, E., Järvenpää, M., & Tervaniemi, M. (2009). The amusic brain: In tune, out of key, and unaware. *Brain: A Journal of Neurology, 132*(Pt 5), 1277–1286.

Peretz, I., Champod, A. S., & Hyde, K. (2003). Varieties of musical disorders. The Montreal Battery of Evaluation of Amusia. *Annals of the New York Academy of Sciences, 999*, 58–75.

Peretz, I., Gagnon, L., & Bouchard, B. (1998). Music and emotion: Perceptual determinants, immediacy, and isolation after brain damage. *Cognition, 68*(2), 111–141.

Peretz, I., Kolinsky, R., Tramo, M., Labrecque, R., Hublet, C., Demeurisse, G., & Belleville, S. (1994). Functional dissociations following bilateral lesions of auditory cortex. *Brain: A Journal of Neurology, 117* (Pt 6), 1283–1301.

Phillips-Silver, J., Toiviainen, P., Gosselin, N., Piché, O., Nozaradan, S., Palmer, C., & Peretz, I. (2011). Born to dance but beat deaf: A new form of congenital amusia. *Neuropsychologia, 49*(5), 961–969.

Samson, S., Zatorre, R. J., & Ramsay, J. O. (2002). Deficits of musical timbre perception after unilateral temporal-lobe lesion revealed with multidimensional scaling. *Brain: A Journal of Neurology, 125*(Pt 3), 511–523.

Särkämö, T., Tervaniemi, M., Soinila, S., Autti, T., Silvennoinen, H. M., Laine, M., & Hietanen, M. (2009). Cognitive deficits associated with acquired amusia after stroke: A neuropsychological follow-up study. *Neuropsychologia, 47*(12), 2642–2651.

Satoh, M., Nakase, T., Nagata, K., & Tomimoto, H. (2011). Musical anhedonia: Selective loss of emotional experience in listening to music. *Neurocase, 17*(5), 410–417.

Schuppert, M., Münte, T. F., Wieringa, B. M., & Altenmüller, E. (2000). Receptive amusia: Evidence for cross-hemispheric neural networks underlying music processing strategies. *Brain: A Journal of Neurology, 123* Pt 3, 546–559.

Tillmann, B., Albouy, P., Caclin, A., & Bigand, E. (2014). Musical familiarity in congenital amusia: Evidence from a gating paradigm. *Cortex; A Journal Devoted to the Study of the Nervous System and Behavior, 59*, 84–94.

Tillmann, B., Gosselin, N., Bigand, E., & Peretz, I. (2012). Priming paradigm reveals harmonic structure processing in congenital amusia. *Cortex; A Journal Devoted to the Study of the Nervous System and Behavior, 48*(8), 1073–1078.

Tillmann, B., Jolicoeur, P., Ishihara, M., Gosselin, N., Bertrand, O., Rossetti, Y., & Peretz, I. (2010). The amusic brain: Lost in music, but not in space. *PloS One, 5*(4), e10173. http://doi.org/10.1371/journal.pone.0010173

Tillmann, B., Lévêque, Y., Fornoni, L., Albouy, P., & Caclin, A. (2016). Impaired short-term memory for pitch in congenital amusia. *Brain Research, 1640*(Pt B), 251–263.

Tillmann, B., Peretz, I., Bigand, E., & Gosselin, N. (2007). Harmonic priming in an amusic patient: The power of implicit tasks. *Cognitive Neuropsychology, 24*(6), 603–622.

Tillmann, B., Schulze, K., & Foxton, J. M. (2009). Congenital amusia: A short-term memory deficit for non-verbal, but not verbal sounds. *Brain and Cognition, 71*(3), 259–264.

Vignolo, L. A. (2003). Music agnosia and auditory agnosia. Dissociations in stroke patients. *Annals of the New York Academy of Sciences, 999*, 50–57.

Wan, C. Y., Bazen, L., Baars, R., Libenson, A., Zipse, L., Zuk, J., . . . Schlaug, G. (2011). Auditory-motor mapping training as an intervention to facilitate speech output in non-verbal children with autism: A proof of concept study. *PloS One, 6*(9), e25505. http://doi.org/10.1371/journal.pone.0025505

Williamson, V. J., Cocchini, G., & Stewart, L. (2011). The relationship between pitch and space in congenital amusia. *Brain and Cognition, 76*(1), 70–76.

Williamson, V. J., McDonald, C., Deutsch, D., Griffiths, T. D., & Stewart, L. (2010). Faster decline of pitch memory over time in congenital amusia. *Advances in Cognitive Psychology / University of Finance and Management in Warsaw, 6*, 15–22.

Zatorre, R. J., Evans, A. C., & Meyer, E. (1994). Neural mechanisms underlying melodic perception and memory for pitch. *The Journal of Neuroscience: The Official Journal of the Society for Neuroscience, 14*(4), 1908–1919.

Ziegler, J. C., Pech-Georgel, C., George, F., & Foxton, J. M. (2012). Global and local pitch perception in children with developmental dyslexia. *Brain and Language, 120*(3), 265–270.

# 20

# ASSISTED MUSIC LISTENING IN HEARING LOSS

*Tonya R. Bergeson and Rachael Frush Holt*

## Introduction

How does hearing loss affect perception and understanding of music? It is not as simple as turning down the volume on sound. Sensorineural hearing loss (with causes ranging from neurotoxic drugs to aging to genetics) involves damage to the inner ear and can result in different degrees and configurations of hearing loss. For example, when people age they might gradually lose high-frequency hearing but have no problem hearing low frequencies. Moreover, the technologies involved with assistive listening devices such as hearing aids and cochlear implants do not simply turn up the volume of sound. These aids can be programmed to process incoming sound in particular ways to amplify certain frequency bands. Hearing aids and cochlear implants were originally designed to benefit speech understanding, but engineers have begun to develop technologies to benefit music listening as well. Although tests of music perception are not included in routine examinations of hearing, clinicians are becoming more interested in how music can enhance quality of life. Finally, studying music perception in people with hearing loss can help answer questions regarding the effects of auditory deprivation on what some call the "universal language."

## Hearing Loss and Assistive Devices

The Centers for Disease Control and Prevention estimates that 2–3 per 1000 children are born with sensorineural hearing loss (CDC, 2010). Approximately 15% of people between 6 and 19 years of age have bilateral sensorineural hearing loss, and the ratio increases as age advances. Sensorineural hearing loss is a permanent condition caused by damage to structures located in the auditory periphery, typically the basilar membrane, which is located in the cochlea. Sensorineural hearing loss can, as the name suggests, be due to damage to the auditory nerve, but routine diagnostic testing does not distinguish between these two sites of lesion. The basilar membrane is organized tonotopically, meaning that it is maximally sensitive to sounds of different frequencies along its length: low frequencies are coded at the apex and high frequencies at the base. Sensorineural hearing loss can range from mild (inability to hear birds chirping, low-intensity, high-frequency sounds such as /f/ and /s/, or the sounds of a flute) to profound (inability to hear a loud motorcycle revving its engine, a rock band, and any speech sounds). Additionally, sensorineural hearing loss generally leads to reduced frequency selectivity because of damage to the cochlea. Specifically, the neural system's ability to operate as a set of auditory filters, which are narrow to carefully analyze sound spectra, change with cochlear damage, becoming broader and less selective. This broadening can result in difficulties perceiving the harmonics in complex sounds, such as musical tones (Moore, 2008a). Moreover, frequencies that would normally stimulate an area of the cochlea that is no longer functional (i.e., "dead region") can instead excite a different region of the cochlea, resulting in a different perception of pitch for those particular frequencies (Moore & Carlyon, 2005). Therefore, listeners with sensorineural hearing loss not only perceive input at reduced sensation levels (if at all), but the input is also distorted.

Deaf individuals often still enjoy music not only with the limited auditory signals they may receive, but also with visual and vibrotactile cues to the music (Good, Reed, & Russo, 2014). For example, famed percussionist Evelyn Glennie, who has had a profound high-frequency hearing loss since the age of 12 years, walks onstage with bare feet and lifts her head so that she can feel the sound vibrations from her feet and neck (Horowitz, 2012, pp. 134–138). Other individuals with hearing loss may choose assistive technologies to enhance the auditory signal. There are two basic categories of assistive devices that individuals with hearing loss can use to improve their auditory input: hearing aids and cochlear implants.

### Hearing Aids

Hearing aids are recommended for hearing losses of all severities. Conventional analog aids amplify all sounds according to a pre-set frequency response that is based on an individual's hearing loss. Some analog aids now also include the ability to program frequency responses according to various listening contexts, such as one-on-one conversation or a noisy cocktail party. Much more common, however, are digital aids, which convert sound into digital signals. Some digital hearing aids have the added benefit of noise reduction algorithms, which allow more control of acoustic feedback and loudness levels; additionally, some can self-adjust based on the acoustic environment. Nevertheless, no hearing aid provides "normal" hearing. And although hearing aids can be programmed to enhance music perception, there are still programming issues that remain, such as allowing listeners larger frequency and dynamic ranges to cover the demands of music, before delivering a normal-sounding musical signal (see Chasin & Russo, 2004 for a review). Finally, hearing aids do not completely ameliorate the reduced frequency selectivity due to sensorineural hearing loss. That is, the impaired ear distorts the sound signal, and the hearing aid effectively alters or distorts it even more (e.g., compression, expansion, etc.). The resulting distorted signal could be particularly problematic for music, where small pitch and timing differences are important in differentiating sequences, patterns, and songs.

### Cochlear Implants

Cochlear implants are auditory prostheses for listeners with the greatest degrees of hearing loss. They include an external microphone that converts sound into an electric signal, a sound processor that typically filters the electrical signal based on our understanding of speech perception, and a transmitter that passes the electrical signal to an internal receiver. This receiver sends the electrical signal to an array of electrodes surgically implanted in the cochlea that stimulate auditory nerve fibers. There is substantial variability in outcomes across cochlear implant recipients, but in general, cochlear implants transmit sound signals in a way that allows for speech and spoken language comprehension. On the other hand, cochlear implants were not designed to transmit suprasegmental information (e.g., pitch and timbre), leading to difficulty perceiving and producing music (Moore & Carlyon, 2005). One reason why cochlear implants are poor at transmitting pitch and timbre is that cochlear implant signal processing strategies have not traditionally conveyed fine spectral detail well, nor are listeners with sensorineural hearing loss able to process temporal fine structure cues well (Moore, 2008b). Another reason for cochlear implants' difficulties with pitch and timbre is that the electrode array cannot be fully inserted into the cochlea. Instead, a typical electrode array will span (at best) 1½ of the possible 2½ turns of the cochlea, beginning at the base. Additionally, it is unlikely that the frequencies in the environment will be properly mapped to their correct respective regions on the tonotypically arranged basilar membrane. In effect, the electrical stimulation to the cochlea is frequency-compressed and frequency-shifted. Finally, there are a comparatively small number of electrodes (up to 24) that provide the stimulation that approximately 13,000 inner hair cells would typically provide in a normal-hearing ear, and adjacent electrodes often stimulate overlapping regions of the basilar membrane.

## Listening to Music with Assistive Devices: Post-Lingually Deafened Adults

Despite the limitations of the assistive devices, hearing aid and cochlear implant users continue to report listening to and participating in music (e.g., Gfeller, Christ, Knutson, Witt, & Mehr, 2003). What do they hear when they listen to music?

### *Pitch*

The broad category of pitch perception includes a range of specific tasks such as pitch discrimination and melody recognition. In the following discussion, performance along particular dimensions of pitch perception for adults with hearing aids and/or cochlear implants is presented when available.

It is worth noting here that almost every study of music perception in listeners with hearing loss shows large individual variability. That is, even though the average performance might be poorer for listeners with hearing loss than normal-hearing listeners, there are often listeners with hearing loss who perform at levels similar to those of their normal-hearing peers.

### *Pitch Discrimination*

When asked to discriminate two 1–second pure tones of different frequencies, normal-hearing adults displayed better discrimination abilities than adults with cochlear implants. Nevertheless, cochlear implant users could discriminate frequency differences less than one semitone (st), one of the building blocks of music (Gfeller et al., 2002). On the other hand, when tested on pitch discrimination for complex tones, normal-hearing adults had an average threshold of 1.1 st; adults with cochlear implants had an average threshold of 7.6 st.

In another study of pitch discrimination, a third group of adults was added: short-electrode cochlear implant users who receive low-frequency acoustic information from residual hearing in addition to the electric input from the cochlear implant (Gfeller et al., 2007). This group of cochlear implant users performed at levels of pitch discrimination similar to the group of normal-hearing adults when presented with low frequencies but not at a higher frequency range. Adults who have profound hearing loss but use hearing aids alone scored 75% correct on a 3-st pitch discrimination task whereas adults with cochlear implants performed at chance (Looi, McDermott, McKay, & Hickson, 2008).

## Contour Perception

In one study of melodic contour perception, Galvin, Fu, & Nogaki (2007) asked adults to identify nine melodic contours (e.g., rising, flat, falling, flat-rising) in five intonation conditions that varied in terms of number of semitones (1–5) between successive notes in each contour. Normal-hearing adults scored 95.8% correct, whereas adults with cochlear implants scored 53.3% correct across the conditions. Other researchers have used the Montreal Battery of Evaluation of Amusias, or MBEA (Peretz, Champod, & Hyde, 2003) to examine contour perception in adults with cochlear implants. In this task participants are presented with a pair of melodies in which one note of one of the melodies may be altered in such a way that it changes the musical contours in that melody. Normal-hearing adults score 84% correct on this test, whereas adults with cochlear implants only achieve 55–61% correct performance (Peterson & Bergeson, 2015; Wright & Uchanski, 2012). Moreover, normal-hearing adults listening to 4- and 6-channel cochlear implantation simulations perform at levels similar to adults who use cochlear implants (Cooper, Tobey, & Loizou, 2008). Finally, when cochlear implant users add a hearing aid, their contour perception performance improves to 73% correct, most likely due to the enhancement of the low frequency information in the signal (Peterson & Bergeson, 2015).

## Consonance and Dissonance

Although understanding of consonance ("pleasant" or "good") and dissonance ("unpleasant" or "grating") has been put to the test in normal-hearing listeners (e.g., Schellenberg & Trainor, 1996), perception of consonance and dissonance is less well understood in listeners with assistive devices. In one study of music perception with cochlear implants, listeners were asked to discriminate whether a sound selection was music or "noise" (Wright & Uchanski, 2012). Normal-hearing adults scored 100% and those with cochlear implants performed slightly worse (92.8%), but still well above chance. This is not a surprising result because cochlear implants are essentially "noise vocoders" that process incoming frequency bands of sound and transmit the amplitude-envelope, via noise bands that match those frequency bands, to the internal electrodes of the implant. The result is a "noisy" signal. However, very little is known about whether listeners can still distinguish consonant and dissonant music under the noisy conditions of a cochlear implant.

## Scale Structure and Musical Key

The little that is known about the perception of scale structure and musical key in adults with hearing loss suggests that adults with hearing loss perform poorly in these areas. Researchers have examined perception of note changes that violate musical scale in pairs of melodies on the MBEA, and found that normal-hearing adults achieve an average score of 91% correct, whereas adults with cochlear implants (with and without hearing aids) as well as normal-hearing adults listening to 4- and 6-channel cochlear implant simulations perform at or near chance levels (Cooper et al., 2008; Peterson & Bergeson, 2015; Wright & Uchanski, 2012).

## Melody Perception

The area of music perception that has been most extensively studied in adults with hearing loss is the perception and recognition of melody. In comparisons of melody recognition without lyrics across different timbres, performance for normal-hearing adults is consistently better than that of adults with cochlear implants (Dorman, Gifford, Spahr, & McKarns, 2008; Drennan et al., 2015). When note durations are equalized so that melodies are isochronous (i.e., no rhythm cues) performance remains near ceiling for normal-hearing adults but range from 12% to 52% for cochlear implants users (Dorman et al., 2008; Drennan et al., 2015; Kong, Stickney, & Zeng, 2005; Wright & Uchanski, 2012). Melody identification with original rhythm cues is better for listeners with hearing aids (91% correct) and listeners with cochlear implants plus hearing aids (57%) than for listeners with cochlear implants alone (17–52% correct) (Looi et al., 2008; Peterson & Bergeson, 2015). Finally, isochronous melody recognition improves for listeners with severe to profound hearing loss when using a hearing aid (average scores range from 45% to 71% correct) or when using a hearing aid in combination with a cochlear implant (average scores range from 55% to 71% correct) (Dorman et al., 2008; Kong et al., 2005). As expected, the more residual hearing a listener has access to (e.g., with a contralateral-side hearing aid, a hybrid device, or a soft-surgical approach that preserves neural structures, etc.), the more that listener can use spectral cues to recognize melodies stripped of temporal and rhythmic cues.

## *Timbre*

In one of the first studies of music perception in adult cochlear implant recipients, Gfeller and Lansing (1991) asked postlingually deafened adults to complete the Musical Instrument Quality Rating task, which assesses perceived quality (e.g., beautiful versus ugly) of melodies played on nine acoustic instruments. There was a wide range in ratings, with approximately 15–85% of participants labeling the instruments "beautiful" or "pleasant." Listeners identified the correct instrument only 13.5% of the time (although the majority were not musically trained and may not have known instrument names or sounds). Several researchers have examined timbre recognition on closed-set tests of 8–9 instruments, with performance for listeners with cochlear implants averaging 37–70% correct (above chance levels) and normal-hearing adults averaging around 82–87% correct (Brockmeier et al., 2011; Drennan et al., 2015; Wright & Uchanski, 2012). Other studies have examined listeners' abilities to differentiate among several instruments playing simultaneously. For example, Brockmeier and colleagues (2011) found that normal-hearing listeners could differentiate up to four instruments, whereas cochlear implant users could differentiate only two instruments and often had the perception of a fused timbre when more than one instrument was playing. Finally, Looi et al. (2008) examined perception of timbre in adults with severe-profound hearing loss who used either hearing aids or cochlear implants. Listeners in both groups performed similarly in an instrument recognition test (HA = 69%, CI = 61%) and an ensemble recognition test (HA = 47%, CI = 43%).

## Timing

In general, adults with cochlear implants and hearing aids perform better on tasks involving perception of timing (tempo, rhythm, meter) compared to those involving pitch and timbre, with comparable performance to that of normal-hearing listeners (Brockmeier et al., 2011; Gfeller & Lansing, 1991; Looi et al., 2008; Peterson & Bergeson, 2015; Wright & Uchanski, 2012).

## Other Factors

### Emotion Perception

Very little is known about the perception of emotion in music by listeners with hearing loss. In one study, adults rated the emotions of several pieces of music on a scale of one (very sad) to ten (very happy) (Brockmeier et al., 2011). Normal-hearing listeners and those with cochlear implants gave similar emotion ratings, and these ratings were highly correlated with tempo (e.g., faster tempo related to higher rating of happiness). Nevertheless, emotions in music are much more complex than simply happy and sad, involving cues such as tempo, rhythm, pitch interval, mode, melody, and amplitude that result in emotional responses ranging from joy and triumph to nostalgia to hostility (see Timmers, this volume; Juslin, & Sloboda, 2011). Future studies are necessary to determine the musical properties that lead to an emotional response in listeners with hearing loss.

### Preference

In a study examining ratings of liking and complexity of classical, country, and pop music, Gfeller and colleagues (2003) found that adults with cochlear implants did not prefer any of the three genres, whereas normal-hearing listeners liked classical music more than pop, and pop more than country. Moreover, normal-hearing listeners, but not listeners with implants, rated familiar items as more likeable than unfamiliar items. Both groups of listeners rated classical music as most complex and country music as least complex. Finally, Gfeller et al. found a positive correlation between liking and complexity for normal-hearing listeners, but a negative correlation for listeners with cochlear implants.

Wright and Uchanski (2012) asked listeners to rate the same musical selections as used in Gfeller et al. (2003). They found that cochlear implant users rated music as more pleasant sounding than their normal-hearing peers listening to cochlear implant simulations. However, both groups rated music as less pleasant sounding than normal-hearing listeners. It is quite possible that if the normal-hearing listeners had more time to accommodate to the simulation they would also find the simulation less harsh and more pleasant.

Although listening to music with hearing aids as opposed to cochlear implants enables better pitch perception (Looi et al., 2008) and melody recognition (Looi et al., 2008; Peterson & Bergeson, 2015), adults who have severe-to-profound hearing loss and use cochlear implants rate music as more pleasant sounding than adults with similar levels of hearing loss who use hearing aids (Looi, McDermott, McKay, & Hickson, 2007). Similar to Gfeller et al. (2003), both groups of listeners rate music with multiple instruments (i.e., more complex) as sounding less pleasant than music with a single instrument (i.e., less complex) (Looi et al., 2007).

Importantly, music perception and music appraisal are distinguishable outcomes following cochlear implantation (Gfeller et al., 2008). Factors such as music listening experience after implantation and performance on a visual cognitive task predicted preferences for instrumental music, whereas music listening experience prior to implantation, use of bilateral implants or a cochlear implant plus a hearing aid, and performance on speech perception in noise predicted preference for music with lyrics. To date, researchers have found no correlation between performance on various music perception tests and music enjoyment in cochlear implant users (Brockmeier et al., 2011; Drennan et al., 2015; Wright & Uchanski, 2012).

## Listening to Music with Assistive Devices: Pre-Lingually Deafened Children

Adults with post-lingual hearing loss have had the opportunity to build their internal representations and understandings of music over years of experience listening to, participating in, and learning music. Children with pre-lingual hearing loss, however, must develop their understanding of aural music using a different set of cues received through hearing aids or cochlear implants. How do children hear music after receiving hearing aids or cochlear implants following congenital and pre-lingual hearing loss? We turn now to an examination of these matters.

### *Pitch*

#### *Pitch Discrimination*

Even though prelingually deafened children have not had the opportunity to develop internal representations of music prior to receiving a cochlear implant, they still show some patterns of music perception similar to adult cochlear implant recipients (Bergeson, Chin, Anderson, Simpson, & Kuhns, 2010; Houston et al., 2012; Nakata, Trehub, Mitani, & Kanda, 2006). Like adult cochlear implant recipients, there is significant variability in children's pitch perception performance, ranging from 9.5% to 92.5% on a pitch discrimination and ranking task (Chen et al., 2010). In studies of pitch discrimination, children with and without hearing loss were asked to determine whether the second in a pair of notes was higher or lower than the first. Normal-hearing children were able to discriminate pairs of tones that were separated by 7 semitones, whereas children with cochlear implants discriminated tones separated by 14 semitones (See, Driscoll, Gfeller, Kliethermes, & Oleson, 2013). Jung et al. (2012) found even better pitch direction discrimination of 3-tone complexes (3 semitones) in children with cochlear implants. When asked to determine whether two tones were different in pitch (regardless of direction), children with cochlear implants can discriminate tones separated by only 0.5 semitones (Vongpaisal, Trehub, & Schellenberg, 2006).

#### *Contour Perception*

See et al. (2013) presented 5- to 10-year-olds with spoken and sung sentences and asked them to determine whether the sentences were statements (falling contour) or questions (rising contour). Normal-hearing children performed better than children with cochlear implants (83% vs. 63% correct). In another study, Bergeson and colleagues (2010) asked children ages 5–15 years to listen to four vocal pitch contours (rising, falling, rising-falling, falling-rising) and then recorded their vocal imitations. Normal-hearing children produced more accurate contours (75% correct) than children with cochlear implants (63% correct), although the latter group still performed recognizable contours for three out of the four contours. Both groups of children performed best for the rising contour, followed by the falling and rising-falling contours, and finally the falling-rising contour.

## Melody Perception

In a study of music recognition, children with cochlear implants identified pop songs just as well as normal-hearing children (Vongpaisal, Trehub, Schellenberg, & Papsin, 2004). When the vocals were removed from the stimuli by using a karaoke version the children with cochlear implants could still identify the songs but were less accurate than normal-hearing children. Their performance dropped significantly as compared to normal-hearing children when the pop songs were presented as piano melodies with no additional cues. Similarly, when other researchers presented young listeners with isochronous melodies, children with cochlear implants achieved only 11% correct performance (Jung et al., 2012).

## Other Measures of Pitch Perception

As of yet, the perception of consonance and dissonance, scale structure, and musical key have not been rigorously studied in children with hearing loss who use cochlear implants and hearing aids.

## Timbre

Jung and colleagues (2012) asked children with cochlear implants to identify musical instruments in a closed-set task. They found that children performed higher than chance level (34% correct). They performed most accurately for the guitar timbre, and often confused flute and violin timbres.

## Timing

Most studies have been conducted on pitch and melody perception rather than timing. However, Nakata, et al. (2006) examined timing in songs of children with and without hearing loss, and found the two groups' timing of performances to be similar to one another.

## Other Factors

### Emotion Perception

Volkova and colleagues (2013) presented children with and without hearing loss with "happy" (major mode, rapid tempo) and "sad" (minor mode, slow tempo) piano pieces and asked the children to point to a picture of a child laughing or crying. Normal-hearing children performed at ceiling (98%). Children with cochlear implants performed more poorly (80%) but still above chance levels.

*Preference*

Although children with cochlear implants perform more poorly than normal-hearing children on a number of music perception tasks, they still participate in music lessons and activities and rate music favorably (e.g., Trehub, Vongpaisal, & Nakata, 2009).

## Discussion

### *The Parts Do Not Equal the Whole*

Although we now know quite a lot about perception of the various components of music by listeners who use hearing aids and cochlear implants, it turns out that there is little to no relationship between the perception of music's component parts and ratings of music enjoyment (Brockmeier et al., 2011; Drennan et al., 2015; Wright & Uchanski, 2012). It is possible that the areas in which there is very little research, such as musical tonality and melodic expectancies, are the "glue" which "holds the parts together" to give a sense of the larger music picture. Further research is needed to determine the role these musical features play in music perception in listeners with assistive hearing devices.

### *The Ear Is Connected to the Brain*

It is also possible that general cognitive skills play a large role in music perception in listeners with hearing loss. Deficits in cognitive skills such as attention, working memory, and executive function, may be a byproduct of a period of auditory deprivation (e.g., AuBuchon, Pisoni, & Kronenberger, 2015; Houston et al., 2012). Indeed, there is evidence that performance on music perception tasks is related to cognitive skills in listeners with hearing loss (Gfeller et al., 2008; Vongpaisal et al., 2004). For example, children with cochlear implants have better pitch discrimination skills in tasks that compare pairs of tones alone rather than in the context of melodies (Vongpaisal et al., 2006). In a study of children's song production, Bergeson et al. (2010) found that children with cochlear implants could sing the beginning of the song "Happy Birthday" with accuracy similar to that of normal-hearing children, but their pitch accuracy decreased after the first phrase. It is possible that the cognitive demands of keeping in mind simultaneously the melody, rhythm, lyrics, and motoric output outpaced the children's cognitive abilities. In fact, music and speech therapists have used music as an integral part of speech therapy for children with hearing loss who use assistive devices (Barton & Robbins, 2015). It is possible that training cognitive skills such as attention, sequence learning, and working memory through music, which has high levels of enjoyment for children, might transfer to other areas such as speech and hearing (e.g., Tierney, Krizman, Skoe, Johnston, & Kraus, 2013).

### *Clinical Assessment of Music*

If perception of the component parts of music and music enjoyment are independent for listeners with hearing loss what is the value of measuring music perception in clinical assessments? Measuring individual features of music is consistent with typical testing of hearing, which isolates frequencies and amplitudes, and testing of speech, which traditionally focuses in on perception of parts of words (e.g., minimal pairs), words, or sentences in quiet or in noise. Most tests of hearing and speech perception do not examine perception of natural conversation with multiple participants, which is more complex and difficult to interpret. It follows, then, that music batteries developed for use in the clinic might focus on the component pieces of music rather than on judgments of larger works of music. Listeners with hearing loss participate in and enjoy music regardless of their relatively poorer performance on music perception tests such as pitch, melody, and timbre. It could be argued that enjoyment of and participation in music are the most clinically relevant aspects of music for listeners with hearing loss.

## Enjoyment of Music

There has been a wave of research and literature breaking down the ways in which music training benefits us in various ways, such as helping to ameliorate the deleterious effects of aging and degraded speech in noise perception (Slater et al., 2015). For the most part, the research on music cognition in listeners with hearing loss follows this line of reasoning. If there are benefits of music for normal-hearing listeners, we should understand how listeners with hearing loss perceive and understand music to determine the comparative benefits. However, this line of reasoning ignores the larger question of music enjoyment. Although there have been some studies that have examined ratings of music appraisal among listeners with hearing loss we still know very little about how music makes listeners with hearing loss *feel*. This spans the range of complex emotions normal-hearing listeners experience while listening to music to the feelings of identifying with lyrics to fitting into a social community. And, of course, we know even less about how all listeners with and without hearing loss, regardless of use of assistive listening devices, feel the physical features of music. As Evelyn Glennie noted, "Music is about communication . . . it isn't just something that maybe physically sounds good or orally sounds interesting; it's something far, far deeper than that" (Humphries, 2001).

## Core Reading

Brockmeier, S. J., Fitzgerald, D., Searle, O., Fitzgerald, H., Grasmeder, M., Hilbig, S., Vermiere, K., Peterreins, M., Heydner, S., and Arnold, W. (2011). The MuSIC perception test: A novel battery for testing music perception of cochlear implant users. *Cochlear Implants International, 12*, 10–20.

Drennan, W. R., Oleson, J. J., Gfeller, K., Crosson, J., Driscoll, V., Won, J. H., Anderson, E. S., &. Rubinstein, J. T. (2015). Clinical evaluation of music perception, appraisal and experience in cochlear implant users. *International Journal of Audiology, 54*(2), 114–123.

Jung, K. H., Won, J. H., Drennan, W. R., Jameyson, E., Miyasaki, G., Norton, S. J., & Rubinstein, J. T. (2012). Psychoacoustic performance and music and speech perception in prelingually deafened children with cochlear implants. *Audiology & Neuro-otology, 17*, 189–197.

Trehub, S. E., Vongpaisal, T., & Nakata, T. (2009). Music in the lives of deaf children with cochlear implants. *Annals of the New York Academy of Sciences, 1169*, 534–542.

Wright, R., & Uchanski, R. M. (2012). Music perception and appraisal: Cochlear implant users and simulated cochlear implant listening. *Journal of the American Academy of Audiology, 23*, 350–365.

## Further References

AuBuchon, A. M., Pisoni, D. B., & Kronenberger, W. G. (2015). Verbal processing speed and executive functioning in long-term cochlear implant users. *Journal of Speech, Language & Hearing Research, 58*(1), 151–162.

Barton, C., & Robbins, A. M. (2015). Jumpstarting auditory learning in children with cochlear implants through music experiences. *Cochlear Implants International, 16*(S3), S51–S62.

Bergeson, T. R., Chin, S. B., Anderson, L. L., Simpson, A. K., & Kuhns, M. J. (2010). *Vocal prosody and song production in children with cochlear implants.* Paper presented at the 11th International Conference on Cochlear Implants and Other Implantable Auditory Technologies, Stockholm, Sweden.

Centers for Disease Control and Prevention (CDC) (2010). Identifying infants with hearing loss—United States, 1999–2007. *Morbidity and Mortality Weekly Report, 59*(8), 220–223.

Chasin, M., & Russo, F. A. (2004). Hearing aids and music. *Trends in Amplification, 8,* 35–47.

Chen, J. K.-C., Chuang, A. Y. C., McMahon, C., Hsieh, J.-C., Tung, T.-H., & Li, L. P.-H. (2010). Music training improves pitch perception in prelingually deafened children with cochlear implants. *Pediatrics, 125,* e793–e800.

Cooper, W. B., Tobey, E., & Loizou, P. C. (2008). Music perception by cochlear implant and normal hearing listeners as measured by the Montreal Battery for Evaluation of Amusia. *Ear & Hearing, 29,* 618–626.

Dorman, M. F., Gifford, R. H., Spahr, A. J., & McKarns, S. A. (2008). The benefits of combining acoustic and electric stimulation for the recognition of speech, voice and melodies. *Audiology & Neurotology, 13*(2), 105–112.

Galvin, J. J., Fu, Q. J., & Nogaki, G. (2007). Melodic contour identification by cochlear implant listeners. *Ear & Hearing, 28,* 302–319.

Gfeller, K., Christ, A., Knutson, J. F., Witt, S., & Mehr, M. (2003). The effects of familiarity and complexity on appraisal of complex songs by cochlear ipmlant recipients and normal hearing adults. *Journal of Music Therapy, 40,* 78–112.

Gfeller, K., & Lansing, C. R. (1991). Melodic, rhythmic, and timbral perception of adult cochlear implant users. *Journal of Speech and Hearing Research, 34,* 916–920.

Gfeller, K., Oleson, J. J., Knutson, J. F., Breheny, P., Driscoll, V., & Olszewski, C. (2008). Multivariate predictors of music perception and appraisal by adult cochlear implant users. *Journal of the American Academy of Audiology, 19,* 120–134.

Gfeller, K., Turner, C., Mehr, M., Woodworth, G., Fearn, R., Knutson, J. F., Witt, S., & Stordahl, J. (2002). Recognition of familiar melodies by adult cochlear implant recipients and normal-hearing adults. *Cochlear Implants International, 3*(1), 29–53.

Gfeller, K., Turner, C., Oleson, J. J., Zhang, X., Gantz, B., Froman, R., & Olszewski, C. (2007). Accuracy of cochlear implant recipients on pitch perception, melody recognition, and speech reception in noise. *Ear & Hearing, 28,* 412–423.

Good, A., Reed, M. J., & Russo, F. A. (2014). Compensatory plasticity in the deaf brain: Effects on the perception of music. *Brain Sciences, 4*(4), 560–574.

Horowitz, S. S. (2012). *The Universal Sense: How Hearing Shapes the Mind.* New York, NY: Bloomsbury.

Houston, D. M., Beer, J., Bergeson, T. R., Chin, S. B., Pisoni, D. B., & Miyamoto, R. T. (2012). The ear is connected to the brain: Some new directions in the study of children with cochlear implants at Indiana University's DeVault Otologic Research Laboratory. *Journal of the American Academy of Audiology, 23,* 446–463.

Humphries, S. (2001, October 12). Glennie creates fresh vibes. *The Christian Science Monitor.* Retrieved from www.csmonitor.com/2001/1012/p20s1-alip.html

Juslin, P. N., & Sloboda, J. A. (2011) (Eds.). *Music and emotion: Theory, research, applications.* New York, NY: Oxford University Press.

Kong, Y.-Y., Stickney, G. S., & Zeng, F.-G. (2005). Speech and melody recognition in binaurally combined acoustic and electric hearing. *Journal of the Acoustical Society of America, 117,* 1351–1361.

Looi, V., McDermott, H., McKay, C., & Hickson, L. (2007). Comparisons of quality ratings for music by cochlear implant and hearing aid users. *Ear & Hearing, 28*(2), 59S–61S.

Looi, V., McDermott, H., McKay, C., & Hickson, L. (2008). Music perception of cochlear implant users compared with that of hearing aid users. *Ear & Hearing, 29,* 421–434.

Moore, B. C. J. (2008a). Basic auditory processes involved in the analysis of speech sounds. *Philosophical Transactions of the Royal Society B, 363*(1493), 947–963.

Moore, B.C. J. (2008b). The role of temporal fine structure processing in pitch perception, masking, and speech perception for normal-hearing and hearing-impaired people. *Journal of the Association for Research in Otolaryngology, 9*, 399–406.

Moore, B.C. J., & Carlyon, R. P. (2005). Perception of pitch by people with cochlear hearing loss and by cochlear implant users. *Springer Handbook of Auditory Research, 24*, 234–277.

Nakata, T., Trehub, S. E., Mitani, C., & Kanda, Y. (2006). Pitch and timing in the songs of deaf children with cochlear implants. *Music Perception, 24*, 147–154.

Peretz, I., Champod, S., & Hyde, K. L. (2003). Varieties of musical disorders: The Montreal Battery of Evaluation of Amusia. *Annals of the New York Academy of Sciences, 999*, 58–75.

Peterson, N. R., & Bergeson, T. R. (2015). Contribution of hearing aids to music perception by cochlear implant users. *Cochlear Implants International, 16*(S3), S71–S78.

Schellenberg, E. G., & Trainor, L. J. (1996). Sensory consonance and the perceptual similarity of complex-tone harmonic intervals: Tests of adult and infant listeners. *Journal of the Acoustical Society of America, 100*, 3321–3328.

See, R. L., Driscoll, V., Gfeller, K., Kliethermes, S., & Oleson, J. J. (2013). Speech intonation and melodic contour recognition in children with cochlear implants and with normal hearing. *Otology & Neurotology, 34*(3), 490–498.

Slater, J., Skoe, E., Strait, D. L., O'Connell, S., Thompson, E., & Kraus, N. (2015). Music training improves speech-in-noise perception: Longitudinal evidence from a community-based music program. *Behavioural Brain Research, 291*, 244–252.

Tierney, A., Krizman, J., Skoe, E., Johnston, K., & Kraus, N. (2013). High school music classes enhance the neural processing of speech. *Frontiers in Psychology, 4*, 855. doi: 10.3389/fpsyg.2013.00855

Volkova, A., Trehub, S. E., Schellenberg, E. G., Papsin, B., & Gordon, K. A. (2013). Children with bilateral cochlear implants identify emotion in speech and music. *Cochlear Implants International, 14*, 81–91.

Vongpaisal, T., Trehub, S. E., & Schellenberg, E. G. (2006). Song recognition by children and adolescents with cochlear implants. *Journal of Speech, Language, and Hearing Research, 49*, 1091–1103.

Vongpaisal, T., Trehub, S. E., Schellenberg, E. G., & Papsin, B. (2004). Music recognition by children with cochlear implants. *International Congress Series, 1273*, 193–196.

# PART 3

# Making and Using Music

# 21

# CREATING MUSIC

## Composition

*Roger T. Dean*

I'm hearing music. Debussy uses the froth of the sea dying on the sands, ebbing and flowing. Bach is a mathematician. Mozart is the impersonal divine. Chopin reveals his most intimate life. Schoenberg, through his self, reaches the classical self of everyone. Beethoven is the stormy human elixir searching for divinity and only finding it in death.

(Lispector, 1978/2004, p. 6)

### Introduction

If composition is as all-embracing as Lispector has it above, what consistent cognitive features can it present? Let us first briefly distinguish composition and improvisation, and then note their underlying links, and the topics of this chapter. Most composition is distinctive in being long-term, discontinuous but recurrent, often mediated by notation (including recording). Composition is usually the endeavor of a single person, though informed by their culture, society and the discipline of music as practiced by their peers (these aspects are indexed in the socio-cultural apex of Figure 21.1, and relate to composer Jonathan Harvey's external "inspiration," see Deliège & Wiggins, 2006). But collaboration is common in popular music composition (Bennett, 2012). To contrast with these facets of composition, improvisation is short-term: The music is sounded at the same time frame it is conceived. Collaboration is routine in improvisation: Improvisers respond fluently to unpredicted events.

This simplistic comparison hides a continuum. No improvisation is removed from present and previous context or experience. And many classical composers of Western Art Music (WAM) were improvisers (e.g. Beethoven, see Kinderman, 2009). Their composing commonly involved "applied improvisation" (Smith & Dean, 1997), where recurrent improvisation solidifies into a reusable composition. Conversely, many improvisers use "referents," pre-organized frameworks for realization with substantial newly improvised components: The framework rarely specifies sounds much, unlike a notated composition, so quite different sounds (e.g. instrumental vs. recorded) may be used. Applied improvisation is used in many arts (e.g. theatre and film by Mike Leigh and Jacques Rivette).

There is also a collaborative creative, somewhat improvisatory role for performers in realizing the generative texts of notated WAM (Cook, 2013). Musical performance is "sociality in sound" Cook says (p. 273), pointing to a post-structural view of listeners as co-creators of musical meaning (Sawyer, 2005). In my view, while hearing a piece, listeners can recurrently delineate for themselves the meaningful components within it, particularly when the piece is stylistically unfamiliar (Dean, 2005). This delineation engenders meaning and affect, which we cannot consider here. In contrast, the idea of WAM composition as converting earlier aural-oral traditions into an aural-literate one, requiring listener expertise (Barrett, 2005), relates composition to "product creativity" (Sawyer, 1995), which demands an output object with prefigured impact for consumption by others, who thus require literacy in the tradition of such outputs, being here compositions.

So we can consider what are the long-term cognitive processes in composition. Problem solving at large may be thought as having multiple dimensions of variation, an extended time frame, and as approachable by empirical more than experimental methods (Newell & Simon, 1972). Such ideas require further investigation. Applying them to composition, I briefly survey composers' views. I push aside ideas of genius or "big Creativity" (with a capital C), focusing on routine professional creativity: composition with a small c. After a broad synopsis, composition since 1950 is emphasized. Next, at a more general level, I address computational inputs to composition in order to approach the central topic of the chapter: empirical studies on cognition within composition. I close with suggestions for future work.

## Composers on Ideas and Mental Processes during Composition: A Synopsis

The Ancient Greeks viewed creativity as a gift of the muses, an instantaneous contribution of the Gods: Sometimes Mozart's compositions are thought comparably immediate. The idea of a dialogue of ideas continuously churning statistically in the mind, with solutions occasionally surfacing, is a contemporary interpretation, of which computational modeling frameworks will allow empirical evaluation (Wiggins & Forth, 2015). The view still presented by some composers that creativity takes an instant, can probably be attributed more to psychological/socio-economic demand in interview, than to realistic retrospection (Burnard in Collins, 2012). Most composers would instead agree that composition is a long term cycle/iteration, akin to that modeled for practice-led research and research-led practice (Smith & Dean, 2009). Consequently, cognitive "regularities" that are routine for most people (not just creative workers) may be important (Bink & Marsh, 2000) and I consider these below.

Surveys of composers' attitudes stem from Bahle's in 1935 (Collins, 2012). I will compare these with models of creativity. Blum summarizes statements by composers/theoreticians across centuries (Blum, 2009): The statements advocate diverse musical systems, tunings, scales, harmonies and performance practice (e.g. those of Zarlino, C. P.E. Bach, Rameau). But our concern is their remarkably consistent thoughts on composition. Blum (2009) quotes:

> Lampadius (1537): CONTRIVE notable phrases in one's mind; WEIGH these judiciously; proceed to WORKING OUT. . . . Busoni (1916): musician improvises; improvisation captured in notation; improvisation reborn through appropriate responses to notated signs. . . . Ishaq al-Mawslii (d. 850 C.E.): male musician creates melody; . . . woman revises and renews the melody.
>
> *(pp. 243, 247)*

A process is shared, and notation is seen as a means of transmission: It can also facilitate manipulation, transformation, and co-relation (Barrett, 2005). As philosopher John Locke appreciated (Dean & Bailes, 2007): "A musician used to any tune will find that, let it but once begin in his head, the ideas of the several notes of it will follow one another orderly in his understanding, without any care or attention" (Book 2, ch. XXXIII, para 6). Locke's ideas lead statistically, implicitly or explicitly by means of notation, to creation of relations between sound structures, movements and meaning. A seemingly inevitable common process is signaled.

In the early 20th century, assumptions of composition were challenged, and broadened. Pioneer American composer Henry Cowell wrote (Cowell, 1996) of the need to use "scientifically co-ordinated materials," and that the new resources he proposed (in pitch, chords, rhythms) "add to the possibilities of musical expression, and are therefore vital potentialities and not merely cold facts" (p.xv). The resources included systematized pitch clusters, rare interval combinations, and complex non-binary rhythms. Many of his ideas were most fully explored by others (for rhythm: Conlon Nancarrow using the piano roll, and much later, computational algorithmic music makers, see Milne & Dean, 2016). Cowell (1926) also contributed to the psychological literature, suggesting that a composer needs to effortfully self-educate his/her imagery, so as to develop a "sound-mind," that can imagine combinations of sounds beyond those of instruments, another challenge to pre-ordained systems.

Overall, composers from aural-oral and aural-literate traditions before 1950 shared ideas quite similar to views of creative processes at large, such as the GENEPLORE model (Finke, 1996), which refers to a repeated cycle: generate/explore/refine/select. To this, I add from an evolutionary and artificial life (aLife[1]) perspective (Whitelaw, 2004) the need to maintain diversity of materials within the system. Our focus is next on later composers' views, many reflecting new technical and socio-economic conditions of music creation.

## Composers Since 1950 on Music Creation

American composer Roger Reynolds has written several books concerning music and its societal context (Reynolds, 2013). He engages with complex sounds, artificial and natural, and their relation to movement, agency and spatial distribution, as much as he engages with the idea of organizing instrumental notes. He references other composers' contributions, such as the "pithy" ideas of Xenakis (1971) that focused on usable mathematical/statistical structures, and on neglected systems of pitch, tuning, rhythm and harmony. Such composers do not simply rely on pre-existing forms, structures, and constraints (such as "grammars"). They create their own boundary conditions, and a "tradition of the moment" (McAdams, 2004). As above, I see this in both improvisation and composition as the creative construction of potentially new fields of signs that may bear meaning (semiotics) and remain responsive to external influences.

Thus Dufourt responds to external influences in the form of paintings, finding movement and instability and needing new musical (dis)continuity, that defines "a world of its own" (p. 643) not reproducing an external reality (Pasler, 2013). This requires transformations and new logical relations (such as equivalence and substitution) on micro- and macro-temporal and spatial scales. Creating new technologies applicable to works beyond the present one is also important.

This is in part because new technologies now inform many visual contexts of composition. In video games, "adaptive" music may be apposite: The composer provides modules that are either triggered by aspects of game progress or arranged adaptively by the video producer (roughly the converse of film procedures). Interesting also is the "app album," or interactive algorithmic composition for tablets: Björk's *Biophilia* was stimulated by touch screen technology, becoming "an artistic vision of the relationships among nature, technology, and music" (Dibben, 2013, p. 686), features it shares with earlier intermedia works in computational aLife (McCormack, 2003). One objective for Björk was music-educative: to encourage non-professionals to make or control music, another transformation of the role of the viewer-listener. Visualization is used by Björk to encourage awareness of musical structures and how to play with them; giving a "curated experience of coherent artistic vision" (Dibben, 2013, p. 688). Related ideas inhabit environmental installation pieces, some with overtly activist agendas.

The new technologies offered by electronic literature (text works including digital media components) are important for composers, though still under-populated, and not widely appreciated by artists of sound and visual art (see the online Collections 1–3 of the premier Electronic Literature Organization). In contrast, the idea that composers might make sound from visual objects is more exploited, e.g. in some of Xenakis' influential work, in software such as MetaSynth, and in the concept of algorithmic synesthesia (Dean et al., 2006).

As a final innovation, let us reconsider the improviser as a technological tool for composers. Duke Ellington emphasized that a jazz composition (in his case, a referent of some detail but certainly not specifying all the notes or sounds that would appear) depends on the particular interpreters for whom it is written. Subsequently, comprovisations (compositions for improvisers) often require the improvisers to fulfill specific creative roles. My late colleague Graham Collier discussed this (Collier, 2009; Dean, 1992), and the title of one CD we made together, *directing 14 Jackson Pollocks*, symbolizes the relationship. As he said, "[W]hat I do as a jazz composer . . . is to work with highly skilled musicians, the 14 . . . of the title, to produce music . . . that . . . happens in real time, once" (2009, p. 342). Similarly, the title work of one of my CDs with austraLYSIS, *History Goes Everywhere,* involves using experienced improvisers' deep knowledge of prior technologies (styles) in jazz and improvisation as referent material.

## Computers as Musical Collaborators

Since the availability of affordable computers, composers (and improvisers) have considered the roles such machines could play as collaborators/partners in music making. Computer- and computer-assisted music necessarily involve different approaches to composition from those engaging conventional notation, permitting a more extensive and rapid generative searching of an available solution space of transformations of a sonic structure (Bainbridge et al., 2010; Dean, 2009). A notable composers' interface, *Polyphony* facilitates the interaction of note, synthesizer, and effect sculpting, and has been used to study 12 experienced composers each making within an hour a 20-second piece related to a specific Webern Bagatelle (Garcia et al., 2014).

In a complementary way, computational models of cognition predict some applications of cognition in composing (Brown et al., 2015). Psychology often contrasts "bottom up" processes, where sensory stimuli have necessary physical impacts on the body and correlated perceptual effects, with "top down" processes, in which learnt experience transforms the cognition of the stimuli. Miranda interprets this dichotomy within computer-assisted composition as Dionysian and Apollonian approaches (in Collins, 2012). Computational systems are used to convert (potentially Dionysian) physical gestures into music, and allow "external" unpredictability in composition (e.g. ENACTIV, Spasov, 2011).

So called *Live algorithms* are computational forms of composition that an interpreter or improviser can use in performance: These are commonly written in MAXMSP or Supercollider, and used in repeated performances, or in long term installations, autonomous or user-driven. A more recent arrival is *Live Coding* (Magnusson, 2014), often involving real-time coding during performance to generate, loop, transform, and overlay sound. Here the algorithm itself is constructed live. The code is often displayed as it is being written and used. Having worked extensively with live algorithms and modestly with live coding, I consider the cognitive demands of conceiving code while predicting and analyzing its consequences (as in live coding) to be even greater than those of live algorithms. Live coders often suggest that their coding fluency increases with experience, perhaps reducing cognitive demands.

## Empirical Investigations of Cognition in Composition

So what does recurrent application to a particular aspect of composition over a period of time allow that is not achievable in a single session, and how? In the Figure, I synthesize the ideas above with my own views as composer/cognitive researcher to offer a process diagram of composition. While long-term memory is a common object of study, like learning, long-term development of ideas and solutions has been less studied given the magnitude/duration of the task, and the case of music is no exception. This section considers some of the published work, opening with a discussion of our intrinsic abilities and potentials.

### *Aptitude*

Musical aptitude may be distinct from other creative aptitude or general cognitive ability. Recent genome-wide linkage analyses indicate that a region on chromosome 4 (4q22.1) may be critical for compositional aptitude, and it overlaps another region of genes involved in general musical potential and appreciation (Oikkonen et al., 2016). While functions of many of these genes are partly understood, it is still difficult to predict compositional abilities from this.

One can say roughly the same of neuroimaging of composition, though with greater temporal/sequential resolution in these analyses in the future, this will surely change. Presently, there is little dynamic neuroimaging of composing rather than improvising (the latter is reviewed in Vuust & Kringelbach, this volume, and elsewhere, e.g. Beaty, 2015). Common to improvisation and composition seems to be a default mode network (DMN), including the dorsal premotor cortical regions (dPMC), and the supplementary and pre-supplementary motor areas (SMA and pre-SMA), as "all imaging studies of musical improvisation to date implicate at least one" (Bashwiner et al., 2016). This statement is taken from a study on brain structure in relation to self-assessed creativity of 239 STEM University students and academics. It correlated surface area or volume of these areas and of emotion-related regions with creativity. "Creativity" here comprised both improvisation and composition. Imaging studies suggest these regions support many of the cognitive processes in Figure 21.1. Note though that a network implied by current dynamic neuroimaging is usually one of coincidence rather than of the sequential and causal interactions cognition requires. Analogously, differences in brain surface/volume may be cause or consequence of creative activity, relating to the activity or compensating for it. EEG studies, including some on people with brain

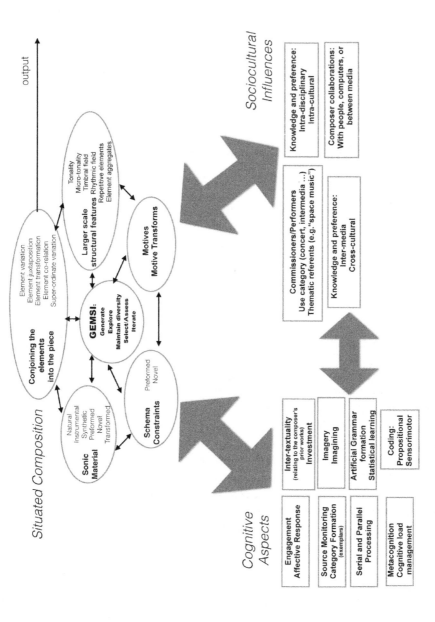

*Figure 21.1* Selective representation of factors playing a role in composition. All compositional processes (top) are inter-related recurrently via GEMSI (centre). No entry point to the compositional processes is indicated, as a composer may enter at any point. The cognitive processes are discussed in the text, and an effort is made there to relate disparate terminologies to those in the figure. Some additional views deserve referencing here: the need for engagement and affective response related to the ongoing composition (Brown, & Dillon in Collins, 2012), and possible limits to perceptible relational complexity (Halford, Wilson, & Phillips, 1998). The chapter does not consider socio-cultural influences indicated on the diagram nor distinctions between experimental and conceptual creativity; also implied by GEMSI (but see Katz in Collins, 2012).

damage, seem to imply a special role of the right hemisphere in generative musical behavior (Brattico & Tervaniemi, 2006). But insecurity of interpretation is acknowledged in these studies.

There is little evidence that composers are any more "creative" in relation to specified tasks than their musical peers such as improvisers. In a study of 150 largely White Caucasians in the USA, general creativity scores were modestly correlated with the number of compositions produced, but comparably so with experience in performing jazz or bluegrass, forms involving some improvisation (Goncy & Waehler, 2006). Might studies of composers' psychological traits provide useful pointers? The use of Catten's 16 feature questionnaire suggests preferential adoption by composers of "expedient" approaches, i.e. the use of heuristics that allow reliable and efficient solutions that may not be optimized (Kemp, 1996). Similarly, it suggested "dominance" as a trait (a wish to control other things). Kemp's findings are roughly consistent with stereotypic ideas of composers as introverted, solitary, divergent in thinking, low in compassion, and suffering almost as much as enjoying their work; but the evidence for this is weak. More recently, Big Five Aspect personality tests of 40 undergraduate composers from Australian higher education institutions (Garrido & Davidson, 2015), revealed trait distinctions between those favoring "handwriting" composition or "technology." Both technology and chance methods aided the latter group, who showed more extraversion. The evidence was mildly supportive of the stereotypic views of (handwriting) composers. Implications for cognitive processes in composers are unclear, but it is encouraging that even short experiential interventions substantially enhance attitudes towards composition in high school and university students (Menard & Rosen, 2016).

### *Cognition During the Compositional Process*

Let us now consider further GEMSI, the Generate-Explore-Select-Iterate framework of Figure 21.1. GEMSI paraphrases GENEPLORE and adds an M step to "maintain diversity." This retains a range of options even while selecting amongst them, and is informed by the necessities of evolution. In biology, maintenance of diversity is important for adaptability and selection and has to be balanced against loss of diversity (similarly in aLife art, McCormack & d'Inverno, 2012; Whitelaw, 2004). The GEMSI process belongs to a line of models of creative processes going back at least to Wallas (1926), who referred to preparation, incubation, illumination and verification, where illumination is akin to forming a Gestalt, or as in the figure, forming manipulable propositions/co-relations.

Arguably (Bink & Marsh, 2000) the cognitive processes in creative activities are domain-general, shared with those in routine, less creatively focused activities (the observed role of the DMN supports this view, which would also imply their origin in evolutionary processes). Such a domain-general argument espouses the GEMSI model, but the tasks generally studied are short term, mostly non-recurrent; nevertheless the source monitoring (discerning the origins or novelty of items) and metacognitive prioritization of components of GEMSI are already present. The implication is that we should consider how people with no special expertise engage in composition, alongside expert composers.

Simonton (2014) reviewed the development of many kinds of creative expertise, implicating diverse factors from genetics, environment, education, and drives to personal learning and broadening. For example, fluid intelligence is needed to create verbal metaphors, which require idea generation and transformation (Silvia & Beaty, 2012), and so it may contribute to musical motive processing. Simonton's review (2014) supports numerous uni- and bi-directional interactions and recurrence with change, as employed in the Figure.

Approaching the development of imagery and imagining from a behavioral perspective, Bailes & Bishop distinguish four levels of imagery in composers differing in abstraction, predictability and non-conscious accessibility, and in their compositional roles (see their chapter in Collins, 2012). These levels may also represent developmental stages of expertise in imagery, which music creators perhaps engage more than other groups. Empirical data on imaging loudness (Bailes et al., 2012) and more complex musical features is developing. Imaging of musical features is not solely motor imaging, though the two often overlap.

Figure 21.1 indicates that composition often commences with making melodies (if pitched and instrumental) or "motives" (in any kind of music, including noise-based, electroacoustic, percussive) that might be further used. So we need to understand motive making itself, and how this changes during development and pedagogical guidance. Composition teaching is limited in schools and higher education, and mostly based on the "eminence" model (imitate eminent examples); but a "craft" based approach like GEMSI, encouraging student-centered developments, is developing in several cultures (Lupton & Bruce, 2010). Bamberger, studying musically untrained students, provided pre-composed "tune-blocks" for sequencing using a computer interface, and efforts towards continuity and whole/part relationships were observed (Bamberger, 1977). Another study compared novices and experts in writing a modulating melody, given some starting material, observing stronger chunking by experts (Davidson & Welsh, 1988). Motive transformation and co-relation within tonal frameworks is facilitated by reduced representations: The sharing of a reduced set of properties can co-relate motives which arose in different transformational paths, perhaps at different stages in the composition (Large et al., 1995). Statistical-cognitive models can also generate tonal melodies acceptable to expert listeners (e.g. Wiggins et al., 2009).

The learning of some other compositional elements has been studied, including young people's devising of melody, harmony and structure (Folkestad et al., 1997), and novice and expert performance in reduced anachronistic tasks, such as completions of a harmonization of a Bach Chorale (Colley et al., 1992). Harmonization has been an informative task for algorithmic composition based on style regeneration (Ebcioğlu, 1988), but it is a narrow task compared with generating motives worthy of creative investment in making a piece. We need more open-ended tasks (without pre-set materials, for example), ideally done in naturalistic environments.

Consequent on these issues, Sloboda suggested that the only way to understand cognition in composition (particularly professional composition) is to discuss out loud during direct engagement with such wide-ranging tasks (Sloboda, 1985, 1988). This has not yet been common, but has taken the form of observation, description (by composer and observer), and sometimes recreation of compositional situations, with discussion by the originating composer of how these could be resolved.

One fascinating case study concerns Reynolds' *Angel of Death* (2002), for piano, chamber ensemble, and computer-processed sound (McAdams, 2004). This presented three categories of problem solving: first, composing motivic material that could be used both by piano and ensemble; second, composing two parts with "similar temporal structures but vastly different ways of traversing the same thematic musical materials" (p. 391); and third, a wish to perform the two major instrumental sections in either order, yet always have the later section accompanied by the computer sound. Reynolds developed microstructures to fill previously conceived macrostructures, in contrast to, e.g. approaches based on removing excess materials from a large starting set. He also used representations (e.g. graphic) to aid solving problems. The study is retrospective, with extensive interviews: It is a small but important part of a project on the piece (occupying an issue of the journal Music Perception), which includes perceptual assessments of and responses to the piece. This work is a counterpoise to that I suggest later in which it would be the composer's own perceptions of the material and processes that are investigated experimentally, since introspection may be misleading.

There are several other interesting longitudinal descriptive/analytic studies of composers in action that follow Sloboda's real-time approach (Collins, 2005), including a three year study of a professional composer working on music for a show-reel for video games. MIDI files were saved incrementally, alongside retrospective verbal reporting on completion of the compositional task, and interview/verification sessions. Periodically but unpredictably "a Gestalt restructuring of the problem" occurred (shown in Figure 21.1 as the proposition (re)formation), with "simultaneous handling of multiple operations" such that "each problem solved generates an ongoing set of sub-goals" (Collins, 2005, p. 18). This corresponds to "parallel processing" in Figure 21.1. Putting it simply, many things happened at once, alongside each other, but periodically there was an abrupt shift in purpose, often affecting many ongoing processes.

A subsequent paper (Donin & Theureau, 2007) concerned Philippe Leroux's electro-acoustic piece *Voi(rex)* (2003). The study occurred a year after the composition, and the researchers repeatedly resituated the composer with stages of his materials/sketches, to reconstruct the processes pursued. Mutable "ideas" for the composition and "appropriation" of tools were observed. Later work (Donin & Féron, 2012) investigated retrospectively a movement for chamber ensemble composed in one day by Stefano Gervasoni: He nicely described an "experimental (gardening) field where different 'cuttings' and 'transplants' would be made" (p. 266). Moving towards more interventionist studies with controlled variables, yet seeking ecological validity, a "re-enactment" of the processes was attempted, using pre-compositional and the newly-generated documents. Here the researcher himself attempted to recreate the composer's processes in notation, receiving feedback mostly when deviating from the composer's expectation/recollection. The paper suggests the utility of abrupt removal/alteration of ongoing constraints (co-relations/propositions in Figure 1). The most recent researcher–single composer interaction studies (Pohjannoro, 2016) similarly applied the term "rational intuition" to the process of elaboration of an "Identity Idea" into a composition.

To close this section, we consider briefly whether involvement in composition has cognitive or well being benefit. Such questions in the arts usually concern broad categories of activity, such as "writing," "image making", or "performing" in music, theatre or dance. But we need studies that concern specific activities, such as improvisation/composition in music. One qualitative study (Habron et al., 2013) investigated five older people collaborating with the Manchester Camerata, UK (a professional chamber music performance group) to "compose" a piece. Though the participants' role in composition seemed subordinate to that of the professionals, positive conclusions were drawn on influences of involvement on well-being, and on representation of "users' feelings and biographies" in the composition. More would be required to allow confidence in such results, or to analyze them in cognitive terms. We do not discuss here the meaning and affect of music, though these may be important for any benefits engendered in people participating in music listening or composition.

## Future Approaches to Some Accessible Questions

Following Sloboda's recommendation of dealing directly with composers, I suggest we need a further empirical step, perturbing the compositional process with related tasks as it unfolds. In considering the overall process, one might compare the ethnographic components of studies involving composers with an auto-ethnographic approach: force a comparison between the process perceived by the participant composer and represented by a researcher-composer, and the one perceived by that researcher-composer as they co-create a piece. We might next suspend our belief in what the composer has to say, and test experimentally whether some sound they anticipate using is indeed being imagined with appropriate features. With composer agreement, we could require the use of materials which are perceptually related to those being developed, but not those at hand, and test the impact of their relatedness. Other questions, such as the creation of co-relations/propositions can be converted into empirical tests also. Furthermore, a composer might be monitored neurophysiologically during the whole of a compositional process or at least a long-term component: in other words, continuously for at least a day. Long term skin conductance measures can be made and these can reveal attentional shifts during music creation, at least in the short term (Dean & Bailes, 2015). Long-term EEG studies are also becoming more common and interpretable. While there may be many non-conscious creative events during composition, these too may be accessible empirically.

Figure 21.1 summarizes our current understanding of cognition in composition, and points to numerous questions. Understanding compositional cognition remains a huge task, but not an impenetrable one.

## Note

1. Put simply, aLife is a range of artificial (computational) endeavors, often artistic in intent, in which computational agents are endowed with behaviors and needs, and compete with one another for limited resources within a finite system, such that pressures and change akin to biological evolution ensue.

## Core Reading

Bink, M. L, & Marsh, R. L. (2000). Cognitive regularities in creative activity. *Review of General Psychology, 4*(1), 59.

Collins, D. (Ed.). (2012). *The act of musical composition: Studies in the creative process.* Farnham, UK: Ashgate Publishing, Ltd.

McAdams, S. (2004). Problem-solving strategies in music composition: A case study. *Music Perception, 21*, 391–429.

## Further References

Bailes, F., Bishop, L., Stevens, C. J., & Dean, R. T. (2012). Mental imagery for musical changes in loudness. *Frontiers in Psychology, 3*, 525. doi: 10.3389/fpsyg.2012.00525

Bainbridge, D., Novak, B. J, & Cunningham, S. J. (2010). A user-centered design of a personal digital library for music exploration. Paper presented at the *10th Annual Joint Conference on Digital Libraries.*

Bamberger, J. (1977). In search of a tune. In D. Perkins & B. Leondar (Eds.), *The arts and cognition* (pp. 284–319). Baltimore, MD: Johns Hopkins University Press.

Barrett, M. (2005). Musical communication and children's communities of musical practice. In D. Miell, R. MacDonald, & D. J. Hargreaves (Eds.), *Musical communication* (pp. 261–280). New York, NY: Oxford University Press.

Bashwiner, D. M, Wertz, C. J, Flores, R. A, & Jung, R. E. (2016). Musical creativity "revealed" in brain structure: Interplay between motor, default mode, and limbic networks. *Scientific Reports, 6*, 20482. doi:10.1038/srep20482

Beaty, R. E. (2015). The neuroscience of musical improvisation. *Neuroscience & Biobehavioral Reviews, 51*, 108–117.

Bennett, J. (2012). Constraint, collaboration and creativity in popular songwriting teams. In D. Collins (Ed.), *The act of musical composition* (pp. 139–169). Farnham, UK: Ashgate.

Blum, S. (2009). Representations of music making. In G. Solis & B. Nettl (Eds.), *Musical improvisation. Art, education, and society.* (pp. 239–262). Urbana, IL: University of Illinois Press.

Brattico, E., & Tervaniemi, M. (2006). Musical creativity and the human brain. In I. Deliège & G. A. Wiggins (Eds.), *Musical creativity* (pp. 290–321). Hove, UK: Psychology Press.

Brown, A. R., Gifford, T., & Davidson, R. (2015). Techniques for generative melodies inspired by music cognition. *Computer Music Journal, 39*(1), 11–26.

Colley, A., Banton, L., Down, J., & Pither, A. (1992). An expert-novice comparison in musical composition. *Psychology of Music, 20*(2), 124–137.

Collier, G. (2009). *The jazz composer. Moving music off the paper.* London: Northway Publications.

Collins, D. (2005). A synthesis process model of creative thinking in music composition. *Psychology of Music, 33*(2), 193–216.

Cook, N. (2013). *Beyond the score. Music as performance.* New York, NY: Oxford University Press.

Cowell, H. (1926). The process of musical creation. *The American Journal of Psychology, 37*(2), 233–236.

Cowell, H. (1996). *New musical resources.* With notes and an accompanying essay by David Nicholls. Original edition 1927. Cambridge: Cambridge University Press.

Davidson, L., & Welsh, P. (1988). From collections to structure: the developmental path of tonal thinking. In J.A. Sloboda (Ed.), *Generative processes in music: The psychology of performance, improvisation and composition* (pp. 260–285). Oxford: Oxford Science Publications.

Dean, R. T. (1992). *New structures in Jazz and improvised music since 1960.* Milton Keynes, UK: Open University Press.

Dean, R. T. (2005). NoiseSpeech, a noise of living bodies: Towards Attali's 'composition'. (Includes a soundwork by the author, Speak Noise Speech, also available online). *Journal of New Media and Culture, 3* (Fall 2004), unpaginated. http://www.ibiblio.org/nmediac/winter2004/NoiseSpc.htm

Dean, R. T. (Ed.). (2009). *The Oxford handbook of computer music.* New York, NY: Oxford University Press.

Dean, R. T., & Bailes, F. (2007). 'Human Understanding' in imagining and organising sound: Some implications of John Locke's Essay for ecological, cognitive and embodied approaches to composition. *Organised Sound, 12*(1), 89–95.

Dean, R. T., & Bailes, F. (2015). Using time series analysis to evaluate skin conductance during movement in piano improvisation. *Psychology of Music, 43*(1), 3–23.

Dean, R. T., Whitelaw, M., Smith, H., & Worrall, D. (2006). The mirage of algorithmic synaesthesia: Some compositional mechanisms and research agendas in computer music and sonification. *Contemporary Music Review, 25*(4), 311–327.

Deliège, I., & Wiggins, G.A. (Eds.). (2006). *Musical creativity: Multidisciplinary research in theory and practice.* Hove: Psychology Press.

Dibben, N. (2013). Visualizing the app album with Bjork's *Biophilia*. In C. Vernallis, A. Herzog, & J. Richardson (Eds.), *The Oxford handbook of sound and image in digital media* (pp. 682–706). New York, NY: Oxford University Press.

Donin, N., & Féron, F-X. (2012). Tracking the composer's cognition in the course of a creative process: Stefano Gervasoni and the beginning of Granigna. *Musicae Scientiae, 16*(3), 262–285.

Donin, N., & Theureau, J. (2007). Theoretical and methodological issues related to long term creative cognition: The case of musical composition. *Cognition, Technology & Work, 9*(4), 233–251.

Ebcioğlu, K. (1988). An expert system for harmonizing four-part chorales. *Computer Music Journal, 12*(3), 43–51.

Finke, R. A. (1996). Imagery, creativity and emergent structure. *Consciousness and Cognition, 5*, 381–393.

Folkestad, G., Lindström, B., & Hargreaves, D. J. (1997). Young people's music in the digital age: A study of computer based creative music making. *Research Studies in Music Education, 9*(1), 1–12.

Garcia, J., Tsandilas, T., Agon, C., & Mackay, W. E. (2014). Structured observation with polyphony: A multifaceted tool for studying music composition. Paper presented at the *2014 Conference on Designing Interactive Systems*.

Garrido, S., & Davidson, J. (2015). The modern composer: Technology and the creative personality. *Journal of Technology in Music Learning, 5*(2), 60–72.

Goncy, E. A., & Waehler, C. A. (2006). An empirical investigation of creativity and musical experience. *Psychology of Music, 34*(3), 307–321.

Habron, J., Butterly, F., Gordon, I., & Roebuck, A. (2013). Being well, being musical: Music composition as a resource and occupation for older people. *The British Journal of Occupational Therapy, 76*(7), 308–316.

Halford, G. S., Wilson, W. H., & Phillips, S. (1998). Processing capacity defined by relational complexity: Implications for comparative, developmental, and cognitive psychology. *Behavioral and Brain Sciences, 21*(6), 803–831.

Kemp, A. E. (1996). *The musical temperament: Psychology and personality of musicians.* Oxford: Oxford University Press.

Kinderman, W. (2009). Improvisation in Beethoven's creative process. In G. Solis, & B. Nettl (Eds.), *Musical improvisation. Art, education and society* (pp. 296–312). Urbana, IL: University of Illinois Press.

Large, E. W., Palmer, C., & Pollack, J. B. (1995). Reduced memory representations for music. *Cognitive Science, 19*(1), 53–96.

Lispector, C. (2004). *A breath of life.* Penguin Books. (Originally published in 1978.)

Lupton, M., & Bruce, C. (2010). Craft, process and art: Teaching and learning music composition in higher education. *British Journal of Music Education, 27*(3), 271–287.

Magnusson, T. (2014). Herding cats: Observing live coding in the wild. *Computer Music Journal, 38*(1), 8–16.

McCormack, J. (2003). Evolving sonic ecosystems. *Kybernetes, 32*(1/2), 184–202.

McCormack, J., & d'Inverno, M. (Eds.). (2012). *Computers and creativity.* Berlin: Springer.

Menard, E. A, & Rosen, R. (2016). Preservice music teacher perceptions of mentoring young composers: An exploratory case study. *Journal of Music Teacher Education, 25*(2), 66–80.

Milne, A. J., & Dean, R. T. (2016). Computational creation and morphing of multi-level rhythms by control of evenness. *Computer Music Journal, 40*(1), 35–53.

Newell, A., & Simon, H. A. (1972). *Human problem solving* (Vol. 104, No. 9). Englewood Cliffs, NJ: Prentice-Hall.

Oikkonen, J., Kuusi, T., Peltonen, P., Raijas, P., Ukkola-Vuoti, L., Karma, K., & Järvelä, I. (2016). Creative activities in music: A genome-wide linkage analysis. *PLoS One, 11*(2), e0148679.

Pasler, J. (2013). Hugues Dufourt's cinematic dynamism: Space, timbre and time in *L'Afrique d'apres Tiepolo*. In C. Vernallis, A. Herzog, & J. Richardson (Eds.), *The Oxford handbook of sound and image in digital media* (pp. 642–662). New York, NY: Oxford University Press.

Pohjannoro, U. (2016). Capitalising on intuition and reflection: Making sense of a composer's creative process. *Musicae Scientiae*, doi: 1029864915625727.

Reynolds, R. (2013). *Mind models.* New York, NY: Routledge.

Sawyer, R. K. (1995). Creativity as mediated action: A comparison of improvisational performance and product creativity. *Mind, Culture, and Activity, 2*(3), 172–191.

Sawyer, R. K. (2005). *Social emergence. Societies as complex systems.* Cambridge: Cambridge University Press.

Silvia, P. J., & Beaty, R. E. (2012). Making creative metaphors: The importance of fluid intelligence for creative thought. *Intelligence, 40*(4), 343–351.

Simonton, D. K. (2014). Creative performance, expertise acquisition, individual differences, and developmental antecedents: An integrative research agenda. *Intelligence, 45*, 66–73.

Sloboda, J. A. (1985). *The musical mind: The cognitive psychology of music.* Oxford: Oxford University Press.

Sloboda, J. A. (1988). *Generative processes in music: The cognitive psychology of music.* Oxford: Clarendon.

Smith, H., & Dean, R. T. (1997). *Improvisation, hypermedia and the arts since 1945.* London: Harwood Academic.

Smith, H., & Dean, R. T. (2009). Practice-led research, research-led practice: Towards the iterative cyclic web. In H. Smith, & R. T. Dean (Eds.), *Practice-led research, research-led practice in the creative arts* (pp. 1–38). Edinburgh: Edinburgh University Press.

Spasov, M. (2011). Music Composition as an Act of Cognition: ENACTIV–interactive multi-modal composing system. *Organised Sound, 16*(1), 69–86.

Wallas, G. (1926). *The act of thought.* London: Watts.

Whitelaw, M. (2004). *Metacreation: Art and artificial life.* Cambridge, MA: MIT Press.

Wiggins, G.A., Pearce, M. T., & Mullensiefen, D. (2009). Computational modeling of music cognition and musical creativity. In R. T. Dean (Ed.), *The Oxford handbook of computer music* (pp. 383–420). New York, NY: Oxford University Press.

Wiggins, G. A, & Forth, J. (2015). IDyOT: A computational theory of creativity as everyday reasoning from learned information. In T. R. Besold, M. Schorlemmer, & A. Smaill (Eds.), *Computational creativity research: Towards creative machines* (pp. 127–148). Berlin: Springer.

Xenakis, I. (1971). *Formalized music.* Bloomington, IN: Indiana University Press.

# 22

# MUSIC IMPROVISATION
## A Challenge for Empirical Research

*Peter Vuust and Morten L. Kringelbach*

*[handwritten: — Improvision / Spontanuity]*

## Introduction

At the heart of many musical genres is the highly valued concept of improvisation; usually understood as shorter or longer periods of time where the musicians play what comes into their minds, creating music *in the moment*. Spontaneous improvisation is seen as a hallmark of musical creativity and as such taken to be highly meaningful and pleasurable. In fact, it could be argued that improvisational elements can be found in all kinds of music making (Brattico & Tervaniemi, 2006). While the importance of improvisation varies across genres, there is at least a touch of improvisation when a string quartet plays Joseph Haydn where notes and note values are fixed, but the phrasing is determined by the musicians, or even when DJs mix tracks into each other. Similarly, when composing a piece of music, which is often described as the opposite process of improvisation, improvisation still plays a significant role when composers try out various alternatives, though this process is free of improvisation's usual temporal constraints. *[handwritten: Improvision seen even when not "supposed to"]*

However, there is a big difference between mere interpretation, or ornamentation, of other people's compositions and the creative processes involved in certain musical genres, where musicians in principle have the liberty to play any given note anytime (Cook, 2014), and where the act of improvisation is the central, defining element in which compositions, if present at all, mainly serve as a framework for soloists to improvise on. This is true for many non-Western styles of music, blues or freestyle rap and in particular for jazz music (Berliner, 1994; Monson, 1997). Here, *free jazz,* without compositions or predefined agreements or starting points, but where the music seems to be happening by itself, is often considered the most radical form.

Musical improvisation can be found in solo performances or in group settings where the improvised artwork takes its form in a dynamic interplay between musicians. Collective musical improvisation has often been linked to the concept of musical communication where music acts as a kind of *emotive* language spoken between the musicians, often with an aesthetic purpose.

The present chapter focuses on existing studies of the behavioral and neural correlates of musical improvisation, discussing the prerequisites for being a skilled improviser. Musical improvisational behavior has been studied through music analyses, mathematical modeling, and using behavioral and neuroscientific experiments; most often using jazz as the prime example. Most of the material covered in this chapter will therefore consider jazz improvisation though many of the aspects and conclusions could perhaps be generalized to improvisation in other styles of music. We will discuss two related questions, central for understanding the cognitive science of music improvisation: To what extent is improvisation in music constrained by context, and can music improvisation be compared to communication or dialogue without words?

## Contextual Constraints on Music Improvisation

Let us begin with the key question for improvisation of whether there exists performance deliberated from musical constraints, not conforming to any predefined musical structure or chord scheme. Take, for example, Keith Jarrett's famous *Köln concert,* which is often taken as an example of improvisation without constraints. This performance is in fact not free but constrained by a large number of factors (Ashley, 2011). First, his instrument, the piano, has certain limitations, such as the missing ability to glide between notes as on a guitar, i.e. the music is limited to the well-tempered scale. Second, even though Jarrett is versatile and technically at an extremely high level, there are still limits to what his motor skills enable him to do. Third, what Jarrett can conceive is bounded by his creative skills, his repertoire, what he has listened to during his career, and what his stylistic preferences allow him to play. Fourth, if Jarrett decides to play in tempo, which happens from time to time during the improvisation, he also performs under the constraint of tempo and musical meter.

### *Modeling Improvisation*

Hence, improvisation is invariably subject to stylistic templates and limitations which become even clearer once we consider the more common situation where jazz musicians improvise over a given melody (Large, Palmer, & Pollack, 1995) with an underlying chord scheme. Here, there are rules that the musicians will obey or diverge from dependent on the specific substyle. These rules are especially evident in bebop, which developed in the 1940s and dominated the jazz of the 1950s and has been a starting point for much jazz pedagogy ever since. Take as an example the tones jazz musicians use when improvising on chord progressions. To each chord, there is a scale that expresses the tonality best; a pool of notes improvisers draw their so-called *target notes* from, notes that are heard as belonging to or extending the harmonies. These may be surrounded by *approach notes* that lead to the target notes but are not necessarily within the scales of the given chord. The improviser can choose to play outside of the harmonies to create an effect of surprise or tension but will most often return to target notes within the chord scales. This process has been modeled for bebop (Toiviainen, 1995), showing that the pitch organization to a certain extent conforms to pitch organization found in Western music as a whole (Jarvinen, 1995).

Because of its strongly rule-based nature bebop has been the object of many modeling attempts. Researchers have created generative grammars for 12-bar blues chord sequences, common in jazz (Steadman, 1984). Johnson-Laird showed that bebop improvisation is more than stringing licks together or following deterministic rules and theorized that bebop improvisation follows Chomskian generative grammars defining permissible

*[handwritten in margin: bebop—starting chord progression in jazz]*

well-formed structures (Johnson-Laird, 1991, 2002). Keller and Morisson (2007) took a turn away from regular grammars by creating software for generating jazz solos automatically, using probabilistic grammars where production rules are assigned weights or probabilities. Recently, Pachet (2012) presented sophisticated computational systems generating highly ecological, virtuoso bebop solos based on a second-order Markov model (meaning that the probability of the next note is determined by the two notes played just before it), but applying various non-Markovian procedures for incorporating, for instance, chromatic side-slips, chord change negotiation, pitch-range constraints, and intentional target pitches.

Studying improvisation by looking at the melodic material, however, captures only one aspect of improvisation. Phrasing and expressive rhythmic timing of the notes by which the performers add emotions to the melodic content (Ashley, 2002) can be used for various purposes, such as to emphasize phrase boundaries, and the emotional responses in listeners may be captured by skin conductance measures (Dean & Bailes, 2015). Notably, the personal phrasing and timing is often what characterizes the individual style of each musician. It is debatable, though, whether the way expressive timing is used by jazz improvisers is different from the way it is used in non-improvisational musical styles. One key aspect of improvisation is, however, that (when used in a group setting) it involves a unique way of interaction and communication between musicians, which may be performed and learned without verbal instruction (Seddon, 2005). In this respect it resembles spoken language.

## Jazz Improvisation as a Form of Communication

The metaphor of music improvisation as a form of language with a generative grammar resonates well with how musicians think about improvising together, namely that they *use* music as a language. This pragmatic aspect of music communication during improvisation was elucidated in a study of the music interactions in Miles Davis's Quintet from the 1960s (Vuust, 2000; Vuust & Roepstorff, 2008) that applied Roman Jacobson's model of verbal communication (Jakobson, 1960). According to this model the *message* (e.g. a musical phrase) is sent from sender to receiver through a channel (live music) in a certain code (jazz) in a certain context (a concert hall in the 1960s). In praxis, since music, in contrast to language, allows for simultaneous playing, the messages constitute more of a patchwork than a sequential conversation.

Hence, music improvisation can be argued to resemble spoken language up to a certain point, not only at a structural level (Besson & Schön, 2001), but also at the pragmatic level in the way it is used in improvising collectives. The communication between jazz musicians is a tool for exchanging musical ideas and fostering creativity, which is not captured well by the recent modeling attempts. However, a number of interaction studies outside the field of music, most relevantly interactive tapping studies, have shown microtiming adjustments as a result of social interaction (Konvalinka, Vuust, Roepstorff, & Frith, 2010). Communication is necessary for making every improvisational performance unique and interesting and dependent on the fact that musical phrases can assume different communicational functions, just like in spoken language. In accordance with the viewpoint held by some ethnomusicologists of music as fundamentally a social activity (McLeod, 1974), to the musicians, the main value of playing jazz may lie in participating in the musical communication process more than in the artwork itself (see also Monson, 1997, chap. 3).

In the following, we shall discuss recent neuroscientific experiments and their consequences for our understanding of music improvisation as a creative and communicational human activity.

## Brain Correlates of Improvisation

Is it possible to find neural correlates of musical improvisation? This question has recently been examined in a number of brain scanning studies which informed this chapter's questions about the contextual constraints and communicational aspects of musical improvisation. They point towards a network consisting of prefrontal brain regions, including the pre-supplementary motor area (pre-SMA), medial prefrontal cortex (MPFC), inferior frontal gyrus (IFG), dorsolateral prefrontal cortex (DLPFC), and dorsal premotor cortex (DPMC). These findings seem reasonable since music improvisation involves motor planning and execution, known to be related to activation in the above mentioned motor areas, some sort of self-generated internal cognitive processes, related to activation of MPFC, and communication, which has been linked to IFG.

### *Improvisation: A Tough Challenge for Cognitive Neuroscience*

The results of the neuroscientific endeavors into improvisation, all of which use functional magnetic resonance imaging (fMRI), however, highlight a general problem with this technique and also point to an unsolved philosophical question about improvisation. In studies of improvisation it has been common to contrast improvisation with a control condition, e.g. memory-retrieval, or to contrast different types of improvisation. The inherent problem using this approach is that whereas memory-retrieval supposedly is a confined task with a clearly defined outcome, improvisation is highly individual (Norgaard, 2011). Therefore, the outcome will differ between participants in which motor sequences that are executed leading to differences in motor activity, which notes are being played entailing different auditory activity, and other cognitive and perceptual differences entailing a much more diverse brain activity during improvisation. Since the brain activity recorded during the improvisation conditions, in the worst case, will be comparable to random noise, the contrast images may reveal something about the control condition but not necessarily be very informative as to understanding the neural underpinnings of improvisation *per se*. Note that this problem is not confined to studies of improvisation but a general problem in all neuroimaging studies, including those on e.g. free will (Brass & Haggard, 2007), creativity (Geake & Kringelbach, 2007) or resting state fMRI (van den Heuvel & Hulshoff Pol, 2010).

### *The Role of the Dorsolateral Prefrontal Cortex (DLPFC) in Improvisation*

One of the first and most notable studies on musical improvisation highlights this inherent problem. Limb and Braun (2008) fMRI scanned six professional jazz musicians playing on an fMRI-compatible piano keyboard contrasting over-learned control conditions with free improvising. In one experiment the improvisation was confined to the notes of a C major scale within one octave while playing the scale up and down one octave acted as the control condition. The other experiment contrasted free improvising on a given chord progression with a memorized novel melody on the same chord progression. The most prominent finding was less activity while improvising in large portions of the frontal lobe, the dorsolateral prefrontal cortex (DLPFC), and the lateral prefrontal regions (LOFC), which in other studies have been related to executive functions, working memory, and cognitive control (Smith & Jonides, 1999). This was paired with an increase of the activity in the medial prefrontal cortex (MPFC), which has been related to introspection (van der Meer, Costafreda, Aleman, & David, 2010).

One interpretation of these results is that improvisers use less neural resources related to cognitive control functions when improvising compared to when playing musical phrases by memory. In other words, the deactivation of the frontal lobe should reflect a suspension of the conscious monitoring and inhibition of the participants' actions. A similar study (Liu et al., 2012) contrasting freestyle rap in twelve freestyle rappers with conventional rehearsed performance similarly found decreases in DLPFC and increases in MPFC in support of Limb & Braun's findings. The authors of this study proposed that this dissociated pattern between MPFC and DLPFC reflects a state in which internally motivated, stimulus-independent behaviors (reflected by the activity in MPFC) are allowed to unfold in the absence of conscious volitional control (reflected as a decrease in DLPFC).

A down-regulation of the prefrontal brain activity in DLPFC resonates well with the way many jazz improvisers describe their mental state while improvising, in that these musicians often point to a deliberate loss of control in order to be able to unfold their creativity freely. Therefore, this has been a credible account of the findings. However, the other possible interpretation, that the musical memory task put stronger demands on networks for memory and cognitive control including the DLPFC is equally likely, and the data at hand do not favor one explanation over the other. Note also that in *real* improvisation overlearned material is widely used, such as when jazz musicians cite previous recordings by other jazz musicians or even themselves (Berliner, 1994), a fact that confounds the contrast between improvisation and memorized material.

Donnay and colleagues (2014), in contrast to Limb and Braun (2008), found activation of DLPFC. They used a particularly ecological approach, scanning subjects while they were *trading fours* playing piano keyboards with the investigators who were situated outside the scanner. Trading fours means that the two musicians alternate playing four bars each, something that happens frequently during jazz improvisation especially between soloists and drummers. Mimicking the earlier study, one experiment contrasted scale improvisation with playing up and down the scale. The other more complex experiment contrasted a memorized jazz composition with improvisation restricted only by having to be monophonic. The main difference between the two studies was that Donnay's study showed interaction between the person in the scanner and the experimenter. This resembles the communication between musicians, which takes place in real jazz performances, but could place greater demands on performance monitoring. Hence, it seems that the relative activation or deactivation of DLPFC is related to the context or difficulty of the tasks involved rather than a specific difference between improvisation and memory retrieval.

## Motor and Language Brain Areas Involved in Improvisation

Another approach for studying improvisation has been to contrast different types of improvisation (Berkowitz & Ansari, 2008, 2010). Using fMRI, de Manzano and Ullén (2012) scanned 18 classical pianists performing melodic and rhythmic improvisation at three different levels of difficulty as well as producing random notes. Comparing the improvisations with random note generation, they found activation of DLPFC, pre-SMA, MPFC, insula, IFG, and the cerebellum. The left IFG is part of Broca's area, which is considered one of the most important language areas implicated in both syntax, semantic processing, and more generally in processing of word order (Burholt Kristensen, 2013). Recently, the IFG has also been implicated in a number of musical studies on melody performance in people suffering from amusia (Mandell, Schulze, & Schlaug, 2007), processing of complex musical rhythms (Vuust, Wallentin, Mouridsen, Ostergaard, & Roepstorff, 2011), and harmony errors (Garza-Villarreal, Brattico, Leino, Ostergaard, & Vuust, 2011). Whereas language predominantly activates the left IFG, music studies often report right or bilateral activation though modulated towards the left hemisphere by musical expertise (Herholz, Lappe, & Pantev, 2009; Vuust, Ostergaard, & Roepstorff, 2006). We may hence speculate that the activation of these language areas in musicians and the left lateralization seen e.g. in de Manzano and Ullén's (2012) study may reflect a more language like use of the musical material, corroborated by the finding of left IFG also in Donnay et al.'s study (2014), which involved actual music interaction. Interestingly, there were only subtle differences between the rhythmic and melodic conditions indicating that these tasks to a large extent draw on similar neuronal resources. Importantly, this study was the first to use a larger sample size of participants, and the statistics were more conservatively corrected for multiple comparisons than previous studies.

## The Influence of Expertise on Brain Processing during Improvisation

One thing that tends to vary across investigations of improvisation is the individual expertise of the participants both with regard to motor abilities, ear training, music theory, and familiarity with improvisation. A few studies have tried to determine the influence of improvisational expertise on brain activity during improvisation. Pinho et al. fMRI scanned 39 pianists with a university degree in either classical or jazz music (Pinho, de Manzano, Fransson, Eriksson, & Ullén, 2014). They computed an index of improvisational experience and correlated it to activation during four slightly different improvisation modes. They found the total hours of improvisation experience to be negatively associated with activity in DLPFC bilaterally and the angular gyrus, consistent with the idea that the more expertise, the less attentional resources needed, which is in line with the lower DLPFC activation in Limb and Braun (2008). In contrast, improvisation training was positively associated with functional connectivity of the bilateral dorsolateral prefrontal cortices, dorsal premotor cortices, and pre-supplementary motor areas, which may reflect a more efficient integration of representations of musical structures at different levels of abstraction, as well as strengthened connectivity between cognitive and sensorimotor aspects of improvisation. Importantly, the effects were significant when controlling for hours of classical piano practice and age. So this study points to more efficient processing in and greater connectivity between the networks required for musical improvisation as a result of improvisational training, which is consistent with models of improvisation (Pressing, 1988) that propose that as expertise increases, processing demands should be minimized so that attention can be allocated to higher order goals and cognitive monitoring. The same conclusion was drawn by Berkowitz and Ansari (2010) in a study that compared classical pianists to non-musicians. They found a deactivation of the right temporoparietal junction during melodic improvisation in musicians only. This brain area is considered part of the so-called attention network, and the data hence suggest that there is an inhibition of stimulus-driven attention, freeing up resources for a more goal-directed performance state that may be beneficial to improvisation.

### Improvisation and Random Number Generation

None of the above mentioned studies on musical improvisation deal convincingly with the fundamental challenge of understanding what actually happens in the minds of participants when they are asked to improvise. In a broader perspective this challenge has been addressed extensively in studies of random number generation. Participants are instructed to say the numbers one to nine in a random fashion for a number of trials in synchrony with a pacing stimulus. This is in some ways similar to improvisation in that it involves efficient control of voluntary goal-directed behaviors and requires suppression of competing or habitual responses so that the appropriate responses are selected. When contrasted to a condition in which the participants are merely counting, there is significant activation of a network, consisting to a great extent of brain areas that also have been implicated in the above studies of improvisation: left DLPFC, the anterior cingulate, the superior parietal cortex bilaterally, the right IFG, and the left and right cerebellar hemispheres (Jahanshahi, Dirnberger, Fuller, & Frith, 2000). Interestingly, when the pace is increased, the regional cerebral blood flow decreases in the left and right DLPFC and the right superior parietal cortex. This is paired with an increasingly more habituated behavior: The subjects tend to *count in ones*. Earlier studies using transcranial magnetic stimulation (TMS) had shown that if you knock out the activity in DLPFC, the most habitual response, *counting in ones*, increases at the expense of the controlled response behavior of *counting in twos* (Jahanshahi & Dirnberger, 1999). The authors therefore concluded that the role of the (left) DLPFC is to suppress habitual counting and that at faster rates, where the synchronization demands take priority, this breaks down evidenced by lower activity in the DLPFC paired with more predictable number sequences.

Translated to improvisation this provides a putative explanation to the apparent discrepancy in activation of the DLPFC observed in the different studies. The consistent pattern in these studies is that participants who are proficient improvisers show deactivation of DLPFC while inexperienced improvisers show activation of the same brain area. Proficient improvisers hence seem to exert less cognitive control and rely more on their automatized motor programs whereas less experienced improvisers may need a strong cognitive control partly to avoid repetitions of the same musical material. Importantly, these studies also tell us something crucial about improvisation, namely that improvisation is not only choices of what to do but also choices about what *not* to do.

### Do Improvising Musicians Process Auditory Input Differently from Others?

The above studies indicate that musical expertise and experience with improvising heavily influence the brain processing associated with improvising. Does this generalize to the way improvisers listen to music? In general, differences in instrumental and stylistic requirements between musicians lead to differences even at the very basic levels of auditory processing of music and sounds. Musicians who need to intone while playing their instrument, such as violinists, display greater sensitivity to small differences in pitch compared to non-musicians

(Koelsch, Schröger, E., & Tervaniemi, 1999) and to other instrumental groups. Similarly, singers respond with a stronger brain response than instrumentalists to small pitch changes (Nikjeh, Lister, & Frisch, 2008), while conductors process spatial sound information more accurately than professional pianists and non-musicians (Münte et al., 2001), and rhythmically skilled jazz musicians respond to rhythmic deviations with a stronger, more left-lateralized and faster brain response than non-musicians (Vuust et al., 2005). Using a novel musical EEG paradigm and behavioral measures, Vuust and colleagues (Vuust, Brattico, Seppänen, Näätänen, & Tervaniemi, 2012a; Vuust, Brattico, Seppänen, Näätänen, & Tervaniemi, 2012b; Vuust, Brattico et al., 2011) recently showed that the style/genre of music professional musicians are engaged with influences their brain responses to changes in acoustically presented melodic lines. In particular, there were larger overall brain responses in jazz musicians compared to classical musicians, rock musicians, and non-musicians across six different sound features (pitch, timbre, location, rhythm, phrasing, and intensity). This indicates a greater overall sensitivity to sound changes in jazz musicians as compared to other types of musicians. These results were paired with the fact that jazz musicians scored higher in musical aptitude tests than rock musicians and non-musicians, especially with regard to tonal abilities. It is therefore reasonable to think that the need for improvising musicians to be able to decipher and respond to what the other musicians are playing and the derived focus on ear training in their daily practice lead to what we observe as enhanced brain responses to unpredictable events in the music they listen to. Hence, the auditory skills and the related pre-attentive brain processing needed for fast communication with the other musicians during musical improvisation seem to be enhanced in improvising musicians.

## Conclusion

The behavioral and neuroscience studies reviewed in this chapter have pointed to two important aspects of improvisation. First, music improvisation in any form is constrained by a number of formalized, unspoken or unconscious contextual factors. Attempts to model music improvisation typically use formalized constraints, such as time signature, key, and chord progression as starting point and can be used for generating solos. These models are most successful in improvisational styles with strong grammars linked to the formalized constraints, such as bebop, whereas it is harder for models to incorporate the unspoken or unconscious contextual factors. These constraints also pose a serious problem to the neuroscience of improvisation. The existing studies use very limited settings where participants, who may not be top-level musicians, improvise on simple chord progressions with one hand on a computer keyboard located at the front end of an MRI scanner. In general, these studies implicate a network consisting of areas related to the motor system, cognitive control, and language processing. However, since contextual factors, skills, and strategy of the improvisers vary so much in different experimental settings, there is substantial variation in brain activation between studies. The most problematic finding is the activation/deactivation of DLPFC since, as the studies on random number generation show, it is heavily dependent on task difficulty. On the other hand, letting go of cognitive control is probably something that many improvisers use as a successful strategy even though this may not be possible to track through brain scanning techniques.

Second, collective improvisation could be thought of as speaking a language that has an esthetic message to deliver, and this is reflected in recruitment of brain areas specialized for language processing. However, the fact that these areas are present does not necessarily mean that music and language are processed similarly by the brain when musicians communicate, but it indicates that music and language brain modules may be overlapping. Especially, the inferior frontal gyrus is increasingly being thought of as a multi-purpose area, or at least involved in a number of cognitive tasks, and is consistently implicated in the reviewed neuroscientific investigations into improvisation. That music improvisation employs networks specialized for other cognitive tasks gives rise to speculations about a putative transfer to other domains (Husain, Thompson, & Schellenberg, 2002; Thompson, Schellenberg, & Husain, 2001). This is an important task for future research to test whether there is a transfer effect of music improvisational skills to other cognitive abilities. As clearly demonstrated by neuro-physiological studies on auditory processing in musicians, there are domain-specific advantages of musical improvisational training. Beaty and colleagues (2013) furthermore showed that semi-professional jazz musicians' scores on general creative thinking ability tests predicted the quality of their improvisations as rated by a team of experts. This points to a potential overlap between the ability to generate creative ideas in general and the ability of jazz musicians to generate novel music sequences. Future studies may show to what extent musical creativity can be trained and whether this training would also enhance creative abilities in general. In relation to this it would also be interesting to understand whether there is a critical period for learning, so that you may need to learn to improvise from an early age.

## Core Reading

Beaty, R. E. (2015). The neuroscience of musical improvisation. *Neuroscience & Biobehavioral Reviews, 51*, 108–117.

Berliner, P. F. (1994). *Thinking in jazz: The infinite art of improvisation.* Chicago, IL: The University of Chicago Press.

Norgaard, M. (2014). How jazz musicians improvise: The central role of auditory and motor patterns. *Music Perception, 31*(3), 271–287.

## Further References

Ashley, R. (2002). Do[n't] change a hair for me: The art of jazz rubato. *Music Perception, 19*, 311–332.

Ashley, R. (2011). Musical improvisation. In S. Hallam, I. Cross, & M. Thaut (Eds.) *The Oxford handbook of music psychology* (pp. 667–679). Oxford: Oxford University Press.

Beaty, R. E., Smeekens, B. A., Silvia, P. J., Hodges, D. A., & Kane, M. J. (2013). A first look at the role of domain-general cognitive and creative abilities in jazz improvisation. *Psychomusicology: Music, Mind, and Brain, 23*, 262–268.

Bengtsson, S. L., Csikszentmihalyi, M., & Ullén, F. (2007). Cortical regions involved in the generation of musical structures during improvisation in pianists. *Journal of Cognitive Neuroscience, 19*(5), 830–842.

Berkowitz, A. L., & Ansari, D. (2008). Generation of novel motor sequences: The neural correlates of musical improvisation. *Neuroimage, 41*(2), 535–543.

Berkowitz, A. L., & Ansari, D. (2010). Expertise-related deactivation of the right temporoparietal junction during musical improvisation. *Neuroimage, 49*(1), 712–719.

Berliner, P. F. (1994). *Thinking in jazz: The infinite art of improvisation.* Chicago, IL: The University of Chicago Press.

Besson, M., & Schön, D. (2001). Comparison between language and music. *Annals of the New York Academy of Sciences, 930*, 232–258.

Brass, M., & Haggard, P. (2007). To do or not to do: The neural signature of self-control. *Journal of Neuroscience, 27*(34), 9141–9145.

Brattico, E., & Tervaniemi, M. (2006). Musical creativity and the human brain. In I. Deliège & G. Wiggins (Eds.), *Musical creativity: Multidisciplinary research in theory and practice* (pp. 289–321). New York, NY: Psychology Press.

Cook, N. (2014). *Beyond the score: Music as performance.* Oxford: Oxford University Press.

De Manzano, O., & Ullén, F. (2012). Goal-independent mechanisms for free response generation: Creative and pseudo-random performance share neural substrates. *Neuroimage, 59*(1), 772–780.

Dean, R. T., & Bailes, F. (2015). Using time series analysis to evaluate skin conductance during movement in piano improvisation. *Psychology of Music, 43*(1), 3–23.

Donnay, G. F., Rankin, S. K., Lopez-Gonzalez, M., Jiradejvong, P., & Limb, C. J. (2014). Neural substrates of interactive musical improvisation: An fMRI study of 'trading fours' in jazz. *PLoS ONE, 9*(2), e88665.

Garza-Villarreal, E. A., Brattico, E., Leino, S., Ostergaard, L., & Vuust, P. (2011). Distinct neural responses to chord violations: A multiple source analysis study. *Brain Research, 1389,* 103–14.

Geake, J., & Kringelbach, M. L. (2007). Imaging imagination: Brain scanning of the imagined future. *Proceedings of the British Academy, 147,* 307–326.

Herholz, S. C., Lappe, C., & Pantev, C. (2009). Looking for a pattern: An MEG study on the abstract mismatch negativity in musicians and nonmusicians. *BMC Neuroscience, 10,* 42–52.

Husain, G., Thompson, W. F., & Schellenberg, E. G. (2002). Effects of musical tempo and mode on arousal, mood, and spatial abilities. *Music Perception, 20,* 151–171.

Jahanshahi, M., & Dirnberger, G. (1999). The left dorsolateral prefrontal cortex and random generation of responses: Studies with transcranial magnetic stimulation. *Neuropsychologia, 37*(2), 181–190.

Jahanshahi, M., Dirnberger, G., Fuller, R., & Frith, C. D. (2000). The role of the dorsolateral prefrontal cortex in random number generation: A study with positron emission tomography. *Neuroimage, 12*(6), 713–725.

Jakobson, R. (1960). Closing statement: Linguistics and poetics. In T. A. Sebeok (Ed.), *Style in language* (pp. 350–377). Cambridge, MA: MIT Press.

Jarvinen, T. (1995). Tonal hierarchies in jazz improvisation. *Music Perception, 12,* 415–437.

Johnson-Laird, P. N. (1991). Jazz improvisation: A theory at the computational level. In P. Howell, R. West, & I. Cross (Eds.), *Representing musical structure* (pp. 291–325). London: Academic Press.

Johnson-Laird, P. N. (2002). How jazz musicians improvise. *Music Perception, 19,* 415–442.

Keller, R. M., & Morrison, D. R. (2007). A grammatical approach to automatic improvisation. In *Proceedings of the 4th Sound and Music Computing Conference* (pp. 330–337).

Koelsch, S., Schröger, E., & Tervaniemi, M. (1999). Superior pre-attentive auditory processing in musicians. *Neuroreport, 10*(6), 1309–1313.

Konvalinka, I., Vuust, P., Roepstorff, A., & Frith, C. D. (2010). Follow you, follow me: Continuous mutual prediction and adaptation in joint tapping. *Quarterly Journal of Experimental Psychology, 63*(11), 2220–2230.

Kristensen, L. B., Engberg-Pedersen, E., Nielsen, A. H., & Wallentin, M. (2013). The influence of context on word order processing—An fMRI study. *Journal of Neurolinguistics, 26*(1), 73–88.

Large, E. W., Palmer, C., & Pollack, J. B. (1995). Reduced memory representations for music. *Cognitive Science, 19*(1), 53–93.

Limb, C. J., & Braun, A. R. (2008). Neural substrates of spontaneous musical performance: An fMRI study of jazz improvisation. *PLoS ONE, 3*(2), e1679.

Liu, S., Chow, H. M., Xu, Y., Erkkinen, M. G., Swett, K. E., Eagle, M. W., Rizik-Baer, D. A., Braun, A. R. (2012). Neural correlates of lyrical improvisation: An FMRI study of freestyle rap. *Scientific Reports, 2,* 834. doi: 10.1038/srep00834

Mandell, J., Schulze, K., & Schlaug, G. (2007). Congenital amusia: An auditory-motor feedback disorder? *Restorative Neurology and Neuroscience, 25*(3–4), 323–334.

McLeod, N. (1974). Ethnomusicological research and anthropology. *Annual Review of Anthropology, 3,* 99–115.

Monson, I. (1997). *Saying something: Jazz improvisation and interaction.* Chicago studies in ethnomusicology. Chicago, IL: The University of Chicago Press.

Münte T. F., Kohlmetz, C., Nager, W., & Altenmüller, E. (2001). Neuroperception: Superior auditory spatial tuning in conductors. *Nature, 409*(6820), 580.

Nikjeh, D. A., Lister, J. J., & Frisch, S. A. (2008). Hearing of note: An electrophysiologic and psycho-acoustic comparison of pitch discrimination between vocal and instrumental musicians. *Psychophysiology, 45*(6), 994–1007.

Norgaard, M. (2011). Descriptions of improvisational thinking by artist-level jazz musicians. *Journal of Research in Music Education, 59*(2), 109–127.

Norgaard, M. (2014). How jazz musicians improvise: The central role of auditory and motor patterns. *Music Perception, 31*, 271–287.

Pachet, F. (2012). Musical virtuosity and creativity. In J. McCormack & M. d'Inverno (Eds.), *Computers and creativity* (pp. 115–146). Berlin: Springer.

Pinho, A. L., de Manzano, O., Fransson, P., Eriksson, H., & Ullén, F. (2014). Connecting to create: Expertise in musical improvisation is associated with increased functional connectivity between premotor and prefrontal areas. *Journal of Neuroscience, 34*(18), 6156–6163.

Pressing, J. (1988). Improvisation: Methods and models. In J. A. Sloboda (Ed.), *Generative processes in music* (pp. 129–178). Oxford: Oxford University Press.

Seddon, F. A. (2005). Modes of communication during jazz improvisation. *British Journal of Music Education, 22*(1), 47–61.

Smith, E. E., & Jonides, J. (1999). Storage and executive processes in the frontal lobes. *Science, 283*(5408), 1657–1661.

Steedman, M. J. (1984). A generative grammar for jazz chord sequences. *Music Perception, 2*, 52–77.

Thompson W. F., Schellenberg E. G., & Husain G.(2001). Arousal, mood, and the Mozart effect. *Psychological Science, 12*(3), 248–51.

Toiviainen, P. (1995). Modeling the target-note technique of bebop-style jazz improvisation: An artificial neural network approach. *Music Perception, 12*, 399–413.

Van den Heuvel, M. P., & Hulshoff Pol, H. E. (2010). Exploring the brain network: A review on resting-state fMRI functional connectivity. *European Neuropsychopharmacology, 20*(8), 519–534.

Van der Meer, L., Costafreda, S., Aleman, A., & David, A. S. (2010). Self-reflection and the brain: A theoretical review and meta-analysis of neuroimaging studies with implications for schizophrenia. *Neuroscience & Biobehavioral Reviews, 34*(6), 935–946.

Vuust, P. (2000). *Polyrhythm and meter in modern jazz—A study of Miles Davis' Quintet from the 1960s (Danish)*. Aarhus, Denmark: Royal Academy of Music.

Vuust, P., Brattico, E., Glerean, E., Seppänen, M., Pakarinen, S., Tervaniemi, M., & Näätänen, R. (2011). New fast mismatch negativity paradigm for determining the neural prerequisites for musical ability. *Cortex, 47*(9), 1091–1098.

Vuust, P., Brattico, E., Seppänen, M., Näätänen, R., & Tervaniemi, M. (2012a). Practiced musical style shapes auditory skills. *Annals of the New York Academy of Sciences, 1252*, 139–46.

Vuust, P., Brattico, E., Seppänen, M., Näätänen, R., & Tervaniemi, M. (2012b). The sound of music: Differentiating musicians using a fast, musical multi-feature mismatch negativity paradigm. *Neuropsychologia, 50*(7), 1432–43.

Vuust, P., Østergaard, L., & Roepstorff, A. (2006). Polyrhythmic communicational devices appear as language in the brains of musicians. *Proceedings from the 9th International Conference on Music Perception and Cognition* (pp. 1159–1167).

Vuust, P., Pallesen, K. J., Bailey, C., van Zuijen, T. L., Gjedde, A., Roepstorff, A., & Østergaard, L. (2005). To musicians, the message is in the meter: Pre-attentive neuronal responses to incongruent rhythm are left-lateralized in musicians. *Neuroimage, 24*(2), 560–564.

Vuust, P., & Roepstorff, A. (2008). Listen up! Polyrhythms in brain and music. *Cognitive Semiotics, 3*, 131–159.

Vuust, P., Wallentin, M., Mouridsen, K., Ostergaard, L., & Roepstorff, A. (2011). Tapping polyrhythms in music activates language areas. *Neuroscience Letters, 494*(3), 211–216.

# 23

# PERFORMING MUSIC
## Written Traditions

*Dorottya Fabian*

### Introduction

In many traditions, music-making is essentially an oral-aural activity. Musicians learn their craft through the apprentice model and performing traditions are passed on orally and through supervised practice or occasions for the community to join the singing and playing. The written traditions are far less ubiquitous, often serving as little more than memory aids, reminding the performer of melody contour, at times perhaps structure and sometimes also duration. These notations, found primarily in the East (e.g. China, India), tend to rely on alphabetic or numeric symbols to indicate pitch, generally through reference to scale degree similar in principle to the Western solfege system. In certain versions the spacing of symbols implies meter or the length of notes (e.g. Chinese *gongche* notation). Drumming patterns (e.g. in Indonesia) also tend to be notated with vocables that are used to remember a sequence. The slightly more complex system of tablature notation is able to indicate pitch as well as duration by notating hand positions on staff representing the strings of the instrument. The horizontal placement of changes implies the temporal unfolding of the music. The Japanese Koto notation similarly indicates primarily means of production and only indirectly the sound produced (Bent et al., 2014). What these notation systems have in common with the Western or European notation tradition is the "prescriptive" rather than "descriptive" nature of the practice (Seeger, 1958). The notation is a visual analogue of sound imagined; a record of the musical piece that the performer should bring to life rather than a transcription of what or how the performer is playing. Although the symbols can be used to transcribe performances, they did not evolve for this purpose and generally remain far too rigid for recording the subtle variations in timbre, pitch, and duration typical of human performance of music. An exception is the Japanese shakuhachi notation tradition. It is entirely different as it reflects playing instructions—what timbre to produce, how to glide from note to note, and so on (Wikipedia, musical notation).

Despite the fascinating diversity in notation systems, my focus will be on Western notation because cognitive studies of music performance tend to study this repertoire. Furthermore, Western notation exemplifies questions and developments relevant for notation systems in general and illustrates well the kinds of problems musicians have to solve when performing notated music. I begin with a brief history of modern Western notation as it

*Focuses more on the actual written language of music than its production* [handwritten annotation]

evolved since circa 1600 to suit changes in social practices of European composed music. This will provide the background for a discussion of contemporary performing practices of Western classical music and the cognitive demands performers of this tradition face. The second half of the chapter will summarize evidence which addresses various processes implicated in the performance of notated music: sight-reading, preparation and memorization; and the matter of expressiveness—namely, the characteristics of musical performance that are not explicitly written in the notation. In doing so, the chapter highlights the various approaches, achievements and limitations of empirical performance research.

## Changing Usages and Interpretations of Western Music Notation

Music notation in Europe dates back to ancient Greece and Egypt but the basics of our current system have been in place only since about the second half of the sixteenth century (Bent et al., 2014). Earlier practices pose problems that are irrelevant for the "common-practice" period that is the domain of cognitive studies in music performance. They are explained in detail by Apel (1961).

During the early decades of the first two hundred years following the emergence of the modern system (ca. 1600–1800), notation became rather skeletal, composers indicating just the bass line and a sketch of the melody, expecting performers to fill in the harmony and decorative detail (Figure 23.1). Notating only basic pitches and rhythm was fine as long as the musicians stayed in the same region throughout their lives and worked in personal proximity of the composer. By the early to mid-1700s progressively more traveling and hiring of primarily Italian musicians weakened national idioms and composers became increasingly concerned with the potential misinterpretation of their music in faraway locations unless it was notated more precisely. A famous case involves Johann Sebastian Bach (1685–1750), who had a reputation for notating out much more than his Italian contemporaries. He was chastised for this practice by the critic and theorist Johann Adolph Scheibe (1708–1776) and defended by the Leipzig law professor Johann Abraham Birnbaum (Wolff, 1998). Bach's notation practices are halfway between being prescriptive and descriptive: A performer needs to know how to read his scores to avoid misinterpreting rhythm and ornaments (Fabian, 2013).

*Figure 23.1* Opening measures of the G minor Sonata for Solo Violin (BWV 1001) by J.S. Bach. The outer staves illustrate how a contemporary Italian composer, like Corelli, would have notated the music (skeletal melody with figured bass). Bach scores a possible performance of such a "sketch," by filling out the basic pitches with melodic embellishments. Accordingly, the rhythm should be understood as approximately reflecting the improvised gesture decorating the underlying harmony and fundamental melodic contour.

Bach not only wrote out the elaboration of melodies and fully realized polyphonic accompaniments but he often indicated articulation and dynamics as well, a practice still very rare throughout the eighteenth century. Until about Beethoven's time (1770–1827), the convention was to indicate only what might be the exception. As normally the opening tempo was lively and the volume *forte*, only *piano* or softer levels tended to be indicated in scores. Character and tempo words, such as *dolce, affettuoso, presto, allegro*, etc. were also rare. Musicians were supposed to deduce the correct tempo and musical character from the combination of time signature and rhythmic values (Houle, 1987). A predominance of shorter notes indicated lighter, more flowing character, so a piece in 3/8 using mostly eighth- and sixteenth-notes called for a less accented if not necessarily faster performance than a piece in 3/4 using similar rhythmic values. At this time tempo words tended to refer to the mood and accentual pattern of a piece rather than tempo *per se*. For instance, a piece in 4/4 and moving mostly by quarter- and eighth-notes labelled *adagio* was less heavily accented (but not necessarily slower or faster) than the same if labelled *lento*, which means "broadly" and thus calls for each quarter-note to be evenly stressed. Most importantly, Common Time (C) was not at all a simple substitute for 4/4. In C there were only two accents per bar on the first and third beats, propelling the music to move forward more flowingly than in 4/4. The information encoded in the choice of time signature in combination with smaller or larger note values had largely been lost by the 1800s and modern musicians have to re-acquaint themselves with these meanings by studying contemporaneous treatises and instrumental tutors if they wish to perform compositions from this period in a manner that is likely to approximate the historical style.

One of the biggest problems of performing notated music of historical times is that the meaning of the signs and symbols has changed (Haynes, 2007). Musicians have to develop an understanding of what they meant at particular time periods or location. Apart from tempo and dynamics, musicians also have to learn how to interpret the articulation markings they find in eighteenth-century scores as opposed to nineteenth or twentieth-century notation. Modern sources compiling historical evidence (Neumann, 1993; Lawson & Stowell, 1999) can aid answering questions like: What is a phrase mark as opposed to a legato sign? When does a slur indicate grouping of notes or playing them in a connected way? How can one transfer the effect, if not the exact execution, of dynamic and articulation marks meant for earlier versions of wind, string, and keyboard instruments? A *sforzando* on a fortepiano with its quick decay will be very different to one performed on a concert grand the sound of which is more resonant. These and many other issues play important parts in decision-making processes, technical solutions involving motor skills, and musical expression with likely implications for performance science. Although much cognitive research has been conducted on mainstream music making, such potential differences between modern and historical practices in preparation, delivery, and expressive goals have been little targeted yet the differences in aesthetic effect are demonstrable (Fabian, 2014) and have been discussed by performers and historical musicologists (Haynes, 2007; Leech-Wilkinson, 2012).

## Interpreting Notation: Sources of Evidence and Information

The most important evidence we have regarding how much people's interpretation of notation has changed over time are sound recordings. The earliest recordings show that musicians born and trained in the nineteenth century performed in a radically different way while later recordings confirm more gradual changes across the twentieth century (Fabian, 2014). Artists making recordings around the 1910s–1920s display many "liberties" or deviations from what the notation implies to us. Pianists commonly rolled notes written as chords without the arpeggio sign. They also often played the melody well after the accompaniment, especially in slow, emotive sections (Peres Da Costa, 2012). The asynchrony of hands can easily be spotted when listening to the performances of Clara Schumann's pupils (e.g. Fanny Davis) and their younger contemporaries (e.g. Jan Paderewsky Ilona Eibenschütz). Such expressive delays of the melody and asynchrony between melody and accompaniment can also be observed in recordings of singers, violinists, and cellists of the same generations. Early recordings show that non-synchrony of vertically aligned parts was common even in string quartet playing and symphonic music yet it is never indicated in notation except in treatises discussing expressive performance (Hudson, 1994; Philip, 1992). Current research on ensemble coordination focuses on mechanisms of playing in synchrony (Keller, 2013) but this has not always been the goal of performers.

Another considerable difference between performances from the beginning of the twentieth century versus those from the second half is the disappearance, around the 1930s, of frequent sliding (*portamento*) between notes (in singing and string playing) and the concurrent appearance of continuous and evenly calibrated vibrato on every note (Philip, 1992). While *portamento* was a common expressive device throughout the 19th century, vibrato was a selectively used ornament not an essential component of sound production as it is today. Such fundamental changes in aesthetics are important to keep in mind when making assumptions about performance based on experimentally derived evidence collected in contemporary research labs.

While sound recordings provide audible testimony regarding how musicians perform contemporaneous music (e.g. Brahms's friend and chamber partner, Joseph Joachim performing Brahms's Hungarian dances, or Béla Bartók his own piano pieces), for earlier periods our only sources of information regarding performance are written documents that are much more open to debate and interpretation (Lawson & Stowell, 1999).

Seventeenth- and eighteenth-century writings discuss figuration and ornamentation at length (Neumann, 1993; Hudson, 1994) because being able to create subdivisions over a given harmony or fill out leaps between melodic pitches were essential skills for performers in the baroque era, as mentioned earlier (Figure 23.1). Unlike today, the study of figuration was embedded in instrumental and vocal learning and went hand in hand with mastering articulation and rhythmic patterns (Houle, 1987). Prior to ca. 1800, musicians performed only in their own contemporary style and the vocabulary of that style became ingrained and procedural knowledge enabling improvisation and the spontaneous addition of embellishments. Today's performers bring modern sensibilities to a broad repertoire covering hundreds of years.

During the nineteenth century, the roles of composer and performer had started to split. While composers left less and less to chance and notated their music with increasing precision and detail, instrumental virtuosity developed to unprecedented levels. This change in required skills is clearly reflected in the treatises. Instead of discussing harmonic embellishments or figuration, nineteenth-century authors dwell on technique and expression, including formulas for virtuosic cadenzas (Lawson & Stowell, 1999).

The extensive literature throughout the centuries on how to perform notated music implies that notation only inadequately transmits what a performer must do to communicate the essence of a score. Or rather, that a score is only an approximation of what the composer had in mind when writing it down.

## *Twentieth-Century Notation*

The twentieth century did not manage to solve this problem. Not even through sound recordings documenting the composer performing his (more rarely her) own music. The modernist stance of the century and also of the 1950s and 1960s brought about an increased emphasis on precise notation. The level of detail in dynamic and articulation markings together with the complexity of rhythm made scores hardly playable accurately due to an overload of information and specific requirements. From a perceptual standpoint there may be little difference between high complexity and randomness (Margulis, this volume). The requirement to play septuplets against sextuplets and quintuplets, sometimes with rests inserted, or to project changing meters of 5/4, 7/6, 9/16 or the like while alternating dynamics of *p*, *sf*, *ff*, and *mp* at high speed is hard to both execute and perceive accurately. It might be worth testing if a simpler notation with *ad lib* or *rubato* or *con espressivo* instruction might create a similar effect while being easier for the performer. In any case, multiple recordings of the same composition by the composer (e.g. Stravinsky conducting his *Firebird*) show that over time they change their interpretation of their own scores and at times they may even alter or omit bars (e.g. Bartók performing his *Allegro barbaro*). Composers' attempts to use metronome markings to prescribe tempo have also failed to be waterproof as their printed indication of duration of sections or their own recordings often deviate, proving Brahms's dictum that "the metronome is of no value. (. . .) I myself have never believed that my blood and a mechanical instrument go well together" (cited in Henschel, 1907, p. 78).

The alternative contemporary experiment in scoring music has been the so-called graphic notation using line drawings, colours, and geometric shapes supplemented by extensive written instructions regarding delivery (e.g. *Aria* by Cage *Játékok* by Kurtág). Just like the existence of performance treatises of earlier times, the need for additional instructions underlines the difficulty of expressing the aural phenomenon of music in the alternate domain of writing, whether words or symbols.

In summary, notation is far less precise in indicating how the playing should unfold than one may assume. Western notation can accurately indicate pitch (as long as it is one of the twelve chromatic semitones) and can approximate note duration fairly well but is silent on timbre, tempo, volume, intensity and all those ineffable aspects that make a performance "musical" or "expressive." Traditionally musicologists have fixated on the score assuming an ontological verisimilitude between it and the composer's idea of the music. This approach has been challenged by theoretical shifts (Cook, 2001) and the rise of performance research that examines the evidence of sound recordings (Leech-Wilkinson, 2012; Cook, 2014; Fabian, 2015). This revisionist approach emphasizes the role of the performer in interpreting the notation; the score is a script for the act of performing. While it can be challenging to balance the requirements of assumed stylistic conventions with personal musical insights, the tension is also the source of the fascinating diversity of interpretations, even within a single time span and single individual.

## Key Cognitive Processes in Performing Notated (Western) Music

Performing written music involves numerous skills, both cognitive and motor. Some, like reading, memorizing or controlling body-movements, are potentially similar to every-day living skills. Others are highly specialised cognitive and motor skills. It is commonly claimed that to attain high proficiency a musician spends an average of 10,000 hours practicing

(Ericsson, Krampe & Tesch-Römer, 1993). Parncutt and McPherson (2002), Gabrielsson (2003) and Parncutt (2016) offer excellent summaries of research on reading, memorization and preparation processes while Keller (2012) and Pfordrescher (2005) cover the role of imagery, feedback, and timing.

## Reading

Learning to perform a piece of written music may start with sight-reading the score and making decisions regarding efficient practice strategies. But first one has to learn how to read music. Mastering the meaning of the multitude of symbols and the underlying theory can cause cognitive overload for young students learning to play a new instrument at the same time. Some pedagogues advocate learning by ear first and only later introducing notation (McPherson & Gabrielsson, 2002).

According to numerous studies, reading notation is similar to reading texts in that both involve reading groups or chunks of information and relying on pattern recognition. The reading is necessarily ahead of playing and requires good instrumental technique as well as rapid processing of input and good working memory (Lehmann & Kopiez, 2016). A good tactile feel of the instrument aids playing from notation: The eyes remain free to focus on reading rather than having to shift from score to instrument/hands and back. As in reading, context influences how far ahead the eye is looking within its skill boundaries. Even highly skilled sight-readers would tend to stop looking further ahead than a musical phrase boundary. Reading music is easier if the style is familiar and if the notation follows appropriate spacing and other conventions (Sloboda, 2005).

## Memorization

Preparing for a performance of notated music generally involves memorization. Although it poses enormous demands on the mental processing of a performer (Aiello & Williamon, 2002) it is considered desirable to allow greater freedom in optimizing the technical and interpretative control and expressive communication (Williamon, 1999). The memorization process tends to be twofold: A rote or kinaesthetic memory is achieved through the sheer practicing of the piece and learning to control its technical demands. A more conscious memorization involves analysing the score, creating mental imagery and noting performance cues that may relate to the interpretive, expression or tactile aspects of the work in question (Chaffin, Imreh, & Crawford, 2002). All sources agree that an implicit (if not necessarily analytical) knowledge of musical structure, including harmony, voice-leading, and form is essential for memorization. Neither aural, nor kinesthetic or visual memory could function reliably without it (Aiello & Williamon, 2002) whether the memorizing is deliberate or not.

Expert memory has been studied extensively since at least the 1970s. The currently accepted skilled memory theory (Chase & Ericsson, 1982) refers to a process of chunking that "allows for rapid categorization of domain-specific patterns" and uses mental representation that "relies on a hierarchically organized set of preformed retrieval cues (based perhaps on the music's formal structure" or style) and mnemonics (Aiello & Williamon, 2002, p. 171). In other words, experts are efficient users of long term memory that tends to be domain specific. The more familiar the style, "vocabulary," or structure, the easier it becomes to memorize it because of the skilled memorizer's method of coding larger "chunks" (i.e. meaningful units such as a harmonic sequence or melodic pattern). When the material is unfamiliar the performer has to work with smaller units or even individual notes making the music more difficult to remember.

## *Imagery*

Performers often report using mental imagery during the performance of a written out composition. The imagery tends to be multi-modal and dependent on individual preferences. Some performers' mental image is reflective of their physical movements developed during repeated practice, or an image of the score; some may focus on their inner hearing, "picturing" the sound ahead of producing it while others prefer metaphorical or emotional images. Such extra-musical analogies can aid the processing of the memory-intensive task of performance (Maes, Giacofci & Lehman, 2005; Saintilan, 2015).

Keller (2012) has focussed attention on the multidimensional and multi-modal representation of music. This shows the complex interaction between various musical skills (theoretical, aural, kinaesthetic, motor), level of expertise, and personal preferences for internal models. The use of mechanisms such as action simulation, inner hearing, and visual imagery facilitates planning and execution.

All this confirms that given the multitude of cognitive and motor skills involved when performing written music, at every stage from sight-reading to memorization performance is considerably aided by a comprehensive approach utilizing the musician's full armoury of varied skills and knowledge base.

## Expression in Musical Performance

The question of how musicians interpret the notated scores in such a way that the performance sounds "expressive" or "musical" has occupied cognitive musicologists for more than a century (Gabrielsson, 2003; Fabian, Timmers, & Schubert, 2014). As discussed earlier, the meaning of signs has changed over time, impacting on stylistic conventions and norms. Apart from matters of musical expression, this has implications for performance decisions including mental imagery. So far empirical and cognitive investigations of performance have largely ignored these historical and cultural dimensions and in this section I focus on some of the arising issues, some important findings related to underlying principles and constraints, and potential future research.

In music psychological research expression is usually defined as micro-deviations from the score (Clarke, 2014) or from a prototypical performance (Repp, 1997). Neither seems to take into account the cultural and historical dimensions that contribute so significantly to performance diversity and changing norms. Musical expressiveness is a value-laden aesthetic category. Whether micro-variations are deemed expressive may depend on consensus or preference.

The training of performers is partly to teach them how to instinctively understand notation and communicate these "written-in" expressive qualities. Their knowledge-base that also helps them sight-read and memorize, as shown in the previous section, comprises of culturally defined information relating to compositional style and performing conventions. Given the changing meaning of signs and the incomplete and imprecise nature of Western music notation, it can become problematic when particular characteristics of micro-variations commonly found in, say, 1980s performances of nineteenth-century repertoire are regarded as universal benchmarks of musical expressiveness.

## *Underlying Principles and Their Constraints*

Cognitive music performance researchers draw a strong link between expressiveness and musical structure (Gabrielsson, 2003). Slowing down at phrase ends, delaying the resolution of a dissonance, hurrying to a melodic climax and so on are means of communicating the music's structure, of creating meaning for the listener. Some of these musical behaviours seem common across cultures and may be related to body movements like gradually slowing to a halt from running.

At the micro-variation level, experimental studies have shown that the perceived expressiveness of note timing depends on overall tempo. Listeners judge artificially manipulated timings as sounding less expressive because of the jarring between these note-timing deviations and a given tempo (e.g. Honing, 2006). Such investigations have also shown that the 3:1 proportional relationship of dotted dyads changes according to tempo. The faster the tempo the closer the proportion shifts to 1:1 because the absolute duration of the notes become closer until they cannot be discerned as separate categories (Friberg & Sundström, 2002). These seem essential physical and acoustical properties rather than features dependent on style or period convention.

These results have assisted computer scientists to create performance rules that enable computers to play notated music in a stylish and expressive manner. One such system has been developed by Anders Friberg and colleagues since the early 1990s (Friberg & Bisesi 2014). The more than twenty original rules are used in an elaborate way; they are additive and applied in a weighted, prescribed order. They have been refined to include stylistic differences as well. The manipulation of rules aids controlled testing of interaction among parameters and their impact on listeners' perception and experience.

On the other hand, the results of historical studies caution against hasty generalizations and rule formulations. The much theorized "phrase-arching" phenomenon (playing progressively faster and louder towards the middle of the phrase and gradually slower and softer towards the end) that is regarded as a basic performance rule has recently been shown to be a characteristic of mid-twentieth-century performance practice (Cook, 2014). In earlier times it was more common to limit rubato to the measure (rather than spread it across four to eight-measures or longer phrases); to use *ritenuto* rather than *rallentando*;[1] to use rapid fluctuations of dynamics and create light-shade effects through tonal inflections (rather than long-range, gradual *crescendos* and *diminuendos*); to use timing stresses rather than dynamic accents; and even to speed up (rather than slow down) towards closures (Fabian, 2014; Hudson, 1994; Peres Da Costa, 2012). Limiting experimental research to current practice is useful only if its results are properly circumscribed. Devising experiments that compare technical differences between historical and contemporary performing styles enlisting specialist performers who are at the forefront of both period and mainstream performance practice would be an important step forward in this line of research. The availability of motion capture technology provides one way of studying differences in motor control/action as well as the resultant sound.

Historical studies also offer important insights into the multi-modal and multidimensional aspect of performing notated Western music. For instance, the interpretation of baroque music was very different when musicians thought of it as being "monumental" (mostly until the 1940s) or "motoric" (most commonly during the 1950s and 1960s). The former view led to large performing forces, intense tone production, legato articulation, long-spun melody lines and ponderous tempos. The latter aimed at stripping the music of "excessive emotional expression" and instead emphasized the repetitive-motor rhythms, playing them fast and with clockwork-like evenness. The historical evidence that much of this music relies on dance rhythms and was supposed to emulate the rhetorical delivery of great orators fostered a different mental imagery that contributed to a radically different way of playing baroque music expressively (Haynes, 2007; Fabian, 2015).

## Conclusions

Performing music in written traditions is much more complex and diverse than might be assumed. Music notation systems tend to be imprecise coding of information that is culturally constructed. Each generation of musicians has to learn to interpret them. This may explain both the remarkable consistency of interpretations by individual musicians of the same piece over long periods of time as well as their ability to radically re-conceptualise it. Cognitive investigations of performing notated music have contributed vastly to our understanding of the multi-modal and multidimensional mental processes involved in musical skills ranging from reading, hearing, and memorizing to acquiring and mastering motor skills and using mental imagery. These studies show that in the case of experienced musicians the decoding of notation to performance is an automated process. As such, it depends, at least partially, on education. Further research could be conducted into the processes that musicians employ to perform according to different stylistic conventions.

## Note

1. *Ritenuto* means holding back and is usually applied to a single note. *Rallentando* means slowing down and is therefore applied to a series of notes.

## Core Reading

Bent, I., Hughes, D., Provine, R., & Rastall, R. (2014). Notation II: Notational systems. *Grove music online.* Oxford Music Online. Oxford University Press. www.oxfordmusiconline.com/subscriber/article/grove/music/20114pg1#S20114.1 (last accessed May 30, 2016).

Clarke, E. (2014). Theories of performance expression. (Section 3 of §IV in D. Deutsch, et al., Psychology of music.) *Grove music online.* Oxford Music Online. Oxford University Press. www.oxfordmusiconline.com/subscriber/article/grove/music/42574pg4 (last accessed January 7, 2016).

Cook, N. (2014). *Beyond the score: Music as performance.* New York, NY: Oxford University Press.

Fabian, D., Timmers, R., & Schubert, E. (Eds.). (2014). *Expressiveness in music performance: Empirical approaches across styles and cultures.* Oxford: Oxford University Press.

Gabrielsson, A. (2003). Music performance research at the millennium. *Psychology of Music, 31,* 221–72.

Haynes, B. (2007). *The end of early music: A period performer's history of music for the twenty-first century.* New York, NY: Oxford University Press.

Keller, P. (2012). Mental imagery in music performance: Underlying mechanisms and potential benefits. *Annals of the New York Academy of Sciences: The neurosciences and music IV: Learning and Memory, 1252,* 206–213.

Lawson, C., & Stowell, R. (1999). *Historical performance practice: An introduction.* Cambridge: Cambridge University Press.

Leech-Wilkinson, D. (2012). Compositions, scores, performances, meanings. *Music Theory Online, 18*(1), 1–17.

Parncutt R., & McPherson, G. (Eds.). (2002). *The science and psychology of music performance: Creative strategies for teaching and learning.* Oxford: Oxford University Press.

Parncutt, R. (Ed.). (2016). Music performance. Part 7 in S. Hallam, I. Cross, & M. Thaut (Eds.), *Oxford handbook of music psychology* (2nd ed.) (pp. 529–649). Oxford: Oxford University Press.

Peres Da Costa, N. (2012). *Off the record: Performing practices in romantic piano playing.* New York: Oxford University Press.

## Further References

Aiello, R., & Williamon, A. (2002). Memory. In R. Parncutt & G. McPherson (Eds.), *The science and practice of music: Creative strategies for teaching and learning* (pp. 167–182). Oxford: Oxford University Press.

Apel, Willi (1961). *The notation of polyphonic music, 900–1600.* (5th ed., rev. with commentary). Cambridge, MA: Mediaeval Academy of America.

Chaffin, R., Imreh, G., & Crawford, M. (2002). *Practicing perfection: Memory and piano performance.* Mahwah, NJ: Lawrence Erlbaum Associates.

Chase, W. G., & Ericsson, K. A. (1982). Skill and working memory. In G. H. Bower (Ed.), *Psychology of learning and motivation* (Vol. 16, pp. 1–58). New York, NY: Academic Press.

Cook, N. (2001). Between process and product: Music and/as performance. *Music Theory Online 7*(2), http://www.mtosmt.org/issues/mto.01.7.2/mto.01.7.2.cook.html (last accessed May 30, 2016).

Ericsson, K.A., Krampe, R.Th., & Tesch-Römer, C. (1993). The role of deliberate practice in the acquisition of expert performance. *Psychological Review, 100*(3), 363–406.

Fabian, D. (2013). Ornamentation in recent recordings of J. S. Bach's solo sonatas and partitas for violin, *Min-Ad: Israeli Studies in Musicology Online, 11*(2), 1–21. http://www.biu.ac.il/hu/mu/min-ad/ (last accessed January 11, 2016).

Fabian, D. (2014). Commercial sound recordings and trends in expressive music performance: Why should experimental researchers pay attention? In D. Fabian, R. Timmers, & E. Schubert (Eds.), *Expressiveness in music performance: Empirical approaches across styles and cultures* (pp. 58–79). Oxford: Oxford University Press.

Fabian, D. (2015). *A musicology of performance: Theory and method based on Bach's solos for violin.* Cambridge: Open Book Publishers.

Friberg, A., & Bisesi, E. (2014). Using computational models of music performance to model stylistic variations. In D. Fabian, R. Timmers, & E. Schubert (Eds.), *Expressiveness in music performance: Empirical approaches across styles and cultures* (pp. 240–259). Oxford: Oxford University Press.

Friberg, A., & Sundström, A. (2002). Swing ratios and ensemble timing in jazz performance: Evidence for a common rhythmic pattern. *Music Perception, 19*(3), 333–349.

Henschel, G. (1907). *Personal recollections of Johannes Brahms.* Boston, MA: R. G. Badger.

Honing, H. (2006). Evidence of tempo-specific timing in music using a web-based experimental setup. *Journal of Experimental Psychology: Human Perception and Performance, 32*(3), 780–786.

Houle, G. (1987). *Meter in music, 1600–1800: Performance, perception and notation.* Bloomington, IN: Indiana University Press.

Hudson, R. (1994). *Stolen time: The history of tempo rubato.* Oxford: Clarendon Press.

Keller, P. (2013). Musical ensemble performance: A theoretical framework and empirical findings on interpersonal coordination. In A. Williamon & W. Goebl (Eds.), *Proceedings of the International Symposium on Performance Science* (pp. 271–285). Brussels, Belgium: European Association of Conservatoires (AEC).

Lehmann, A., & Kopiez, R. (2016). Sight-reading. In S. Hallam, I. Cross & M. Thaut (Eds.), *Oxford handbook of music psychology* (2nd ed.) (pp. 547–559). Oxford: Oxford University Press.

Maes, P-J., Giacofci, M., & Lehman, M. (2015). Auditory and motor contributions to the timing of melodies under cognitive load. *Journal of Experimental Psychology: Human Perception and Performance, 41*(5), 1336–1352.

McPherson, G., & Gabrielsson, A. (2002). From sound to sign. In R. Parncutt, & G. McPherson (Eds.), *The science and psychology of music performance: Creative strategies for teaching and learning* (pp. 99–115). Oxford: Oxford University Press.

Neumann, F. (1993). *Performance practices of the seventeenth and eighteenth centuries.* New York, NY: Schirmer.

Pfordrescher, P. Q. (2005). Auditory feedback in music performance: The role of melodic structure and musical skill. *Journal of Experimental Psychology: Human Perception and Performance, 31*(6), 1331–1345.

Philip, R. (1992). *Early recordings and musical styles: Changing tastes in instrumental performance.* Cambridge: Cambridge University Press.

Repp, B. (1997). The aesthetic quality of a quantitatively average music performance: Two preliminary experiments. *Music Perception, 14*, 419–44.

Saintilan, N. (2015). The use of imagery during the performance of memorized music. *Psychomusicology: Music, Mind, and Brain, 24*(4), 309–314.

Seeger, C. (1958). Prescriptive and descriptive music-writing. *The Musical Quarterly 44*(2), 184–195.

Sloboda, J. (2005). *Exploring the musical mind: Cognition, emotion, ability, function.* Oxford: Oxford University Press.

Wikipedia, *Musical notation.* https://en.wikipedia.org/wiki/Musical_notation (last accessed May 30, 2016).

Williamon, A. (1999). The value of performing from memory. *Psychology of Music 27*(1), 84–95.

Wolff, C. (Ed.). (1998). *The new Bach reader—A life of Johann Sebastian Bach in letters and documents.* New York, NY and London: Norton.

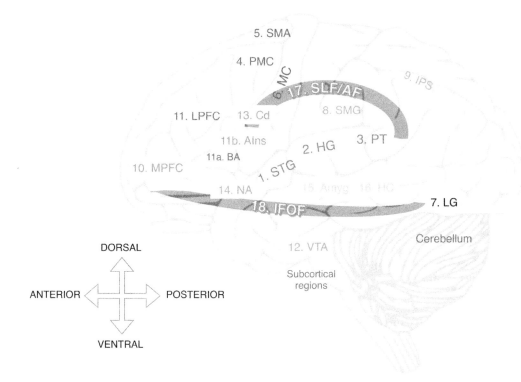

*Figure 2.1*  Anatomical locations of some grey matter regions involved in music perception and cognition. Shaded grey regions represent mesial structures, i.e., areas that are seen in cross-section rather than in the present surface view of the brain. Shaded orange regions represent white matter pathways. Colors of text represent general areas of the brain: Blue = temporal lobe; red = frontal lobe; brown = occipital lobe; green = parietal lobe; pink and violet = subcortical structures. See page 14.

1.  STG: Superior temporal gyrus
2.  HG: Heschl's gyrus
3.  PT: Planum temporale
4.  PMC: Premotor cortex
5.  SMA: Supplementary motor area
6.  MC: Motor cortex
7.  LG: Lingual gyrus
8.  SMG: Supramarginal gyrus
9.  IPS: Intraparietal sulcus
10.  MPFC: Medial pretrontal cortex
11.  LPFC: Lateral prefrontal cortex

    a.  BA: Broca's area
    b.  AIns: Anterior insula

12.  VTA: Ventral tegmental area
13.  Cd: Caudate
14.  NA: Nucleus accumbens
15.  Amyg: Amygdala
16.  HC: Hippocampus
17.  SLF/AF: Superior Longitudinal Fasciculus/Arcuate Fasciculus
18.  IFOF: Inferior Frontal-Occipital Fasciculus

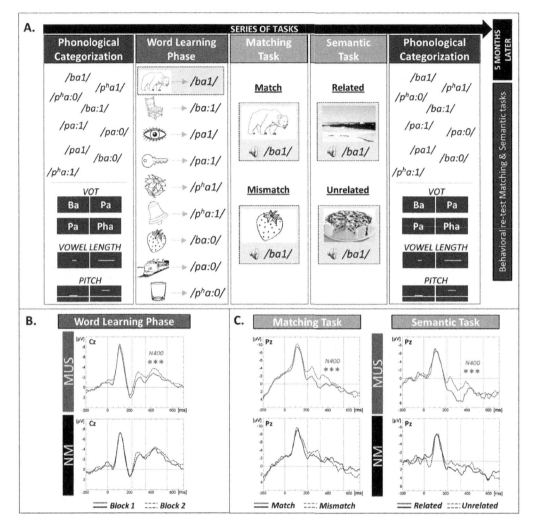

*Figure 4.1* (A) Illustration of the series of tasks used in the experiment. Phonological categorization task of mono-syllabic words based on pitch, vowel length, and voice-onset-time (VOT). In the word learning phase, participants learned the meaning of new words through picture-word associations. In the matching task, participants were asked to decide whether picture-word pairs matched or mismatched those from the learning phase and, in the semantic task, if novel pictures were semantically related or unrelated to the newly learned words. Finally, the matching and semantic tasks were performed again five months later in a subset of participants to test for long-term memory. (B) The increase in N400 amplitude from the first to the second part of the learning phase (block 1 vs. block 2) was larger in musicians than in non-musicians. (C) The differences between match/semantically related and mismatch/semantically unrelated words were also larger in musicians than in non-musicians. See page 41.

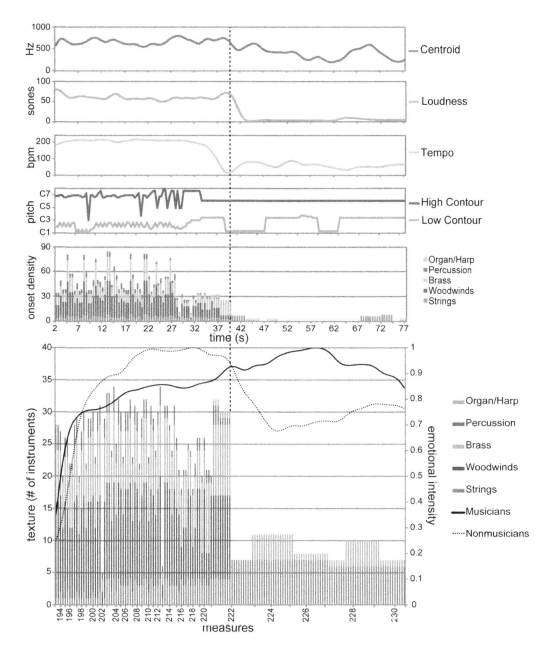

*Figure 11.1* Visualization of Holst, *The Planets*, "Uranus," mm. 193–236, with score-based features (instrumental texture, onset density, and melodic contour), performance-based features (loudness, spectral centroid, and tempo), and average emotional intensity ratings for musician and non-musician listeners. See page 136.

From Goodchild (2016), Fig. A.10.

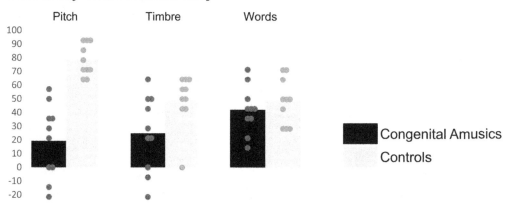

*Figure 19.1* Group data for congenital amusic and control participants presented together with individual data points (black: amusics, grey: controls) for the following tests: **A.** MBEA (Peretz et al., 2003), expressed as numbers of correct responses (maximum score = 30). Scores are presented for the entire battery (cut-off for amusia diagnosis = 23/30) and two of the six subtests (scale and rhythm, maximum score = 30 in each case). **B.** Pitch Discrimination Thresholds (as measured in Tillmann et al., 2009) in semitones (for the same participants as in Figure 19.1A, N_amusics=34, N_controls=34). **C.** Performance (presented in terms of percentage of Hits-False Alarms) in auditory short-term memory tasks for pitch (melodies), musical timbre, and word materials (data from Tillmann et al., 2009, N_amusics=10, N_controls=10). See page 228.

*Figure 30.2* Three frames from an action sequence in *Minority Report* (Twentieth Century Fox and Dreamworks, 2002). See endnote 5 for details on the selected scene and film. See page 371.

# 24

# PERFORMING MUSIC
## Oral and Improvising Traditions

*Nikki Moran*

## Introduction

This chapter addresses the cognitive processes that are understood to underlie musical performance in oral and improvising traditions. In relation to music, the idea of an oral tradition refers broadly to musical practices whose means of transmission (of musical ideas and activities—including repertoires, performance conventions, techniques) do not rely on written or printed notation. Improvisation in music, meanwhile, broadly describes the material process and aesthetic consequence where musicians generate organized, meaningful sounds "in the course of performance" (Nettl & Russsell, 1998). In the past, musical improvisation has also been defined primarily through its relation to conventional, scored composition (Nettl, 2005). The title of the chapter thus encompasses a vast array of musical practices, essentially describing all types of performance which are not considered to be part of a highly literate tradition, namely those associated with classical Western art music.

Two bodies of literature in particular are relevant for the discussion of performance in the context of non-notated music. Firstly, there is a considerable body of psychological research on music performance; secondly, ethnomusicological research has investigated oral traditions and practices from around the world. Since the field of music psychology has largely—though not exclusively—offered explanations of cognitive processes behind perceptual phenomena which relate directly to Western classical art music, academic discourse on music cognition has been shaped to some extent by knowledge of the formal practices and theoretical concepts associated with this particular conception of music-making. Accordingly, the field has yielded substantial bodies of literature devoted to self-evidently exclusive topics, such as sight-reading, or the perception of Western classical tonality. An indirect consequence of this particular focus has been to influence the extent to which scientists have been able to conceptualize and investigate music as performance and social behavior. Thus, knowledge and understanding of music cognition in oral and improvising traditions requires the evidence and insight offered from the fields of ethnomusicology and sociology in order to balance the picture gleaned through psychological research methods. This has lately resulted in more attention to a wider range of musical traditions and situations—which in turn helps to inform the study of performance within the dominant Western art music tradition since performers in this tradition also rely on orally-learned, cultural knowledge to complete their interpretation of a notated score. For a fruitful discussion of performance processes in the context of oral traditions, I will borrow from both psychological and anthropological perspectives in this chapter, seeking deliberately to synthesize evidence from distinct disciplinary traditions.

Psychological research into music performance has a core literature following some forty years of increasingly concerted scholarship. Readers unfamiliar with this literature can look to the reviews by Gabrielsson (2003); Palmer (1997, 2013); and the collection of chapters in the section on performance of the *Oxford Handbook of Music* (Hallam, Cross, & Thaut, 2016), and *The Science and Psychology of Music Performance* (Parncutt & McPherson, 2002). These each provide their own overview of the topic, revealing the scale and multidimensionality of the scientific endeavor that it demands. They report empirical measurement of psychological tendencies and behavioral constraints in various aspects of musical performance-related tasks, such as sight-reading, memorization, performance planning, motor processes, and comparative measurements of expressive variation, focusing typically on sound production discrepancies within a repertoire or between performers (see also Fabian, this volume).

As noted earlier, however, oral and improvised performance is by no means the primary focus of this literature. For an introduction to the range of insights brought to the study of music cognition from ethnomusicological accounts of music performance—predominantly focusing on oral musical cultures—see Ramnarine (2009). Two further, key pieces of literature for the topic of cognition in oral music traditions include the most recent cross-cultural music perception review article by Stevens (2012), and Ashley's (2016) entry on the psychology of improvisation for *The Oxford Handbook of Music Psychology*. As Ashley notes (2016, p. 669), a significant cognition and psychology literature now deals with musical improvisation—albeit with a bias towards Euro-American jazz, which is likely to skew the field towards Western-centric research questions and explanations of performance. Described by Averill (2004) as a "Euro-American fetish for sophistication" (p. 97), this tendency continues to orient studies towards a limited canon of intellectualized musical forms, with a predominance of attention to Asian court musics and also to jazz. The chapter by Vuust and Kringelbach (this volume) deals exclusively with the psychology of musical improvisation, and reports on the most current developments in the field.

The concepts of orality and improvisation address different concerns, and yet these concepts are strongly associated. Music performance organized within oral traditions can involve varying degrees and sorts of extemporization. Our first task is then to consider the concept of orality a little more fully in order to understand its relationship with the notion of improvisation, before continuing with the main topic of this chapter. There, the focus will be on relating oral performance traditions conceived within varying socio-cultural contexts with extant music cognition research, whose focus is predominantly on notated music, exploring implications as well as discrepancies.

Oral (or, more precisely, oral–aural) musical tradition can be taken to describe specifically the perpetuation of specific cultural knowledge, combining both abstract forms and material practices. Such knowledge is learned and shared through processes of face-to-face communication, involving the activities of listening and memorizing through replication and repetition. In this way, oral–aural musical traditions are sustained through the participation of individuals and their memorization of particular musical compositions, forms, and texts—and also through these individuals' practice-based acquisition of multimodal music production and perception skills. Ethnomusicological literature describes how the conceptualization of oral music traditions may come about through prescriptive teaching and learning processes, resulting in a systematic and thorough means of conservation of repertoire and style (Wade, 2004, p. 17). Such transmission processes are generally understood to preserve musical works through a process of slow but constant change (Nettl, 2005, p. 297).

The formality and prescriptiveness of the transmission process, however, does not imply that all resulting performances will be acoustically equivalent. Thus, a particular song or tune may be learned aurally to a high level of acoustic verisimilitude—exactly the same notes, sung with the same words and pronunciation, in the same key, at the same tempo. Alternatively, the same song may be learned aurally but developed during the event of performance into a novel reworking: some aspect of its structure, such as its scale-form, text, harmonic organization, or melodic patterning may be treated as a point of departure for a never-to-be-repeated, improvised performance. Improvised performance, in this sense, is clearly differentiated from the performance of music that has been memorized either "by ear"—as in informal learning of popular music, for example—or learned "by heart" from notation, as is more typical for performances of classical Western art music. Differences between these forms of learning lead us to expect differences in the memorization procedures used, their cognitive representation and organization as units and structures, and in the choices made by performers when they must subsequently deploy known units and structures in the act of musical performance. Of course, what dimensions of perceived musical structure happen to be considered as "the same" or "different" within a given musical system is a complex and culturally-differentiated matter. Musical scores tend to make a restricted array of musical features (e.g. harmonic structure, metric organization, narrative coherence) appear as definitive structures, whilst aspects such as timbre and groove, or cyclical forms—which may just as well be considered as the primary conceptual structures in a given musical system—are less apparent in notation. What is deemed to be a faithful and accurate rendition of a particular item of repertoire within an oral tradition may in some cases involve an entirely new melodic line; or the "same song" may have brand new words. Nettl again: "No doubt, the particular view that a society has of change and the nature of music plays a greater role than any law of human behavior" (2005, p. 297).

In addressing music cognition of oral performing traditions, we will first consider variations in music's roles and functions and the varying demands and expectations these impose on music performance, as well as variations in performance contexts. This is followed by more specific consideration of cognitive aspects of performance including memory, cognitive schemata and multimodality in performance; and finally, rhythm, meter, and expressive timing.

## Sociocultural and Sociomusical Expectations of Performers

Ethnomusicologists and music sociologists have demonstrated the multiplicity of music's social and personal functions. Clayton (2016) reports that music plays a part in many profound and vital social transactions, such as in ceremony and ritual, where musically organized behaviors may induce states of trance, possession, and ecstasy, which may be directly associated with healing or other fundamental matters of wellbeing. At the level of individual taste and preference, music is also implicated in the construction of a socio-cultural identity, including differentiations in gender, age, ethnicity, and social history. At a wider level, the adoption and adaptation of musical genres by globally dispersed communities may also contribute to the collective construction of cultural identity. This array of functions of musical performance functions makes it obvious that a musician is more than just a sound-maker. Musicians take on both social and creative roles, negotiating their actions with audiences and fellow musicians through events of performance. The goals, organization and criteria for success of a performance vary as a consequence.

To consider what constitutes a successful music performance, one might ask: On what grounds do we judge technical and aesthetic proficiency? Who judges it and how does this shape performance? We know that specialist training in musical performance is not essential for everyone, since profoundly affective musical experiences are available to so-called non-musicians who have not received specific musical training. Our focus on music as oral tradition offers particular insight into the world of pre- or non-expert performance. Ethnomusicologist Jankowsky (2010) describes, for example, ritual healing events enacted by Stambeli musicians in Tunisia, which are deliberately structured in order to permit participation by non-musicians alongside the expert Stambeli. Or, one could consider the case of more routine, day-to-day music-making such as choir singing or singing along with music in the car. From an anthropological perspective, the criteria for "success" in a music performance must vary according to the time, place and function of performance in all forms: amateur and professional, popular and classical, formal and informal.

These varied sociocultural contexts of music-making draw attention to the multiple ways that participants within a musical culture acquire their skills, through both formal and informal means (Green, 2002; Green & Smart, this volume). Processes of enculturation into oral music traditions have been recorded through countless ethnomusicological research projects, but the topic has certainly not yet been exhausted by music psychologists. A recent example of a comparative anthropological approach is available in the "Growing into music" project, whose output includes a 68-minute ethnographic film documenting musical enculturation across a number of oral traditions in West Africa, Cuba, Venezuela, North India, Rajasthan and Azerbaijan (Durán, Magriel, & Baker, 2011). The impact of such an ambitious project has been, so far, to foster greater awareness of and interest in oral transmission in the countries featured in the study; such a corpus may yet be used as a resource for psychological enquiry into the acquisition of musical performance skills in the context of oral musical traditions.

Of course, the particularities in each case of musical enculturation present a methodological challenge to the design of psychological studies. However, when we seek out pragmatic commonalities in the attributes and knowledge which constitute musicianship across oral and literate cultures, human relationships and interactions lie at the heart of musical practice. In psychological research, the dimension of interpersonal interaction in joint performance has been explored through studies of co-ordination and synchrony among ensemble musicians (see Wöllner & Keller, this volume). Intuitively-designed studies have explored the relationship of "leader" to "follower," picking up on the conventional role-based hierarchies that classical art music performance lends itself to. However, systematic investigation of detailed timing evidence has revealed that the achievement of musical synchrony is not as simple as this role-based account might suggest: Counter to their designated roles, "leaders" consistently concede to the behavior of their "followers" in the course of musical performance. "Thus, adaptation to the timing of one's partner in a musical ensemble seems to transcend influences of musical roles and any biomechanical differences" (Palmer, 2013, p. 416). For any musical tradition which involves some degree of extemporization or deviation from a learned script, and more than one performer, communication skills, including sensitivity to others' actions and—crucially—the capacity to adapt one's own behavior to match these—are of utmost importance. In the next section, we will also see how certain performance contexts further promote a mutual relationship between performers, and between performers and their audiences.

## Performance Contexts and Communication

Performance context affects the organization of interpersonal interaction within a performance event, and therefore it is likely to impact on the psychological demands for performing musicians and audience alike. To illustrate the influence of performance context, consider, on the one hand, performers in purpose-built concert halls—or at a large music festival—who tend to tend to be physically separated from their audience by the staging and architecture. They may also need to accommodate amplification equipment, or the conventions of orchestral ensemble configurations, so that their interactions with one another are physically limited—perhaps hindered further by the presence of music stands. Such events may still be abundantly interactive and engaging, but it is possible to imagine the material content of the performance transported from one venue to another with little change. At the other extreme, in one specific example, the case of Afro-Brazilian Congado offers an entirely different view. In this religious performance, the contextual and environmental dimensions are themselves drawn into play, since the congadeiro (musician) procession must shape the dynamics of their continuous, cyclical performance according to the demands and possibilities of each place or ritual (Lucas, 2013).

Ethnomusicological examples of secular music performance, too, describe the extent to which context and audience role may shape the outcome of the musical performance. Describing his own experience as a performer of secular Arabic music, ethnomusicologist Racy (1998) reports an occasion on which "the physical presence of a large group of individuals unable to respond idiomatically to my improvisation [felt like] a musical liability" (p. 106). This sentiment is echoed by North Indian sitar maestro, Pandit Budhaditya Mukherjee:

> The artist is there—he's the person responsible for creating the beauty, which is expected of him. But give him a chance! So for the first ten or fifteen minutes, it is the audience's most respectful duty to support the artist in whatever he's doing. If he can't grab the attention of the audience in those fifteen minutes initially, then they're free to talk or leave the place!
>
> *(Moran, 2007, p. 84)*

We can hear in these accounts a social conception of music, where the responsibility for what material emerges comes from the time and place of the performance, implicating the audience, too, as contributors.

At a pragmatic level, the way in which musicians and their audiences organize and orient themselves in relation to one another has received some attention in music psychology performance research, mainly via studies addressing matters of communication and interaction in the case of classical Western music interpretation. Such research reveals the range of negotiations made by singers and instrumentalists in the course of resolving pragmatic and aesthetic concerns, such as King and Ginsborg's (2011) investigation of gestures and glances by ensemble musicians, and Kawase's (2014) study of piano duos' use of mutual gaze to support their co-ordination. Researchers who have set out to explain the cognition behind performance structures in oral (particularly improvised) music also make reference to dimensions of interpersonal interaction, often drawing on analogies to speech-like or conversational episodes. Sloboda (1985, p. 139), for example, compares the process of melodic improvisation to the verbal skills demonstrated in storytelling. Ashley (2016) later draws attention to the similarity between musical improvisation and conversational speech production, pointing out the need for musical improvisers to articulate their musical utterances within the constraints of both larger-scale, discourse-like structures but also in tight temporal concert with other performers, although he adds that this is "unlike speech, where the norm is one speaker at a time" (Ashley, 2016, p. 668).

Following this analogy, it is worth noting the complexity of those social cues which permit coherent turn-taking and which facilitate a narrating speaker's utterance production: Face-to-face or conversational interaction depends on a strongly collaborative process. In fact, the attention of the listener is vital in face-to-face story-telling. Bavelas and colleagues (2002) asked experimental participants to tell informal "close-call" stories to a confederate. When the confederate listeners withheld their demonstration of attention by averting their gaze at key moments, the narrator's stories were curtailed. Similar dependencies between actor and co-actor can be expected in musical interactions, such as between soloists and their accompanists or between two (improvising) soloists. Investigating the implicit support between performers, Moran, Hadley, Bader, and Keller (2015) investigated the extent to which improvising musician duos appear as a coherent social "unit" to observers in an experimental study, using 10-second audio-visual stimuli depicting improviser instrumentalist duos as motion-captured point light displays. These stimuli—created from episodes of the recorded performances in which one musician improvised a solo whilst their partner instrumentalist was temporarily silent—simulated a conversation-like scenario within musical interaction. The results of the study indicated that the sample of sixty participants were not differentiated by music training backgrounds in their ability to distinguish the original free-improviser duos from manipulated stimuli, in which the soloist and listener were switched between different duos. Such evidence supports the view that musicians behave responsively to their partners on the level of social and musical behavioral cues. The implication is as well to suggest an elevated role for the audience's role in music performance reception, since they may apparently draw on their general abilities of social perception to make pertinent musical judgments.

## Structuring Performance: The Role of Memory, Cognitive Schemata and Multimodality

Psychological research into music performance provides a picture of various interlinked cognitive systems (e.g. associative, schematic and procedural memory systems), which together account for the extraordinary and wide-ranging feats of memory demonstrated by performing musicians (Chaffin, Logan, & Begosh, 2008). In order to participate in "a community of musicians who share a common purpose, set of skills and musical vocabulary" (Ashley, 2016, p. 674), oral or improvising musicians must usually have learned a certain amount of content, such as a corpus of songs. Such repertoire knowledge is in this sense a cornerstone for stylistic development. Ethnomusicological texts such as the authoritative, ten-volume *Garland Encyclopedia of World Music* (Nettl & Stone, 1998–2002) document repertoire as a matter of disciplinary routine. And yet, this is not a simple act of taxonomy: most such repertoires are neither transmitted nor acquired via cleanly indexed books like jazz real-books. Even in traditions where such commodities are available, the reality is far messier, as Faulkner and Becker's (2009) ethnography shrewdly reveals, referring to "the jazz repertoire" as "the mixture of jazz, popular songs, ethnic music, and whatever else ordinary musicians might learn through their experiences playing in public" (p. 16).

Musical performance that takes place without recourse to either a sight-read or pre-learned script is of course characterized by skills of recall and reproduction: but also by fundamentally generative processes of sound production. Performers themselves must supply, at the point of performance, the ongoing material content (in other words, the music!). Studies in the cognitive psychology of oral tradition and memory account for particular memorization and recall processes associated with song and chant (Rubin, 1997). For example, the cuing effect of rhythmic performance facilitates learning and recall through mechanisms to do with constraints imposed by the temporal position of items (e.g. word or melody-choice at a given moment), and durational limits (e.g. long-short patterning). Repetition in the structure of songs and chants also aids memorization, particularly where this reinforces hierarchical and episodic organization (McLucas, 2011, pp. 43–5). Sloboda (1985) argues that memory mechanisms in both oral and literate contexts share such processes in common, since both are based on "the ability to extract higher-order structure from sequences of notes. In an oral context, the musician uses a stored structure to generate different, but structurally linked, note sequences on different occasions" (Sloboda, 1985, p. 246).

Sloboda's (1985) influential text on music cognition, *The Musical Mind*, proposed some key similarities and distinctions between specifically precomposed and improvised (namely, jazz) performance. With reference to *schemas*—our recognition of patterned information through representations held in long-term memory—Sloboda describes improvisation as a process in which "formal constraints . . . comprise a 'blueprint' for performance," in place of a fully composed and revised musical score (1985, p. 139). Ethnomusicologists typically urge a more circumspect consideration of the intersection between improvisation and pre-composition, emphasizing the relationship between the two concepts along a full spectrum of pre-scripted, to prompted, to (ostensibly) free-form musical forms. However, this model is consistent with a number of descriptive and empirical accounts of music performance. Nettl's (2005) analogy between Western serialist composition and Native American Peyote song, for example, compares the serialist composer's manipulation of materials according to explicit rules, and the performance of Peyote song, which involves "using and abiding by general structural principles . . . musically making clear a number of intricate inter-relationships, deriving new phrases from earlier ones, all within a rather rigidly defined framework" (p. 29).

In order to carry out such principles in live music performance, musicians are required to have at their fingertips a range of learned motor patterns. The design and execution of these sub-units of performance material reflects (and, by processes of feedback, informs) the performer's own understanding of the musical organization that they are generating. In contrast to some styles of Western music pedagogy where patterns are learned in connection to a highly literate theoretical system of harmonic interrelationships, music performance supported by a predominantly oral tradition is more likely to be learned through functional performance units. For example, it is common to hear students of classical music practicing major scales from tonic to tonic, which reinforces the key's theoretical unity—but not its typical deployment in performance. In the case of our two best-documented improvisational genres, jazz musicians know the value of rehearsing complete *licks*, and North Indian sitarists work to perfect their *tans*; these are both examples of transposable melodic formulas which are consciously overlearned in order that they serve as stock-phrases, allowing performers to "keep it going" during performance (Slawek, 1998). Berkowitz's (2010) detailed account of learning to improvise at the keyboard within the classical Western tradition reports a similar process of internalizing through embodied memory particular cadence patterns, harmonic relationships, and idiomatic melodic movements.

The way in which such knowledge is acquired is a key factor in determining the likely organization and subsequent usage of that knowledge. The degree to which traditions make knowing use of a theoretical foundation varies, ranging from informal, implicit learning (linked to complete items of repertoire and therefore particular patterns), to an explicit, highly specified basis that allows for theoretical rather than intuitive generation of new material. Knowledge of repertoire and its underlying schemata does not need to be abstract or purely auditory. In contrast, it is likely to be intrinsically linked to motor expertise. All music-specialist performance skills rest on technical skills at producing and modulating sound, whether as extemporized or pre-learned material. The intentional control of an instrument of any sort (including the internally-housed apparatus used by singers) requires fine motor control, expert temporal co-ordination of independent movements between limbs or parts, and the assimilation of feedback between aural and motor processes at a very high temporal resolution. It is well known that expert performance of Western classical music requires "the precise execution of very fast and, in many instances, extremely complex physical movements that must be structured and coordinated with continuous auditory, visual, and somatosensory feedback" (Altenmüller & Furuya, 2016, p. 529).

Performance of non-Western classical music at the expert level requires similarly skillful, multimodal and temporally integrated technical proficiencies, whether the performance is initiated and acted out according to the memorization of a precomposed work, or whether it is generated extemporaneously according to learned formal constraints. One of the most documented examples comes again from the study of North Indian classical music, a predominantly oral and highly formalized tradition. The acquisition of highly controlled motor patterns is of no less importance to the sitarist than to the violinist. North Indian classical musicians acquire their skills within a tradition which upholds punishingly high expectations of skillfulness and dexterity, achieved through rigorous over-learning of schematic patterns within overarching modal, rhythmic and melodic systems (Neuman, 1980). Similarly, following Berliner's (1994) identification of "licks," "crips" and "schemas," Biasutti and Frezza (2009) emphasize how much value jazz musicians assign to consummate mastery of idiomatic sound production. Ashley (2016) explains how such internalization of physical patterns and behaviors through dedicated hours of intentional practice and repetition leads to procedural (as opposed to declarative) knowledge, which is what seems to provide "a set of pre-existing materials which serve as a vocabulary or lexicon from which they [improvisers] can select and on which transformations can be effected" (p. 670).

Based on his research into Afghan lute performance, and with the advantage of his own status as an expert performer, ethnomusicologist and psychologist, John Baily has argued that one of the most important conceptual models for improvised performance is "a spatial model in which movements are planned and experienced in visual, kinesthetic, and tactile terms" (Baily, 1992, p. 150). His introspectively-driven account emphasizes the role of motor pattern learning and feedback in the generative work of creating large-scale, coherent musical structures in the course of performance, which chimes with the personal report of many practicing musicians. Although the study of the relationship of motor systems to memory is not yet a mature field (Chaffin, Logan, & Begosh, 2008, p. 355), the multimodality of musical performance—its demand for simultaneous activity across, for example, auditory, motor, visual and emotional systems—is understood to provide great opportunity for learning and the creation of retrieval cues.

## Rhythm, Meter and Expressive Timing

In performance, musicians make decisions that serve to emphasize what is salient according to their own estimation and comprehension of the underlying musical structures. Such expressive decisions may distinguish amateur from expert performers; their detection and reception by audience members can also separate the cultural outsiders from the insiders. Conceived as a particular sub-domain of empirical performance research (Gabrielsson, 2003), *expressiveness* in performance research describes a topic staked out according to musicological efforts to explore the non-textual elements so apparent in music listening and performance but which are hidden in score-based study: the sum effect of nuances of phrasing, intonation and delivery which can distinguish one musical performance from another. Fabian, Timmers, and Schubert (2014) provide a collection of chapters which present the music psychology community with the broadest consideration of this topic to date, including discussion of expressiveness in Estonian song and in Central African polyphony from the Cameroonian Bedzan community, as well as examples from popular, funk, jazz and Indian classical music. The chapters by Ashley (2014) and Bauer (2014) highlight particularly the importance of groove and microtiming as expressive features identified in popular and jazz music.

The study of groove and microtiming has accelerated as a consequence of the availability of high quality timing data from audio recordings. This area of research is extremely important for the study of oral music cultures: High quality recordings and, specifically, timing data provides an empirical alternative to the score, and a redistribution of the attention formerly focused on melodic transcription. An example of the insights to be gained from such a perspective comes from recent research on Mande drumming (Polak & London, 2014). The basic roles taken up by members of Mande drumming ensembles include a core metrical accompaniment, a performer who provides the characteristic "hook," and an improvising and regulative lead drummer. Polak and London's (2014) analysis reveals that performers show individual microtiming patterns, whilst the collective ensemble generates a non-isochronous metrical structure and continuous accelerando. Performers negotiate this structural acceleration, which means that successful ensemble playing in this context cannot rely on a stable reference tempo, but one that is characterized by continuous directional change. Such long-term changes in tempo are central to various oral traditions, including Japanese Gagaku and Tibetan monastic music as described by Huron (2006).

## Conclusions

Even where music is routinely notated in some fashion, an individual musician or music student always acquires the practical skills of music-making orally, through their relationships with other people: In this sense, orality is a key component of every musical performance tradition. But the matter of notated versus non-notated music performance raises some issues for music psychology. Two important and related questions which have a particular bearing on music perception and cognition research are: Firstly, how do we determine which structural or formal components can be considered as fixed features, and are central to the perceived organization of musical phenomena? Secondly, how is such knowledge articulated and transmitted amongst its proponents? These are important considerations to take on board when interpreting evidence from scientific research, whose ultimate aim, of course, is not to document individual cases and distinctiveness but to find collective and generalizable underlying features. For reasons already discussed at length, not all topics reported in mainstream music psychology performance research have an obvious bearing on oral or improvised performance (for example, the psychology of sight-reading); and yet many issues (such as the nature and diversity of underlying musical schema, or the relationship of motor systems to musical perception and memorization) are clearly deserving of the increasing and comparative attention that they now receive.

## Core Reading

Ashley, R. (2016). Musical improvisation. In S. Hallam, I. Cross, & M. Thaut (Eds.), *The Oxford handbook of music psychology* (2nd ed., pp. 667–679). Oxford: Oxford University Press.

Berkowitz, A. (2010). *The improvising mind: Cognition and creativity in the musical moment.* Oxford: Oxford University Press.

Berliner, P. (1994). *Thinking in jazz: The infinite art of improvisation.* Chicago, IL: Chicago University Press.

McLucas, A.D. (2011). *The musical ear: Oral tradition in the USA.* Farnham, UK: Ashgate.

Nettl, B., & Russell, M. (1998). *In the course of performance: Studies in the world of musical improvisation.* Chicago, IL: University of Chicago Press.

Stevens, C. J. (2012). Music perception and cognition: A review of recent cross-cultural research. *Topics in Cognitive Science, 4*(4), 653–667. doi: 10.1111/j.1756–8765.2012.01215.x

## Further References

Altenmüller, E., & Furuya, S. (2016). Planning and performance. In S. Hallam, I. Cross, & M. Thaut (Eds.), *The Oxford handbook of music psychology* (2nd ed., pp. 529–545). Oxford: Oxford University Press.

Ashley, R. (2014). Expressiveness in funk. In D. Fabian, R. Timmers, & E. Schubert (Eds.), *Expressiveness in music performance: Empirical approaches across styles and cultures.* Oxford: Oxford University Press.

Averill, G. (2004). "Where's 'one'?": Musical encounters of the ensemble kind. In Solís T. (Ed.), *Performing Ethnomusicology: Teaching and Representation in World Music Ensembles* (pp. 93–112). Berkeley and Los Angeles, CA: University of California Press.

Baily, J. (1992). Music performance, motor structure, and cognitive models. In U. Wegner, M. P. Baumann, & A. Simon (Eds.), *European studies in ethnomusicology: Historical developments and recent trends* (pp. 142–158). Wilhelmshaven, Germany: Noetzel.

Bauer, W. R. (2014). Expressiveness in jazz performance. In D. Fabian, R. Timmers, & E. Schubert (Eds.), *Expressiveness in music performance: Empirical approaches across styles and cultures.* Oxford: Oxford University Press.

Bavelas, J. B., Coates, L., & Johnson, T. (2002). Listener responses as a collaborative process: The role of gaze. *Journal of Communication, 52*(3), 566–580.

Biasutti, M., & Frezza, L. (2009). Dimensions of music improvisation. *Creativity Research Journal, 21*(2–3), 232–242.

Chaffin, R., Logan, T. R., & Begosh, K. T. (2008). Performing from memory. In S. Hallam, I. Cross, & M. Thaut (Eds.), *The Oxford handbook of music psychology.* Oxford: Oxford University Press.

Clayton, M. R. L. (2016). The social and personal functions of music in cross-cultural perspective. In S. Hallam, I. Cross, & M. Thaut (Eds.), *The Oxford handbook of music psychology.* (2nd ed.) Oxford: Oxford University Press.

Durán, L., Magriel, N., & Baker, G. (2011). Growing into music: Musical enculturation in oral traditions. Retrieved 9 June, 2016, from http://growingintomusic.co.uk/

Fabian, D., Timmers, R. & Schubert, E. (Eds.). (2014). *Expressiveness in music performance: Empirical approaches across styles and cultures*. Oxford: Oxford University Press.

Faulkner, R. R., & Becker, H. S. (2009). *"Do you know . . . ?": The jazz repertoire in action*. Chicago, IL: University of Chicago Press.

Gabrielsson, A. (2003). Music performance research at the millennium. *Psychology of Music, 31*(3), 221–272.

Green, L. (2002). *How popular musicians learn: A way ahead for music education*. Aldershot, UK: Ashgate Publishing, Ltd.

Hallam, S., Cross, I., & Thaut, M. (Eds.) (2016). *The Oxford handbook of music psychology* (2nd ed.). Oxford: Oxford University Press.

Huron, D. B. (2006). *Sweet anticipation: Music and the psychology of expectation*. Cambridge, MA: MIT Press.

Jankowsky, R. C. (2010). *Stambeli: Music, trance, and alterity in Tunisia*. Chicago, IL: University of Chicago Press.

Kawase, S. (2014). Gazing behavior and coordination during piano duo performance. *Attention, Perception, & Psychophysics, 76*(2), 527–540.

King, E., & Ginsborg, J. (2011). Gestures and glances: Interactions in ensemble rehearsal. In Gritten A., King E. (Eds), *New perspectives on music and gesture* (pp. 177–201). Farnham, UK: Ashgate.

Lucas, G. (2013). Performing the rosary. In M. R. L. Clayton, B. Dueck, & L. Leante (Eds.), *Experience and meaning in music performance* (pp. 86–106). New York, NY: Oxford University Press.

Moran, N. (2007). *Measuring musical interaction: Analysing communication in embodied musical behaviour*. (PhD). Milton Keynes, UK: Open University.

Moran, N., Hadley, L. V., Bader, M., & Keller, P. E. (2015). Perception of 'back-channeling' nonverbal feedback in musical duo improvisation. *Plos One, 10*(6), e0130070.

Nettl, B. (2005). *The Study of ethnomusicology: 31 issues and concepts*. Urbana-Chicago, IL: University of Illinois Press.

Nettl, B., & Stone, R. (Eds.) (1998–2002). *Garland encyclopedia of world music*. New York, NY: Garland, Routledge.

Neuman, D. M. (1980). *The life of music in North India*. Chicago, IL: University of Chicago Press.

Palmer, C. (1997). Music performance. *Annual Review of Psychology, 48*, 115–138.

Palmer, C. (2013). Music performance: Movement and coordination. In D. Deutsch (Ed.), *The psychology of music* (3rd ed., pp. 405–422). San Diego, CA: Academic Press/Elsevier.

Parncutt, R., & McPherson, G. (Eds.). (2002). *The science and psychology of music performance: Creative strategies for teaching and learning*. Oxford & New York, NY: Oxford University Press.

Polak, R., & London, J. (2014). Timing and meter in Mande drumming from Mali. *Music Theory Online, 20*(1): 20.1.1.

Racy, A. J. (1998). Improvisation, ecstasy, and performance dynamics in Arabic music. In B. Nettl & M. Russell (Eds.), *In the course of performance: Studies in the world of improvisation* (pp. 95–112). Chicago, IL: University of Chicago Press.

Ramnarine, T. K. (2009). Musical performance. In J. Harper-Scott, P. Edward, & J. Samson (Eds.), *An introduction to music studies* (pp. 221–235). Cambridge: Cambridge University Press.

Rubin, D. C. (1997). *Memory in oral traditions: The cognitive psychology of epic, ballads, and counting-out rhymes*. Oxford: Oxford University Press.

Slawek, S. (1998). Keeping it going: Terms, practices, and processes of improvisation in Hindustani instrumental music. In B. Nettl, & M. Russell (Eds.), *In the course of performance: Studies in the world of musical improvisation* (pp. 335–368). Chicago, IL: University of Chicago Press.

Sloboda, J. A. (1985). *The musical mind: The cognitive psychology of music*. Oxford: Clarendon Press.

Wade, B.C. (2004). *Thinking musically: Experiencing music, expressing culture*. New York, NY: Oxford University Press.

# 25

# PERFORMING MUSIC
## Humans, Computers, and Electronics

*Elaine Chew and Andrew McPherson*

## Introduction

Performing music, communication through music, is a ubiquitous human activity. As tools to assist in human activities have evolved from the mechanical to the electronic, music making has not escaped the relentless tide of technological innovation. This chapter explores forms of *technology-mediated performance*, and the ways in which the intervention of computers and electronics has changed, and continues to change, our processes and understanding of music making. Advances in computing power and speed now allow machines to simulate aspects of human-like intelligence and behavior so that computers can more closely and dynamically partner with humans in creative performance, improvisation, and composition. Technological innovations have led to new instruments and traditional instruments augmented by electronics that lead to new ways of performing, improvising, and composing.

The technologies considered are broadly divided into two categories: *digital instrument systems* that extend the sound-producing capabilities of the performer, and *generative* or *intelligent systems* that offer control at a higher level of musical abstraction, extending the mind of the performer and/or composer. The two categories, the first of which draws on a combination of hardware and software and the second of which is primarily software-based, are far from clear divisions. Music software is inextricably tied to electronic capabilities and not infrequently coupled with physical instruments. Many digital music instruments embed and take on the capacity of intelligent software. The physical manifestations and constraints of an instrument necessarily impact mental representations of the music; and, the desired high-level representations and handles on musical parameters inevitably shape the design of an instrument. What is clear is that the advent of electronics and computers has introduced profound shifts in musical thought, changing our understanding of the performer's, composer's, and listener's roles and our ideas of what an instrument should be, what a performance can be, and the very notion of creativity itself. The two categories will be treated in sequence in the following sections.

## Extending the Musician's Body: Electronic and Digital Instruments

Through the ages, human invention has adapted the tools at its disposal to serve artistic purposes. The rise of digital technology has led to *digital musical instruments* (DMIs), also known as *new interfaces for musical expression* (NIMEs) after the conference of the same name (Jensenius & Lyons, 2017), and traditional instruments augmented by electronics. This section will cover trends and innovations in the design and use of digital musical instruments, with a particular focus on tools which fit a traditional instrumental paradigm where physical actions and sounds are closely coupled in time and energy.[1] The history of music-making with electronics—see Chadabe (1997), Miranda and Wanderley (2006), and Emmerson (2013)—is a story of technical innovation, competing artistic forces of tradition and experimentation, and creative appropriation of technology in often unexpected ways. Jordà (2004) describes the process of creating DMIs as *digital lutherie:* not a strict science but "a sort of craftsmanship that sometimes may produce a work of art, no less than music."

## Technical Foundations

Here we summarize common technical principles and taxonomies in digital musical instrument design before moving on to human factors in the next section. The archetypical DMI consists of *sensor inputs*, *output parameters* (usually sonic, though sometimes including modalities such as visuals or haptics), and a *mapping layer* (Wanderley & Depalle, 2004). The mapping layer attracts particular interest (e.g. Hunt, Wanderley, & Paradis, 2003, Magnusson, 2009): On acoustic instruments, the action-sound relationship is fixed by mechanical design, but DMIs allow arbitrary relationships to be created, including complex mappings involving stochastic or generative processes, or mapping-by-demonstration using machine learning (e.g. Fiebrink, 2011).

Several taxonomies of DMIs have been proposed, with a distinction often made between *instruments*, which integrate the input, mapping and output into a single system, and *controllers*, which perform input and mapping only and leave the sound generation to an external device. The MIDI (Musical Instrument Digital Interface) standard, published in 1983, remains the dominant protocol for digital controllers, even though its keyboard-focused paradigm makes assumptions that are not valid for all music.[2] Controllers can be versatile, but they lack the tactile or kinesthetic feedback of acoustic instruments (Jordà, 2004), and frequently changing mappings can be an impediment to developing expertise.

Wanderley and Depalle (2004) classify DMIs according to their relationship to traditional musical instruments and playing techniques. *Instrument-like controllers* (say, MIDI keyboards and electronic drum pads) inherit the form and playing interface of familiar acoustic instruments while replacing the means of sound production with an electronic process. *Instrument-inspired controllers* borrow aspects of a familiar instrument interface but seek a fundamentally different musical purpose. *Alternate controllers* do not deliberately resemble traditional instruments.

The final category in Wanderley and Depalle's classification, *extended instruments* (also known as *augmented instruments*), comprises of existing familiar instruments fitted with new sensors and actuators to extend their capabilities. The typical goal of an augmented instrument is to maintain all the capabilities and nuances of the underlying instrument while enlarging the musical vocabulary. Augmentations have been developed of most common Western instruments including piano (McPherson, 2015), guitar (e.g. Lähdeoja, 2015), violin (Overholt, 2012) and trumpet (Thibodeau & Wanderley, 2013). Augmentations typically take two forms: sensors on the instrument that control digital audio processing or synthesis, and electromechanical actuation of the instrument's resonating structures. Actuation is often applied to the body of the instrument through embedded loudspeakers or vibration transducers, or it can be applied to vibrating metal strings using electromagnets (Overholt, Berdahl, & Hamilton, 2011).

## Human Factors

What makes a "good" instrument depends less on any particular technical specification and more on a player's ability to make creative use of it. This section considers the relationship between player and instrument in DMI performance.

On acoustic instruments, performers commonly experience the feeling "that the musical instrument has become part of the body" (Nijs, Luc, Lesaffre, & Leman, 2009). The theory of embodied music cognition (Leman, 2008) holds that the musical instrument is a "mediation technology" between the mind and a musical environment. At expert levels, the instrument becomes transparent to the performer; the bodily operations of manipulating the instrument become automatic, so the performer's full attention can focus on the action of creating music. In other words, the challenge of understanding performer-instrument interaction is precisely that the performer is *not* consciously thinking about the instrument while playing.

An open question in DMI design, aesthetically and cognitively, is the amount of control the instrument should give to the performer. It is far easier to make a computer system capable of controlling many simultaneous sonic dimensions than it is for a performer to learn to play it. Momeni and Wessel (2003) suggest that three simultaneous dimensions are the limit of what is easily controlled in real time, although many DMIs possess more degrees of freedom in practice. Adding more control dimensions, possibly even extending the instrument to control multiple media, does not necessarily improve the artistic result (Tanaka, 2000). On the contrary, the role of constraints in fostering creativity has long been noted. In one study of a simple DMI (Zappi & McPherson, 2014), a version of the instrument with two degrees of freedom resulted in *less* diverse usage and more negative performer feedback than an otherwise identical instrument with only a single degree of freedom.

Another important consideration is the learning curve for a new instrument. Wessel and Wright (2002) propose that the ideal instrument should have a "low entry fee with no ceiling on virtuosity," but how one reliably achieves such an outcome remains unknown. Given the importance of extended practice in acquiring instrumental expertise, it is unlikely that shortcuts exist to performer virtuosity on a new and unfamiliar instrument. Building on existing instrumental expertise through augmented instruments or instrument-inspired controllers is one possible approach. An open challenge here is to develop strategies for maximizing musical novelty while minimizing the amount of re-learning that is required to achieve proficiency.

## Cultural Considerations

A DMI's technical design or even its relationship to the performer tells but part of the story. Broader cultural factors, including repertoire, pedagogy, and the existence of well-known virtuoso players can be crucial to the instrument's success. For the most groundbreaking instruments, a creative tension emerges over how much to embrace or challenge established musical culture. A microcosm of such creative tensions can be found in the theremin, an early 20th-century instrument played by waving the hands in the air without touching the instrument, and its contemporary the Ondes Martenot, where pitch is controlled by either a keyboard or a sliding ring worn on the finger. Partly on account of its striking technical innovation, the theremin remains better-known in popular culture, while the Ondes Martenot maintains a regular presence in the concert hall through its championing by Olivier Messiaen and other composers.

One of the most surprising developments in popular electronic music emerged from the use of the turntable (Katz, 2010). Originally designed as a home playback device, hip-hop DJs reimagined it as a performance tool for constructing music from repeated loops of recorded material. Many present-day digital performance tools draw on metaphors from this practice. The turntable's emergence as a musical instrument highlights two important phenomena about technology in music. First, nearly anything can become a musical instrument in the right hands, from a washboard to a pair of spoons to an oil drum (the Caribbean steelpan). Instruments may also be used in ways their creator did not imagine, as with the growling tones and pitch bends used by jazz saxophonists, or distortion and feedback on the electric guitar. New techniques are passed from one player to the next, often through emulating role models (see Moran, and Green & Smart, this volume), such that techniques that were once unusual or even subversive quickly become widespread.

The turntable-as-instrument is also an example of how no tool or technology can be aesthetically neutral. Magnusson (2009) observes

> the piano keyboard "tells us" that microtonality is of little importance . . .; the drum-sequencer that 4/4 rhythms and semiquavers are more natural than other types; and the digital audio workstation, through its affordances of copying, pasting and looping, assures us that it is perfectly normal to repeat the same short performance over and over in the same track.
>
> *(p. 171)*

In this sense, observing the construction and evolution of digital musical instruments can yield insight into the artistic values and priorities of the people creating them.

## *Instrument or Composition?*

Many DMIs maintain the familiar paradigm of acoustic instruments, where a single action produces a single sound. However, unlike acoustic instruments, some DMIs give the user control over higher-level musical structures rather than individual events. Magnusson (2009) calls such instruments "epistemic tools," explaining that the performer can delegate part of the cognitive process to the instrument ("extensions of the mind rather than the body"). The symbolic instructions of the machine, rather than the resonating body or quality of sound production, form the musical core of these instruments. Accordingly, the performer's interaction takes place on a symbolic rather than embodied level.

No musical instrument design can claim to be aesthetically neutral. But the aesthetic intention of the design perhaps becomes more explicit when moving to more abstract levels of musical control. Schnell and Battier (2002) discuss the idea of "composed instruments" which incorporate complex artistic processes into the instrument design. Playing such an instrument is akin to navigating a route through a particular piece, representing cooperation between composer and performer on different terms than traditional acoustic instruments.

In the next section, we will consider more such composed instruments, along with other systems in which musical events are generated or shaped at a higher level of abstraction by the human musician through a computer.

## Extending the Musician's Mind: Generative and Intelligent Systems

Before the advent of the first computers, when Babbage conceived of the general-purpose computing machine, Lovelace (1843) predicted that computers would one day be capable of creative intelligence, that they would be able to compose "elaborate and scientific pieces of music of any degree of complexity or extent" (p. 694). From the era of the first computers, Hiller and Isaacson (1958) composed a string quartet, the Illiac Suite, using material generated by the ILLIAC I. The same year also marked the birth of computer performance of music, when Max Mathews' Music I program played a 17-second composition on an IBM 704.[3] Thus began explorations into the digital computer as a musical instrument and as a composer (Mathews, 1963). Inventions of fast computer chips and algorithms like that for FM synthesis (Chowning, 1973) made it possible to perform computations to synthesize musical notes and timbres in less than the time it takes to play them. Such responsiveness has enabled the design of interactive systems that can participate in live performance.

Early notions of computational intelligence ascribe this ability only to creative systems capable of generating music. Increasingly, the ability to perform, to interpret and shape, scripted (or generated) or improvised music is also recognized as musically intelligent, even creative. Intelligent systems come in many forms: from those that synthesize music from scratch to those that emulate style, from systems that generate a simple motif to those that create orchestrated pieces, from systems that can entrain to a pulse to those that can engage in ensemble dialog, from conducting systems to those that mimic performance style. This section discusses three classes of generative and intelligent systems: conductor programs, accompaniment systems, and improvisation systems. While the role of intelligent systems in composition, improvisation, and performance is surveyed elsewhere (e.g. de Mantarras & Arcos, 2002, see also Dean, this volume), the focus here is on interactive systems deployed in performance.

### *Conductor Programs*

Machines built to control the playback of music date back to the middle ages, when music box-like devices were used to drive organs and harmoniums—see review by Malinowski (2016). Known as *conductor programs*, these machines extend the performer's mind, allowing users to control expressive parameters such as tempo, timing, and dynamics.

For the discussion, we shall borrow some of Rowe's terminology. In his seminal book on interactive music systems, Rowe (1993, Chapter 1) describes them as systems "whose behavior change in response to musical input." He further classifies interactive music systems along three dimensions: *score-driven* (aligns events to score representation) vs. *performance-driven* (responds to performed properties); *transformative* (transformations applied to input), *generative* (serial procedures applied to elementary material), or *sequenced* (playback of pre-recorded fragments); and, as following the *player paradigm* (for ensemble results) or *instrument paradigm* (producing solo performances). In Rowe's terminology, conductor programs constitute score-driven, sequenced-response, instrument paradigm systems.

Conductor programs allow performers to focus on the timing and other expressive factors without having to worry about getting the notes right. Composers may determine the pitches—the "most important musical parameter" but "the least expressive factor" (Mathews, 1991, in title)—but it is performers who shape expressive factors and control the music experience. For example, prompted by Pierre Boulez's request for an interface to control the playback speed of tape recordings, Max Mathews invented the Radio Baton, a wireless three-dimensional controller based on technology developed by robotics engineer Bob Boie that can shape the timing and dynamics of music performance in real time. The decoupling of parameters through the use of two independent batons allows for fine expressive control, such as of individual note shapes and extraordinary time suspensions.

Traditionally, physical skill at an instrument is gained through years of practice. By removing the need for dexterity at the instrument, conductor programs allow their users to bypass these years of grind to focus early on higher-level issues of musical control and musicality. This control can be realized through known gestures or by creating new mappings. In Borchers, Lee, Samminger, Mühlhäuser's (2004) Personal Orchestra, the user controls the tempo, dynamics, and instrument emphasis of the video playback of a Vienna Philharmonic performance with an infrared baton, while the Air Worm by Dixon, Goebl, and Widmer, (2005) uses Langner's two-dimensional perceptual space to control tempo and loudness. To preserve micro expressive nuances that are still difficult for machines to synthesize, the program flattens then re-introduces tempo and loudness properties, leaving intact details such as articulation, chord asynchronies, and inter-voice dynamics. Leveraging the analogy between music and motion, Chew, François, Liu, and Yang's (2005) Expression Synthesis Project (ESP) takes the driving metaphor for music performance to the next level to create a driving (wheel and pedals) interface for controlling expressive parameters through driving on a virtual road.

Conducting programs' focus on direct control over expressive nuance presents immediate impact on music pedagogy. Following the Radio Baton's event triggering paradigm, Schnell (2013) with the *Atelier des Feuillantines* uses a chess game to enact a performance of Bach's *Goldberg Variation 18* ("Canone a la Sesta")—alternating chess moves correspond to half-bar onsets. In another game, players catching a ball trigger pizzicato chords in the orchestra accompaniment in Bach's *Concerto in F-minor* (2nd movement). Similarly, Wang's (2014) *Magic Piano* uses finger taps on falling balls of light on an iPad or iPhone to trigger notes in a piece of music. These new interfaces nudge the performer's role closer to active listening, but with relatively less physically engagement, and raise natural questions on the roles instrumental virtuosi play in the digital age.

## Accompaniment Systems

Like conductor programs, *automated accompaniment systems* control the playback of music, except they do this through an instrument rather than through a digital interface. The live instrumentalist thus serves as the conductor. Automated accompaniment systems are considered intelligent because, distinct from their precursor the music-minus-one system, they can entrain with the soloist so as to synchronize with the live performer, like traditional accompanists. According to Rowe's (1993) terminology, these systems constitute score-driven, sequenced-response, player paradigm systems.

There are a number of real challenges to machines synchronizing to humans in scripted performance. In practice, note-perfect performances are rare except for the simplest pieces, and performance errors and other deviations can make MIDI note or audio input-to-score alignment imprecise. In Vercoe's (1984) *Synthetic Performer*, an instinctive listening model extracted a sense of tempo from audio and sensor input for linking between performer and machine. Dannenberg (1984) experimented with real-time score-matching algorithms that allowed for extra and missing notes. In Raphael's (2010) *Music Plus One* (MPO) system, rehearsals allow the system to learn probable expressions and a Kalman filter-like algorithm predicts timings for the near future. Cont's (2008) *Antescofo* was created originally for Marco Stroppa's ". . . of Silence" for saxophone and chamber electronics. Designed for synchronization and interaction between an electronic score and live player, the electronic score may embed generative sequences or transformations triggered by live events. Further systems are reviewed in Rowe (1993, chapter 3), Cont 2004, and Dannenberg and Raphael (2006).[4]

## Improvisation Systems

*Improvisation systems* generate music on the fly in collaboration with live performer(s). They represent, in Rowe's parlance, performance-driven, player paradigm systems, and their responses can be transformative or generative. Traditional composition and improvisation both involve creating new music material, but differ in terms of the immediacy of the output, and in the time allowed to review, reflect, and revise decisions. When computers are involved, it takes little to no time to generate new material and all options can be evaluated in the blink of an eye. Thus, while the capabilities may resemble that of composition, the speed with which computers are able to produce music makes their creating more akin to improvising, thus blurring the line between improvisation and composition. However, because the ability to reason and make common sense judgments still eludes even the best computer algorithms, computers still lag behind humans when it comes to the ability to reflect on and revise past decisions.

Improvising machines typically perform with a live musician(s). In *human-machine improvisation*, the performance results from in-the-moment dialog between the live player(s) and the machine. Lewis' (2000) *Voyager* represents one such interactive experiment. Voyager analyses the musician's input to generate complex musical responses based on the playing as well as rules encoding domain-specific knowledge. This is an example of an *expert system*-type approach to intelligent music systems, where the programmer hard codes specific rules that represent aspects of music knowledge into the system. This is in contrast to *data analytics*-type approaches, which includes machine learning, in which the system automatically derives insights from data for decision making. The logical and systematic structure of Voyager's program leads Lewis to refer to it as a composition.

Later systems sought to emulate improvisation styles as encapsulated by note sequences, learning from human input through a data analytics approach (see also Vuust & Kringelbach, this volume). The *OMax* family of systems (Assayag, Bloch, Chemillier, Cont, & Dubnov, 2006) accomplishes this by reducing improvised music sequences to factor oracles, a data structure capturing repeated patterns and continuation links; traversing the resulting network recombines the patterns to generate believable sequences resembling the original input. An independent operator determines system parameters such as the sampling area of the network and the recombination rate, which determines the degree of novelty of the output. Pachet's (2003) *Continuator* uses Markov models to represent style; traversing the networks of the Markov models then produces sequences having the same statistical properties as the input. Interactions with *OMax* and the Continuator tend to be reactive as it is hard to predict the system's output until it has sounded; the musician must then adapt rapidly to make the performance a success. *Mimi* by François, Chew, and Thurmond (2011) allows for a more reflective mode of interaction by providing visual feedback; the improviser also controls Mimi's parameters, including when she learns, plans, plays, and starts afresh.

Structure is widely regarded to be a desirable musical trait; compositions are typically associated with form and structure, and improvisation with lack of structure (Lewis, 2000). However, analyses of improvisations produced with *Mimi* showed that the system's functions and constraints result in music following common classical forms (Schankler, Chew, & François, 2014). The creation of structure in improvised performance is further reinforced in experiments with *Mimi4x* (François, Schankler, & Chew, 2013), which allows users to engage directly with high-level structural improvisation, thereby taking on some of the role of the composer.

Although some improvisations have been transcribed for re-performance, the spontaneity of improvising means that most improvisations have traditionally been far removed from notation. Advances in computing technologies now allow compositions to be generated and notated on the fly for live performance. In Didkovsky's (2004) "Zero Waste," the pianist starts by reading an initial difficult-to-read two bars of music; each subsequent set of two bars are based on the sight reading of the previous two bars like a game of "Chinese whispers". In Hoadley's (2012) "Calder's Violin," the violin part is generated and notated in real-time so that the details of the piece change with each performance. Such serendipitous and ephemeral real time scores are starting to close the traditional gap between improvisation and composition, creating what Hajdu (2016) calls a breed of "comprovisations."

Numerous variations on the human-machine collaborative improvisation paradigm exist. In live coding, the computer program itself is generated on the fly, and the programmer becomes both performer and composer (see Collins, McLean, Rohrhuber, & Ward, 2003; Wang & Cook, 2004). Robotic improvisation takes place when the performance of the machine-generated music is realized through an anthropomorphic robot (e.g. Weinberg & Driscoll, 2006). When, in addition, the audience is allowed to influence the generated outcomes (see Freedman, 2008), listeners also serve the function of the composer.[5]

## Conclusions

The chapter has covered a spectrum of machine interventions in musical performance ranging from electronic and digital instruments that extend the musician's body to generative and intelligent systems that extend the musician's mind, showing the wealth of creative possibilities engendered by computers and electronics.

The new interaction paradigms call to question the roles of the performer, composer, improviser, and computer, and the distribution of creativity amongst the various agents involved in music making. When a live musician partners with a computer to make music, is the computer a (co-)creative agent? Is the programmer the creative agent? Is the computer a sophisticated mirror for the performer's intentions? If some degree of intelligence is embedded in the system, is this done using an expert system approach incorporating the programmer's music knowledge, or a data analytics approach where the computer assumes some of the roles usually associated with musical insight? If the computer is simply executing pre-coded instructions, or even if it is autonomously recognizing patterns, does that represent true creative intelligence? These are but some of the questions that have emerged in the age of musical interaction with computers.

What might the future hold? Forecasting may be hard, but one thing is for sure: Musical styles do not remain fixed over time; they respond to external forces such as the available tools for musical expression, and constantly evolve and adapt to new opportunities and situations. We may be designing digital tools to push the envelope with regard to existing genres and scenarios, but the most artistically transformative uses of digital technology may be yet to come.

## Notes

1. This chapter will not examine the tools used to create electronic dance music, though this is an area of significant technical and artistic innovation; further discussion on the aesthetics of those genres can be found in Demers (2010).
2. For example, MIDI assumes that music can be divided into discrete notes, each at a particular semitone with a discrete onset and release. Continuous, independent control within each note is a persistent challenge which there have been periodic attempts to solve—the most of recent of which is the Multidimensional Polyphonic Expression (MPE) extension to the MIDI standard.
3. From Max Mathews' summary of his work in computer music for the program for the festival "Horizons in Computer Music," held 8–9 March, 1997, at the Simon Recital Center of the School of Music, Indiana University, Bloomington, Indiana.
4. This chapter does not cover harmonization systems, which are largely composition systems although some are realized as on-the-fly systems for specific classes of music. For a review that is part of an overview of music generation systems, see Herremans, Chuan, & Chew (under review).
5. This chapter does not cover Internet performance where network delay affects both performance and composition (see Carôt, Rebelo, & Renaud, 2007) and performers can become the instrument (Hajdu, 2007).

## Core Reading

Assayag, G., Bloch, G., Chemillier, M., Cont, A., & Dubnov, S. (2006). Omax brothers: A dynamic topology of agents for improvisation learning. In X. Amatriain, E. Chew, J. Foote (Eds.), *Proceedings of the Workshop on Audio and Music Computing for Multimedia, Association for Computing Machinery (ACM) Multimedia* (pp. 125–132). Santa Barbara, California. New York, NY: ACM.

Jensenius, A. R., & Lyons, M. (Eds.) (2017). *A NIME reader—Fifteen years of new interfaces for musical expression.* Berlin: Springer.

Jordà, S. (2004). Instruments and players: Some thoughts on digital lutherie. *Journal of New Music Research, 33,* 321–341.

Lewis, G. (2000). Too many notes: Computers, complexity and culture in Voyager. *Leonardo Music Journal, 10,* 33–39.

Magnusson, T. (2009). Of epistemic tools: Musical instruments as cognitive extensions. *Organised Sound, 14*(2), 168–176.

Mathews, M. (1991). The Radio Baton and conductor program, or: Pitch, the most important and least expressive part of music. *Computer Music Journal, 15*(4), 37–46.

Rowe, R. (1993). *Interactive music systems: Machine listening and composing,* Cambridge, MA: MIT Press.

Schankler, I., Chew, E., & François, A. R. J. (2014). Improvising with digital auto-scaffolding: How Mimi changes and enhances the creative process. In N. Lee (Ed.), *Digital Da Vinci* (pp. 99–125). Berlin: Springer Verlag.

Wanderley, M. M., & Depalle, P. (2004). Gestural control of sound synthesis. In *Proceedings of the Institute of Electrical and Electronic Engineers (IEEE)*, 92(4), 632–644.

Wessel, D., & Wright, M. (2002). Problems and prospects for intimate musical control of computers. *Computer Music Journal*, 26(3), 11–22.

## Further References

Borchers, J., Lee, E., Samminger, W., & Mühlhäuser, M. (2004). Personal orchestra: A real-time audio/visual system for interactive conducting. *Multimedia Systems*, 9(5), 458–465.

Carôt, A., Rebelo, P., & Renaud, A. (2007). Networked music performance: State of the art. In *Proceedings of the Audio Engineering Society (AES) 30th International Conference: Intelligent Audio Environments* (pp. 16–22). Saariselka, Finland. Audio Engineering Society.

Chadabe, J. (1997). *Electric sound, the past and promise of electronic music*. New York, NY: Prentice-Hall, Inc.

Chew, E., François, A. R. J., Liu, J., & Yang, A. (2005). ESP: A driving interface for expression synthesis. In *Proceedings of the International Conference on New Interfaces for Musical Expression (NIME)* (pp. 224–227). Vancouver, B.C.

Chowning, J. (1973). The synthesis of complex audio spectra by means of frequency modulation. *Journal of the Audio Engineering Society*, 21(7), 526–534.

Collins, N., McLean, A., Rohrhuber, J., & Ward, A. (2003). Live coding in laptop performance. *Organised Sound*, 8(3), 321–330.

Cont, A. (2004). *Improvement of observation modeling for score following*. PhD dissertation, Université Pierre et Marie Curie, PARIS VI, France.

Cont, A. (2008). ANTESCOFO: Anticipatory synchronization and control of interactive parameters in computer music. In *Proceedings of the International Computer Music Conference (ICMC)*, (pp. 33–40). Belfast, Ireland. International Computer Music Association.

Dannenberg, R. (1984). An on-line algorithm for real-time accompaniment. In *Proceedings of the International Computer Music Conference (ICMC)* (pp. 193–198). IRCAM, France. International Computer Music Association.

Dannenberg, R., & Raphael, C. (2006). Music score alignment and computer accompaniment. *Communications of the Association for Computing Machinery (ACM)*, 49(8), 38–43.

Demers, J. (2010). *Listening through the noise: The aesthetics of experimental electronic music*. New York, NY: Oxford University Press.

Didkovsky, N. (2004). Recent compositions and performance instruments realized in Java Music Specification Language. In *Proceedings of the International Computer Music Conference (ICMC)*. Miami, USA. International Computer Music Association.

Dixon, S., Goebl, W., & Widmer, G. (2005). The "air worm": An interface for real-time manipulation of expressive music performance. In *Proceedings of the International Computer Music Conference (ICMC)*. Barcelona, Spain. International Computer Music Association.

Emmerson, S. (2013). *Living electronic music*. Farnham, UK: Ashgate Publishing Ltd.

Fiebrink, R. (2011). *Real-time human interaction with supervised learning algorithms for music composition and performance*. PhD dissertation, Princeton University, New Jersey, USA.

François, A. R. J., Chew, E., & Thurmond, D. (2011). Performer-centered visual feedback for human-machine improvisation. *Association for Computing Machinery (ACM) Computers in Entertainment*, 9(3). DOI: 10.1145/2027456.2027459

François, A. R. J., Schankler, I., & Chew, E. (2013). Mimi4x: An interactive audio-visual installation for high-level structural improvisation. *International Journal of Arts and Technology*, 6(2), 138–151.

Freedman, J. (2008). Extreme sight-reading, mediated expression, and audience participation: Real-time music notation in live performance. *Computer Music Journal*, 32(3), 25–41.

Hajdu, G. (2007). Playing performers—Ideas about mediated network music performance. In *Proceedings of the Music in the Global Village Conference* (pp. 41–42). Budapest, Hungary.

Hajdu, G. (2016). Disposable music. *Computer Music Journal*, 40(1), 25–34.

Herremans, D., Chuan, C.-H., & Chew, E. (under review). A functional taxonomy of music genera-tion systems. *Association for Computing Machiner (ACM) Computing Surveys.*

Hiller, L. A., & Isaacson, L. M. (1958). Musical composition with a high speed digital computer. *Journal of the Audio Engineering Society, 6(3),* 154–160.

Hoadley, R. (2012). Calder's violin: Real-time notation and performance through musically expres-sive algorithms. In *Proceedings of the International Computer Music Conference (ICMC)* (pp. 188–193). Ljubljana, Slovenia. International Computer Music Association.

Hunt, A., Wanderley, M. M., & Paradis M. (2003). The importance of parameter mapping in elec-tronic instrument design. *Journal of New Music Research 32*(4), 429–440.

Katz, M. (2010). *Groove music: The art and culture of the hip-hop DJ.* New York, NY: Oxford University Press.

Lähdeoja, O. (2015). An augmented guitar with active acoustics. In *Proceedings of the International Con-ference on Sound and Music Computing.*

Leman, M. (2008). *Embodied music cognition and mediation technology.* Cambridge, MA: The MIT Press.

Lovelace, A. A. (1843). Notes by the translator of "Sketch of the Analytical Engine Invented by Charles Babbage, Esq." by L. F. Menabrea of Turin, Officer of the Military Engineers. In R. Taylor (Ed.), *Scientific Memoirs, Selected from the Foreign Academies of Science and Learned Societies and from Foreign Journals.* London: Richard and John E. Taylor.

Malinowski, S. (2016). *The conductor program—Computer-mediated musical p[erformance.* Url: www.musanim.com/tapper (accessed 8 August 2016).

de Mantarras, R. L., & Arcos, J. L. (2002). AI and music: From composition to expressive performance. *Artificial Intelligence (AI) Magazine, 23*(3), 43–57.

Mathews, M. (1963). The digital computer as a musical instrument. *Science, 142,* 553–557.

McPherson, A. (2015). Buttons, handles, and keys: Advances in continuous-control keyboard instruments. *Computer Music Journal, 39*(2), 28–46.

Miranda, E. R., & Wanderley, M. M. (2006). *New digital musical instruments: control and interaction beyond the keyboard* (Vol. 21). AR Editions, Inc.

Momeni, A., & Wessel, D. (2003). Characterizing and controlling musical material intuitively with geometric models. In *Proceedings of the International Conference on New Interfaces for Musical Expres-sion (NIME)* (pp. 54–62). Singapore, Singapore.

Nijs, Luc, Lesaffre, M., & Leman, M. (2009). The musical instrument as a natural extension of the musician. In *Proceedings of the 5th Conference of Interdisciplinary Musicology* (pp. 132–133). Paris: LAM-Institut Jean Le Rond d'Alembert.

Overholt, D. (2012). Advancements in violin-related human–computer interaction. *International Jour-nal of Arts and Technology 2,* 7(2–3), 185–206.

Overholt, D., Berdahl, E., & Hamilton, R. (2011). Advancements in actuated musical instruments. *Organised Sound, 16*(2), 154–165.

Pachet, F. (2003). The continuator: Musical interaction with style. *Journal of New Music Research, 32,* 333–341.

Raphael, C. (2010). Music Plus One and machine learning. In *Proceedings of the 27th International Conference on Machine Learning* (pp. 21–28). Haifa, Israel.

Schnell, N. (2013). *Playing (with) sound.* PhD dissertation, University of Music and Performing Arts Graz, Austria.

Schnell, N., & Battier, M. (2002). Introducing composed instruments, technical and musicological implications. In *Proceedings of the International Conference on New Interfaces for Musical Expression (NIME)* (pp. 1–5). Singapore, Singapore.

Tanaka, A. (2000). Musical performance practice on sensor-based instruments. In M. M. Wanderley and M. Battier (Eds.), *Trends in Gestural Control of Music* (pp. 389–405). Paris, France. IRCAM.

Thibodeau, J., & Wanderley, M. M. (2013). Trumpet augmentation and technological symbiosis. *Computer Music Journal,* 37(3), 12–25.

Vercoe, B. (1984). The synthetic performer in the context of live performance. In *Proceedings of the International Computer Music Conference (ICMC)* (pp. 199–200). IRCAM, France. International Computer Music Association.

Wang, G. (2014). Principles of design for computer music. In *Proceedings of the International Computer Music Conference (ICMC)* (pp. 391–396). Athens, Greece. International Computer Music Association.

Wang, G., & Cook, P. (2004). On-the-fly programming: Using code as an expressive musical instrument. In *Proceedings of the International Conference on New Interfaces for Musical Expression (NIME)* (pp. 138–143). Hamamatsu, Japan.

Weinberg, G., & Driscoll, S. (2006). Toward robotic musicianship. *Computer Music Journal, 30*(4), 28–45.

Zappi, V., & McPherson, A. (2014). Dimensionality and appropriation in digital musical instrument design. In *Proceedings of the International Conference on New Interfaces for Musical Expression (NIME)* (pp. 455–460). London, United Kingdom.

# 26

# MUSIC WITH OTHERS

## Ensembles, Conductors, and Interpersonal Coordination

*Clemens Wöllner and Peter E. Keller*

### Introduction

Music making is fundamentally a social activity. Musicians perform together and strive for temporal synchronization, shared expressive musical intentions, and sound qualities or greater intensity through a higher number of instruments or voices. Ensemble music consists of, and affords, social interactions and interpersonal relations. Evolutionary theories of musical origins assume that enhanced coordination in bodily movement was among the key advantages of joint music making (Merker, 2000); For instance, various types of labor are carried out more efficiently if they are rhythmically synchronized. The discovery of several instruments such as bone flutes at prehistoric sites suggests that music making has long been a group activity, undoubtedly also including vocal and percussion performances (Huron, 2001).

These group interactions are apparent in collective bodily movements, and close links between dance and music have been reported for various cultures (Baily, 1985). Individuals also make music with others for nonmusical purposes relating to social cohesion in a community, fostering friendships or further psychosocial benefits. Music is typically performed to be heard by listeners, which further points to the social goal of making music *for* others.

Ensemble performance can be seen as a microcosm of human interactions (d'Ausilio et al., 2015). Empirical research has studied ensemble performance in relatively controlled contexts, investigating multilayered group processes as well as dyadic joint actions with real or virtual partners, and the insights these offer into nonverbal communicative behavior. Questions tackled in relevant research include how musicians prepare for ensemble performance and how they negotiate between individual anticipation, and the monitoring of group processes in order to achieve a coherent and synchronized performance. What roles do they take in ensembles; for example, is a leader necessary? Approaching these questions, the chapter provides an overview of empirical findings on musical ensemble performance, discussing underlying psychological processes with a particular focus on adaptation, anticipation and leadership in ensembles for attaining musical coherence.

## Diversity of Ensemble Playing and Musical Interactions

Ensemble performance as a social activity has been shaped by the society and the epoch in which the music was composed or improvised. In most cultures, music is indeed performed with others in various places, social contexts and for different functions. Differences in types, sizes, and relationships within ensembles have been suggested to be reflective of the diversity in functions, contexts and social relationships it is associated with, to the extent that metaphors of ensembles as a microcosm of society were proposed (Lomax & Berkowitz, 1972). For instance, the classical Western orchestra may mirror the hierarchy found at feudalist courts (Spitzer & Zaslaw, 2004), with defined roles, deputy leaders and several layers of dependencies.

A basic definition of ensemble refers to two or more people making music together. More refined definitions may categorize ensembles according to *instruments and technology* (e.g., big bands, piano duos, gamelan, computer music ensemble), *genre* (e.g., world music ensemble, jazz combo, Barbershop chorus), *professionalism* (e.g., amateurs, semi-professionals, professionals), *aim and function* (e.g., community and senior citizen choirs, touring rock band, school orchestra). These examples demonstrate the great variety in which music is performed with others, be it primarily for the enjoyment of audiences, for the social benefits of those making music together, for educational purposes or a combination of these reasons.

With the rise of radio technology and the Internet, individuals became fascinated by making music with others even over large distances. Technology offers not only the sharing of musical play-lists and preferences, but also of music making. Networked music performances, as long as technical issues of stable information transfer and latency are controlled, enable feelings of connectedness and presence of multiple individuals (cf. Hajdu, 2017), while at the same time the virtual situation has also been described to be less body-related. Ensembles are thus not confined to playing at the same location—a fact that has long been realized in the recording industry with subsequent recordings of different ensemble members, but is now increasingly found for real-time networked performances.

A crucial yet simple way of differentiating between ensembles lies in the number of musicians involved. Rasch (1988) modeled the asynchronies between instruments in relation to the number of musicians in an ensemble, which is hypothetically at 18 ms for two musicians and higher for greater numbers of musicians. According to this model, synchronization in small ensembles of up to nine musicians is better when they synchronize with each other, while larger ensembles benefit from an external conductor. A subsequent survey (ibid.) of classical chamber music confirmed his model with regard to the employment of conductors. This result was replicated in an unpublished study by the second author, who surveyed concert programs (between 1980 and 1997) by the Australia Ensemble, with only 8 out of 301 (3%) works for nine or fewer instrumentalists being led by a conductor and 12 out of 22 (55%) performances with 10 or more musicians featuring a conductor (see below for further discussion of leadership by conductors).

## Psychological Investigations of Ensemble Rehearsal and Performance

The psychological underpinnings of ensemble performance have been studied in controlled laboratory paradigms involving simple movements (e.g., finger tapping) or, at the other end of the spectrum, real musical performances with audience interactions. While most of the empirical research presented here deals with Western classical and jazz music, there is reason to argue that some of the fundamental psychological processes also apply to other musical cultures. As an example, musical ensemble performance places exceptional demands upon the mental and physical capacities of co-performers. Among these demands is the balance that individuals are able to achieve between temporal precision and flexibility in interpersonal coordination. Empirical research on ensemble performance has addressed how the ability to do so is influenced by strategies that are used to prepare for performance, as well as psychological mechanisms that underpin interpersonal coordination during performance, and intrinsic (personal) and extrinsic (contextual) factors that affect the implementation of these strategies and mechanisms (reviewed in Keller, 2014).

### *Attaining a Coherent Performance*

Musicians prepare for performance through a combination of individual private practice and collaborative group rehearsal. Collaborative rehearsal is typically aimed at developing a shared performance goal (Keller, 2008; King & Ginsborg, 2011; Williamon & Davidson, 2002). Shared goals are pursued during rehearsal through a process by which ensemble musicians become familiar with the structure of each other's parts and also the expressive manner in which these parts will be played (Ragert, Schroeder & Keller, 2013). This process is primarily based on nonverbal communication through body movements and musical sounds, and, depending on the familiarity of the ensemble members with each other, more or less verbal communication (Price & Byo, 2002).

To reach ensemble cohesion, expressive performance parameters need to be coordinated including timing, intensity, articulation, and intonation (Keller, 2014). A mixture of social, conventional, and pragmatic considerations govern this process of negotiation. Social factors—including personality, pre-existing interpersonal relationships, verbal and nonverbal communication styles, gender and instrument stereotypes—all impact upon the manner of information exchange during rehearsal (Davidson & Good, 2002; Ginsborg, Chaffin & Nicholson, 2006; Goodman, 2002; King, 2013; Williamon & Davidson, 2002). Practical issues such as the size of the group further affect negotiations by influencing for example the need for clear leadership and explicit decision-making.

The similarity of mental representations of the music residing in each performer's memory to those of other performers is presumably an important determinant of how unified an ensemble will sound. Consistent with this assumption, similarity in idiosyncratic performance styles is a reliable predictor of the quality of interpersonal coordination in ensembles (see Keller, Novembre, & Loehr, 2016).

Musicians employ these mental representations to select performance plans that guide the motor processes that link goal representations with body movements required to produce the musical sound (Palmer, 2013). In these mental representations, performance cues play an important role by defining features of the music that group members collectively attend to during performance (Ginsborg, Chaffin, & Nicholson, 2006).

Successful ensemble performance is facilitated by cognitive and motor skills that enable performers to anticipate, attend, and adapt to each other's actions in real time (Keller, 2008; Keller, Novembre, & Hove, 2014). In other words, ensemble performance consists of a combination of prepared and online processes. Anticipatory processes reliant on established mental representations and likely experienced as mental imagery (Keller, 2012) are involved in planning a performer's own actions and predicting other ensemble members' actions

(Pecenka & Keller, 2011; Wöllner & Cañal-Bruland, 2010). Online assessment of the performance plan requires attention to be divided between one's own actions and those of others while monitoring the overall, integrated ensemble output (Keller, 2001). Furthermore, adaptive mechanisms allow performers to react to intentional and unintentional variations in each other's action timing as well as other performance features (Repp & Keller, 2008; Wing, Endo, Bradbury & Vorberg, 2014). Laboratory tasks involving finger tapping or drumming in time with computer-controlled auditory sequences have revealed that anticipatory and adaptive processes work in tandem to facilitate precise synchronization (e.g., Mills, van der Steen, Schultz & Keller, 2015). The interaction between these processes is formalized in the ADaptation and Anticipation Model (ADAM) of sensorimotor synchronization (van der Steen & Keller, 2013; van der Steen, Jacoby, Fairhurst, & Keller, 2015), which provides a means for quantifying individual differences in ensemble skill (van der Steen, Schwartze, Kotz, & Keller, 2015).

Collectively, cognitive-motor skills related to anticipation, attention, and adaptation allow performers to communicate their intentions concerning musical structure and stylistic expression via the auditory modality (through variations in timing, intensity, intonation, articulation, and timbre) and the visual modality (through gestures, eye gaze, and large-scale movements such as body sway) (Keller, 2014). The degree to which mutual anticipation, attention, and adaptation are required varies with the momentary demands of the music (e.g., steady vs. changing tempo), the degree to which music is rehearsed, as well as contextual factors such as ensemble size.

The requirement to align performance parameters related to basic and expressive properties of sounds across ensemble members means that musicians may produce the same phrase differently depending on whether it is played solo or in an ensemble and may deliberately reduce expressive variation (Goodman, 2002). In ensemble playing, performers thus simplify interpersonal coordination by making actions easier to predict, for example, by using less *rubato* or by exaggerating their body movements (Glowinski, Mancini, Cowie, Camurri, Chiorri, & Doherty, 2013; Goebl & Palmer, 2009). In this way, co-performers may transcend their individual musical identities to achieve a group identity and an inherently social form of expression.

### Social Processes in Musical Interactions

The social interactions in ensembles have been studied with a variety of qualitative and quantitative approaches including video observation (e.g., Davidson & Good, 2002), content analysis of rehearsal talk (e.g., Ginsborg, Chaffin, & Nicholson, 2006), personality inventories (e.g., Cameron, Duffy, & Glenwright, 2015), motion capture (e.g., Badino, d'Ausilio, Glowinski, Camurri, & Fadiga, 2014; Luck, 2011) and neurophysiological methods (e.g., Babiloni, Buffo, Vecchio et al., 2012; see below). Findings suggest that the roles members take in an ensemble as well as social relationships between musicians shape musical and audiovisual performance parameters, and ultimately the degree to which collective musical goals can be reached. Personality, empathy and individual differences are hence relevant factors in ensemble synchronization.

Evidence suggests that the social dimension of communicating musically with each other in ensembles is related to concepts of interpersonal empathy. The ability to take someone's perspective and to "feel into" another person—according to cognitive and affective definitions of empathy—facilitate successful group processes in ensembles.

Responding to the fellow musicians' timing and spontaneous improvisations appears to be particularly relevant for jazz ensembles, where this process has been termed "empathic attunement" (Seddon, 2005, p. 56). Jazz musicians respond to nuances in the performance and are able to differentiate between imitated and improvised melodies as shown by Engel and Keller (2011). They found that perspective taking was related to the musicians' differentiation accuracy, indicating that this component of empathy may modulate the sensitivity in responding to other musicians' play. Similarly, research suggests that audience members' empathy is related to perceiving the musicians' expressive intentions (Wöllner, 2012). When musicians perceive a recording of their own ensemble, empathic attunement is also present (Babiloni, Buffo, Vecchio et al., 2012). In this study, EEG was measured in jazz ensembles during a performance and during a subsequent presentation of the recording to them. Jazz musicians' individual empathy scores were related to higher activations in a frontal brain region, indicating increased neural activity when observing their own ensemble play.

Research on pianists (Novembre, Ticini, Schütz-Bosbach, & Keller, 2012) and individuals tapping along with a partner (Pecenka & Keller, 2011) further revealed that the ability to predict or simulate the actions of others via perspective taking facilitates synchronization. This indicates that links between personality traits and basic cognitive-motor skills can affect the real-time dynamics of interpersonal coordination. Related work has shown that another aspect of personality, locus of control (the degree to which life events are perceived to be a result of one's own actions), is associated with the degree to which an individual adapts to a virtual partner's timing (Fairhurst et al., 2014). Specifically, individuals who generally attribute the cause of events to their own actions engaged in less adaptive timing than individuals who attribute events to external factors. Personality may thus affect how an individual both predicts and reacts to others during interpersonal coordination, and thereby predispose him or her towards playing certain roles in ensembles (e.g., leader vs. follower; soloist vs. accompanist; independent vs. doubled voice). A pedagogical implication of these links between social-psychological factors and interpersonal interaction style is that it may be prudent to take personality into account when developing ensemble skills tailored to individuals.

The aforementioned view of musical ensembles as social microcosms has attracted researchers from management and business studies. Gilboa and Tal-Shmotkin (2012) proposed that string quartets exhibit self-managing strategies that have much in common with the teamwork in business contexts (cf. Murnighan & Conlon, 1991). In a recent study investigating the economics of musical teamwork of popular rock bands from 1965–2005 (Phillips & Strachan, 2016), external financial incentives played an important role in remaining together as a band even in difficult phases, since most musicians were more successful in their band than as soloists or in other formations. Staying in their original band was more lucrative for most of the musicians, and rock bands in later decades disbanded less often than they used to before.

## Leadership and Conducting

### *Leader–Follower Relations, Synchrony, and Groove*

In musical traditions such as the rhythmically complex Balinese gamelan, performances are coordinated without a visual leader. The music is rather led by the musician playing the kendhang drums, who coordinates up to 40 musicians by auditory and visual cuing, both keeping the tempo and indicating changes in the musical structure. In small Western chamber ensembles working without conductors, leader–follower roles have been identified in visual social communication and analyses of the ensembles' timing.

Case studies of selected ensembles indicate that leaders precede the followers in vocal ensembles (Palmer, Spidle, Koopmans, & Schubert, 2013), thus attaining higher synchrony in unison singing. However the exact synchronization strategy may depend on the ensemble and its leadership style. In a study of professional string quartets (Wing, Endo, Bradbury, & Vorberg, 2014), the mean timing difference between the first violin and the other three musicians was found to average 11.7 ms in one string quartet and 3.2 ms in the other. This was coupled with the finding that in the latter, the first violinist corrected asynchronies as well—possibly pointing to a more team-oriented leadership style in the second string quartet.

String quartets are typically coordinated by the first violinist, who also plays a lead role in chamber orchestra formations, based on the prominent musical function of the melody lead instrument. These conventions are not always kept, especially for contemporary music without clear melodic lines assigned to certain instruments of the ensemble. For instance, in the Arditti Quartet's rehearsals and their world premiere of Ferneyhough's sixth string quartet, the violist temporally coordinated the quartet rather than Arditti himself at the first violin (Archbold & Still, 2012). In jazz ensembles, on the other hand, leader–follower relations may not coincide with temporal leading, since the melody instruments occasionally lag behind the other instruments in order to achieve a relaxed or grooving sound quality (Friberg & Sundström, 2002). In other cases, there may be a lead vocalist, while the drum or bass may function as a temporal reference. Exact adaption to each other's timing may thus not always be a shared goal across musical genres. In duos and other small ensembles, bidirectional temporal adaptations can be more successful than only following one lead instrument (Timmers, Endo, Bradbury, & Wing, 2014).

Asynchronies related to leader–follower relations tend to be relatively small compared to expressive uses of temporal displacement such as in jazz performances (cf. Ashley, 2002). Such systematic and intentional deviations from strict synchrony may give music a vital drive, or "groove," that can induce a pleasurable urge to move in simple and more complex rhythms (Janata, Tomic, & Haberman, 2012; Keil, 1995). The degree of asynchrony that is considered desirable or appropriate varies across musical traditions. For example, the tight interlocking of parts in African polyrhythm and Balinese gamelan music is eschewed in Indian raga (Clayton, 2007; Clayton, Sager, & Will, 2005), as well as in some Western contemporary art music and freely improvised music (Smith & Dean, 1997). In the extreme case of carnival competitions and some religious rituals (e.g., Brazilian congado), separate groups exert their identity by exhibiting tight within-group coordination while attempting to avoid coordination between groups (Lucas et al., 2011). Differences in the dynamics of interpersonal coordination are not only related to aesthetic ideals, but also to social function—whether the goal is to encourage reflective listening, to support coordinated activity such as dance, or to signal group cohesion to others (Lomax & Berkowitz, 1972).

The social dimension of leadership may affect ensemble motivation. In student quartets of various instruments, clear definitions of leadership roles were perceived to be more efficient (King, 2006), as less time was spent on debates in rehearsals. The roles of ensemble members may contribute to the overall musical success. In the Western musical tradition, the apparent power of conductors as musical leaders has been criticized repeatedly (Schumann, 1888; Adorno, 1962). Performing orchestral music without a conductor may however not always succeed. For example, the "Persymphan" (Russian acronym for "First symphonic ensemble" without a conductor), established in the first years of the Soviet Union, soon realized that collective and more "democratic" ways of coordination were not possible for symphonies of the 19th century (Kondrashin, 1989). After a short experimentation phase, the Persymphan was abrogated.

### Individual versus Prototypical Conductors

Music performance, in accordance with many forms of art in the Western tradition, highly values individual approaches. Audiences expect to perceive personal intentions and expressive individual messages from the performers. Conductors in particular are expected to embody the ideas expressed in the music while at the same time conveying their own individual musical intentions to achieve a unique but coherent musical interpretation. This focus on individual music making occasionally stands in conflict with the basic need for clear coordination. It is not uncommon that renowned conductors lead orchestras all over the world, typically with limited time for rehearsal. It has been observed that orchestras adjust to the gestural language of each conductor in a very short time (Kondrashin, 1989). Although no empirical study has so far systematically investigated the communicative processes in "first encounters" between orchestras and conductors, a number of characteristics may contribute to the quick understanding of conductors' gestural and facial communication, including expressive body language related to basic emotions that are understood cross-culturally (Ekman & Friesen, 1969), for example expressions of surprise by widely opened eyes. Similarly, cross-modal correspondences between movements and sounds are readily understood, such as relationships between size of motion and the intensity of sound. This is coupled with a relatively small set of conventionalized conducting gestures, for instance to indicate the different beats in a bar (Rudolf, 1995; Scherchen, 1929) and the employment of prototypical gestures that are learned through experience. These prototypes refer to gestures typically and often used by various conductors. Orchestra musicians, based on their experience with many different conductors, construct representations of such prototypical gestures, comparable to prototypes in other domains (Rubenstein, Kalakanis, & Langlois, 1999).

   In a study with orchestra conductors, we investigated the role of movement prototypes for synchronization (Wöllner, Deconinck, Parkinson, Hove & Keller, 2012). Twelve conductors performed standard four-beat movements to a metronome while being recorded with a motion capture system. Point-light displays of their movements were created, presenting videos with markers at relevant body parts, thus not showing other bodily features of the conductors (Figure 26.1). Three types of prototypical point-light videos were produced: 2D averaged movements of all conductors, of the experts only and of the novice conductors. In subsequent experimental sessions, participants who were not familiar with the conductors tapped along with the point-light movements of the individual conductors and the prototypes. Analyses revealed that, in relation to the original metronome, tapping asynchronies were smaller for the prototypes, particularly for the averaged movements of expert conductors. Furthermore, variance in tapping was smaller with the prototypes. Ratings of the movements showed that prototypical movements were perceived to be more conventional, whereas individual movements appeared to be more expressive. Taken together,

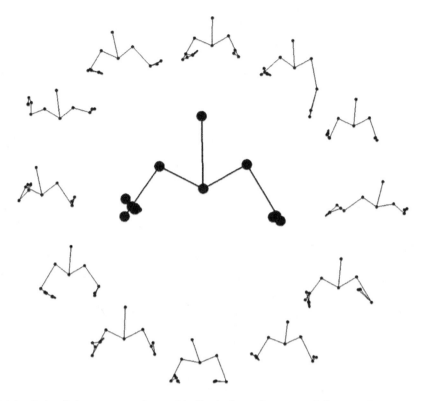

*Figure 26.1*   Point-light representations of individual conductors and the grand average morph at the center.

Wöllner et al., 2012, p. 1394.

these findings indicate that participants found it easier to synchronize with the averaged conducting movements, providing evidence that prototypes afford relevant cues for action coordination.

## Conclusions

Ensemble performance is at the core of musical activities in many cultures. A growing body of research has investigated the psychological and social processes involved in establishing shared performance goals, collective action plans, and sensorimotor correction and prediction mechanisms for attaining high-tuned coordination among individuals. In particular, the temporal dynamics and expressive characteristics of a performance need to be controlled. How this is done may depend on the constitution of an ensemble and the musical and social roles that ensemble members fulfill. Conductors are only needed for a relatively small musical repertoire—although widely played internationally mainly as a Western heritage of the 19th century. Different approaches to performance coordination are applicable in the context of, among others, non-Western musical cultures, smaller ensembles and for networked performances involving computing technology.

The interactive processes when making music with others are related to fundamental psychological and social processes that stem from beyond the domain of music. Ensembles mirror to some extent the social situations of their times (Spitzer & Zaslaw, 2004), and may resemble ways of team working in the business sector (Gilboa & Tal-Shmotkin, 2012). Indeed, an individual's actions in an ensemble may be shaped by his or her typical behavior outside music (Kawase, 2015), with personality characteristics and empathy influencing musical interactions. Therefore, it is justified to see ensemble performance as actions that are closely related to other human activities, and to investigate music in relation to comparable processes in nonmusical domains, as exemplified in the timing of turn-taking in speech conversation and duo music (see Hadley, Novembre, Keller, & Pickering, 2015). More research could scrutinize these fundamental domain-independent dimensions in human interactions such as the timing of collective behavior, whilst, on the other hand, specify advantageous characteristics that enable successful interaction within a given domain, including experience, training and personality. It could be particularly beneficial for future work to draw parallels with social interaction domains where rehearsal is not relevant such as conversation or (untrained) social dancing. In comparison, "first encounters" between musicians can be investigated, highlighting coordination strategies in the context of limited rehearsal time and spontaneous group interactions. Finally, taking into account a greater variety of musical traditions and genres as well as a greater variety of expressive parameters including timbre, dynamics and intonation is crucial to expanding and deepening our knowledge of music as a social activity.

## Core Reading

Davidson, J.W. (2009). Movement and collaboration in musical performance. In S. Hallam, I. Cross, & M. Thaut (Eds.), *The Oxford handbook of music psychology* (pp. 364–376), Oxford, Oxford University Press.

Keller, P.E. (2008). Joint action in music performance. In F. Morganti, A. Carassa, & G. Riva (Eds.), *Enacting intersubjectivity: A cognitive and social perspective to the study of interactions* (pp. 205–221). Amsterdam: IOS Press.

Keller, P.E. (2014). Ensemble performance: Interpersonal alignment of musical expression. In D. Fabian, R. Timmers, & E. Schubert (Eds.), *Expressiveness in music performance: Empirical approaches across styles and cultures* (pp. 260–282). Oxford: Oxford University Press.

Price, H.E., & Byo, J.L. (2002). Rehearsing and conducting. In R. Parncutt, & G.E. McPherson. (Eds.), *The science and psychology of musical performance: Creative strategies for teaching and learning* (pp. 335–351). Oxford: Oxford University Press.

## Further References

Adorno, T.W. (1962/1997). *Einleitung in die Musiksoziologie* (Gesammelte Schriften 14) [Introduction to Music Sociology]. Frankfurt/M · Suhrkamp.

Archbold, P., & Still, C. (DVD producers) (2012). *Climbing a mountain: Arditti Quartet rehearse Brian Ferneyhough "String Quartet no. 6"* (DVD Documentary). University of London: Institute of Musical Research.

Ashley, R.D. (2002). Do[n't] change a hair for me: The art of jazz rubato. *Music Perception, 19,* 311–332.

Babiloni, C., Buffo, P., Vecchio, F., Marzano, N., Del Percio, C., Spada, D., Rossi, S., Bruni, I., Rossini, P.M., & Perani, D. (2012). Brains "in concert": Frontal oscillatory alpha rhythms and empathy in professional musicians. *Neuroimage, 60,* 105–116.

Badino, L., d'Ausilio, A., Glowinski, D., Camurri, A., & Fadiga, L. (2014). Sensorimotor communication in professional quartets. *Neuropsychologia, 55,* 98–104.

Baily, J. (1985). Music structure and human movement. In P. Howell, I. Cross, & R. West (Eds.), *Musical structure and cognition* (pp. 237–258). London: Academic Press.

Cameron, J. E., Duffy, M., & Glenwright, B. (2015). Singers take center stage! Personality traits and stereotypes of popular musicians. *Psychology of Music, 43,* 818–830.

Clayton, M. (2007). Observing entrainment in music performance: Video-based observational analysis of Indian musicians' tanpura playing and beat marking. *Musicae Scientiae, 11,* 27–59.

Clayton, M., Sager, R., & Will, U. (2005). In time with the music: The concept of entrainment and its significance for ethnomusicology. *European Meetings in Ethnomusicology, 11,* 3–142.

d'Ausilio, A., Novembre, G., Fadiga, L., & Keller, P. E. (2015). What can music tell us about social interaction? *Trends in Cognitive Sciences, 19,* 111–114.

Davidson, J. W., & Good, J. M. M. (2002). Social and musical co-ordination between members of a string quartet: An exploratory study. *Psychology of Music, 30,* 186–201.

Ekman, P., & Friesen, W. (1969). *The repertoire of nonverbal behavior.* Berlin: de Gruyter.

Engel, A., & Keller, P. E. (2011). The perception of musical spontaneity in improvised and imitated jazz performances. *Frontiers in Psychology, 2*:83. doi: 10.3389/fpsyg.2011.00083

Fairhurst, M. T., Janata, P., & Keller, P. E. (2014). Leading the follower: An fMRI investigation of dynamic cooperativity and leader-follower strategies in synchronization with an adaptive virtual partner. *NeuroImage, 84,* 688–697.

Friberg, A., & Sundström, A. (2002). Swing ratios and ensemble timing in jazz performance: Evidence for a common rhythmic pattern. *Music Perception, 19,* 333–349.

Gilboa, A., & Tal-Shmotkin, M. (2012). String quartets as self-managed teams: An interdisciplinary perspective. *Psychology of Music, 40,* 19–41.

Ginsborg, J., Chaffin, R., & Nicholson, G. (2006). Shared performance cues in singing and conducting: A content analysis of talk during practice. *Psychology of Music, 34,* 167–192.

Glowinski, D., Mancini, M., Cowie, R., Camurri, A., Chiorri, C., & Doherty, C. (2013). The movements made by performers in a skilled quartet: A distinctive pattern, and the function that it serves. Frontiers in Psychology. *Auditory Cognitive Neurosciences, 4,* 841. doi: 10.3389/fpsyg.2013.00841

Goodman, E. (2002). Ensemble performance. In J. Rink (Ed.), *Musical performance: A guide to understanding* (pp. 153–167). Cambridge, UK: Cambridge University Press.

Goebl, W., & Palmer, C. (2009). Synchronization of timing and motion among performing musicians. *Music Perception, 26,* 427–438.

Hadley, L., Novembre, G., Keller, P. E., & Pickering, M. J. (2015). Causal role of motor simulation in turn-taking behaviour. *The Journal of Neuroscience, 35,* 16516–16520.

Hajdu, G. (2017). Embodiment and disembodiment in networked music performance. In C. Wöllner (Ed.), *Body, sound and space in music and beyond. Multimodal explorations.* Farnham, UK: Ashgate.

Huron, D. (2001). Is music an evolutionary adaptation? *Annals of the New York Academy of Sciences, 930,* 43–61.

Janata, P., Tomic, S. T., & Haberman, J. M. (2012). Sensorimotor coupling in music and the psychology of the groove. *Journal of Experimental Psychology: General, 141,* 54–75.

Kawase, S. (2015). Relationships between performers' daily social skills, social behaviors in ensemble practice, and evaluations of ensemble performance. *Musicae Scientiae, 19,* 350–365.

Keil, C. (1995). The theory of participatory discrepancies: A progress report. *Ethnomusicology, 39,* 1–19.

Keller, P. E. (2001). Attentional resource allocation in musical ensemble performance. *Psychology of Music, 29,* 20–38.

Keller, P. E. (2012). Mental imagery in music performance: Underlying mechanisms and potential benefits. *Annals of the New York Academy of Sciences, 1252,* 206–213.

Keller, P. E., Novembre, G., & Hove, M. J. (2014). Rhythm in joint action: Psychological and neurophysiological mechanisms for real-time interpersonal coordination. *Philosophical Transactions of the Royal Society B, 369*: 20130394. doi: 10.1098/rstb.2013.0394

Keller, P. E., Novembre, G., & Loehr, J. (2016). Musical ensemble performance: Representing self, other, and joint action outcomes. In E. S. Cross, & S. S. Obhi (Eds.), *Shared representations: Sensorimotor foundations of social life* (pp. 280–310). Cambridge: Cambridge University Press.

King, E.C. (2006). The roles of student musicians in quartet rehearsals. *Psychology of Music, 34*, 263–283.

King, E.C. (2013). Social familiarity: Styles of interaction in chamber ensemble rehearsal. In: E. King & H. Prior (Eds.), *Music and familiarity: Listening, musicology, performance* (pp. 253–270). Farnham: Ashgate.

King, E.C., & Ginsborg, J. (2011). Gestures and glances: Interactions in ensemble rehearsal. In A. Gritten & E. King (Eds.), *New perspectives on music and gesture* (pp. 177–201). Aldershot, UK: Ashgate Press.

Kondrashin, K. (1989). *Die Kunst des Dirigierens* [The art of conducting, E. Heresch, Trans.]. Munich, Germany: Piper.

Lomax, A., & Berkowitz, A.L. (1972). The evolutionary taxonomy of culture. *Science, 177*(4045), 228–239.

Lucas, G., Clayton, M., & Leante, L. (2011). Inter-group entrainment in Afro-Brazilian Congado ritual. *Empirical Musicology Review, 6*, 75–102.

Luck, G. (2011). Quantifying the beat-inducing properties of conductors' temporal gestures, and conductor-musician synchronization. In I. Deliege & J. Davidson (Eds.), *Music and the Mind: Essays in Honour of John Sloboda*. Oxford: Oxford University Press.

Merker, B. (2000). Synchronous chorusing and human origins. In N.L. Wallin, B. Merker, & S. Brown (Eds.), *The origins of music* (pp. 315–327). Cambridge, MA: The MIT Press.

Mills, P.F., van der Steen, M.C., Schultz, B.G., & Keller, P.E. (2015). Individual differences in temporal anticipation and adaptation during sensorimotor synchronization. *Timing & Time Perception, 3*, 13–31.

Murnighan, K.J., & Conlon, D.E. (1991). The dynamics of intense work groups: A study of British string quartets. *Administrative Science Quarterly, 36*, 165–186.

Novembre, G., Ticini, L.F., Schütz-Bosbach, S., & Keller, P.E. (2012). Distinguishing self and other in joint action. Evidence from a musical paradigm. *Cerebral Cortex, 22*, 2894–2903.

Palmer, C. (2013). Music performance: Movement and coordination. In D. Deutsch (ed.), *The psychology of music* (3rd ed.). Amsterdam: Elsevier.

Palmer, C., Spidle, F., Koopmans, E., & Schubert, P. (2013). Temporal coordination in vocal duet performances of musical rounds. In R. Bresin & A. Askenfelt (Eds.), *Proceedings of the Stockholm Music Acoustics Conference* (pp. 678–682). Stockholm: KTH Royal Institute of Technology.

Pecenka, N., & Keller, P.E. (2011). The role of temporal prediction abilities in interpersonal sensorimotor synchronization. *Experimental Brain Research, 211*, 505–515.

Phillips, R., & Strachan, I.C. (2016). Breaking up is hard to do: The resilience of the rock group as an organizational form for creating music. *Journal of Cultural Economics, 40*, 29–74.

Ragert, M., Schroeder, T., & Keller, P.E. (2013). Knowing too little or too much: The effects of familiarity with a co-performer's part on interpersonal coordination in musical ensembles. *Frontiers in Psychology*, 4:368. doi: 10.3389/fpsyg.2013.00368

Rasch, R.A. (1988). Timing and synchronization in ensemble performance. In J.A. Sloboda (Ed.), *Generative processes in music: The psychology of performance, improvisation, and composition* (pp. 70–90). Oxford: Clarendon Press.

Repp, B.H., & Keller, P.E. (2008). Sensorimotor synchronization with adaptively timed sequences. *Human Movement Science, 27*, 423–456.

Rubenstein, A.J., Kalakanis, L., & Langlois, J.H. (1999). Infant preferences for attractive faces: A cognitive explanation. *Developmental Psychology, 35*, 848–855.

Rudolf, M. (1995). *The grammar of conducting: A comprehensive guide to baton technique and interpretation* (3rd ed.). New York, NY: Schirmer.

Scherchen, H. (1929). *Lehrbuch des Dirigierens* [Handbook of conducting]. Mainz: Schott.

Schumann, R. (1888). Schwärmbriefe, Eusebius an Chiara. In H. Simon (Hrsg.), *Gesammelte Schriften über Musik und Musiker, Bd. 1*. Leipzig: Reclam.

Seddon, F.A. (2005). Modes of communication during jazz improvisation. *British Journal of Music Education, 22*, 47–61.

Smith, H., & Dean, R. T. (1997). *Improvisation, hypermedia and the arts since 1945*. London: Harwood Academic.

Spitzer, J. & Zaslaw, N. (2004). *The birth of the orchestra: History of an institution, 1650–1815*. Oxford: Oxford University Press.

Timmers, R., Endo, S., Bradbury, A., & Wing, A.M. (2014). Synchronization and leadership in string quartet performance: A case study of auditory and visual cues. *Frontiers in Psychology, 5,* 645. doi: 10.3389/fpsyg.2014.00645

Van der Steen, M.C., Jacoby, N., Fairhurst, M. T., & Keller, P. E. (2015). Sensorimotor synchronization with tempo-changing auditory sequences: Modeling temporal adaptation and anticipation. *Brain Research, 1626,* 66–87.

Van der Steen, M.C. & Keller, P.E. (2013). The Adaptation and Anticipation Model (ADAM) of sensorimotor synchronization. *Frontiers in Human Neuroscience, 7,* 253. doi: 10.3389/fnhum.2013.00253

Van der Steen, M. C., Schwartze, M., Kotz, S. A., & Keller, P. E. (2015). Modeling effects of cerebellar and basal ganglia lesions on adaptation and anticipation during sensorimotor synchronization. *Annals of the New York Academy of Sciences, 1337,* 101–110.

Williamon, A., & Davidson, J. (2002). Exploring co-performer communication. *Musicae Scientiae, 6,* 53–72.

Wing, A.M., Endo, S., Bradbury, A., & Vorberg, D. (2014). Optimal feedback correction in string quartet synchronization. *Journal of the Royal Society Interface, 11*:20131125. doi: 10.1098/rsif.2013.1125

Wöllner C. (2012). Is empathy related to the perception of emotional expression in music? A multimodal time-series analysis. *Psychology of Aesthetics, Creativity, and the Arts, 6,* 214–233.

Wöllner, C., & Cañal-Bruland, R. (2010). Keeping an eye on the violinist: Motor experts show superior timing consistency in a visual perception task. *Psychological Research, 74*(6), 579–585.

Wöllner, C., Deconinck, F. J. A., Parkinson, J., Hove, M. J., & Keller, P. E. (2012). The perception of prototypical motion: Synchronization is enhanced with quantitatively morphed gestures of musical conductors. *Journal of Experimental Psychology: Human Perception and Performance, 38,* 1390–1403.

# 27

# MUSIC ALONE AND WITH OTHERS
## Listening, Sharing, and Celebrating

*Alexandra Lamont*

While making music is a common part of all cultures around the world, listening to music is also a ubiquitous human phenomenon (Boschi, Kassabian, & Quiñones, 2013). In Western industrialized society, technology enables us to be listening to music in virtually any situation. Boschi et al. outline a fictional "average person" whose day might begin by being woken by a spaghetti-Western-themed polyphonic ring tone, getting a coffee on the way to work from a café accompanied by suitably selected exotic music, working at her desk to the accompaniment of iTunes, shopping in a department store surrounded by arias like "Nessun Dorma" from *Turandot,* working out at the gym to carefully selected appropriately paced music, having dinner with friends in an Indian restaurant with Bollywood music playing, and later going to see a film with a carefully matched soundtrack. In the course of a given day, the average Western listener will be experiencing a bewilderingly wide array of different kinds of music, some self-chosen, others chosen more for the environment than the music, and still others entirely unchosen; some alone and others shared.

One of the pressing challenges for music cognition is to establish the what, when, who and where of everyday music listening, and a second is to try to address the why (cf. North, Hargreaves, & Hargreaves, 2004). To explore this in a rich and valid way, an emerging tradition of experience sampling research in music was begun by Sloboda, O'Neill, and Ivaldi (2001). This technique had been extensively used with more observable leisure and work activities (Csikszentmihalyi & Lefevre, 1989), and Sloboda et al. were the first to apply it to music *listening* to try to uncover what people did with music. They asked eight adult "non-musicians" (without formal music training) to carry a pager for a week, and paged them at random intervals during the day to find out what they were doing, how they were feeling, and, importantly, whether music was being heard and if so how it affected the situation. Sloboda and colleagues found 44% of episodes either contained music (23%) or music had been heard since the last prompt, i.e. some time within the past two to four hours (21%). Analyzing what people were doing while listening, music was found to be an accompaniment to a wide range of other activities including personal maintenance, travel, work, forms of leisure such as reading or playing sport, and socializing. Their results highlighted the emotional impact of the music in these real-life experiences as making listeners more positive, more alert, and more focused in the present.

This technique has subsequently been applied by a range of other researchers (e.g. Greasley & Lamont, 2011; Juslin, Liljeström, Västfjäll, Barradas, & Silva, 2008). With advances in technology North et al. (2004) carried out a similar study with 346 participants who were prompted once a day for 14 days about their music use, and similar studies have followed this approach (see e.g. Krause, North, & Hewitt, 2015). Although not directly comparable due to differences in data collection, the figures for music being heard at the time of prompting or in the few hours beforehand range from 44% in Sloboda et al.'s (2001) first study up to 68% in North et al.'s (2004) study. Out of the possible response categories for whether the music was heard alone or with others, solitary listening experiences accounted for 38.6% of the total of music episodes in North et al.'s (2004) data, while the remainder with others were mostly with friends, then with spouse/partner, family, or work colleagues. Listening with strangers was one of the smallest response categories in this data at 2.5% of the total.

Music listening has been shown to have many functions beyond simple aesthetic pleasure. Research has explored the effects of listening to different types of music on cognition and emotion during travel, brain work, body work, emotional work, and social encounters such as concert attendance which I will briefly review below (for more detail see Lamont, Greasley, & Sloboda, 2016). Many adults are highly conscious of their own deliberate music choices and how these work in the music-listener-context dynamic (Hargreaves, Hargreaves, & North, 2012). Self-chosen music is indeed found to have a greater impact on listeners than non-chosen music (Sloboda et al., 2001). Emotional impact is one of the most frequently cited reasons for listening (Juslin et al., 2008) alongside using it for other physical, psychological, emotional, and social functions. In this chapter I cover how music listening works for the solitary listener, for listening as a social activity, and the ways in which the two interrelate in individuals' lives, focusing on the purposes music listening fulfils.

## Solitary Music Listening, Flow, and Emotional Self-Regulation

Csikszentmihalyi describes an example of intense listening to self-chosen music, which gives a starting point for considering factors involved in listening to music alone.

> Those who make the most of the potential for enjoyment inherent in music have strategies for turning the experience into flow. They begin by setting aside specific hours for listening. When the time comes, they deepen concentration by dousing the lights, by sitting in a favorite chair, or by following some other ritual that will focus attention. They plan carefully the selection to be played, and formulate specific goals for the session to come.
>
> *(Csikszentmihalyi, 2002, p. 110)*

Csikszentmihalyi goes on to describe three components to the focused listening experience: The sensory (focusing on qualities of sound), the analogic (evoking feelings and images based on sound patterns, shapes and gestures), and the analytic (recognizing the structure and order underlying the work). This represents the most idealized form of music listening: Intentional, deliberate, controlled, and with the potential to be highly engaging. While these experiences are rare in everyday life for many people (Sloboda et al., 2001), they can be far-reaching in terms of their impact. Gabrielsson's (2011) extensive in-depth investigation of people's strongest and most intense memories of music generated a range of accounts which included a high proportion of listening memories, and some solitary experiences amongst them. For instance, one middle-aged woman recalled how self-chosen individual listening successfully took her to a different mental state:

> I had been involved in something that made me sad several days afterwards. So I wasn't at all in the mood to listen to music . . . A few days earlier, I had recorded a live broadcast . . . Beethoven's Piano Concerto No. 3 in C minor . . . that I put on one afternoon. What happened when I started to listen didn't feel like a separate physical or mental sensation, more like that every single tone corresponded directly with my own state of mind. Starting from the beginning of the first movement, it felt as if I sank all the deeper into a great and universal concentration. All my senses were directed in towards the music. I was completely plugged into it, body and soul, and nothing could disturb the wholeness that the music and me consisted of. I didn't feel consoled, rather it felt as I got this deep experience despite the mood I was in. Nor do I think that art offers, or can offer, consolation, or that it can be used for therapy. At any rate that has never worked for me. Nevertheless, then and there, every part of the music that reached my ears became a part of me.
>
> *(Gabrielsson, 2011, p. 85, abridged quote)*

From over a thousand accounts gathered over many years, Gabrielsson generated seven categories of strong experiences with music (Gabrielsson & Lindström, Wik, 2003): general characteristics, physical reactions (goosebumps, shivers down the spine), perception, cognition, emotion/feeling, existential and transcendental elements, and personal and social elements. The quote above exemplifies a sense of transcendence in becoming at one with the music, and clearly illustrates the state of flow and engaged listening that Csikszentmihalyi (2002) referred to. What is also notable is that although the participant was aware of how self-chosen music listening normally worked for her and what to expect from it, the experience overtook her and took her somewhat unaware.

Solitary music listening is frequently a context for emotional self-regulation or self-care (e.g. Juslin & Laukka, 2004). Saarikallio (2011) identified the different emotional strategies that music listening can serve for adults as happy mood maintenance, revival, strong sensation, diversion, discharge, mental work, solace, and "psyching up." To give just one example of this, revival refers to finding a way of recharging when tired and includes the idea of taking a break, detaching, and gaining new strength, as Ann (aged 63) reported:

> I used to come home from work, and then you sit on a rocking chair, lift your feet up on a chair, and there's good music, then after 10 minutes you feel as if half of your housekeeping work has already been done, even though it has not.
>
> *(Saarikallio, 2011, p. 312)*

Mood regulation and the role of music listening has been further explored by van Goethem and Sloboda (2011). From a diary and interview study, they were able to confirm that music was a successful mood regulation device across a range of different situations. Participants were attempting to deal with everyday life affects including motivation, frustration, worry and boredom with music. The most popular mood states created through listening were happiness and relaxation. In terms of the affect regulation strategies involved—how exactly the music worked to regulate mood—music was found to help to distract the listener from the situation, allow them to reflect on the situation, and generate active coping strategies to deal with the situation. Introspection, venting and rational thinking also occurred, but far less often. Looking at negative emotions and music, people who show high tendencies towards reflectiveness can use sad music effectively as a tool to process their negative emotions (Garrido & Schubert, 2011), although listening to sad music often does depress listeners' moods in the short term (Garrido & Schubert, 2015). Looking specifically at sad music experienced after adverse negative events, listeners tended to carefully select the music that would meet their goals (van den Tol & Edwards, 2015). Cognitive reappraisal and distraction were most commonly experienced prior to mood enhancement through listening, and mood enhancement under these circumstances was more likely to happen when the music had been chosen for its high aesthetic value to the listener—i.e. chosen to experience its beauty.

## The Effects of Musical Training and Engagement on Music Listening

Does musical training and engagement with music affect the ways in which we listen to music when alone, and the functions music fulfills? Gabrielsson's (2011) participants were more musically experienced in terms of prior and ongoing training and performing than would be expected from a general population, due in no small part to the method of recruitment—through newspaper advertisements asking people to write about musical experiences. In an experience sampling study targeting a broad student population, we found evidence for differences in behaviors between more and less engaged music listeners, who also varied in their musical training (Greasley & Lamont, 2011). Across all participants, there was a wide variety of contexts and situations that music listening occurred in, a broad range of styles, and a great deal of variation in the ways in which people used music. For example, some participants needed to study with music as an accompaniment while others found it very distracting. There was a high incidence in this data of solitary listening at 55%, perhaps due to the undergraduate student sample, with more musically engaged listeners spending slightly more time listening to music than less engaged listeners.

Looking at the influence of musical background on the functions of music, we found that more engaged listeners heard more self-chosen music and were more likely to use music for the purposes of evoking moods and enhancing an activity. More engaged listeners also chose more potential reasons for and effects of listening (up to 12, compared to 1–5 for the less engaged participants). For instance, a 19-year-old female, Melissa, had chosen music at home while studying for the purposes of helping her concentrate, helping her carry out the activity, helping create the right atmosphere, creating an emotion/mood, because she liked listening and out of habit. After this episode, she reported that the music had helped her concentrate, relax, and carry out the activity, brought back memories, created and accentuated an emotion/mood, she liked it, it helped pass the time and it helped her feel less alone. While more engaged listeners chose more intended functions, when it comes to outcomes, there were no differences. Solitary music listening in this data was most likely to fulfill the functions of passing the time, enjoyment, aiding concentration, and mood regulation.

## The Use of Technology

Our students (Greasley & Lamont, 2011) reported listening to music on their computers 39% of the time. Technology clearly provides many opportunities for listeners to find the appropriate music in solitary listening situations. Advances in technology have played a major part in enabling listeners to curate and manipulate the soundtrack to their everyday lives. MP3 is now the second most popular format to access music after the radio (Krause et al., 2015). Whether accessed through dedicated music players or increasingly via other multipurpose devices such as smartphones, MP3 has facilitated almost instant access to vast playlists and music libraries, which need not even be purchased or downloaded (services such as Last.fm and Spotify provide subscriptions to extremely large online libraries). These technological advancements seem likely to lead to substantial changes to the way people interact with music (Baym, 2010; Liebowitz, 2004), which research needs to keep track of.

The portability and availability of music enables a counterbalance to the deep and intense focused listening described earlier. Listeners are now able to plug in their own music to almost every scenario imaginable, and background music need not be attended to in order to have effects (see Dibben, this volume). Looking at the more self-chosen and deliberate use of music in everyday settings, Bull (2007) studied the use of personal music players in a travelling context in busy urban environments. He found that people used their own music as a way of blocking out the rest of the world, creating a little auditory bubble, a "zone of immunity and security" (Bull, 2006, p. 3). Similarly, Skånland (2011) explored the MP3 player in relation to coping with stress, interviewing users of MP3 players who worked or lived in urban environments. Participants talked about the ability to play their music—the phrase "my music" crops up throughout the interviews—in different situations as a very effective coping strategy that could sometimes even prevent stress from setting in. This distancing and coping with noise appears to be a valuable function in high-density environments, but we observed that a high proportion of students on our university campus also wore headphones while making very short journeys, typically on foot, across fields and paths surrounded by birds and trees (Heye & Lamont, 2010). Exploring their behavior by stopping people with headphones and asking questions, we discovered that rather than simply habit, the music was perceived to fulfill a number of functions also found in other research, including enjoyment, passing the time, accentuating an emotion, and fading out disturbing noises. Even in more relaxed settings, being more secure and in one's own "little world" seemed to be a very positive element of music listening. Thus technology does not seem to have watered down the nature of the listening experience, but rather brought it to a wider range of settings.

As with other areas of music listening research, such as the more and less engaged listeners studied by Greasley and Lamont (2011), there are indications of different styles when it comes to engaging with technology. In our study of campus-based travelers (Heye & Lamont, 2010), we found a difference between technology "users" and technology "consumers." Technology users had more music on their mobile device, often carefully organized into playlists, and were able to rapidly identify and locate desired music. Technology consumers made more use of automatic playlists and were typically less aware of the technological capabilities of their equipment. Interestingly, both reported the need to have control and autonomy over their listening experiences, but achieved it through different approaches. Krause and Hargreaves (2012) also found differences in engagement with the functions technology provides in their two groups which they termed "music practitioners" and "music consumers." The consumers, who were less experienced, were less likely to use (self-created) playlists. People with more musical experience who counted music as more important in their lives were more likely to mention computer-related devices such as iPods (Krause et al., 2015), which are associated with having more choice and control over the music heard and the effects it has.

Technology may have enabled listening in more settings and given easier access to a wider range of music, but one argument sometimes leveled is that it has also encouraged solitude and loneliness. Csikszentmihalyi (2002) makes some very strong arguments about humans' need to be social and interact with others, suggesting that when we are alone we experience mild sensory deprivation and a lack of challenge. Music listening alone is a way of minimizing or preventing this, as shown by the research on mood regulation discussed earlier, but engaging with music is also a highly social experience, as the next section will show. Solitary music listening, paradoxically, also forms the basis for social interaction, and technology has aided that. Our research with young adults shows they are able to share much more of their music than ever before (Greasley, Lamont, & Sloboda, 2013), and people note that their music preferences serve the purpose of social engagement (Schäfer & Sedlmeier, 2009).

## Listening with Others

As noted earlier, most music listening, whether deliberate or in the background, is shared, and music listening is an inherently social activity. From the very earliest experiences that infants may have of music being performed for them and around them, they begin to attune themselves to what they hear and respond accordingly in a process of communicative musicality (Malloch & Trevarthen, 2009). In adulthood, the vast majority of listening experiences occur with people with whom we have some kind of relationship (North et al., 2004), and thus provide opportunities to share and to form important bonds with others.

Social experiences of music listening can happen in a broad range of contexts. Background music is heard in shops, the workplace, and social gatherings, and deliberate shared music listening includes attending live musical events. Self-reported strong experiences of music with others overwhelmingly happen in live settings (75% in Gabrielsson, 2011). I found an even greater proportion of over 80% social experiences in a replication of Gabrielsson's approach with a smaller sample of university students (Lamont, 2011). Attending a musical event is seen to be a highly valued and keenly anticipated occasion, as one of my participants, Sue, explained:

> I have been a big fan of the Chilis' music for a long time and I was extremely excited about seeing them perform live. The atmosphere in the arena was electric before they came on stage as the majority of people had been waiting, like us, for about 4 hours in the arena to see them. The most intense experience came before you could see the Chilis on stage when everything was dark and the crowd was silent with anticipation and then John played the opening riff to 'Can't Stop' and the lights came up to reveal the band and the crowd in the arena went wild. It was an amazing moment.
>
> *(Lamont, 2011, p. 239)*

In many of these contexts, the listening experience itself is premeditated: As people deliberately attend live events they may be primed to have highly intense experiences (cf. DeNora, 2000). Thompson (2007) uncovered three pre-event factors that made a difference to listeners' subsequent enjoyment of a live concert, including musical anticipation (looking forward to the program, knowing the music), features to do with the listener's personal state and general wellbeing (feeling relaxed and being in a good mood), and the environment (knowledge of the performers and the venue). Being with friends in this study was included alongside the musical anticipation factors rather than the listener's personal state or the environment, indicating that attending the event with other people might actually heighten the expectation of the music itself.

The importance of the social in live events is found in different settings. For instance, Packer and Ballantyne (2011) identified interpersonal relationships as one of the influential psychological factors leading to greater social wellbeing in young music festival attendees. In my strong experiences data (Lamont, 2011), there were many examples of group listening situations, and their social nature served to enhance the emotions of the experience. One participant, Tom, explained this succinctly: "Listening to them [Radiohead] on CD is one thing, but when thousands of people surround you, singing to every word like you, the atmosphere electric, there's no other feeling as strong, or intense, as that" (Lamont, 2011, p. 240). Shared experiences are responsible for engendering a feeling of community through the use of music in social events such as weddings, funerals, and community celebrations. Gabrielsson (2011) found many examples of what he termed religious experiences, where fellowship and communion with others feature strongly. However, these are only one amongst many other types of experiences mentioned by his participants, and the transcendence and connection with others seen in many of the accounts came from quite different and less frequent live events such as concerts rather than highly ritualized events such as regular worship.

Interaction with others as well as simply being in the same place at the same time can be important. Thompson (2007) identified the importance of engagement between the performers and the audience during the event, and engagement with the audience has been found in a range of more qualitative enquiries of different live events (e.g. Brand, Sloboda, Saul & Hathaway, 2012; Pitts & Burland, 2013). The social interactions that are possible with other audience members and with the musicians involved also add considerable value to the experience (Dobson & Sloboda, 2014). In research on experienced opera goers, O'Neill, Edelman and Sloboda (2016) found the theme of "Other People" to be important. While their participants initially emphasized the more individual nature of their preferences for the opera and going to the opera, they often went on to talk about being introduced to the art form by others, discussing opera with others to enhance their interest and knowledge, and bolstering their sense of identity through opera-going. When asked about what they loved about opera, many references were made to other people and the sense of communality and shared experience was very prominent.

While memorable experiences tend to occur most frequently at live music events, these are relatively rare in listeners' lives and a large proportion of everyday music listening with others occurs with recorded music. In our student data (Greasley & Lamont, 2011), we found that less engaged listeners were more likely to be listening to music as a result of someone else, and evidently the majority of these episodes took place in a social setting. When listening with others, choices have to be made about what to listen to. One of our participants, Naomi (aged 26), talked about the process of negotiation that took place in the car with her partner travelling for a wedding in two episodes we captured. On the way to the wedding Naomi noted listening to her partner's music, with the effect that her partner liked it. She subsequently told us that she disliked the music and that it reduced the conversation between her and her partner because it was all she could think about (Greasley, 2008). On the way back, there was more negotiation: They tried some of his preferred music (Elton John and Queen), some of her preferred music (Evanescence), and then settled on music neither of them particularly liked as a compromise (ABBA, Cher, and Bryan Adams). This led to more positive outcomes of listening for Naomi herself, including relaxation and passing the time.

Talking about music is another aspect of shared experience through music which was mentioned in the opera-goers' data (O'Neill et al., 2016) and talking about music also crops up frequently in research with adolescents and young adults. As noted earlier, when asked what purpose music listening fulfils, the social dimension features prominently (Schäfer & Sedlmeier, 2009). In a more detailed study Schäfer, Sedlmeier, Städtler and Huron (2013) further explored social relatedness. This included in particular a range of aspects related to social bonding and affiliation: E.g. music makes me feel connected to my friends and others who like the same music, music tells me how other people think, helps me show I belong to a given social group, helps me form friendships, enables me to learn something about other people. This confirms findings that music is useful for making social connections: It is one of the first things young adults talk about when trying to get to know one another (Rentfrow & Gosling, 2006) and conversations about music can be involved in shaping friendships in adulthood (Groarke & Hogan, 2016).

## Music Alone and Together: Combining Solitary and Social Experiences

Groarke and Hogan (2016) have recently developed a model of how music listening alone and together might serve the aims of enhancing wellbeing. They began with a very simple query to their participants: "Why do you listen to music?" Group discussions with younger and older adults revealed a range of different functions of music listening they believed to be important. In relation to the topics discussed above, there were age differences in what was felt to be most important. Younger adults (aged 18–30) prioritized the functions of affect regulation (which required personal space) and of social connections, highlighting the importance of both personal and social aspects in their musical engagement. These were sometimes intimately interconnected: One young female participant reported, "I think reminiscence probably just makes you happy, and then you're more inclined to be sociable because you're happy" (Groarke & Hogan, 2016, p. 777). However, older adults (aged 60–85) focused more on personal features of music to create what they call "transportation," or being able to transcend everyday experiences, and again highlighted the importance of strong emotional experiences. Nonetheless, social connections were still present in this group, particularly in relation to reminiscence. Their results confirm those from Schäfer et al. (2013), who took a different approach in asking their participants to rate 500 statements about why they listened to music but also highlighted the importance of self-awareness, social relatedness, and arousal and mood regulation as the primary themes in people's understandings of why they listen to music.

Looking at the combination of personal and social settings specifically, Batt-Rawden and DeNora (2005) carried out a year-long study with adults aged 34–65 years old with chronic illness. Starting from music which was important for the primary researcher (Batt-Rawden), they asked participants to engage with this in terms of emotions and feelings. Participants then generated their own compilations of music that was emotionally significant for them, which were shared amongst the other participants (the self-chosen CD titles included "My Mood," "Feeling At Your Best," and "All Time Best"). This intervention helped participants to connect or reconnect with music to help deal with their chronic illness. Participants created their own music and also shared music with others virtually, thus fulfilling some sense of creating a community. What was important throughout this project was the personal nature of the music used, whether it belonged to the researcher, the participant, or other participants. Equally important was the sense of community and the discussion around their own and other people's music. This project brought together the positive effects of simply listening to music and the additional benefits gained from social interaction around music for patients with chronic conditions. The results are likely to apply to other clinical and non-clinical populations.

## Conclusion

Thinking about music listening choices using Hargreaves' (2012) reciprocal feedback model provides a way of thinking about how to optimize experience. In essence, Hargreaves identified a distinction between the *music*, the *listener*, and the *situations* and contexts of music. All three of these are involved, through a process of reciprocal feedback, in shaping the outcomes of and responses to musical experiences, and all three need to be taken into account when thinking about what these experiences might mean.

Considering the music, it is clear that there is an enormous diversity in the types of music that people use for particular effects. While some research has suggested that there are general features of music that might be more or less effective in given situations, such as faster music during exercises but slower music after exercise (North & Hargreaves, 2000), research on everyday listening suggests that the most important factor is the value the listener places on the music. As noted earlier, self-chosen music is typically likely to be responded to more strongly. As van den Tol and Edwards' (2015) results highlight, music that listeners feel to be of aesthetic value is likely to create mood enhancement in a negative setting, but there is no attempt in this or any other research to define what kind of music this might be: This is left up to the listeners themselves. A simple recommendation here is that the actual music (art music, popular music, well-known, famous, world music, improvised music) is the listener's choice, and aesthetic value and meaning can be found in all musical styles.

Considering the listener, Thompson's findings (2007) suggest that anticipating and looking forward to the event can lead to greater enjoyment (see also Lamont, 2011). Being in the appropriate frame of mind to engage with music is generally important, and most deep experiences of listening are likely to result from planned, anticipated, and shared events. Focusing on the listening in a deep analogic and analytic way also has the potential, as Csikszentmihalyi (2002) noted, to evoke a sense of flow, so taking time to really engage with listening from time to time may help deepen the impact of the experience, whether this is in one's own living room, on the move, or at a live event. Somewhat unsurprisingly, research has shown that the more one is involved in music and the technology around it, the greater its potential impact and the wider the range of functions it can fulfill.

Concerning the context, it is clear that a wide range of settings are being used on a daily basis to experience music, from the bedroom to the concert hall, from the train or car to the workplace, from the gym to the music festival. Mobile technology has considerably widened the places and spaces to which we can bring our own music, and this ability to bring "my music" to a range of context including stressful situations such as commuting is clearly valued by today's listeners. While people often choose music that they like in a general sense across a range of settings, such as listening to music in the car which is liked and listened to in other situations (Dibben & Williamson, 2007), some situations require highly specialized music, such as fast-paced tempo for exercise. Music listening has been shown to enhance the surroundings as well as block them out (Heye & Lamont, 2010).

Trying different music out in different situations can be a way of finding out more about the fit between music and situation (cf. North & Hargreaves, 2000): An explicit contrast can sometimes reveal more about both the music and the situation and help transport the listener to a different mood state entirely.

## Core Reading

Gabrielsson, A. (2011). *Strong experiences with music: Music is much more than just music*. Oxford: Oxford University Press.

Greasley, A. E., & Lamont, A. (2011). Exploring engagement with music in everyday life using experience sampling methodology. *Musicae Scientiae, 15*(1), 45–71.

Groarke, J. M., & Hogan, M. J. (2016). Enhancing wellbeing: An emerging model of the adaptive functions of music listening. *Psychology of Music, 44*(4), 769–791.

Lamont, A. (2011). University students' strong experiences of music: Pleasure, engagement, and meaning. *Musicae Scientiae, 15*(2), 229–249.

Saarikallio, S. (2011). Music as emotional self-regulation throughout adulthood. *Psychology of Music, 39*(3), 307–327.

Schäfer, T., Sedlmeier, P., Städtler, C., & Huron, D. (2013). The psychological functions of music listening. *Frontiers in Psychology, 4*, 1–33. doi: 10/3389/fpsyg.2013.00511.

## Further References

Batt-Rawden, K., & DeNora, T. (2005). Music and informal learning in everyday life. *Music Education Research, 7*, 289–304.

Baym, N. (2010). *Personal connections in the digital age*. Cambridge: Polity Press.

Boschi, E., Kassabian, A., & Quiñones, M. G. (2013). Introduction: A day in the life of a ubiquitous musics listener. In: M. G. Quiñones, A. Kassabian & E. Boschi (Eds.), *Ubiquitous musics: The everyday sounds that we don't always notice* (pp. 1–12). Basingstoke, UK: Ashgate.

Brand, G., Sloboda, J.A., Saul, B., & Hathaway, M. (2012). The reciprocal relationship between jazz musicians and audiences in live performances: A pilot qualitative study. *Psychology of Music, 40*(5), 635–651.

Bull, M. (2006). Investigating the culture of mobile listening: From Walkman to iPod. In K. O'Hara, & B. Brown (Eds.), *Consuming music together: Social and collaborative aspects of music consumption technologies* (pp. 131–149). London: Springer.

Bull, M. (2007). *Sound moves: iPod culture and urban experience*. New York, NY: Routledge.

Csikszentmihalyi, M. (2002). *Flow: The classic work on how to achieve happiness*. London: Rider.

Csikszentmihalyi, M., & Lefevre, J. (1989). Optimal experience in work and leisure. *Journal of Personality and Social Psychology, 56*, 815–822.

DeNora, T. (2000). *Music in everyday life*. Cambridge: Cambridge University Press.

Dibben, N., & Williamson, V. (2007). An exploratory survey of in-vehicle music listening. *Psychology of Music, 35*(4), 571–590.

Dobson, M., & Sloboda, J.A. (2014). Staying behind: Explorations in post-performance musician-audience dialogue. In K. Burland, & S. Pitts (Eds.), *Coughing and clapping: Investigating audience experience* (pp. 159–174). Aldershot, UK: Ashgate.

Gabrielsson, A., & Lindström Wik, S. (2003). Strong experiences related to music: A descriptive system. *Musicae Scientiae, 7*(2), 157–217.

Garrido, S., & Schubert, E. (2011). Individual differences in the enjoyment of negative emotion in music: A literature review and experiment. *Music Perception, 28*(3), 279–295.

Garrido, S., & Schubert, E. (2015). Moody melodies: Do they cheer us up? A study of the effect of sad music on mood. *Psychology of Music, 43*(2), 244–261.

Greasley, A. E. (2008). *Engagement with music in everyday life: An in-depth study of adults' musical preferences and listening behaviour*. Unpublished doctoral thesis. Keele University, UK.

Greasley, A. E., Lamont, A., & Sloboda, J. A. (2013). Exploring musical preferences: An in-depth qualitative study of adults' liking for music in their personal collections. *Qualitative Research in Psychology, 10*(4), 402–427.

Hargreaves, D. J. (2012). Musical imagination: Perception and production, beauty and creativity. *Psychology of Music, 40*(5), 539–557.

Hargreaves, D. J., Hargreaves, J. J., & North, A. C. (2012). Imagination and creativity in music listening. In D. Hargreaves, D. Miell, & R. A. R. MacDonald (Eds.), *Musical imaginations: Multidisciplinary perspectives on creativity, performance and perception* (pp. 156–172). Oxford: Oxford University Press.

Heye, A., & Lamont, A. (2010). Mobile listening situations in everyday life: The use of MP3 players while travelling. *Musicae Scientiae, 14*(1), 95–120.

Juslin, P. N., & Laukka, P. (2004). Expression, perception and induction of musical emotions: A review and a questionnaire study of everyday listening. *Journal of New Music Research, 33*, 217–238.

Juslin, P. N., Liljeström, S., Västfjäll, D., Barradas, G., & Silva, A. (2008). An experience sampling study of emotional reactions to music: Listener, music, and situation. *Emotion, 8*(5), 668–683.

Krause, A. E., & Hargreaves, D. J. (2012). myTunes: Digital music library users and their self-images. *Psychology of Music, 41*(5), 531–544.

Krause, A. E., North, A. C., & Hewitt, L. Y. (2015). Music-listening in everyday life: Devices and choice. *Psychology of Music, 43*(2), 155–170.

Lamont, A., Greasley, A., & Sloboda, J. A. (2016). Choosing to hear music: Motivation, process, and effect. In S. Hallam, I. Cross, & M. Thaut (Eds.), *The Oxford handbook of music psychology* (2nd Edition, pp. 711–724). Oxford: Oxford University Press.

Liebowitz, S. (2004). Will MP3 downloads annihilate the record industry? The evidence so far. *Advances in the Study of Entrepreneurship, Innovation, and Economic Growth, V*(15), 229–260.

Malloch, S., & Trevarthen, C. (2009). *Communicative musicality: Exploring the basis of human companionship.* Oxford: Oxford University Press.

North, A. C., & Hargreaves, D. J. (2000). Musical preferences during and after relaxation and exercise. *American Journal of Psychology, 113*, 43–67.

North, A. C., Hargreaves, D. J., & Hargreaves, J. J. (2004). Uses of music in everyday life. *Music Perception, 22*, 41–77.

O'Neill, S., Edelman, J., & Sloboda, J. A. (2016). Opera and emotion: The cultural value of attendance for the highly engaged. *Participations: Journal of Audience & Reception Studies, 13*(1), 24–50.

Packer, J., & Ballantyne, J. (2011). The impact of music festival attendance on young people's psychological and social well-being. *Psychology of Music, 39*(2), 164–181.

Pitts, S. E., & Burland, K. (2013). Listening to live jazz: An individual or social act? *Arts Marketing: An International Journal, 3*(1), 7–20.

Rentfrow, P. J. & Gosling, S. D. (2006). Message in a ballad: The role of musical preferences in interpersonal perception. *Psychological Science, 17*(3), 236–242.

Schäfer, T., & Sedlmeier, P. (2009). From the functions of music to music preference. *Psychology of Music, 37*(3), 279–300.

Skånland, M. S. (2011). Use of MP3 players as a coping resource. *Music and Arts in Action, 3*(2), 15–33.

Sloboda, J. A., O'Neill, S. A., & Ivaldi, A. (2001). Functions of music in everyday life: An exploratory study using the Experience Sampling Method. *Musicae Scientiae, 5*, 9–32.

Thompson, S. (2007). Determinants of listeners' enjoyment of a performance. *Psychology of Music, 35*(1), 20–36.

Van den Tol, A. M., & Edwards, J. (2015). Listening to sad music in adverse situations: How music selection strategies relate to self-regulatory goals, listening effects and mood enhancement. *Psychology of Music, 43*(4), 473–494.

Van Goethem, A., & Sloboda, J. A. (2011). The functions of music for affect regulation. *Musicae Scientiae, 15*, 208–228.

# 28

# MUSIC AND TEXT

## Vocal Musicianship

*Annabel J. Cohen*

## Introduction

From infancy to senior years, singing provides human beings the opportunity for making music. Typically combining music and text, singing engages mental capacities underlying both music and speech production and perception. While many adults sing from time to time, and some belong to choirs, often they prefer to listen to professional performers like Adele or Bruno Mars in the pop world, or Renee Fleming or Plácido Domingo in the classical realm. This chapter reviews aspects of the development of singing as both an ordinary capacity as well as an extraordinary skill of the professional musician. Recent neuroscience research is reviewed with a focus on how the brain adapts to the complexity of dealing with text and melody. The benefits of choral singing for group cohesion and community-building are reviewed as are the benefits of singing in early life for pre-literacy skills, and for the amelioration of certain language disorders. The chapter ends with suggestions for future acceleration of understanding in this somewhat neglected but fruitful area of music psychology.

  Much research in music psychology concerns instrumental music, and musicians are often thought of as those who play musical instruments. Yet a great deal of the music that the average person listens to is song—instrumental music that partners with text. Moreover, singing is the music that most people actually engage in, at birthday celebrations, religious services, special events, in the shower or in choirs of various types (Cohen, 2011). By asking a wide range of people to sing particular familiar songs and subsequently analyzing their accuracy, Dalla Bella, Giguère, and Peretz (2006) concluded that the ability to reproduce pitch patterns through singing is normally distributed across populations. Other researchers emphasize the inaccuracy of the majority of singers (Pfordresher, Brown, Meier, Belyk, & Liotti, 2010). Such inaccuracy is not surprising given the degree of sensory-motor co-ordination involved in producing a single pitch, let alone producing lyrics along with sequential temporal and tonal structures associated with melody and rhythm of song. Perhaps in sympathy with the complexity of singing as compared to playing an external musical instrument, humans are more tolerant of out-of-tune singing than out-of-tune violin performance (approximately one-third of a semitone difference, Hutchins, Roquet, & Peretz, 2012).

Singing just a single tone entails activation and co-ordination of a large skeletal-musculature involving the lungs as the source of breath, the vocal cords as the source of the pitch of the voice, and finally the vocal tract (including the infinitely variable oral cavity of the mouth area) whose shapes filter the pitch source so as to create phonemes (vowels and consonants) and many aspects of vocal quality (Sundberg, 2013). This three-part vocal source/filter production system partners with a sensory-cognitive feedback system that compares vocal output to a mental image of the desired pitch/time outcome, and also includes matching internal motor commands and their kinesthetic consequences. Several models of the production-and-feedback system have been recently proposed (Keough & Jones, 2011; see also Tsang, Friendly, & Trainor, 2011). Current neural network models of speech motor acquisition also apply to singing (cf., Kleber & Zarate, 2014), and the first model of speech production of Gunnar Fant directly influenced the pioneering research on the science of the singing voice of Sundberg (1987, 2013).

## Development of Vocal Musicianship

Song is "one of the few aspects of human musicality that virtually all commentators agree is universally found in all human cultures" (Fitch, 2015, p. 4). Typically linking two conceptually separable vocal production systems (i.e., melody and speech), singing represents an integrated motor and mental feat of astounding complexity, yet one that children can accomplish seemingly without much difficulty.

Every child learns to sing at the same time as learning to speak. The prolongation of vowels distinguishes singing from speech, at a low level of analysis; at a higher level, singing reflects musical and linguistic rules of the culture. Note-by-note analyses of recordings of children singing, have led Stefanie Stadler Elmer (2011) to distinguish children raised in an environment that is musically rich compared to one that offers little exposure to music. She concludes that children who are raised in a musically enriched environment are generally able to reproduce or produce a melody and can create songs that match well with the culture-specific musico-linguistic rules. Such children's songs reflect the musical elements of melodic contour, phrase segmentation, metric and rhythmic patterns, repetition and variation, as well as syllable formation. Linguistic features such as word formation, however, may be less prominent or even absent. As well, rhythmic rules provide a temporal framework for regular motor movements and for filling in linguistic elements that still may lack semantic meaning. According to Stadler Elmer, songs of children from musically impoverished environments may lack these features and instead their melodic patterns of extended vowels will sound more speech-like.[1]

Vocal utterances of toddlers may be ambiguous with respect to being song-like or speech-like. Adachi and Falk (2012) explored the extent to which adults from Japan and Germany agree on whether the recorded vocalizations of a Japanese toddler were either speech or song. Adults from both countries generally agreed on their classifications of song and speech, but tended to use different cues. Because parental–infant turn taking in vocalization is a natural phenomenon of temporal co-ordination (Trehub & Trainor, 1998), it can be surmised that parents who hear their infants "speaking" will tend to speak back on their turn, whereas parents who hear their infant as "singing" will tend to sing back. Exposure to a language is critical to language development, and it seems logical that the same is true for development of singing. In a six-month longitudinal study of two children in pre-school music play sessions, Valerio, Seaman, Yap, Santucci, & Tu (2006) observed increased toddler vocalizations when adults provided tonal and rhythmic pattern improvisations (see also Forrester & Borthwick-Hunter, 2015). Children who are sung to and raised in a musical environment show early learning of the culture's musicolinguistic conventions of song. Additional research is required however to support the seemingly obvious view that children who are not sung to may be deprived of stimulation that would normally inspire the development of singing ability and potentially have other consequences.

Infants can discriminate singing from speaking and find singing directed to them as particularly rewarding. For example, infant distress (evidenced as an infant's frowning facial expression) was delayed by more than three minutes when presented with infant-directed singing as compared to infant-directed speech, regardless of whether the lyrics were in a familiar or unfamiliar language (Corbeil, Trehub, & Peretz, 2015). Trehub and Gudmunds-dottir (2015) suggest that through singing to infants, mothers initially provide emotional support, but ultimately mothers become "singing mentors" using singing to facilitate language ability. This makes sense given research that shows that singing draws attention to vocal pattern, and the acoustical features of the speech signal are slowed as compared to their presentation rate in speech. Bergeson and Trehub (1999) noted the greater distinctiveness of word articulation in the singing to pre-school children as compared to infants, consistent with the notion of the changing role of singing from emotional support to cognitive-linguistic training.

A series of studies tested the hypothesis that both infants and mothers are attuned to small integer frequency relations in singing (e.g., Van Puyvelde Loots, Gillisjans, Pattyn, & Quintana, 2015). The researchers analyzed the pitch of continuous mother-infant vocal interchanges. One study in Belgium and Mexico revealed that both infants and mothers, regardless of culture/language, produced melodies that emphasized small integer ratios, and as well, small ratios characterized the relation between the last pitch produced by one member of the mother-infant dyad and the first pitch produced by the other member. The rationale behind this work is founded in basic acoustics: Every sound of the human voice (like most musical instruments) represents a regular harmonic complex (harmonics related by small integer ratios) created at the vocal cords which undergoes filtering by the resonances of the vocal tract.

It is speculation that an infant capable of vocal imitation may choose to match his or her voice to the nearest audible harmonic. Perhaps infants prefer sounds that are harmonically related, or further, perhaps small integer ratios are simpler to encode being periodic as compared to aperiodic. Developmental psychologists, Papoušek and Papoušek (1981) noted that recorded vocal improvisations of their one-year-old daughter often contained successive small integer ratio relations, such as the major triad (*do mi sol*), consistent with van Puyvelde et al.'s (2015) observations in the Belgian and Mexican infants. Nevertheless, Dowling's (1984) analysis of more than 500 songs of his two daughters between the ages of 1 and 3.5 years, revealed no particular emphasis on simple ratio relations.

Dowling's observations are consistent with Rutkowski's (2015) proposal that children's singing can be categorized into several stages, from speech-like vocalization to being able to carry a melody, rather than beginning with a tonal foundation. The voice range of male and female children is roughly the same and both increase similarly in range until puberty. Rutkowski (p. 286) defined specific note ranges and behaviors characterizing nine stages of development of the child's singing voice. Her system has been used by a number of researchers and has been influential in practice. She points out the impossibility of singing the right notes if they are outside one's range. Only if a melody is within the voice range is it possible to determine whether the voice range is the problem for poor singing or whether the problem is more general. Children who are able to sing in the high range of A4 and B♭4 are somewhat arbitrarily referred to by Rutkowski (p. 285) as "singers."

While some children may show a limited singing voice early on as described by Rutkowski, perhaps you know of very young children who sing pop songs or children's songs with amazing accuracy and emotion. Such examples can be found on YouTube, generally uploaded by adoring parents. One can imagine that their children have been raised on lullabies, play songs, and a rich musical environment. Somewhat remote from the field of music psychology, the field of political studies tells us that socioeconomic status is directly correlated with the amount of time parents have for social interaction or "Goodnight Moon" time (Putnam, 2015). Children of college-educated parents receive 50% more time for talking, reading, playing (and presumably singing) than children of less educated parents, in a society where education is equated with social class and prosperity (Putnam, 2015). Studies of children's singing as a function of social class have yet to be conducted, however, differences in language skill and vocabulary as a function of socioeconomic class are evident at 18 months (Fernald, Marchman, & Weisleder, 2013).

## Group Singing and Social Cohesion

Singing, however, may be the exception to the notion of a correlation between socioeconomic status and time spent with family. As much as singing is a comfort for infants, it has been a comfort for people of all ages in dire circumstances. For example, during the Great Depression of the late 1920s and early 1930s, the Southern Gospel Music Industry flourished.[2] Bailey and Davidson (2005) reported research on the benefits of singing for a group of homeless persons. Fitch (2015, p. 7) noted that "music performed in groups is a far more typical expression of human musicality than solo performance." The motoric synchronization or mutual entrainment, which Fitch notes is also found in the non-human species, and is referred to as "chorusing" even when not necessarily vocal (as in the case of coordinated flashing of fireflies). Singing in a group can provide evidence of strength to an outgroup (Pearce et al., 2016).

Pearce, Launay and Dunbar (2015) studied whether group singing, as compared to other extracurricular group activities, led to a greater sense of closeness with a collection of relative strangers. Participants in three group activities—choral singing, crafts, creative writing—were asked to rate the extent of closeness that they felt toward the persons in their group. Ratings were made at the beginning and end of the class/rehearsal early in the seven-month term, in the middle, and at the end. By the seventh month, the average closeness felt by the members in each group had greatly increased and to the same level for all three activity groups. However, at the beginning of the term, the singing group showed the greatest increase in judged closeness. The researchers termed this the "ice-breaker" effect of group singing whereby singing facilitates the fast bonding of large human groups of relative strangers "which bypasses the need for personal knowledge of group members gained through prolonged interaction" (p. 1). Weinstein, Launay, Pearce, Dunbar, and Stewart (2016) showed that the sense of group cohesion through singing arises with members of choirs as large as 200 members.

The studies of group singing suggest that everyday examples of group participation in singing, for example, at sporting events, in religious congregations, and for birthday celebrations, are not simply a ritual but rather an opportunity for building community and trust.

The power can be harnessed for both noble and ignoble causes, and effects may be intentional or unintentional. As far back as Ancient Greece, Plato wrote of the dangers of certain musical modes (Norton, 2016), and in more modern times, for example, parent groups have expressed concern for the content of lyrics of songs to which their children could be exposed. The combined effect of the emotion of music and the verbal messages may be stronger than either alone. As an example of the power of lyrics, Pearce et al. (2016) noted that all members of a British college fraternity typically learned a common repertoire of songs that would differ across fraternities, while the nested groups (called "Cliques") within the fraternity had their own unique repertoire. The authors suggest that for the songs of the larger group "the language used and the concepts depicted in the lyrics . . . could potentially refocus awareness away from Clique disparities and towards a shared superordinate category" (p. 4).

## Singing and Text

Lyrics are typically integral to most songs, in regard to their sound patterns and meaning. Theoretical and pedagogical debates concern the integration of words and melody in learning a song (Morrongiello & Roes, 1990). According to the neuroscientific Shared Syntactic Integration Resource Hypothesis (SSIRH, Patel, 2003), musical and linguistic sequences are integrated into higher order structures based on acquired syntactic rules. Syntactic rule representations are domain-specific (e.g., subject, verb, object for language differs from dominant-to-tonic chord progression in music). SSIRH however proposes that execution of these rules (required to accurately process the sequential information) places a demand on the single syntactic resource. The need to encode both musical and language structure within a song may stress the syntactic processor.

Using sung sentences as stimuli, an fMRI study directly localized the interaction of music and language syntax in Broca's area in the left inferior frontal gyrus (Kunert, Willems, Casasanto, Patel, & Hagoort, 2016), a finding of interest given the often found greater activation of the right hemisphere for various aspects of music processing. The stimuli represented the combination of simple or complex syntactic sentence structure (associated with a relative clause structure) and three kinds of music structure (all tones of a melody belonged to the same key, all but one tone belonged to the key, or all tones belonged to the key but one tone was louder). The loudness cue served as a control condition, ruling out simple attentional effects. The melodies differed from the experimental standpoint only in terms of the pitch (in-key/out-of key) or loudness of the tone sung on the stressed syllable of a disambiguating word that characterized the linguistic structure as simple or complex.[3] Listeners in the fMRI scanning machine were presented with the sung melodies, asked to focus on the sentence meanings, and respond to a question about the meaning. The fMRI results reflected increased activity in the frontal lobe in the vicinity of Broca's area in response to the complex as compared to the simple language syntax, but only under the complex music structure condition. The authors concluded that the study confirmed the connection between Broca's area and the hypothesized syntactic resource that processes syntactic relations between tones in music and words in speech, and that these processes are not wholly independent.

The stimulus materials in this study were *sung* sentences that followed typical conventions of Western tonal music. The results may provide an explanation both for some behavioral findings concerning the independence and integration of lyrics and melody in songs and for the general pedagogical view that in teaching songs there is an advantage to focusing on lyrics and melody separately to reduce cognitive load, and then bringing the two together. Nevertheless, some music educators believe that this approach may take away some of the musical appeal of singing, and that the whole song should be taught at once. The debate is reminiscent of that in the realm of reading pedagogy regarding whole word versus phonetics.

Berkowska and Dalla Bella (2009) asked occasional singers to perform well known songs both with the words and on the syllable *la*. Reducing linguistic information increased singing proficiency, consistent with the shared syntactic resource hypothesis described above. Racette and Peretz (2007) also reported that learning the words of an unfamiliar folk song was enhanced when the participants spoke rather than sang the words, regardless of whether the words were initially presented as sung or spoken lyrics. The results also indicated the surprising finding that whether the melody had been accompanied by lyrics or not made no difference to recall of the melody, suggesting that melody and lyrics were processed independently.

Learning songs from cultures different than one's own is a valued aspect of choral and music pedagogy, but with increasing globalization its value may also be increasing as a means of establishing common ground (see also reference to the ice-breaker effect earlier discussed, Pearce et al., 2015). The challenges of learning a song presented in a foreign language should not be underestimated. When university students of two language groups (Chinese and North American) were asked to sing back a new song on the syllable *la* (without words), hearing the song in their *native* language as compared to a *foreign* language led to significantly higher scores (Cohen, Pan, Stevenson, & McIver, 2015). These results again support the common practice in non-professional settings of teaching songs by initially training lyrics and melody individually.

Ginsborg and Sloboda (2007) explored the need to separately train lyrics and melody for persons who can read music. Professional musicians and amateurs studied the music notation and lyrics for a period of 20 minutes under one of three conditions: music notation first, then lyrics alone, and then together; lyrics first, then music notation, and then together; or finally, music notation and lyrics simultaneously. Participants also had access to an audio-recorded model of either the melody or the melody plus lyrics, associated with the respective conditions. Measures of errors and fluency indicated that only the most highly trained group benefitted from studying the integrated materials from the start.

Wilson, Abbott, Lusher, Gentle, and Jackson (2011) approached the question of integration of lyrics and melody in singing through two covert tasks while participants (differing in level of vocal performance ability) underwent fMRI. In one task, the participant imagined speaking words that began with a particular letter, and in the other, the participant imagined singing a well-known song. The two tasks elicited activity in neural networks that were close to each other. Non-expert singers as compared to expert singers showed greater activation of their language network during the covert singing task and more right-hemisphere activation. Experts showed greater activation of the left hemisphere and greater distinction in the activation for the verbal and singing tasks. Decoupling singing from the language network was thus associated with vocal training. Returning to Kunert et al.'s (2015) fMRI examination of the shared syntax resource hypothesis using sung sentences, it is interesting to note that untrained participants localized musico-linguistic structural influences in the left hemisphere frontal lobe, although left hemisphere effects were associated with music training in Wilson et al.'s (2015) study. Future fMRI studies using the methodology of Kunert et al. (2015) might well examine music training with the possibility of increasing the relatively weak but significant effects shown.

## *Intelligibility of Lyrics*

While lyrics are generally integral to singing, their intelligibility is challenged by competing melody. Condit-Schultz and Huron (2013) assessed the intelligibility of brief musical excerpts representing 12 song genres. They asked participants to record the words during presentation of the excerpts. Mean accuracy was lowest for classical music (48%) and highest for jazz (96%), and listeners who reported that lyrics were personally important to them were a little better at deciphering lyrics, regardless of genre. In a follow-up study, the opportunity to rehear the songs slightly increased the intelligibility scores but reached asymptote by the third hearing. Condit-Shultz and Huron (2017) further showed that intelligibility of lyrics also depends on the number of voices singing, though the best by far is the solo voice.

An extensive survey regarding the importance of intelligibility of lyrics and the potential factors associated with ease of intelligibility concluded that "[E]nhancing sung text intelligibility is thus perceived to be within the singer's control, at least to some extent, but there are also many factors outside their control" (p. 1) and more empirical work to explore the factors influencing intelligibility was needed for the benefit of vocal pedagogy, choral directors, and composers (Fine & Ginsborg, 2014).

## The Impact of Singing Training on Brain Development

While neural syntactic resources for the music and text of song may be found in Broca's area, and the fMRI data of Wilson et al. (2011) suggest use of the left hemisphere by expert singers, in a comparison of classically trained singers and age-matched adults without singing training, voxel-based morphometry (VBM)[4] revealed increased grey matter in several areas of the right hemisphere (Kleber et al., 2016). An increase in gray-matter in the ventral primary somatosensory cortex (larynx S1) was associated with the degree of training after the age of 14 years. In other words, for vocalists who began singing prior to the age of 14 years, the years of training before the age of 14 had no further effect. The authors suggest that until the age of 14 years, the priority for brain development is speech acquisition. Only after reaching this milestone, ending the critical period for language development, does practice in singing begin to have an impact on brain development in at least this one part of the brain.

This time-point coincides also with the age of the voice change due to maturation in males but also females to some extent. The voice change requires recalibration of the sensory-motor feedback system. It is as if the brain has evolved so as to waste little space on a system that will require recalibration; when the vocal system approaches a mature state, then special training is associated with increased grey matter dedicated to the laryngeal motor representation.

Earlier research of Kleber, Zeitouni, Friberg and Zatorre (2013) compared fMRI responses of trained singers and non-singers who were asked to sing musical intervals under an unusual condition . . . that of anesthetized vocal cords. Anesthesia affected singers' accuracy of production less than non-singers, indicating that long-term vocal training led to autonomy of the motor system and a prominent feed-forward system. The anesthesia appeared to influence the right anterior insular cortex (AIC) where decreased activity was noted for singers and increased activity for non-singers. It was concluded that "right AIC and sensory-motor areas play a role in experience-dependent modulation of feedback integration for vocal motor control during singing" (p. 670). Kleber, Veit, Birbaumer, Gruzelier, and Lotze (2010) earlier compared fMRI brain activation patterns during singing of a famous Italian aria in three groups differing in degree of classical vocal training (professional level, conservatory students, non-singer students). Those with classical training had increased activation in the area representing the larynx and the somatosensory association cortex in the parietal lobe. In studies that distorted auditory feedback via headphones, Zarate and Zatorre (2008, as described by Kleber & Zarate, 2014) noted recruitment of different networks by musicians compared to non-musicians, and short term training of the non-singers was insufficient to change their activation pattern, further implying the impact of long term vocal training and practice.

Another line of research associated with singing training arises from performance science and the focus on preparation for a performance. The methodology employed relies on introspection and retrospection, and identifies the performance cues (e.g., for interpretation and expression) considered during rehearsal and performance, (Ginsborg & Chaffin, 2011).

## Singing as a Facilitation of Language Capabilities

While singing is intrinsically valuable as a means of musical engagement, its integration of speech and musical pattern has benefits for various language skills. Within the scope of this chapter, it is only possible to mention several avenues without going into great detail. First, the "Every Child Ready to Read" research-based program of the American Library Association names singing as one of five practices of early literacy (i.e., singing, talking, reading writing, and playing), includes it in community library programs for infants, toddlers, and preschoolers, and encourages parents to do likewise at home (Celano & Neuman, 2015). Second, several studies have shown the value of singing for learning aspects of a second language (Ludke, Ferreira, & Overy, 2014). Third, while anecdotal research has suggested the value of singing to assist reduction of stuttering, Falk, Maslow, Thum, and Hoole (2016) have shown how singing training can increase control over verbal timing which may help stuttering. Fourth, melodic intonation therapy has a long history of application to the problems of aphasia, and while there is some question about the exact aspect of the therapy that benefits the patient, the therapy has provided positive results in a number of cases (Merrett, Peretz, & Wilson, 2014; Schlaug, Norton, Marchina, Zipse & Wan, 2010; Thaut, Thaut, & McIntosh, 2014). The most well-known example is American politician Gabrielle Giffords who survived a gun-shot wound to the left temporal lobe in a 2011 attempted assassination. Her speaking improved but even six years later, with more continuous speech therapy than most people receive, speaking remains a great challenge, falling far below her abilities for verbal comprehension. It needs to be clear that melodic intonation therapy was only a part of her therapy program. Finally, as one of many other possible examples, singing provides a means for communicating with persons with Alzheimer's disease, and evidence of this success has led to the suggestion of incorporating singing into the curriculum for nurses and those receiving caregiver training (Götell, Brown, & Ekman, 2009).

## Future Directions for Research on Vocal Musicianship: Music and Text

While hundreds of studies have been conducted on the acquisition of speech, relatively few have been conducted on the acquisition of singing. This chapter has reviewed a large number of informative studies on vocal musicianship; however, it can be argued that much more data are needed to truly understand how singing develops under the many influences of culture, language, socio-economic status, age, musical aptitude, and personality variables. Singing is not just one skill, but many. Basic data on the separate skills are needed. The AIRS (Advancing Interdisciplinary Research in Singing) Test Battery of Singing Skills (ATBSS) was developed for this purpose (Cohen, 2015; Cohen, Armstrong, Lannan, & Coady, 2009). It tests such skills as the ability to sing a familiar melody, learn a new melody, compose an ending to a melody, improvise an entirely new melody, produce the highest and lowest note, and imitate melodic fragments. It also entails several verbal tasks. An on-line version is available in several languages, and data have been collected in the USA, Canada, and China. The data from such a test are extremely rich, and full analysis of a large sample could take a lifetime. Yet by making the data available to other researchers through a digital library, analyses can be conducted on particular aspects of the data by researchers anywhere. An analogous example from child language is provided by CHILDES (Child Language Data Exchange System) (MacWhinney & Snow, 1985), which led to over 3000 publications. A database for singing presents challenges that go beyond those for language, but new technological developments have overcome former impediments (Cohen & Ludke, in press). Worldwide cross-sectional and longitudinal studies with data accessible in a shared repository with a strict protocol (as in the case of CHILDES) could lead to a very bright future for the understanding of vocal musicianship, a most fertile area for the future of the psychology of music. Studies of the acquisition of singing of the youngest children, including infants and toddlers, will probably be the most informative and more studies at these ages are needed.

## Acknowledgement

The support of the Social Sciences and Humanities Research Council (SSHRC) for the Advancing Interdisciplinary Research in Singing (AIRS) Major Collaborative Research Initiative Program, the University of Prince Edward Island, and the work of the AIRS Co-investigators and Collaborators are gratefully acknowledged.

## Notes

1. Stadler Elmer, S., & Muzzulini, D. (2012). Early song singing infants discover a rule-based system. Paper presented at the AIRS 4th Annual Meeting, Charlottetown.
2. MacDonald, C.M. (2016). Embodying Faith and Fandom: Songs of Identity in Depression-Era Gospel Singing Communities. Presentation to the American Musicological Society, Vancouver.
3. The study ruled out the possibility that the effect was related to general attention resources because the control condition entailing an anomalous intensity pattern did not have the same effect as a melodic tonal anomaly. The control condition did however activate the right hemisphere homologue of Broca's area.
4. Voxel-based morphometry unlike traditional morphometry registers every brain to a template removing information that is common to all brains and leaving what is unique, that can subsequently be measured voxel by voxel to some extent. An early application showed an increase in size of a portion of the hippocampus of London taxi drivers who are thought to have unusual spatial memory, a skill associated with the hippocampus.

## Core Reading

Ludke, K.M., Ferreira, F., & Overy, K. (2014). Singing can facilitate foreign language learning. *Memory & Cognition, 42*, 41–52.

Pearce, E., Launay, J., & Dunbar, R.I.M. (2015). The ice-breaker effect. Singing mediates fast social bonding. *Royal Society Open Science, 2*, 150221. doi: 10.1098/rsos.150221

Stadler Elmer, S., (2011). Human singing: Towards a developmental theory. *Psychomusicology: Music, Mind & Brain, 21*, 13–30.

Trehub, S. E., & Gudmundsdottir, H. R. (2015). Mothers as singing mentors for infants. In G. F. Welch, D. M. Howard, & J. Nix (Eds.), *Oxford handbook of singing*. Oxford: Oxford University Press. Advance online publication. doi: 10.1093/oxfordhb/9780199660773.013.25

Wilson, S. J., Abbott, D. F., Lusher, D., Gentle, E. C., & Jackson, G. F. (2011). Finding your voice: A singing lesson from functional imaging. *Human Brain Mapping, 32*, 2115–2130.

## Further References

Adachi, M., & Falk, S. (2012). Does native language influence the mother's interpretation of an infant's musical and linguistic babblings? In E. Cambouropoulos, C. Tsougas, P. Mavromatis, & K. Pastiadis (Eds.), *Proceedings of the 12th International Conference on Music Perception and Cognition and the 8th Triennial Conference of the European Society for the Cognitive Sciences of Music.* New York, NY: Routledge.

Bailey, B. A., & Davidson, J. W. (2005). Effects of group singing and performance for marginalized and middle-class singers, *Psychology of Music, 33*, 269–303.

Bergeson, T., & Trehub, S. E. (1999). Mothers' singing to infants and preschool children. *Infant Behavior & Development, 22*, 51–64.

Berkowska, M., & Dalla Bella, S. (2009). Reducing linguistic information enhances singing proficiency in occasional singers. *Annals of the New York Academy of Science, 1169, The Neurosciences and Music III-Disorders and Plasticity*, 108–111.

Celano, D. C., & Neuman, S. B. (2015). Libraries emerging as leaders in parent engagement. *Kappan, 96*, 30–35.

Cohen, A.J. (2011). Research on singing: Development, education and well-being—Introduction to the special volume on 'singing and psychomusicology'. In A. J. Cohen, & S. E. Trehub (Eds.). Singing and psychomusicology. *Psychomusicology: Music, Mind, & Brain, 21*, 1–5.

Cohen, A. J. (2015). The AIRS Test Battery of Singing Skills: Rationale, item types, and lifespan scope. *Musicae Scientiae, 19*, 238–264.

Cohen, A. J., Armstrong, V. L., Lannan, M. S., & Coady, J. D. (2009). A protocol for cross-cultural research on the acquisition of singing. In S. Dalla Bella, N. Kraus, K. Overy, K., Pantev, J. S. Snyder, M. Tervaniemi, B. Tillmann, & G. Schlaug (Eds.), *The neurosciences and music III: Disorders and plasticity (Annals of the New York Academy of Science, 1169*, 112–115). New York, NY: New York Academy of Sciences.

Cohen, A. J., & Ludke, K. M. (2016 on-line, in press). Digital libraries for singing: the example of the AIRS project. In G. Welch, D.M. Howard, & J. Nix (Eds.). *The Oxford handbook of singing*. Oxford, UK: Oxford University Press. DOI: 10.1093/oxfordhb/9780199660773.001.0001

Cohen, A.J., Pan, B-Y., Stevenson, L., & McIver, A. (2015). Role of native language on memory for an unfamiliar song: A comparison of native English and native Chinese students on the AIRS Test Battery of Singing Skills. *Musicae, Scientiae, 19*, 301–324.

Condit-Schultz, N., & Huron, D. (2013). Catching the lyrics: Intelligibility in twelve song genres. *Music Perception, 32*, 470–483.

Condit-Schultz, N., & Huron, D. (2017). Word intelligibility in multi-voice singing: The influence of chorus size. *Journal of Voice, 31*(1), 121.e1–121.e2.

Corbeil, M., Trehub, S.E., & Peretz, I. (2015). Singing delays the onset of infant distress. *Infancy, 21*, 373–391.

Dalla Bella, S., Giguere, J., & Peretz, I. (2006). Singing proficiency in the general populations. *Journal of the Acoustical Society of America, 121*(2), 1182–1189.

Dowling, W. J. (1984). Development of musical schemata in children's spontaneous singing. In W. R. Crozier, & A. J. Chapman (Eds.), *Cognitive processes in the perception of art* (pp. 145–163). Amsterdam: Elsevier Science.

Falk, S., Maslow, E., Thum, G., & Hoole, P. (2016). Temporal variability in sung productions of adolescents who stutter. *Journal of Communication Disorders, 62*, 101–114.

Fernald, A., Marchman, V. A., & Weisleder, A., (2013). SES differences in language processing skill and vocabulary are evident at 18 months. *Developmental Science, 16*, 234–248.

Fine, P., & Ginsborg, J. (2014). Making myself understood: Perceived factors affecting the intelligibility of sung text. *Frontiers in Psychology, 5*, DOI: 10.3389/fpsyg.2014.00809

Fitch, W. T. (2015). Four principles of bio-musicology. *Philosophical Transactions. Royal Society, B*, 370: 20140091. http://dx.doi.org/10.1098/rstb.2014.0091

Forrester, M. A., & Borthwick-Hunter, E. (2015). Understanding the development of musicality: Contributions from longitudinal studies. *Psychomusicology: Music, Mind & Brain, 25*, 93–102.

Ginsborg, J., & Chaffin, R. (2012). A singer's thoughts while singing Schoenberg. *Psychomusicology: Music, Mind, & Brain, 21*, 137–158.

Ginsborg, J., & Sloboda, J. (2007). Singers' recall for the words and melody of a new, unaccompanied song. *Psychology of Music, 35*, 421–440.

Götell, E., Brown, S., & Ekman, S.-L. (2009). The influence of caregiver singing and background music on vocally expressed emotions and moods in dementia care. *International Journal of Nursing Studies, 46*, 422–430.

Hutchins, S., Roquet, C., & Peretz, I. (2012). The vocal generosity effect: How bad can your singing be? *Music Perception, 30*, 147–159.

Keough, D., & Jones, J. A. (2011). Contextual cuing contributes to the independent modification of multiple internal models for vocal control. *Journal of Neurophysiology, 105*, 2448–2456.

Kleber, B., Veit, R., Birbaumer, N., Gruzelier, J., & Lotze, M. (2010). The brain of opera singers: Experience-dependent changes in functional activation. *Cerebral Cortex, 20*, 1144–1152.

Kleber, B., Veit, R., Moll, C. V., Gaser, C., Birmaumer, & Lotze, M. (2016). Voxel-based morphometry in opera singers: Increased gray-matter volume in right somatosensory and auditory cortices. *NeuroImage, 133*, 477–483.

Kleber, B., & Zarate, M. J. (2014). The neuroscience of singing. In G. Welch, & J. Nix (Eds.). *The Oxford handbook of singing*. Oxford, UK: Oxford University Press. DOI: 10.1093/oxfordhb/9780199660773.013.015

Kleber, B., Zeitouni, A.G., Friberg, A., Zatorre, R. J. (2013). Experience-dependent modulation of feedback integration during singing: role of the right anterior insula. *Journal of Neuroscience, 33*, 6070–6080.

Kunert, R., Willems, R.M., Casasanto, D., Patel, A.D., & Hagoort, P. (2016). Music and language syntax interact in Broca's area: An fMRI study. *PLOS One. 10*(11): e0141069. doi:10.1371/journal.pone.0141069

MacWhinney, B. & Snow, C. (1985). The child language data exchange system. *Journal of Child Language, 12*, 271–295.

Merrett, D. L., Peretz, I., & Wilson, S. J. (2014). Neurobiological, cognitive, and emotional mechanisms in Melodic Intonation Therapy. *Frontiers of Human Neuroscience, 8*:401. http://dx.doi.org/10.3389/fnhum.2014.00401

Morrongiello, B. A., & Roes, C. L. (1990). Children's memory for new songs: Integration or independent storage of words or tunes. *Journal of Experimental Child Psychology, 50*, 25–38.

Norton, K. (2016). *Singing and wellbeing: Ancient wisdom, modern proof.* New York, NY: Routledge.

Papoušek, M., & Papoušek, H. (1981). Musical elements in the infant's vocalization: Their significance for communication, cognition and creativity. In L. P. Lipsitt & C. K. Rovee-Collier (Eds.), *Advances in infancy research* (Vol. 1, pp. 163–224). Norwood, NJ: Ablex.

Pearce, E., Launay, J., van Duijn, M., Rotkirch, A., David-Barrett, T., & Dunbar, R.I.M. (2016, online-first). Singing together or apart: The effect of competitive singing on social bonding within and between sub-groups of a university Fraternity. *Psychology of Music*, DOI: 10.1177/0305735616636208.

Pfordresher, P. Q., Brown, S., Meier, K. M., Belyk, M., & Liotti, M. (2010). Imprecise singing is widespread. *Journal of the Acoustical Society of America, 128*, 2182–2190.

Putnam, R. D. (2015). *Our kids: The American dream in crisis.* New York, NY: Simon & Schuster.

Racette, A., & Peretz, I. (2007). Learning lyrics: To sing or not to sing? *Memory and Cognition, 35*, 242–253.

Rutkowski, J. (2015). The relationship between children's use of singing voice and singing accuracy. *Music Perception, 32*, 283–292.

Schlaug, G., Norton, A., Marchina, S., Zipse, L., & Wan, C.Y. (2010). From singing to speaking: Facilitating recovery from nonfluent aphasia. *Future Neurology, 5,* 657–665.

Sundberg, J. (1987). *The science of the singing voice.* Dekalb, IL: Northern Illinois University Press.

Sundberg, J. (2013). The perception of singing. In D. Deustch (Ed.), *The psychology of music* (3rd ed., pp. 69–106). London: Academic Press.

Thaut, M. H., Thaut, C. P., & McIntosh, K. (2014). Melodic intonation therapy (MIT). In M. H. Thaut and V. Hoemberg (Eds.). *Handbook of neurologic music therapy* (pp. 140–145). Oxford, UK: Oxford University Press.

Trehub, S. E., & Trainor, L. J. (1998), 'Singing to infants: Lullabies and playsongs'. *Advances in Infancy Research, 12,* 43–77.

Tsang, C. D., Friendly, R. H., & Trainor, L. J. (2011). Singing development as a sensorimotor interaction problem. *Psychomusicology: Music, Mind, & Brain, 21,* 45–53.

Valerio, W. H., Seaman, M. A., Yap, C.C., Santucci, P. M., & Tu, M. (2006). Vocal evidence of toddler music syntax acquisition: a case study. *Bulletin of the Council for Research in Music Education, 170,* 33–45.

Van Puyvelde, M., Loots, G., Gillisjans, L., Pattyn, N., & Quintana, C. (2015). A cross-cultural comparison of tonal synchrony and pitch imitation in the vocal dialogs of Belgian Flemish-speaking and Mexican Spanish-speaking mother-infant dyads. *Infant Behavior and Development, 40,* 41–53.

Weinstein, D., Launay, J., Pearce, E., Dunbar, R. I., & Stewart, L. (2016). Singing and social bonding: Changes in connectivity and pain threshold as a function of group size. *Evolution and Human Behavior, 37,* 152–158.

Zarate, J. M., & Zatorre, R. J. (2008). Experience-dependent neural substrates involved in vocal pitch regulation during singing. *Neuroimage, 40*(4), 1871–1887.

# 29

# MUSIC AND MOVEMENT
## Musical Instruments and Performers

*Laura Bishop and Werner Goebl*

## Introduction

Music and movement are intrinsically bound. When we make music, we carry out sequences of controlled movements with the aim of producing certain sounds. Playing the piano, for instance, involves moving your hands and fingers in a way that allows you to press the keys in a specific order. Of course, pianists make many other movements as they play—the arms, head, upper body, legs, and feet are often in near-constant motion. These movements may not be directly involved in producing sound, but they have both technical and communicative functions, shaping the tone that is produced, helping us coordinate with our co-performers if we are playing in a group, and communicating our expressive intentions to the audience.

Movement is tied to music perception just as it is tied to music production (Phillips-Silver, 2009). When we experience another person's performance, we hear the sounds that result from that person's movements. Our perception of expression in the sounded performance is shaped by the type and quality of movements used. Our perceptions of performance expression also depend on whether we can see as well as hear the musicians playing. Musicians' body movements—even those movements not directly involved in sound production—communicate a great deal of information (Wanderley et al., 2005; Moran et al., 2015). Body movements help to indicate performers' interpretations of the music, while also giving clues as to their intentions, allowing both audience members and co-performers to predict when the next note is going to come and how it is going to sound.

Thus, both sound and movement are critical means of musical communication. The link between music and movement is particularly significant, since, in most musical genres, movement is required to produce sound, and it is only by carrying out precise and controlled movements that performers can produce sounded music that fits with their intentions. In this chapter, the role of movement as a means of musical communication is discussed. We examine the functions of performers' body movements, with a focus on how these movements are controlled and how they contribute to performers' realization of their expressive intentions. We begin in the next section with a discussion of the methods that can be used to investigate performers' body movements.

## Methods for Mapping and Measuring Body Movements

Researchers studying musicians' body movements require recording techniques that capture movement information as precisely as possible, while interfering as little as possible with the movements themselves (see Goebl, Dixon, & Schubert, 2014 for a review of movement analysis techniques). Video recording, which is unobtrusive and relatively inexpensive, is often used (e.g. Tsay, 2013; Wanderley et al., 2005; Williamon & Davidson, 2002). Audio and video recordings can be aligned with high precision, making video recording an effective means of capturing motion that will be analyzed qualitatively (e.g. by categorizing gesture types; relating motion to sounded music) or used for perceptual experiments (e.g. assessing tolerance for audiovisual asynchrony; examining the influence of gesture observation on the perception of sounded music). Some kinematic analysis of body movements in video data is also possible using recently developed movement tracking and recognition algorithms (Castellano et al., 2008).

Three-dimensional motion capture systems present an alternative to video recording. Despite some disadvantages—they are expensive, require substantial technical knowledge, and are difficult to transport between performance spaces—they are capable of mapping the trajectories of performers' body joints with very high spatial and temporal precision. Motion capture systems use infrared cameras to track the movement of markers through three-dimensional space. Markers are affixed to specific locations on the performer's body and either reflect light (in the case of passive systems) or emit an infrared signal (in the case of active systems). Active systems use markers that are attached to cables, so passive systems are often preferred in situations where cables would interfere with the performer's movement. However, active systems are better than passive systems at re-identifying markers that reappear after briefly disappearing from the cameras' fields of view (which can happen when, for instance, a moving limb obstructs the line of sight). Passive systems require post-processing to ensure that pre- and post-disappearance trajectories are linked to the same marker.

Data collected via motion capture systems can be used for detailed analyses of body kinematics. Large-scale movements, like instrumentalists' head nods or body sway, as well as small-scale movements, like the motion of pianists' fingers on the keyboard, can be analyzed. As we see throughout the remainder of this chapter, such fine-grained analyses provide a critical basis for determining the functions of performers' body movements.

## Performance Gestures: What Purpose Do They Serve?

In the literature on human movement, the term "gesture" is used to describe a body movement that carries meaning (Jensenius et al., 2010; Kendon, 2004; Leman, 2008). A movement does not have to produce a meaningful outcome, such as a sounded word or tone, to constitute a gesture (though sound-producing movements are gestures as well). Rather, it is the movement itself that is meaningful. The musical gestures used in performance include facial expressions, body sway, and head nods, as well as sound-producing movements like the drop of a hand onto piano keys or the sweep of a bow across violin strings.

There has been some debate about whether a movement has to be intentional (i.e. executed deliberately) to count as a gesture, and likewise, whether it is only a gesture if its meaning is understood by observers. In this chapter, the movements of performers that we refer to as "gestures" have only the potential to be correctly interpreted by observers (see Ashley, Chapter 39, this volume). Part of what makes music an artform rather than a systematic transfer of specific information is that performers' gestures, as well as the sounded music they produce, are ambiguous, to a degree, and interpreted in different ways by different people. We also suggest that many of the gestures a performer makes are not themselves intentional. Instead, the performer has an underlying intention to communicate particular ideas, and it is this intention that shapes the gestures that are made, while the performer focuses attention primarily on anticipating the sounds that they aim to produce.

Performance gestures can be grouped into categories according to the functions they fulfill (Dahl et al., 2010):

1. Sound-producing gestures are directly involved in producing or modifying sounded tones (e.g., blowing into the mouthpiece of a clarinet).
2. Sound-facilitating gestures support the production of sound without producing sound themselves (e.g., changing posture of the body to help in playing at a higher sound level).
3. Communicative gestures are those performers direct at others to emphasize their inter-pretation or help coordinate their playing (e.g., nodding to a co-performer).
4. Sound-accompanying gestures are made in response to sounded music (e.g., dancing).

These categories are not intended to be discrete, but rather, overlapping, as most performance gestures serve multiple purposes. When performers are drawn by the sound of the music to tap their feet to the beat, for example, they might be simultaneously responding to the music they hear, supporting the maintenance of a steady tempo in their own performance, and emphasizing the beat structure for the audience. Attempting to segment performers' move-ments into meaningful units can be a difficult task anyway, since performers are in constant motion. Multiple gestures are often coarticulated (i.e. joined together and overlapping in time; Godøy, 2010); some align precisely with a particular level of the temporal framework in the sounded music, while others align with a different level or do not align with the tem-poral framework at all (Demos, Chaffin, & Kant, 2014). The way a gesture is performed is subject to the influence of other overlapping gestures as a result.

Music performance is therefore a very complex task motorically. Many different move-ments must be made in parallel, along different timescales, and with high precision. Success on such a task would not be possible if it were necessary to focus attention and deliber-ately control each movement that had to be made. Instead, music performance research has shown that most sub-tasks proceed automatically, without the performer focusing attention on them or attempting to control them (Palmer, 1997). This raises an interesting question: If performers are not constantly focusing on the execution of their movements, what are they attending to instead? In the next section, we discuss how skilled musicians' focus on anticipating the effects of their actions helps them carry out their expressive intentions successfully.

## Controlling Performance Gestures through Anticipation

Skilled musicians report using a mental image of the sound they want to produce to help guide their performance. Their descriptions of a guiding mental image have been supported by empirical research, which suggests that musicians anticipate the effects that they intend their actions to have through a process referred to as anticipatory imagery (Keller, Dalla Bella, & Koch, 2010).

The ability to anticipate the effects of your actions develops as you gain experience in performing those actions and perceiving the consequences that they have on the world (Hommel et al., 2001). Action–effect associations form in the brain and strengthen with increasing expertise. Student pianists, for example, learn to associate different hand motions on the keyboard with different sound qualities in piano tone. According to theories of internal models, these action–effect associations can activate bidirectionally: Via forwards activation, motor commands are provided to incite the performance of an action, while via inverse activation, an expected effect primes the action necessary to achieve it (Jeannerod, 2003). In this way, performers' attention to the expected effects of their actions can enable automatic selection and performance of the movements necessary to achieve those effects.

During expressive performance, musicians must control many aspects of the sound they are producing, including (depending on the constraints of their instruments) pitch, timing, articulation, dynamics, and timbre. People can imagine all of these parameters offline (i.e. not concurrently with performance; Janata & Paroo, 2006). Online (i.e. during performance), research has shown that at least pitch, timing, articulation, and dynamics are imagined. Some studies, for instance, have compared expressive performances given in silence (e.g., on a keyboard with the sound turned off) to baseline performances given under normal audio conditions. Pianists maintain expressive parameters such as dynamics and articulation when performing in silence—as well as maintaining accuracy in pitch and timing—suggesting that anticipatory imagery guides their movements even when no sound is produced (Bishop et al., 2013).

Research on perceptual-motor expertise suggests that experts perform better when attending to an anticipatory image than when focusing on movement execution. Novices, in contrast, perform better when they focus on executing movements. This contrast was observed in a study with expert and novice soccer players: Experts performed better on a dribbling task under dual-task conditions (while simultaneously monitoring a stream of sounded words for a particular target) than under skill-focused conditions (while monitoring their foot movements and indicating verbally at regular intervals which part of their foot had last touched the ball). Thus, if the unrelated word-monitoring task interfered with experts' dribbling performance, the degree of interference was less than that caused by attending to foot movements. Novices showed the opposite results, performing better under skill-focused conditions than under dual-task conditions (Beilock et al., 2002).

The optimal method for performance may therefore differ between experts, for whom anticipatory imagery is strong and movements are largely automatized, and novices, for whom anticipatory imagery is less well-developed and movements require deliberate control. It is important to acknowledge, however, that attention is constantly in flux during performance, and usually distributed among a number of cognitive processes. Performers' awareness of their own body gestures changes from moment to moment, as does the degree of deliberate control that they exert over those gestures (Toner & Moran, 2014). At times, it is beneficial for experts to direct their attention towards the execution of their gestures; for instance, when refining movements during practice.

In the next sections, we focus on how anticipation underlies the use of two types of performance gestures: 1) sound-producing gestures and 2) communicative gestures that help performers maintain interpersonal coordination when playing together. The aim of the first section is to illustrate how performers' control over their technical movements helps them achieve their expressive intentions. The aim of the second section is to show how performance gestures help ensemble musicians anticipate one another's actions and coordinate their playing.

## Playing Technique under the Magnifier

Sound-producing gestures are the movements that enable musicians to create sounds on their musical instruments. They are goal-directed, in that their aim is to generate or modify sound in a refined and controlled way. These gestures vary greatly with the particular instrument played, as tone production depends on the properties of instruments' acoustical systems and the control parameters available.

For example, on bowed string instruments, different movements are performed by the left and right hand: The right moves the bow against the strings to generate sound, while the left controls pitch and vibrato by pressing against the fingerboard. Left and right hand movements have to be coordinated with high precision (Baader, Kazennikov, & Wiesendanger, 2005). On keyboard instruments, in contrast, the two hands—even the individual fingers—produce different sounds independently, and, therefore, may exhibit different degrees of coordination. Musicians refer to these movements and their acquisition and development generally as playing technique.

### *Individualism in Expert Playing Technique*

As musicians acquire their personal movement strategies—via a learning process that takes many years of practice (Krampe & Ericsson, 1996; Thompson, Mosing, & Ullén, this volume; Green & Smart, this volume)—they gain the ability to repeat movement patterns with high reliability. At the same time, their playing gestures may differ increasingly from those of other musicians, despite generating sometimes identical sounds. Looking at finger-tip kinematics of skilled pianists, Dalla Bella and Palmer (2011) were able to train a neural-network classifier to successfully recognise a particular pianist just by finger velocity and acceleration patterns, a result recently confirmed with skilled flute players (Albrecht et al., 2014).

Individual movement strategies may also be related to timing quality and maximum tempo. Goebl and Palmer (2013) measured the entire kinematic chain from the fingertip to the forearm of the right hands of a dozen skilled pianists, who were asked to play a short melody in as many tempo conditions as possible, starting from a medium tempo and increasing to fast tempi. The pianist who was able to perform most precisely and accurately across tempo conditions, and who was also the only participant able to perform in the fastest tempo condition (16 tones per second), showed the most efficient keystrokes, based on an efficiency measure that combines all joint angle trajectories during a single keystroke. Conversely, pianists with keystrokes of lower efficiency showed performances that were less precise, and had lower maximum tempi. These findings suggest that despite a wide range of possible ways of executing sound-producing movements (degrees of freedom problem in motor control; Kay, Turvey, & Meijer, 2003), there are certain movement characteristics that better support fast, precise and accurate performance. Musicians have to find the optimal movement strategies that best fit the desired sounding goal.

The properties of sound-producing movements change systematically with performance tempo. At slow tempi, the gestures are usually well separated from one another (e.g., with hovering phases in between active keystrokes on the piano, Goebl and Palmer, 2009). As the tempo increases, the movement duration takes larger parts of the inter-onset intervals, and those movements start to overlap and form one compound movement (Kay, et al., 2003). Pianists raise their fingers higher above the keyboard at faster tempi, which is in contrast to recommendations of educators to strive to play as closely to the keys as possible (Bernstein, 1981). Similar observations were made with clarinetists who raise their fingers higher (Palmer, Koopmans, Loehr, & Carter, 2009), even though educators recommend keeping the fingers close to the keys. However, clarinetists also use less force on the keys at faster tempi (Hofmann & Goebl, 2016), which is again in line with such recommendations.

Different ways of executing sound-producing movements usually lead to differences in the sounds produced. On the piano, the main acoustical parameter of dynamics is shaped by the speed with which the hammer hits the strings. It has long been believed that piano sounds produced with identical hammer velocities sound identical, even if they have been played with entirely different keystroke movements. Recent research, however, has shown that different ways of touching piano keys (e.g., pressing or striking them; see Furuya & Kinoshita, 2008) produce differences in piano timbre that are well-discriminated by listeners, even though hammer velocities are identical (Goebl, Bresin, & Fujinaga, 2014). Conversely, there are systematic modifications of sound-producing movements that do not affect the sound; for example, clarinet keys have to be closed to modify the pitch, making any additional finger force against the keys superfluous. However, clarinetists' finger forces on the ring keys of a clarinet clearly vary: Clarinetists press harder at slower tempi, at higher registers, at louder dynamics, and when they perform with more expression (Hofmann & Goebl, 2016).

Sound-producing movements are optimized in expert performers. Experts usually show a more economical approach in their movement properties than do student-level or amateur musicians. For example, professional pianists exhibit smaller angular finger joint activity and lower muscular load while performing fast alternating tone sequences than do amateur pianists (Furuya et al., 2011). Professional players also show lower peak finger forces compared to student players on the clarinet (Hofmann & Goebl, 2016) and on the piano (Parlitz, Peschel, & Altenmüller, 1998). However, professional pianists use more covariation between fingers that possess an innate connectivity between them, such as the ring and little finger, while amateurs work against those conditions (Winges & Furuya, 2014).

## Motor Feedback from Sound-Producing Gestures

Sound-producing movements also yield non-auditory sensory feedback that facilitates control of the produced sequences (Palmer, 2013). For example, a kinematic landmark occurs when the finger touches the piano key surface during a keystroke, reflected in a large change in the acceleration trajectory that may be used as tactile information by the pianist to control the timing of the sequence. These finger-key landmarks occur more often and are more pronounced when pianists play faster and louder (Goebl & Palmer, 2008). Moreover, the magnitude of these landmarks is related to the timing accuracy of the subsequent event, suggesting that pianists use this tactile feedback to improve their timing control.

This finding was replicated in a kinematic analysis of skilled clarinet performances (Palmer, Koopmans, Loehr, & Carter, 2009). However, the fingers control timing on the clarinet only in legato articulation. In other articulation types (portato, staccato), the tongue controls timing together with the fingers, or sometimes independently of the fingers (tone repetitions). In a study that investigated the coordination of tongue and finger forces on the clarinet, Hofmann and Goebl (2016) found that timing control of the tongue alone was more precise than timing control of fingers alone. Combined tongue and finger control enabled well-stabilized and accurate timing.

## Visual Communication for Ensemble Synchronization

Ensemble musicians must align their individual interpretations to produce a coherent joint performance. Each ensemble member maintains an image of how his or her own part should be performed, as during solo performance; however, it is also important that all members share a joint goal image of what they want to achieve as a group (Loehr et al., 2013). To maintain a shared goal image, ensemble musicians must be able to interpret their co-performers' intentions. Performers thus try to be as predictable as possible to each other without sacrificing the expressiveness of their performance. Visual communication can be an important means of exchanging information about one another's interpretation and improving predictability.

## Predicting the Outcomes of Observed Gestures: When Is It Useful?

For the most part, ensemble musicians can predict their co-performers' intentions based purely on the sound of their playing. Depending on the structure of the music and how strictly the ensemble follows a steady beat, visual contact between performers may not even be needed for a coherent performance to be achieved (Ragert, Schroeder, & Keller, 2013). These expectations develop automatically as a result of familiarity with the musical genre (Ockelford, 2006).

In less predictable musical contexts, visual communication becomes critical. During improvisation, or when playing notated music with large temporal fluctuations, long pauses, or abrupt changes in tempo, it can be more difficult to predict co-performers' upcoming actions based on the sound of their playing alone (Kawase, 2013). Ensemble musicians then attend to their co-performers' body movements for clarification of their intentions.

A study of ours investigated pianists' use of visual communication across different structural contexts (Bishop & Goebl, 2015). Recordings were made of skilled pianists and violinists performing the primo part to three piano duets (with live accompaniment, which was recorded separately). The duets that we selected included some potential challenges for synchronization (e.g., a slow, free tempo; long pauses). We assessed pianists' synchronization with these recordings as their access to audio and visual communication channels was manipulated: In an audio-visual condition, pianists could see and hear the primo playing, while in an audio-only condition they could hear but not see the primo, and in a visual-only condition they could see the primo but not hear his or her playing.

Pianists were little affected by the removal of incoming video, with synchronization equally precise in audio-visual and audio-only conditions. Synchronization was worse in the visual-only condition, indicating that accompanists rely primarily on incoming audio to coordinate their playing with that of a soloist. In audio-visual and audio-only conditions, asynchronies were larger following phrases that ended on a fermata than they were mid-phrase, while in visual-only conditions, asynchronies were larger mid-phrase than they were at these phrase boundaries. This finding suggests that the gestures given at re-entry points (i.e., following long pauses) are particularly meaningful and communicate performers' intentions more effectively than do the gestures given elsewhere in the piece. Performers probably also attend more closely to each other's gestures at re-entry points, since timing is imprecisely specified by the score and they are less certain of each other's intentions.

## Communicating the Concept of Time through Performance Gestures

Ensemble musicians aim to coordinate a number of musical parameters, but paramount among these is timing. How is information about piece timing encoded into performers' gestures? A few studies investigating different types of musical gestures have examined which gesture features indicate beat position to observers. In one study, people were asked to synchronize key-presses with conductor gestures (Luck & Sloboda, 2009). Observers used either peak velocity or peak acceleration as a reference for beat position, depending on the size of the radius of curvature in the baton movements. In another study, people judged the audio-visual synchrony between sounded rhythms and point-light representations of a bouncing human figure (Su, 2014). These observers used peak velocity as a reference for beat position in the bouncing movements.

Thus, the gesture features that indicate beat position seem to be temporal rather than spatial, even when the gestures follow a repetitive, predictable spatial trajectory, as with the bouncing movements. These findings suggest that the processes underlying visual beat perception are not specific to individual gesture types. Different gestures may follow very different spatial trajectories, but that should not impede beat perception if the position of the beat is determined by temporal features.

A recent study of ours examined the gestures that instrumentalists use to cue each other at the beginnings of pieces (Bishop & Goebl, in press). Visual communication is particularly important at the start of pieces, since there is no prior sound to help performers determine when their notes should be played. Cueing-in gestures are usually given by a designated leader (e.g. the first violinist in a string quartet) and need to communicate the temporal placement of the first beat as well as the starting tempo of the piece.

Piano and violin duos played through short pieces as their head movements were tracked with Kinect sensors and accelerometers. On each trial, one performer or the other was designated the leader and asked to cue their partner in, without speaking, at a tempo selected by the experimenters. Both leaders' and followers' first note onsets coincided with instances of peak head acceleration, suggesting that head acceleration acts as a reference for beat position (Figure 29.1). Periodicity in head acceleration related to piece tempo. Thus, information about both beat position and tempo seem to be encoded in the temporal features of instrumentalists' cueing-in gestures.

## Interpreting Incoming Visual Signals

As described earlier in this chapter, learned associations between actions and their perceptual consequences enable performers to anticipate what the effects of their own actions will be. These same associations are activated when people see others performing those actions, allowing observers to anticipate the effects of others' actions (Cross et al., 2009). This process, termed action simulation, is thought to underlie the prediction of both observed and sounded action outcomes (Jeannerod, 2003).

In support of this theory, people are particularly successful at predicting patterns of movement that are similar to those they would perform themselves. For example, pianists synchronize more precisely when accompanying recordings of their own performances than

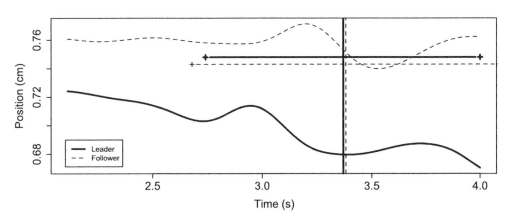

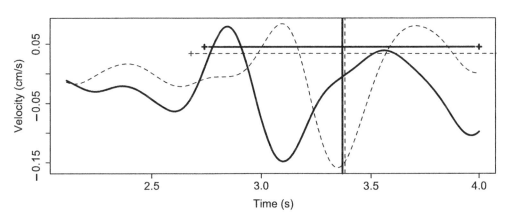

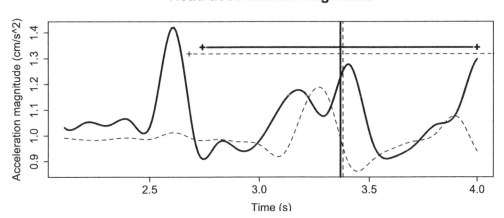

*Figure 29.1* Head position, velocity, and acceleration magnitude for a violin (leader)—piano (follower) duo in the seconds prior to piece entry. Performers' first note onsets and tempi were very well-synchronized in this trial. The follower's head movements mimicked the leader's, with a slight temporal lag—a common occurrence across the trials we recorded.

when accompanying recordings of others' performances (Keller, Knoblich, & Repp, 2007). People are also particularly successful at predicting movements that they have prior experience in performing themselves. Extensive visual exposure to particular movements also improves prediction, but to a lesser extent (Wöllner & Cañal-Bruland, 2010).

Our research has tested how instrument-specific performance expertise affects prediction and synchronization in music ensembles. Do pianists synchronize more successfully with other pianists than with string players, and do string players synchronize more successfully with each other than with pianists? In our study investigating ensemble musicians' cueing-in gestures (Bishop & Goebl, in press; discussed above), synchronization was worse for piano–violin duos than for either piano–piano or violin–violin duos (who performed similarly to each other). On average, asynchronies were highest for the first note of a piece and improved rapidly across the next few notes. This pattern was observed for all instrument pairings, but for piano–violin duos, the asynchrony for the first note was greater than for the other groups, and the improvement across the first three notes was less. Thus, the musicians in this study benefitted from playing with a same-instrument partner both at the first note (which required synchronizing with an observed gesture) and through the body of the passages (which required effective use of combined audio and visual cues).

## Conclusions

This chapter has focused on the movements involved in producing, shaping, and coordinating sounds during music performance. We describe the sound-producing gestures used by different varieties of instrumentalists, as well as the features of communicative gestures that musicians use to indicate their intended timing to their co-performers. We also discuss how a distal focus, directed to the expected outcome of sound-producing gestures, can benefit skilled performance, and we show how anticipation of others' movements enables coordination between ensemble performers.

Though the audience's perspective of performance gestures was not the focus here, both the observation of performance gestures and a familiarity with the sorts of gesture that underlie sound-production shape the audience's experience. At times, the audience's perception of performance gestures can even sway their perception of the sounded music (Tsay, 2013). Movement underlies most of the music that people experience on a daily basis. However, we might also wonder about music that has been made without the use of the gestures that have traditionally been required to produce musical sound. Such cases can arise when a human performer is replaced by a computer system, when human musical performances are recorded and then altered to include acoustic effects that could not have been produced by performing on an existing instrument, or when computer music is designed to incorporate environmental or digitally-constructed sounds that listeners would not attribute to human movements.

An aim of future research should be to determine how divorcing music from sound-producing and communicative movements affects the experience of both performers and listeners. For example, do musicians have more difficulty coordinating with computer co-performers than with human co-performers? How are listeners' perceptions of expression in sounded music affected by the inclusion of sounds that are not associated with physical movements?

The link between music and movement has long been acknowledged, and as discussed in this chapter, researchers continue assessing and defining the movements involved in producing sounded music. At the same time, recent developments in machine learning and audio engineering are expanding the opportunities available for creating and/or performing music that does not draw on human movement. Such developments provide researchers with valuable new genres of material to consider. Systematic study of the forms of music that draw little or not at all on human movement, alongside continued study of performance gestures, may enable an improved understanding of how critically bound music and movement are.

## Core Reading

Bishop, L., & Goebl, W. (2015). When they listen and when they watch: Pianists' use of nonverbal audio and visual cues during duet performance. *Musicae Scientiae, 19*(1), 84–110.

Bishop, L., & Goebl, W. (in press). Beating time: How ensemble musicians' cueing gestures communicate beat position and tempo. *Psychology of Music*.

Dahl, S., Bevilacqua, F., Bresin, R., Clayton, M., Leante, L., Poggi, I., & Rasamimanana, N. (2010). Gestures in performance. In R. I. Godøy, & M. Leman (Eds.), *Musical gestures: Sound, movement, and meaning* (pp. 36–68). New York, NY, London: Routledge.

Palmer, C. (2013). Music performance: Movement and coordination. In D. Deutsch (Ed.), *The Psychology of music* (3rd ed.) (pp. 405–422). Amsterdam: Elsevier Press.

Palmer, C. (1997). Music performance. *Annual Review of Psychology, 48*(1), 115–138.

Phillips-Silver, J. (2009). On the meaning of movement in music, development and the brain. *Contemporary Music Review, 28*(3), 293–314.

## Further References

Albrecht, S., Janssen, D., Quarz, E., Newell, K. M., & Schöllhorn, W. I. (2014). Individuality of movements in music—Finger and body movements during playing of the flute. *Human Movement Science, 35*, 131–144.

Baader, A., Kazennikov, O., & Wiesendanger, M. (2005). Coordination of bowing and fingering in violin playing. *Cognitive Brain Research, 23*(2–3), 436–443.

Beilock, S., Carr, T. H., MacMahon, C., & Starkes, J. L. (2002). When paying attention becomes counterproductive: Impact of divided versus skill-focused attention on novice and experienced performance of sensorimotor skills. *Journal of Experimental Psychology: Applied, 8*(1), 6–16.

Bernstein, S. (1981). *With your own two hands: Self-discovery through music*. London: Schirmer Books and Collier Macmillan.

Castellano, G., Mortillaro, M., Camurri, A., Volpe, G., & Scherer, K. (2008). Automated analysis of body movement in emotionally expressive piano performances. *Music Perception, 26*, 103–120.

Cross, E. S., Kraemer, D. J. M., Hamilton, A., Kelley, W. M., & Grafton, S. T. (2009). Sensitivity of the action observation network to physical and observational learning. *Cerebral Cortex, 19*, 315–326.

Dalla Bella, S., & Palmer, C. (2011). Rate effects on timing, key velocity, and finger kinematics in piano performance. *PLoS ONE, 6*(6), e20518. doi:10.1371/journal.pone.0020518

Demos, A. P., Chaffin, R., & Kant, V. (2014). Toward a dynamical theory of body movement in musical performance. *Frontiers in Cognitive Science, 5*, 477. doi: 10.3389/fpsyg.2014.00477

Furuya, S., Goda, T., Katayose, H., Miwa, H., & Nagata, N. (2011). Distinct inter-joint coordination during fast alternate keystrokes in pianists with superior skill. *Frontiers in Human Neuroscience, 5*, 50 doi:10.3389/fnhum.2011.00050

Furuya, S., & Kinoshita, H. (2008). Expertise-dependent modulation of muscular and non-muscular torques in multi-joint arm movements during piano keystroke *Neuroscience, 156*(2), 390–402.

Godøy, R., Jensenius, A. R., & Nymoen, K. (2010). Chunking in music by coarticulation. *Acta Acustica, 96*(4), 690–700.

Goebl, W., Bresin, R., & Fujinaga, I. (2014). Perception of touch quality in piano tones. *Journal of the Acoustical Society of America, 136*(5), 2839–2850.

Goebl, W., Dixon, S., & Schubert, E. (2014). Quantitative methods: Motion analysis, audio analysis, and continuous response techniques. In D. Fabian, R. Timmers, & E. Schubert (Eds.), *Expressiveness in music performance—Empirical approaches across styles and cultures* (pp. 221–239). Oxford: Oxford University Press.

Goebl, W., & Palmer, C. (2008). Tactile feedback and timing accuracy in piano performance. *Experimental Brain Research, 186*(3), 471–479. doi:10.1007/s00221-007-1252-1

Goebl, W., & Palmer, C. (2009). Synchronization of timing and motion among performing musicians. *Music Perception, 26*(5), 427–438.

Goebl, W., & Palmer, C. (2009). Finger motion in piano performance: Touch and tempo. In A. Williamon, S. Pretty, & R. Buck (Eds.), *Proceedings of the International Symposium on Performance Science 2009* (pp. 65–70). Utrecht: European Association of Conservatoires.

Goebl, W., and Palmer, C. (2013). Temporal control and hand movement efficiency in skilled music performance. *PLOS ONE, 8*(1), e50901, doi:10.1371/journal.pone.0050901.

Hofmann, A., & Goebl, W. (2016). Finger forces in clarinet playing. *Frontiers in Psychology. Performance Science.*

Hommel, B., Müsseler, J., Aschersleben, G., & Prinz, W. (2001). The theory of event coding (TEC): A framework for perception and action planning. *Behavioural and Brain Sciences, 24,* 849–937.

Janata, P., & Paroo, K. (2006). Acuity of auditory images in pitch and time. *Perception & Psychophysics, 68*(5), 829–844.

Jeannerod, M. (2003). The mechanism of self-recognition in humans. *Behavioural Brain Research, 142,* 1–15.

Jensenius, A. R., Wanderley, M. M., Godøy, R. I., & Leman, M. (2010). Musical gestures. Concepts and methods in research. In R. I. Godøy, & M. Leman (Eds.), *Musical gestures: Sound, movement, and meaning* (pp. 12–35). New York, NY, London: Routledge.

Kawase, S. (2013). Gazing behavior and coordination during piano duo performance. *Attention, Perception, & Psychophysics, 76,* 527–540.

Kay, B. A., Turvey, M. T., & Meijer, O. G. (2003). An early oscillator model: Studies on the biodynamics of the piano strike (Bernstein & Popova, 1930). *Motor Control, 7*(1), 1–45.

Keller, P. E., Dalla Bella, S., & Koch, I. (2010). Auditory imagery shapes movement timing and kinematics: Evidence from a musical task. *Journal of Experimental Psychology: Human Perception and Performance, 36*(2), 508–513.

Keller, P. E., Knoblich, G., & Repp, B. (2007). Pianists duet better when they play with themselves: On the possible role of action simulation in synchronization. *Consciousness and Cognition, 16,* 102–111.

Kendon, A. (2004). *Gesture: Visible action as utterance.* Cambridge: Cambridge University Press.

Krampe, R. T., & Ericsson, K. A. (1996). Maintaining excellence: Deliberate practice and elite performance in young and older pianists. *Journal of Experimental Psychology: General, 125*(4), 331–359.

Leman, M. (2008). *Embodied music cognition and mediation technology.* Cambridge, MA: MIT Press.

Loehr, J. D., Kourtis, D., Vesper, C., Sebanz, N., & Knoblich, G. (2013). Monitoring individual and joint action outcomes in duet music performance. *Journal of Cognitive Neuroscience, 25*(7), 1049–1061.

Luck, G., & Sloboda, J. (2009). Spatio-temporal cues for visually mediated synchronization. *Music Perception, 26*(5), 465–473.

Moran, N., Hadley, L. V., Bader, M., & Keller, P. E. (2015). Perception of 'back-channeling' nonverbal feedback in musical duo improvisation. *PLoS ONE, 10*(6), e0130070. doi: 10.1371/journal.pone.0130070

Ockelford, A. (2006). Implication and expectation in music: A zygonic model. *Psychology of Music, 34*(1), 81.

Palmer, C., Koopmans, E., Loehr, J. D., & Carter, C. (2009). Movement-related feedback and temporal accuracy in clarinet performance. *Music Perception, 26,* 439–450.

Parlitz, D., Peschel, T., & Altenmüller, E. (1998). Assessment of dynamic finger forces in pianists: Effects of training and expertise. *Journal of Biomechanics, 31*(11), 1063–1067.

Ragert, M., Schroeder, T., & Keller, P. E. (2013). Knowing too little or too much: The effects of familiarity with a co-performer's part on interpersonal coordination in musical ensembles. *Frontiers in Auditory Cognitive Neuroscience, 4,* 368. doi: 10.3389/fpsyg.2013.00368

Su, Y. (2014). Peak velocity as a cue in audiovisual synchrony perception of rhythmic stimuli. *Cognition, 131*(3), 330–344.

Toner, J., & Moran, A. (2014). In praise of conscious awareness: A new framework for the investigation of "continuous improvement" in expert athletes. *Frontiers in Psychology, 5,* 769. doi: 10.3389/fpsyg.2014.00769

Tsay, C. J. (2013). Sight over sound in the judgment of music performance. *Proceedings of the National Academy of Sciences, 110*(36), 14580–14585.

Wanderley, M. M., Vines, B. W., Middleton, N., McKay, C., & Hatch, W. (2005). The musical significance of clarinetists' ancillary gestures: An exploration of the field. *Journal of New Music Research, 34*(1), 97–113.

Williamon, A., & Davidson, J. W. (2002). Exploring co-performer communication. *Musicae Scientiae, 6*(1), 53–72.

Winges, S. A., & Furuya, S. (2014). Distinct digit kinematics by professional and amateur pianists. *Neuroscience, 284,* 643–652.

Wöllner, C., & Cañal-Bruland, R. (2010). Keeping an eye on the violinist: Motor experts show superior timing consistency in a visual perception task. *Psychological Research, 74,* 579–585.

# 30

# SCENE AND HEARD

## The Role of Music in Shaping Interpretations of Film

*Siu-Lan Tan*

> Each musical soundtrack creates its own particular type of film and plot.
> (Bullerjahn & Güldenring, 1994, p. 112)

Billy Wilder's film *The Lost Weekend* (1945) opens with a panoramic shot of the New York City skyline in the 1940s, and continues panning across the back of a brick building, passing by two windows and stopping at the last window. Inside, a man is packing a suitcase and pausing as if to reflect. *What could this man be thinking? What are his life circumstances? What could happen next?* These were the questions Vitouch (2001) asked participants to answer as they wrote continuations of the plot.

Viewers who watched the excerpt with the original soundtrack to the film, which includes a score by Miklós Rózsa (consisting of pleasant and lush orchestral music, with a few strains of a theremin at the open window), tended to provide positive or ambivalent story continuations. For instance: "The man is in a good mood, has a secure and well-paid job, and is just preparing a meal for his new love (candle-light dinner for two). Then they go for a walk and explore the beauties of this city" (Vitouch, 2001, p. 76). Those who viewed an altered version of the film produced by pairing the same film clip with an excerpt of Barber's *Adagio for Strings* that had been shown to evoke "sadness" and "melancholy" in previous studies (e.g., Krumhansl, 1997) produced more negative story continuations. For example: "The man has been left by his wife. He's visiting the places where he thinks she could be. When he finally finds her together with another man, he shoots him." (Vitouch, 2001, p. 76)

The content analysis of the participants' written responses revealed that the music even seemed to alter the perception of the weather and impression of the cityscape, with some participants describing "lovely weather" and "beautiful surroundings" (with Rózsa's score) versus "all gray and desperate" and "the city looks depressing, without a perspective for the future" (with Barber's music) (p. 79). Overall, Vitouch found a close match between the participants' description of the music and the character or mood of their story continuations, even though each participant saw only one version of the film and was not told that the focus of the study was on the music.

In his book *The Art of Film Music,* the late musicologist and film composer George Burt wrote of the vital role of the score in storytelling:

> Music has the power to open the frame of reference to a story and to reveal its inner life in a way that could not have been fully articulated in any other way. In an instant, music can deepen the effect of a scene or bring an aspect of the story into sharper focus. It can have a telling effect on how the characters in the story come across—on how we perceive what they are feeling or thinking—and it can reveal or expand upon subjective aspects and values associated with places and ideas intrinsic to the drama . . . accenting this or that instant or event to help bring out the connections and divergent points of view.
>
> *(1994, pp. 4–5)*

These words were penned by Burt in 1994, the same year that the journal *Psychomusicology* published a special issue described by guest editor Annabel Cohen as "the first collection of articles devoted entirely to the experimental psychology of film music" (Cohen, 1994, p. 2), written by contributors who were "pioneers in a new field" (p. 7). Prior to this, the role of music in film had been the focus of only a few empirical investigations, in spite of its constant presence in film, in live keyboard and orchestral accompaniment in so-called "silent" films in the early 1900s and since the early days of sound film in the 1920s. Almost two decades after the *Psychomusicology* monograph, the first book consolidating the scientific research on music in film and other media was published, entitled *The Psychology of Music in Multimedia,* a volume edited by Tan, Cohen, Lipscomb, & Kendall (2013).

As the present chapter will show, *every line* of George Burt's statement has been supported by one or more studies in the still modest, but steadily growing area of empirical work focusing on film music. Other reviews explore the various functions music serves in film (Cohen, 1999) and emotional dimensions of film music (Cohen, 2010) or provide general surveys of film music research methods and findings (e.g., Cohen, 2014; Tan, 2016; Tan, in press). The present chapter does not duplicate these efforts but sets out to examine the role of music in shaping viewers' interpretation of film scenes and the evolving storyline. The focus of the chapter is on the *epic* or *narrative function* of music in film as described by Bullerjahn, which refers to the way film music supports the narrative course (as cited in Kuchinke, Kappelhoff, & Koelsch, 2013, p. 127).

## The "Unheard Melodies" of Cinema

Film music presents a compelling case for psychological study as music plays an integral role in film and has been shown to have profound effects on many facets of the film viewing experience, without being in the "spotlight" of our attention for very long. This paradox inspired film music theorist Claudia Gorbman's title for her influential 1987 book, *Unheard Music: Narrative Film Music.* In most narrative films, the storytelling is foregrounded, whereas stylistic elements—such as camera movement, editing, and the musical score—are often intended to serve the narrative without drawing much attention to themselves.[1] For instance, there are 1,000 to 2,000 film edits in a typical 90-minute Hollywood movie but most viewers do not notice the majority of the cuts. Psychologists attribute this "edit blindness" to effective film editing practices designed to bind separate shots together,[2] to coincidences with eye blinks and saccades, and especially to inattentional blindness as attention is focused elsewhere on characters, action, and story (Smith & Henderson, 2008).

Similarly, most viewers have only a momentary or fleeting awareness of the score while watching a film. And when the music credits roll, most viewers do not recall having heard most of the pieces—even if the music is familiar, such as in a compilation score. Conversely, in a pilot study, my colleagues and I found that two-thirds of our 31 participants reported having heard music in one or more of six film clips when in fact there was no music at all (Tan, Spackman, & Bezdek, 2007). How can music significantly influence and even alter viewers' perception of film when we are only momentarily aware of its presence (or absence)? This paradox underlies many film music studies and has yet to be fully resolved (see Cohen, 2014).

Our apparent lack of awareness of the film score, relative to the visual component of film, is not merely anecdotal. The phenomenon of *visual dominance*—which refers to how visual input often overrides information from other senses—has been widely demonstrated in studies on perception and memory (e.g., Posner, Nissen, & Klein, 1976; Spence, 2009). More specifically, when it comes to audiovisual contexts, attention is often prioritized to the visual component when both auditory and visual stimuli are present. To cite a musical example, Schutz and Lipscomb (2007) showed that the perceived duration of a tone produced by a marimba can be altered by showing a video of the marimba player striking the key with a long or short arm gesture. Much less frequently, *auditory dominance* has also been demonstrated. For instance, in the sound-induced flash illusion or SIFI, a single flash of light accompanied by two beeps in rapid succession is often perceived as two flashes (e.g., Shams, Kamitani, & Shimojo, 2000). Some studies show that auditory information may be dominant in audiovisual presentations of stimuli with emotional or affective components (see Kuchinke et al., 2013, for a review).

Most investigations of visual dominance employ speeded discrimination tasks with simple stimuli such as tones and flashing lights. Film music provides a context for studying multi-modal processing with more meaningful materials of longer duration, often with a strong emotional component. The participants' attention is often directed to the film and the focus on the music is typically concealed from the participants, so as not to bring more attention to the music track than when viewing a film in real-world contexts (see Tan, in press). Yet clear patterns often emerge between the responses of participants watching the same film clip with different music tracks. Music even influences viewers' perception of the intensity of emotional interactions when participants are instructed to focus only on the video (e.g., Bolivar, Cohen, & Fentress, 1994) and incidental learning of (mood-congruent) musical soundtracks has occurred in a memory task, even when participants were instructed to memorize only the visual component of the film (Boltz, 2004). When it comes to film music, the motivating force for researchers is not so much to discover whether visual or auditory dominance prevail, but to better understand how information from multiple senses is integrated to construct meanings that amount to more than each sense can singly or jointly contribute.

## The Focus of Attention

For many, the earliest experiences of the storytelling power of a pictorial image can be traced back to a parent pointing to objects or figures in a picture book and commenting on them, shaping selective attention and attaching fragments of narrative to the shared focus of interest. Likewise, directing the viewer's attention to particular elements of a film scene and ascribing meaning to those elements is fundamental to the comprehension of a scene and to the shaping of an unfolding story in the conscious mind. Can music play such a role in our experience of a film—and if so, how?

## Temporal Congruence

In a landmark study in 1988, Marshall and Cohen added two different music tracks to a silent black-and-white animation of geometric shapes, and found that the music changed viewers' interpretations of some elements of the film. For instance, a small triangle was rated as significantly more "active" when accompanied by what they called "strong" music (in a minor key, played in octaves and chords in the lower register, with a slow but accelerating tempo) than when accompanied by "weak" music (in a major key, with a single line melody played in an upper register, and an unchanging moderate tempo). It is notable that the music tracks in Marshall and Cohen's (1988) study did not have sweeping effects on the participants' impression of all elements in the animation in a wholesale fashion, but altered the perception of only specific elements of the scene. The researchers speculated that some features of the "strong" music must have directed attention to the small triangle. They proposed that structural accents in this particular piece of music happened to coincide with many movements of the small triangle, directing attention to it because of its temporal correspondence to the music. Further, the music was strong and lively in character, and thus the characteristic of being "active" became attributed to the focus of attention (i.e., the small triangle).

In sum, two mechanisms were proposed: congruence and association. (1) *Congruence:* When the structure of the music coincides with events on screen, the eye is drawn to points of temporal (i.e., time-based) matching. Marshall and Cohen referred to this as "*temporal* congruence" (1988, p. 18). Even infants look longer at video screens that match the timing of a soundtrack than one that is mismatched (e.g., Spelke, 1976), suggesting that humans have a tendency to seek meaningful congruencies among incoming data from different senses. (2) *Association:* The meaning of the music then becomes ascribed to the focus of attention; that is, the "connotations" of the music become attached to these elements, thus shaping our interpretation of the scene. These two ideas laid the foundations for the Congruence-Associationist Model or CAM (e.g., Cohen, 2013a), a cognitive theory of music in multimedia that is discussed later in this chapter.

Eye-tracking represents a potentially fruitful way to test the proposition of temporal congruence in film viewing, as this technique involves recording the movement of the eyes, and monitoring *fixations* (points in space where the eyes stabilize momentarily), *saccades* (movements involved as the eyes shift from one fixation to another), and *scanpaths* (the pattern or sequence of fixations and saccades over time). This technology has been used to study gaze behavior while viewing dynamic scenes, although only a handful of studies have examined how music may influence visual attention while viewing films (e.g., Auer et al., 2012; Mera & Stumpf, 2014; Smith, 2014; Wallengren & Strukelj, 2015).

In one study, Mera and Stumpf (2014) selected a scene[3] from Michel Hazanavicius' silent film *The Artist* (2011) and added music tracks intended to either direct attention toward the main characters or to diffuse the focus. The selected clip was two and a half minutes long, and showed two characters (George and Peppy) crossing paths on a multilevel staircase with many other people passing by, thus providing multiple competing visual

*Figure 30.1*   Scene from *The Artist* with many visual points of interest (Studio 37 Orange, 2011). See endnote 3 for details on the selected scene and film.

points of interest (as shown in Figure 30.1). The "focusing" music track was selected to direct attention to "the interplay between the central characters with melodic, textural, and orchestrational materials that change[d] . . . fluidly to match the narrative dynamics of the scene" (2014, p. 8). In contrast, the "distracting" music track was designed to disperse attention to the many possible focal points of the scene, and consisted of fast, lively music in 2/2 time with relentless high energy, avoiding audiovisual connections between the music and key elements in the scene. Consistent with the proposition of temporal congruence, Mera and Stumpf (2014) found that participants who watched the version with the "focusing" music track engaged in the lowest number of shifts in gaze and longest gaze duration, compared to those who had watched the version with the "distracting" music track or the (original) "silent" version.

Of further interest was a scene at the end of the clip, in which the main focus of interest (George) appears very small in an extreme wide-shot, and he is standing still while several passersby are moving at other points on the staircases. The "focusing" music was meant to draw attention to George's motionless presence with a sudden shift from full orchestration to a single sustained note played by the violins (a common "focusing" device used in film scoring) and the tempo and meter also change suddenly at this point to mark a shift in focal point from the previous shot. Indeed, those in the "focusing" music condition took the shortest time to fixate on George (2.66 seconds from the beginning of that particular scene, compared to 3.76 and 5.02 seconds for "distracting" and silent versions respectively, though this finding did not reach statistical significance).

## Semantic Congruence

Marshall and Cohen's initial (1988) study focused on *temporal congruence*, or attention to matching parts of a scene due to perceived *time-based* (synchronized) correspondences between some aspect of the moving image and the structure of the music. Another type of audiovisual matching is *semantic congruence*—which is based on matching of meanings—such as when the meaning of the music draws viewers' attention to an object or a part of the scene. Boltz et al. (1991) and Bolivar et al. (1994, p. 32) first shed light on this type of congruence, and focused on *affective* meaning.

For example, the idea of semantic congruence may explain the divergent perceptions of the city and weather in the opening scene of *The Lost Weekend*, as described in Vitouch's (2001) study in the beginning of this chapter. The peaceful, cheerful mood of Rózsa's score may have drawn viewers' attention to buildings in the foreground that seemed to be swathed in faint sunshine, whereas the somber and melancholic excerpt of Barber's music may have drawn more attention to the gray skies and drab buildings in the distance. Thus, viewers may perceive the same cityscape to be either lightly sunlit or set in a gloomy fog, due to the tendency for viewers to focus mostly on parts of the film images that seem to match the affective meaning of the music—as conveyed by features such as mode, tempo, and harmony (see Gabrielsson & Lindström, 2010). Had one of the music tracks consisted of Grieg's "Morning Mood" from the *Peer Gynt* suite, another kind of semantic congruence might have come into play. If the viewer recognizes this piece of music, attention might then be drawn to aspects of the scene linked to the idea of morning, such as the faint sunlight on the buildings and windows thrown open to let in the fresh morning air. In each case, the music conveys something that orients a viewer's attention, and the meaning of the music may then become ascribed to the focus of attention, framing the scene and its story in a particular way.

An early eye-tracking pilot study on film music used a 10-second film clip from John Curran's *The Painted Veil* (2006), which showed a young couple riding in a small boat on a river. Auer et al. (2012) showed this scene to participants paired with either calm orchestral music, suspenseful music from a horror film, or without any music. Participants who saw the film with the "calm" track tended to gaze mostly at the rowboat in the center of the screen.[4] However, those who saw the film paired with the "horror" music spent significantly more time looking at a dark patch of the water in the left corner of the screen.

Although the researchers did not set out to test semantic congruence, this finding could be interpreted in this way: The genre (horror) or emotion (scary, chilling) of the music may have directed participants' attention to the dark patch, where something may be lurking. The composition of the shot is quite symmetrical and there is little camera movement to guide the eye, and no dialogue or narration in this scene. Therefore, the shift in gaze to the left corner seems to have been directed by the music. The two music tracks elicited two different focal points of attention in this scene, and essentially generated two different sets of expectations and stories for the scene.

## The Unfolding Scene and Storyline

### *The Working Narrative*

The physical elements of film are light waves and sound waves impinging on our sense organs in a darkened room. How is this sensory information eventually translated into meaningful scenes and storylines that engage us in a film?

This is what Cohen aims to explain in the *Congruence-Associationist Model (CAM)*, a multi-level framework for representing the cognitive processing of music and film information. A discussion of the full model lies beyond the scope of this short chapter; readers are referred to chapters and articles by Cohen providing thorough descriptions of CAM (e.g., Cohen, 2013a, which traces the development of CAM and includes a link to an animated version of the model narrated by Annabel Cohen herself). Given its relevance to the interpretation of scenes, this section provides only an outline of the "working narrative" level in the center of the model.

Briefly, Cohen (2014) proposes that we make use of two main sources of information in multimedia contexts such as film viewing: lower-order sensory input and higher-order knowledge.

(a) *Lower-order input from the senses:* In CAM, this sensory input (light waves, sound waves, etc.) comes through two visual channels (visual, text) and three auditory channels (music, speech, sound effects). Recently, a sixth channel has been added to encompass sensory input of a kinesthetic nature, such as MX4D and D-Box theater seats with motion effects (and vibrotactile and other sensations) synchronized with the movie action. In Cohen's (2013a, 2014) view, the immediate sensory analysis of information includes the discovery of cross-channel congruencies. These structural correspondences or redundancies lead to prioritization of the cross-modally matched information for processing over other information. (In this chapter, we focus on the connections between the music and visual channels, but congruencies can occur between information from all channels—with the visual channel often, but not always, being prioritized).

(b) *Higher-order knowledge stored in long-term memory:* This includes autobiographical memory (i.e., recollection of episodes from one's experience similar to what is being viewed on screen), knowledge of the grammar of story construction, knowledge about social rules and conventions, and all other information pertinent to building expectations and predictions about a particular unfolding scene and story. This source of higher-order knowledge is activated in top-down fashion when some of this pre-attentively assessed information from the lower-order input "leaks through" via fast bottom-up processes sufficiently to serve as clues for the generation of expectations or hypotheses about the narrative.

In Cohen's view (2014), the best match between these two main sources of information at each point in the evolving film is what gives rise to the "working narrative." Thus, the working narrative can be described as the viewer's conscious, moment-to-moment, multi-modal experience of the film as it is unfolding. Previously referred to as "visual narrative" in earlier formulations of the model, this phrase was replaced with the "working narrative" "because the conscious representation of a film narrative is transient and is always a work in progress, and because of possible connections to Baddeley's (1986) model of working memory" (Cohen, 2013a, p. 31). Thus, CAM serves as a broad cognitive framework for understanding how we make sense of information in multimedia contexts, which continues to expand and respond to advancements in empirical findings and in cinema and theater technology.

## Inferences and Expectations

The discussion thus far has focused on how music plays a role in directing attention to particular elements within a film scene, thus influencing the course of the working narrative. However, music can also suggest ideas that cannot always be depicted on screen such as the internal states of characters (i.e., their motives, thoughts, emotions, and desires) and the nature of the relationship between the characters and intentions toward one another (e.g., Boltz, 2001; Bullerjahn & Güldenring, 1994; Hoeckner, Wyatt, Decety, & Nusbaum, 2011; Tan, Spackman, & Wakefield, in press; Vitouch, 2001). Further, the music track may also guide inferences that extend to future events in the form of expectations and predictions, as described in Vitouch's *The Lost Weekend* study reviewed in the beginning of this chapter. (See also Boltz, 2001; Boltz et al., 1991; Bullerjahn & Güldenring, 1994; Tan et al., 2007.)

In one study, Boltz (2001) showed three ambiguous film excerpts accompanied by music with a "positive" mood (pieces in major mode, with a clear melodic line, and strong metrical structure), or music with a "negative" mood (pieces in minor mode, with a lot of dissonance, fragments rather than a clear melody, and less predictable metrical structure), or no music. One of the three excerpts was a scene from Paul Schrader's film *Cat People* (1982), in which a brother and sister reunite after a long separation, and peruse a closet of old circus toys that they had played with when they were children. Boltz found that the majority of participants who viewed the scene accompanied by music conveying a "positive" mood tended to interpret the reunion as the start of a happy life together. In contrast, the majority of participants who viewed the same scene with music conveying a "negative" mood were more likely to believe that the brother will harm or kill the sister. Positive music also led to more positive descriptions of the brother's traits (e.g., kind, loving, protective), whereas more negative personality descriptions were ascribed to him (e.g., deranged, evil, manipulative) when the scene was accompanied by negative music.

Further, the music track also affected the accuracy of participants' recall for whether particular items had appeared in a film scene or not, when given a surprise memory test one week later. For example, those who had watched the scene described earlier with "positive" music correctly recognized more "positive"-themed objects that had been featured in the scene such as old family photographs, juggling balls, and a feathered boa, than those who had viewed the scene without music (control condition). Similarly, those who watched with "negative" music correctly recognized more "negative"-themed objects such as storm clouds and a full moon, a human skull, statues of demons, than those who had viewed the scene without music. Thus it seemed that music directed more attention to items that were congruent with the character or mood of the music (semantic congruence), leading to better recall for these items.

Most surprisingly, participants who watched the film excerpt with "positive" music also *falsely* recognized more "positive" objects that had not been shown in the film clip—such as a music box, locket, and wrapped gifts. Similarly, those who watched with "negative" music *falsely* recognized more negative-themed objects, such as a large hunting knife, a book of witchcraft, and a bottle of poison, none of which had appeared in the film scene. Thus, the music may also have evoked associations with items that were congruent with the music, suggesting embellishments or elaborations to the scene that were consistent with these schemas. Boltz concluded that music "exert[s] a direct influence on the cognitive processing of a film by guiding selective attending toward mood-consistent information and away from other information that is inconsistent with its affective valence" (2001, p. 446). Although Boltz interpreted the results in the context of schematic influence, the findings are also consistent with CAM as the affect of the music seemed to direct attention to congruent visual properties of the film, thus influencing the working narrative.

### Mood Congruence and Incongruence

A number of studies have examined the effects of mood-congruent versus mood-incongruent music on viewers' perceptions of a film scene. Compared to music that is incongruent with the emotional tone and action of a scene, congruent music has been shown to have a stronger intensifying effect on perceived emotions of interactions (e.g., Bolivar et al., 1994, expt. 3), to be more absorbing and to draw more attention to central elements of a scene (Cohen & Siau, 2008), and to strengthen memory for the details of a mood-congruent scene, even when attention is directed away from the audio (Boltz, 2004).

Thus far, the studies reviewed in this chapter all employed *non-diegetic music* (or a *dramatic score*), as the standard method in film music research is based on selecting film scenes that have no inherent music or dialogue so that they can be paired with different background music tracks (Tan, 2016; Tan, in press). Non-diegetic music accompanies a scene but is external to the fictional world of the film, such as music that punctuates the action and mirrors the mood and tension of a high-speed car chase. Empirical studies have very rarely focused on *diegetic music*, which refers to music presented as if originating from a source inside the fictional world of the film—such as music that the characters produce (e.g., by singing or playing), or control (e.g., by switching on a radio), or can hear because it is supposedly playing within their environment. Pertinent to this discussion, diegetic music is often used to interject music that is incongruent to the mood or events in a scene in a way that may give the impression of being incidental.

In an exploratory study, my colleagues and I examined the effects of presenting a piece of incongruent music diegetically or non-diegetically on viewers' interpretation of the characters and scenario (Tan, Spackman, & Wakefield, in press). We selected a scene[5] from Steven Spielberg's *Minority Report* (2002) in which a man and woman make their way hurriedly through a shopping mall, pursued by a troop of armed police (as shown in Figure 30.2). This tense scene is accompanied by a slow, gentle ballad (Henry Mancini's "Moon River") that sounds like it is playing distantly over the loudspeakers inside the mall. Thus, the music

*Figure 30.2* Three frames from an action sequence in *Minority Report* (Twentieth Century Fox and Dreamworks, 2002). See endnote 5 for details on the selected scene and film. See insert for color figure.

in the original scene is diegetic and mood-incongruent. We created an alternate version by mixing a recording of Mancini's "Moon River" music at a louder level in relation to the dialogue and sound effects in order to suggest a non-diegetic dramatic score accompanying the scene.

The relationship and intentions of the two characters, and many aspects of the scenario, are somewhat open to interpretation for those who have not seen the film. My colleagues and I found that viewers who watched the altered version (with mood-incongruent music that we mixed to suggest *non-diegetic* music accompanying the scene) perceived the scene to be less tense and less suspenseful, assumed a less hostile and antagonistic relationship between the two characters, and believed them to be less fearful and suspicious of each other and less intent to harm each other, compared to those who watched the original Spielberg version (with diegetic mall music). Participants also perceived the male character to be experiencing less fear and more romantic interest in the other character when watching the scene with non-diegetic music, than those who watched the original Spielberg scene with music sounding like it was playing inside the shopping mall. It is possible that the gentle ballad music sustains the tension in a suspenseful action sequence if it sounds like incidental music that happened to be playing inside the mall (diegetic). However, the same mood-incongruent ballad may be assumed to be a commentary on the scene when presented as the non-diegetic dramatic score, thus having a softening or mollifying effect with romantic undertones.

We may posit that along with knowledge of story grammar in the "higher-order knowledge" level of the CAM model, one might include knowledge of musical conventions and film grammar, which studies have shown are assimilated at a young age through exposure to film, television, video games, and other narrative multimedia (e.g., see Wingstedt, Brandstrom, & Berg, 2008). Interestingly, systematic differences between the interpretations of the *Minority Report* scene for the diegetic and non-diegetic music versions were found even among participants who were unable to correctly recall whether the music had been presented as if playing inside the shopping mall or as part of the dramatic score. Future research may bear out whether the diegetic or non-diegetic nature of the music is registered at the pre-attentive level of CAM or later in the process.

## *Placement of Music*

Thus far, most of the research studies reviewed in this chapter focused on the effects of simultaneous presentation of music and moving images. However, the music track may also influence the perception of images not shown concurrently with the music.

For instance, my colleagues and I found that music does not have to accompany a character in order to influence our interpretation of the characters' emotions (Tan, Spackman, & Bezdek, 2007). We selected four film clips to which we added 15 seconds of music, either ending just as a character entered a scene or beginning just after a character had left the scene. Even though the music was not played during the close-ups of the faces (selected through pilot testing to display neutral affect) and only overlapped a few seconds with the entrance of the character, the viewers' interpretation of the film characters' emotions tended to "migrate" toward the emotion expressed by the music. A surprising finding was that even music played *after* the character left the scene colored viewers' perceptions of what they had already seen. We interpreted this as a case of *backward priming*, in which "the evaluative prime *succeeds* the target stimulus and possibly influences *ongoing* target processing" (Fockenberg, Koole, & Semin, 2006, p. 800, emphases provided).

Our findings highlight the constantly evolving and non-linear nature of the working narrative in CAM as evaluation does not end with the presentation of a stimulus; viewers continuously update the working narrative with new information they encounter, including cues from the musical score. Music may prime the affective tone of images that follow it, or reframe a prior action or event, just as narration may frame the meaning of a scene that follows it or modify the meaning of a prior action or event earlier in the story.

The placement of the music may also affect the strength of our memory for a scene. In a study focusing on the role of music in foreshadowing film events, it was found that memory for 3- to 4-minute suspenseful film sequences differed, depending on the placement of the music in relation to the resolution of the scene (Boltz, Schulkind, & Kantra, 1991). Specifically, when music *foreshadowed* the resolution of a scene, participants' memory of the sequence was better if the affect of the music (sad or happy/positive or negative) was *incongruent* with the resolution of the scene. On the other hand, if the music *accompanied* the resolution, memory for the sequence was enhanced when the affect of the music *matched* the positive or negative resolution of the scene. Boltz et al. concluded that music that accompanies or foreshadows the outcome of a scene engages different attentional mechanisms that enhance the memorability of the film clip. Namely, music accompanying a scene enhances memory by directing attention to corresponding mood-congruent aspects of a scene (i.e., semantic congruence, based on the affective meaning of the music) whereas musical foreshadowing with mood-incongruent music may enhance memory by drawing attention to the discrepancy between one's expectations and the outcome, in line with research showing that expectancy violations are recalled more accurately than information conforming to expectations (e.g., Maki, 1990).

## *Sense of Closure*

Finally, music may also influence the degree to which a scene may feel completed or closed. In a series of studies, Thompson, Russo, and Sinclair (1994) found that viewers generally perceive film scenes to have ended with greater closure if paired with a musical soundtrack that resolves to the tonic (e.g., ending on a C chord if in the key of C) than when accompanied by exactly the same musical score but not resolving to the tonic (e.g., ending on the dominant or G chord in the key of C). Further, the perception of completion was stronger for scenes accompanied by tonally closed music with a clear metrical structure and a final melodic note that ended on a strong beat. Most of the participants in Thompson et al.'s experiments had little to no musical training, so these effects do not seem to rely on formal musical knowledge.

The findings were clear for a simple and brief film clip, showing a face emerging from a painting and back again. However, the effects are not always simple: For more elaborate film clips created by third author Sinclair or excerpts from the Hollywood film *Clue* (1985), tonally closed music increased viewers' perception of closure of the events in some scenes, whereas for other film clips, musical closure had no effect or even decreased the impression of scene closure. On this question and many others reviewed in this chapter, there is still much to explore and understand with respect to how music interacts with numerous audio and visual elements to shape viewers' experience of rich and complex film scenes.

## Conclusion

Film music provides a compelling case for psychological investigation in many domains, especially music cognition. In spite of our often fleeting awareness of music accompanying a film, the systematic variations in participants' responses to different musical tracks paired with the same film scene suggest that viewers must be processing some salient characteristics of the music—such as tempo, mode, dynamics, register, consonance/dissonance, timbre and instrumentation, tonal closure, and other parameters of music that have been shown to either express or induce emotions (Gabrielsson & Lindström, 2010). According to the Congruence-Associationist Model, meanings conveyed by the music then become attached to focal points of the visual scene that are structurally congruent in temporal and/or semantic ways.

In sum, music accomplishes much more than simply mirroring the action and emotion of a film scene, or intensifying the effects of the moving images. By directing attention, guiding inferences and suggesting elaborations, foreshadowing future events and reframing scenes we have already seen, and influencing the degree of perceived openness or closure of scenes, music plays an essential role in shaping the audience's interpretation of the unfolding storyline of a film.

## Acknowledgments

The author is grateful to Elizabeth A. Penix (Kalamazoo College and Walter Reed Army Institute of Research, Center for Military Psychiatry and Neuroscience) and Miguel Mera (Department of Music at the City University of London) for helpful comments on an earlier draft and kind assistance with a figure.

## Notes

1. See chapter 2 in Audissino, E. (2014). *John Williams' film music*. Madison, WI: University of Wisconsin Press.
2. For instance, see Bordwell and Thompson on continuity editing on pages 232–255 in Bordwell, D., & Thompson, K. (2012). *Film art*. New York, NY: McGraw-Hill.
3. The selected scene begins at 35 minutes and 26 seconds into the film and is 158 seconds in duration: Langmann, T. (Producer), & Hazanavicius, M. (Director). (2011). *The artist* [DVD]. France: Studio 37 Orange.
4. This is common, as a center-of-screen bias has been shown in many eye-tracking studies of dynamic scenes. See Mital, P. K., Smith, T. J., Hill, R. M., & Henderson, J. M. (2010). Clustering of gaze during dynamic scene viewing is predicted by motion. *Cognitive Computation, 3*, 5–24.
5. The selected scene can be found at 1:35:33 to 1:36:57 in the film and is 84 seconds in duration: Molen, G. R., Curtis, B., Parkes, W. F., de Bont, J. (Producers), & Spielberg, S. (Director). (2002). *Minority report* [DVD]. United States: 20th Century Fox and DreamWorks.

## Core Reading and Film

Boltz, M. G. (2001). Musical soundtracks as a schematic influence on the cognitive processing of filmed events. *Music Perception, 18*, 427–454.
Cohen, A. J. (2013b). Film music from the perspective of cognitive science. In D. Neumeyer (Ed.), *The Oxford handbook of film music studies* (pp. 96–130). Oxford: Oxford University Press.
Schrader, M. (Director), & Kraft, R., Willbanks, J., Thompson, T., Holmes, K., Gold, N., & Chavarria, C. (Producers). (2016). *Score: A film music documentary* [Motion picture]. United States: Epicleff.

(Features interviews with over 50 Hollywood composers, tracing the history and process of film scoring. Duration: 94 minutes.)

Tan, S.-L., Cohen, A. J., Lipscomb, S. D., & Kendall, R. A. (2013). *The psychology of music in multimedia.* Oxford: Oxford University Press.

## Further References

Audissino, E. (2014). *John Williams' film music.* Madison, WI: University of Wisconsin Press.

Auer, K., Vitouch, O., Koreimann, S., Pesjak, G., Leitner, G., & Hitz, M. (2012, July). *When music drives vision: Influences of film music on viewers' eye movements.* Paper presented at the 12th International Conference on Music Perception and Cognition and the 8th Triennal Conference of the European Society for the Cognitive Sciences, Thessaloniki, Greece.

Baddeley, A. (1986). *Working memory.* New York, NY: Oxford University Press.

Bolivar, V. J., Cohen, A. J., & Fentress, J. C. (1994). Semantic and formal congruency in music and motion pictures: Effects on the interpretation of visual action. *Psychomusicology, 13,* 28–59.

Boltz, M. G. (2004). The cognitive processing of film and musical soundtracks. *Memory & Cognition, 32,* 1194–1205.

Boltz, M., Schulkind, M., & Kantra, S. (1991). Effects of background music on the remembering of filmed events. *Memory & Cognition, 19,* 593–606.

Bordwell, D., & Thompson, K. (2012). *Film art.* New York, NY: McGraw-Hill.

Bullerjahn, C., & Güldenring, M. (1994). An empirical investigation of effects of film music using qualitative content analysis. *Psychomusicology, 13,* 99–118.

Burt, G. (1994). *The art of film music.* Boston, MA: Northeastern University Press.

Cohen, A. J. (1994). Introduction to the special volume on psychology of film music. *Psychomusicology, 13,* 2–8.

Cohen, A. J. (1999). The functions of music in multimedia: A cognitive approach. In S. W. Yi (Ed.), *Music, mind, and science* (pp. 53–69). Seoul, Korea: Seoul National University Press.

Cohen, A. J. (2010). Music as a source of emotion in film. In P. N. Juslin, & J. A. Sloboda (Eds.), *Handbook of music and emotion: Theory, research, applications* (pp. 879–908). New York, NY: Oxford University Press.

Cohen, A. J. (2013a). Congruence-Association Model of music and multimedia: Origin and evolution. In S.-L. Tan, A. J. Cohen, S. D. Lipscomb, & R. A. Kendall (Eds.). *The psychology of music in multimedia* (pp. 17–47). Oxford: Oxford University Press.

Cohen, A. J. (2014). Resolving the paradox of film music. In J. C. Kaufman & D. K. Simonton (Eds.), *The social science of cinema* (pp. 47–83). New York, NY: Oxford University Press.

Cohen, A. J., & Siau, Y.-M. (2008). The narrative role of music in multimedia presentations: The Congruence-Association Model (CAM) of music and multimedia. In K. Miyazaki, Y. Hiraga, M. Adachi, Y. Nakajima, & M. Tsuzaki (Eds.), *Proceedings of the 10th International Conference on Music Perception and Cognition (ICMPC10) Sapporo, Japan* (pp. 77–82). Adelaide, Australia: Causal Productions.

Fockenberg, D., Koole, S., & Semin, G. (2006). Backward affective priming: Even when the prime is late, people still evaluate. *Journal of Experimental Social Psychology, 42,* 799–806.

Gabrielsson, A., & Lindström, E. (2010). The role of structure in the musical expression of emotions. In P. N. Juslin, & J. A. Sloboda (Eds.), *Handbook of music and emotion* (pp. 367–400). New York, NY: Oxford University Press.

Gorbman, C. (1987). *Unheard melodies: Narrative film music.* Bloomington, IN: Indiana University Press.

Hoeckner, B., Wyatt, E. M., Decety, J., & Nusbaum, H. (2011). Film music influences how viewers relate to movie characters. *Psychology of Aesthetics, Creativity, and the Arts, 5,* 146–153.

Krumhansl, C. L. (1997). An exploratory study of musical emotions and psychophysiology. *Canadian Journal of Experimental Psychology, 51,* 336–353.

Kuchinke, L., Kappelhoff, H., & Koelsch, S. (2013). Emotion and music in narrative films: A neuroscientific perspective. In S.-L. Tan, A. J. Cohen, S. D. Lipscomb, & R. A. Kendall (Eds.), *The psychology of music in multimedia* (pp. 118–138). Oxford: Oxford University Press.

Langmann, T. (Producer) & Hazanavicius, M. (Director). (2011). *The artist* [DVD]. France: Studio 37 Orange.

Maki, R. H. (1990). Memory for script actions: Effects of relevance and detail expectancy. *Memory & Cognition, 18*, 5–14.

Marshall, S. K., & Cohen, A. J. (1988). Effects of musical soundtracks on attitudes toward animated geometric figures. *Music Perception, 6*, 95–112.

Mera, M., & Stumpf, S. (2014). Eye-tracking film music. *Music and the Moving Image, 7*, 3–23.

Mital, P. K., Smith, T. J., Hill, R. M., & Henderson, J. M. (2010). Clustering of gaze during dynamic scene viewing is predicted by motion.

Molen, G. R., Curtis, B., Parkes, W. F., de Bont, J. (Producers), & Spielberg, S. (Director). (2002). *Minority report* [DVD]. United States: 20th Century Fox and DreamWorks.

Posner, M. I., Nissen, M. J., & Klein, R. M. (1976). Visual dominance: An information-processing account of its origins and significance. *Psychological Review, 83*, 157–171.

Schutz, M., & Lipscomb, S. (2007). Hearing gestures, seeing music: Vision influences perceived tone duration. *Perception, 36*, 888–897.

Shams, L., Kamitani, Y., & Shimojo, S. (2000). Illusions: What you see is what you hear. *Nature, 408*, 788.

Smith, T. J. (2014). Audiovisual correspondences in Sergei Eisenstein's Alexander Nevsky: A case study in viewer attention. In T. Nannicelli, & P. Taberham (Eds.), *Cognitive Media Theory* (pp. 85–105). New York, NY: Routledge.

Smith, T. J., & Henderson, J. M. (2008). Edit blindness: The relationship between attention and global change blindness in dynamic scenes. *Journal of Eye Movement Research, 2*, 1–17.

Spelke, E. S. (1976). Infants' intermodal perception of events. *Cognitive Psychology, 8*, 553–560.

Spence, C. (2009). Explaining the Colavita visual dominance effect. *Progress in Brain Research, 176*, 245–258.

Tan, S.-L. (2016). Music and the moving image keynote address 2015: The psychology of film music: Framing intuition. *Music and the Moving Image, 9*, 23–38.

Tan, S.-L. (in press). From intuition to evidence: The experimental psychology of film music. *The Routledge companion to screen music and sound*. Abingdon, UK: Routledge.

Tan, S.-L., Spackman, M. P., & Bezdek, M. A. (2007). Viewers' interpretations of film characters' emotions: Effects of presenting film music before or after a character is shown. *Music Perception, 25*, 135–152.

Tan, S.-L., Spackman, M. P., & Wakefield, E. M. (in press). The effects of diegetic and nondiegetic music on viewers' interpretations of a film scene. *Music Perception*.

Thompson, W. F., Russo, F. A., & Sinclair, D. (1994). Effects of underscoring on the perception of closure in filmed events. *Psychomusicology, 13*, 99–118.

Vitouch, O. (2001). When your ear sets the stage: Musical context effects in film perception. *Psychology of Music, 29*, 70–83.

Wallengren, A.-K., & Strukelj, A. (2015). Film music and visual attention: A pilot experiment using eye-tracking. *Music and the Moving Image, 8*, 69–80.

Wingstedt, J., Brändström, S., & Berg, J. (2008). Narrative music, visuals and meaning in film. *Visual Communication, 9*, 193–210.

# 31

# MUSIC AS ENABLING

## Enhancing Sport, Work, and Other Pursuits

*Nicola Dibben*

The idea that music is "enabling" is firmly rooted in popular consciousness through its presence in commercial, community and health settings, and in a wealth of research attesting to music's ubiquity, functionality and contribution to human flourishing. Psychological research in this topic attempts to discover and understand when, why and how humans experience music as facilitating activities which it accompanies. Indeed, the topic is so diverse that it is necessary to identify some boundaries in the context of this volume. First, I briefly consider the particular contexts and activities in which we find music, and the enabling effects which arise in them, examined through three specific examples. Second, I review the underlying routes by which music enables and offer a new synthesis. I end by questioning the dominance of research into music's enabling effects: I consider the extent to which music may be "disabling," thereby pointing towards a more critical and reflective psychological approach to understanding music in everyday life.

## Functional Niches of Music Listening

The numerous accounts of music's functions in everyday life point to a variety of contexts for music listening. This chapter is primarily concerned with the enabling effects of listening to recorded music in the context of non-musical everyday activities without formal therapeutic or pedagogic purpose, as is found in music listening during office work, exercising, or travelling, for example.[1] One feature of research into music's enabling capacities is that contexts of music listening are often treated separately, resulting in a disorienting panoply of investigations into a myriad of everyday contexts. One successful remedy to this has been to group these into "functional niches" (categories of non-musical activities that music accompanies and enhances). In their overview of self-selected listening, Sloboda, Lamont, and Greasley (2009) identify six such niches: travel (e.g. the benefits of music for driver attention and mood), physical work (e.g. energizing and giving meaning to daily chores), what they term "brain work" (e.g. contexts for improving productivity and creativity), body work (e.g. enhancing the intensity and enjoyment of exercise), emotional work (e.g. regulating mood states), and attendance at live music events as an audience member, which could be broadened to include music in screen media.[2] To these six, I add two additional categories which appear in the literature associated with imposed music listening: Music in commerce and marketing, and "social" work encompassing identity, self-exploration and self-expression, collective action, and social cohesion (DeNora, 2000). Rather than attempt to discuss all these contexts, I examine three functional niches to exemplify the evidence for music's benefits and the commonalities which cut across them.

## Examples of Music Enabling

### *Music Enabling Cognitive Work*

Many people listen to music while working or studying. In the early-twentieth century music was sometimes broadcast in factories as a means of increasing productivity and morale, whereas in the twenty-first century individualized music listening is the norm due to availability of mobile music listening technologies, and changes to production economies meaning an increase in office- and computer-based work. A qualitative study of music in two British office workplaces indicated that a large proportion of employees listened to music for much of their working time, generally while carrying out low-demand, solitary tasks with respondents reporting that it improved concentration, reduced stress, relieved boredom, was a way of exerting agency in the workplace, and of creating private space within the public office (Dibben & Haake, 2013). Similarly, adults and children frequently listen to music while studying, citing their belief that it increases focus (by blocking noise and stopping their mind from wandering), reduces boredom and increases motivation (by helping "pass the time"), and reduces stress and anxiety (via mood regulation).

However, self-report evaluations of auditory distraction can be inaccurate (Ellermeier & Zimmer, 1997), and the evidence is contradictory as to whether music is always beneficial to cognitive tasks. Some studies show that music may benefit mental tasks under certain circumstances, revealing improvements for attention, memory, mental arithmetic and learning (for example, Hallam, Price, & Katsarou, 2002). Other research suggests that music increases cognitive demands in a way which may be deleterious to certain tasks as described below.

This contradictory evidence can be explained by models of memory and attention, which have been brought to bear on studies of the Irrelevant Sound Effect (ISE): This is the well-established phenomenon in which serial recall performance is poorer in the presence of background sound than in a quiet condition (Sörqvist & Rönnberg, 2014). First, the ISE is characterized by the need to maintain order information in the focal task, and this seriation is a common feature of short-term memory tasks such as serial and free recall, mental arithmetic, and language learning. For tasks not involving maintenance of order information, such as those reported in Hallam et al. (2002) above, music is less disruptive. Second, for the ISE to be observed the sound must contain acoustical change between successive sound items. More steady-state sound (e.g. where there are few dramatic changes in the acoustic features of the music) is less disruptive. In this context working memory can be understood as the way attention is used to maintain or suppress information and avoid distraction, although there is still disagreement about the precise mechanisms responsible.

Individual differences in working memory can account for variations between individuals' susceptibility to distraction in the presence of music. Researchers have used complex-span tasks (serial recall tasks interleaved with irrelevant processing tasks such as reading sentences) to measure working memory capacity (WMC) and correlated this with person-specific measures of distractibility. This shows that individuals with high-WMC are less susceptible to the effects of background noise on memory and reading comprehension, and therefore that age-related differences in distractibility can be explained by life-span changes in WMC, and differences between personality types can be explained by higher WMC amongst certain personalities (Sörqvist & Rönnberg, 2014). It appears that individuals with high-WMC have more effective gating of auditory-perceptual information at subcortical and cortical processing stages than do those with low capacity. In contrast to music heard prior to a task, where music can improve performance by changing emotional state (Schellenberg, Nakata, Hunter, & Tamoto, 2007), liking for background music does not influence serial recall performance. Indeed, disliked, unfamiliar music can even produce better performance than liked, familiar music if the disliked music is steady-state (Perham & Sykora, 2012). In summary, music's effects on a concurrent task are dependent on contextual factors, including the cognitive demands of the particular task, individual differences in cognitive capacities, and characteristics of the music.

Music does seem beneficial for creative tasks. Research on the effects of mood on creativity suggest that creativity is enhanced by positive, activating mood states, which have an "approach motivation," i.e. you do something because you think something good will happen (Baas, De Dreu, & Nijstad, 2008). Meta-analyses, such as that of Baas et al., indicate that these mood states may have a variety of effects: Positive moods may influence insight and originality by increasing cognitive flexibility (e.g. the ability to switch quickly from thinking about one dimension (e.g. color) to another (e.g. shape) and to think about more than one concept at the same time), while other moods may impact by increasing cognitive persistence (focused attention).

### Music Enabling Exercise

Music is commonly used to accompany exercise (e.g. in group aerobic sessions, or individual running routines) and to accomplish clinical goals in health-related physical activities. Music's influence on movement involves cognitive, sensory-motor and psycho-emotional processes: Music has been found to divert attentional focus away from feelings of fatigue, encourage more rhythmic and efficient movements, induce a state of flow, and evoke useful memories, moods and emotions, including feelings of motivation and reward (Clark, Baker, & Taylor, 2016). Better understanding of the benefits of music for exercise and their causes, could enable more systematic applications, both in sport and in therapeutic settings.

The complexity of the topic is heightened by the different ways in which music is incorporated into exercise routines: Specifically, whether used before after or during exercise, and whether or not exercise movements are deliberately synchronized with the music. Used prior to or after exercise music can optimize arousal levels and attentional focus, whereas during exercise its contribution includes ergogenic as well as psychological effects. Use of music in synchrony with exercise movements as opposed to music which is rhythmically asynchronous with movements also has distinct benefits: Music which is not synchronized with movements is associated with psychological effects such as distraction from fatigue and increased positive affect, whereas music which is synchronous with repetitive endurance exercise also has positive ergonomic effects both for deliberate and spontaneous synchronization.

In one of the most comprehensive reviews of the topic, Karageorghis and Priest (2012a, 2012b) identified three main effects of music in exercise: Synchronization with the pulse of music can increase work output for sub-maximal exercise (ergogenic effects), music can reduce perceived exertion for sub-maximal exercise (psychophysical effects), and it can enhance positive affective states for exercise of medium and high levels of intensity (psychological effects). The ways in which music can influence positive affect are well documented in detail elsewhere (Juslin, 2013) so I briefly discuss psychophysical and ergonomic effects here instead.

Music's ability to reduce perceptions of effort and fatigue in exercise, and consequently to increase work output, endurance and enjoyment, have been construed as a distraction mechanism by researchers in sports psychology (Karageorghis & Priest, 2012b). Neurophysiological evidence shows that when individuals perform movements, premotor and motor areas of the brain related to voluntary muscle contractions are active, and the sense of effort the individual perceives correlates with this central motor command (Morree, Klein, & Marcora, 2012). The cognitive explanation for music's capacity to divert attention from physical effort is based on an information processing model of attention, which proposes that multiple sources of information (emotional and sensory) are processed in parallel at a pre-conscious stage, but at a conscious stage one focus of attention dominates. Hence, the perception of music during exercise and the perception of physical exertion compete for the same focal attention and so music prevents perception of fatigue being brought into focal awareness, until such time as the effects of exertion overpower the attentional draw of the music. However, given that even high intensity exercise can feel more pleasant in the presence of music, some aspects of music involved in positive affective states and reward may involve subcortical processing (the anterior cingulate cortex and amygdala), and by implication may be less influenced by attentional capacity.

The effectiveness of music's temporal qualities for entrained movements (i.e. deliberately synchronized movements) is evident from studies of treadmill exercise, running and cycling. These show that participants exercise for longer in the presence of "motivational" synchronous music compared to no music, or a non-motivational music control, that the accuracy of the movements is improved, and is associated with improved energy efficiency (lower oxygen consumption, lower blood lactate levels), and work ouput (Karageorghis & Priest, 2012b). The neuropsychological explanation for these benefits highlights the role of brain structures involved in auditory-motor processing (cerebellum, basal Ganglia and motor cortex). The consensus is that music with a constant meter provides a repeating time measure providing an inter-beat reference against which the timing of movements can be iteratively judged and planned, enabling error correction and execution of precise and accurate movements (Thaut, 2015). Music also provides a motivational quality (Bood, Nijssen, Van Der Kamp, & Roerdink, 2013)—a meaningful and rich auditory context for this temporal pattern, rendering it more effective than a simple metronomic beat.

Research into the sonic characteristics of music associated with people exercising harder, for longer and with more enjoyment, has primarily focused on tempo, and used self-report instruments such as the Brunel Music Rating Inventory (Karageorghis, Priest, Terry, Chatzisarantis, & Lane, 2006). More recently attention has turned to understanding the role of additional sonic features via the theoretical perspective of embodied cognition. This offers a holistic framework, in which the relationships between musical features such as rhythm, tension, and relaxation, and spontaneous motoric and muscular changes, are viewed as facilitating effects of music on effort and speed. This approach frames the effects of music in terms of entrainment of "vigor," attributable to particular acoustic features of experimental stimuli (the presence of a clear 4/4 meter beat, chord changes every 4 bars, and mean energy in particular frequency bands; Buhmann, Desmet, Moens, Van Dyck, & Leman, 2016). Much work remains to be done identifying the acoustic features of "motivational" music.

The importance of self-selection and the role of individual differences (age and gender) and social and cultural context as factors influencing the effectiveness of music in exercise have now begun to be explored and form part of theoretical frameworks (Clark et al., 2016).

### *Music Enabling Commerce*

Music's occurrence in commercial settings is associated with a range of functions, including engaging consumers in adverts, improving recall for advert content, activating relevant knowledge to create meanings for the product, creating positive attitudes towards the advert and content, influencing message processing (Tan, Cohen, Lipscomb, & Kendall, 2013), and ultimately influencing product choice and expenditure (North & Hargreaves, 2008). The classical conditioning model proposes that when a positive stimulus, such as liked music, is paired with a neutral stimulus, the positive affect for the liked stimulus becomes associated with the neutral stimulus, increasing liking for it and positive judgments of it. In addition, environments and products associated with liked music appear to increase "approach" behaviors. There is also evidence that music can activate consumers' knowledge in such a way as to influence product selection: In a field study (North, Hargreaves, & McKendrick, 1999) stereotypical French or German music played at a wine stall increased sales of French or German wine respectively.

Another way in which music can have commercial utility is by influencing consumers' motor behavior: Music with more energizing potential (faster/louder) is associated with increased speed of movement in stores, online retail environments, eating in restaurants, and drinking in bars (see for a review North & Hargreaves, 2008). However, the identification of musical characteristics associated with these effects requires more systematic investigation, as discussed in relation to exercise above.

These examples of music enhancing cognitive work, exercise and commerce illustrate some of the interrelationships between music's enabling effects. In other words, whether music is beneficial for some other activity or not depends on a range of contextual factors. While some music can distract the listener from a concurrent task (e.g. disrupt reading comprehension), other music can enhance focus on that task (e.g. by providing a relatively stable sound environment which masks other changing background sound); and while in some circumstances distraction may be a cause of impairment to a concurrent task, in others, it can be a positive aid (e.g. distraction from exercise fatigue); and while in some situations liking for the music is necessary for music's positive effects, in others (such as certain concurrent cognitive tasks) liking has no bearing on performance.

These examples highlight common musical, socio-cultural, psychological, biopsychological, neurochemical and neurophysiological systems underlying music's ability to enhance other activities. Indeed, in addition to conceptualizing music listening's enabling effects in terms of the "functional niches" in which it happens, one can look across these individual contexts and effects to the processes which underlie them.

### Underlying Routes by which Music Enables

Based on existing literature and their explanatory frameworks, I identify four routes by which music listening facilitates concurrent tasks: perceptuo-cognitive, affective, attentional, and perceptuo-motor. These correspond to the functions of self-chosen music use identified by Sloboda, Lamont, and Greasley (2009, p. 431) (meaning enhancement, entrainment, distraction and energizing) but differ from previous formulations in two ways: The perceptuo-motor category comprises both motor entrainment and un-entrained effects on "vigor," consistent with an approach informed by embodied cognition; this allows the "affective" category to include effects of mood valence and not just the arousal (energy) dimension of mood.

## *Perceptuo-Cognitive*

Music is heard as having historically and culturally specific associations due to the history of use of its "materials" (melodies, harmonies, timbres, rhythms, etc.) which listeners pick up through exposure and informal and formal training. Hence, when an enculturated listener hears music, that music can activate associated knowledge (Dibben, 2001; Tagg & Clarida, 2003), e.g. a leaping brass motif is associated with heroic masculinity, historically in military and hunting contexts, and more recently in the theme tunes accompanying film heroes such as James Bond. From a psychological perspective such knowledge activation by music is a form of implicit memory recall and has been investigated using priming paradigms, and brain imaging studies which show that even brief, isolated musical sounds can activate semantic meanings (Painter & Koelsch, 2011). These implicit associations activated by music influence the meanings and values attributed to advertisements, brands and the products they promote, perception of physical and online environments, interpretation of television and film narratives, product choice and even other people. We may identify with the meanings and values expressed by a certain artist or kind of music, and use the music as part of a larger process of identity construction. In turn, branding companies use these meanings of music to endow products with particular appeal.

This affiliation with certain musics and avoidance of others is sometimes deployed as a tool to influence patronage and people's behavior in particular places: For example, in the broadcast media, radio programming is designed to attract particular sectors of society who are the target consumers for relevant advertisers; in retail environments "youth music" might be played in a clothes shop aimed at an adolescent consumer group; and conversely, easy listening or classical music might be broadcast in a public space such as a metro station to deter adolescents from loitering (Hirsch, 2007). Moreover, the extent of "fit" between these meanings of the music and another product with which it is associated can indirectly influence our judgments of that product: A message (in an advert for example) is more persuasive when music activates information/associations which fit the advertised product (Kellaris, Cox, & Cox, 1993).

One additional consequence of music's meanings for listeners is that music can influence perception in other sensory modalities (and vice versa). This includes the ways in which music influences visual perception in musical multimedia—film, television, gaming and mobile media (Tan et al., 2013; Tan, this volume), smell and taste (Spence, 2011). Cross-modal correspondences offer opportunities to design music to enhance experiential qualities of environments and products, such as odors, flavors and associated gustatory experiences, as well as visual and arguably motion-oriented experiences we may be more familiar with.

## *Affective*

Music's ability to influence affective states of listeners points to the utility of music as a tool for mood regulation, whether informal (e.g. part of a deliberate self-chosen mood regulation strategy; Saarikallio, 2011), or formal (e.g. a therapeutic intervention; Thaut, 2015). Music-induced changes in the arousal and valence of listeners' mood states have been implicated in improvements to cognitive performance on tasks heard subsequent to music listening as described earlier. Music's effects on mood also influence decision-making and evaluation, and it is these which are put to the service of influencing others in their evaluations of environments, products, and adverts (North & Hargreaves, 2010), such as in the classical conditioning example mentioned above. Indeed, music's valence has been shown to influence evaluation not just of neutral or positive products and messages, but acceptance of unethical messages, and compliance with a request which could harm a third person (Ziv, 2016). It is beyond the scope of this chapter to go into further explanation but as in other instances, what seems to be going on is a series of cascade reactions to music: Music influences mood which itself impacts on other processes, which leads to, in this case, acceptance of messages.

### *Attention*

Background music is by definition heard in the presence of some other activity to which it is ultimately unnecessary; therefore many of music's effects can be attributed to its impacts on attention. Up until fairly recently background music's distracting capacity was attributed to its "complexity," loosely defined in terms of information load. More recently, specific psychoacoustic parameters have been identified which increase potential for distraction dependent upon task, music characteristics, and working memory capacity of the individual. For example, fluctuation strength (Ellermeier & Zimmer 2014)—how much the sound varies over time—is thought to interfere with a concurrent temporally structured task (such as verbal short-term memory tasks, mental arithmetic, and reading tasks). Conversely, music with more stable temporal characteristics can be used to mask more unpredictable environmental sounds, since the unvarying background music is less likely to capture focal attention, as when people use music to create an "auditory bubble." It remains to be determined whether the measure of fluctuation strength is, by itself, an adequate predictor of the distraction potential of music, or whether other psychoacoustic and musical indices, such as dissonance loudness and tempo also contribute beyond fluctuation strength.

Music's effects on attention also explain some of music's persuasive effects: For example, the elaboration likelihood model of persuasion (Cacioppo & Petty, 1984) argues that a stimulus (in this case music) accompanying a message that causes attention to be diverted away from the content of a message makes individuals become more prone to use peripheral routes to make judgments (such as liking for the music).

### *Perceptuo-Motor*

Music is often experienced in terms of its ability to induce a pleasurable desire to move, and the ability of music to influence human movement is well established in research. Music is effective in cueing periodic movement in healthy populations, and in people with movement disorders where it can influence the timing, spatial and force dynamics of movements (Thaut, 2015).

Tapping or moving along to a musical beat appears to be a simple task requiring little effort for the vast majority of people, yet the brain mechanisms underlying it involve a variety of functions ranging from basic timing processes to sensorimotor coupling and are distributed across neural regions. Even listening to music, without moving to it, involves neural processes and activates brain regions associated with the motor system, including premotor cortices, supplementary motor areas, cerebellum and the basal ganglia (Zatorre, Chen, & Penhune, 2007).

There is some debate over which musical features determine music-induced movement. A meta-analysis of empirical studies of impacts of background music revealed that the tempo of music influences the speed of actions performed in its presence (Kämpfe, Sedlmeier, & Renkewitz, 2011). However, the extent to which music's effects on motor movement can be attributed to tempo alone are debatable, especially given the variability with which tempo has been manipulated in previous research (both in terms of bpm and in terms of isolating effects of tempo from other musical parameters; Bramley, Dibben, & Rowe, 2014) and evidence that walking speed varies systematically with changes in musical features other than tempo (Leman et al., 2013). One of the key characteristics appears to be the psychological construct of "groove," namely that aspect of the music which induces a pleasant sense of wanting to move along with the music ("sensorimotor synchronization") and in which the coupling feels easy (Janata, Tomic, & Haberman, 2012). Music which induces this pleasurable desire to move is characterized by four common features: beat salience and event density, repetition (which enhances predictability, with consequent improvements to sensorimotor synchronization) and an optimal level of syncopation determined by an inverted-U curve relationship between increasing rhythmic complexity on the one hand and experienced pleasure and self-reported desire to move on the other (Witek, Clarke, Wallentin, Kringelbach, & Vuust, 2014).

Some researchers understand sensorimotor coupling as an embodied enactment of musical meter in which the desire to move to syncopated music is a *response* to this *invitation* and the pleasure which is experienced is a result of the fulfilled desire (Witek et al., 2014; Janata et al., 2012). From the perspective of clinical applications of music-cued movement, sensorimotor coupling to music relies on associations between rhythm perception and brain areas responsible for motor perception and action. It has been argued that auditory rhythm and music trigger firing rates of auditory neurons, which entrain the firing patterns of motor neurons (Thaut, 2015). As a consequence, auditory stimulation is thought to prime the motor system, which increases the quality of the movement, and provides a specific period forming a stable anticipatory time reference, which optimizes motor planning, and execution (Thaut, 2015). Music's ability to instill a pleasurable desire to move is recruited to enhance sports performance, speed of movements in retail environments, work tasks involving movement, and movement therapies where it is used to enhance gait and upper body training.

## A Vision for Research into Music as Enabling

### *Modeling the Enabling Capacity of Music*

The discussion of three specific examples of "functional niches" in which music operates, and the summary of processes underlying them illustrates three important points for research in this area. First, any specific niche where music may appear can entail a number of different benefits, which may draw on any or all of the underlying processes. This highlights the necessity of identifying the specific phenomena to be understood, and drawing on the relevant psychological theories and evidence to better understand them. Second, music's effects are contextual on the concurrent task or activity, characteristics of the music, and capacities and goals of the individual or group. Third, a consequence of this is that research in this area needs to recognize the mutuality inherent in the affordances offered to individuals/groups by music rather than a linear model in which music "produces" effects on listeners—a conceptualization which can fail to recognize the contingency of any such effects on other factors. The review above highlights the need to better understand the role of specific musical characteristics and indicates the current neglect of new modes of listening to and sharing music online, of multimedia and participatory experiences enabled by digitalization and social media, and the potential to use analysis of "big data" in research (audio analysis of music corpus, streaming usage, and social media) to better understand ways in which recorded music benefits listeners.

## A Critical Perspective on Music Consumption

As this summary suggests, "ubiquitous" music has commonly been viewed by the social sciences as an enabling resource, or, from a more functionalist perspective, as a tool to improve human functioning. Indeed, the word "enabling" used in the title to this chapter has the neutral meaning "to allow" or "facilitate," yet its everyday usage in relation to music psychology research is often taken to mean something unquestionably positive. A more critical perspective highlights the potentially negative ways in which music may be involved in human experience, and the need for a broader conception of the role of music in human flourishing.

A critique of psychological approaches to music in everyday life (Hesmondhalgh, 2013, pp. 35–42) notes the predominantly positive formulations of human agency implied in much research on musical participation, community music, and individualized music listening for mood regulation or other affective and social ends. We might also add to this list, the positive formulation of research into music in commercial applications such as retail environments and advertising where the rhetoric is one of using music to benefit industry. Hesmondhalgh points out that while many people often do have the opportunity to exert agency through musical engagement, they can also be limited in their capacity to do so by virtue of social, historical and biographical constraints. Given music's evident involvement in social processes of a modern society marked by inequalities and exploitation, the effects of musical engagement are highly unlikely to be somehow free of these more negative aspects of modern life. Supporting evidence for Hesmondhalgh's assertion comes from music psychology studies on more or less deliberate attempts to influence the behavior, subjective experience and thinking of other people, or oneself. Music's capacity to influence others is deliberately deployed in ways which are morally dubious or unethical: Music can enhance acceptance of unethical messages and compliance (Ziv, 2016); it can encourage detrimental patterns of consumption such as the speed of bet placement in online gambling (Bramley et al., 2014); music broadcast in public places can deter specific groups of "unwanted" people from those sites (Hirsch, 2007); music is used by military personal to help produce aggressive mental and physical states appropriate to combat, and even as part of a portfolio of torture techniques (Cusick, 2008). Even our own, self-selected uses of music may be less helpful to our individual flourishing than we realize: For example, some listening behaviors may be maladaptive in so far as they facilitate mood regulation strategies such as rumination, venting or suppression which can be injurious to mental health (Saarikallio, 2011), or interfere with a cognitive task when we think it is helping. Lastly, Hesmondhalgh argues that psychological approaches ignore the role of aesthetic experience in daily life, and he calls for a broader stance on the role of music in human flourishing. This broader approach is not (just) a psychology of happiness, of pleasure or of wellbeing, but a fuller account of music's role in attaining fundamental human "capabilities."

The overview provided in this chapter attests to the many specific contexts of use for music in the early 21st century. The ubiquity of (recorded) music in daily life, both personalized and broadcast via mass media, can be expected to grow further given the increasing ownership of mobile listening devices (smartphones in particular), screen-based media (to which music is an audio adjunct), and internet-based on-demand music access. Research has evidenced a diverse range of "effects" of music listening and has started to link these to underlying psychological processes, and to specific musical and psychoacoustic features. However, this review also points to the need to better understand the specific mechanisms implicated in particular activities and effects. Doing so will inform sound/music design and automated music selection, increase awareness of maladaptive or unethical uses of music, and point the way to a fuller understanding of the value of music to human flourishing.

## Notes

1  See chapters elsewhere in this volume for discussions of the enabling potential of music-making (e.g., improvisation and performance), music's contribution to general intellectual functioning ("cognitive transfer effects"), and health and wellbeing. These are discussed in chapters surveying music and cognitive abilities (Gordon & Magne, this volume), and community music, therapy and their contribution to health, social functioning, cohesion, and identity (see Fachner, this volume, Saarikallio, this volume; Lamont, this volume; Vuoskoski, this volume).
2  The enabling effects of music in screen media (e.g., film, television, and computer gaming) are not examined here. Readers are referred to Tan (this volume) and Tan, et al. (2013).

## Core Reading

DeNora, T. (2000). *Music in everyday life*. Cambridge: Cambridge University Press.
Hesmondhalgh, D. (2013). *Why music matters*. John Wiley & Sons.
North, A., & Hargreaves, D. (2008). *The social and applied psychology of music*. Oxford: Oxford University Press.

## Further References

Baas, M., De Dreu, C. K., & Nijstad, B. A. (2008). A meta-analysis of 25 years of mood-creativity research: Hedonic tone, activation, or regulatory focus? *Psychological Bulletin, 134*(6), 779.
Bood, R. J., Nijssen, M., Van Der Kamp, J., & Roerdink, M. (2013). The power of auditory-motor synchronization in sports: Enhancing running performance by coupling cadence with the right beats. *PloS ONE, 8*(8), e70758.
Bramley, S., Dibben, N., & Rowe, R. (2014). The influence of background music tempo and genre on virtual roulette. *Journal of Gambling Issues, 29*, 1–12.
Buhmann, J., Desmet, F., Moens, B., Van Dyck, E., & Leman, M. (2016). Spontaneous velocity effect of musical expression on self-paced walking. *PloS ONE, 11*(5), e0154414.
Cacioppo, J. T., & Petty, R. E. (1984). The elaboration likelihood model of persuasion. *Advances in Consumer Research, 11*, 673–675.
Clark, I. N., Baker, F. A., & Taylor, N. F. (2016). The modulating effects of music listening on health-related exercise and physical activity in adults: A systematic review and narrative synthesis. *Nordic Journal of Music Therapy, 25*(1), 76–104.
Cusick, S. G. (2008). "You are in a place that is out of the world . . . ": Music in the detention camps of the "Global War on Terror." *Journal of the Society for American Music, 2*(1), 1–26.

Dibben, N. (2001). What do we hear, when we hear music?: Music perception and musical material. *Musicae Scientiae, 5*(2), 161–194.

Dibben, N., & Haake, A. B. (2013). Music and the construction of space in office-based work settings. In G. Born (Ed.), *Music, sound and the space: Transformations of public and private experience,* (pp. 151–168). Cambridge: Cambridge University Press.

Ellermeier, W., & Zimmer, K. (1997). Individual differences in susceptibility to the "irrelevant speech effect." *The Journal of the Acoustical Society of America, 102*(4), 2191–2199.

Ellermeier, W., & Zimmer, K. (2014). The psychoacoustics of the irrelevant sound effect. *Acoustical Science and Technology, 35*(1), 10–16.

Hallam, S., Price, J., & Katsarou, G. (2002). The effects of background music on primary school pupils' task performance. *Educational Studies, 28*(2), 111–122.

Hirsch, L. E. (2007). Weaponizing classical music: Crime prevention and symbolic power in the age of repetition. *Journal of Popular Music Studies, 19*(4), 342.

Janata, P., Tomic, S. T., & Haberman, J. M. (2012). Sensorimotor coupling in music and the psychology of the groove. *Journal of Experimental Psychology: General, 141*(1), 54.

Juslin, P. N. (2013). From everyday emotions to aesthetic emotions: Towards a unified theory of musical emotions. *Physics of Life Reviews, 10*(3), 235–266.

Kämpfe, J., Sedlmeier, P., & Renkewitz, F. (2011). The impact of background music on adult listeners: A meta-analysis. *Psychology of Music, 39*(4), 424–448.

Karageorghis, C. I., Priest, D. L., Terry, P. C., Chatzisarantis, N. L., & Lane, A. M. (2006). Redesign and initial validation of an instrument to assess the motivational qualities of music in exercise: The Brunel Music Rating Inventory-2. *Journal of Sports Sciences, 24*(8), 899–909.

Karageorghis, C. I., & Priest, D. (2012a). Music in the exercise domain: A review and synthesis (part I). *International Review of Sport Exercise Psychology, 5*, 44–66.

Karageorghis, C. I., & Priest D. (2012b). Music in the exercise domain: A review and synthesis (part II). *International Review of Sport Exercise Psychology, 5*, 67–84.

Kellaris, J. J., Cox, A. D., & Cox, D. (1993). The effect of background music on ad processing: A contingency explanation. *The Journal of Marketing, 57,* 114–125.

Leman, M., Moelants, D., Varewyck, M., Styns, F., van Noorden, L., & Martens, J. P. (2013). Activating and relaxing music entrains the speed of beat synchronized walking. *PloS ONE, 8*(7), e67932.

Morree, H. M., Klein, C., & Marcora, S. M. (2012). Perception of effort reflects central motor command during movement execution. *Psychophysiology, 49*(9), 1242–1253.

North, A. C., & Hargreaves, D. J. (2010). Music and marketing. In P. N. Juslin, & J. A. Sloboda (Eds.), *Handbook of music and emotion: Theory, research, applications* (pp. 909–930). Oxford: Oxford University Press.

North, A. C., Hargreaves, D. J., & McKendrick, J. (1999). The influence of in-store music on wine selections. *Journal of Applied Psychology, 84*(2), 271.

Painter, J. G., & Koelsch, S. (2011). Can out-of-context musical sounds convey meaning? An ERP study on the processing of meaning in music. *Psychophysiology, 48*(5), 645–655.

Perham, N., & Sykora, M. (2012). Disliked music can be better for performance than liked music. *Applied Cognitive Psychology, 26*(4), 550–555.

Saarikallio, S. (2011). Music as emotional self-regulation throughout adulthood. *Psychology of Music, 39*(3), 307–327.

Schellenberg, E. G., Nakata, T., Hunter, P. G., & Tamoto, S. (2007). Exposure to music and cognitive performance: Tests of children and adults. *Psychology of Music, 35*(1), 5–19.

Sloboda, J. A., Lamont, A., & Greasley, A. (2009). Choosing to hear music: Motivation, process and effect. In S. Hallam, I. Cross, & M. Thaut (Eds.), *The Oxford handbook of music psychology* (pp. 431–440). New York, NY: Oxford University Press.

Sörqvist, P., & Rönnberg, J. (2014). Individual differences in distractibility: An update and a model. *PsyCh Journal, 3*(1), 42–57.

Spence, C. (2011). Crossmodal correspondences: A tutorial review. *Attention, Perception, & Psychophysics, 73*(4), 971–995.

Tagg, P., & Clarida, B. (2003). *Ten little title tunes. Towards a musicology of the mass media.* Montreal and New York, NY: The Mass Media Music Scholars' Press.

Tan, S. L., Cohen, A. J., Lipscomb, S. D., & Kendall, R. A. (Eds.). (2013). *The psychology of music in multimedia.* Oxford: Oxford University Press.

Thaut, M. H. (2015). The discovery of human auditory–motor entrainment and its role in the development of neurologic music therapy. *Progress in Brain Research, 217,* 253–266.

Witek, M. A., Clarke, E. F., Wallentin, M., Kringelbach, M. L., & Vuust, P. (2014). Syncopation, body-movement and pleasure in groove music. *PloS ONE, 9*(4), e94446.

Zatorre, R. J., Chen, J. L., & Penhune, V. B. (2007). When the brain plays music: Auditory–motor interactions in music perception and production. *Nature Reviews Neuroscience, 8*(7), 547–558.

Ziv, N. (2016). Music and compliance: Can good music make us do bad things? *Psychology of Music, 44*(5), 953–966.

# PART 4

# Developing Musicality

# 32

# MUSIC ACROSS THE SPECIES

*Bruno Gingras*

The comparative study of music perception and cognition across animal species, sometimes termed "zoomusicology" or "biomusicology," is a relatively young field of research (Doolittle & Gingras, 2015; Gingras, 2014; Hoeschele, Merchant, Kikuchi, Hattori, & ten Cate, 2015). Musicians, including celebrated composers such as Janequin or Messiaen, have evoked or imitated birdsong for a long time, and scholars regularly transcribed birdsongs using musical notation. However, it is only since the last century that the scientific study of animal sound production and perception has flourished, thanks largely to the development of modern recording and audio analysis techniques, as well as the emergence of the discipline of comparative psychology in the wake of Charles Darwin's influential contributions. Today, it is a thriving research area which, along with the closely allied field of evolutionary musicology, seeks to identify possible biological bases of musicality and to propose a plausible, empirically supported account of the origins of music.

For a number of reasons, caution is required when broaching the topic of "animal music." First of all, it is notoriously difficult to come up with an all-encompassing definition of human music, let alone non-human music, considering that not all music makes use of discrete pitches, a regular pulse, or even sound in the case of John Cage's *4'33"* (Bispham, 2009). Nevertheless, for practical purposes, we will take as a starting point Brown and Jordania's (2013) "conserved universals" across human musical traditions, which include the use of discrete pitches, octave equivalence, transposability, and the presence of common sound-based arousal-inducing parameters such as tempo, amplitude, and register. Second, the conceptual possibility of non-human music remains a point of contention among scholars: Some argue that only humans can decide "what is and is not musical, even when the sound is not of human origin" (Nattiez, 1990), while others consider that any sound patterning, including those of animal origin, should be treated as music (Herzog, 1941). Along these lines, some authors distinguish between the musical interpretation of animal-produced sounds from a human perspective, which is considered the realm of zoomusicology (Martinelli, 2008), and the ability to perceive and produce musical sounds, termed *musicality* (Honing, ten Cate, Peretz, & Trehub, 2015), whose biological basis is the focus of biomusicology. Third, a few behavioral researchers have pointed out that "human" music, which is typically used in research on animal musicality, may not be ecologically relevant for other species. Thus, it might be more sensible to investigate animals' responses to sound patterns designed to take into account species-specific auditory perceptual capacities (Snowdon & Teie, 2010). While this is a valid caveat, it can be argued that fundamental research focusing on the perception of basic auditory processes which play a central role in music still has its place in the field (Hoeschele et al., 2015).

In this chapter, I provide an overview of the music-like behaviors associated with sound perception and production in non-human animals, with an emphasis on cross-species comparisons. I begin with a review of animal responses to music, focusing on pitch and rhythm perception, before examining animal song and outlining its commonalities with human music. The development of the emerging disciplines of zoomusicology and biomusicology is situated in a historical context and current perspectives are briefly outlined.

## Animal Responses to Music

Although the empirical study of sound and music perception in animals is a recent phenomenon, scholars have speculated about the potential effects of music on animals for centuries. For instance, the 11th-century Arabic writer Ibn al-Haytham (Alhazen) claimed, in a *Treatise on the Influence of Melodies on the Souls of Animals* (for which we have no extant copies), that music could affect a camel's pace, persuade horses to drink, charm reptiles, and lure birds (Farmer, 1997). However, it was not until Darwin, who credited birds with "strong affections, acute perceptions, and a taste for the beautiful" (Darwin, 1871), that the topic of animal responses to music was taken up in earnest by the scientific community.

Besides the pioneering work of Reinert (1957, 1960), which unfortunately has been largely ignored by English-speaking scholars, one of the first modern experiments to address this issue was conducted by Porter & Neuringer (1984), who showed that pigeons (*Columba livia*) could be trained to discriminate between Baroque and 20th-century music in a manner comparable to that of college students. Similar results were obtained with Java sparrows (*Padda oryzivora*, Watanabe & Sato, 1999), whereas an analogous study showed that koi fish (*Cyprinus carpio*) could discriminate between recordings of blues and classical music (Chase, 2001). Needless to say, while these reports suggest that non-human species possess the necessary auditory and neural apparatus to distinguish between different musical styles, they do not demonstrate that these species use the same acoustical features as humans to do so. Thus, rather than studying higher-order tasks such as the ability to categorize musical styles, other researchers have examined the issue from a more fundamental perspective, investigating lower-level auditory processes such as pitch perception, octave generalization and the discrimination between consonance and dissonance. Let us therefore review the extant research on these perceptual abilities before briefly discussing emotional responses to music.

### *Pitch Perception*

The ability to discriminate between sounds along a frequency dimension, and more specifically to perceive pitch, presumably constitutes an essential prerequisite for any meaningful discussion of music cognition in non-human animals, considering that the use of discrete pitches is one of Brown and Jordania's "conserved universals" in music. In experiments using pure tones, rats (*Rattus norvegicus*) (Blackwell, & Schlosberg, 1943), pigeons (Jenkins, & Harrison, 1960), starlings (*Sturnus vulgaris*) (Cynx, 1993), and goldfish (*Carassius auratus*) (Fay, 1992) were shown to possess a perceptual dimension corresponding to sound frequency, suggesting that it is a widespread ability among non-human species.

The sensation of pitch can also be evoked by complex tones, that is, harmonic (or periodic) sounds whose acoustic energy is mostly located at frequencies that are integer multiples of a common fundamental frequency (F0). Given that most animal vocalizations exhibit a harmonic structure (Roederer, 2008), such sounds are particularly relevant from a biological standpoint. In humans, harmonic sounds evoke the perception of a single sound source for which the pitch is matched to F0, as do harmonic sounds containing no acoustic energy at F0, a phenomenon known as the "pitch of the missing fundamental" (Plack, Oxenham, Fay, & Popper, 2005). A similar phenomenon has been shown in cats (*Felis catus*) (Heffner, & Whitfield, 1976), rhesus monkeys (*Macaca mulatta*) (Tomlinson, 1988), and starlings (Cynx & Shapiro, 1986). Buttressing these earlier findings, a recent study showed that the perceptual mechanisms responsible for the pitch sensations evoked by complex tones are shared among humans and common marmosets (*Callithrix jacchus*), a new World monkey (Song, Osmanski, Guo, & Wang, 2015). Taken together, these findings suggest that pitch attribution for complex tones is likely based on similar neural mechanisms among birds and mammals, including humans.

### Relative Pitch and Octave Generalization

Relative pitch is a central property of "human" musicality, in that it is associated with the capacity to encode a melody as a set of intervallic relationships, which remains perceptually invariant when transposed to a different pitch. With respect to tones presented simultaneously, several bird species (e.g., Brooks & Cook, 2010; Hulse, Bernard, & Braaten, 1995), as well as Japanese monkeys (*Macaca fuscata*) (Izumi, 2000), have been shown to be able to discriminate between chord types and to generalize to different transposition levels. However, this ability may be based on the degree of consonance or sensory roughness (see section "Consonance versus Dissonance") rather than on relative pitch *per se*. With respect to tones presented sequentially, a bottlenose dolphin (*Tursiops truncatus*) (Ralston & Herman, 1995), as well as two ferrets (*Mustela putorius*) (Yin, Fritz, & Shamma, 2010) were successfully trained to discriminate between short sequences using only pitch contour cues. Otherwise, evidence of relative pitch processing with tone sequences is sparse in non-human species, especially for birds, which appear to rely on spectral shape rather than on pitch cues (Bregman, Patel, & Gentner, 2016).

Octave generalization constitutes a restricted version of relative pitch, insofar as it concerns itself solely with the perceptual equivalence of melodies transposed by one or more octaves. In mammals, D'Amato (1988) did not find any evidence for octave generalization in cebus monkeys (*Cebus apella*). On the other hand, Wright et al. (2000) reported octave generalization in rhesus monkeys, but only for melodies using pitches from the diatonic scale and not for atonal melodies, a result which is in line with the earlier observation that humans are also generally better at recognizing transpositions of tonal melodies (Cuddy, Cohen, & Mewhort, 1981). Other results obtained with rats (Blackwell & Schlosberg, 1943) and bottlenose dolphins (Richards, Wolz, & Herman, 1975) imply, but do not unambiguously demonstrate, octave generalization in these species. Hulse and Cynx (1985) reported that starlings did not show any capacity for octave generalization, and the available evidence to date suggests that this is also the case for other bird species.

## Consonance versus Dissonance

Notwithstanding cultural influences on the categorization of sounds into consonant and dissonant ones, the perception of consonance is based, at least in part, on the physical properties of tone combinations. These properties include sensory roughness, which occurs when the frequency components of a sound are too close to be properly resolved on the basilar membrane, and harmonicity, which is related to the degree to which the frequency components of a complex tone are related by simple integer ratios (McDermott, Lehr, & Oxenham, 2010). Japanese monkeys can learn to discriminate between consonant and dissonant intervals (Izumi, 2000), and there is some evidence that songbirds can also discriminate between consonant and dissonant complex tones (Hulse et al., 1995). However, preference for consonant over dissonant sounds, which is displayed by two-month-old infants (Trainor, Tsang, & Cheung, 2002), is not universal across species: Whereas newborn chicks (*Gallus gallus*) prefer consonant music (Chiandetti & Vallortigara, 2011), other species, such as cotton-top tamarins (*Saguinus oedipus*), show no such preference (McDermott & Hauser, 2004).

## Timbre

Relatively few studies have examined timbre perception in non-human species. A few reports suggest that birds are comparatively more sensitive than humans to mistunings of single harmonics in complex tones (Lohr & Dooling, 1998) and other timbral differences (Amagai, Dooling, Shamma, Kidd, & Lohr, 2000). Among birds, zebra finches (*Taeniopygia guttata*) are sensitive to prosodic features of human speech and can recognize words produced by different speakers (male or female), indicating an ability to recognize common phonetic features across timbral and frequency changes (Ohms, Gill, Van Heijningen, Beckers, & ten Cate, 2010). On the other hand, black-capped chickadees (*Poecile atricapillus*) do not recognize a chord as being the same when played in a different timbre (Hoeschele, Cook, Guillette, Hahn, & Sturdy, 2014). Data on mammalian species remains scarce at the moment, although an early study reported that an Asian elephant (*Elephas maximus*) could recognize a melody across different instrumental timbres (Reinert, 1957).

## Perception of Rhythmic Patterns

Besides the ubiquity of periodic biological patterns, such as respiration, heartbeat, gait, and brain activity, the presence of an isochronous pulse is a "predominant feature" of human music according to Brown and Jordania (2013). As such, the ability to detect an isochronous pulse, as well as recurring patterns of rhythmic accentuation, constitutes a basic feature of "human-like" musicality, along with pitch perception. Equally fundamental is the perception of event rate or tempo. However, in contrast to pitch perception, research investigating rhythmic behaviors in non-human species has mostly focused on "production" aspects such as synchronization and entrainment (Patel, 2014), which I discuss below (see "Music-Like Behaviors and Singing in Non-Human Species"), and few studies have considered rhythm perception in isolation. Nonetheless, the available evidence indicates that jackdaws (*Corvus monedula*) (Reinert, 1960), starlings (Hulse & Kline, 1993), pigeons (Hagmann & Cook, 2010), as well as two monkey species (McDermott & Hauser, 2007), can discriminate between slow and fast tempi, indicating that this ability is likely to be common among higher vertebrates. Moreover, starlings can discriminate between isochronous and non-isochronous sequences

(Hulse, Humpal, & Cynx, 1984), a feat that could not be achieved by pigeons, implying that the latter may simply judge the average rate of auditory events without detecting periodicity (Hagmann & Cook, 2010).

### *Emotional Responses*

More than a century after Darwin outlined his theory of animal aesthetics (Darwin, 1871), little is known about the emotional or affective responses evoked by music or animal song in non-human species. However, we do know that the same brain circuit activated in human listening to pleasant music, namely the mesolimbic reward pathway (Blood & Zatorre, 2001), is also activated in female birds listening to birdsong, whereas the amygdala, associated with responses to unpleasant music in humans, is activated in male birds in the same context (Earp & Maney, 2012). Other findings suggest species-specific musical inclinations: Cotton-top tamarins, while preferring slow- to fast-tempo music, choose silence over music (McDermott & Hauser, 2007) and are mostly unresponsive to "human" music, but show increased emotional responses to music incorporating features based on tamarin vocalizations (Snowdon & Teie, 2010). These and other findings have led some researchers to highlight the signaling function of music and animal song, as well as emphasize the tight link between specific acoustical forms of the signals and the behavioral responses they evoke in listeners or recipients (Bryant, 2013).

### Music-Like Behaviors and Singing in Non-Human Species

Unlike perceptual responses to music, behaviors associated with singing are generally more difficult to study in experimentally controlled conditions (although creative scientists are devising ingenious ways to do so—see Rothenberg et al., 2014, for a review), and investigation relies to a larger extent on field observations and analysis of recordings. Up to now, the study of music-like behaviors in non-human species has typically gravitated towards the identification of potential commonalities between human music and animal song.

Animal song was, until recently, largely seen as a purely functional behavior: as summarized by McDermott and Hauser (2007), it was thought that animals did not sing for their enjoyment, that singing was almost exclusively associated with mate selection and territorial defense, and that it was essentially a male prerogative. However, Fitch (2006) and others noted that male–female duets are common among tropical songbirds, and that birds actually "practice" their songs. Moreover, neurochemicals implicated in the regulation of reward-seeking behaviors have been found to promote both undirected singing (what we might consider "practice") and female-directed singing in songbirds (Riters, 2011), implying that birds may in fact derive pleasure from singing.

### *Songs, Calls, and Vocal Learning*

Not all animal vocalizations are considered to be songs, although the distinction between "songs" and "calls" remains somewhat unsettled. Among earlier scholars, Tinbergen (1939) emphasized functional aspects, associating songs with territorial defense and courtship, and calls with other contexts such as food or predator alarms, whereas Thorpe (1956) differentiated between songs and calls on the basis of duration and complexity, with songs being longer and more elaborate than calls. More recently, Fitch (2006) suggested that, rather than functionality or complexity, the defining property of animal song was that it was a learned behavior, unlike calls, which are innate vocalizations. This "vocal learning" model has gained traction in recent years, notably because the relatively few animal clades capable of vocal learning and imitation (among mammals, humans, cetaceans, pinnipeds, elephants, and bats, and among birds, parrots, hummingbirds, and oscine songbirds) are generally among those that display music-like behaviors. Indeed, Patel (2006) surmised that vocal learning abilities, which are associated with specific neural pathways not found in non-vocal learning species (Jarvis, 2007), may also underpin the ability to synchronize movements with an isochronous external pulse (see paragraph "Rhythmic Entrainment and Coordination").

Much like humans learning to speak, songbirds first go through a "babbling" phase before developing the species-typical adult song. This learning phase, already described by Barrington (1773), was investigated more thoroughly in recent decades by Thorpe (1956), as well as by Marler (1970) and Nottebohm (1969). One byproduct of songs being a learned behavior, rather than an instinctual one, is that a number of songbirds display geographically based dialects. This geographic variation, noticed by von Pernau as early as 1720 (Stresemann, 1947), was examined in greater detail by Marler and Tamura (1962). An analogous phenomenon was described in humpback whales (Megaptera *novaeangliae*) (Payne, & Guinee, 1983), whose songs tend to be similar within a group but vary across geographic areas. Unlike songbirds, adult humpback whales do not settle on a stable, species-typical, song repertoire, but instead gradually reshape their songs over time, leading to a continuously evolving "song culture."

## Song Structure and Pitch Organization

Many animal songs are highly structured, some in ways that overlap with human musical forms. For example, humpback whales sing series of "rhyming" phrases, which begin differently and end with the same pattern (Guinee & Payne, 1988). Other structural commonalities between human and animal songs may be explained by analogous motor constraints on song production mechanisms, as for instance the preference for descending pitch contours and longer final notes found in both human and avian song (Tierney, Russo, & Patel, 2011). On the other hand, songbirds' ability to maintain separate tensions on the left and right pair of labia in the syrinx (vocal organ of songbirds) enables them to achieve large pitch jumps more frequently than human singers.

As mentioned previously, some non-human species, such as chicken, display a perceptual preference toward consonant intervals. Thus, an interesting question is whether this perceptual bias is complemented by a preference for producing sequential pitch intervals corresponding to harmonically-related frequencies. In songbirds, the only group for which this issue has been extensively investigated so far, the results are mixed. No evidence of the use of low-integer frequency ratios (e.g., 2:1 or 3:2), which generally correspond with consonant or harmonically-related pitches, was found in nightingale wrens (*Microcerculus philomela*) (Araya-Salas, 2012) or in white-throated sparrows (*Zonotrichia albicollis*) (Dobson, & Lemon, 1977). On the other hand, the songs of hermit thrushes (*Catharus guttatus*) (Doolittle, Gingras, Endres, & Fitch, 2014) are based on pitches that are harmonically related to a fundamental frequency (which is itself not sung), whereas musician wrens (*Cyphorhinus* arada) (Doolittle & Brumm, 2012) favor pitch intervals corresponding to low-integer frequency ratios. Outside the avian kingdom, yellow fever mosquitoes (*Aedes aegypti*) engage in courtship duets in which their buzzing frequencies (flight tones) converge to a 3:2 frequency ratio (perfect fifth) before mating (Cator, Arthur, Harrington, & Hoy, 2009). Altogether, there is some evidence that a preference for producing consonant or harmonically related intervals is not unique to humans, but the fragmented results published so far suggest that this bias is far from being universal.

### *Rhythmic Entrainment and Coordination*

Rhythmic entrainment, the ability to synchronize action or sound production to an external isochronous pulse, was long seen as uniquely human. Yet, evidence of rhythmic entrainment has surfaced in two parrot species (Hasegawa, Okanoya, Hasegawa, & Seki, 2011; Patel, Iversen, Bregman, & Schulz, 2009), which belong to a vocal-learning clade, as well as in Californian sea lions (*Zalophus californianus*) (Cook, Rouse, Wilson, & Reichmuth, 2013), whose status as a non-vocal learning species may need to be reevaluated (Patel, 2014). Furthermore, there is some anecdotal evidence of entrainment in elephants (Schachner, Brady, Pepperberg, & Hauser, 2009). Other behaviors involving rhythmic coordination, though not necessarily entrainment, can be observed among various species. For instance, synchronized chorusing, as seen in some frogs, or synchronized flashing found in fireflies (Buck, 1988), also requires the ability to detect a regular pulse and to synchronize to it. Additionally, a number of tropical bird species sing rhythmically coordinated duets involving mating pairs (Farabaugh, 1982).

Although drumming bouts in great apes have been proposed as a precursor to analogous human behaviors (Fitch, 2006), chimpanzees (*Pan troglodytes*), which are non-vocal learners, have shown only a limited capacity to entrain to an external pulse (Hattori, Tomonaga, & Matsuzawa, 2013). Nevertheless, the latest evidence, including a report of spontaneous isochronous drumming in a chimpanzee (Dufour, Poulin, Curé, & Sterck, 2015), suggests that the differences in rhythmic abilities between vocal non-learners and vocal learners may not be systematic (Wilson & Cook, 2016).

### Current Perspectives and Implications for Evolutionary Musicology

With the quest for human musical universals an ever-present concern among evolutionary musicologists (Brown & Jordania, 2013), cross-species comparisons provide researchers with an opportunity to generalize even further by investigating whether these universals also extend to non-human species. In doing so, such studies may reveal which principles are unique to human music, and which ones are shared with other species, ultimately leading to a better understanding of the nature of human music. Perhaps more importantly, cross-species comparative research offers a means to empirically test hypotheses regarding the origins and possible adaptive functions of proto-musical behaviors in humans and in their ancestors by examining analogous behaviors in animals. For instance, cross-species investigations currently focus on pitch processing and rhythmic entrainment, two central components of musicality, with the aim of identifying their biological basis and suggesting a plausible evolutionary history. To be sure, this methodological approach suffers from potential drawbacks related to the ecological validity of the stimuli and experimental settings, as well as the tendency to generalize from data obtained on a small number of species. Thus, researchers have emphasized the need to examine a greater diversity of species and to combine field observations and controlled laboratory experiments in order to accurately assess a species' abilities (Hoeschele et al., 2015; Wilson & Cook, 2016). Finally, owing to the rapid development of the field, animal musicality is quickly becoming a topic of interest in its own right, leading some scholars to advocate a "biocentric" approach to zoomusicology rather than an anthropocentric one, and ultimately to question the conventional definitions of music, culture, and aesthetics (Mâche, 1992; Martinelli, 2008).

## Acknowledgments

I thank Marisa Hoeschele, Manuela Marin, Renee Timmers, and an anonymous reviewer for providing useful suggestions on an earlier draft of this chapter.

## Core Reading

Doolittle, E. L., & Gingras, B. (2015). Quick guide: Zoomusicology. *Current Biology, 25*(19), R819–820.

Fitch, W. T. (2006). The biology and evolution of music: A comparative perspective. *Cognition, 100,* 173–215.

Gingras, B. (2014). Cross-species comparisons. In W. F. Thompson (Ed.), *Music in the social and behavioral sciences: An encyclopedia* (Vol. 1, pp. 287–290). Thousand Oaks, CA: SAGE Publications.

Hoeschele, M., Merchant, H., Kikuchi, Y., Hattori, Y., & ten Cate, C. (2015). Searching for the origins of musicality across species. *Philosophical Transactions of the Royal Society of London B,* 370:20140094. doi: 10.1098/rstb.2014.0094

Martinelli, D. (2008). *Of birds, whales and other musicians: An introduction to zoomusicology.* London: University of Scranton Press.

Rothenberg. D, Roeske, T. C., Voss, H. U., Naguib, M., & Tchernichovski, O. (2014). Investigation of musicality in birdsong. *Hearing Research, 308,* 71–83.

## Further References

Amagai, S., Dooling, R. J., Shamma, S., Kidd, T. L., & Lohr, B. (2000). Detection of modulation in spectral envelopes and linear-rippled noises by budgerigars (Melopsittacus undulatus). *Journal of the Acoustical Society of America, 105,* 2029–2035.

Araya-Salas, M. (2012). Is birdsong music? Evaluating harmonic intervals in songs of a neotropical songbird. *Animal Behavior, 84,* 309–313.

Barrington, D. (1773). Experiments and observations on the singing of birds, by the Hon. Daines Barrington, Vice Pres. RS in a letter to Mathew Maty, MD Sec. RS. *Philosophical Transactions (1683–1775), 63,* 249–291.

Bispham, J. C. (2009). Music's "design features": Musical motivation, musical pulse, and musical pitch. *Musicae Scientiae, 13,* 41–61.

Blackwell H. R., & Schlosberg, H. (1943). Octave generalization, pitch discrimination, and loudness thresholds in the white rat. *Journal of Experimental Psychology, 33,* 407–419.

Blood, A. J., & Zatorre, R. J. (2001). Intensely pleasurable responses to music correlate with activity in brain regions implicated in reward and emotion. *Proceedings of the National Academy of Sciences of the USA, 98,* 11818–11823.

Bregman, M. R., Patel, A. D., & Gentner, T. Q. (2016). Songbirds use spectral shape, not pitch, for sound pattern recognition. *Proceedings of the National Academy of Sciences of the USA, 113*(6), 1666–1671.

Brooks, D. I., & Cook, R. G. (2010). Chord discrimination by pigeons. *Music Perception, 27,* 183–196.

Brown, S., & Jordania, J. (2013). Universals in the world's musics. *Psychology of Music, 41,* 229–248.

Bryant, G. A. (2013). Animal signals and emotion in music: Coordinating affect across groups. *Frontiers in Psychology,* 4:990. doi: 10.3389/fpsyg.2013.00990

Buck, J. (1988). Synchronous rhythmic flashing in fireflies. II. *Quarterly Review of Biology, 63,* 265–289.

Cator, L. J., Arthur, B. J., Harrington, L. C., & Hoy, R. R. (2009). Harmonic convergence in the love songs of the dengue vector mosquito. *Science, 323,* 1077–1079.

Chase, A. R. (2001). Music discriminations by carp (Cyprinus carpio). *Animal Learning & Behavior,* *29*(4), 336–353.

Chiandetti, C., & Vallortigara, G. (2011). Chicks like consonant music. *Psychological Science, 22,* 1270–1273.

Cook, P., Rouse, A., Wilson, M., & Reichmuth, C. (2013). A California sea lion (Zalophus californianus) can keep the beat: Motor entrainment to rhythmic auditory stimuli in a non vocal mimic. *Journal of Comparative Psychology, 127,* 412–427.

Cuddy, L. L., Cohen, A. J., & Mewhort, D. J. K. (1981). Perception of structure in short melodic sequences. *Journal of Experimental Psychology: Human Perception and Performance, 7,* 869–883.

Cynx, J. (1993). Auditory frequency generalization and a failure to find octave generalization in a songbird, the European starling (*Sturnus vulgaris*). *Journal of Comparative Psychology, 107*(2), 140–146.

Cynx, J., & Shapiro, M. (1986). Perception of missing fundamental by a species of songbird (Sturnus vulgaris). *Journal of Comparative Psychology, 100,* 356–360.

D'Amato, M. R. (1988). A search for tonal pattern perception in Cebus monkeys: Why monkeys can't hum a tune. *Music Perception, 5,* 453–480.

Darwin, C. (1871). *The descent of man and selection in relation to sex.* London: Murray.

Dobson, C. W., & Lemon, R. E. (1977). Bird song as music. *Journal of the Acoustical Society of America, 61*(3), 888–890.

Doolittle, E. L., & Brumm, H. (2012). O Canto do Uirapuru: Consonant intervals and patterns in the song of the musician wren. *Journal of Interdisciplinary Music Studies, 6,* 55–85.

Doolittle, E. L., Gingras, B., Endres, D. M., & Fitch, W. T. (2014). Overtone-based pitch selection in hermit thrush song: Unexpected convergence with scale construction in human music. *Proceedings of the National Academy of Sciences of the USA, 111*(46), 16616–16621.

Dufour, V., Poulin, N., Curé, C., & Sterck, & E. H. M. (2015). Chimpanzee drumming: A spontaneous performance with characteristics of human musical drumming. *Scientific Reports, 5,* 11320.

Earp, S. E., & Maney, D. L. (2012). Birdsong: Is it music to their ears? *Frontiers in Evolutionary Neuroscience,* 4:14. doi: 10.3389/fnevo.2012.00014

Farabaugh, S. M. (1982). The ecological and social significance of duetting. In D. E. Kroodsma, & E. H. Miller (Eds.), *Acoustic communication in birds* (Vol. 2, pp. 85–124). New York, NY: Academic Press.

Farmer, H. G. (1997). Studies in oriental music: reprints of writings published in the years 1925–1966. In E. Neubauer (Ed.), *History and theory* (Vol. 1, pp. 240–241). Frankfurt am Main: Institute for the History of Arabic-Islamic Science.

Fay, R. R. (1992). Analytic listening by the goldfish. *Hearing Research, 59*(1), 101–107.

Guinee, L. N., & Payne, K. B. (1988). Rhyme-like repetitions in songs of humpback whales. *Ethology, 79(4),* 295–306.

Hagmann, C. E., & Cook, R. G. (2010). Testing meter, rhythm, and tempo discriminations in pigeons. *Behavioral Processes, 85,* 99–110.

Hasegawa, A., Okanoya, K., Hasegawa, T., & Seki, Y. (2011). Rhythmic synchronization tapping to an audio-visual metronome in budgerigars. *Scientific Reports, 1,* 120.

Hattori, Y., Tomonaga, M., & Matsuzawa, T. (2013). Spontaneous synchronized tapping to an auditory rhythm in a chimpanzee. *Scientific Reports, 3,* 1566.

Heffner, H., & Whitfield, I. C. (1976). Perception of the missing fundamental by cats. *Journal of the Acoustical Society of America, 59,* 915–919.

Herzog, G. (1941). Do animals have music? *Bulletin of the American Musicological Society, 5,* 3–4.

Hoeschele, M., Cook, R. G., Guillette, L. M., Hahn, A. H., & Sturdy, C. B. (2014). Timbre influences chord discrimination in black-capped chickadees but not humans. *Journal of Comparative Psychology, 128,* 387–401.

Honing, H., ten Cate, C., Peretz, I., Trehub, S. E. (2015). Without it no music: Cognition, biology and evolution of musicality. *Philosophical Transactions of the Royal Society B,* 370: 20140088. doi:10.1098/rstb.2014.0088.

Hulse, S. H., Bernard, D. J., & Braaten, R. F. (1995). Auditory discrimination of chord-based spectral structures by European starlings (Sturnus vulgaris). *Journal of Experimental Psychology, 124,* 409–423.

Hulse, S. H., & Cynx, J. (1985). Relative pitch perception is constrained by absolute pitch in songbirds (Mimus, Molothrus, and Sturnus). *Journal of Comparative Psychology, 99*, 176–196.

Hulse, S. H., Humpal, J., & Cynx, J. (1984) Discrimination and generalization of rhythmic and arrhythmic sound patterns by European starlings (Sturnus vulgaris). *Music Perception, 1*, 442–464.

Hulse, S. H., & Kline, C. L. (1993). The perception of time relations in auditory tempo discrimination. *Animal Learning & Behavior, 21*, 281–288.

Izumi, A. (2000). Japanese monkeys perceive sensory consonance of chords. *Journal of the Acoustical Society of America, 108*, 3073–3078.

Jarvis, E. D. (2007). Neural systems for vocal learning in birds and humans: A synopsis. *Journal of Ornithology, 148*(Suppl. 1), S35–S44.

Jenkins, H. M., & Harrison, R. H. (1960). Effect of discrimination training on auditory generalization. *Journal of Experimental Psychology, 59*(4), 246–253.

Lohr, B., & Dooling, R. J. (1998). Detection of changes in timbre and harmonicity in complex sounds by zebra finches (Taeniopygia guttata) and budgerigars (Melopsittacus undulatus). *Journal of Comparative Psychology, 112*, 36–47.

Mâche, F. B. (1992). *Music, myth and nature.* Translated by Susan Delaney. Switzerland: Harwood Academic Publishers.

Marler, P. (1970). A comparative approach to vocal learning: Song development in white-crowned sparrows. *Journal of Comparative and Physiological Psychology, 71*, 1–25.

Marler, P., & Tamura, M. (1962). Song "dialects" in three populations of white-crowned sparrows. *Condor, 64*(5), 368–377.

McDermott, J. H., & Hauser, M. (2004). Are consonant intervals music to their ears? Spontaneous acoustic preferences in a nonhuman primate. *Cognition, 94*, B11–B21.

McDermott, J. H., & Hauser, M. D. (2007). Nonhuman primates prefer slow tempos but dislike music overall. *Cognition, 104*, 654–68.

McDermott, J. H., Lehr, A. J., & Oxenham, A. J. (2010). Individual differences reveal the basis of consonance. *Current Biology, 20*, 1035–1041.

Nattiez, J. J. (1990). *Music and discourse: Towards a semiology of music.* Princeton, NJ: Princeton University Press.

Nottebohm, F. (1969). The "critical period" for song learning. *Ibis, 111*, 386–387.

Ohms, V. R., Gill, A., Van Heijningen, C. A. A., Beckers, G. J. L., & ten Cate, C. (2010). Zebra finches exhibit speaker-independent phonetic perception of human speech. *Proceedings of the Royal Society B, 277*, 1003–1009.

Patel, A. D. (2006). Musical rhythm, linguistic rhythm, and human evolution. *Music Perception, 24*, 99–104.

Patel, A. D. (2014). The evolutionary biology of musical rhythm: was Darwin wrong? *PLoS Biology, 12*(3): e1001821. doi:10.1371/journal.pbio.1001821

Patel, A. D., Iversen, J. R., Bregman, M. R., & Schulz, I. (2009). Experimental evidence for synchronization to a musical beat in a nonhuman animal. *Current Biology, 19*, 827–830.

Payne, R. S., & Guinee, L. N. (1983). Humpback whale songs as an indicator of "stocks." In R. Payne (Ed.), *Communication and Behavior of Whales* (pp. 333–358). Boulder, CO: Westview Press.

Plack, C. J., Oxenham, A. J., Fay, R. R., & Popper, A. N. (2005). *Pitch: Neural coding and perception.* Berlin, Germany: Springer.

Porter, D., & Neuringer, A. (1984). Music discrimination by pigeons. *Journal of Experimental Psychology: Animal Behavior Processes, 10*, 138–148.

Ralston, J. V., & Herman, L. M. (1995). Perception and generalization of frequency contours by a bottlenose dolphin (Tursiops truncatus). *Journal of Comparative Psychology, 109*, 268–277.

Reinert, J. (1957). Akustische Dressurversuche an einem Indischen Elefanten. *Zeitschrift für Tierpsychologie, 14*, 100–126.

Reinert, J. (1960). Unterscheidungsvermögen einer Dohle für verschieden schnelle Metronom-Schlagfolgen. *Zeitschrift für Tierpsychologie, 17*, 114–124.

Richards, D. G., Wolz, J. P., & Herman, L. M. (1975). Vocal mimicry of computer-generated sounds and vocal labeling of objects by a bottlenosed dolphin, Tursiops truncates. *Journal of Comparative Psychology, 98,* 10–28.

Riters, L. V. (2011). Pleasure seeking and birdsong. *Neuroscience & Biobehavioral Reviews, 35,* 1837–1845.

Roederer, J. (2008). The physics and psychophysics of music: An introduction. New York, NY: Springer-Verlag.

Schachner, A., Brady, T. F., Pepperberg, I. M., & Hauser, M. D. (2009). Spontaneous motor entrainment to music in multiple vocal mimicking species. *Current Biology, 19,* 831–866.

Snowdon, C. T., & Teie, D. (2010). Affective responses in tamarins elicited by species-specific music. *Biology Letters, 6,* 30–32.

Song, X., Osmanski, M. S., Guo, Y., & Wang, X. (2015). Complex pitch perception mechanisms are shared by humans and a New World monkey. *Proceedings of the National Academy of Sciences, 113*(3), 781–786. doi: 10.1073/pnas.1516120113

Stresemann, E. (1947). Baron von Pernau, pioneer student of bird behavior. *Auk, 64,* 35–52.

Thorpe, W. H. (1956). The language of birds. *Scientific American, 195,* 128–138.

Tierney, A. T., Russo, F. A., & Patel, A.D. (2011). The motor origins of human and avian song structure. *Proceedings of the National Academy of Sciences, 108*(37), 15510–15515.

Tinbergen, N. (1939). The behavior of the snow bunting in spring. *Transactions of the Linnaean Society of New York, 5,* 1–95.

Tomlinson, R. W. W. (1988). Perception of the missing fundamental in nonhuman primates. *Journal of the Acoustical Society of America, 84,* 560–565.

Trainor, L. J., Tsang, C. D., & Cheung, V. H. M. (2002). Preference for sensory consonance in 2- and 4-month-old infants. *Music Perception, 20,* 187–194.

Watanabe, S., & Sato, K. (1999). Discriminative stimulus properties of music in Java sparrows. *Behavioral Processes, 47,* 53–57.

Wilson M., & Cook P. F. (2016). Rhythmic entrainment: Why humans want to, fireflies can't help it, pet birds try, and sea lions have to be bribed. *Psychonomic Bulletin & Review.* Advance online publication. doi:10.3758/s13423-016-1013-x.

Wright, A. A., Rivera, J. J., Hulse, S. H., Shyan, M., & Neiworth, J. J. (2000). Music perception and octave generalization in rhesus monkeys. *Journal of Experimental Psychology: General, 129,* 291–307.

Yin, P., Fritz, J. B., & Shamma, S. A. (2010). Do ferrets perceive relative pitch? *The Journal of the Acoustical Society of America, 127*(3), 1673–1680.

# 33

# MUSIC COGNITION
## Developmental and Multimodal Perspectives

*Sandra E. Trehub and Michael W. Weiss*

## Introduction

In this chapter, we describe aspects of music processing in three phases of childhood: infancy (0 to 2 years), the preschool period (2 to 5 years), and the primary school years (6 to 10 years of age). In each developmental phase, we depict age-related changes in music cognition and the *ecology* of children's musical lives—facets that contribute to socialization in family and community and to the acquisition of culture-specific musical knowledge and skill. Multimodality and social contexts are the hallmarks of children's everyday musical experiences. Insights from laboratory research, which are based largely on Western, middle-class populations, reveal the abilities of very young infants and the subsequent acquisition of implicit and explicit musical knowledge. Systematic musical exposure or training is presumed to have more potent effects in earlier than in later developmental periods. We conclude with a suggestion of further lines of research that could enhance our understanding of musical development.

## The Musical Ecology of Infancy

Young infants, especially those in Western middle-class cultures, are not part of the larger society around them. Instead, they inhabit a micro-culture that is influenced by societal conventions but uniquely implemented by primary caregivers who prioritize face-to-face interactions. Such caregivers talk a great deal, providing irrelevant content in a melodious, affectively positive, and engaging manner. Because mothers usually fulfill the role of primary caregivers in infancy and are the focus of most research on caregiving, we use the terms *mothers* and *maternal* to refer more broadly to primary caregivers and their activities.

Mothers sing much less than they talk to infants, but they usually sing several times daily from a small repertoire of play songs (for a review, see Trehub & Gudmunstdottir, 2015). Repeated singing of specific songs enhances their familiarity and appeal for infants and their utility as sources of comfort. The maternal style of singing to infants differs from the same person's informal singing style by being higher in pitch, slower in tempo, and more emotionally expressive. In fact, mothers sing more expressively in face-to-face contexts than when infants are equally close but obscured from view (Trehub, Plantinga, & Russo, 2016). They perform each song in a highly stereotyped manner, with pitch level, tempo, and expressive style largely preserved from one occasion to the next (see Trehub & Gudmundsdottir, 2015). Maternal singing is visually as well as vocally distinctive because mothers smile almost continuously while singing but only intermittently while speaking (Trehub et al., 2016), often swaying or nodding rhythmically as they sing. Infants are mesmerized by these sung performances, gazing adoringly at the singer for extended periods, often without moving.

Even for decontextualized audio recordings of songs by unfamiliar singers, infants are more engaged by emotive infant-directed (ID) versions than by non-ID versions, the latter being more neutral in emotional tone. Although audio versions of ID singing and speech are equally effective for *capturing* infants' attention, the sung versions are considerably more effective for *sustaining* infants' composure and delaying the onset of distress (Corbeil, Trehub, & Peretz, 2016). Specifically, 7- to 10-month-old infants who were exposed to recordings of ID singing or speech in an unengaging environment (dimly lit room, no toys, parent out of sight) fretted or cried after 9 minutes of listening to a Turkish children's song but after 4 minutes of listening to a spoken (ID) rendition of the lyrics. The findings were similar for native-language (French) ID materials, highlighting the importance of maternal singing for affect and attention regulation.

Mothers' propensity to smile while singing enhances its appeal. Indeed, silent videos of ID singing elicit greater infant attention than silent videos of ID speech (Trehub, et al., 2016). Not surprisingly, infants are most responsive to vocalizations in live, multimodal contexts. For distressed infants, multimodal maternal singing (face-to-face, including touch and movement) is more effective than multimodal maternal speech in reducing arousal and distress (Ghazban, 2013). Infants may become entrained internally (rather than externally) to maternal singing because of its temporal regularity, one consequence of which is distraction from states of discontent.

From about 6 months of age, infants become increasingly engaged in exploration and toy play. Mothers talk about the objects and events that are the focus of infants' attention, but they continue to sing face-to-face and make greater use of action songs (e.g., *Itsy, Bitsy Spider*). Inspired, perhaps, by mothers' rhythmic movement to music, infants begin moving rhythmically to music (Zentner & Eerola, 2010). From about 9 months of age, Western infants experience music from new technologies as well as from interpersonal interactions (Young, 2008). Rather than replacing active musical engagement with passive consumption, these technologies supplement the ways in which infants engage with music.

## Infants' Sensitivity to Musical Structure

Although infants might be expected to have a relatively blank musical slate, their music perception skills parallel those of adults in many respects, with some intriguing differences. From their earliest visits to music perception laboratories (usually 5 months of age or older), infants exhibit sensitivity to transposition (i.e., pitches changed but pitch relations preserved), melodic contour (i.e., pattern of directional changes in pitch) and, at times, interval size (i.e., precise pitch distances between adjacent notes) (see Trainor & Hannon, 2013; Trehub & Degé, 2016 for reviews). Infants are also sensitive to scale structure, detecting changes more readily in scales with unequal intervals (e.g., the whole- and half-steps of the major scale), which are prevalent across cultures, than in scales with equal intervals, which seem to be absent or rare across cultures (see Trehub & Degé, 2016). Although infants are sensitive to consonance and dissonance, there is no consensus about whether *preferences* for consonance, commonly observed in Western cultures but not in some non–Western cultures, are innate or acquired (Plantinga & Trehub, 2014). Infants are also sensitive to grouping structure, detecting rhythmic changes, categorizing patterns on the basis of their rhythms, and imposing subjective grouping on isochronous sequences or those with equally timed notes (see Trainor & Hannon, 2013; Trehub & Degé, 2016).

Infants' ignorance of culture-specific musical conventions occasionally results in greater infant than adult sensitivity to culturally atypical musical materials. For example, infants detect subtle pitch changes in scales with unequal intervals, whether real (e.g., the major scale) or invented, in contrast to adults, who are successful only in the context of familiar scales (see Trehub & Degé, 2016). Similarly, infants detect melodic changes equally well in music based on the Indonesian *pelog* scale or the Western major scale, in contrast to adults, who have difficulty with the foreign *pelog* scale (see Trehub & Degé, 2016). Even in familiar musical contexts, implicit musical knowledge sometimes interferes with the detection of differences. For example, adults more readily detect a one-semitone change that goes outside the key of a melody than a four-semitone change that remains within the key and implied harmony; infants detect both changes equally well, reflecting their insensitivity to key membership and harmony (see Trainor & Hannon, 2013).

Similar infant processing advantages are evident in the temporal domain. For example, Western 6-month-olds detect metrical changes in the context of complex meters, which are common in non–Western music, and in the context of simple meters, which prevail in Western music (see Trehub & Degé, 2016). By contrast, adults fail to detect metrical changes in patterns with complex meter. By 12 months of age, Western infants exhibit adult-like processing biases for simple meters, which implies that musical enculturation is well under way (see Trehub & Degé, 2016). After limited exposure to music with complex meter, however, 12-month-olds overcome their difficulty with complex meters, but adults do not. In such circumstances, infants profit from their inexperience and perceptual flexibility.

Stimulation in one modality often affects perception in another modality. The tight coupling of our auditory and motor systems results in reciprocal influences between sound and movement, even in infancy. For example, infants' perception of a metrically ambiguous pattern is influenced by the movement experienced while listening. When bounced on every second beat, infants perceive the auditory pattern in duple meter; when bounced on every third beat, they perceive the same pattern in triple meter (Phillips-Silver & Trainor, 2005).

There are important social consequences of synchronized musical behavior that are first evident in infancy. For example, 14-month-olds who are bounced to music in the presence of a synchronously bouncing adult are more helpful to that adult than to an adult whose bouncing is not synchronous (Cirelli, Einarson, & Trainor, 2014). The prosocial consequences of interpersonal synchrony do not result from overall enhancement in arousal or positive affect because they are directed selectively to the synchronous bouncer and her friends (Cirelli, Wan, & Trainor, 2016).

Familiar songs can also promote favorable social responses to unfamiliar individuals. For example, 5-month-olds are more attentive to an unfamiliar woman who previously sang a familiar song than to one who sang an unfamiliar song but only if maternal singing was the source of familiarization (Mehr, Song, & Spelke, 2016). In other words, the songs that mothers sing acquire positive qualities that generalize to other singers of those songs. Although infants remember songs presented repeatedly from a toy or other singer (by video link), such exposure has no effect on their social preferences.

Infants' inclination to move to music, which is readily observable at home, has also been documented in the laboratory. Because multimodal renditions of vocal music are captivating, they often lead to movement suppression rather than activation. Nevertheless, audio recordings of rhythmic vocal and instrumental music elicit rhythmic but not synchronous movement in infants 5 to 24 months of age (Zentner & Eerola, 2010). ID speech, by contrast, does not elicit rhythmic movement.

Infants also exhibit long-term memory for music (see Trehub & Degé, 2016). After at-home exposure to Mozart sonatas, they distinguish actual excerpts from novel excerpts. Similar at-home exposure to a synthesized piano melody reveals memory for the melody but not for its pitch level. By contrast, they remember the pitch level of expressively sung lullabies, which implies richer encoding and retention of ecologically valid music. Remarkably, after one or two weeks of at-home exposure to a vocal melody, infants recognize it 8 months later (Mehr et al., 2016).

Various parent-infant music programs report musical as well as non-musical gains, but few feature random assignment to training and control conditions. As a result, such gains may be attributable to other factors such as the higher levels of education and affluence of families who opt for such programs. One study with random assignment compared outcomes in infants who participated (with parents) in a 6-month program featuring interactive musical experiences (movement, singing, percussion instruments) or an alternative program that featured passive exposure to music during toy play. The program with active musical exposure resulted in enhanced music perception, gestural communication, and social behavior relative to the one with passive musical exposure (Gerry, Unrau, & Trainor, 2012). Similarly, a 12-session program for 9-month-olds that emphasized coordinated movement to music resulted in enhanced neural processing of temporal structure in speech and music relative to infants who completed a play intervention without music (Zhao & Kuhl, 2016). It remains to be determined whether the favorable consequences of such early musical interventions are temporary or enduring.

In short, infants' impressive sensitivity to musical structure indicates that they can profit from their rich, highly social, and multimodal musical environment. It is impossible to distinguish the contributions of nature from those of nurture because musical exposure and learning begin in the prenatal period. It is notable, however, that the brains of sleeping newborns are sensitive to the beat of music and to pitch direction well before comparable sensitivities are demonstrable behaviorally (see Trehub & Degé, 2016). At the very least, musical exposure in the postnatal period reinforces and extends initial sensitivities while also enhancing infants' interest in music.

Remarkably, attunement to culture-specific aspects of musical structure begins in infancy. Moreover, the relative ease with which 12-month-olds learn about foreign musical structure and adults' difficulty in this regard may implicate greater plasticity in young brains and interference from entrenched knowledge in older brains.

## The Musical Ecology of the Preschool Period

Middle-class parents provide a range of informal musical experiences for preschoolers. Although they sing less than they do for infants, they continue to sing conventional, improvised, and invented songs during caregiving (bedtime, mealtime, bathtime) and play routines

(Custodero, 2006; Lamont, 2008). Preschoolers reproduce their caregivers' songs as well as creating their own songs. In addition, children of preschool age may experience music in semi-structured settings such as nursery schools or daycare centers where music scaffolds play and learning routines and children use coordinated movement and vocalization to gain the attention of peers.

Technology also figures prominently in preschoolers' musical experiences. Roughly a third of the musical episodes of UK preschoolers involve entertainment media (Lamont, 2008). Many Western preschoolers make use of devices such as smartphones, tablets, and TVs, to play interactive musical games or to find music and dance routines for imitative play. Despite ever-increasing "screen time," there is no indication that it is supplanting musical interactions with parents or peers. Instead, technology may be responsible for more diverse musical input, perhaps enhancing rather than diminishing preschoolers' musical engagement.

Preschoolers sing while they play alone or with others, frequently moving as they sing or listen to music. For obvious reasons, it is difficult to assess their singing proficiency from invented or improvised songs. With conventional songs, one can quantify their deviations from notated versions or adult norms, but such measures provide little insight into their capabilities. Only with the onset of formal schooling or music instruction do children become fully aware of conventional standards of pitch accuracy. Contrary to the prevailing view that preschoolers master the words and rhythms of songs but not the tunes, many 2-year-olds produce recognizable versions of songs with conventional pitch range, contours, and rhythms (see Trehub & Gudmundsdottir, 2015). Moreover, higher levels of singing accuracy are evident in home recordings of spontaneous singing than in laboratory or preschool recordings of experimenter-selected songs (Trehub & Gudmundsdottir, 2015). In general, however, recognizable lyrics and rhythms emerge before recognizable melodies.

## Preschoolers' Sensitivity to Musical Structure

There is less research on music perception in the preschool period than in infancy and that research is largely restricted to Western samples. What is clear, however, is that greater incidental exposure to music and greater cognitive maturity promote incremental gains in musical understanding. Unlike infants, who are insensitive to key membership (i.e., comparable detection of in-key and out-of-key changes to melodies), 4- and 5-year-olds more readily detect out-of-key than in-key changes, but their understanding of Western tonality is incomplete (see Trainor & Hannon, 2013).

The preschool phase often invites consideration of critical or sensitive periods for musical development (Trainor, 2005)—phases of life or states of the brain when exposure or training is maximally effective, with potentially enduring consequences. For example, many notable musicians began their training in the preschool period, raising questions about sensitive or optimal periods for the onset of training. Links between early training and later achievement are complicated by potentially confounding effects of musically talented parents (i.e., genetic contributions) and musically rich environments (i.e., informal musical exposure). Moreover, many celebrated musicians began their training beyond the putative sensitive period. If sensitive periods for musical development are real, they may be restricted to absolute pitch (Trainor, 2005) and sensorimotor synchronization (Penhune, 2011).

Absolute pitch (AP), or the ability to recognize musical pitches in isolation, is thought to depend not only on the early onset of music training but also on training in the context of a fixed-*do* system, ongoing use of a fixed-pitch instrument, and genetic predispositions, as reflected in a family history of AP (Wilson et al., 2012). The necessity of early training is based largely on retrospective analyses of musicians with AP. In one prospective study, Japanese children who began their training at 4 years of age in a program that involved piano, singing, pitch naming, and a fixed-*do* system exhibited gradual improvement in naming white-key pitches until 7 years of age and naming black-key pitches until 8 years of age but no improvement thereafter (Miyazaki & Ogawa, 2006). Although this research revealed varying degrees of AP following appropriate early exposure, it did not establish the necessity of exposure in the preschool period. Pitch naming was relatively inaccurate and highly variable (i.e., large individual differences) at 5 and 6 years of age, raising the possibility that training onset at 6 years would have yielded comparable AP skills. However, another study in which 3- to 4-year-olds, 5- to 6-year-olds, and adults received 3 weeks of training to distinguish a "special note" ($C_5$) from a set of alternatives ($G_4, A_5, B_4, D_5, E_5,$ and $F_5$) revealed highest identification accuracy for 5- to 6-year-olds, which is consistent with a privileged period for acquiring note names (Russo, Windell, & Cuddy, 2003). Nevertheless, special conditions such as congenital blindness seem to obviate the need for early training, which implies that experiential as well as maturational factors are implicated in optimal periods for learning.

Because of its pitch-naming requirements, AP is necessarily limited to those who receive music training. Musically untrained individuals, however, can remember the pitch level of highly familiar musical material such as the theme music of popular television programs (Schellenberg & Trehub, 2003), which confirms their representation of absolute aspects of pitch. This ability, often termed *implicit, residual,* or *latent AP,* is also evident and of comparable accuracy in children between 4 and 12 years of age (Jakubowski, Müllensiefen, & Stewart, 2017). The implication is that the presumed sensitive period is relevant for pitch naming but not pitch memory.

Another developmentally significant domain is synchronization to music, which is considered a cornerstone of our musicality. Entrainment or synchronization to music depends on perceptual skills, motor skills, and sensorimotor coordination. Children's optimal tempo for attention, discrimination, and spontaneous tapping (without sound) decreases progressively from 4 years of age until adulthood, while the range of accessible tempi expands over the same period (McAuley et al., 2006). In general, synchronized movement to music is not evident until about 4 years of age. Younger children sometimes synchronize their movements to music, but they do so only within the range of their spontaneous or preferred tempo. Social factors also influence synchronization accuracy. For example, preschoolers more readily synchronize their drumming with a social partner than with a mechanical drummer (Kirschner & Tomasello, 2009). On the basis of comparisons of adult musicians with early or late onset of music lessons, the sensitive period for optimal sensorimotor coordination is presumed to close at roughly 7 years of age (Penhune, 2011). It remains to be determined whether training during a specific age range results in more rapid acquisition of rhythmic skills, or short-term benefits, than training outside of that age range.

Children's explicit understanding of emotional expressiveness in music changes during the preschool period. For example, 3- and 4-year-olds are unable to classify instrumental excerpts varying in tempo (fast, slow) and mode (major, minor) as happy or sad. By contrast, 5-year-olds' judgments are influenced by tempo but not mode, and 6-year-olds' judgments are influenced by tempo and mode (Dalla Bella, Peretz, Rousseau, & Gosselin, 2001). With music from the children's repertoire, however, 4-year-olds judge fast versions as happy and slow versions as sad (Mote, 2011). Preschoolers' implicit knowledge of expressive musical conventions is evident in more natural tasks with vocal rather than instrumental music. When singing a familiar song to make a listener happy or sad, the happy renditions of children as young as 4 are faster, louder, and at a higher pitch level than their sad renditions (Adachi & Trehub, 1998).

Music listening habits or tastes in adolescence or adulthood often influence social judgments, distinguishing in-group members from out-group members. Preschoolers' social judgments are also affected by shared musical experiences. For example, they prefer to socialize with unfamiliar children who share their knowledge of specific songs rather than those who know different songs (Soley & Spelke, 2016).

In sum, the expansion of preschoolers' social lives, in conjunction with increasing cognitive and motor skill, accelerates the process of musical enculturation. This period, which is dominated by multimodal musical activities, reveals impressive gains in children's implicit knowledge of musical structure and expressive conventions. Preschoolers exhibit rudimentary forms of AP and the potential, with appropriate training, for acquiring *pure AP*. Their movement to music is not merely pleasurable, as it was previously; it also becomes increasingly coordinated with music and with others, favorable social outcomes being one consequence and enhanced temporal coordination being another.

## The Musical Ecology of the Primary School Period

By the time children begin formal schooling, their musical experiences are influenced by a range of identities linked to school, home, community, and culture, each with its own constraints—for example, curricular constraints in classrooms and social constraints in schoolyards and playgrounds. Just as parents use specific songs for playtime, bedtime, and diaper-changing in infancy, children use chanting or singing rituals to choose team members for ad-hoc games or to designate the chaser (i.e., the person who is "it") in a game of tag (Countryman, 2014). At home, children gain access to music on the internet and mp3 players, their musical tastes being increasingly influenced by peers rather than parents.

Social and cultural factors figure prominently in school-age children's musical experiences, influencing the developing identity and attitudes of those from mainstream, minority, or immigrant backgrounds. For example, there are various attempts to elevate and preserve traditional music, as in Aotearoa/New Zealand schools that use Māori music in everyday lessons (Bodkin-Allen, 2013). Cross-cultural materials are being added to music curricula in the United States, Canada, and Europe in an effort to enhance children's understanding of other cultures and their immigrant peers.

Middle-class parents typically value formal music instruction more highly than musical play, especially in the school years, but some children may feel otherwise. In developing countries, the boundaries between music instruction and play are often more fluid than they are in developed countries. In Bali, for example, young children experience the music and dance of their culture at home, but they also participate in more formal performances at cultural and religious events (Dunbar-Hall, 2011).

Children's musical experiences, regardless of culture, are mostly social and playful. Musical playground games feature multimodality (e.g., clapping and singing games), improvisation (e.g., creation of novel lyrics and rhythms), and blurred distinctions between performer and audience (Marsh, 2009). Vocalizations during such play are simple and repetitive, at times, and elaborate at other times. Children compose in the moment, adapting or modifying music from school, pop culture, and other sources to fit their immediate needs. Polyrhythmic clapping and chanting of school-age girls are especially notable for their complexity and precision. Musical play is not limited to playgrounds, extending to the home where children sing and dance with friends and siblings.

## Primary Schoolchildren's Sensitivity to Musical Structure

Laboratory research, focused primarily on Western music, has revealed progressively increasing sensitivity to Western tonality (see Trainor & Hannon, 2013). Such improvement arises largely from incidental exposure to music, although formal training accelerates the pace of improvement. Adult-like sensitivity is typically attained by 10 or 11 years, but earlier sensitivity is evident with implicit rather than explicit measures.

Surprisingly, Western listeners' explicit preference for consonant over dissonant intervals emerges as late as 9 years of age, and such preferences only become adult-like at about 12 years of age for those without music training (Valentine, 1962). These findings are at odds with so-called "natural" preferences for consonance, being consistent instead with experiential accounts (Plantinga & Trehub, 2014).

As noted, children are sensitive to absolute as well as relative aspects of pitch, but the salience of these aspects of pitch processing changes with age. In one study (Stalinski & Schellenberg, 2010), adults and children between 5 and 12 years of age rated the degree of similarity of pairs of seven-tone melodies in which some comparison melodies featured a four-semitone transposition (relative pitch preserved) and others featured a melodic change (five internal pitches reordered) that preserved the overall (mean) pitch level. For 5- to 9-year-olds, pitch level made greater contributions to similarity judgments than did relative pitch (transposition); pitch level and relative pitch made equal contributions in 10- to 12-year-olds; and relative pitch made greater contributions to adults' similarity judgments. In short, relative pitch processing becomes increasingly dominant.

Temporal processing skills seem to be acquired more rapidly than pitch processing skills, but the ease of learning novel or foreign temporal structures decreases in the school years, in line with a sensitive period perspective. Just as 12-month-old infants acquire sensitivity to foreign (non-isochronous) metrical structure more readily than adults, so do 5-year-old children, but the ability to acquire such sensitivity from passive exposure decreases progressively with increasing age (Hannon, Vanden Bosch der Nederlanden, & Tichko, 2012).

With respect to production, children's spontaneous tempo decreases from the preschool years through the school years, while synchronized movement to music becomes more accurate and less variable (McAuley et al., 2006). It is possible, however, that typical synchronization tasks, such as finger-tapping to simple auditory patterns, exaggerate the differences between younger and older children. Singing accuracy also changes dramatically during the school years. For example, there is substantial improvement in the reproduction of single pitches, intervals, and four-pitch sequences between 5 and 11 years of age; by college age, interestingly, performance often regresses to kindergarten levels (Demorest & Pfordresher, 2015). It would seem that those who sing most—usually school-age children—sing best.

Children's sensitivity to musical emotions also exhibits further progress. As noted, Western 6-year-olds reliably link the major mode to happiness and the minor mode to sadness (Dalla Bella et al., 2001). By 11 years of age, they identify a broader range of emotional intentions—scary and peaceful as well as happy and sad (Hunter, Schellenberg, & Stalinksi, 2011).

Despite their sensitivity to emotion in music, children can be distracted by the lyrics of songs. When asked to ignore the lyrics and judge a singer's happy or sad feelings solely from the sound of her voice, adults base their judgments on tempo (fast, slow) and mode (major, minor), but 5- to 10-year-olds focus on the emotional implications of the lyrics (Morton & Trehub, 2007). Their sensitivity to the musical cues is evident, however, when the same tunes are sung with meaningless syllables (*da da da*). With more ecologically valid stimuli such as familiar songs (tunes and lyrics) sung by same-age children, children are not only adept at differentiating happy from sad performances; they also outperform adults (Adachi, Trehub, & Abe, 2004).

For young children, emotion may be identified more readily from body movements than from musical cues just as emotion is more readily identified from facial than from vocal cues. For example, children as young as 4 differentiate the emotional implications of dance movements (joy, anger, fear, and sadness) above chance levels, and 8-year-olds perform as well as adults (Lagerlöf, & Djerf, 2009). As is the case for music, the tempo of movement is critical to emotion identification, but the force or intensity of movement is also relevant.

In short, the musical play that dominates the preschool years continues, in somewhat altered form, in the school years, but there are increasing opportunities for systematic exposure and learning, whether in classrooms, school choirs or bands, or music lessons. There are gains in culture-specific knowledge of music, both implicit and explicit, with corresponding losses in sensitivity to foreign musical structure. Nevertheless, children's implicit musical knowledge does not yet match that of adults.

## Conclusions and Unanswered Questions

From infancy through the elementary school years, children's engagement with music is multimodal, social, playful, and pleasurable. Infants' repeated exposure to caregivers' lively play songs and soothing lullabies—expressive music in conjunction with expressive gestures—intensifies the ties between caregiver and infant and the links between music and contentment. These early experiences with music may set the stage for its life-long role as a potent social and emotional regulator and vehicle for learning. Exposure to maternal singing may also influence music perception and production in infancy. Just as greater exposure to ID speech is linked to enhanced language processing and production, so greater exposure to ID singing may be linked to enhanced music processing (e.g., greater accuracy on perception tasks) and production (e.g., age of onset of singing). It would be of interest to ascertain whether early music and language processing skills are correlated or independent, implicating domain-general or domain-specific processes, respectively.

Preschoolers' spontaneous singing in peer contexts has social goals, in contrast to their spontaneous singing in solitary contexts, which has emotional self-regulatory goals. One would therefore expect greater reliance on songs learned from caregivers in conjunction with self-regulatory intentions and songs learned in peer contexts in conjunction with social regulatory intentions, an issue that could be explored in future research.

The most striking developmental proposals involve the onset, in the preschool years, of a sensitive period for aspects of musical development, notably AP (Miyazaki & Ogawa, 2006; Trainor, 2005) and synchronization to music (Penhune, 2011), and the presumed closure of that sensitive period in the early school years. These claims are based primarily on the higher incidence of AP and enhanced synchronization in musicians with early training onset relative to those with later training onset. It is important to gain further insight into age-related changes in the rate of learning in these domains (e.g., Russo et al., 2003) and the requisite circumstances for retaining the advantages of early learning. Most musicians undergo continuous training for many years, so it is not surprising that they maintain or improve the skills acquired early. For children with AP who discontinue music training, are there progressive decreases in AP skills like the progressive losses in native-language skills when a second language replaces the first? Do early trained children retain their sensorimotor integration advantages if they discontinue training?

There are age-related changes in children's musical experiences—from the intimate, dyadic interactions of infancy to the varied musical experiences of later school years—which are likely to have consequences for music processing. It is possible, for example, that infants would not connect synthesized instrumental renditions of a familiar song (e.g., "Twinkle, Twinkle, Little Star") with the sung renditions heard at home even though they recognize the song when sung by another woman. By contrast, older children who regularly experience music in multiple forms and contexts are more likely to perceive similarity across diversity. Documenting age-related changes in the nature and generality of children's representations of music is an important challenge for future research.

Finally, it must be acknowledged that developmental research on the acquisition of musical structure has relied on samples of convenience, consisting largely of children from middle-class Western environments. It is important to understand the ways in which different musical and parenting practices affect the nature and pace of acquisition.

## Acknowledgments and Authors' Note

The preparation of this chapter was assisted by funding from the Natural Sciences and Engineering Research Council of Canada and the Social Sciences and Humanities Research Council of Canada. Requests for information can be addressed to sandra.trehub@utoronto.ca or michael.william.weiss@gmail.com

## Core Reading

Marsh, K. (2009). *The musical playground: Global tradition and change in children's songs and games*. Oxford: Oxford University Press.

Trainor, L. J., & Hannon, E. E. (2013). Musical development. In D. Deutsch (Ed.), *The psychology of music* (3rd ed., pp. 423–497). San Diego, CA: Academic Press.

Trehub, S. E., & Gudmundsdottir, H. R. (2015). Mothers as singing mentors for infants. In G. Welch, & J. Nix (Eds.), *Oxford handbook of singing*. Oxford: Oxford University Press.

Trehub, S. E., & Degé, F. (2016). Reflections on infants as musical connoisseurs. In G. E. McPherson (Ed.), *The child as musician: A handbook of musical development* (2nd ed., pp. 31–51). Oxford: Oxford University Press.

## Further References

Adachi, M., & Trehub, S. E. (1998). Children's expression of emotion in song. *Psychology of Music, 26*, 133–153.

Adachi, M., Trehub, S. E., & Abe, J. (2004). Perceiving emotion in children's songs across age. *Japanese Psychological Research, 46*, 322–336.

Bodkin-Allen, S. (2013). The interweaving threads of music in the Whariki of early childhood cultures in Aotearoa/New Zealand. In P. S. Campbell, & T. Wiggins (Eds.), *The Oxford handbook of children's musical cultures* (pp. 387–401). Oxford: Oxford University Press.

Cirelli, L. K., Einarson, K. M., & Trainor, L. J. (2014). Interpersonal synchrony increases prosocial behavior in infants. *Developmental Science, 17*, 1003–1011.

Cirelli, L. K., Wan, S. J., & Trainor, L. J. (2016). Social effects of movement synchrony: Increased infant helpfulness only transfers to affiliates of synchronously moving partners. *Infancy, 21*, 807–821.

Corbeil, M., Trehub, S. E., & Peretz, I. (2016). Singing delays the onset of infant distress. *Infancy, 21*, 373–391.

Countryman, J. (2014). Start-up games on school playgrounds: Instances of ceremonial rituals. *Bulletin of the Council for Research in Music Education, 202*, 7–27.

Custodero, L. A. (2006). Singing practices in 10 families with young children. *Journal of Research in Music Education, 54*, 37–56.

Dalla Bella, S., Peretz, I., Rousseau, L., & Gosselin, N. (2001). A developmental study of the affective value of tempo and mode in music. *Cognition, 80*, B1–B10.

Demorest, S. M., & Pfordresher, P. Q. (2015). Singing accuracy from K – adult: A comparative study. *Music Perception, 32*, 293–302.

Dunbar-Hall, P. (2011). Children's learning of music and dance in Bali: An ethnomusicological view of the cultural psychology of music education. In M. S. Barrett (Ed.), *A cultural psychology of music* (pp. 17–40). New York, NY: Oxford University Press.

Gerry, D., Unrau, A., & Trainor, L. J. (2012). Active music classes in infancy enhance musical, communicative and social development. *Developmental Science, 15*, 398–407.

Ghazban, N. (2013). Emotion regulation in infants using maternal singing and speech. Unpublished doctoral dissertation, Ryerson University, Toronto.

Hannon, E. E., Vanden Bosch der Nederlanden, C. M., & Tichko, P. (2012). Effects of perceptual experience on children's and adults' perception of unfamiliar rhythms. *Annals of the New York Academy of Sciences, 1252*, 92–99.

Hunter, P. G., Schellenberg, E. G., & Stalinski, S. M. (2011). Liking and identifying emotionally expressive music: Age and gender differences. *Journal of Experimental Child Psychology, 110*, 80–93.

Jakubowski, K., Müllensiefen, D., & Stewart, L. (2017). A developmental study of latent absolute pitch memory. *Quarterly Journal of Experimental Psychology, 70*, 434–443.

Kirschner, S., & Tomasello, M. (2009). Joint drumming: Social context facilitates synchronization in preschool children. *Journal of Experimental Child Psychology, 102*, 299–314.

Lagerlöf, I., & Djerf, M. (2009). Children's understanding of emotion in dance. *European Journal of Developmental Psychology, 6*, 409–431.

Lamont, A. (2008). Young children's musical worlds: Musical engagement in 3.5-year-olds. *Journal of Early Childhood Research, 6*, 247–261.

McAuley, J. D., Jones, M. R., Holub, S., Johnston, H. M., & Miller, N. S. (2006). The time of our lives: Life span development of timing and event tracking. *Journal of Experimental Psychology: General, 135*, 348–367.

Mehr, S. A., Song, L. A., & Spelke, E. S. (2016). For 5-month-old infants, melodies are social. *Psychological Science, 27*, 486–501.

Miyazaki, K., & Ogawa, Y. (2006). Learning absolute pitch by children. *Music Perception, 24*, 63–78.

Morton, J. B., & Trehub, S. E. (2007). Children's expression of emotion in song. *Psychology of Music, 26*, 133–153.

Mote, J. (2011). The effects of tempo and familiarity on children's affective interpretation of music. *Emotion, 11*, 618–622.

Penhune, V. B. (2011). Sensitive periods in human development: Evidence from musical training. *Cortex, 47*, 1126–1137.

Phillips-Silver, J., & Trainor, L. J. (2005). Feeling the beat: Movement influences infant rhythm perception. *Science, 308*, 1430.

Plantinga, J., & Trehub, S. E. (2014). Revisiting the innate preference for consonance. *Journal of Experimental Psychology: Human Perception and Performance, 40*, 40–49.

Russo, F. A., Windell, D. L., & Cuddy, L. L. (2003). Learning the "special note": Evidence for a critical period for absolute pitch acquisition. *Music Perception, 21*, 119–127.

Schellenberg, E. G., & Trehub, S. E. (2003). Good pitch memory is widespread. *Psychological Science, 14*, 262–266.

Soley, G., & Spelke, E. S. (2016). Shared cultural knowledge: Effects of music on young children's social preferences. *Cognition, 148*, 106–116.

Stalinski, S. M., & Schellenberg, E. G. (2010). Shifting perceptions: Developmental changes in judgments of melodic similarity. *Developmental Psychology, 46*, 1799–1803.

Trainor, L. J. (2005). Are there critical periods for musical development? *Developmental Psychobiology, 46*, 262–278.

Trehub, S. E., Plantinga, J., & Russo, F. A. (2016). Maternal vocal interactions with infants: Reciprocal visual influences. *Social Development, 25,* 665–683.

Valentine, C. W. (1962). Musical intervals and attitudes to music. In C. W. Valentine (Ed.), *The experimental psychology of beauty* (pp. 196–227). London, UK: Methuen.

Wilson, S. J., Lusher, D., Martin, C. L., Rayner, G., & McLachlan, N. (2012). Intersecting factors lead to absolute pitch acquisition that is maintained in a "fixed do" environment. *Music Perception, 29*, 285–296.

Young, S. (2008). Lullaby light shows: Everyday musical experience among under-two-year-olds. *International Journal of Music Education, 26*, 33–46.

Zentner, M., & Eerola, T. (2010). Rhythmic engagement with music in infancy. *Proceedings of the National Academy of Sciences of the United States of America, 107*, 5768–5773.

Zhao, T. C., & Kuhl, P. K. (2016). Musical intervention enhances infants' neural processing of temporal structure in music and speech. *Proceedings of the National Academy of Sciences of the United States of America, 113*, 5212–5217.

# 34

# MUSICAL EXPERTISE
## Genetics, Experience, and Training

*William Forde Thompson, Miriam A. Mosing, and Fredrik Ullén*

Research into the environmental and genetic foundations of expert performance has attracted attention across several domains of skill, reflecting the applied and scientific implications of this topic. Superior performance is a desirable achievement across domains; those who acquire expertise are esteemed and act as role models for others. Research on expertise also has the potential to inform organizations and industries that rely upon the acquisition of exceptionally high levels of skill by developing evidence-based training protocols and assessment tools. Furthermore, the study of superior performance can tell us about the role of experience and training in brain plasticity, which has implications for our understanding of learning and cognitive transfer. For example, we have the potential to understand whether engaging in specific forms of skills training (e.g., learning a musical instrument) may yield cognitive and physical benefits that extend beyond the domain of training. Finally, by examining individual differences in the acquisition of superior performance—including variables such as personality, physical traits, intelligence, motivation, and social environment—we can elucidate the developmental antecedents of elite levels of performance, and the role of genetic predispositions and gene-environment interactions. It has long been known that expert performance runs in families (e.g., Galton, 1869), but until relatively recently it has been difficult to tease apart the environmental and genetic factors responsible for this tendency.

In this chapter, we address the role of genetics, experience, and training in the acquisition of expert music performance. Central to this chapter is the evaluation of evidence that genetic predispositions are relevant to expertise—perhaps more so than previously assumed. We begin by discussing how the construct of expertise is defined across domains of performance, and thereafter review research on the acquisition of musical expertise, including work on musical prodigies who acquire high levels of expertise at very rapid rates. The role of practice and other traits for skill acquisition is discussed next, beginning with an overview of existing meta-analyses on practice-skill associations. In the final section, outline the strategies and logic used within the field of behavior genetics, and conclude by discussing the evidence that genetic factors play a significant role in the acquisition of expertise, including the motivation to engage in the persistent and deliberate practice that is needed to achieve exceptional musical skill.

## What Is Musical Expertise?

In most Western industrialized societies, expertise is understood to be a valued skill that is difficult to acquire, requires high levels of dedication, and is achieved by a small percentage of the population. Although many forms of expertise have practical value for individuals and society (e.g., leadership skills and medical expertise), other forms of expertise are valued because of their *exceptionality*. The rare ability of a chess player to recognize hundreds of board configurations is more likely to attract attention than the prosaic ability of expert car mechanics to recognize hundreds of engine parts, even though both accomplishments reflect expertise and are likely to recruit similar brain regions dedicated to object and pattern recognition.

From the perspective of cognitive neuroscience, it is often difficult to distinguish "rare" skills associated with elite professionals from commonplace skills employed by individuals in their daily lives. Whether driving a vehicle, navigating a complex environment, playing a computer game, or reading a book, expertise is widespread. We may be fascinated by skills that are only rarely developed by members of a population, but the underlying cognitive and motor processes may be similar to those employed on a daily basis by most members of the population.

Expertise can be observed across a wide array of activities, and include skills of surgery, navigation, leadership, memory, athletic pursuits, art, and music, among others. In many cases, expert skills become internalized and automatic, and not easily accessible to introspection. They are also highly specialized. Whereas elite aircraft pilots must learn to detect and respond rapidly and accurately to task-relevant perceptual cues (signals) in dynamic and uncertain environments containing multiple irrelevant cues (noise), performing musicians must nurture technical and expressive motor skills in order to create an aesthetic experience that is appreciated by perceivers of these artworks.

Within the domain of musicianship, specialist skills differentiate types of musicians, whether composers, performers, or conductors (Quinto, Ammirante, Connors, & Thompson, 2016; Quinto & Thompson, 2013). In traditions that rely on notation to share musical ideas, performers and composers collaborate in a joint act of aesthetic communication, combining their unique capabilities. Performers of music from the Western canon exert considerable control over the degree of energy or arousal experienced by listeners, as this dimension of emotionality is carried by acoustic attributes under their expressive control, such as tempo and intensity (see Timmers, this volume). Performers have more limited control over the positive or negative dimension of experience (valence), which is strongly determined by the pitch and rhythmic structure of compositions. In short, the skills needed to become a musician depend, at least partly, on the activity being pursued.

Most research on musical expertise has focused on skills possessed by accomplished performers (e.g., Brown, Zatorre, & Penhune, 2015). These skills include superior auditory processing (Kraus, Skoe, Parbery-Clark, & Ashley, 2009), skills of coordination and synchronization (Keller, 2014a, 2014b), exceptional domain-specific long-term and working memory (Palmer, 2006), enhanced skills of musical imagery (Gelding, Thompson, & Johnson, 2015), motor control and planning (Palmer & Drake, 1997), and the ability to introduce subtle expressive variation in timing, intensity, and intonation. The latter skills, collectively termed *performance expression*, function to highlight musical structure, communicate emotional meaning, and convey stylistic norms (Thompson, 2014; Fabian, Timmers, & Schubert, 2014; Fabian, this volume).

How are musical skills acquired in development, and which ones emerge in the absence of formal training? At early stages of development, infants exhibit sensitivity to subtle changes in melodies (reflected in measures such as head-turn responses, looking time, and sucking rate). Sensitivity to contour emerges before the age of one year, and may assist infants in decoding emotional messages conveyed in speech intonation (Thompson, 2014, ch. 5; Trehub & Weiss, this volume). Although infants may not show a difference in preference between consonant and dissonant sounds (Plantinga & Trehub, 2014), they certainly exhibit this sensitivity later in development (between the ages of 6 and 9 years, Valentine, 1962). More generally, school-age children respond to music in ways that reflect passive enculturation to music conventions. Western children exhibit sensitivity to musical key by the age of five, and sensitivity to the implied harmony of melodies by the age of seven, reflecting a gradual appreciation of regularities in Western music (see Trehub & Weiss, this volume). Some children, notably music prodigies, reach these milestones earlier.

Progress in performance ability is often monitored by evaluating several distinct skills, such as performing rehearsed music, sight-reading, playing from memory, playing by ear, and improvising. In an examination of the development of performance skill across three years of music lessons among children aged 5–7 years, McPherson (2005) reported improvement in all of the above measures across three years. Progression on the five skills was relatively smooth, improving from year to year. However, by the third year only 68% had continued with their lessons. More generally, there were large differences between performance abilities of the children across the five measures. Presumably, such discrepancies are the result of differences in practicing styles, environmental factors, genetic predispositions, and interactions among these factors.

In order to investigate the role of environmental and genetic influences on musical expertise, it is necessary to have valid and reliable measures of the skills that differentiate high and low levels of achievement. Measuring expertise in an objective manner is challenging though, as even experienced adjudicators adopt idiosyncratic criteria for assessing performance excellence (e.g., Thompson, Diamond, & Balkwill, 1998) and are susceptible to adjudication biases (McPherson & Thompson, 1998). For example, the body movements and facial expressions of performers have a surprising impact on the judged expressive and technical caliber of a music performance (e.g., Platz & Kopiez, 2012; Thompson, Graham, & Russo, 2005). Given that non-auditory signals impact upon assessments of performance excellence, including evaluations by highly experienced adjudicators, many musicians consciously develop skills at using ancillary body movements to support their expressive intentions and supplement the auditory dimension of a performance (Rodger, Craig, & O'Modhrain, 2012).

One strategy of investigating musical expertise is to consider the environmental circumstances and individual characteristics of exceptional musicians. The study of child prodigies is especially revealing given that their expertise is, by definition, achieved over a short period of time (McPherson, 2016). Because prodigies develop expertise at such a rapid pace over a brief period of time, their examination may provide a magnified picture of the influences and antecedents of advanced musical skills. Most research on prodigies involves "case studies" and suggests that prodigious skill arises when natural abilities interact with environmental and intrapersonal catalysts in optimal ways. These natural abilities include high levels of intellectual functioning, creative ability, social skills, and perceptual capacities, along with advantageous physical traits such as muscular ability and motor control. Environmental catalysts include physical, cultural, social, and familial milieu, support and encouragement from peers, teachers, and mentors, and access to resources. Intrapersonal catalysts include temperament, personality, resilience, self-awareness, motivation, and perseverance.

Such factors characterize many prodigies. For example, Mozart, Beethoven, Mendelssohn, Glenn Gould, André Mathieu, and Alma Deutscher all came from musical families and had access to resources and support needed to advance their musical development. Nonetheless, case studies of musical savants with autism indicate that expertise can sometimes develop in spite of intellectual and/or social challenges (Ockelford, 2016).

A second strategy of investigating musical expertise is to compare the characteristics of adult nonmusicians and musicians (e.g., Gaser & Schlaug, 2003; Kraus et al., 2014; Zatorre, 1998). Such an approach gives rise to correlational data, making causal inferences difficult. Ideally, individuals should be assigned randomly to conditions so that the effects of musical practice can be evaluated independently of preexisting individual differences (see Schellenberg & Weiss, 2013, for a review). Without such random assignment, correlational data based on unrelated individuals are difficult to interpret given that "children seek out environments, including those with music lessons, which are consistent with predispositions" (Schellenberg, 2015, p. 170).

Among studies that compare musicians and nonmusicians in a quasi-experimental design, additional tests may be conducted to refine the measurement of expertise, by testing individual skills of musicianship such as pitch discrimination (e.g., Doelling & Poeppel, 2015) and sight-reading ability (e.g., Lehmann & Ericsson, 1993; Kopiez & Lee, 2008). Quantitative measures of expertise have also included ratings of performances by expert adjudicators (Meinz, 2000; Meinz, & Hambrick, 2010; Tuffiash, 2002), and rankings of performers by music teachers or entrance adjudicators (Ruthsatz, Detterman, Griscom, & Cirullo, 2008).

## Practice

Practice is characterized by persistent goal directed activities aimed at enhancing skills and knowledge. Teaching, in turn, involves employing systematic strategies for training individuals to acquire specialized competencies. Performance is known to depend crucially on practice, and this dependency has been formalized into the "deliberate practice theory" (Ericsson, Krampe, & Tesch-Römer, 1993; Ericsson & Smith, 1991; Ericsson & Ward, 2007). A central premise of this framework is that deliberate practice is both necessary and sufficient for the acquisition of elite levels of performance skill.

Consistent with deliberate practice theory, high levels of musical expertise are associated with individual differences in regional brain anatomy for motor and premotor areas, Broca's area, auditory areas, the cerebellum, and white matter pathways such as the corpus callosum, the superior longitudinal fasciculus, and the pyramidal tracts (for a detailed review see Ullén Mosing, & Madison, 2015; see also Loui & Przysinda, this volume). For example, Amunts, et al. (1997) reported a correlation of between .60 and .63 (Spearman rho) between the size of motor cortex and age of commencement of music training. For experts who rely on rapid and highly specialized visual recognition, the fusiform face area (FFA) may become adapted for holistic processing of domain-specific visual information, such as chess-game positions

(Bilalić, Langner, Ulrich, & Grodd 2011). There have also been reports of differences in regional neuroanatomy among other expert groups such as taxi drivers, jugglers, and painters (Maguire et al., 2000; Draganski et al., 2004; Lorains, Ball, & MacMahon, 2013). Such findings indicate that intensive engagement in practice can lead to neuroanatomical changes that support increased levels of skill, particularly during sensitive periods of development (Knudsen, 2004; Shavinina, 2016).

Such anatomical changes are correlated with higher levels of achievement, as well as with a streamlining of cognition and action (Vandervert, 2016). For example, one mechanism by which practice may lead to higher levels of achievement is by progressive increases in the efficiency of neural pathways in the cerebellum dedicated to the execution of movements and accompanying thought processes (Ito, 2005, 2008; Stoodley, Valera, & Schmahmann, 2012; Strick, Dum, & Fiez, 2009).

The importance of practice for the acquisition of expertise is further supported by positive correlations between estimates of lifetime deliberate practice and measures of expertise. In a meta-analysis across a wide array of domains, Macnamara and colleagues (2014) found that deliberate practice on average explained 12% of the variance in expert performance. This association was stronger for the domains of music (21%), games (26%), and sports (18%), but considerably weaker for educational (4%) and professional (1%) forms of expertise.

In another meta-analysis of 13 studies (N=788), Platz and colleagues (2014) reported that deliberate practice accounted for roughly 36% of the variance in musical expertise ($r = .61$), where expertise in music performance was assessed using various strategies and for different forms of expertise such as sight reading, musical memory, overall technical skill, and timing accuracy. In a third meta-analysis of eight studies employing continuous measures of musical expertise, the amount of deliberate practice (measured by responses to surveys administered to performers) explained approximately 30% of the reliable variance in music performance (Hambrick et al., 2014). In short, even accounting for errors in the measurement of expertise, it appears that deliberate practice is an important factor in the development of expertise, but it still leaves a considerable proportion of the variance unexplained.

## Genetic Influences on Expert Music Performance

Although it is obvious that practice is needed to achieve high levels of music performance skill, evidence suggests that musical expertise cannot be explained solely by practice. Other environmental factors (e.g., family and peer support), together with genetic predispositions, make interactive contributions to the acquisition of expertise. For example, genetic predispositions may mediate the motivation and inclination to engage in extensive deliberate practice that, in turn, amplifies other individual predispositions that support the ability to engage in expert musicianship. Indeed, once genetic factors are statistically controlled, the correlation between deliberate practice and some aspects of expertise may be considerably attenuated or disappear entirely (Mosing, Madison, Pedersen, Kuja-Halkola, & Ullén, 2014). To understand this evidence, a brief overview is provided of strategies used to estimate the influence of genetic factors on a trait.

Twin and adoption studies are most commonly used to estimate the relative influence of genetic and environmental factors on a trait, and to distinguish environmental influences that are shared within families from those that are not shared. The classical twin design is based on comparing the within-pair similarities of monozygotic (MZ) and dizygotic (DZ) twins. While both MZ and DZ twins have a shared environment of upbringing, MZ twins also share all of their genes, while DZ twins share on average only half of their segregating genes (Plomin, DeFries, Knopik, & Neiderheiser, 2013). A higher within-pair similarity for a given phenotype[1] in MZ twins than in DZ twins therefore indicates a genetic influence on that phenotype. In quantitative terms, the classical twin model divides variance in a phenotype (Vp) into three latent (estimated) factors, referred to as additive genetics (A), common or shared environment (C), and non-shared environment (E), so that:

$$Vp = A + C + E$$

C is an estimate of environmental influences that account for resemblances between family members (*shared environment*), such as socioeconomic status and family traditions such as giving children music lessons and instilling certain values or ambitions. E includes environmental effects that make family members different from one another (*non-shared environment*), such as influences from the unique peers that individuals within a family may have, but will also include measurement error.

These variance components are estimated using approaches based on Structural Equation Modeling (SEM) (Rijsdijk & Sham, 2002). The SEM framework allows for estimation of the contribution of genetic effects not just to a single trait (i.e. its heritability), but also to the covariation between phenotypes, as well as for calculation of confidence intervals on parameters, inclusion of covariates, and model comparison. Most commonly, SEM is used to explore complex relationships between observed (measured) and unobserved (latent) variables and also between two or more latent variables. SEM also allows for the explicit modeling of effects of covariates (e.g. sex and age) and interaction effects. The parameters of the structural equation model (e.g. phenotypic means and genetic and environmental variance components) can be estimated using for example maximum likelihood estimation of the parameter values that best explain the observed pattern of MZ and DZ variances and co-variances.

At the present time, a large body of evidence suggests that most, if not all, complex human traits are partly heritable, including those associated with expertise (Polderman et al., 2015). A reasonable hypothesis is therefore that expertise in music performance is similarly influenced by genetic predispositions. Indeed, in the last few years more and more evidence has come from twin studies. This evidence, combined with gene finding research, suggests that individual differences in music expertise are to a considerable degree genetically influenced. Here we will focus on twin-research, as most of the gene-finding results are based on small samples and have not been replicated as yet. For a review of gene-finding studies exploring the genetic background of individual differences in music related traits, see Tan et al. (2014).

One early example is a study by Coon and Carey (1989) on a sample of over 800 same-sex twin pairs which reported that the heritability (i.e. proportion of total variance explained by genetic influences) of self-reported musical achievement (out-of-school music performances) was 38% for males and 20% for females. In line with these estimates, a more recent twin study also on self-reported music accomplishment, reported a heritability of 26% across males and females (Hambrick & Tucker-Drob, 2015). A recent study using a much larger twin sample of 1,685 twin pairs (Vinkhuyzen, van der Sluis, Posthuma, &

Boomsma, 2009) explored the heritability of self-rated aptitude (three categories: less competent than others, as competent as most people, and more competent than most people) and exceptional talent (comparing ability in the normal range vs. exceptionally skilled) in music. Heritability estimates for self-rated musical aptitude was 66% for males and 30% for females with additional shared environmental influences of 8% and 54%, respectively, while exceptional musical talent showed heritability as high as 86%. Finally, the largest twin study on self-rated music achievement to date (i.e. success in the music world on a seven-point scale ranging from not involved in music to (inter)nationally acclaimed) reported a heritability of 57% in males and only 9% in females (non-significant), with an additional 46% of shared environmental influences in females (Mosing et al., 2015). These four studies suggest that individual differences in (self-rated) overall musical accomplishment are at least partly determined by genetic factors. At present, it is difficult to account for the differences in heritability estimates for males and females, which vary across studies, indicating the need for more research on this issue.

Similarly, moderate heritability estimates have been shown for more objective measures of musical expertise. For example, Drayna and colleagues (2001) reported that 71–80% of the variation in performance on the Distorted Tunes Test, which requires the participant to identify incorrect pitches from familiar melodic stimuli, was due to genetic influences. In line with that, more recently, a large Swedish twin study showed that individual differences in rhythm, melody and pitch discrimination skills (based on the Swedish Musical Discrimination Test) are also moderately heritable with 50%, 59%, and 12–30% of the variance being due to genetic influences, respectively (Ullén, Mosing, Holm, Eriksson, & Madison, 2014). Interestingly, recent evidence from twin studies suggests that not only is expert performance heritable; the inclination to practice also seems to be partly heritable. For example, two recent studies reported heritabilities between 38% and 70% for music practice (Hambrick, & Tucker-Drob, 2015; Mosing, et al., 2014). Although heritability estimates vary between studies, presumably reflecting the use of different samples and measures, It is increasingly clear that genetic factors can account for both expert performance and the willingness to practice in a particular field (i.e., music).

Recent research exploring the association between practice and music skills using genetically informative samples suggests that genetic pleiotropy (i.e. the same genes influencing different phenotypic traits,) explains much of the association (Mosing et al., 2014). Consistent with this finding, there was no skill difference between the more trained twin and their less trained, genetically identical co-twin for either musical discrimination (Mosing et al., 2014) or accuracy of motor timing (Ullén, Mosing, & Madison, 2015) suggesting that the associations between practice and these skills were not causal. Similarly, it seems that contrary to previous proposals (Ericsson & Smith, 1991), music practice does not decrease the genetic influences on music skills (Verweij et al., 2016) or self-reported musical accomplishment (Hambrick & Tucker-Drob, 2015). Instead, estimates of heritability tend to increase with music practice, suggesting that genetic influences may play a more important role with accumulated practice hours.

The studies discussed above suggest that variation in practice behavior, often interpreted as an environmental influence used to circumvent the need for talent (i.e. with enough practice anyone can become an expert), is to a large degree influenced by genes. Thus, individuals will tend to persist in an area they can succeed, and this inclination to persist is strongly influenced by genetic factors.

In short, musical expertise must be regarded as a multifactorial phenomenon. Although practice is clearly essential, one central tenet of deliberate practice theory (i.e. that long-term practice is in itself sufficient to explain expert performance, with a limited role for talent or genetic endowment) is not supported by the available data. For music, estimates of the influence of cumulative practice explain a moderate proportion of the variance in expert performance (Macnamara et al., 2014; Platz et al., 2014) and traits such as cognitive abilities correlate with expert performance even when controlling for practice (see e.g. Meinz & Hambrick, 2010). Moreover, genetic factors influence both practice itself and its relationship with different aspects of musical expert performance (Mosing et al., 2014; Ullén et al., 2015), as well as musical interests (Butković, Ullén, & Mosing, 2015).

Stimulated by these developments in expertise research, we have recently proposed a model for expert performance, called the multifactorial gene-environment interaction model (the MGIM), which synthesizes existing findings and provides a useful basis for future experimental work (Figure 34.1; Ullén, Hambrick, & Mosing, 2016). In accordance with deliberate practice theory, the MGIM includes practice as an important predictor of expert performance, and assumes that this association in part reflects causal effects of practice on skill. However, in the MGIM, expert performance can also be influenced by physical and psychological traits, independently of practice. For music, this could

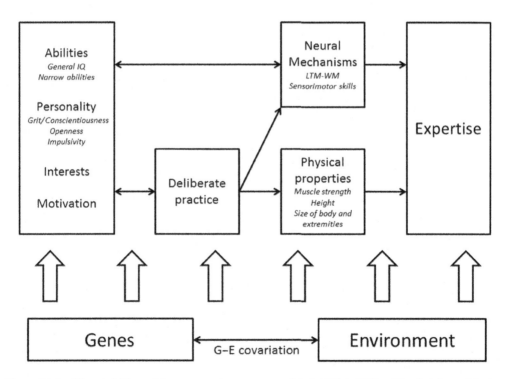

*Figure 34.1* The multifactorial gene–environment model (MGIM; Ullén, Hambrick, & Mosing, 2016) illustrating the various different factors influencing individual differences in expertise. Reprinted from Ullén, Hambrick, and Mosing, 2016, with permission.

include instrument-specific physical traits influencing, e.g. voice quality or hand dexterity (Wagner, 1988), as well as relevant cognitive abilities, including working memory (Meinz & Hambrick, 2010) and musical auditory discrimination (Ullén et al., 2014). Second, the MGIM differs from deliberate practice theory in that it includes effects of genetic factors and gene-environment interactions on practice itself, expert performance, other expertise related traits, and the covariations between these variables (Figure 34.1). A final point of particular interest, in relation to the exceptionally fast progress of prodigies, is that the multifactorial nature of the MGIM allows the possibility of complex non-linear interactions between predictors as well as simple additive effects. In this framework, the effect of each practice hour could thus vary depending on genetic factors, trait variables such as the capacity for sustained attention and metacognition, as well as environmental support and coaching.

## Conclusion

Expertise in music has been investigated using a range of experimental strategies, including comparisons of musicians and nonmusicians on behavioral or neuroscientific measures, case studies of music prodigies, and twin studies. This research suggests that musical expertise is acquired through an interaction between genetic predispositions and environmental catalysts. Until recently, much of the existing theory has been based on correlational data derived from quasi-experimental designs, making it difficult to draw strong conclusions and encouraging high levels of theoretical speculation. However, recent approaches have integrated cognitive modeling of expert performance with behavior genetics and neurobiological investigations, yielding a rich body of evidence that can be used to evaluate complex models of expertise and skill. An important general conclusion from these findings is that musical expertise depends causally on multiple factors, in addition to practice, which is clearly essential. For music, these factors are likely to include both physical traits of importance for playing a particular musical instrument and psychological traits such as personality, interests, and cognitive abilities. Furthermore, genetic factors play an important role for musical expertise acquisition by influencing both practice itself and its covariation with other expertise-related variables. These recent advances in the neuropsychology of musical expertise have been instrumental in the development of multifactorial theoretical frameworks for expertise, such as the MGIM model, and highlight the importance of including individual and environmental non-practice variables as well as genetically informative samples in future expertise research.

## Note

1. Phenotype refers to the characteristics of an individual. Genotype refers to an individual's genetic identity.

## Core Reading

Brown, R. M., Zatorre, R. J., & Penhune, V. B. (2015). Expert music performance: Cognitive, neural, and developmental bases. *Progress in Brain Research, 217,* 57–86.

Hambrick, D. Z., Oswald, F. L., Altmann, E. M., Meinz, E. J., Gobet, F., & Campitelli, G. (2014). Deliberate practice: Is that all it takes to become an expert? *Intelligence, 45,* 34–45.

Platz, F., Kopiez, R., Lehmann, A. C., & Wolf, A. (2014). The influence of deliberate practice on musical achievement: A meta-analysis. *Frontiers in Psychology, 5,* 646.

Tan, Y. T., McPherson, G. E., Peretz, I., Berkovic, S. F., & Wilson, S. J. (2014). The genetic basis of music ability. *Frontiers in Psychology, 5,* 658.

Ullén, F., Hambrick, D. Z., & Mosing, M. A. (2016). Rethinking expertise: A multifactorial gene-environment interaction model of expert performance. *Psychological Bulletin, 142,* 427–46.

## Further References

Amunts, K., Schlaug, G., Jäncke, L., Steinmetz, H., Schleicher, A., Dabringhaus, A., & Zilles, K. (1997). Motor cortex and hand motor skills: Structural compliance in the human brain. *Human Brain Mapping, 5,* 206–215.

Bilalić, M., Langner, R., Ulrich, R., & Grodd, W. (2011). Many faces of expertise: Fusiform face area in chess experts and novices. *The Journal of Neuroscience, 31,* 10206–10214.

Butković, A., Ullén, F., & Mosing, M. A. (2015). Personality and related traits as predictors of music practice: Underlying environmental and genetic influences. *Personality and Individual Differences, 74,* 133–138.

Coon, H., & Carey, G. (1989). Genetic and environmental determinants of musical ability in twins. *Behavior Genetics, 19*(2), 183–193.

Doelling, K. B., & Poeppel, D. (2015). Cortical entrainment to music and its modulation by expertise. *Proceedings of the National Academy of Sciences, 112*(45), E6233–E6242.

Draganski, B., Gaser, C., Busch, V., Schuierer, G., Bogdahn, U., & May, A. (2004). Neuroplasticity: Changes in grey matter induced by training. *Nature, 427*(6972), 311–312.

Drayna, D., Manichaikul, A., de Lange, M., Snieder, H., & Spector, T. (2001). Genetic correlates of musical pitch recognition in humans. *Science, 291*(5510), 1969–1972.

Ericsson, K. A., Krampe, R. T., & Tesch-Römer, C. (1993). The role of deliberate practice in the acquisition of expert performance. *Psychological Review, 100,* 363–406.

Ericsson, K. A., & Smith, J. (Eds.). (1991). *Toward a general theory of expertise: Prospects and limits.* New York, NY: Cambridge University Press.

Ericsson, K. A., & Ward, P. (2007). Capturing the naturally occurring superior performance of experts in the laboratory: Toward a science of expert and exceptional performance. *Current Directions in Psychological Science, 16,* 346–350.

Fabian, D., Timmers, R., & Schubert, E. (2014). *Expressiveness in music performance: Empirical approaches across styles and cultures.* Oxford: Oxford University Press.

Galton, F. (1869). *Hereditary genius: An inquiry into its laws and consequences.* London: Macmillan.

Gaser, C., & Schlaug, G. (2003). Brain structures differ between musicians and non-musicians. *Journal of Neuroscience, 23,* 9240–9245.

Gelding, R., Thompson, W. F. & Johnson, B.W. (2015). The pitch imagery arrow task: Effects of musical training, vividness, and mental control. *PLoS ONE, 10*(3): e0121809.

Hambrick, D. Z., & Tucker-Drob, E. M. (2015). The genetics of music accomplishment: Evidence for gene-environment correlation and interaction. *Psychonomic Bulletin & Review, 22,* 112–120.

Ito, M. (2005). Bases and implications of learning in the cerebellum: Adaptive control and internal model mechanism. In C. I. De Zeeuw, & F. Cicirata (Eds.), *Creating Coordination in the Cerebellum* (pp. 95–109). Amsterdam: Elsevier.

Ito, M. (2008). Control of mental activities by internal models in the cerebellum. *Nature Reviews Neuroscience, 9,* 304–313.

Keller, P. E. (2014a). Ensemble performance. In Thompson, W. F. (Ed.). *Music in the social and behavioral sciences: An encyclopedia* (pp. 396–399). New York City, NY: Sage.

Keller, P. E. (2014b). Ensemble performance: Interpersonal alignment of musical expression. In D. Fabian, R. Timmers, & E. Schubert (Eds.), *Expressiveness in music performance: Empirical approaches across styles and cultures* (pp. 260–282). Oxford: Oxford University Press.

Knudsen, E. (2004). Sensitive periods in the development of brain and behavior. *Journal of Cognitive Neuroscience, 16,* 1412–1425.

Kopiez, R., & Lee, J. I. (2008). Towards a general model of skills involved in sight reading music. *Music Education Research, 10,* 41–62.

Kraus, N., Skoe, E., Parbery-Clark, A., & Ashley, R. (2009). Experience-induced malleability in neural encoding of pitch, timbre, and timing: Implications for language and music. *Annals of the New York Academy of Sciences, 1169*, 543–557.

Kraus, N., Slater, J., Thompson, E. C., Hornickel, J., Strait, D. L., Nicol, T., & White-Schwoch T. (2014). Music enrichment programs improve the neural encoding of speech in at-risk children. *Journal of Neuroscience, 34*, 11913–11918.

Lehmann, A. C., & Ericsson, K. A. (1993). Sight-reading ability of expert pianists in the context of piano accompanying. *Psychomusicology: A Journal of Research in Music Cognition, 12*, 182–195.

Lorains, M., Ball, K., & MacMahon, C. (2013). An above real time training intervention for sport decision making. *Psychology of Sport and Exercise, 14*, 670–674.

Macnamara, B. N., Hambrick, D. Z., & Oswald, F. L. (2014). Deliberate practice and performance in music, games, sports, education, and professions: A meta-analysis. *Psychological Science, 25*(8), 1608–1618.

Maguire, E. A., Gadian, D. G., Johnsrude, I. S., Good, C. D., Ashburner, J., Frackowiak, R. S., & Frith, C. D. (2000). Navigation-related structural change in the hippocampi of taxi drivers. *Proceedings of the National Academy of Sciences, 97*, 4398–4403.

McPherson, G. (2005). From child to musician: Skill development during the beginning stages of learning an instrument. *Psychology of Music, 33*, 5–35.

McPherson, G. (2016). *Musical Prodigies: Interpretations from Psychology, Music Education, Musicology and Ethnomusicology.* Oxford: Oxford University Press.

McPherson, G., & Thompson, W. F. (1998). Assessing music performance: Issues and influences. *Research Studies in Music Education, 10*, 12–24.

Meinz, E. J. (2000). Experience-based attenuation of age-related differences in music cognition tasks. *Psychology and Aging, 15*, 297–312.

Meinz, E. J., & Hambrick, D. Z. (2010). Deliberate practice is necessary but not sufficient to explain individual differences in piano sight-reading skill: The role of working memory capacity. *Psychological Science, 21*, 914–919.

Mosing, M. A., Madison, G., Pedersen, N. L., Kuja-Halkola, R., & Ullén, F. (2014). Practice does not make perfect: No causal effect of music practice on music ability. *Psychological Science, 25*(9), 1795–1803.

Mosing, M. A., Verweij, K. J. H., Madison, G., Pedersen, N. L., Zietsch, B. P., & Ullén, F. (2015). Testing predictions from the sexual selection hypothesis of music evolution using a large genetically informative sample of over 10,000 twins. *Evolution and Human Behavior, 36*(5), 359–366.

Ockelford, A. (2016). Prodigious musical talent in blind children with autism and learning difficulties: Identifying and educating potential musical savants. In G. McPherson (Ed.), *Musical prodigies: Interpretations from psychology, music education, musicology and ethnomusicology* (pp. 471–495). Oxford: Oxford University Press.

Palmer, C. (2006). The nature of memory for music performance skills. In E. Altenmueller & M. Wiesendanger (Eds.), *Music, motor control and the brain* (pp. 39–53). Oxford: Oxford University Press.

Palmer, C., & Drake, C. (1997). Monitoring and planning capacities in the acquisition of music performance skills. *Canadian Journal of Experimental Psychology, 51*, 369–384.

Plantinga, J., & Trehub, S. E. (2014). Revisiting the innate preference for consonance. *Journal of Experimental Psychology: Human Perception and Performance, 40*, 40–49.

Platz, F., & Kopiez, R. (2012). When the eye listens: A meta-analysis of how audio-visual presentation enhances the appreciation of music performance. *Music Perception, 30*(1), 71–83.

Plomin, R., DeFries, J. C., Knopik, V. S., & Neiderheiser, J. M. (2013). *Behavioral genetics* (6th ed.). New York, NY: Worth Publishers.

Polderman, T. J., Benyamin, B., de Leeuw, C. A., Sullivan, P. F., van Bochoven, A., Visscher, P. M., & Posthuma, D. (2015). Meta-analysis of the heritability of human traits based on fifty years of twin studies. *Nature Genetics, 47*(7), 702–709.

Quinto, L., Ammirante, P., Connors, M. H., & Thompson, W. F. (2016). Prodigies of music composition: Cognitive abilities and developmental antecedents. In G. McPherson (Ed.), *Musical prodigies: Interpretations from psychology, music education, musicology and ethnomusicology* (pp. 358–377). Oxford: Oxford University Press.

Quinto, L., & Thompson, W.F. (2013). Composers and performers have different capacities to manipulate arousal and valence. *Psychomusicology: Music, Mind and Brain, 23*(3), 137–150.

Rijsdijk, F.V., & Sham, P.C. (2002). Analytic approaches to twin data using structural equation models. *Briefings in Bioinformatics, 3*(2), 119–133.

Rodger, M.W.M., Craig, C.M., & O'Modhrain, S. (2012). Expertise is perceived from both sound and body movements of musical performance. *Human Movement Sciences, 31*(5), 1137–1150.

Ruthsatz, J., Detterman, D.K., Griscom, W.S., & Cirullo, B.A. (2008). Becoming an expert in the musical domain: It takes more than just practice. *Intelligence, 36*(4), 330, 338.

Schellenberg, E.G. (2015). Music training and speech perception: A gene-environment interaction. *Proceedings of the National Academy of Sciences, 1337,* 170–177.

Schellenberg, E.G., & Weiss, M.W. (2013). Music and cognitive abilities. In D. Deutsch (Ed.), *The psychology of music* (3rd edition) (pp. 499–550). Amsterdam: Elsevier.

Shavinina, L.V. (2016). On the cognitive-developmental theory of the child prodigy phenomenon. In G. McPherson (Ed.), *Musical prodigies: Interpretations from psychology, music education, musicology and ethnomusicology* (pp. 259–278). Oxford: Oxford University Press.

Stoodley, C., Valera, E., & Schmahmann, J. (2012). Functional topography of the cerebellum for motor and cognitive tasks: An fMRI study. *NeuroImage, 59,* 1560–70.

Strick, R., Dum, R., & Fiez, J. (2009). Cerebellum and nonmotor function. *Annual Review of Neuroscience, 32,* 413–434.

Thompson, W.F. (2014). *Music, thought and feeling: Understanding the psychology of music,* 2nd edition. New York, NY: Oxford University Press.

Thompson, W.F., Diamond, C.T.P., & Balkwill, L. (1998). The adjudication of six performances of a Chopin Etude: A study of expert knowledge. *Psychology of Music, 26,* 154–174.

Thompson, W.F., Graham, P., & Russo, F.A. (2005). Seeing music performance: Visual influences on perception and experience. *Semiotica, 156*(1/4), 203–227.

Tuffiash, M. (2002). Predicting individual differences in piano sight-reading skill: Practice, performance, and instruction (unpublished master's thesis). Tallahassee, FL: Florida State University.

Ullén, F., Mosing, M.A., Holm, L., Eriksson, H., & Madison, G. (2014). Psychometric properties and heritability of a new online test for musicality, the Swedish Musical Discrimination Test. *Personality and Individual Differences, 63,* 87–93.

Ullén, F., Mosing, M.A., & Madison, G. (2015). Associations between motor timing, music practice, and intelligence studied in a large sample of twins. *Annals of the New York Academy of Sciences, 1337,* 125–129.

Valentine, C.W. (1962). Musical intervals and attitudes to music. In C.W. Valentine (Ed.), *The experimental psychology of beauty* (pp. 196–227). London: Methuen & Co. Ltd.

Vandervert, L. (2016). The brain's rapid encoding of rule-governed domains of knowledge: A case analysis of a musical prodigy. In G. McPherson (Ed.), *Musical prodigies: Interpretations from psychology, music education, musicology and ethnomusicology* (pp. 245–258). Oxford: Oxford University Press.

Vinkhuyzen, A.A., van der Sluis, S., Posthuma, D., & Boomsma, D.I. (2009). The heritability of aptitude and exceptional talent across different domains in adolescents and young adults. *Behavior Genetics, 39*(4), 380–392.

Wagner, C. (1988). The pianist's hand: Anthropometry and biomechanics. *Ergonomics, 31*(1), 97–131.

Zatorre, R.J. (1998). Functional specialization of human auditory cortex for musical processing. *Brain, 121,* 1817–1818.

# 35

# LEARNING MUSIC
## Informal Processes and Their Outcomes

*Lucy Green and Tim Smart*

### Informal Learning: A General Overview

Human beings learn everywhere, all the time, through their dealings with other people and the environment around them; and through processes that can be intentional and conscious, or unintentional and beyond the realms of conscious awareness. It is hardly surprising that there has long been research on learning and how best to foster it in formal educational environments. But there is today a growing recognition, as Werquin (2010, p. 14) puts it, "that individuals are capable of accumulating knowledge, skills and competencies throughout their lifetime, well beyond their organized learning in formal settings, such as school, university or structured vocational training." Increased attention from educationalists and other researchers regarding the characterization of learning that takes place outside formal education, and the learning outcomes that result, has resulted in a fast-developing field of enquiry. Work exists in generic educational studies, fields such as sociology, anthropology, and psychology (for example, Eraut, 2000, 2004; Merriam, Caffarella, & Baumgartner, 2009; Werquin, 2010) and music (e.g. Finnegan, 1989; Green, 2002; McCarthy, 1999).

Current generic conceptualizations of different approaches to learning are summarised by Werquin (2010) as located on a continuum, with the concepts of "formal" and "informal" learning at opposite poles and "non-formal" learning located between the two. (For similar formulations in relation to music, see Green, 2002, pp. 5–6; Folkestad, 2006; Smilde, 2012; and Veblen, 2012). There are a number of differentials that characterize types of learning along this continuum, including for example: how, where and why the learning takes place; the levels of conscious awareness of learning and intentionality to learn on the part of the learner; the presence of oversight in the form of quality assurance or input from a recognised teacher, or the input of others such as peers and family; and the perceptions of the learning environment of the people who are involved in it.

In general, "formal" learning refers to learning that takes place in or under the auspices of recognised and purposive educational establishments such as schools and universities. The process is usually regarded as intentional, and learners as being consciously aware of learning or attempting to learn. It is associated with recognised and qualified teachers, organized curricula and often, syllabi, examinations and accredited qualifications. Within the context of music, such learning mainly takes place in schools, universities, conservatoires, or other educational institutions. Individual or small-group instrumental lessons with a recognized teacher, especially when linked with a wider curriculum and/or accredited assessments such as grade exams, are often also a part of institutional provision and in this sense fall under the formal umbrella.

"Non-formal" learning is a standard term in the wider literature as well as the field of music, and refers to intentional learning which occurs as a result of organized provision, but which usually takes place outside educational institutions, and in many cases voluntarily. Non-formal music learning contexts would include community and youth music programs, as well as some practices that occur within the school or higher education setting such as extra-curricular activities. Instrumental teaching which is undertaken on a private basis aside from provision by an institution would, in that case, often come under this category, especially when it does not involve exams or accreditation.

Learning that falls outside of these two general areas (i.e. "formal" and "non-formal") can be characterised as "informal." Schugurensky (2000, p. 2) notes that *non*-formal learning is a residual category, referring to "things that are not formal learning." By extension, he defines informal learning as a residual category of a residual category, being "everything that is neither formal nor non-formal." As he notes, it is in these areas where "most of the significant learnings [sic] that we apply to our everyday lives are learnt" (2000, p. 2). This points to a hugely influential range of learning types and contexts, which we will examine in more detail below.

It is important to recognise that a learning situation may have the potential to be characterized in different ways, depending upon a number of variables. For example, in relation to music, as we noted above, an instrumental lesson might be seen as "formal" or "non-formal," depending on the nature of the provision and context. A learning situation may also include multiple categories of learning (Schugurensky, 2002, p. 2). For example informal learning may take place within formal establishments, but independently of the intended goals of the curriculum.

Beyond the relatively broad strokes of the three overarching labels that are often used—formal, non-formal and informal—as Werquin notes, the fine detail of the interactions and overlaps between different forms of learning means that defining the terms too rigidly is likely to be of limited utility (2010, p. 24). He instead suggests that key terms be defined by the context in which they operate, an approach that we adopt as we look towards informal learning in general, and then informal learning in music.

## Informal Learning: Conceptualizations

Schugurensky (2000, p. 3) offers a three-part characterization of informal learning. "Self-directed" informal learning is defined as "learning projects" that learners engage in while being both conscious of learning and intending to learn. This occurs without oversight from a recognised teacher or instructor, although the presence of a more able "resource person" is a noted feature of this characterization, as long as they do not see themselves, nor are seen by others, as an "educator." Such "self-directed" informal learning may encompass both individual and group learning. So this characterization would include, for example, a group of musicians engaged in peer learning in the environment of a "garage band" rehearsal, even if one of the members of the band is more highly skilled than the others and is guiding the others. Secondly, "incidental" informal learning occurs when a learning experience happens unintentionally, but is nonetheless consciously recognized as being of value, either at the time or afterwards. Finally, Schugurenskyy uses the term "socialization" to describe the process of informal learning that takes place both unintentionally and nonconsciously, for example through the process of enculturation. In such a case the learner would be unaware of the learning that is taking place, and would persist in this lack of awareness beyond the experience itself.

Bennett (2012) considers Schugurensky's characterizations, and proposes modification and extension. In place of Schugurensky's third term "socialization," she prefers the term "tacit" informal learning, to capture learning that takes place for the learner on their own as well as in a social setting, and linking with research on implicit learning and processing (for example, Reber, 1993; Berry and Dienes, 1993). She also suggests extending Schugurensky's model with the additional recognition of "integrative" informal learning. This type of learning is an intentional practice, but involves non-conscious processes, for example the recognition of the value of learning from "experience," even when the specifics of how this learning takes place are not necessarily apparent. Bennett summarises the model thus:

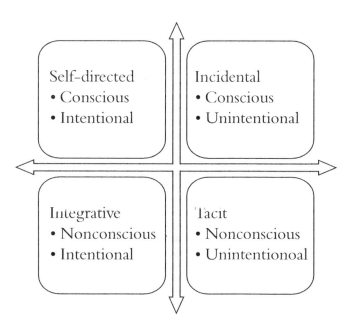

*Figure 35.1*   Bennett's reconceptualization of the model of informal adult learning.

Bennett, 2012, p. 27.

Within the four subsets of "informal" learning outlined in Bennett's model, there is recognition that the characterization of an informal learning situation might flow freely from one subset to another as learning takes place (Bennett, 2012, p. 27). One key differentiating factor in the categorization of informal learning situations is how the learners themselves view the situation or the processes involved (their "intentionality"). Thus any change in awareness of potential learning outcomes associated with specific situations or processes may alter the characterization of learning that one might apply. For clarity of expression from here we use the phrase "informal learning processes" throughout our discussion, with acknowledgement of the different learning practices, situations, levels of awareness and intentionality that this encompasses. (Also see Smart and Green (in press) for further discussion of the use of key terms.)

Various informal learning processes and their outcomes are often undervalued by the people engaged in them, and indeed by educational institutions and society at large (Werquin, 2010, p. 18). A central thread within informal learning research has been to raise the visibility of learning in these ways, and the learning outcomes that they yield, in order to appreciate the value of these approaches alongside other forms of learning, and to support a more balanced and inclusive understanding of learning as it occurs in all settings. Mirroring wider findings in learning studies, informal learning by musicians has until recently, tended to be undervalued by educationalists and governmental educational policy-makers, and indeed the musicians themselves, relative to the more recognised processes and outcomes of formal learning. Over the last couple of decades, by highlighting the outcomes of informal learning, and the processes that support the learning, research in music education has raised the visibility of learning in these ways, and challenged many of the assumptions and value systems previously attached to them. In the field of music education, one result of this has been the relatively recent adaptation and incorporation of some informal learning practices into the formal educational environment (see e.g. Chua & Ho, 2013; D'Amore, 2011; Green, 2008; Jeanneret, McLennan, & Stevens-Ballenger, 2011; Lebler, 2007; Wright, 2011, 2016).

In the discussion that follows, we firstly give a broad overview of the main musical informal learning processes employed by novice learners, then examine how these, and others, feature in the lives of more advanced musicians including professionals, throughout the life-course. Into our discussion, we thread a consideration of the range of overall skills and knowledge—that is, learning outcomes—which are reported to be highly valued by different individuals across different musical styles, from beginner to advanced standard. As will be seen, many aspects of these skills and knowledge are, and in some cases can only be, acquired informally; and this is often the case also for musicians who have undergone extensive formal training. Our discussion also considers the development of the musician through life experiences that go beyond "mere" musical learning processes and situations. Research on informal learning in music has tended to focus on a variety of what can be called "vernacular musicians" in different parts of the world. These have been highly relevant populations to study, as in many cases, from popular musicians working in the recording industry, to children in the Venda tribe in South Africa, much of their learning falls broadly into the realms of the informal.[1] However, as we hope to demonstrate in the remainder of this chapter, informal learning can be seen as a part of the learning profile of musicians from far wider than these vernacular fields. The concept of lifelong learning has strong resonances with informal learning, and if all musicians, like everyone else, learn constantly (Werquin, 2010, p. 14), a vast amount of this learning must take place informally over the lifespan.

This would be the case even for those, such as classical musicians, who have had an extensive formal learning profile. We suggest that widening the potential field of study to include *all* musicians may have beneficial effects for the overall study of informal learning in music, and learning in music as a whole.

## Informal Music Learning: Basic Characteristics[2]

At a general level it is possible to encapsulate the basic characteristics of informal music learning which would likely be present across many, if not most, contexts. One essential characteristic is that the music being learnt is nearly always already familiar to the learner. This could be a familiarity engendered through enculturation in the musical environment of the family or community, as in a typical folk or traditional music setting; through the general sound-scape of the family house or car; through a friendship group which may or may not exclude others outside the group, as would be typical of a teenage-subculture for example; or indeed through a listener's individual and even isolated practices. Very often the learners, whether as part of a social group or alone, experience high levels of enjoyment in listening to the music they are learning, and can have a strong affinity and identity with it. This is rather different from what normally happens in formal education, where teachers or other experts usually choose the music for the learners, and where the music is likely to be unfamiliar and may not be enjoyable for them. The ramifications of learning to create music with which the learner is already familiar, and to which the learner enjoys listening, are profound. Regarding familiarity, learning to play unfamiliar music ideally involves the need to at least become acquainted with "how the music should go," whereas when the learner is already encultured (an informal, unconscious and unintentional learning process) into the music, that acquaintance knowledge is already given. Regarding enjoyment, whether or not a learner likes the music they are learning to play can have a significant effect on motivation (as has been shown in school classroom research, e.g. Green, 2008). Being familiar with and enjoying listening to music play a crucial, indeed possibly the most fundamental part of informal learning, at a number of different levels which we go on to examine.

Another common and very important characteristic of the informal realm, and one which relies on listening, is that the music is usually (but not necessarily, as we mention later) learnt by ear. We refer to a range of practices involved in this as "ear-playing" (see e.g. Johansson, 2004; McPherson, 1995; McPherson, Bailey, & Sinclair, 1997; McPherson & Gabrielsson, 2002). Amongst its many implications for the learner, ear-playing necessarily pays close attention to a number of musical parameters that are left unaddressed by notation: such as playing with "feel," "swing," "sensitive phrasing," "sensitive touch," or just the ephemeral notion of "playing musically," which we examine later. Ear-playing can involve a range of approaches, including aural copying by listening to live or recorded music then attempting to play it, playing along simultaneously to live or recorded music in order to copy it, playing along without any intention to copy, and improvising. Below we break down these practices into some of their inter-related components.

Aural copying by listening first and then playing afterwards tends to be associated more with non-formal and formal modes of transmission than informal ones, although not exclusively. For example, in much Indian music a master-musician will often provide a musical model that the learner is expected to emulate. In aural tests for classical grade exams, one of the most common tasks is for the learner to listen to a segment of music and then play or sing it back afterwards. In the informal realms where no dedicated expert or teacher is present, this could happen via a peer or relative, or via a recording. However it is less likely to be used in this sphere.

More common within our broad definition of informal learning is playing along simultaneously with music. In a live music-making setting, this is of course the main way in which music has been transmitted from generation to generation since the dawn of civilization. It has always occurred with members of the family, community, or friends, and continues today across many arenas, particularly traditional musics. Since the invention of recording technology at the turn of the 20th century, the audio recording has added a new resource to this practice, enabling a learner to play along when completely alone. This has gone on almost since recording technology began. Video recordings came later, and nowadays the internet is making the practice of not only aural but visual learning by playing along with recorded material very common.

It is important to distinguish two main approaches to the practice of playing along. We will firstly consider these in relation to playing along with a recording. In one approach, the part being played by the learner is missing from the recording. This approach has been used for many decades in classical music, with the availability of, for example, backing tracks such as "Music Minus One," or piano accompaniments to classical songs or sonatas. In other styles, today there are thousands of karaoke backing tracks, and applications such as iReal Pro, which offer electronically programmed versions of backing tracks that are able to change key or tempo at the click of a few buttons. In all these cases, the recording plays the role of a "mere" accompaniment.

In the other approach to playing along, the part being played by the learner is not missing, but the recording contains the complete piece of music, and the part is doubled by the live player. Playing along to a complete recorded track has long been associated with the practices of popular as well as jazz musicians, and is increasingly used in other styles as wide apart as, for example, Irish traditional music or Karnatic Indian music (Grimmer, 2011), where ear-playing was the main transmission medium before recording was invented. However, it is also nowadays being taken up in Western classical music realms where it supports the use of notation, or in some cases, substitutes for it: For example singalongs feature in the amateur choral world, where audio materials of standard works are available, with options to increase the volume of an individual part to aid the listening ear.[3] Some amateur choir singers rely entirely on recorded materials to learn their parts, and some choral directors systematically provide such materials for this purpose.

The two approaches—playing along to a mere accompaniment track and playing along to a complete recording—tend to involve quite different learning experiences. In the former case it is likely, indeed usually necessary, that the notes themselves have already been learnt (either by ear or notation), or that the basic chord progression is known and understood at least to a point where it is possible to play along with it. There is no model to emulate on the recording, but the focus is on getting the "feel and flow" of playing in time with the accompaniment, without being "put off" by, for example, any unexpected events in the accompaniment. In the latter case, the point of playing along is very often simply to "get the notes" themselves in the first place; and thereafter to continue playing along only if the player wishes to focus further on "feel and flow."

Similar issues to those above also apply to playing along with live, rather than recorded music. In a traditional pub session of folk music, for example, it is likely that more than one instrument will have the same tune, and a player learning that tune will do so by playing along with a part that he or she is doubling. However, in a jazz setting a learner may be playing along, not in order to copy the same tune played by another player, but in order to improvise their own part.

It can be helpful to conceive of the listening skills involved in the practice of ear-playing along on a continuum from purposive to distracted listening (Green, 2002). At one extreme, in purposive listening, the learner has the conscious purpose of copying or in some other way putting to practical instrumental use, the music to which they are listening. At the other extreme, in distracted listening they are mentally taking in the music without any conscious purpose or even without any conscious awareness, as part of their musical enculturation. Yet the familiarity engendered by this will affect the way they later play not only that particular music but music in general.

It is during ear-playing, particularly whilst playing along, that improvisation enters the fray. As distinct from *aural copying* whilst playing along, *improvisation* whilst playing along relies on a deep familiarity, not only with the given chord progressions and the most likely chord variants, but beyond that with the relevant musical styles and conventions at a level of detail such as where exactly to "put the beat," how to bend a note, and many other aspects (e.g. Smart and Green, in press). This familiarity is, again, acquired first and foremost by listening, not only whilst playing but also separately from doing so.

Improvisation may be more likely to develop from aural copying than from using notation. McPherson (1995) studied the relationships between sight-reading, ear-playing, playing from memory, improvising, and performing rehearsed music. His findings showed that ear playing exerted a direct influence on enhancing improvising, sight reading and playing from memory, and an indirect influence on enhancing the performance of rehearsed music (also see Green, 2014). The reasons why ear-playing may enhance improvisation are partly to do with the development of a facility to play without notation, an experience often found strange by those who are only accustomed to playing from notation (Green, 2014). In addition, with aural copying there is no fixed instruction as to which notes are "right" or "wrong" such as there is in notation. Thus what would be counted as a "mistake" when reading from notation could more easily be understood as an "embellishment" or "creative improvisational idea" when music is being copied aurally. Improvisation then grows almost organically out of this (Green, 2014; McPherson, 1995).

Another characteristic of informal music learning concerns the organization, or lack of organization, of progression in the learning trajectory. In many formal, and to some extent non-formal music learning situations, musical leaders will typically break down skills, tasks, and indeed music itself into component parts, in order to enable learners to climb up a ladder starting with easier and more accessible steps, and becoming progressively harder. However, in many informal contexts, the learner starts with "whole," "real-world" pieces of music. Rather than being led through a series of carefully worked-out steps, each individual finds their own route through the learning; thus, skills and knowledge tend to be assimilated in holistic, and often haphazard ways. Again, the learners may receive help from others, who could be peers, family or community members, they may work entirely alone, or a combination of the two.

As is already clear, informal approaches generally tend to involve the integration of listening, performing, and improvising throughout the learning process. This is rather different from what happens in formal music education, where teachers or others are liable to split skills up into different lessons or sections of lessons.

Although we have suggested that informal music learning tends to be heavily associated with ear-playing, using notation is of course not ruled out by any definition of informal learning, since a learner may, for example, decide to download a "How-to-read-music" text or video, say, and study it of their own accord; or they may get help in notation-reading from a parent or other person, thus fulfilling many of the criteria associated with informal as well as non-formal learning as discussed above. Similarly an informal learner may decide to use texts or other materials which break down tasks progressively, and in that way, they are able to structure their learning into simple tasks followed by gradually more complex ones, rather than starting with whole pieces. However such approaches are not so common in the informal context as the formal.

## Informal Music Learning as a Life-Long Process: Advanced Musicians

The informal learning processes discussed so far are typical across a range of contexts involving novice learners, but many of them continue to be used by those who go on to become advanced musicians. In some cases, advanced musicians who are highly trained in the formal sphere, and who may not have engaged with the processes above, come to a later discovery of them. We now go on to consider some of the likely outcomes of informal learning, and how these are valued by musicians themselves. Whilst many of these outcomes and values are held in common across novice and advanced learners, here we focus on the perspectives of advanced musicians, citing examples of musicians' own words from three sources (Green, 2002; Cottrell, 2004; and Smart, unpub., but see also Bennett, 1980; Berliner, 1994; Finnegan, 1989).

Technical skill, that is, the motor-coordination involved in playing an instrument, is clearly a crucial element in the creation of a successful musical event, but this skill is often not regarded as sufficient for a good performance. Instead, musicians recognise the necessity for a range of attributes that are commonly referred to as being "musical," playing with "feel" or being able to put some individual expression into the musical interpretation, although these qualities can be difficult to describe in words:

> They can come and play a concerto and they might be superficially very efficient players, great facility. I think there's a great concentration on facility, on notes in other words, rather than the musical aspects.
>
> *(Professional musician cited in Cottrell, 2004, p. 35)*

> I think with all music, it's the feel that makes the music, you know, you could be technically brilliant and as boring as anything. I think it's what people put into it really.
>
> *(Professional drummer cited in Green, 2002, p. 108)*

Different musical contexts have specific requirements in terms of appropriate musical behaviours. Appropriate responses are likely to vary between a theatre pit, an orchestral concert, a big band stage, a wedding function, a brass band or improvising jazz group, or indeed across the recording studio and live performance environments (see e.g. Becker, 1963; Bennett, 2008; Cottrell, 2004; Green, 2002; O'Flynn, 2009). Thus, knowledge of the nature and demands of the context that the individual musician is operating in are of high importance, as this allows the musician to respond in the most appropriate fashion.

> I think the skills are important but I think that you can have the skills and not necessarily *use* them correctly. [. . .] It's about having the tools but knowing when to use them, and how to use them.
>
> *(Professional pianist/composer cited in Smart, unpub.)*

Such aspects also require the musician to possess an awareness of the musical input of other participants, and how their roles interact with the whole:

> You get certain people and they're really soloistic and that doesn't work, and you get certain people who are timid and that doesn't work. But somehow when you get someone who's so in touch with the whole thing, they just slot in . . .
>
> *(Professional musician cited in Cottrell, 2004, p. 86)*

The ability to respond appropriately applies not only to a musical context, but also to social contexts. A musician rehearsing with an already-established string quartet for the first time, for example, will have to adapt their behaviour and decisions to reflect the nature of the group and their own relative inexperience in that particular environment. This will include being sensitive to inter-personal interactions with other members of the group in terms of, for example, leadership, artistic input and even things like who makes the coffee or buys a round in the pub after the rehearsal. Learning about many of these aspects is often recognised as being a function of informal learning:

> There are lots of social skills about being in an orchestra that you're not really trained to do, you just pick them up bit by bit.
>
> *(Professional musician cited in Cottrell, 2004, p. 82)*

> I think the personality is in some ways the most important thing, because some of the most awkward and difficult people, really however wonderfully they have played, have been a complete menace in an orchestra.
>
> *(Professional musician cited in Cottrell, 2004, p. 110)*

Such informal learning also reaches out beyond the socio-musical group itself:

> College is a great base to learn from, but you need to go on and learn about yourself and life and it is only with the onset of real life and real stress and playing and understanding of real situations [that you develop further].
>
> *(Professional tubist cited in Smart, unpub.)*

One central informal learning process that carries on throughout life-long learning is simply listening to a wide range of music. This is valued not only as an end in itself, but also through a tacit process of "widening your experiences, like travelling to a different country" (professional guitarist, cited in Smart, unpub.). Listening to music is seen as a method of creating an internal bank of knowledge that informs a knowledge of repertoire, as well as crucially influencing "feel" and "expression" through interpretative and stylistic decisions, defining what is played, and how.

> I'm playing some Schumann, and I've decided what I want to express in this beautiful moment, I know, because I've heard a lot of people do Schumann, I know what

to do at that moment, and it's not a conscious decision, it isn't "Ah, I must do that" but you know from your internal archive, you know what is going to get the effect that you want.

*(Professional oboist, cited in Smart, unpub.)*

Interacting with fellow musicians away from music-making itself also offers crucial incidental learning experiences that may occur in some unusual settings, for example in social gatherings, long car journeys, and, as below, in hotel bars.

A lot of realisations about improving as a musician I have had in Travelodges at 3am with Steve Pearce and Trevor Barry and Ralph Salmins [highly regarded professional freelance musicians in London]. I have learnt a phenomenal amount from talking to these people and gauging their approach. I remember Steve talking to me about where he puts the beat depends on whom he is playing with, he consciously knows where he is going to put the beat, and that information is priceless. So I'd say that my development as a musician over the last 10 years has been characterised by little nuggets of information at 4am at a hotel in Bristol, and that has gradually worked in. You think about it, and then you are aware of it on a gig, and it goes in.

*(Professional guitarist, cited in Smart, unpub.)*

There is also recognition of the impact of other non-musical aspects of personal development on specific aspects of music making:

Might be getting off the subject, but things like playing in time, I've noticed that the older I have got, the more relaxed as a person I have become and the more comfortable, the more I feel comfortable in my own skin, so I think that has resulted in my time getting better, it's kind of an esoteric concept but it has a physical result because if I turn up on a session and I have a click going on, I am more relaxed, because you get older, you know people and you are comfortable in your environment, where you place the beat is more relaxed. I think when I was younger I was a bit pushy on the beat, and now as a result, not of technical skill, as a result of the things that I have just talked about, now it's a bit further back, where I would like it to be. [. . .] I think that it was an emotional thing, an emotional thing that has nothing to do with music.

*(Professional guitarist, cited in Smart, unpub.)*

Skills and knowledge of the kind discussed here are amongst those that are likely to be most highly valued by musicians (including in most cases novices, see Green 2002). They include listening to a wide range of music with understanding and appreciation, the ability to play "musically"; being sensitive to both the musical and the personal input and roles of other musicians, interacting with other musicians not only as part of the music-making experience, but beyond it, and even learning "about yourself and life." These skills and knowledge are usually picked up through various kinds of informal learning in a range of contexts. They are not, and in many cases never could be, fully addressed by formal education (see e.g. Bennett, 2008; Green, 2002; Odam & Bannan, 2005; Rogers, 2002; Smilde, 2012). Most notably, not only young, dedicated informal learners in vernacular musics, but many musicians across a wide range of styles recognise and engage with the informal learning processes which can lead to such outcomes.

## Conclusion

As mentioned earlier, one aim of research in informal learning is to raise the visibility and recognition of the outcomes of informal learning, as well as the processes that produce them, in order to foster a more inclusive viewpoint of different processes that underpin and drive all human learning. We have offered a glimpse of the main characteristics of informal music learning cutting across a range of musical styles. We have referred to musicians' descriptions of some of their most valued skills, which tend to be the kinds of skills that are acquired informally. This includes many situations in which learning takes place through tacit, incidental, integrative, and self-directed processes. Both the learning outcomes and the informal processes that are seen to support them often transcend what is normally conceived as being part of formal music education, a factor recognised by research and musicians themselves. Thus beyond the boundaries of formal music education, an extensive range of attributes, in combination with the lifelong dedication to learning of musicians, mean that even musicians with advanced formal training have many elements of their knowledge-base informed and developed by informal learning. The field undoubtedly requires further research into the fine grains of characterising this learning, and making more visible both the outcomes of this learning and the processes that develop these outcomes, along with recognizing the interplay of these different forms of learning in the trajectory of any individual musician.

## Notes

1. It is important to note that this does not apply to all "world music" since traditions such as Indian classical music or gamelan are associated with rigorous approaches to training which would fall more happily under the "formal" categorisation, and others such as Ghanaian drumming might be seen as "non-formal" in many ways, according to the broad definitions above.
2. From here when we refer to "playing" we also include singing, and when we refer to "musical instruments," we also include the voice as an instrument, unless the context demands specificity.
3. These include www.learnchoralmusic.co.uk/, www.choraline.com/ and many others. [accessed September 1, 2015].

## Core Reading

Finnegan, R. (1989). *The hidden musicians: Music-making in an English town*. Cambridge: Cambridge University Press.

Green, L. (2002). *How popular musicians learn*. Aldershot: Ashgate.

Smilde, R. (2012). Lifelong learning for professional musicians. In G. McPherson and G. Welch (Eds.), *The Oxford handbook of music education* (Vol. 2., pp. 289–302). Oxford: Oxford University Press.

Veblen, K. (2012). Adult music learning in formal, non-formal and informal contexts. In G. McPherson and G. Welch (Eds.), *The Oxford handbook of music education* (Vol. 2., pp. 243–256). Oxford: Oxford University Press.

## Further References

Becker, H. (1963). *Outsiders*. New York: The Free Press of Glenco.

Bennett, D. (2008). *Understanding the classical music profession: The past, the present and strategies for the future*. Aldershot, UK: Ashgate.

Bennett, E. E. (2012). A four-part model of informal learning: Extending Schugurensky's conceptual model. In J. Buban & D. Ramdeholl (Eds.), *Proceedings of the 53 Adult Education Research Conference May 31–June 3, 2012* (pp. 24–31). Saratoga Springs, NY: SUNY Empire State College. Retrieved April 10, 2016, from www.adulterc.org/proceedings/2012/papers/bennett.pdf

Bennett, H. S. (1980). *On becoming a rock musician.* Amherst, MA: University of Massachusetts Press.

Berliner, P. (1994). *Thinking in jazz: The infinite art of improvisation.* Chicago, IL: Chicago University Press.

Berry, D.C., & Dienes, Z. (1993). *Implicit learning: Theoretical and empirical issues.* Hove, UK: Lawrence Erlbaum Associates.

Chua S. L., & Ho H. P. (Eds.) (2013). *Connecting the stars: Essays on student-centric music education* (pp. 87–97). Singapore: Singapore Teachers' Academy for the Arts, Ministry of Education. Retrieved April 18, 2016, from www.star.moe.edu.sg/resources/star-research-repository

Cottrell, S. (2004). *Professional music-making in London.* Aldershot, UK: Ashgate.

D'Amore, A. (Ed.) (2011). *Musical futures: An approach to teaching and learning: Resource Pack, 2nd Edition.* London: Paul Hamlyn Foundation.

Eraut, M. (2000). Non-formal learning and tacit knowledge in professional work. *British Journal of Educational Psychology, 70,* 113–136.

Eraut, M. (2004). Informal learning in the workplace. *Studies in Continuing Education 26*(2), 247–273.

Folkestad, G. (2006). Formal and informal learning situations or practices versus formal and informal ways of hearing. *British Journal of Music Education, 23*(2), 135–145.

Green, L. (2008). *Music, informal learning and the school.* Aldershot, UK: Ashgate.

Green, L. (2014). *Hear, listen, play: How to free your students' aural, improvisation and performance skills.* New York, NY: Oxford University Press.

Grimmer, S. (2011). Continuity and change: The *guru-shishya* relationship in Karnatic classical music training. In L. Green (Ed.), *Learning, teaching and musical identity: Voices across cultures* (pp. 91–108). Bloomington, IN: Indiana University Press.

Jeanneret, N., McLennan, R., & Stevens-Ballenger, J. (2011). *Musical futures: An Australian perspective: Findings from a Victorian pilot study.* Melbourne: University of Melbourne.

Johansson, K. (2004). What chord was that? A study of strategies among ear players in rock music. *Research Studies in Music Education, 23,* 94–101.

Lebler, D. (2007). Student as master? Reflections on a learning innovation in popular music pedagogy. *International Journal of Music Education, 25*(3), 205–221.

McCarthy, M. (1999). *Passing it on: The transmission of music in Irish culture.* Cork, Ireland: Cork University Press.

McPherson, G. (1995). Five aspects of musical performance and their correlates. *Bulletin of the Council for Research in Music Education, 127,* 115–121.

McPherson, G., Bailey, M., & Sinclair, K. (1997). Path analysis of a theoretical model to describe the relationship among five types of musical performance. *Journal of Research in Music Education, 45*(1), 103–129.

McPherson, G., & Gabrielsson, A. (2002). From sound to sign. In R. Parncutt, & G. McPherson (Eds.), *The science and psychology of music performance: Creative strategies for teaching and learning* (pp. 99–116). New York, NY: Oxford University Press.

Merriam, S. B., Caffarella, R. S., & Baumgartner, L. M. (2009). *Learning in adulthood: A comprehensive guide* (3rd ed.). San Francisco, CA: Jossey-Bass.

Odam, G., & Bannan, N. (Eds.) (2005). *The Reflective conservatoire: Studies in music education.* Aldershot, UK: Ashgate.

O'Flynn, J. (2009). *The Irishness of Irish music.* Farnham, UK: Ashgate Press.

Reber, A. S. (1993). *Implicit learning and tacit knowledge: An essay on the cognitive unconscious.* New York, NY: Oxford University Press.

Rogers, R. (2002). *Creating a land with music: The work, education and training of professional musicians in the 21st century.* London: Youth Music.

Schugurensky, D. (2000). *The forms of informal learning: Towards a conceptualization of the field.* Toronto: Ontario Institute for Studies in Education of the University of Toronto

Smart, T., & Green, L. (in press). Informal learning and music performance. In J. Rink, H. Gaunt, & A. Willamon (Eds.), *Musicians in the making: Pathways to creative performance.* Oxford: Oxford University Press.

Smart, T. (unpub.). Unpublished interviews from PhD research. UCL Institute of Education.

Werquin, P. (2010). *Recognising non-formal and informal learning.* Paris: OECD.

Wright, R. (2011). Musical futures: A new approach to music education. *Canadian Music Educator, 53*(2), 19–21.

Wright, R., Younker, B. A., & Beynon, C. (Eds.) (2016). *21st century music education: Informal learning and non-formal teaching approaches in school and community contexts.* Research to practice: Vol. 7. S. A. O'Neill (Senior Editor). Waterloo, ON: Canadian Music Educators' Association.

# 36

# MUSIC AND SOCIAL COGNITION IN ADOLESCENCE

*Susan A. O'Neill*

## Introduction

The concept of *adolescence* is a familiar one, and, yet, the limits are expansive. There is no single way to characterize the many discursive constructions that shape what it means to be a *young person* growing up in today's complex, technological, and globalized world. From a research perspective adolescence tends to be considered a psychological and social transition period between late childhood and early adulthood. Individuals enter this phase of development having acquired social-cognitive abilities during childhood—ways of orienting, constructing, and understanding the social world they inhabit—based on everyday life experiences at home, school, and through the media. During adolescence, social relationships and identity development are particularly salient. As adolescents interact increasingly with others in different physical and virtual life spaces, they find themselves "facing the external world" and meeting "diverse views" about the thoughts and emotions that are considered "'reasonable,' 'appropriate,' or 'expected'" (Brizio, Gabbatore, Tirassa, & Bosco, 2015, p. 1).

Understanding the complex social world of adolescence requires an integrated approach to social cognition that is capable of addressing "real-world" issues in adolescents' everyday life experiences (Augoustinos, Walker, & Donaghue, 2014, p. 6). For example, over the past 15 years, researchers have focused increasing attention on the relationships young people have with music and what this can tell us about their social worlds. Music has been shown to be an influential medium in areas such as emotion and mood regulation, and peer-group affiliation. Add to this the digital landscape where adolescents engage increasingly in self-directed and collaborative music activities with an unprecedented amount of autonomy through the use of technological advances, information sharing, and social media. Of interest is how young people engage with music to enhance their sense of wellbeing. Another key concern of current research is the identification of what constrains and enables adolescents' choices and engagement in music activities within complex personal and social situations (O'Neill, 2017).

This chapter examines two main areas and several influential studies that shed light on the links between music and social cognition in adolescence: music listening and participation in organized music activities in everyday life, and the influence of music on emotion, mood regulation and socio-emotional communication. It begins with a brief overview of how social cognition has influenced our understanding of adolescence. This is followed by a discussion of the major developmental changes and challenges adolescents face as they embark on a key transition period into what is often referred to as emerging adulthood. Given that the present generation of the world's population has the largest number of 10 to 19 year olds in recorded history (1.2 billion or nearly a quarter of the world's population) (WHO, 2016), there is a sense of urgency in gaining a deeper understanding of adolescence in relation to multiple contexts of youth development and the transition to emerging adulthood. Add to this the notion that music is a prevalent activity in adolescents' everyday lives (North, Hargreaves, & O'Neill, 2000), and we gain a sense of the importance of research on the capacity of music to make a positive difference in the lives of young people.

## *Social Cognition in Adolescence*

Social cognition is the means through which adolescents make sense of themselves, others, and the world around them. The phrase "make sense of" is crucial in distinguishing social cognition from a mere behavioral focus and in shifting the emphasis to psychological approaches that are embedded within particular social contexts. Brizio and colleagues (2015) argue that the literature on social cognition in adolescence is "scarce and scattered" (p. 1) with few empirical studies and no unitary theoretical framework. They claim that adolescent development is best described as a "yet-to-be-understood mix of biological and cultural factors" (p. 1), which makes context-free studies impossible to devise when researchers attempt to explain how adolescents "experience and enact their social life" (p. 10). They suggest phenomenological approaches are needed and that these are best captured in narrative form as researchers attempt to understand the life events of adolescents within "the situated, embedded, embodied, autobiographically rich first person" (p. 1). Other approaches to social cognition in adolescence focus on dynamic models of human development and emphasize the importance of relations between people and their "real world" ecological settings for understanding variations that promote future options, opportunities and trajectories (Silbereisen & Lerner, 2007).

Social cognition also "functions as a form of acting and as a mediator of action and development" during social interactions where "individuals engage dialogically with other *persons* through the use of *mediational means*" (Mascolo & Margolis, 2004, p. 289, original emphasis). Mediational means include cultural tools such as music and dialogical or relational social interactions that take place within different sociocultural, economic, and educational contexts. These social interactions are interpreted through different lenses of cultural knowledge and social realities. As a result, the field of social cognition in adolescence has become increasingly diversified and complex. In particular, adolescents' "everyday life" experiences combined with cultural factors have expanded the contemporary research landscape. Researchers in social cognition and related areas of psychology are uniquely placed among diverse academic perspectives "to advance understanding of the integrated biopsychosocial nature of humans and how they manage and shape the everyday world around them" (Bandura, 2001, p. 18). However, a key criticism associated with the majority of research and theory in social cognition is that it is "driven by an overwhelmingly individualistic orientation that forgets that the contents of cognition originate in social life, in human interaction and communication" (Augoustinos et al., 2014, p. 7). Although there appears to be a changing landscape of theorizing and research in adolescent social cognition, there is still much work to be done to encourage researchers, including those with interests in music-related areas, to examine aspects of adolescence as a dynamic and context-dependent process whereby individuals are continually engaged in a process of making sense of how they experience and enact their social life.

As this chapter unfolds, we will consider how music-related research has contributed to a changing research landscape. We will explore how various social cognition perspectives have advanced our understanding of how adolescents draw on music to negotiate aspects of their everyday life, such as regulating their mood, coping with personal challenges, identifying with and evaluating themselves in relation to others, and creating an identity and making an external impression on others.

### *Transitions to Adolescence and Emerging Adulthood*

Adolescence is considered a transitional period between childhood and adulthood with two major transitional phases. The beginning of adolescence is associated with puberty as a complex biological transition. There has been much research devoted to maturational changes associated with the onset of puberty and increased levels of distress during the transition to early adolescence as well as impacts on social and emotional well-being (Sawyer et al., 2012). The second transitional phase is from late adolescence to early adulthood or what is often referred to as emerging adulthood. Both of these transitional phases may take on different meanings depending on the groups and society in which individuals live (Brizio et al., 2015).

Due to increased fragmentation, mobility, and uncertainty in the world today, adolescents face considerable developmental changes and challenges in what Larson (2011) refers to as "coming of age in a disorderly world" (p. 330). As adolescents prepare to embark on emerging adulthood, they are "setting the stage for continued development through the life span as individuals begin to make choices and engage in a variety of activities that are influential on the rest of their lives" (Zarrett & Eccles, 2006, p. 13). During this transitional phase, which often coincides with the completion of compulsory schooling, adolescents move into a period marked by decisions that include "education or vocational training, entry into and transitions within the labor market, moving out of the family home, and sometimes marriage and parenthood" (p. 13). The transition to emerging adulthood is also marked by increased independence and greater responsibility as young people take a more active role in their own life course.

Some attention has been given to how adolescent music learners negotiate the transition to young adulthood (Davidson & Faulkner, 2016; Evans & McPherson, 2016). Much of this work focuses on changes in adolescent identity development drawing on an Eriksonian (Erikson, 1986) view of identity formation and extensions of this work by Marcia (1980). A key finding from this approach is that "adolescence involves a process of continually exploring various identities, and making decisions and commitments to those in which one identifies" (Evans & McPherson, 2016, p. 215).

This chapter continues by examining two main areas and several influential studies that shed light on the links between music and social cognition in adolescence: music listening and participation in organized music activities in everyday life, and the influence of music on emotion, mood regulation and well-being.

## Adolescents and Music in Everyday Life

Music is ubiquitous in adolescents' everyday lives; it enables them to portray an "image" of themselves to the outside world and satisfy emotional needs (North et al., 2000). In considering the influence of music in how adolescents manage and shape their everyday lives, studies at the end of the 1990s began to explore the reasons for adolescents' music consumption (Zillmann & Gan, 1997). As Boekhoven (2016) explains, music was found to assist adolescents in many aspects of their lives such as communication, connection, representation, comfort, identity and rebellion (Campbell Connell, & Beegle, 2007). Earlier research helped to establish links between social factors and everyday life experiences of music with psychosocial development and adolescent identity (Larson, 1995). Participation in music activities was also found to support identity exploration, personal goals, agency and self-determination (Denny, 2007). Although many adolescents engage in both playing and listening to music, the trajectories of these activities are divergent. Time spent listening to music tends to increase during the adolescent years, while interest in music as a subject at school tends to decline (McPherson & O'Neill, 2010).

In the sections that follow, three key features of adolescents' experience of music in their everyday lives will be considered: music preferences, musician role models, and music participation in organized activities. Each of these music-related activities offer different perspectives on understanding the capacity of music to make a difference in the lives of young people.

### *Music Preferences*

Music preferences reflect and shape young people's values, conflicts, and development (Schwartz & Fouts, 2003). Friendships based on shared musical tastes are particularly important during adolescence (O'Neill, 2005). In considering the importance of music preferences, several previous studies employed the uses and gratification approach (Rubin, 1994)—a theory developed to explain how and why people make different media choices depending on personal characteristics and needs. For example, adolescents tend to gravitate toward particular kinds of music based on personality characteristics, issues, and/or needs that are either reflected in the music they choose or that the music satisfies (see Bosacki & O'Neill, 2012). Adolescents' music preferences have been found to be related to issues of identity, dependence–independence, and separateness–connection (Avery, 1979; Mainprize, 1985); values, images, beliefs, and identifications (Arnett, 1995; Larson, 1995). Steele and Browne's (1995) "media practice model" for adolescents incorporates identity, music selection, and social interaction to describe the nature of their involvement with media that, in turn, shapes their sense of themselves. Lull (1987) concluded, "young people use music to resist authority at all levels, assert their personalities, develop peer relationships and romantic entanglements, and learn about things that their parents and the schools aren't telling them" (p. 152).

The effects of shared music preferences on intergroup bias in adolescence were the focus of a study of 97 adolescents in England (Bakagiannis & Tarrant, 2006). Drawing on social identity theory, the researchers assigned participants to one of two social groups that were told had similar or different music preferences compared to a control group who were not told anything about the music preferences of the groups. Next, participants completed measures designed to assess their perceptions of the ingroup and outgroup (by rating trait adjectives referred to as an intergroup discrimination measure) and to rate how their group was perceived by the outgroup (referred to as a meta-stereotyping measure). The results indicated that when participants perceived that the ingroup and outgroup had similar music preferences, there were lower levels of intergroup discrimination. The authors concluded that "adolescents' preferences that their own groups and outgroups have similar musical preferences can facilitate the development of positive intergroup relations" (Bakagiannis & Tarrant, 2006, p. 134). In other words, it appears that music preferences can indeed bring adolescents together.

Research also indicates that music listening preferences can be a resource for adolescents' self-evaluations. In a study by Kistler and colleagues (2010), social cognitive theory was used to interpret the pathways between early adolescents' music media consumption and three domains of self-concept (physical appearance, romantic appeal, and global self-worth). SCT suggests that adolescents are "likely to remember and create mental representations of (i.e., retain) music media images when they connect personal meaning to them" (Kistler et al., 2010, p. 617). Since media portrayal of music artists tends to depict them "as powerful, attractive, or successful" (p. 618), adolescents' "self-appraisals against the norms projected through music media" may influence their self-concepts. The findings indicated a mediational model whereby higher consumption of music media was associated with "perceiving one's self as less physically attractive (i.e., having less competency in the physical appearance domain) and having a lower overall opinion of one's self (global self-worth)" (p. 627). According to the authors, the results suggest "that through involvement processes with music media characters, adolescents may use music media as a venue for social comparison against which they evaluate their own physical attractiveness and self-worth" (p. 616). This notion of identity and social comparison is explored further in the next section on adolescents' identification of musician role models.

### Musician Role Models

Role models play a large part in adolescents' understanding of themselves and the social and media worlds in which they live. In the 1990s, research demonstrated that adolescents tend to identify celebrities as their role models rather than non-famous people (Bromnick & Swallow, 1999; Duck, 1990). Role models were defined as "adults who are worthy of imitation in some area of life" (Pleiss & Feldhusen, 1995, p. 163) or as "someone to look up to and base your character, values or aspirations on" (Gauntlett, 2002, p. 211). And yet, even if adolescents admire the same role model, they might vary in the extent to which they expect or aspire to become similar to that particular person.

In a study of adolescents' choice of musician role models, we asked 381 adolescents (aged 13–14 years) to identify the musicians they admired the most and the reasons why (Ivaldi & O'Neill, 2008). Our findings indicated that the majority of adolescents identified famous figures as role models and most of these were male singers of popular music styles. The three main reasons adolescents gave for admiring a role model were dedication, popular image, and ability. The adolescents also mentioned that whether or not the role model played a musical instrument was of little importance when identifying a famous musician. We concluded that high levels of media exposure experienced by adolescents is likely to influence their preferences not only for musical styles but also for the musician role models that they admire.

In a follow-up based on this study, we drew on social identity theory to examine how adolescents talked about musician role models during focus groups (Ivaldi & O'Neill, 2008).

Through their talk, we found that adolescents constructed and negotiated a complex understanding of musical subcultures, whereby high levels of expertise and success were perceived within the notion of privilege. For example, when discussing a photo of one young classical musician, one adolescent participant said "he just looks like rich and posh and got whatever he wanted" and another replied "because if you're playing the cello when you're six it just seems like you know, you're really posh." The adolescents talked about being "posh" as an undesirable characteristic that is an inevitable consequence of having money and high social status. These findings suggest that adolescents' perceptions of privilege may act as a barrier or constraint to their exploration of alternative conceptualizations of musical expertise and success, thereby limiting their own musical potential. We concluded with a call for further research to explore practical ways to assist young people in critical reflections about what it means to be a musician to assist them in overcoming possible barriers or constraints to their own musical aspirations.

## *Music Participation in Organized Activities*

Music is a commonly chosen organized or extracurricular activity that is associated with numerous positive personal and social benefits to adolescents including the development of music and performance skills, opportunities to develop discipline and commitment, increased communication, connections and cooperation with peers and adults, enhanced creativity, and increased initiative and perseverance in the face of challenges (Boekhoven, 2016). Organized activities are characterized by "structure, adult supervision, and an emphasis on skill-building" and are "generally voluntary, have regular and scheduled meetings, maintain developmentally based expectations and rules for participants, offer supervision and guidance from adults, and are organized around developing particular skills and achieving goals" (Mahoney, Larson, Eccles, & Lord, 2005, p. 4).

One approach to participation in organized activities that has gained increasing momentum over the past two decades in developmental psychology draws on the concept of positive youth development (PYD) (Seligman & Csikszentmihalyi, 2000). PYD offers an alternative approach to previous deficit-based models of adolescence by emphasizing instead the "manifest potentialities rather than the incapacities of young people" (Damon, 2004, p. 15). Past PYD research has focused on the outcomes of adolescents' participation in extracurricular activities such as music (Fredricks et al., 2002). For many young people, music participation is the most favored leisure activity (Lonsdale & North, 2011) and is associated with both personal and social benefits such as opportunities for young people to define and express their identity (O'Neill, 2002; O'Neill, Ivaldi & Fox, 2002). For example, wearing a band or choir jacket during high school is often a source of pride that symbolizes identification and belonging for many young people (O'Neill, 2005). Other benefits include emotional understanding, development of life-skills, and increased social skills (Barrett & Bond, 2015).

In this section, we examined the relationships young people have with music and what this can tell us about their social worlds. We gained some insights into what constrains and enables adolescents' choices and engagement in music activities within complex personal and social situations. In the next section, we examine the capacity of music as an influential medium in areas such as emotion and mood regulation, and as a coping strategy that influences adolescents' sense of well-being.

## Emotion, Mood Regulation and Socio-Emotional Communication

A growing corpus of research suggests that adolescents use music purposefully to express and regulate their emotions (Miranda & Claes, 2009; Saarikallio, Vuoskoski, & Luck, 2014), and that emotion-related abilities and competencies, such as emotion recognition and empathy, are key factors in adolescents' development of social communication and well-being. According to MacDonald (2013), everyday uses of music "may be uniquely suited to managing or regulating emotions and stress in everyday life since it has the capacity to both distract and engage listeners in a variety of ways" (p. 4). Well-being tends to be broadly defined in most studies of music and adolescents and tends to refer to positive psychological functioning and experience. In youth development research, four concepts of wellbeing are especially prominent: life satisfaction, positive affect, confidence, and future orientation (Jose, Ryan, & Pryor, 2012). Music-related research has tended to focus on the positive affect of music in everyday life for monitoring the self and mood maintenance "as a form of psychological self-help" (MacDonald, 2013, p. 4). Music is second only to exercise in being the most commonly used mood regulation strategy among young people (Thayer, Newman, & McClain, 1994).

### *Emotion and Mood Regulation*

In a noteworthy study, Saarikallio and Erkkilä (2007) explored the role of music in adolescents' mood regulation in an in-depth qualitative research study of eight adolescents. The authors focused on the concept of mood regulation rather than emotion regulation arguing that "moods are generally differentiated from emotions by their longer duration and lack of specific cause" (p. 89). Mood regulation was thought to be linked more to music experiences in everyday life by "regulating undifferentiated mood states and subjective experiences rather than regulating behaviour, or specific emotional responses to specific events" (p. 90). Participants were divided into two groups and attended two interview sessions, one week apart, where their music activities, preferences, and experience were discussed. During the intervening week, participants were asked to complete a form each time they engaged in a music activity to describe the affective experience (pleasantness and energy level) and reflect on the affective experience. The findings indicated seven processes of mood regulatory strategies. These were: entertainment, revival, strong sensation, diversion, discharge, mental work, and solace. Engaging in music activities to increase positive moods was particularly salient and the authors proposed that the "pleasures of musical experiences may produce a sense of well-being, stability, wholeness and purpose in life" (p. 104). According to one young female in the study, "If you're in a terribly depressed mood, then, in my view, it's much nicer to start listening to something uplifting" (p. 99).

### *Coping and Socio-Emotional Communication*

To investigate further music as a coping resource in adolescence, Miranda and colleagues (2010) followed 336 adolescents over a six-month period to examine whether three styles of coping by music listening (emotion oriented, problem oriented, and avoidance/disengagement oriented—based on a measure developed by Miranda and Claes, 2009), could predict changes in levels of neuroticism (based on an eight-item measure). The results indicated a modest short-term effect of coping by music listening as a predictor of neuroticism in both a positive (adaptive/protective factor) and negative (maladaptive/risk factor) direction. Specifically, problem-oriented coping predicted lower neuroticism in adolescents who were high in neuroticism (at baseline) and low in avoidance-oriented coping. In contrast, adolescents who were high in neuroticism (at base-line) and showed high avoidance-oriented coping, predicted higher levels of neuroticism. The results are intriguing as they indicate a complex interplay of mediating and moderating factors in considering how adolescents use and respond to music as a coping strategy and pressing need for future research in this area.

In a preliminary study considering the link between musical behavior and adolescents' social-emotional communication, Saarikallio and colleagues (2014) investigated emotion perception and expression on music-related tasks and self-report measures of empathy and externalized behaviors (conduct problems) among 61, 14-year-olds in Finland. Participants were asked to listen to 50 music excerpts and rate emotion words on a 7-point scale for each. The musical task was designed to measure the ability to accurately recognize emotions expressed by music. The authors emphasized the importance of choosing stimuli "that could be considered indisputably expressive of the intended emotion" (p. 6). They reported choosing carefully five basic emotions used most in music research: happiness, sadness, anger, fear, and tenderness. The results suggest that sensitivity to music may provide an indicator of broader socio-emotional communication abilities. Perspective taking (the cognitive component of empathy) was related to the accurate recognition of tenderness in music and the expression of anger. Empathic concern (the affective component of empathy) was related to a general tendency to perceive fear in the music and to music expressing sadness (with slow tempo) and anger (with loud volume). Conduct problems (features relating to psychological maladjustment) were associated with participants' recognition of incongruent (opposing) patterns (dull timbre for anger and staccato articulation for sadness). Despite the support for their hypotheses, the authors call for caution in interpreting the results as more studies are needed to understand these links as well as other emotional-related competencies. The authors concluded that, "the results preliminarily support the idea of using musical behavior as an indicator of the broader socio-emotional communication abilities, which in turn play a major role in adolescent adjustment and wellbeing" (p. 1).

Although more research is needed, there is growing evidence that music can be used "to enhance relationships, immerse in emotions, modify emotions and modify cognitions in young people" (Papinczak, Dingle, Stoyanov, Hides, & Zelenko, 2015, p. 1131). However, the complex findings by Miranda et al. (2010) also remind us that music may not be beneficial for all adolescents in all situations. More research is needed to increase our understanding of the links between music, emotion and mood regulation and coping strategies and the extent to which music provides a protective factor or benefits the well-being of emerging adults within the context of their everyday lives.

## Conclusion

Drawing on a range of influential studies that shed light on links between music and social cognition in adolescence, this chapter provides an overview of current thinking about how adolescents draw on music to negotiate aspects of their everyday life, such as regulating their mood, coping with personal challenges, and evaluating themselves in relation to others. Findings of studies reviewed here suggest how music shapes the ways young people orient, construct, negotiate, and understand themselves and the social world they inhabit. We saw in this chapter how music preferences and musician role models can serve as symbolic representations of what matters to young people as they use music to communicate their values, attitudes and opinions to others. We also saw how increased media consumption among adolescents can impact negatively on their perceptions of themselves and others, for example resulting in lower self-evaluations of their attractiveness and self-worth. As well as music serving as a vehicle for self-expression, adolescents also use music in their private lives to help them reflect on thoughts and emotions and to accompany various moods and activities. And, as a commonly chosen extracurricular or organized activity, music participation brings positive personal and social benefits to adolescents.

The key role that music plays in the lives of adolescents may serve important functions during this transitional phase of their development when social relationships and identity development are especially salient. Advancing our understanding of the role of music in the lives of adolescents appears to be moving towards an increasingly integrated perspective whereby social cognition research examines the thoughts, feelings, and behaviors of individuals within different life places and spaces.

Beyond considerations of identity formation and self-determination, few theoretical approaches provide insights into the affordances and constraints that young people experience as they encounter music across different activities and resources, with different companions, and in different places and spaces over time. There is a need for future research examining the trajectories of relationships and outcomes in adolescence and situations where young people's changing lives and a changing society converge with important implications for their musical development. There is also a need for research focused on interventions that might assist young people in understanding media influences on their beliefs about themselves and others, perhaps involving techniques such as critical reflection and cognitive reappraisal. According to Papinczak et al. (2015), "music provides one way through which young people could be taught to regulate their emotions to enhance well-being." (p. 1131). Within the dynamics of person-environment relations, transitions to adolescence and young adulthood are impacted in ways that are likely to create musical opportunities for some and barriers and constraints for others. Since music is a resource that serves a variety of functions in the everyday lives of adolescents, future research is likely to benefit from a consideration of music as both constitutive and functional in how adolescents experience and understand themselves in their social world.

## Core Reading

Kistler, M., Boyce Rogers, K., Power, T., Weintraub Austin, E., & Griner Hill, L. (2010). Adolescents and music media: Toward an involvement-mediational model of consumption and self-concept. *Journal of Research on Adolescence, 20*(3), 616–630.

Saarikallio, S., Vuoskoski, J., & Luck, G. (2014). Adolescents' expression and perception of emotion in music reflects their broader abilities of emotional communication. *Psychology of Well-Being: Theory, Research and Practice, 4*, 21. doi: 10.1186/s13612-014-0021-8

## Further References

Arnett, J. J. (1995). Adolescents' uses of media for self-socialization. *Journal of Youth and Adolescence, 7*, 313–331.

Augoustinos, M., Walker, I., & Donaghue, N. (2014). *Social cognition: An integrated introduction,* 3rd edn. Los Angeles, CA: Sage.

Avery, R. (1979). Adolescents' use of the mass media. *American Behavioral Science, 23,* 53–70.

Bakagiannis, S., & Tarrant, M. (2006). Can music bring people together? Effects of shared musical preference on intergroup bias in adolescence. *Scandinavian Journal of Psychology, 47,* 129–136.

Barrett, M.S., & Bond, N. (2015). Connecting through music: The contribution of a music programme to fostering positive youth development. *Research Studies in Music Education, 37*(1), 37–54.

Boekhoven, B. (2016). *The relation between adolescents' music activity participation and character development.* Unpublished Doctoral Dissertation, Carleton University, Ottawa, Canada.

Bosacki, S.L., & O'Neill, S.A. (2012). Youth culture, personal identity, relationships and emotional competence in adolescents: Implications for music learning. In S.A. O'Neill (Series Ed. & Vol. Ed.), *Research to practice:Vol. 5. Personhood and music learning: Connecting perspectives and narratives* (pp. 135–152). Waterloo, ON: Canadian Music Educators' Association.

Brizio A., Gabbatore I., Tirassa M., & Bosco F. M. (2015). "No more a child, not yet an adult": Studying social cognition in adolescence. *Frontiers in Psychology, 6,* 1011. doi: 10.3389/fpsyg.2015.01011

Bromnick, R.D., & Swallow, B.L. (1999). I like being who I am: A study of young people's ideals. *Educational Studies, 25,* 117–129.

Campbell, P.S., Connell, C., & Beegle, A. (2007). Adolescents' expressed meanings of music in and out of school. *Journal of Research in Music Education, 55*(3), 220–236.

Damon, W. (2004). What is positive youth development? *The Annals of the American Academy of Political and Social Science, 591,* 13–24.

Davidson, J., & Faulkner, R. (2016). The transition from adolescent to adult music learner. In G. McPherson (Ed.), *The child as musician: A handbook of musical development* (2nd ed., pp. 626–638). New York, NY: Oxford University Press.

Denny, E. (2007). To what extent does participation in extracurricular music affect the future aspirations of 11–12 year olds? A small scale investigation. *British Journal of Music Education, 24*(1), 99–115.

Duck, J.M. (1990). Children's ideals: The role of real-life versus media figures. *Australian Journal of Psychology, 42,* 19–29.

Erikson, E.H. (1986). *Identity, youth, and crisis.* New York, NY: Norton.

Evans, P., & McPherson, G.E. (2016). Process of musical identity consolidation during adolescence. In R. MacDonald, D.J. Hargreaves, & D. Miell (Eds.), *Oxford handbook of musical identities* (pp. 213–231). New York, NY: Oxford University Press.

Fredricks, J.A., Alfield-Liro, C., Hruda, L.Z., Eccles, J.S., Patrick, H., & Ryan, A.M. (2002). A qualitative exploration of adolescents' commitment to athletics and the arts. *Journal of Adolescent Research, 17*(1), 68–97.

Gauntlett, D. (2002). *Media, gender and identity.* London: Routledge.

Hargreaves, D.J., & North, A.C. (1999). The functions of music in everyday life: Redefining the social in music psychology. *Psychology of Music, 27*(1), 71–83.

Ivaldi, A., & O'Neill, S.A. (2008). Adolescents' musical role models: Whom do they admire and why? *Psychology of Music, 36*(4), 395–415.

Jose, P.E., Ryan, N., & Pryor, J. (2012). Does social connectedness promote a greater sense of well-being in adolescence over time? *Journal of Research on Adolescence, 22*(2) 235–251.

Larson, R. (1995). Secrets in the bedroom: Adolescents' private use of media. *Journal of Youth and Adolescence, 24*(5), 535–550.

Larson, R.W. (2011). Positive development in a disorderly world. *Journal of Research on Adolescence, 21*(2), 317–334.

Londsdale, A.J., & North, A.C. (2011). Why do we listen to music? A uses and gratification analysis. *British Journal of Psychology, 102*(1), 108–134.

Lull, J. (1987). Listeners' communicative uses of popular music. In J. Lull (Ed.), *Popular music and communication* (pp. 140–174). Newbury Park, CA: Sage.

MacDonald, R. (2013). Music, health, and well-being: A review. *International Journal of Qualitative Studies on Health and Well-being, 8,* 20635. doi: 10.3402/qhw.v8i0.20635.

Mahoney, J. L., Larson, R. W., Eccles, J. S., & Lord, H. (2005). Organized activities as developmental contexts for children and adolescents. In J. L. Mahoney, R. Larson, & J. S. Eccles (Eds.), *Organized activities as contexts of development: Extracurricular activities, after school and community programs* (pp. 3–22). Mahwah, NY: Lawrence Erlbaum Associates.

Mainprize, S. (1985). Interpreting adolescents' music. *Journal of Child Care, 2,* 55–62.

Marcia, J. E. (1980). Identity in adolescence. In J. Adelson (Ed.), *Handbook of adolescent psychology* (pp. 159–187). New York, NY: Wiley.

Mascolo, M. F., & Margolis, D. (2004). Social cognition as a mediator of adolescent development: A coactive systems approach. *European Journal of Developmental Psychology, 1*(4), 289–302.

McPherson, G. E., & O'Neill, S. A. (2010). Students' motivation to study music as compared to other school subjects: A comparison of eight countries. *Research Studies in Music Education, 32*(2), 1–37.

Miranda, D, Gaudreau, P., & Morizot, J. (2010). Blue notes: Coping by music listening predicts neuroticism changes in adolescence. *Psychology of Aesthetics, Creativity, and the Arts, 4*(4), 247–253.

Miranda, D., & Claes, M. (2009). Music listening, coping, peer affiliation and depression in adolescence. *Psychology of Music, 37,* 215–233.

North, A. C., Hargreaves, D. J., & O'Neill, S. A. (2000). The importance of music to adolescents. *British Journal of Educational Psychology, 70,* 255–272.

O'Neill, S. A. (2002). The self-identity of young musicians. In R. A. R. MacDonald, D. J. Hargreaves, & D. Miell (Eds.), *Musical identities* (pp. 79–96). Oxford: Oxford University Press.

O'Neill, S. A. (2005). Youth music engagement in diverse contexts. In J. L. Mahoney, R. Larson, & J. S. Eccles (Eds.), *Organized activities as contexts of development: Extracurricular activities, after school and community programs* (pp. 255–273). Mahwah, NY: Lawrence Erlbaum Associates.

O'Neill, S. A. (2017). Young people's musical lives: Learning ecologies, identities, and connectedness. In R. MacDonald, D. J. Hargreaves, & D. Miell (Eds.), *Handbook of musical identities* (pp. 79–104). New York, NY: Oxford University Press.

O'Neill, S. A., Ivaldi, A., & Fox, C. (2002). Exploring the identity and subjectivity of "talented" adolescent girls. *Feminism and Psychology, 12*(2), 153–159.

Papinczak, Z. E., Dingle, G. A., Stoyanov, S. R., Hides, L., & Zelenko, O. (2015). Young people's uses of music for well-being. *Journal of Youth Studies, 18*(9), 1119–1134.

Pleiss, M., & Feldhusen, J. (1995). Mentors, role models and heroes in the lives of gifted children. *Educational Psychologist, 30,* 159–169.

Rubin, A. M. (1994). Media uses and effects: A uses-and-gratifications perspective. In J. Bryant, & D. Zillman (Eds.), *Media effects: Advances in theory and research* (pp. 417–436). Hillsdale, NJ: Erlbaum.

Saarikallio, S., & Erkkilä, J. (2007). The role of music in adolescents' mood regulation. *Psychology of Music, 35*(1), 88–109.

Sawyer, S. M., Afifi, R. A., Bearinger, L. H., Blackmore, S. J., Dick, B., Ezeh, A. C., et al. (2012). Adolescence: A foundation for future health. *Lancet, 379,* 1630–1640.

Schwartz, K. D., & Fouts, G. T. (2003). Music preferences, personality style, and developmental issues of adolescents. *Journal of Youth and Adolescence, 32*(3), 205–213.

Seligman, M. E. P., & Csikszentmihalyi, M. (2000). Positive psychology: An introduction. *American Psychologist, 55*(1), 5–14.

Silbereisen, R. K., & Lerner, R. M. (Eds.) (2007). *Approaches to positive youth development.* New York, NY: Sage.

Steele, J. R., & Browne, J. D. (1995). Adolescent room culture: Studying the media in the context of everyday life. *Journal of Youth and Adolescence, 24*(5), 551–576.

Thayer, R. E., Newman, R., & McClain, T. M. (1994). Self-regulation of mood: Strategies for changing a bad mood, raising energy, and reducing tension. *Journal of Personality and Social Psychology, 67*(5) 910–925.

World Health Organization (WHO) (2016). *Adolescents: Health risks and solutions.* [Fact Sheet No. 345]. www.who.int/mediacentre/factsheets/fs345/en/

Zarrett, N., & Eccles, J. (2006). The passage to adulthood: Challenges of late adolescence. *New Directions for Youth Development, 111*, 13–28. doi: 10.1002/yd.179

Zillmann, D., & Gan, S. (1997). Musical taste in adolescence. In D. J. Hargreaves, & A. C. North (Eds), *The social psychology of music* (pp. 61–87). Oxford: Oxford University Press.

# 37

# MUSICAL PREFERENCE
## Personality, Style, and Music Use

*Jonna K. Vuoskoski*

## Introduction

Liking or disliking a piece of music is perhaps our most common affective response to music (e.g., Brattico & Jacobsen, 2009). But why do we like the music that we like? Although certain general features of music—such as its familiarity and complexity—can be used to explain why we like or dislike certain pieces of music, our music preferences are largely shaped by our social and cultural surroundings. Consistent with the idea that individual differences are inherent to matters of taste, music preferences tend to vary greatly from one individual to the next. In fact, it is a commonly held belief that an individual's music preferences can reveal salient information about their personality to others (Rentfrow & Gosling, 2003). Indeed, empirical findings have established that there is a consistent pattern of correlations between our personality dispositions and the kinds of music we enjoy listening to. Different personality traits are associated with different emotional, social, and cognitive needs and motives (e.g., Olson & Weber, 2004). Importantly, music listening has the ability to fulfill a wide variety of functions in everyday life (e.g., Sloboda, O'Neill, & Ivaldi, 2001; North, Hargreaves, & Hargreaves, 2004), and consequently it has been postulated that people may enjoy listening to the kinds of music that best help them to fulfill their psychological needs (e.g., Chamorro-Premuzic, Fagan, & Furnham, 2010). Taken together, music can function to both reflect and reinforce aspects of people's personalities, self-views, and values. In this chapter, I will first outline some general principles and theories that have been proposed to account for listeners' liking and disliking responses to music. I will then introduce some key concepts from personality psychology before proceeding to explore the contribution of personality traits to music preferences in more detail.

## Complexity, Familiarity, and "Arousal Potential"

Certain general principals and patterns can be found in listeners' liking and disliking responses to music. The influential theory by Berlyne (1971) applied a psychobiological approach to aesthetics, emphasizing the role of "arousal potential" in liking/disliking responses to artistic stimuli such as music. Music's "arousal potential" is positively associated with features such as tempo, volume, and complexity, and negatively associated with familiarity. In other words, music that is fast, loud, unfamiliar, surprising, and complex has more arousal potential than music that is slow, soft, familiar, simple, and predictable. According to Berlyne, there is an inverted-U relationship between arousal potential and liking. Thus, music with an intermediate degree of arousal potential is liked best, while music with very high or very low arousal potential is disliked. Indeed, empirical studies have repeatedly found inverted-U relationships between musical complexity and liking (e.g., McMullen, 1974; for a review, see Hargreaves, 1986), most recently by Witek and colleagues (2014), who discovered that drum breaks with an intermediate degree of syncopation were liked best and evoked "groove" more effectively than drum breaks with a high or low degree of syncopation. However, the point of "optimal" arousal potential may be partly dependent on the situation; in high-arousal situations, for example, more low-arousal music may be preferred (and high-arousal music in low-arousal situations) in order to achieve an overall state of moderate arousal (for a review, see Konečni, 1982).

It has also been argued that mere repeated exposure to a stimulus (such as music) will increase liking (Zajonc, 1968). However, as familiarity is inversely associated with music's arousal potential, it could be expected that—once the level of optimal arousal potential has been reached—further repetitions would lead to a decline in liking. Indeed, empirical studies have provided evidence for both a positive and an inverted-U relationship between familiarity and liking (e.g., Hargreaves, 1986), showing that overexposure to a piece of music will eventually lead to a decrease in liking (Hunter & Schellenberg, 2011). This initial positive relationship between exposure and liking helps to illustrate how our musical environment shapes our music preferences. For example, when a new song gets played on the radio we may start liking it merely because of repeated exposure. However, repeated exposure might lead to a decline in liking once the peak level of preference has been reached.

North and Hargreaves (2008) have argued for the need to distinguish between objective and subjective complexity of music. Objective complexity can be viewed as a feature of the music itself, and is influenced by factors such as variability, predictability, and event density. However, subjective complexity refers to the degree of complexity perceived by the *listener*. Most importantly, this subjective complexity can be reduced through repeated exposure. Once a piece of music becomes familiar to a listener, it will appear more predictable and less surprising, and thus has less subjective arousal potential. According to this view, musical pieces with high objective complexity will require more repetitions in order to achieve an optimal arousal potential, while liking for pieces with low objective complexity will start to decrease already after a few repetitions (North & Hargreaves, 2008).

Although there may indeed exist an interaction between music's complexity and familiarity with regard to liking and arousal potential, this relationship is probably more complex in real life. One significant feature of some of the most pleasurable experiences evoked by music (such as chills or shivers down the spine) is that they are typically elicited by familiar music. In fact, neuroimaging studies have shown that anticipation of the specific pleasure-evoking passages plays an important role in these responses (Salimpoor et al., 2011). Interestingly, the musical passages that evoke pleasurable chills often contain a sudden or unprepared change, such as the entry of one or more instruments or voices, the return of a melody or theme, an abrupt change in tempo or rhythm, a new or unprepared harmony, abrupt modulation, or a sudden change of texture (Panksepp, 1995). In other words, pleasure-evoking musical passages are characterized by a sudden, significant change that the listener has learned to anticipate and predict through repeated listening. It has been hypothesized that—since accurate prediction is a beneficial ability from an evolutionary perspective—our brains may have developed special structures that reward accurate prediction (Huron, 2006; Granot, this volume). It may also be that familiarity and anticipation reduce the arousal potential of sudden and surprising musical events to an optimal level, leading overall to a pleasurable experience.

In sum, although factors such as complexity and familiarity can be used to explain broad trends in people's liking and disliking responses to musical stimuli, the defining aspect of music preferences is one of inter-individual variability. Thus, the next section will proceed to examine some of the variables consistently associated with this inter-individual variability.

## Individual Differences in Music Preferences

Although individual differences in music preferences have attracted research interest since the 1950's (e.g., Cattell, & Saunders, 1954), the number of studies focused on the topic has increased rapidly during the last two decades. Understanding which factors contribute to music preferences—and how—can help us understand why different people enjoy listening to different kinds of music, and what kinds of psychological functions music helps to serve in people's daily lives. Music preferences are a complex phenomenon that emerges from an interaction between an individual's personality characteristics and their social and cultural environment. Our musical environments and past listening experiences contribute significantly to the development of our music preferences, but there is also an important social element to the process. Shared musical taste plays an important role in the membership of groups and subcultures, and adolescents in particular often use music as a "badge" to communicate their values, attitudes, and opinions to others (e.g., North & Hargreaves, 2008). Moreover, adolescence and early adulthood appear to be critical periods for the formation of music preferences, affecting the preferred styles of music in later adulthood. A study by Holbrook and Schindler (1989) illustrates this by showing that participants (aged 16–86; mean age 54.3) most preferred musical pieces that were popular when they were young adults, peaking at 23.5 years.

Empirical work has shown that people often use their music preferences to communicate information about their personalities to strangers (Rentfrow & Gosling, 2006). Individuals can also use music to reaffirm their own identity, selecting musical styles that reinforce their self-views or remind them of who they were at a certain moment in time (DeNora, 1999). Furthermore, it appears that music preferences do in fact communicate salient information about people's personalities to others, as observers are surprisingly accurate in judging targets' personality traits based on their favorite music (Rentfrow & Gosling, 2006). But what are the overall correspondences between music preferences and personality traits, and how do they fit together with personality theory?

### *Personality*

Individuals differ from each other in terms of their patterns of thought, emotions, and behavior. Personality traits—understood as dispositions to behave in a particular way in a range of situations—are one way of describing, conceptualizing, and measuring individual differences in human functioning. In everyday language, hundreds of trait descriptors such as shy, friendly, or assertive are used to describe an individual's personality. Based on the premise that the most salient individual differences will become encoded as single words in language, these types of everyday trait words have been used as the basis for constructing broader personality factors (e.g., McCrae & Costa, 1987). Different types of traits and trait structures have been suggested throughout the 20th century, but during the recent decades an increasing consensus has emerged regarding the Five-Factor Model of personality (also known as the "Big Five"; see John, Naumann, & Soto, 2008). The five broad personality factors included in the model are Extraversion, Neuroticism, Agreeableness, Conscientiousness, and Openness to Experience.

Extraversion can be defined as a tendency to be outgoing, sociable, assertive, energetic, and enthusiastic (John et al., 2008). In more biological approaches to personality traits (e.g., Eysenck, 1967), Extraversion is also associated with sensitivity to arousal and stimulation. Those scoring low in Extraversion (i.e., introverts) are thought to have a lower threshold for arousal than those scoring high, and to react with greater responsiveness to external stimulation (Eysenck, 1967). This also means that extraverts require a higher degree of stimulation in order to reach an optimal arousal level, while introverts perform better under lower stimulation. While Extraversion is commonly associated with positive emotionality, Neuroticism, on the other hand, is understood as the tendency to experience negative emotions such as anxiety, worry, and tension, and to be moody and emotionally unstable (John et al., 2008; Reisenzein & Weber, 2009). Indeed, a large body of research has established that people scoring high in Extraversion tend to experience positive emotions more often and more intensely, while people scoring high in Neuroticism are more prone to experiencing negative emotions (for a review, see Reisenzein & Weber, 2009).

Agreeableness is viewed as a prosocial trait related to kindness, tender-mindedness, trust, and modesty (John et al., 2008). Agreeableness has previously been associated with the motivation to control negative emotions in communication situations (Tobin et al., 2000), and a tendency to be less anger-prone (Kuppens, 2005). Conscientiousness is a trait characterized by socially prescribed impulse control, and is associated with task- and goal-directed behaviors such as planning, organizing, and delaying gratification. Finally, Openness to Experience can be defined as the tendency to be imaginative and curious, to have wide interests, and to appreciate arts and aesthetic experiences (John et al., 2008). Indeed, people scoring high on Openness to Experience tend to be more sensitive to aesthetic emotions, and they experience more "chills" or "shivers down the spine" in response to aesthetic stimuli such as music (McCrae, 2007; Nusbaum & Silvia, 2011).

## Other Traits

In addition to the more "global" approach to individual differences represented by the Five-Factor Model of personality, other, more specific traits such as Empathy have also been investigated in the context of music preferences. In its broadest sense, Trait Empathy can be described as an individual's general responsiveness to the observed experiences of others, involving both perspective-taking capabilities/tendencies and emotional reactivity (see e.g., Davis, 1980). In other words, Trait Empathy is an individual difference construct related to the tendency to put oneself in the "shoes" of another, and the tendency to respond emotionally (either with the same emotion as observed in another, or with sympathy) to the experiences of others. A specific component of Trait Empathy—*Fantasy* (Davis, 1980)—reflects empathic engagement in fictional contexts, and may also be associated with sensitivity to certain music-induced emotions (Vuoskoski et al., 2012). In fact, it has been proposed that empathy may be one of the mechanisms through which music evokes emotions in listeners (e.g., Scherer & Coutinho, 2013; Timmers, this volume), and thus Trait Empathy may have relevance for emotion-related music preferences as well.

## Explaining Individual Differences in Music Preferences

The following section will outline findings from studies that have investigated the contribution of personality dispositions—the Big Five traits as well as Trait Empathy—to music preferences. These studies are grouped in terms of their approach to music preferences: 1) Genre-based approaches, 2) Emotion-focused approaches, and 3) Functional approaches. Genre-based approaches refer to studies that have characterized and measured people's music preferences in terms of liking for specific genre categories. Emotion-focused approaches, on the other hand, comprise studies that have categorized musical examples with regard to the emotional tone conveyed by the music. Finally, Functional approaches concern studies where music preferences have been examined with regard to the function that the music is used for.

### *Genre-Based Approaches*

Musical genres seem like practical units of analysis when studying music preferences, since people often define and describe their musical taste in terms of preference for specific genres. Studies investigating the connection between genre preferences and personality traits have typically adopted one of two main approaches to measuring genre preferences: asking people to rate their liking for a selection of music excerpts representing different genres, or simply asking people to indicate their liking for a list of musical genres. The former approach has the limitation that a limited number of musical examples chosen by researchers are considered representative of entire genres or musical styles, whereas the latter approach is constrained by the fact that the definition of genres is subjective and changes over time. Furthermore, it may be difficult to determine the extent to which self-reported music genre preferences are related to the intrinsic properties of particular styles of music, or whether these types of ratings are more strongly affected by the social connotations that are attached to specific genres (cf. Rentfrow & Gosling, 2007). However, both types of studies have yielded converging evidence, indicating that people are drawn to musical styles that are congruent with their personality traits.

Using a questionnaire-based measure of music genre preferences, the Short Test of Music Preferences, Rentfrow and Gosling (2003) carried out one of the first large-scale investigations (3000+ participants across several studies) on the associations between personality traits and genre preferences. They found that the structure of music preferences (for 14 genres) could be described in terms of four underlying factors: Reflective & Complex (including blues, jazz, and classical), Intense & Rebellious (rock, heavy metal, and alternative), Upbeat & Conventional (e.g., pop, soundtrack, and country), and Energetic & Rhythmic (rap/hip-hop, soul/funk, and electronica/dance). Across two different samples, several statistically significant correlations emerged between the Big Five personality traits and the four music preference factors. Extraversion was positively associated with preference for Upbeat & Conventional and Energetic & Rhythmic music styles, while Openness to Experience was positively associated with preference for Reflective & Complex and Intense & Rebellious music styles. Both Conscientiousness and Agreeableness were positively correlated with liking for Upbeat & Conventional music styles, but no consistent correlations emerged with regard to Neuroticism. This pattern of correlations is in line with the idea that people tend to prefer and select music that reflects their personalities. For example, extraverts—who are active, outgoing, and tend to experience positive emotions—are drawn to music that reflects and reinforces these characteristics (i.e., Energetic & Rhythmic and Upbeat & Conventional musical styles). Similarly, those scoring high in Openness to Experience—who are curious and value arts and new experiences—tend to appreciate music that satisfies their curiosity and appetite for novelty and strong aesthetic experiences (i.e., Reflective & Complex and Intense & Rebellious music styles).

The broader factor structure underlying music genre preferences suggests that individual differences in music preferences may be better explained by more fundamental features of music—such as its acoustic and emotional characteristics—rather than the rather fuzzy and variable genre categories. Indeed, Rentfrow and Gosling (2003) touched upon this possibility, and explored it in more detail in their later work (Rentfrow, Goldberg, & Levitin, 2011; Greenberg et al., 2015). In a 2011 study, Rentfrow, Goldberg, and Levitin asked participants to rate their liking for 146 unfamiliar music excerpts (using different subsets in different experiments) representing 26 different genres and subgenres. The authors also asked a group of musically untrained judges to rate the 146 music examples in terms of music-specific (e.g., distorted, fast, and percussive) and psychologically/emotionally oriented (e.g., aggressive, inspiring, and sad) attributes. Across three different experiments, the underlying structure of music preferences was best represented by five factors: Mellow/relaxing, Urban/danceable, Sophisticated/aesthetic, Intense/aggressive, and Campestral/sincere (forming the acronym "MUSIC"). Using multiple hierarchical regression analyses, the authors tested whether a musical piece's loadings on the five MUSIC factors were more strongly related to its genre, or its attributes (as rated by the judges). They found that both genres and attributes contributed significantly to the MUSIC factor loadings, suggesting that music preferences are influenced by specific auditory and emotional features as well as the social connotations of music.

### Emotion-Focused Approaches

Since emotional dispositions are so central to many of the Big Five traits as well as to Trait Empathy, approaching individual differences in music preferences from an emotion-focused angle may shed more light on the associations between personality traits and music genre preferences. It should be noted that the focus of this section is on *perceived* rather than *felt* emotions; i.e., what the music sounds like rather than how the listener feels (for more information on music and emotions, see Timmers, this volume). Using 50 short film music excerpts representing different discrete emotions (happiness, sadness, fear, anger, and tenderness) Vuoskoski and Eerola (2011) investigated whether listeners' personality traits were associated with their preference for excerpts expressing particular emotions. They found that the pattern of correlations between preference ratings and personality traits reflected the emotion-related dispositions inherent in the different traits: Extraversion was positively associated with liking for happy-sounding music, while Openness to Experience was positively correlated with preference for sad- and fearful-sounding music. Furthermore, Agreeableness was positively associated with liking for happy- and tender-sounding music, and negatively with liking for angry- and fearful-sounding music. Similar findings have been obtained in studies using musical stimuli from different genres, confirming an association between Extraversion and liking for happy-sounding music (e.g., Chamorro-Premuzic, Fagan, &

Furnham, 2010) and between Openness to Experience and liking for sad-sounding music (Ladinig & Schellenberg, 2012; Vuoskoski, Thompson, McIlwain, & Eerola, 2012).

Another trait that has been found to be associated with liking for sad-sounding music is Trait Empathy (Garrido & Schubert, 2011; Vuoskoski et al., 2012). Using excerpts of film music as stimuli, Vuoskoski and colleagues (2012) discovered that Trait Empathy (especially the Fantasy and Empathic Concern—subscales of the Interpersonal Reactivity Index, see Davis, 1980) was positively correlated with liking for sad- and tender-sounding excerpts. Later work has provided support for these findings using more diverse musical material: Building on the work of Rentfrow, Goldberg and Levitin (2011), Greenberg and colleagues (2015) investigated the extent to which Trait Empathy was associated with preference scores for the five broad MUSIC factors. They discovered that Trait Empathy was positively associated with preference for Mellow/relaxing music, and negatively with preference for Intense/aggressive music. These findings were replicated across three different samples using different musical materials. When they explored the underlying emotional attributes in more detail, they found that those with high Trait Empathy particularly liked music that was tender, reflective, and sad. This pattern of correlations suggests that—as empathic people have a stronger tendency to empathize with those undergoing negative emotions and to experience sympathy and concern (e.g., Davis, 1980)—empathic people may be more open to engage and empathize with sad-sounding music, and more likely to resonate with music expressing warm, compassionate feelings such as tenderness. Furthermore, since Openness to Experience has also been consistently associated with liking for sad-sounding music, it appears that enjoyment of sad music may be related to aesthetic appreciation as well as emotional engagement.

## Functional Approaches

Music listening occurs in many different situations and contexts, and several studies have shown that music has the ability to fulfill a wide variety of functions in everyday life (e.g., North et al., 2004; Sloboda, O'Neill, & Ivaldi, 2001). As different personality traits are associated with different psychological needs and motivations to varying degrees (e.g., Olson & Weber, 2004), it is not surprising that people with different personalities also tend to use music for different functions and in different situations (Chamorro-Premuzic & Furnham, 2007; Chamorro-Premuzic et al., 2009, 2010; Johansson, Vuoskoski, & Eerola, submitted). Moreover, certain types of music are more suited than others for particular uses. Thus, one potentially fruitful method to tackle individual differences in music preferences is to approach the phenomenon from the perspective of the different uses and functions afforded by different types of music.

Chamorro-Premuzic and colleagues (2009) investigated the potential connections between personality traits and different uses of music. They assessed music use in terms of three broad factors—Emotional, Cognitive and Background—which were determined using the "Uses of Music Inventory" (UMI), a 15-item self-report measure specifically designed for a previous study (Chamorro-Premuzic & Furnham, 2007). Their questionnaire data from 245 respondents showed that Cognitive (i.e., intellectual and rational) use of music was related to Openness to Experience, while Emotional use of music was positively associated with Neuroticism and Extraversion. Extraversion was also associated with Background/social uses of music. Although these findings are in line with predictions arising from personality theory, it should be noted that many of the items in the UMI appear to measure music-related attitudes and reactions rather than actual music use.

In a later follow-up study, Chamorro-Premuzic and colleagues (2010) replicated their earlier findings, and extended them to encompass music preferences. They found that Background use of music was positively associated with preference for "social" and happy music, while Emotional use was positively associated with liking for sad music. Furthermore, they discovered that while personality traits such as Extraversion and Openness to Experience were directly associated with liking for happy and complex music (respectively), the relationship between personality and music preferences was also mediated by the different music uses. Similar findings were obtained by Johansson and colleagues (submitted), who explored the relationships between personality traits, music genre preferences, and the use of music for different functions and in different situations. They found that Extraversion was associated with a variety of different uses, but most notably with background uses and mood enhancement. Moreover, Openness to Experience was strongly associated with the use of music for aesthetic experiences and self-expression. Similarly to Chamorro-Premuzic and colleagues (2010), they found that music uses were associated with music preferences, and that personality contributed to music preferences both directly and via music uses. For example, the relationship between Openness to Experience and preference for intense music styles (e.g., heavy, alternative, and soundtrack) was modulated by the use of music for aesthetic experiences and self-expression.

The finding that Extraversion appears to be associated with background use of music is in line with theoretical notions that people with high Extraversion should prefer environments with a higher degree of sensory stimulation (see e.g. Eysenck, 1967), as well as with empirical findings showing that extraverts perform well in tasks such as reading comprehension in the presence of background music (Daoussis & McKelvie, 1986). Considering that music is rarely the primary focus of listeners' attention, it seems likely that extraverts—who have been shown to prefer states of greater sensory stimulation—might use music to maintain an optimal level of arousal while carrying out other activities.

Finally, there is experimental evidence suggesting that the relationship between familiarity/exposure and liking might depend on certain personality traits. Those scoring high in Openness to Experience tend to appreciate novelty, and are more tolerant of ambiguity (McCrae & Costa, 1997; McCrae, 2007). Thus, it may be that this trait modulates the relationship between novelty, arousal potential, and liking also in the context of music listening. Indeed, Hunter and Schellenberg (2011) obtained support for this notion, demonstrating that Openness to Experience moderated the effect of exposure on liking ratings. High Openness to Experience was associated with higher liking ratings for novel music, while low Openness to Experience was associated with higher liking ratings for over-exposed music. These findings may also explain why high Openness to Experience has been consistently associated with preference for diverse and complex music styles (i.e., music characterized by higher novelty and arousal potential).

## Discussion

The body of research reviewed in this chapter shows that people's personality traits are consistently reflected in their music preferences—regardless whether they are characterized in terms of genres or emotional attributes. Nevertheless, it should be emphasized that our personality traits do not directly determine the types of music that we like; rather, our music preferences are the product of a complex interaction between our individual characteristics, musical experiences, and cultural and social environments. Indeed, one of the main limitations of the present chapter is that—due to its focus on individual differences in music preferences—the complex yet significant role of social and cultural factors in the formation of musical preferences was only briefly hinted at. Furthermore, this chapter focused only on a limited selection of potential individual difference variables associated with inter-individual variability in music preferences, namely Big Five personality traits and Trait Empathy. The contribution of other relevant variables such as age, gender, and musical training is, however, reviewed in detail elsewhere (see e.g., North & Hargreaves, 2008). Another limitation of the present chapter is related to the emotional aspects of music preferences, which were only discussed with respect to perceived emotions. It should be noted that *felt emotions* may also contribute significantly to liking and disliking responses (or vice versa), as several studies have reported significant positive relationships between liking and the intensity of felt emotions (e.g., Ladinig & Schellenberg, 2012; Vuoskoski et al., 2012). However, these relationships might be even more complex than one might expect initially, as music-induced feelings of sadness can be associated with either liking or disliking responses, for example (e.g., Ladinig & Schellenberg, 2012; Eerola, Vuoskoski, & Kautiainen, 2016).

Finally, some of the more recent research reviewed in this chapter suggests that—beyond the associations between specific personality traits and music genre preferences—may lie a pattern of correspondences between particular psychological needs and the types of uses afforded by different kinds of music. However, these preliminary studies have only scratched the surface, using quite simplified questionnaire measures of everyday music use and music genre preferences. Modern technologies, such as research-targeted smartphone applications that enable the study of actual music use in everyday life (e.g., Randall & Rickard, 2013) may hold the most promise for a more thorough understanding of the intricate web of associations between music use, musical style, and individual differences.

## Core Reading

North, A., & Hargreaves, D. (2008). *The social and applied psychology of music.* Oxford: Oxford University Press.

Rentfrow, P. J., Goldberg, L. R., & Levitin, D. J. (2011). The structure of musical preferences: A five-factor model. *Journal of Personality and Social Psychology, 100*(6), 1139–1157.

Rentfrow, P. J., & Gosling, S. D. (2003). The Do Re Mi's of everyday life: The structure and personality correlates of music preferences. *Journal of Personality and Social Psychology, 84*, 1236–1256.

Vuoskoski, J. K., Thompson, W. F., McIlwain, D., & Eerola, T. (2012). Who enjoys listening to sad music and why? *Music Perception, 29*(3), 311–317.

## Further References

Berlyne, D. E. (1971). *Aesthetics and psychobiology* (Vol. 336). New York, NY: Appleton-Century-Crofts.

Brattico, E., & Jacobsen, T. (2009). Subjective appraisal of music. *Annals of the New York Academy of Sciences, 1169*(1), 308–317.

Cattell, R. B., & Saunders D. R. (1954). Musical preferences and personality diagnosis: A factorization of one hundred and twenty themes. *Journal of Social Psychology, 39*, 3–24.

Chamorro-Premuzic, T., Fagan, P., & Furnham, A. (2010). Personality and uses of music as predictors of preferences for music consensually classified as happy, sad, complex, and social. *Psychology of Aesthetics, Creativity, and the Arts, 4*(4), 205–213.

Chamorro-Premuzic, T., & Furnham, A. (2007). Personality and music: Can traits explain how people use music in everyday life? *The British Journal of Psychology, 98*, 177–185.

Chamorro-Premuzic, T., Gomà-i-Freixanet, M., Furnham, A., & Muro, A. (2009). Personality, self-estimated intelligence, and uses of music: A Spanish replication and extension using structural equation modeling. *Psychology of Aesthetics, Creativity and the Arts, 3,* 149–155.

Daoussis, I., & McKelvie, S. (1986). Musical preferences and effects of music on a reading comprehension test for extraverts and introverts. *Perceptual and Motor Skills, 62,* 283–289.

Davis, M. H. (1980). A multidimensional approach to individual differences in empathy. *JSAS Catalog of Selected Documents in Psychology, 10,* 85.

DeNora, T. (1999). Music as a technology of the self. *Poetics, 27,* 31–56.

Eerola, T., Vuoskoski, J. K., & Kautiainen, H. (2016). Being moved by unfamiliar sad music is associated with high empathy. *Frontiers in Psychology: Auditory Cognitive Neuroscience, 7,* 1176. doi: 10.3389/fpsyg.2016.01176

Eysenck, H. J. (1967). *The biological basis of personality.* Springfield, IL: C.C. Thomas.

Garrido, S., & Schubert, E. (2011). Individual differences in the enjoyment of negative emotion in music: A literature review and experiment. *Music Perception, 28*(3), 279–296.

Garrido, S., & Schubert, E. (2013). Adaptive and maladaptive attraction to negative emotions in music. *Musicae Scientiae, 17*(2), 147–166.

Greenberg, D. M., Baron-Cohen, S., Stillwell, D. J., Kosinski, M., & Rentfrow, P. J. (2015). Musical preferences are linked to cognitive styles. *PloS ONE, 10*(7), e0131151.

Hargreaves, D. J. (1986). *The developmental psychology of music.* Cambridge: Cambridge University Press.

Holbrook, M. B., & Schindler, R. M. (1989). Some exploratory findings on the development of musical tastes. *Journal of Consumer Research, 16*(1), 119–124.

Hunter, P. G., & Schellenberg, E. G. (2011). Interactive effects of personality and frequency of exposure on liking for music. *Personality and Individual Differences, 50*(2), 175–179.

Huron, D. B. (2006). *Sweet anticipation: Music and the psychology of expectation.* Cambridge, MA: MIT Press.

Johansson, K., Vuoskoski, J. K., & Eerola, T. (submitted). Choosing to listen: The role of personality in the uses of music in everyday life. Manuscript submitted for publication.

John, O. P., Naumann, L. P., & Soto, C. J. (2008). Paradigm shift to the integrative Big Five trait taxonomy. In L. A. Pervin, & O. P. John (Eds.), *Handbook of personality: Theory and research (Third Edition)* (pp. 114–158). New York, NY: Guilford Press.

Konečni, V. J. (1982). Social interaction and musical preference. In D. Deutsch (Ed.), *The Psychology of Music* (pp. 497–516). New York, NY: Academic Press.

Kuppens, P. (2005). Interpersonal determinants of trait anger: Low agreeableness, perceived low social esteem, and the amplifying role of the importance attached to social relationships. *Personality and Individual Differences, 38*(1), 13–23.

Ladinig, O., & Schellenberg, E. G. (2012). Liking unfamiliar music: Effects of felt emotion and individual differences. *Psychology of Aesthetics, Creativity, and the Arts, 6*(2), 146–154.

McCrae, R. R. (2007). Aesthetic chills as a universal marker of openness to experience. *Motivation and Emotion, 31,* 5–11.

McCrae, R. R. & Costa, P. T., Jr. (1987). Validation of the five-factor model of personality across instruments and observers. *Journal of Personality and Social Psychology, 52,* 81–90.

McCrae, R. R., & Costa, P. T., Jr. (1997). Conceptions and correlates of Openness to Experience. In R. Hogan, J. A. Johnson, & S. R. Briggs (Eds.), *Handbook of personality psychology* (pp. 825–847). Orlando, FL: Academic Press.

McMullen, P. T. (1974). Influence of number of different pitches and melodic redundancy on preference responses. *Journal of Research in Music Education, 22*(3), 198–204.

North, A., Hargreaves, D., & Hargreaves J. (2004). Uses of music in everyday life. *Music Perception, 22*(1), 41–77.

Nusbaum, E. C., & Silvia, P. J. (2011). Shivers and timbres: Personality and the experience of chills from music. *Social Psychological and Personality Science, 2*(2), 199–204.

Olson, K. R., & Weber, D. A. (2004). Relations between big five traits and fundamental motives. *Psychological Reports, 95*(3), 795–802.

Panksepp, J. (1995). The emotional sources of "chills" induced by music. *Music Perception, 13*(2), 171–207.

Randall, W. M., & Rickard, N. S. (2013). Development and trial of a mobile experience sampling method (m-ESM) for personal music listening. *Music Perception, 31*(2), 157–170.

Reisenzein, R., & Weber, H. (2009). Personality and emotion. In P. J. Corr & G. Matthews (Eds.), *Cambridge handbook of personality psychology* (pp. 54–71). Cambridge: Cambridge University Press.

Rentfrow, P. J., & Gosling, S. D. (2006). Message in a ballad: The role of music preferences in interpersonal perception. *Psychological Science, 17*, 236–242.

Rentfrow, P. J., & Gosling, S. D. (2007). The content and validity of music-genre stereotypes among college students. *Psychology of Music, 35*(2), 306–326.

Salimpoor, V. N., Benovoy, M., Larcher, K., Dagher, A., & Zatorre, R. J. (2011). Anatomically distinct dopamine release during anticipation and experience of peak emotion to music. *Nature Neuroscience, 14*(2), 257–262.

Scherer, K. R., & Coutinho, E. (2013). How music creates emotion: A multifactorial process approach. In T. Cochrane, B. Fnatini, & K. R. Scherer (Eds.), *The emotional power of music* (pp. 121–145). Oxford: Oxford University Press.

Sloboda, J. A., O'Neill, S. A., & Ivaldi, A. (2001). Functions of music in everyday life: An exploratory study using the Experience Sampling Method. *Musicae Scientiae, 5*(1), 9–32.

Tobin, R. M., Graziano, W. G., Vanman, E. J. & Tassinary, L. G. (2000). Personality, emotional experience, and efforts to control emotions. *Journal of Personality and Social Psychology, 79*, 656–669.

Vuoskoski, J. K., & Eerola, T. (2011). The role of mood and personality in the perception of emotions represented by music. *Cortex, 47*(9), 1099–1106.

Vuoskoski, J. K., Thompson, W. F., McIlwain, D., & Eerola, T. (2012). Who enjoys listening to sad music and why? *Music Perception, 29*(3), 311–317.

Witek, M. A. G., Clarke, E. F., Wallentin, M., Kringelbach, M. L., & Vuust, P. (2014). Syncopation, body-movement and pleasure in groove music. *PLoS ONE, 9*(4), e94446.

Zajonc, R. B. (1968). Attitudinal effects of mere exposure. *Journal of Personality and Social Psychology, 9*(2 part 2), 1–27.

# PART 5

# Musical Meanings

# 38

# MUSIC COGNITION
## Investigations Through the Centuries

*Kyung Myun Lee*

### Introduction

Music cognition involves research on human beings who listen to, enjoy, and perform music. Given the long human history of music, as evidenced by the earliest musical instrument, made some 40,000 years ago (Higham et al., 2012), it is no surprise that questions about the human experience of music have also long been discussed. Indeed, the history of thought regarding music cognition goes back to ancient Greece. Whereas current studies on music cognition investigate how people process music in the auditory system and brain, using advanced technological tools and scientific methods, early studies depended solely on the observation of phenomena or the introspection of mental and physical states. Scientific and experimental methods have been used to examine cognition of music since their development in the 17th century (Cohen, 2010). The history of music cognition is closely related to the history of both physics and psychology, as scientific understandings of both sound and humans contribute to the field. By reviewing studies of music cognition from ancient Greece to early 20th century, this chapter will describe how research on music cognition has developed, and how its topics and methods have changed.

### Music Cognition in the Ancient Period

Perhaps the earliest question about the human experience of music which drew scholarly attention is that of consonance and dissonance—what people *feel* when two tones are *heard* together, and why certain musical intervals heard as more consonant than the others. The ancient Greek mathematician Pythagoras (*c.* 582 BC–*c.* 497 BC) answered this question by examining numerical relationships—ratios—and consonance. He compared the weights of various hammers and the sounds they produced. Although Pythagoras did not leave any written record of his investigations, they were described by Nicomachus of Gerasa (*c.* AD 60–*c.* AD 120) as follows:

> Pythagoras was plunged one day in thought and intense reasoning, to see if he could devise some instrumental aid for the hearing which would be consistent and not prone to error, in the way that sight is assisted by the compasses, the measuring

rod and the dioptra, and touch by the balance and by the devising of measures; and happening by some heaven-sent chance to walk by a blacksmith's workshop, he heard the hammers beating iron on the anvil and giving out sounds fully concordant in combination with one another, with the exception of one pairing; and he recognized among them the consonance of the octave and those of the fifth and the fourth. He noticed that what lay between the fourth and the fifth was itself discordant, but was essential in filling out the greater of these intervals. Overjoyed at the way his project had come, with god's help, to fulfillment, he ran into the smithy, and through a great variety of experiments he discovered that what stood in direct relation to the difference in the sounds was the weight of the hammers, not the force of the strikers or the shapes of the hammer-heads or the alteration of the iron which was being beaten. He weighed them accurately, and took away for his own use pieces of metal exactly equal in weight to the hammers.

*(Barker, 2004, p. 256)*

In the period of the ancient Greeks, the octave, perfect fifth, and perfect fourth were categorized as perfect consonant intervals. What is attributed to Pythagoras is the assertion that the weights of hammers producing those intervals corresponded to certain integer ratios. Thus, the octave results from a 1:2 ratio, while the perfect fifth and perfect fourth arise from 2:3 and 3:4 ratios (Boethius, 1989; Crocker, 1963; Palisca, 2001); we will return to this conclusion later in this chapter. After Pythagoras, the emphasis shifted from ratios of weights to those of lengths of vibrating strings. Thus, on the monochord, an ancient instrument having one string fixed at both ends over a resonating box, placing your finger in the middle of the string divides the length of the string in half, and the produced sound is one octave higher than the original string sound: The octave results from the 1:2 ratio of the whole to stopped string lengths.

So, even though this question about consonance and dissonance was concerned with the human experience of musical intervals, in ancient Greek thought the most important issue was the set of numerical relationships symbolized by music, not the psychology or physiology related to humans listening to musical intervals. For Pythagoras and his followers, numbers were of great interest *per se*; the structure of the universe itself was explained with numbers. It was suggested that celestial bodies, such as the Sun, Moon, and planets, are in mathematical relations and their movements could be heard as the "music of the spheres" (Godwin, 1992). This numerical symbolism of music was criticized for its lack of empirical evidence by Aristoxenus (flourished 4 BC), a pupil of Aristotle's. In his *Elementa harmonica*, Aristoxenus suggested that the account of music should deal with the phenomena and principles of sounds perceived by the ear (Zbikowski, 2002). Thus, he held that the flow of a melody as sensed by the ear is more important for musical judgments than the mathematical relation of musical intervals. These two opposing points of view on consonance were reconciled by Ptolemy (Zbikowski, 2002). Ptolemy's treatise on consonance proposed that the Pythagorean explanation of consonance is not actually incompatible with Aristoxenus' explanation; rather, the one naturally follows the other, because consonant intervals having integer ratios are naturally heard as more pleasant and harmonious by the ear. The significance of music as a psychological and mental phenomenon sensed by the ear became more and more important for scholars considering music, and led, by the mid-16th century, to the doorway of a modern science of music cognition.

## Music and the Scientific Revolution

Whereas scholars in the Greek period used only *in situ* observations for research, experimental methods have been considered as necessary since the beginning of the scientific revolution in the 17th century. The use of controlled experimental approaches was a key element differentiating modern science from medieval natural philosophy. It was researchers such as Francis Bacon (1561–1626), Galileo Galilei (1564–1642), and Sir Issac Newton (1642–1727), who made significant contributions to this change from observation-based to experiment-based empiricism. In his book *Opus Majus* (1998/1928), Bacon (1214–1292) said, "He therefore who wishes to rejoice without doubt in regard to the truths underlying phenomena must know how to devote himself to experimentation" (p. 584). While previous scholars sought to arrive at the truth by reason and by observing natural phenomena, the empiricists of the 17th century sought evidence gathered from scientifically designed and controlled experiments. Beyond the physical sciences, the introduction of experimental methods also had a great influence on music cognition research. Vincenzo Galilei (*ca.* 1520–1591), the father of Galileo Galilei, is remembered as one of the member of the Florentine Camerata and a supporter of the Baroque monody style—the foundation of early opera—but he was also famous for a number of experiments that he conducted in acoustics. To investigate how the material and tension of a vibrating string influence its pitch, he used various strings made of gut and steel and found the errors which existed in the Pythagorean theory about weight (mass) and consonance (Cohen, 2010). Specifically, Galilei found that the ratios between strings producing a consonant musical interval change depending on their material and tension. For example, an octave generated by a string with different tension could be the result of the ratio 1:4 instead of 1:2. Whereas Pythagoras explained that all physical components of vibrating objects—such as the weight of a hammer, the weight and length of a string, and the diameter and length of a pipe—corresponded to a 1:2 ratio for octave, Galilei showed that a 1:2 ratio is applicable only to the length of string, not to other factors such as weight of a hammer or diameter of a pipe. This topic was pursued by others, including Marin Mersenne (1588–1648), supporting the relationship between pitch and a vibrating string's length.

Experimental and scientific research on sound was first categorized under the label of *acoustics*. Phenomena such as pitch, musical intervals, and scales began to be investigated as topics in acoustics instead of speculative music theory. Following in the footsteps of his father Vincenzo, Galileo Galilei (1564–1642) also employed the methods of experimental science and examined the relationships between pitch and frequency. He suggested that sounds are generated by pulses, which he called "shocks" or "percussions." According to Galileo, the vibration of a string makes successive pulses, which are transmitted through the air to the ear and finally are sensed as sounds (Cohen, 2010). Focusing on the physical transformation of sound pulses to the response of the ear, not on the mathematical relations of strings, his study laid an early foundation for research on the sensation and perception of sound (a topic which was to be intensively examined in the 19th century). During the eighteenth century the discipline of physical acoustics continued to evolve, with the development of better tools for precise, objective measurements and experimental techniques, and made significant progress. Sauveur (1653–1716) first discovered the harmonics of a complex tone. The mathematicians Daniel Bernoulli (1700–1782) and Leonard Euler (1707–1783) analyzed the vibrations of sound waves and Joseph-Louis Lagrange (1736–1813) suggested the theory of the propagation of sound. Joseph Ernst Chladni (1756–1827) measured harmonics by using the movement of sand on a vibrating sound-board or elastic surface. Charles Cagniard de la Tour (1777–1859) contributed to the absolute measurement of pitch by inventing a disk siren, in which a certain pitch was generated by the rotation of the disk.

## From Sounds to the Ear in the 19th Century

After the 17th century, the natural sciences continued to develop rapidly, and it became possible to think that science would have the power to explain all natural phenomena (Cohen, 2010). The basic scientific idea of this period was that of *mechanism*—the universe is like a great machine, with its smallest constituent components consisting of atoms. According to this framework, if we know the laws by which atoms work, we are able to predict how the machine will behave (Westfall, 1971). While the physical aspects of sounds were actively investigated by researchers in acoustics in this period, the sensation and perception of sounds was not a parallel research area, because it was thought that human nature is not subject to the same, mechanical laws as hold in the physical world. However, in the 19th century, experimental methods that had proven themselves successful for the natural sciences were adapted and applied to the study of humans. In particular, psychophysicists such as Ernst Weber (1795–1878) and Gustav Theodor Fechner (1801–1887) showed that psychological phenomena, including sensation and perception of weight and touching, could be mathematically quantified as a function of physical phenomena. Experimental, objective, and mathematical approaches to mental phenomena were promoted with the rapid development of biology in the late 18th century and early 19th. In addition, interest in the sensing organs of the human body rapidly increased. It was thought that the perfect understanding of musical experiences would not be possible without also understanding the sensation and perception of sounds. The first step researchers took in knowing how humans sense and perceive sounds was to explore the "ear"—the peripheral auditory system. Thus, in this period, research on sound was associated with the physiology of the ear.

In Germany, the growth in universities made possible the progressive development of science and promoted interdisciplinary research on music and science through the association of psychoacoustics and physics. Hermann von Helmholtz (1821–1894), a German physicist and physiologist, was of great importance for research connecting the ear and sound. His extensive *On the Sensation of Tone as a Physiological Basis for the Theory of Music* (1954/1877) explained how the ear responds to sounds through the analysis of different frequencies, and how this process is related to the more phenomenological experiences and feelings accompanying the perception of music. Helmholtz also tried to answer the issue of consonance and dissonance of musical intervals in terms of the mechanism of the ear. Instead of relying solely on the ratios of numbers attributed to musical sounds, he claimed that dissonance is caused by low frequency amplitude fluctuations that occur when two tones of a dissonant interval are close in frequency to one another. When a musical interval produces such an amplitude fluctuation approximately 33 times per second, the effect is perceived as "roughness," and it is this roughness, arising from wave interferences, which makes musical intervals sound dissonant (Helmholtz, 1954/1877, p. 181). In such explanations, which connected the physiology of the ear with the physical properties of sounds, Helmholtz was a great pioneer, bridging the divide between music and science.

As a physicist and physiologist, Helmholtz made a significant contribution to psychological research by showing how to use experiments to investigate psychological phenomena. However, Helmholtz didn't think of psychology as an independent field of research; it was Wilhelm Wundt (1832–1920) who built up psychology as an independent scientific discipline. After graduating as doctor of medicine from Heidelberg, Wundt gained experience in physiological experiments as an assistant to Helmholtz and founded a laboratory in 1879 at the University of Leipzig, which was considered to be the world's first devoted to psychology. By compiling experimental approaches and theories about mental phenomena, Wundt contributed to the foundation of psychology as a discipline distinct from philosophy. Many students were trained in Wundt's laboratory and some of them became renowned psychologists, leading the next generation of research. Wundt was interested in analyzing the components and elements composing consciousness, an approach which his student, Edward Titchener (1867–1927) termed *structuralism*. It was during this time that scientific research on psychological aspects of human nature began to take root and grow.

The other important German figure of music cognition in the 19th century is Carl Stumpf (1848–1936), a musicologist as well as a psychologist. Stumpf played an important role in establishing psychology as an independent discipline by founding a psychology laboratory in Berlin; he made numerous contributions to the discipline beyond those dealing with music. As a musicologist, he was a pioneer in the field of comparative musicology (*vergleichende Musikwissenschaft*) publishing significant works, including his influential *Origins of Music* (2012/1911). Stumpf discussed the issue of consonance and dissonance from a different point of view from Helmholtz. When we argue why certain musical intervals sound more consonant than others, "nature or nurture" is an important issue. Some claim that the human ear and brain are pre-wired to hear and prefer consonance, whereas others insist that a preference for consonance is the product of enculturation, because we are frequently exposed to consonant relations of pitches. These contrasting positions are represented by Helmholtz and Stumpf. Stumpf foregrounded the effects of experience and cultural context on consonance and dissonance, whereas Helmholtz explained consonance from the perspectives of acoustics and physiology. That is, for consonance, Stumpf emphasized the judgment or opinion (*Urteil*) of listeners, whereas Helmholtz focused on the sensation (*Empfindungen*) of sound. By conducting behavioral experiments, in which participants were asked to decide how well two tones of each interval fused together ("*Verschmelzung*"), Stumpf tried to explain consonance and dissonance as the products of cognitive, mental processing (Stumpf, 1898). From this perspective, the *sensation* of sound is related to a lower level of auditory processing occurring in the ear, but the *judgment* of sound is related to a higher level of processing occurring in the brain. The higher the level of auditory processing, the more important the effects of experience and training become. Given that Stumpf himself was a trained musician and knew very well the phenomenology of hearing musical intervals, it seems natural that he emphasized the role of experience and training. Stumpf influenced research on musical talent in the next generation of psychologists. These included Géza Révész (1878–1955), who studied musical aptitude by observing the pianist Erwin Nyiregyházi (1903–1987) and based the book *The Psychology of a Musical Prodigy* (1970/1925) on Nyiregyházi's development from the ages of 6 to 12.

## The Pioneer of American Music Psychology: Seashore and Functionalism

The motivating framework for psychology in the early 20th century was *functionalism*, which was concerned with the ways in which mental processes adapt to a changing environment

(Schultz, 1981). Functionalism's emphasis on practical aspects of human thought and behavior naturally led to an interest in the application of psychological research to real-world settings. Introspection, a method previously used for research, was supplemented by new methods in functionalism, including mental tests, questionnaires, and objective descriptions of behavior (Schultz, 1981).

Among early 20th-century psychologists interested in music, Carl Seashore was the most significant researcher in America. Seashore, who immigrated to the United States from his native Sweden as a child, was the first recipient of a PhD in psychology from Yale University (Devonis, 2012). After graduation, he returned to Iowa and in the 1920s developed one of the most productive laboratories working in music psychology, at the University of Iowa. With his notable accomplishments and highly influential record of publication, he became Dean of the Graduate School at Iowa in 1908 and held this position until 1936 (Devonis, 2012). As an experimentalist, Seashore was interested in the measurement of vision, audition and learning; He invented many devices for accurate measurement of sensation and perception. By applying his experimental apparatus to the measurement of sound, Seashore pioneered psychological research on music performance. With specially designed equipment and tools which permitted tracking the real-time changes of musical sounds as produced by performers, Seashore analyzed pitch and intensity changes to investigate such phenomena as tempo rubato and vibrato. His studies—carried out in an era without the benefits of computer technologies—measured and analyzed piano, violin and vocal performance, and vastly improved the level of music performance research.

Another line of Seashore's research involved the evaluation of musical ability through systematic testing. Merged with his talent for music, his interest in the measurement of individual differences and intelligence naturally led to the development of his groundbreaking tests for musical aptitude and skill: the Seashore Tests of Musical Ability. These tests provided a concise way to assess musical ability and have been widely used in elementary and secondary schools. Seashore's approach was to treat musical ability as related to auditory acuity, and his tests measured such acuity by asking a listener to compare pairs of sounds with regard to their pitch, timbre, duration, and rhythmic patterning. Ultimately, this kind of high auditory sensitivity to sound was found to be not sufficient for becoming a good musician (Mursell, 1937a); nevertheless, in spite of their limitations, Seashore's tests were particularly valuable in suggesting the use of scientific principles and objective measurements to assess music-related aptitude. The rhythm part of the test is still used as part of the assessment test for brain injuries (Burger, Denney, & Lee, 2000). Seashore's seminal book *The Psychology of Music* (1938) summarized his research including music performance, the measurement and analysis of musical talent, the development of musical skills, learning in music, and mental images of music.

One year before Seashore published *The Psychology of Music* (1938), James Mursell (1893–1963) published a book with the same title (1937b). Although both Mursell and Seashore's books reviewed the perception of basic components of music, including rhythm, melody, and tonality, their views on musicality differed significantly. As a music educator, Mursell thought musicality to be "a complex syndrome in the sense that it represents and is indexed by a wide array of acoustical, physiological, psychological, and socio-cultural factors," (Jorgensen, 2013, p. 69), whereas Seashore viewed musicality "as a simple construct discrete from other aptitudes and abilities, represented and indexed by a person's aptitude for and ability in aural discrimination" (ibid, p. 69). By considering the "awareness of relatedness among tones" rather than "pitch discrimination" (Mursell, 1937b, p. 326), Mursell addressed music in a more holistic way and supported the Gestalt approach to music, to which we turn shortly.

## From *Tonpsychologie* to Music Psychology

Although "music cognition" is a current term for psychological and scientific research on music, emphasizing its cognitive aspects, the terms "psychology of music" and "music perception" were more often used in the 1980s and 1990s. These were broad terms, encompassing research on many aspects of how music is heard and understood by human beings. In the second half of the 20th century, music psychology research often adopted an approach derived from information-processing frameworks. In such approaches, the process of perceiving and comprehending music could be divided into two stages. The earlier stage is that of sensation and perception, dealing with the processing of fundamental components of sounds, such as pitch, loudness, and duration; such processing was seen to be mainly occurring at the "ear" (the peripheral auditory system) and the lower, subcortical parts of the central nervous system. The later stage is that of cognition, where more strictly musical parameters and components, such as melody, rhythm, harmony, and tonality are processed. Although both of these stages are important for understanding music listening, research in music psychology from the 19th century to the middle of the 20th mainly focused on the early stage of musical processing—that is, the processing related to sensation and perception. The stimuli used for these perceptual, experimental studies were typically simple tones that were hard to be heard as music. Thus, the German word *Tonpsychologie*, "the psychology of tones," which was the title of Stumpf's *magnum opus* (1890), would still be a proper name for some studies researching music perception. The necessity for music psychology to address the higher cognitive level of musical processing became increasingly important in the 1930s. Early in that decade, the monograph *Musikpsychologie* (1931) by Ernst Kurth (1886–1946) presented what may be considered a shift in focus away from *tone* psychology to *music* psychology. The more cognitive the level of musical processing is, the more complex it is to be elucidated, because more various factors, such as individual differences caused by cultural experiences or training, should be considered. By stating the relation of music and exterior variables involved in music psychology, Kurth distinguished music psychology from tone psychology (Gjerdingen, 2012).

The early decades of the 20th century also saw a new approach to psychology, the Gestalt school. The German word *Gestalt* means "shape" or "configuration." The well-known sentence, "the whole is different from the sum of its parts" clearly shows the concept of Gestalt psychology. In the Gestalt approach, an additive sensing of each element does not straightforwardly lead to the perception of the whole; the processing of a whole shape is totally different from the sensing of components. In 1923, the German psychologist Max Wertheimer (1880–1943) suggested Gestalt principles, or "laws," of perceptual organization evidenced by experimental data: Proximity, Similarity, Closure, Prägnanz, and Good Continuation (Wertheimer, 1938/1923). The law of *Proximity* predicts that parts of a percept very close to one another in time or space tend to group together. The law of *Similarity* states that parts which are similar in shape, size, or color tend to be seen as belonging together in a group. The law of *Closure* is a tendency to complete figures even when the part of the figure is missing, as for example when there is a momentary break in an otherwise continuous line. The law of *Prägnanz* reflects the perceptual tendency to avoid ambiguity, seeking to interpret stimuli in simpler rather than more complicated ways; for example, given a figure which can be interpreted as a single complicated shape with many angles or two simpler shapes superimposed on one another, we prefer the latter. The principle of *Good Continuation* describes that "in designing a pattern, for example, one has a feeling how successive parts should follow one another; one knows what a "good" continuation is, how "inner coherence" is to be achieved, etc.; one recognizes a resultant "good Gestalt" simply by its own "inner necessity" (Wertheimer, 1938/1923, p. 325). The Gestalt movement started and thrived at first in Germany, but with the rise to power of the Nazis, moved in large part to the United States, brought there by eminent Gestalt psychologists including Max Wertheimer (1880–1943, the New School for Social Research in New York City), Kurt Koffka (1886–1941, Smith College in Horthampton) and Wolfgang Köhler (1887–1967, Swarthmore College in Pennsylvania).

Although the first generation of Gestalt psychologists did not consider music as a topic of research, music provides good examples of Gestalt theory: Listening to an individual tone, or a series of individual tones, is different from listening to the melodic shape or contour formed by series of tones. In the 1960s and 1970s, music psychologists, such as Leonard B. Meyer (1918–2007, University of Chicago and University of Pennsylvania), Diana Deutsch (1938–, the University of California at San Diego), W. Jay Dowling (1941–, the University of Texas at Dallas), and Albert Bregman (1936–, McGill University) all based significant aspects of their approaches to perception and grouping mechanisms of melody and rhythm on the Gestalt principles. Some of these have become widely accepted: In melody perception, there is a tendency to group tones with close pitches together (Proximity); tones with similar timbres tend to be heard as one melodic line (Similarity); and a relatively larger musical interval or gap within a melody tends to be heard with filling it (Closure) (Dowling & Harwood, 1986). The Gestalt approach to psychology has greatly influenced the field of music psychology and served as the precursor of the coming cognitive revolution by emphasizing the role of consciousness and mental process beyond the level of auditory sensation.

## From Music Psychology to Music Cognition

In the early 20th century, behaviorism suggested that all psychological phenomena could be explained by the objective observation of overt behavior responding to stimuli, while rejecting the study of consciousness. However, after World War II, psychologists realized that complex human behaviors could not be explained with extremely simple stimulus and response relations as traditional behaviorism suggested. Psychologists began to understand how people actively encode, process, and manipulate incoming information, instead of simply passively reacting to stimuli. By examining attention, memory, and decision-making processes, the newly emerging "cognitive" psychology tried to reveal the mechanisms of information processing in the human mind, with concepts and methods drawn from related fields including information theory, linguistics, and computer science (Bechtel, Abrahamsen, & Graham, 2001). "Mind" and "consciousness" came back to the field of psychology and became the main issue to be discussed. In his influential book *Cognitive Psychology* (1967), Ulrich Neisser suggested that cognitive psychology "refers to all processes by which the sensory input is transformed, reduced, elaborated, stored, recovered, and used."

In the field of music psychology, the cognitive era saw researchers change their emphasis from sensation to cognition of music. Two famous postwar scholars who examined music from the cognitive point of view were Robert Francès (1919–2012) and Leonard B. Meyer (1918–2007). Both were influenced by Gestalt psychology and investigated the mechanisms of music listening and its induction of emotion in the mind. As a psychologist, Francès used advanced experimental methods to obtain listeners' responses to music, while Meyer, as a humanist, employed an interdisciplinary approach influenced not only by psychology, but also by music theory and aesthetics (Gjerdingen, 2006).

*Emotion and Meaning in Music* (Meyer, 1956), building in part on earlier theories by William James and others regarding the psychology and physiology of emotion in humans, connected musical structures and a listener's prior experience with such structures in a psychological framework, and argued that the emotion raised by the unexpected or delayed progress of music toward some structural goal is related to the meaning of music. In this book Meyer explained that "Affect or emotion-felt is aroused when an expectation—a tendency to respond—activated by the musical stimulus situation, is temporarily inhibited or permanently blocked" (Meyer, 1956, p. 31), setting the stage for a vast empirical literature on musical affect (see Timmers, this volume). Musical meaning was also central to Meyer's thought; in a strikingly modern passage even today, he states "Embodied musical meaning is, in short, a product of expectation. If, on the basis of past experience, a present stimulus leads us to expect a more or less definite consequent musical event, then that stimulus has meaning" (p. 35; for more on meaning, see Clarke, this volume).

In his book *La perception de la musique* (1988/1958), Francès said, "We must distinguish between the effects of acculturation—unreflective, involuntary, and resulting from almost passive familiarity with works—and the effects of education, where perceptual development is supported by the acquisition of concepts and symbols that provide for the definition of forms, their elements and articulations" (Francès, 1988/1958, pp. 2–3). By conducting sixteen musical experiments, Francès tried to disentangle the effects of acculturation and education on music listening. The results of these experiments indicated that listeners develop mental schemas for music from their experience. Through repeated exposure to music, listeners build expectancies to musical events (Francès, 1958/1988). This idea is consistent with Meyer's theory of expectation: "The norms and deviants of a style upon which expectation and consequently meaning are based are to be found in the habit responses of listeners who have learned to understand these relationships . . . dispositions and habits are learned by constant practice in listening and performing, practice which should, and usually does begin in early childhood" (Meyer, 1956, p. 61).

As reviewed in this chapter, the broad sweep of the history of music cognition moves from mathematics and acoustics to "tone psychology" to music psychology—from sound to sensation to cognition. While tone psychology focuses on "bottom up" processing, proceeding from the acoustic signal to sensation, music psychology also deals with "top-down" processing at cognitive levels, where cortical functions are at the forefront. Of course, for a more complete understanding of the musical mind, both bottom-up and top-down processes must be explained. The significance of top-down factors has long been appreciated, as shown by the work of Stumpf and others. In the modern era, the approaches of Francès and Meyer are valuable in seeking a full explanation of music processing, encompassing both bottom-up and top-down aspects. In particular, they identified the role of top-down factors in the process of music by highlighting the effects of experience, acculturation and education. These effects of experience, culture and education on music continue to be better understood through ever-more sophisticated investigations by current cognitive psychologists and neuroscientists.

## Conclusion

This chapter has given a broad overview of the history of music cognition. We see that questions about music and the musical experience which were asked in ancient Greece are still being discussed at the present time, but framed in very different ways and using very different methods of investigation. Questions of the nature and qualia of musical intervals—our starting point with Pythagoras—are still under active investigation. Recent studies still ask why certain musical intervals are more consonant, but also why people prefer consonance and how education and acculturation influence consonance preference (Lee, Skoe, Kraus, & Ashley, 2015; McDermott, Schultz, Undurraga, & Godoy, 2016). We have seen that these questions were first raised by philosophers in ancient Greece, later were investigated by physicists, and are now discussed by psychologists as well as music theorists. In the 21st century, the science of mind has developed rapidly and research on the brain has increased explosively. Advanced technologies to explore the brain open up new possibilities to discuss questions of music cognition (Bigand, & Tillmann, 2015) and guarantee that we will be provided with endlessly news ways to further our insight into age-old questions.

## Core Reading

Gjerdingen, R. (2006). The psychology of music. In T. Christensen (Ed.), *The Cambridge history of western music theory* (pp. 956–981). Cambridge: Cambridge University Press.

Gjerdingen, R. (2012). Psychologists and musicians: Then and now. In D. Deutsch (Ed.), *The psychology of music* (pp. 683–707). New York, NY: Academic Press.

Helmholtz, H. von. (1954). *On the sensations of tone as a physiological basis for the theory of music* (A. J. Ellis, Trans.). New York, NY: Dover. (Original work published in 1877).

Meyer, L. B. (1956). *Emotion and meaning in music.* Chicago, IL: University of Chicago Press.

Seashore, C. E. (1938). *Psychology of music,* New York, NY: McGraw-Hill.

## Further References

Bacon, R. (1998). *Opus majus* (R. B. Burke, Trans.) Philadelphia, PA: University of Pennsylvania Press. (Original work published in 1928.)

Barker, A. (2004). *Greek musical writings: Harmonic and acoustic theory* (Vol. 2). Cambridge, UK: Cambridge University Press.

Bechtel, W., Abrahamsen, A., & Graham, G. (2001). Cognitive science: History, In N. J. Smelser, & P. B. Baltes (Eds.), *International encyclopedia of the social & behavioral sciences* (pp. 2154–2158). Amsterdam: Elsevier.

Boethius, A. M. S. (1989). *Fundamentals of music* (C. M. Bower, Trans. with introduction and notes; C. V. Palisca, ed.). New Haven, CT: Yale University Press.

Cohen, H. F. (2010). *How modern science came into the world: Four civilizations, one 17th-century breakthrough.* Amsterdam: Amsterdam University Press.

Crocker, R. L. (1963). Pythagorean mathematics and music. *Journal of Aesthetics and Art Criticism,* 22(2), 189–198.

Devonis, D.C. (2012). Carl Seashore. In R. Rieber (Ed.), *Encyclopedia of the history of psychological theories* (pp. 984–986). New York, NY: Springer.

Dowling, W. J., & Harwood, D. L. (1986). *Music cognition.* Orlando: Academic Press.

Francès, R. (1988). *The perception of music* (W. J. Dowling, Trans.) Hillsdale, NJ: Lawrence Erlbaum. (Original work published in 1958).

Godwin, J. (1992). *The harmony of the spheres: The Pythagorean tradition in music.* Rochester, Vermont: Inner Traditions International.

Higham, T., Basell, L., Jacobi, R., Wood, R., Ramsey, C. B., & Conard, N. J. (2012). Testing models for the beginnings of the Aurignacian and the advent of figurative art and music: The radiocarbon chronology of Geißenklösterle. *Journal of Human Evolution, 62*(6), 664–676.

Kurth, E. (1931). *Musikpsychologie.* Bern: Krompholz.

Lee, K., Skoe, E., Kraus, N., & Ashley, R. (2015). Neural transformation of dissonant intervals in the auditory brainstem. *Music Perception, 32*(5), 445–459.

McDermott, J. H., Schultz, A. F., Undurraga, E. A., & Godoy, R. A. (2016). Indifference to dissonance in native Amazonians reveals cultural variation in music perception. *Nature, 535*(7613), 547–550.

Mursell, J. (1937a). What about music tests? *Music Educators Journal, 24*(2), 16–18.

Mursell, J. (1937b). *The psychology of music.* New York, NY: W. W. Norton.

Neisser, U. (2014). *Cognitive psychology: Classic edition.* New York, NY: Psychology Press. (Original work published in 1967.)

Palisca, C. V. (2001). Consonance: 1. History. In S. Sadie, & J. Tyrrell (Eds.), *The new Grove dictionary of music and musicians* (2nd ed.). London: Macmillan.

Révész, G. (1970). *The psychology of a musical prodigy.* New York, NY: Johnson Reprint Corp. (Original work published in 1925.)

Schultz, D. (1981). *A history of modern psychology.* New York, NY: Academic Press.

Stumpf, C. (1890). *Tonpsychologie.* Leipzig: S. Hirzel.

Stumpf, C. (1898). Konsonanz und dissonanz. *Beiträge zur Akustik und Musikwissenschaft, 1,* 1–108.

Stumpf, C. (2012). *The origins of music* (D. Trippett, Trans.). Oxford: Oxford University Press. (Original work published in 1911.)

Wertheimer, M. (1938). Gestalt theory. In W. Ellis (Ed.), *A source book of Gestalt psychology* (pp. 71–88). London: Routledge & Kegan Paul. (Original work published in 1923.)

Westfall, R. S. (1971). *The construction of modern science: Mechanisms and mechanics.* Cambridge, UK: Cambridge University Press.

Zbikowski, L. M. (2002). *Conceptualizing music: Cognitive structure, theory, and analysis.* New York, NY: Oxford University Press.

# 39

# MUSIC AND COMMUNICATION

*Richard Ashley*

## Introduction

That music communicates in some way or other is a commonplace—but what does this mean and how does this process of communication operate? When we speak of communication we always work in the shadow of language as the touchstone of human communication—and clearly, however one defines music, it differs greatly from language. To work through this question and to disentangle music as communication from language as communication, this chapter will provide a framework for considering human communication broadly, and then locate musical behaviors more specifically within that framework. We will need to consider many topics covered in this *Companion* (see, *inter alia,* those by Clarke, Eitan, Fachner, Gjerdingen, Henry & Grahn, Margulis, Timmers, and Zbikowski) from the standpoint of communication, limiting ourselves largely to Western tonal music for tractability's sake.

## Framing Human Communication

Communication takes place through action; thus, the overall stance of this *Companion*—that music is best understood as varieties of human action (Small, 1998)—opens the door to seeing music as communicative in a distinctively human way (Blacking, 1973; but see also Gingras, this volume). Many species of animals communicate, for example using vocal calls or visual displays. Yet, communication between humans is of a different order from the communicative actions found in other species, even our closest primate relatives. What about human communication is special?

The definition of communication I will use here is *action intended to bring about alignment or coordination of states between individuals.* This definition may benefit from some unpacking through examples. Alignment of states can mean understanding the same set of facts, for example by me telling you "My daughter's birthday was yesterday"; after I have done this, you and I share a common knowledge state and our views of the world, at least with respect to my daughter's birthday, are aligned. Alternately, I can communicate my mood to you by sighing, having a morose facial expression, and slumping my shoulders; here you may not know precisely what I am feeling or why, but you are able to observe my appearance and make inferences about my affective state; your view of my emotions, if not your own feeling state, is becoming aligned with my mood. Or, I can indicate that you should move to some location, whether I indicate this through words or some visual means, such as pointing or gesturing. When you in fact move to that location, your behavior aligns your spatial and movement states with my intentions. In some situations, as for example basketball players seeking to score points, where one player moving in a certain manner toward a location on the court communicates to a teammate where and how he should move, the process need not be face to face and highly channeled.

In all these situations, it is *recognition that some actions are intended to be communicative* that allows communication to in fact take place. *Understanding the intentions of a communicating partner* is the essential element of human communication. An eminent researcher in human and primate communication writes: "The proposal is thus that human cooperative communication—whether using 'natural' gestures or 'arbitrary' conventions—is one instance, albeit a special instance, of uniquely human cooperative activity relying on shared intentionality" (Tomasello, 2008, p. 7). There is a venerable history of thought centering on the centrality of intention, cooperation, and coordination to human communication; a brief discussion follows.

### Communication, Cooperation, and Coordination

Tomasello's statement, above, foregrounds *cooperation* as the touchstone of human communicative activity. Humans communicate to enable cooperation with one another, and do so effectively. What does "cooperation" mean in this context? It means to *act jointly in the service of achieving mutual goals.* Communication is thus inherently a multiagent activity carried out in real time, with incomplete knowledge of the situation. Part of the challenge of communication is to get communicative partners to adequately share knowledge states, or "common ground" (Clark, 1996). If common ground is sufficient, communication and coordination can take place with minimal interactions. For example, if two persons are told they shall be rewarded if they pick the same square from a board with three blue squares and one red square, the odds are they will, even without discussing the matter, pick the red square, as it is most different and therefore salient. The structure of the visual environment, available to both players, provides the needed assistance and common ground for communicative cooperation to occur.

Many current approaches to communication-as-cooperation stem from the work of H. Paul Grice (collected in Grice, 1989). An early topic for Grice was meaning. Grice distinguished between *natural* meaning, for example "those spots mean she has measles" or "those clouds mean that it will rain," and *non-natural* meaning, for example "I mean that you'll be cold dressed like that." In natural meaning, we notice or infer states of affairs in the world but do not ascribe communicative intent to some agent, whereas such communicative intent is the crux of non-natural meaning; most normal communicative actions seek to make themselves, and their intention to communicate, clearly known, or *ostensive* (Sperber & Wilson, 1985). A later topic, for which Grice is best known, is the *Cooperative Principle* and the maxims of communicative behavior that accompany it. The Cooperative Principle states that one should "Make your contribution such as is required, at the stage at which it occurs, by the accepted purpose or direction of the talk exchange in which you are engaged." The natural setting for this advice is spoken dialog between two or more people, but Grice allows for nonverbal situations as well, such as cooking or repairing a car, where one's contribution can be handing a partner an appropriate implement or tool, without speaking. Appropriate actions—communicative in nature—are taken at the right time and in the right manner to further common goals.

Methods of communication may be *ad hoc*, as with hand gestures accompanying speech which are unrehearsed and carry no culturally conventional set meanings (Kendon, 2004), or they may utilize highly conventionalized means, including languages. The ways in which actions and signals are conventionalized by humans to further cooperation have long been noted, as for example by Hume (1739):

> When this common sense of interest is mutually express'd, and is known to both, it produces a suitable resolution and behaviour. And this may properly enough be call'd a convention or agreement betwixt us, tho' without the interposition of a promise; since the actions of each of us have a reference to those of the other, and are perform'd upon the supposition, that something is to be perform'd on the other part. Two men, who pull the oars of a boat, do it by an agreement or convention, tho' they have never given promises to each other.

More modern treatments of this topic have developed these notions considerably (e.g. Lewis, 1969), including conditions that enable and enhance human interaction. Levinson outlines his view of the "human interaction engine," and what makes it work:

> . . . responses are to actions or intentions, not to behaviors . . . a simulation of the other's simulation of oneself is also involved . . . language does not actually code the crucial actions being performed—these are nearly always inferred, or indirectly conveyed . . . interaction is characterized by action chains and sequences . . . is characterized by expectation of close timing . . . is governed not by rule but by expectation.
> *(Levinson, 2006, pp. 45–46)*

Levinson is not discussing music in his chapter, but the connections with music are obvious: the primacy of intending and recognizing intention, the non-necessity of language compared to processes of inference, and the dynamic nature of actions, sequences, and expectations.

## Music, Language, and Communication

With human communication thus framed as the promotion of cooperation and coordination between people in interaction, both language and music fall neatly into place as potentially communicative. There are significant overlaps between music and language, including the neural systems that subserve them, their use of deliberate and contrastive pitch trajectories, and the use of timing to communicate structural divisions in sound sequences (Patel, 2008; Besson, Barbaroux, & Dittenger, this volume). Musical structure, like language, is complicated in its sequencing and organization, but there are also nontrivial differences between the two.

The most striking difference between language and music is the absence, in music, of *propositional* or *semantic content*—that aspect of meaning in language that lets us make statements about states of affairs, and evaluate the truth of such statements. In language we speak of this as *reference*—the use of language to indicate or point to states of affairs. The ability of a speaker to precisely orient the knowledge states of other persons and thus influence, direct, and delimit the actions predicated on such knowledge states, is a highly evolved function of human languages. It is through language that our intentions may be most clearly and unambiguously expressed. Music's lack of semantic content gives rise to what Cross has notably called music's "floating intentionality" (Cross, 2005), and this lack of semantic content has always been a problem for some wishing to understand music as communication; here, however, semantic aspects of language are understood as a means to an end, rather than the end itself (cf. Austin, 1962; Searle, 1969; Sperber & Wilson, 1985; Clark, 1996). Whatever "sense" there is in music, then, it is not denotative but connotative, and is ambiguous rather than precise. It is this ambiguity that allows music to be flexible in how listeners interpret it, and in that way is more like the allusive and evocative language of poetry than it is like finely honed prose.

A second way in which music and language differ is in the status of grammar or syntax. Syntax is essential for the precise sense-making aspects of language to work properly. Such seemingly simple matters as knowing which noun is the subject and which is the object in a sentence are of critical importance, and a syntactic error can render an utterance either wrong or unintelligible. In the case of Western tonal music, it is much less clear what syntax or grammar may entail, and to what degree it matters. The reader is encouraged to compare the varied ways in which the three chapters of this *Companion* (by Shanahan, Gjerdingen, and Temperley & De Clerq) dealing with the structure of tonal music describe musical syntax, which when put in dialog with one another raise a number of important questions. Are musical structures to be understood as primarily predicated on rules about chord progressions? If so, what do we make of the differences between the progressions found in "classical" music and those found in rock? Is syntax in music conventionally fixed, or is it more fluid and probabilistic? Whatever musical syntax and grammar may be, it is clear that they are less determinate and less determinative than in language; a wrong note or chord may be glossed over or forgotten quickly as the music proceeds on its way, but a wrong word may render a sentence unintelligible in a manner which damages all comprehension of the following discourse.

## Musical Structure and Communication

Music may lack precise meaning and determinate syntax, but like language it allows people to find and make use of common ground. The position taken here is that this is the primary purpose of musical structure: to allow all of the participants in a musical environment the ability to perceive or discover ways they have of aligning and coordinating with one another, and to act upon those possibilities. If musical structure communicates, we confront a paradigmatic case of musical communication: a composer (or improviser), who, like a speaker in language, communicates to a listener (Cone, 1974). The composer provides musical structures to the listener, and wishes the listener to make use of, to follow along with, and so to comprehend these structures, in all likelihood intuitively rather than analytically. Let us consider some aspects of musical structure that facilitate these kinds of alignments and coordination between the minds of composer and listener.

### *Melodic Structures*

Western music's structure makes use of both general principles and style-specific materials and processes, both of which contribute to a listener's ability to understand the music.

For example, basic melodic tendencies facilitate perception and allow listeners to predict continuations, tuning into a melody: A melodic move up by step from a first note to a second one implies that the third note will be higher than its predecessor, and will be a small distance—perhaps a step—away from it. Contrastingly, a large leap up from the first to the second note implies that the third note will be lower than the second, thus filling in the registral gap created by the leap. Such melodic tendencies (Narmour, 1990; Shanahan, this volume) can be found in many styles of music and listeners become acquainted with them from early in life. They may be ultimately grounded in a balance-point between the possibilities and limits of the vocal system, where some sound sequences are simply easier or harder to produce than others, and the need to create the acoustic contrasts on which patterns in both speech and music are predicated. These basic melodic tendencies are everywhere present to the infant and the child, in the same way as the natural phenomena Grice uses in discussing non-natural meaning. All composers and listeners have mutual access to them and can use them in their musical sense-making. Eventually they become highly overlearned and serve as the foundation for listeners' ability to comprehend novel melodies, and their expectations of the norms of melodic structure. Beyond these basic or primal structural principles, listeners experienced in specific styles will become well-versed in the patterns used in those styles, whether the formulaic cadences of Western art music or the syncopated, angular rhythms of a jazz composition by Thelonius Monk. The gradual learning of such stylistic conventions—like the acquisition of a language and its conventional forms—allows them to also be used in the construction of common ground (Gjerdingen, this volume).

## Sequential Structures

Musical structure is more complicated than note-to-note melodic successions. Tonality provides for a sense of departure from, and return to, points of stability and patterns of tension and release. The possibilities so afforded by tonality, in interaction with rhythmic structure, allow composers to build hierarchic structures of considerable complexity. These structures potentially provide listeners with the means by which they may keep themselves abreast of where they are in the music's hierarchical organization. However, as surveyed in my other chapter in this *Companion*, listeners are quite constrained in their cognitive abilities to follow the development of such larger structures, leading some to propose that all musical listening is local in scope. These limitations are ameliorated, however, by listeners' abilities to use features like cadential formulas and other stylistically conventionalized patterns indicating formal functions such as beginnings, middles, or ends of musical sections. A listener may not know how she got to a closing point, but she knows she's there, with the help of such musical conventions.

## Contrapuntal Structures

One immediately apparent difference between speech and music lies in their typical density or texture—to use musical terms, speech is monophonic and music is polyphonic. Attention is a scarce cognitive resource, and communication through speech typically maximizes attention by the mechanism of turn taking, where only one participant speaks at a time; exceptions to this are rare (interruption, talking over someone, and the like, which are contraventions of polite verbal behaviors). The timing of turn taking provides evidence of the role of expectation in dialog, as one speaker typically begins after his interlocutor concludes, with hardly a gap (Sacks, Schegloff, & Jefferson, 1974). In music, where simultaneity of voices or lines is the typical rather than the exceptional case, the problem of hearing multiple voices is not avoided through monophony but rather is solved through differentiating voices by rhythm, spacing in the frequency domain, providing each voice with a predictable melodic path, and sometimes other factors such as different timbres (see chapters by Gjerdingen, Shanahan, and McAdams & Goodchild, this volume).

Such compositional techniques make it possible for a listener's attention to weave through multivoice textures—but what sense do these textures make? One approach is to view such textures as a kind of play, or interplay, between musical events conceived of as either active agents themselves or as quasi-linguistic units functioning in ways parallel to the usage of rhetorical units in language (McCreless, 2002). The interpretation of individual parts or lines as active agents in the musical texture is in part contextual. In a simple case, listeners take music-as-sound as evidence of ostensive display by participants in a musical "conversation." In many musical contexts, different lines in the texture are performed by different musicians; this has its Western origins in the grand tradition of vocal polyphony. Even when technologies (such as keyboard or plucked string instruments) permit a single performer to produce multiple lines simultaneously, the mapping of one line (voice) to one performer (voice) remains strong. String quartet members speak of their ensemble interaction as a "conversation," despite the fact that much of *what* they do is given in the musical score, with their role focused on the *how* of the musical utterance (Blum, 1996). A yet more straightforward parallel to linguistic conversation is found in jazz improvisation, where the interactions between players bring together practiced behaviors and spontaneous responses to one another (Berliner, 1994; Monson, 1997; Vuust & Kringelback, this volume). From the relatively clear case of jazz musicians responding to one another's flourishes and feints, to the "virtual performers" one may hear in the diverse contrapuntal lines of a Bach keyboard movement, listeners respond to the energy and vitality of musical lines interacting as if they were the result of intentionally guided ensemble music making. The patterns we hear in a musical style have their roots in embodied acts of music making over the centuries, even if the music we hear is far removed from the physical presence and action of performers (cf. Brøvig-Hanssen & Danielsen, this volume).

## Musical Structure and Emotion

It is in the domain of emotion that a case for musical communication may most perhaps easily be made, which has been done by many scholars in in many ways. Timmers (this volume) provides an excellent introduction; here we engage only some important aspects of music and emotion. We begin by recognizing that listeners routinely report that music represents, expresses, or communicates emotions, sometimes resulting in very powerful experiences (Dissanayake, 2009; Gabrielsson, 2011), and we seek the reasons for this first of all in aspects of musical structure—the "what" of a musical signal. The communicator here is understood to be the composer, who is intending to send an emotionally communicative message to the listener via the music. When a composer makes certain choices, the emotional "cast" of the music begins to be framed quickly. Mode (major vs. minor) and tempo (faster vs. slower) are two of the most influential aspects of a work's structure determining its attributed or experienced affect; the role of such compositional choices on the perceived or felt affect of music has been discussed in depth since the *Affektenlehre* of the 1700s. *Ceteris paribus*, minor mode and/or slower tempo are indicative of negative valence, as opposed to positive valence with major mode and/or faster tempo. Such responses can be found even when the processing of other aspects of musical structure is compromised, for example by brain damage (Peretz, Gagnon, & Bouchard, 1998).

However, mode and tempo are broad-brush aspects of music indeed, and a wealth of musical details are enclosed within such parametric wrappers. These may include important, perceptually salient musical intervals that have either "innate" or culturally-conventional communicative connotations (Cooke, 1959; Curtis & Bharucha, 2010). On a somewhat larger scale are musical motifs or gestures which serve as either frequent but not invariable associations or signs in the semiotic/Peirceian sense, pointing to some clear referent which would be known to a listener (Hatten, 1994; Mirka & Agawu, 2008). Scholars of Western art music sometimes call these stylistically lexicalized materials "topics," which include the "heroic" and the "pastoral" (Mirka, 2016), but music for film and television contains rich inventories as well (Tagg, 1979); such signs or topics suggest, but are not limited to, emotional connotations which go beyond simple valenced responses. This is certainly the case for music which might invoke the pastoral or heroic—complex notions, culturally and emotionally.

The other great role of musical structure in creating emotion lies in the interplay between structure's implications and a listener's expectations (Meyer, 1956). Interaction, including communicative interaction, involves expectation (as in the quote above from Levinson). Musical structure sets up certain implications for what events should come next, and when they should occur, as in the simple melodic example presented earlier in the chapter. The way a composer (or performer) plays with such implications and their realizations engages the listener in many ways, including psychophysiologically through the reward systems of the brain. This topic is dealt with by other chapters of this Companion (see those by Granot, Timmers, and Margulis) and has been refined greatly in the years since Meyer's pioneering essay (cf. Huron, 2006). The reader is directed to these sources for further treatment; here we note only that the listener recognizes the composer's intent to create emotion through structuring the music's twists and turns, struggles and resolutions.

## Musical Performance and Communication

The other paradigmatically communicative situation in music is that of the performer (speaker) playing for an audience (listeners). We will consider musical performance as communicating about musical structure and musical emotion, beginning with structure.

One role of performers is to *communicate information about musical structure* to listeners. Music is structured rather than random; without some implicit or explicit understanding of that structure, listeners may be disinterested, frustrated, or "lost" (Margulis, this volume). For listeners to be aligned with the process of the music, they must be able to follow its structure and flow. Performers facilitate this process by their actions, which serve to clarify the music's structure for the listener. What this means is that performers are constantly inflecting and modulating the salience of details in the music musical surface through changes in the loudness, duration, and timbre of musical events. Even though some of these variations are simply the result of random factors, like the "noise" or variability in any sequence of human actions (Henry & Grahn, this volume), performers are able to be intentional about their actions with regard to musical structure in ways that clarify that structure (Palmer, 1997).

An obvious way in which performers clarify musical structure is by playing the more important line in a texture more loudly; even young musicians, such as those in school bands, are instructed in this. On a more sophisticated level, one effective and well-researched technique used by performers to clarify musical structure for the listener is through timing: altering the nominal, notated, or "mathematically precise" rhythm of the music (Martens & Benadon, this volume). Systematic, as well as random, variation in rhythmic interpretation is one of the best-attested aspects of expressive performance, not only at the note-to-note level but also at higher levels of structure. In hierarchically structured works like of those of the Western art music tradition, this evidences itself in a performer's slowing of the tempo as the end of a section of the music is approaching. The degree of slowing may vary with the hierarchic importance of the ending, with more slowing being one way, although neither definitive nor obligatory, of indicating the ends of larger, more structurally important time spans. Changes in duration at smaller timescales also help to indicate meter, where different positions in the metric cycle are lengthened or shortened systematically, communicating the cycle as well as the tactus or pulse. And, in jazz, where a melody is played with rhythmic freedom over a steady beat, rhythmic variations serve to clarify motivic structure, by transforming the rhythm of recurring motives in the same way, enhancing their categorical similarities to one another, and also by marking phrase and section endings. Through these variations in performance, the soloist is helping the listener keep track of the music's underlying structure while enjoying the flux and flow of the musical surface (Ashley, 2002).

The bodily movements of performers can also provide information to an audience in the form of expressive or ancillary movements, those which are not essential for the production of sounds (see Bishop & Goebl, this volume). Both local details, such as dissonant nonharmonic tones, and larger structural features, such as phrase endings, can be and often are communicated in the visual modality through bodily movements, providing a multimodal, multichannel communicative stream to the listener parallel in some ways to that seen with speech and gesture (Kendon, 2004). And, of course, visual cues from a performer's body give information not only about structure, but also about affect; processes of empathy and emotional contagion always take place when we can interpret someone's face or body as reflective of an affective state (Juslin & Västfjäll, 2008).

## Music and Interpersonal Coordination

To conclude this survey of musical communication, we note another everyday way in which music is deemed communicative: its ability to let people feel that they are "in touch" with each other. Entrainment—aligning the movement of one's body with an external pulse (see Henry and Grahn, this volume)—is one of the most obvious and interesting ways in which music enables interpersonal coordination, as individuals line up their motor systems with one another, through dance, bobbing heads, participating in a drum circle, or other activities, whether overt or inner. Although some nonhuman species can entrain to music, this ability is not widespread in the animal kingdom (Gringas, this volume), and evidently has a genetic basis. Some scholars have seen connections between mutual entrainment—the rhythmic alignment and interplay of two or more human bodies—to what has come to be called *communicative musicality* (Dissanayake, 2009). This framework has its roots in theories of the psychological and emotional connections between mothers and their infants, where various actions—vocalizations, movements of the limbs, breathing—are all intertwined and temporally connected with one another. The human capacity for entrainment—aligning with the rhythmic aspects of an external stimulus—thus is seen at the earliest stages of life. The evolutionary advantages of a mother feeling so connected to her infant as they interact, by movement or by vocalizations, as with infant-directed speech, are obvious in our species, where the young are unable to care for themselves for so much of their lives.

One need not be moving along with music in the company of others in order to feel connected and aligned with them. In their studies of adolescents' use of music for self-regulation, Saarikallio and Erkkilä (2007) define a number of regulatory strategies which emerged from the comments of their informants. Among these was "solace," where a young person, listening alone to music would feel understood and comforted: ". . . when you feel that I have experienced so much the same as him [the singer], then they kind of fit into my life, too, and then like comfort in some way" (Saarikallio & Erkkilä 2007, p. 100)—even though the composers or performers were personally unknown to the listener, and were nowhere in sight. Such is the power of music to create a sense of interpersonal alignment and connection, despite distance in space and time and incomplete knowledge of the other person. More broadly, the potential for music to facilitate a sense of unity among people has been proposed as important for the development of our species as a whole (Mithen, 2005) and continues to fascinate researchers interested in social cohesion (Koelsch, & Stegemann, 2012).

## Conclusions and Further Directions

In the earlier decades of research in music cognition, investigators primarily focused on perception of carefully controlled stimuli with little communicative potential. More recently, the use of more ecologically realistic materials has opened the door for studies of musical communication. This chapter has identified a number of primary aspects of such communication which have been focal, particularly the communication of musical structure and of emotion. We have learned much from these studies, and yet the interactive aspect of musical communication has been but little examined. Broadly speaking, the cognitive sciences are beginning to address cognition beyond the soundproof booth in the laboratory, where people respond to one another and are co-participants in culture, including musical culture (Lamont, this volume). To more fully understand music as communication, research paradigms are needed which conceive of communication less as one-way channeling of information from composers or performers to listeners and more as active, foraging behaviors by listeners (Clarke, this volume). The reader who explores the chapters of this *Companion* with that thought in mind will find a multitude of possibilities suggested for such investigations, including music alone and with others, "own" vs. "other" musical cultures, and the multiplicity of understandings and meanings even one listener can find in only one piece of music.

## Core Reading

Blacking, J. (1973) *How musical is man?* Seattle, WA: University of Washington Press.

Grice, H. P. (1989). *Studies in the way of words*. Cambridge, MA: Harvard University Press.

Juslin, P., & Västfjäll, D. (2008). Emotional responses to music: The need to consider underlying mechanisms. *Behavioral and Brain Science, 31*, 559–621.

Kendon, A. (2004*). Gesture: Visible action as utterance*. Cambridge: Cambridge University Press.

Levinson, S. C. (2006). On the human "interaction engine." In: N. J. Enfield, & S. C. Levinson (Eds.), *Roots of human sociality: Culture, cognition and interaction* (pp. 9–69). Oxford: Berg.

Small, C. (1998). *Musicking: The meanings of performing and listening*. Middletown, CT: Wesleyan University Press.

Tomasello, M. (2008). *Origins of human communication*. Cambridge, MA: MIT Press.

## Further References

Ashley, R. (2002). Do[n't] change a hair for me: The art of jazz rubato. *Music Perception, 19* (3), 311–332.

Austin, J. L. (1962). *How to do things with words.* Oxford: Oxford University Press.

Berliner, P. (1994). *Thinking in jazz: The infinite art of improvisation.* Chicago, IL: University of Chicago Press.

Blum, D. (1986) *The art of quartet playing: The Guarneri Quartet in conversation.* New York, NY: Alfred Knopf.

Clark, H. (1996). *Using language.* Cambridge: Cambridge University Press.

Cone, E. (1974) *The composer's voice.* Berkeley, CA: University of California Press.

Cooke, D. (1959). *The language of music.* Oxford: Oxford University Press.

Curtis, M. E., & Bharucha, J. J. (2010). The minor third communicates sadness in speech, mirroring its use in music. *Emotion 10,* 335–348.

Cross, I. (2005). Music and meaning, ambiguity and emotion. In D. Miell, D. Hargreaves, & R. Macdonald (Eds.). *Musical communication* (pp. 27–34). Oxford: Oxford University Press.

Dissanayake, E. (2009) Root, leaf, blossom, or bole: Concerning the origin and adaptive function of music. In S. Malloch, & C. Trevarthen (Eds.), *Communicative musicality* (pp. 17–30). Oxford: Oxford University Press.

Gabrielsson, A. (2011) *Strong experiences with music.* Oxford: Oxford University Press.

Hatten, R. (1994). *Musical meaning in Beethoven: Markedness, correlation, and interpretation.* Bloomington, IN: Indiana University Press.

Hume, D. (1739). *A treatise of human nature.* London: John Noon.

Huron, D. (2006). *Sweet anticipation: Music and the psychology of expectation.* Cambridge, MA: MIT Press.

Koelsch, S., & Stegemann, T. (2012). The brain and positive biological effects in healthy and clinical populations. In R. McDonald, G. Kreutz, & L. Mitchell (Eds.), *Music, health, and wellbeing* (436–456). Oxford: Oxford University Press.

Lewis, D. (1969). *Convention.* Cambridge, MA: Harvard University Press.

McCreless, P. (2002). Music and rhetoric. In T. Christensen (Ed.), *Cambridge history of Western music theory* (pp. 845–879). Cambridge: Cambridge University Press.

Meyer, L. (1956). *Emotion and meaning in music.* Chicago, IL: University of Chicago Press.

Mirka, D. (Ed.) (2016). *Oxford handbook of topic theory.* Oxford: Oxford University Press.

Mirka, D., & Agawu, K. (Eds.) (2008). *Communication in eighteenth-century music.* Cambridge: Cambridge University Press.

Mithen, S. (2005). *The singing Neanderthals: Origins of music, language, mind, and body.* London: Weidenfeld and Nicolson.

Monson, I. (1997). *Saying something: Jazz improvisation and interaction.* Chicago, IL: University of Chicago Press.

Narmour, E. (1990) *The analysis and cognition of basic melodic structures.* Chicago, IL: University of Chicago Press.

Palmer, C. (1997). Music Performance. *Annual Review of Psychology, 48,* 115–138.

Patel, A. (2008). *Music, language, and the brain.* Oxford: Oxford University Press.

Peretz, I., Gagnon, L., & Bouchard, B. (1998). Music and emotion: perceptual determinants, immediacy and isolation after brain damage. *Cognition, 68,* 111–141.

Saarikallio, S., & Erkkilä, J. (2007). The role of music in adolescents' mood regulation. *Psychology of Music, 35(1),* 88–109.

Sacks, H., Schegloff, E., & Jefferson, G. (1974). A simplest systematics for the organization of turn-taking for conversation. *Language 50,* 696–735.

Searle, J. (1969). *Speech acts: An essay in the philosophy of language.* Cambridge: Cambridge University Press.

Sperber, D., & Wilson, D. (1985). *Relevance: Communication and cognition.* Oxford: Blackwell.

Tagg, P. (1979). *Kojak: 50 Seconds of television music.* Goteborg, Sweden: University of Goteborg.

# 40

# EMOTION IN MUSIC LISTENING

*Renee Timmers*

It is hard to imagine listening to music without somehow being affected by it and experiencing a change in attention, attitude or physical arousal. Whether it is due to culture, biology or an interaction between the two, our listening to music is closely coupled with an affective-bodily experience that may lead us to say that we feel touched, lifted, transported, or otherwise moved or affected by the music. This is often in a positive way, making us feel better than before, but sometimes also affects us negatively. Perhaps we are conditioned to judge whether or not we recognize and like the music that we hear, inferring what the music means to us, and how we relate to it. Perhaps, as well, we are so used to moving along with music that we can't help but feel aroused or calmed by it.

While this is a very broad description of responses to music, it contains a number of characteristics that suggest the involvement of emotion, if we assume that emotion is a valenced (i.e. positive or negative) appraisal of a stimulus (in this case music and events in it), accompanied by an action-readiness of the body (and mind) to respond.

More precisely, Scherer (2005) distinguished five components, whose inter-play and synchronized occurrence characterize emotion, including a) cognitive-appraisal, b) neurophysiological, c) motor, d) motivational, and e) subjective feeling components. Importantly, engagement with music seems to *simultaneously involve several* of these components. For example, music and its characteristics are evaluated (appraised) as e.g. pleasant, soothing, shocking, or novel; features of the music may trigger (or perhaps better *afford*) bodily and physiological responses (e.g. dancing and a faster heart-beat); encountering the music may draw us in (e.g. dancing together) or repel us; and this whole experience may give rise to feelings of happiness or otherwise.

These examples give an initial indication of how it is possible that music evokes feelings of emotion in listeners who engage with music, which has been one of the questions central to emotion in music research. Other central concerns have been to clarify *what* emotions are perceived and felt in music, and *how* music can be heard as expressive of certain emotions. A distinction is made in the literature between *perceived* emotions in music and *felt* emotions, acknowledging the independence of these two responses (Gabrielsson, 2002). Furthermore, one of the central objectives of research in music and emotion has been to uncover the roles of the compositional structure and the manner of performance (see relevant chapters in Juslin & Sloboda, 2010) in the experience of emotion in music. It is assumed that all three (composition, performer and listener) play a role, in addition to factors related to the context in which the music is heard.

Most of this chapter will be dedicated to these central questions, starting with considering what emotions are perceived in music and how they are perceived, and continuing with the discussion of what, and how emotions are felt in response to music. Additionally, I will consider a recent development in research that investigates the role of emotions in the music listening process—do emotions influence the way we perceive and remember music? The focus in this chapter will be on emotions in response to Western tonal music, in particular "classical" music, as this has been the central domain for music and emotion research, but I will also deal with film music. References to cross-genre variations and generalities will be made where available and appropriate.

## Perception of Emotion in Music

In an important summary of research on emotion perceived in music, Gabrielsson and Juslin (2003) found the perception of certain basic categories of emotions in music to be particularly reliable. Listeners agree when deciding whether a musical excerpt sounds "happy," "sad," "fearful," or "angry," in contrast to more subtle distinctions (e.g. between sad or melancholy) or more abstract emotions (e.g. surprise). Arguing for a special status of basic emotions in the communication of emotion in music, Juslin and Laukka (2003) summarized parallels between the expression of basic emotions in speech by actors and in music by performers. They argued that musicians shape particular acoustical features in performance so as to communicate a particular emotion, which is similar to the way actors portray emotional speech. The effectiveness of this ability to express basic emotions through sound may have a biological origin: From an evolutionary perspective, it is beneficial to be able to effectively communicate and perceive emotional states, and vocal expressions are an important form of such communication. Specialized forms of expression may have consequently arisen for so called primary emotions. Evidence in favor of this hypothesis comes from cross-cultural investigations (Laukka, Eerola, Thingujam, Yamasaki, & Beller, 2013) and comparisons between expressions in speech and music (Juslin & Laukka, 2003; Bowling, Sundararajan, Han, & Purves, 2012).

Nevertheless, despite compelling evidence and sound arguments, empirical data exploring these predictions often show less clear-cut communication of discrete emotions, with considerable variation in the ways emotions are expressed and confusions between emotions (e.g. sad and tender). Therefore, rather than expecting categorically different expressions corresponding to basic emotions, it may be that the relationship between emotion and vocal acoustic characteristics originates at a more general level: Physiological and motor patterns (e.g. smiling and tensing muscles) that are part of emotional responses also affect vocal expressions (Scherer, 1986; Banse & Scherer, 1996). This means that the expressions depend on the state associated with the experienced emotion, which varies with e.g. the intensity of the felt emotion.

In either case, it is clear that emotional expressions in music are not restricted to basic emotions, nor are expressive cues restricted to cues with a biological origin. Exploring the first question of what emotions are expressed in music, Schubert (2003) asked participants to rate the suitability of 91 emotion terms to "describe any kind of music." Analysis of the terms that were considered to be suitable to describe music revealed nine clusters. Highest scoring terms were bright, lyrical, graceful, dreamy, dark, majestic, tragic, tense, and dramatic. More typical emotion terms were part of these clusters including (in the same cluster order) happy, humorous, tender, sentimental, sad, vigorous, agitated, and passionate/exciting. This suggests that music-emotional expression is a combination of musical character (i.e. lyrical, dreamy) and emotion. This indicates perhaps stylized emotion (Schubert & Fabian, 2014) or emotion expressed in a broader meaning-bearing context (see also Clarke, this volume).

This focus on the communication of emotion categories may give the misleading impression that the goal of music is to convey a precise emotion. However, if precision is the goal, we would be better off with words! Indeed, Cross (2008) refers to music as having "floating intentionality," emphasizing the indeterminacy of its meaning. Recognition of particular emotions may be part of a sense-making process where acoustic and music structural characteristics are interpreted within a contextual framework. In this explanation, the acoustic and structural characteristics of music convey emotional qualities in a broad manner, the meaning of which is further specified by the context (see Cross, 2008 for some interesting examples).

Dimensional models of emotion have been used to capture variations in broad emotional qualities, most frequently as a two-dimensional model of emotional valence (pleasant-unpleasant) and emotional arousal (sleepy-awake/aroused) (Russell, 2003). A three-dimensional model including potency/power as an additional dimension may provide a more complete characterization of emotions and emotional expressions (e.g. Goudbeek & Scherer, 2010). Moreover, empirical findings point towards the need to differentiate two types of arousal in characterizing emotions—"energetic arousal" as in active vs. calm and "tense arousal" as in frustrated vs. relaxed (Schimmack, & Rainer, 2002).

Dimensional models of emotion have been used to capture moment-to-moment variations in emotional expression as perceived or experienced in response to music (Schubert, 2004). Indeed, music seems well suited to convey varying degrees of emotional arousal and valence (Schubert, 2004), as well as tension (Ilie & Thompson, 2006). Of these, variations in emotional arousal appear to be communicated relatively robustly through music, showing unambiguous correlations with parameters including intensity, tempo and rhythmic articulation (Schubert, 2004; Gomez & Danuser, 2007; Timmers, 2007a). Similar correlations are found between acoustical features and emotional arousal in speech (Ilie & Thompson, 2006; Coutinho & Dibben, 2013). Variations in emotional arousal are recognized not only by enculturated listeners, but also by participants without prior exposure to the musical style in question (e.g. Congolese Pygmies listening to Western music, see Egermann, Fernando, Chuen, & McAdams, 2014).

Associations between physiological arousal and changes in vocal expressions were mentioned above as a possible underlying factor contributing to the perception of emotional arousal. A second contributing factor may be an association between temporal aspects of the music and a sense of movement, physical or imagined. Indeed, it has been suggested that emotional experiences of music are closely linked to experiences of motion (Molnar-Szakacs & Overy, 2006). Widening the scope of this approach further, cross-modal correspondences with musical parameters—including associations with force, magnitude, size or elevation—may mediate or contribute to the emotional character we perceive in a musical passage. Dancers might translate certain musical characteristics into lightness or heaviness, bodily fluidity or tension; listeners may understand these characteristics as implying different bodily and emotional states. A close association between cross-modal correspondences and emotion is also apparent from the clusters of musical descriptors referred to above

(Schubert, 2003), in which emotion terms are clustered together with visual and physical imagery terms. Examples of a three-fold relationship between emotion, cross-domain mappings of physical attributes, and acoustical parameters can be found in speech and music (for a review see Eitan, Timmers, & Adler, in press; Eitan, this volume).

Experienced emotional valence may be successfully predicted on the basis of acoustical parameters to a certain degree (Coutinho & Dibben, 2013), but models formulated for particular examples do not generalize well to other examples (Coutinho & Dibben, 2013; Eerola, 2011; Timmers, 2007a). To vary emotional valence effectively, it is necessary to adjust aspects of the music's compositional structure in addition to varying the music's acoustic dimensions, such as intensity and tempo, in performance (Quinto, Thompson, & Taylor, 2014). A powerful way to vary emotional valence is to manipulate the inclusion of consonant/dissonant musical chords (Blood, Zatorre, Bermudez, & Evans, 1999). Despite this robust effect, familiarity with dissonant chords moderates the degree of perceived dissonance, making this a cultural as well as a psychoacoustic phenomenon (Arthurs & Timmers, 2016).

Varying the mode of a composition (major/minor) is another common way to vary its emotional valence. Children's sensitivity to this manipulation of emotional valence develops with age, in particular where melodic sequences without supporting chords are concerned (Dalla Bella, Peretz, Rousseau, & Gosselin, 2001). The origin of this culturally supported association between mode and emotional valence has been the topic of considerable debate. Parncutt (2014) outlined six possible contributing factors: 1) The minor triad is more dissonant than the major triad; 2) it is less common and therefore marked as different; 3) it is more ambiguous in tonality and can be perceived as uncertain; 4) it is less familiar and so gains less positive associations; 5) it is more salient in timbre within its harmonic context; 6) and there is a parallel with (sad) speech in that the minor triad has a lower (or more subdued) pitch than expected (see e.g. Bowling et al., 2012). Parncutt (2014) refers to a number of relevant phenomena: Repeated exposure/greater familiarity is associated with increases of positive affect (Zajonc, 2001); prediction is a fundamental cognitive function and closely associated with affective response reinforcing learning (Bechara, Damasio, Tranel, & Damasio, 1997) and contextual presentation strongly influences connotations (Walker, 2016). Following Meyer (1956) and Huron (2006), Parncutt (2014) argues that (tonal) uncertainty and violation of expectancies induce a sense of negative valence.

It seems that our perceptual processing of structural and acoustical characteristics of music have affective implications. This may be through associations with vocal expressions, movement patterns, or physical and cognitive phenomena, or is perhaps intrinsic to the processing of musical materials themselves—i.e. expectations are confirmed or violated, an expected resolution is delayed, a musical passage comes to a halt, changes suddenly, is complex or easy to predict.[1] Sounds and musical structures set up contexts with varying coloration (e.g. bright–dark), physical implications (e.g. strong–weak), and degrees of stability and predictability. The emotion we perceive in a musical passage is informed by these implications but also depends on the way we engage with the music, conceptualize emotions, and conceptualize what we hear (see for a discussion Moran, this volume). For example, when we visually perceive movement and facial expression, this informs us about expressed emotions, as well as the intensity of these emotions (e.g., Thompson, Russo, & Quinto, 2008; Vines, Krumhansl, Wanderley, Dalca, & Levitin, 2011). Furthermore, appraisals of emotion in music show influences of personal background, including influences of familiarity with the music, age, mood and personality traits (Laukka et al., 2013; Lima & Castro, 2011; Vuoskoski &

Eerola, 2011). These inter-subjective differences become even more apparent when we look at felt rather than perceived emotional responses.

## Felt Emotion in Response to Music

Feeling the emotion expressed in music can occur through a process of "emotional contagion"—one of the mechanisms included in Juslin and Västfjäll's (2008) review on emotion induction in music listening. In their model, emotional contagion happens through internal mimicry of vocal expressions, which is seen as the primary source for perceived emotion in music (see also Juslin, 2013). Others interpret emotional contagion more broadly, including contagion through motor mimicry (e.g. Scherer & Coutinho, 2013). Contagion is related to empathy, but the two are not synonymous. In the latter, listeners imagine the experience of emotions felt by other actors, such as performers and composers. This difference becomes blurred, however, if we perceive emotion in music as deriving from a virtual musical agent or persona, where music is perceived as human expression without the need to attribute it to a particular person (composer, performer or conductor) (see for empirical support e.g. Watt & Ash, 1998). Still, we can imagine that empathy for (for example) a young soloist performer may lead to different emotional experiences than a focus on the perceived emotion in the music.

In cases of emotional contagion, one expects similar emotions to be felt in response to music as perceived, and perceived emotion to be stronger than felt emotion—which is indeed often the case (Schubert, 2013). Other emotion induction processes may, however, give rise to mixed or unmatched relationships, for example when some positively valenced musical passage reminds listeners of a negative period in their life (Gabrielsson, 2002; Schubert, 2013). With the aim to investigate what emotions are experienced in music listening situations, Zentner, Grandjean, and Scherer (2008) started with a list of 515 general terms, which were presented to participants who indicated for each term whether they would use the term to describe feelings of emotions they experience. Based on the results, the list was reduced to 146 "affect terms," including 89 emotion terms that were reported to be perceived or felt with some frequency by participants in relation to music. After deleting synonyms, a list of 66 "musical emotion" terms was presented to 800 volunteers attending a music festival, who indicated their experience of these emotions during the festival. Analysis of the responses indicated 9 dimensions or groups of emotion terms. Six of these were positive in affect, including wonder, transcendence, tenderness, peacefulness, power, and joyful activation, while two were negative (tension and sadness) and one ambiguous in valence (nostalgia). Similarly, an experience sampling study investigating emotions experienced during everyday life episodes including music found a predominance of positive emotions, in this case including calmness, happiness, interest, and pleasure. Two groups of negative emotions were identified—sadness and anger-irritation—and the same ambiguously valenced emotion—nostalgia (Juslin, Liljeström, Västfjäll, Barradas, & Silva 2008). Differences between the findings of these studies suggest an influence of listening context (everyday life or concert experience) on emotional responses, although these differences may also be due to other methodological details.

Zentner and colleagues (2008) observed several differences between emotions reported to be frequent in music listening and frequent in everyday life. Negative emotions such as dysphoria (unease) and sadness were more often experienced in daily life than in music listening. Emotions more often experienced in music depended on the musical genre. For classical music and jazz, frequent responses were amazement and peacefulness, while for

Latin music and Techno, they included activation and (for Latin) joy. In their experience sampling study, Juslin and colleagues (2008) also found a greater prevalence of negative emotions in episodes of everyday life without music, while episodes with music included more often experiences of happiness-elation and nostalgia-longing.

A debate is ongoing regarding the ways in which those emotions experienced in aesthetic response to music (and other art) differ from those experienced in day-to-day activities. "Musical emotions" are similar to otherwise evoked emotions in showing similar and equally strong brain activations and physiological responses (Koelsch, 2014). On the other hand, these emotions may differ in being more intrinsically driven and less goal-directed (Scherer, 2005). This doesn't mean that musical emotions do not serve a purpose. In contrast, listeners often choose to listen to music with a certain purpose in mind (e.g. relaxation, motivation, and encouragement): The emotional effect of music is an important means to obtain this goal (see also Dibben, this volume, and Saarikallio, this volume). An association has been found between emotions experienced, music selected, and the context of listening (Juslin et al., 2008).

A further outstanding issue concerns responses to "sad" music. "Sadness" is reported relatively frequently when listening to classical music (Zentner et al., 2008), and yet such listening may be enjoyable. This sad-but-enjoyable response seems to depend on personality characteristics of the listeners: Listeners who enjoy listening to sad music tend to score relatively high in introversion, openness to experience and empathy (Ladinig & Schellenberg, 2012; Vuoskoski, this volume). In summarizing descriptions that listeners gave of experiences with sad music, Peltola and Eerola (2016) distinguished positive experiences of sad music (sweet sorrow), from two types of negative experiences (grief and melancholy). Indeed, they found different attitudes towards sad music, including "avoidance," "appreciation," "revival," "amplification," and "intersubjective" (Eerola, Peltola, & Vuoskoski, 2015), reflecting different ways in which participants conceptualized sad music and its effects. For example, participants reported to feel less alone in their grief when experiencing sad music (intersubjective); sad music strengthened awareness of the value and purpose of life (appreciation); or sad music made them feel sad (amplification). Providing a theoretical framework for responses to sad music and individual differences between listeners, Huron (2011) argued that listeners differ in the degree to which they empathize with the emotion expressed in the music, and also in the degree to which they are able to cognitively reassure themselves that the sad-inducing stimulus is fictional.

The example of experiencing sad music highlights the individual and contextual nature of emotional responses to music, in addition to feeling the emotion expressed in the music. As discussed above, this latter process of "emotional contagion" is one of the best-recognized induction mechanisms (Juslin et al., 2008), among several other mechanisms through which emotion may be induced. The best-known summary of emotion induction processes comes from the work by Juslin and colleagues (Juslin & Västfjäll, 2008; Juslin, 2013) and includes eight emotion induction mechanisms, abbreviated as BRECVEMA: Brainstem response, Rhythmic entrainment, Evaluative conditioning, Contagion, Visual imagery, Episodic memory, Musical expectancy, and Aesthetic judgment. Scherer and Coutinho (2013) also include these mechanisms in their summary of emotion induction processes. However, they frame them into four possible routes for felt emotion, each of which include multiple mechanisms, which offers fruitful avenues for further investigation. The first route, "appraisal," is controversial in the sense that it is subsidiary for felt emotion in music according to

Juslin (2013), while for Scherer and Coutinho (2013) it is central. The controversy arises partly from different interpretations regarding what "appraisal" entails. According to Scherer and Coutinho (2013), appraisal includes low-level, automatic evaluation of properties of stimuli as well as higher-level cognitive evaluations of the implications of stimuli for a person's goals. The novelty (i.e. predicted, unexpected, sudden), urgency (i.e. loud), and intrinsic pleasantness (i.e. consonant or dissonant) of musical sounds are examples of low-level appraisals. This means that in Scherer and Coutinho's (2013) framework both "Musical expectancy" and "Brainstem response" contribute to the appraisal route. This deviates from Juslin's (2013) interpretation of appraisal as primarily referring to higher-level cognitive evaluations, which would have limited relevance for musical emotions because "music as such rarely has implications for life goals" (Juslin, 2013, p. 239). Nevertheless, as argued above, it is likely for the emotional effect of music to depend on both listening context and a listener's relationship to the music. Support for this hypothesis is for example found in a study investigating physiological responses to music (in this case, the occurrence of a "chill" response). Grewe, Nagel, Kopiez, and Altenmüller (2007) explain that it is not sufficient to look for musical triggers "causing" the response. Instead, the response depends on listeners' attitude and attention towards the music. For Grewe et al. (2007), "it is not so much the distinct musical feature, but the focus of [evaluative] attention on the music that is important for arousing chills" (p. 312).

An assessment of quality or aesthetic value of music is key to Scherer and Coutinho's (2013) account of appraisal. Indeed, perceived quality and felt emotion have been found to be highly correlated in listeners' judgments of musical performances (e.g. Timmers, 2007b; Schubert & Fabian, 2014). A close association between the two is also central to some theoretical accounts of expressiveness in music performance. As Doğantan-Dack (2014) argues, "there is one particular feature that subsumes all those who engage with an expressive music performance, and this is the affective involvement that it elicits" (p. 16). This affective experience is related to "the value attributed to the performance and the performer, who may or may not set out to express or communicate the same or a similar affective content" (p. 15).

The second aspect of Scherer and Coutinho's (2013) multifactorial process model is the "memory" route. This includes both episodic and associative memory. Emotions may arise through episodic memory, when listeners are reminded of previous emotional encounters with the music. In addition to specific reminders of autobiographical episodes, music may evoke non-episodic associations, including in the form of visual and auditory imagery. Indeed, much of music's meaning may be learned through cultural exposure, through which musical patterns and structures become emotionally loaded.

Scherer and Coutinho's third route, "entrainment," refers to psychophysiological responses to musical characteristics, including but not restricted to motor responses to musical rhythms. It is not just that emotional responses trigger changes in physiological arousal: Physiological states dynamically interact with emotional response (for a musical example, see Dibben, 2004). Finally, as mentioned earlier, "emotional contagion" refers to a process whereby listeners internally mimic or experience emotions they observe or perceive, while in "emotional empathy," listeners are empathetic towards emotions felt by other actors (e.g. performers and composer).

The complexity of emotion induction by music is amplified further by the interrelationships and interactions between different processes. For example, motor entrainment is a source for changes in physiological arousal. Additionally, if the music has a strong steady pulse, it is a source for prediction of musical events. Such accurate prediction may induce a positive appraisal (Huron, 2006), which may be stronger in cases when the prediction is challenging rather than simple (and perhaps when a listener is more invested in predicting the music). This question of the relationship between complexity, entrainment and experienced pleasure is relevant, for example, to the experience of "groove" music (Witek, Clarke, Wallentin, Kringelbach, & Vuust, 2014).

A considerable number of questions remain unanswered with respect to felt emotions, including the effect of variations across musical genres, with age and personality, and also those brain structures supporting various emotion mechanisms. The complexity of felt emotions is now being handled with increasing sophistication in empirical investigations. To allow for "ambiguous" emotions or the simultaneous experience of different emotions (such as sad AND happy), several authors have adopted the evaluative space model of emotion (Cacioppo & Berntson, 1994) that proposes that negative and positive evaluations may be coupled in a reciprocal or coactive manner or uncoupled and be activated independently. Progress has been made in defining those emotions relevant for music listening, and in characterizing processes that play a role in emotion induction. These include an interesting mix of emotions and processes relevant for emotion in general, but also some domain-related specializations. Music as a source for pleasure and aesthetic reward is a considerable contributor to emotional response. Understanding music as an aesthetic reward in an individualized manner and relating this coherently to the proposed emotion processes will be an important challenge for coming research (see Juslin, 2013).

## Interactions between Cognition and Emotion in Music

Given the frequency of perceived and felt emotions in music, we may wonder what implications they have for the listening process. Are emotions only a consequence of listening to music, or do they also interact with this listening process—influencing and shaping it in some way? Interactions between emotion and cognition are well evidenced outside of the musical domain. A few studies have begun to investigate this question empirically with respect to music cognition. One of the effects of emotion evoked in music listening is that it can influence memory for music. Houston and Haddock (2007) demonstrated that depending on the mood state (positive or negative) of listeners when learning a set of melodies, those melodies in major mode or minor mode were better remembered. It is also likely that strong emotional experiences with music strengthen memory for that music.

Another effect of emotion during music listening is that it may influence our perception of music and our expectations concerning the characteristics that music may have. Boltz and colleagues (2009) showed that the presentation of emotional visual stimuli alongside music influenced the perception of emotional as well as non-emotional attributes, including judgments of the tempo of music—tunes were judged to be faster in the context of positive affect compared to negative affect. Similarly setting up an emotional context using visual images, Timmers and Crook (2014) demonstrated that emotions influence musical expectations: depending on the emotional context, listeners expected the music to go up rather than down, or to continue with larger rather than smaller intervals. Such expectations may additionally change the way we attend to music. For example, we may focus more strongly on melodic movement in a lower pitch range in a sad context, while attending to a higher pitch range in a happy context (Timmers, Crook, & Morimoto, 2012).

While this is a recent area of research, several studies have offered implicit evidence of the influence of emotion on the perception of music. For example, studies have demonstrated the influence of visually expressed emotion on the perception of a musical performance (e.g. Vines et al., 2011). It is likely that interactions between emotion and cognition of music play a greater role than generally acknowledged. Emotions have been shown to play a role in musical preference and uses of music (see Vuoskoski, this volume; Dibben, this volume), but they should also be considered when investigating memory for music, attention to music and perception of music. Music may be chosen for its emotional effect, but also better remembered for it. Moreover, moments marked emotionally draw our attention, and our emotional experience of the music influences what musical aspects we focus on and how we perceive the music.

## Conclusion

Emotion in music has attracted considerable research attention in recent years and this body of research continues to grow. This includes behavioral studies of emotional effects of music in everyday life, laboratory studies of emotional responses to music with various characteristics, neuroscientific investigations, therapeutic uses of music and emotion, and larger-scale survey studies that allow investigation of individual differences and cross-cultural differences, among others. Central to research in music and emotion is the assumption that listeners (but also performers and composers) perceive music as a means to express emotion, and as a means to feel emotion. The types of emotions perceived and felt may vary, and not all music may be equally "emotional." Variations across different genres are one of the promising areas for further investigation. Despite these variations, there is evidence for a biological basis for emotional responses to sound and music associated with vocalizations of emotion, which helps to explain communication of emotions in early infancy and across cultures. Other physical and biological processes further inform and constrain expression and perception of emotion, including learned and structural correspondences between sensory and kinesthetic domains. Cross-domain correspondences may also be a precondition for motor entrainment to arise (Patel, 2014), which seems in turn central to emotion perception and experience. However, cognitive and cultural factors also play an important role, as emotional responses to music tend to vary strongly across individuals, contexts, and occasions. Moreover, it seems that the ways we use music (e.g. in film, theatre, church, or privately) affect the kinds of emotions expressed and experienced through music, which is itself culturally shaped. At an individual level, we may have certain expectations concerning emotions evoked by music depending on the way we use and engage with music, but also depending on the way we normally express and experience emotions. It is interesting to consider that our engagement with music may reflect many dimensions of our lives, including aspects of our emotional personality, and how we employ music listening in guiding and informing our inner, emotional selves and narratives.

## Note

1. Confirmation and violation of expectations are generally primarily included as sources of "felt" emotion. However, it is likely that these aspects also influence listeners' accounts of perceived emotion.

## Core Reading

Eerola, T. (2011). Are the emotions expressed in music genre-specific? An audio-based evaluation of datasets spanning classical, film, pop and mixed genres. *Journal of New Music Research, 40,* 349–366.

Juslin, P. N. (2013). From everyday emotions to aesthetic emotions: Towards a unified theory of musical emotions. *Physics of Life Reviews, 10*(3), 235–266.

Juslin, P. N., & Sloboda, J. A. (Eds.) (2010). *Handbook of music and emotion: Theory, research, applications.* Oxford: Oxford University Press.

Koelsch, S. (2014). Brain correlates of music-evoked emotions. *Nature Reviews Neuroscience, 15*(3), 170–180.

Laukka, P., Eerola, T., Thingujam, N. S., Yamasaki, T., & Beller, G. (2013). Universal and culture-specific factors in the recognition and performance of musical affect expressions. *Emotion, 13*(3), 434–449.

Scherer, K. R., & Coutinho, E. (2013). How music creates emotion: A multifactorial process approach. In T. Cochrane, B. Fantini, & K. R. Scherer (Eds.), *The emotional power of music* (pp. 121–145). Oxford: Oxford University Press.

Zentner, M., Grandjean, D., & Scherer, K. R. (2008). Emotions evoked by the sound of music: Characterization, classification, and measurement. *Emotion, 8*(4), 494–521.

## Further References

Arthurs, Y., & Timmers, R. (2016). On the fluidity of consonance and dissonance: The influence of musical context. *Psychomusicology: Music, Mind, and Brain, 26,* 1–14.

Banse, R., & Scherer, K. R. (1996). Acoustic profiles in vocal emotion expression. *Journal of Personality and Social Psychology, 70,* 614–636.

Bechara, A., Damasio, H., Tranel, D., & Damasio, A. R. (1997). Deciding advantageously before knowing the advantageous strategy. *Science, 275,* 1293–1295.

Blood, A. J., Zatorre, R. J., Bermudez, P., & Evans, A. C. (1999). Emotional responses to pleasant and unpleasant music correlate with activity in paralimbic brain regions. *Nature Neuroscience, 2*(4), 382–387.

Boltz, M. G., Ebendorf, B., & Field, B. (2009). Audiovisual interactions: The impact of visual information on music perception and memory. *Music Perception, 27,* 43–59.

Bowling, D. L., Sundararajan, J., Han, S. E., & Purves, D. (2012). Expression of emotion in Eastern and Western music mirrors vocalization. *PLoS ONE, 7*(3), e31942.

Cacioppo, J. T., & Berntson, G. G. (1994). Relationship between attitudes and evaluative space: A critical review, with emphasis on the separability of positive and negative substrates. *Psychological Bulletin, 115,* 401–423.

Cross, I. (2008). Musicality and the human capacity for culture. *Musicae Scientiae, 12*(1 suppl), 147–167.

Coutinho, E., & Dibben, N. (2013). Psychoacoustic cues to emotion in speech prosody and music. *Cognition & Emotion, 27,* 658–684.

Dalla Bella, S., Peretz, I., Rousseau, L., & Gosselin, N. (2001). A developmental study of the affective value of tempo and mode in music. *Cognition, 80*(3), B1–B10

Dibben, N. (2004). The role of peripheral feedback in emotional experience with music. *Music Perception, 22,* 79–115.

Doğantan-Dack, M. (2014). Philosophical reflections on expressive music performance. In D. Fabian, R. Timmers & E. Schubert (Eds.) *Expressiveness in music performance: Empirical approaches across styles and cultures* (pp. 3–21). Oxford: Oxford University Press.

Eerola, T. (2011). Are the emotions expressed in music genre-specific? An audio-based evaluation of datasets spanning classical, film, pop and mixed genres. *Journal of New Music Research, 40*(4), 349–366.

Eerola, T., Peltola, H. R., & Vuoskoski, J. K. (2015). Attitudes toward sad music are related to both preferential and contextual strategies. *Psychomusicology: Music, Mind, and Brain, 25*(2), 116–123.

Egermann, H., Fernando, N., Chuen, L., & McAdams, S. (2014). Music induces universal emotion-related psychophysiological responses: Comparing Canadian listeners to Congolese Pygmies. *Frontiers in Psychology, 5*, 1341. http://doi.org/10.3389/fpsyg.2014.01341

Eitan, Z., & Granot, R. Y. (2006). How music moves. *Music Perception, 23*, 221–248.

Eitan, Z., Timmers, R., & Adler, M. (in press). Cross-modal correspondences in a Schubert song. In D. Leech-Wilkinson and H. Prior (Eds.), *Music and shape*. Oxford and New York, NY: Oxford University Press.

Gabrielsson, A. (2002). Emotion perceived and emotion felt: Same or different? *Musicae Scientiae, 5*, 123–147.

Gabrielsson, A., & Juslin, P. N. (2003). Emotional expression in music. In R. J. Davidson, K. R. Scherer, & H. H. Goldsmith (Eds.), *Handbook of affective sciences* (pp. 503–534). Oxford: Oxford University Press.

Gomez, P., & Danuser, B. (2007). Relationships between musical structure and psychophysiological measures of emotion. *Emotion, 7*(2), 377–387.

Goudbeek, M., & Scherer, K. (2010). Beyond arousal: Valence and potency/control cues in the vocal expression of emotion. *The Journal of the Acoustical Society of America, 128*(3), 1322–1336.

Grewe, O., Nagel, F., Kopiez, R., & Altenmüller, E. (2007). Listening to music as a re-creative process: Physiological, psychological, and psychoacoustical correlates of chills and strong emotions. *Music Perception, 24*, 297–314.

Houston, D., & Haddock, G. (2007). On auditing auditory information: The influence of mood on memory for music. *Psychology of Music, 35*, 201–212.

Huron, D. B. (2006). *Sweet anticipation: Music and the psychology of expectation*. Cambridge, MA: MIT Press.

Huron, D. (2011). Why is sad music pleasurable? A possible role for prolactin. *Musicae Scientiae, 15*, 146–158.

Ilie, G., & Thompson, W. F. (2006). A comparison of acoustic cues in music and speech for three dimensions of affect. *Music Perception, 23*, 319–330.

Juslin, P. N., & Laukka, P. (2003). Communication of emotions in vocal expression and music performance: Different channels, same code? *Psychological Bulletin, 129*(5), 770–814.

Juslin, P. N., & Västfjäll, D. (2008). Emotional responses to music: The need to consider underlying mechanisms. *Behavioral and Brain Sciences, 31*, 559–575.

Juslin, P. N., Liljeström, S., Västfjäll, D., Barradas, G., & Silva, A. (2008). An experience sampling study of emotional reactions to music: Listener, music, and situation. *Emotion, 8*(5), 668–683.

Ladinig, O., & Schellenberg, E. G. (2012). Liking unfamiliar music: Effects of felt emotion and individual differences. *Psychology of Aesthetics, Creativity, and the Arts, 6*(2), 146–154.

Laukka, P., Eerola, T., Thingujam, N. S., Yamasaki, T., & Beller, G. (2013). Universal and culture-specific factors in the recognition and performance of musical affect expressions. *Emotion, 13*(3), 434–449.

Lima, C. F., & Castro, S. L. (2011). Emotion recognition in music changes across the adult life span. *Cognition and Emotion, 25*(4), 585–598.

Meyer, L. B. (1956). *Emotion and Meaning in Music*. Chicago, IL: University of Chicago Press.

Molnar-Szakacs, I., & Overy, K. (2006). Music and mirror neurons: From motion to "e"motion. *Social Cognitive and Affective Neuroscience, 1*(3), 235–241.

Patel, A. D. (2014). The evolutionary biology of musical rhythm: Was Darwin wrong?. *PLoS Biology, 12*(3), e1001821.

Parncutt, R. (2014). The emotional connotations of major versus minor tonality: One or more origins? *Musicae Scientiae, 18*, 324–353.

Peltola, H.-R., & Eerola, T. (2016). Fifty shades of blue: Classification of music-evoked sadness. *Musicae Scientiae, 20*, 84–102.

Quinto, L., Thompson, W. F., & Taylor, A. (2014). The contributions of compositional structure and performance expression to the communication of emotion in music. *Psychology of Music, 42*, 503–524.

Russell, J. A. (2003). Core affect and the psychological construction of emotion. *Psychological Review, 110*(1), 145–172.

Scherer, K. R. (1986). Vocal affect expression: A review and a model for future research. *Psychological Bulletin, 99*(2), 143–163.

Scherer, K. R. (2005). What are emotions? And how can they be measured? *Social Science Information, 44*(4), 695–729.

Scherer, K. R., & Coutinho, E. (2013). How music creates emotion: A multifactorial process approach. In T. Cochrane, B. Fantini, & K. R. Scherer (Eds.), *The emotional power of music* (pp. 121–145). Oxford: Oxford University Press.

Schimmack, U., & Rainer, R. (2002). Experiencing activation: Energetic arousal and tense arousal are not mixtures of valence and activation. *Emotion, 2,* 412–417.

Schubert, E. (2003). Update of the Hevner adjective checklist. *Perceptual and Motor Skills, 96,* 1117–1122.

Schubert, E. (2004). Modeling perceived emotion with continuous musical features. *Music Perception, 21*(4), 561–585.

Schubert, E. (2013). Emotion felt by the listener and expressed by the music: Literature review and theoretical perspectives. *Frontiers in Psychology, 4,* 837. doi:10.3389/fpsyg.2013.00837

Schubert, E., & Fabian, D. (2014). A taxonomy of listeners' judgements of expressiveness in music performance. In D. Fabian, R. Timmers, & E. Schubert (Eds.), *Expressiveness in music performance: Empirical approaches across styles and cultures* (pp. 283–303). New York, NY: Oxford University Press.

Thompson, W. F., Russo, F. A., & Quinto, L. (2008). Audio-visual integration of emotional cues in song. *Cognition and Emotion, 22,* 1457–1470.

Timmers, R. (2007a). Vocal expression in recorded performances of Schubert songs. *Musicae Scientiae, 11,* 237–268.

Timmers, R. (2007b). Perception of music performance on historical and modern commercial recordings. *The Journal of the Acoustical Society of America, 122*(5), 2872–2880.

Timmers, R., Crook, H. L., & Morimoto, Y. (2012). Emotional influences on attention to auditory streams. *Proceedings of the 12th ICMPC.* Thessaloniki, Greece.

Timmers, R., & Crook, H. (2014). Affective priming in music listening: Emotions as a source of musical expectation. *Music Perception, 31,* 470–484.

Vines, B. W., Krumhansl, C. L., Wanderley, M. M., Dalca, I. M., & Levitin, D. J. (2011). Music to my eyes: Cross-modal interactions in the perception of emotions in musical performance. *Cognition, 118*(2), 157–170.

Vuoskoski, J. K., & Eerola, T. (2011). The role of mood and personality in the perception of emotions represented by music. *Cortex, 47*(9), 1099–1106.

Walker, P. (2016). Cross-sensory correspondences: A theoretical framework and their relevance to music. *Psychomusicology: Music, Mind, & Brain, 26,* 103–116.

Watt, R. J., & Ash, R. L. (1998). A psychological investigation of meaning in music. *Musicae Scientiae, 2*(1), 33–53.

Witek, M. A. G., Clarke, E. F., Wallentin, M., Kringelbach, M. L., & Vuust, P. (2014) Syncopation, body-movement and pleasure in groove music. *PLoS ONE, 9*(4): e94446. doi:10.1371/journal.pone.0094446

Zajonc, R. B. (2001). Mere exposure: A gateway to the subliminal. *Current Directions in Psychological Science, 10*(6), 224–228.

Zentner, M., Grandjean, D., & Scherer, K. R. (2008). Emotions evoked by the sound of music: Characterization, classification, and measurement. *Emotion, 8*(4), 494–521.

Zentner, M. R., & Kagan, J. (1998). Infants' perception of consonance and dissonance in music. *Infant Behavior and Development, 21,* 483–492.

# 41

# MUSIC, ANALOGY, AND METAPHOR

*Lawrence M. Zbikowski*

Within this volume, music has been connected with physical movement, other communicative media, various technologies, and other domains of human experience or endeavor. Such connections could be seen to implicate a cognitive capacity that contributes much to the distinctive character of human thought processes: analogy. At its core, analogy involves drawing correlations between elements and relationships from two different domains as part of a process of reasoning about the organization or features of one of the domains. Thus knowledge about physical gestures could be used to structure the understanding of a conjunct sequence of musical events, leading to the notion of a "musical gesture."

The first section that follows reviews recent research on analogy with the aim of assessing its role in musical understanding and its potential to provide a means of addressing a number of issues of long standing, including that of the relationship between language and music. The second section explores work on a cognitive process related to but in some measure distinct from analogy: metaphor. Beginning in the 1980s a number of researchers proposed that metaphor was a fundamental structure of human thought, and this proposal has influenced the work of scholars of music cognition. Both analogy and metaphor have affiliations with cross-modal correspondences exemplified by synaesthesia (and which, as recent research has demonstrated (Spence, 2011), are broadly demonstrated in human cognition), and in the concluding section I shall briefly turn my attention to how such cross-modal correspondences relate to analogy and metaphor.

## Analogy

### *Analogy and Understanding*

Analogy, as it has been studied by cognitive scientists over the past few decades, can be conceived of as a reasoning process based on an apprehended match in relational structure between two apparently different objects or phenomena. As an example, consider an analogy between a stalk of broccoli and a deciduous tree. There are similarities of shape (a central stalk supporting a rounded crown), structure (branches which build out from the central stalk), and life-form (both objects under consideration are plants), all of which might lead one to draw inferences between the two. For instance, since broccoli is grown from a seed one might expect that trees are also be grown from seeds. (Despite the obviousness of such an inference, it seems fair to say that most individuals' knowledge about growing things from seeds is based on their experience with garden plants rather than with trees.) And because the structure of a tree is relatively hardy (allowing it to flourish as a plant, and withstand the weather) one might expect that broccoli has adopted a similar shape for similar reasons. It bears mention that differences between correlated objects or phenomena are equally important for analogical reasoning: The fact that a stalk of broccoli is *not* a tree (it cannot be climbed by young children, it endures for only a single planting season) is itself productive for the process of analogy (Gentner & Markman, 1994). There is more to say about analogy as a cognitive process, but for the moment it will be sufficient to note that the emphasis here is on analogy as a species of reasoning that takes as its point of departure similarities and differences between two domains of knowledge.

To illustrate the role of analogy in musical thought and set the stage for a fuller discussion of analogical reasoning, let me offer a brief musical example. The introduction to Franz Schubert's "Der Lindenbaum" (shown in Figure 41.1) opens with a rapidly oscillating pattern of sixths that circulate around E4 and that suddenly break off, in measure 2, with an arrival on the dominant, an arrival emphasized through a melodic leap into the upper register. This figure, which is expanded and modified over the next six measures, has suggested to a number of commentators the rustling of a linden tree's leaves (e.g., G. Johnson & Wigmore, 2014, vol 3: pp. 648–649). From the perspective I shall develop here, such suggestions are based on an analogy between the musical materials of Schubert's introduction and the sounds produced when the leaves of a mature deciduous tree are stirred by the wind.

As noted, analogical reasoning exploits similarities between the constituent elements of disparate domains. In the case of the introduction to "Der Lindenbaum," the rising and falling pitch of the right-hand's figuration is similar to the increase and decrease in sound volume that occurs as leaves are stirred by a breeze (a similarity strengthened by Schubert's dynamic markings); the sequences of triplet sixteenth-notes, bound together under a single phrasing slur, summon a sonic image of continuity quite similar to the sighing of boughs shaken by the wind; and the complexities of air flow (giving rise to gusts and eddies) create interacting layers of sound as various boughs are shaken, layers that can also be found in the push and pull between the left hand and right hand in measure 5 as Schubert builds tension in anticipation of the arrival on the dominant in measure 7.

While observations about similarities like these provide an anchor for the process of analogy, such observations by themselves cannot explain the sophisticated reasoning that follows. This reasoning builds on a two-part correlation: between the constituent elements of two different domains, and between relationships among the elements within each domain; the latter are called "second-order" relations by researchers on analogy (Gentner & Markman, 1997, p. 47). In the case of the analogy activated by the introduction to "Der Lindenbaum," the relevant second-order relations have to do with what might be broadly construed as agency: In the natural domain occupied by the tree, the agent is a powerful physical force (the wind) that animates innumerable objects (the leaves of the tree) to create a distinctive sound; in the musical domain of the song, the agent is the individual responsible for the sounds that make up by the introduction. Although this individual could simply (and quite logically) be identified with the composer, in performance the individual might also be understood to be the pianist or the singer (at whose behest the pianist plays).

A key feature of analogical reasoning illustrated by this example is the role of contextual goals in drawing analogical correspondences. There are, for instance, any number of

*Figure 41.1*  Franz Schubert, "Der Lindenbaum," (Song 5 from *Winterreise*, D. 911; Op. 89), measures 1–12. Text by Wilhelm Müller; translation: "By the well, before the gate, stands a linden tree."

similarities between the introduction to "Der Lindenbaum" and various extra-musical phenomena: Schubert's introduction could, for instance, represent the scurrying of a small animal or the rising emotions consequent to hearing a random snatch of a beloved companion's voice. The correlation of the musical sounds with the sonic image of a rustling linden fits, of course, with the title of the song and with the picture of rustic solitude sketched by the opening lines of Wilhelm Müller's poem. More broadly, however, this correlation fits with the notion that songs like "Der Lindenbaum" are expressive utterances: confronted with a sequence of musical sounds such as that represented by Figure 41.1, it is quite natural to look for a reason behind the production of these sounds ("an evocation of the rustling of the leaves of a tree") and to attribute it to some individual (variously, the composer, pianist, or singer). The alignment of features and structure that typifies analogy is thus constrained by contextual goals that are distinct from the analogical process proper (Holyoak & Thagard, 1995, pp. 6–12). Were the context different, the music of Figure 41.1 might well be heard to represent the hurried movements of a small animal or the surge of emotion consequent to a glimpse of one's beloved.

Making analogies is something that is virtually effortless for humans. Motivated by this fact, Douglas Hofstadter and Emmanuel Sander have argued that analogy, as the means by which concepts are assembled and connected to one another, is at the very core of human cognition (2013). At the very least, there is considerable overlap between judgments of similarity, making analogies, and processes of categorization, all of which contribute to the distinctiveness of human intelligence (Medin, Goldstone, & Gentner, 1993). Perhaps more striking is that the capacity for analogy is apparently unique to our species. Although other species are able to make some very sophisticated similarity judgments, current evidence indicates that no other species comes close to making or using analogies with the facility and speed of humans (Call & Tomasello, 2005; Gentner, 2003). And this capacity is available from a very early age: Children as young as ten months are able to solve problems by analogy (Chen, Sanchez, & Campbell, 1997), and by the age of three years analogical abilities are quite robust (Goswami, 2001; Gentner, 2003).

The ability to map systematic structural relationships between disparate domains bears witness to a capacity for abstract thought—for thinking about relations between relations—of enormous flexibility and wide application. Analogy has been recognized as a key factor in human creativity (Fauconnier & Turner, 2002, p. 14) and has been linked to the conceptual flights of fancy and processes of meaning construction created through metaphor and metonymy (Holyoak & Thagard, 1995, pp. 213–223). Given evidence of the capacity for analogy demonstrated by pre-linguistic children, it also seems apparent that being able to reason with analogy does not require the use of language, opening up the possibility of musical analogies that bypass language entirely.

Despite its importance to human thought there has at present been relatively little research on music and analogy (but see Kielian-Gilbert, 1990; Bar-Yosef, 2007; and Eitan & Granot, 2007). This is not to say, however, that analogical thought in the service of musical understanding is difficult to discover. As but one example, the music theorist David Lewin illustrated a rather abstract relationship between two transformational graphs with an analogy to the different ways a person might appear in a formal setting (for instance, discharging a solemn professional duty) and an informal setting (at a picnic in the park, where he or she is surrounded by friends and family). Just as we would understand that, despite appearances, the same person was involved in both of these activities, so we should understand that two apparently different transformational graphs manifest the same essential musical relationships (Lewin, 1987, p. 171). There are, additionally, intra-musical analogies associated with compositional practice. For instance, within the innumerable theme and variation sets produced by Western European musicians during the late eighteenth century (which, incidentally, exemplify a practice common throughout the world's musics) each variation can be conceived of as an analog for the theme (as well as for other variations), a relationship fuelled by the similarities and differences between theme and variation as well as by differences in the expressive import of individual variations (such as those cast in a minor key). Analogical relationships such as these can also be seen in the many different guises thematic materials can take over the course of a musical composition or improvisation.

## Analogical Reference and Musical Communication

In recent work I have used research on analogy as a basis for the notion of analogical reference (Zbikowski, 2012b, p. 127). This form of reference is effected through structural similarities between the symbolic token and the thing to which it refers (and is thus allied with what C.S. Peirce called an icon (1955, p. 104)) and can be used to explain how sequences of musical sound refer to other phenomena. In Schubert's "Der Lindenbaum," for instance, the music of measures 1–8 provides a sonic analog for the dynamic process associated with leaves rustling in the wind. It is important to note that, while the dynamic process that is analogized here is itself associated with sonic phenomena ("the rustling of the leaves of a tree"), the sounds produced by the piano do not have to faithfully reproduce those sounds. Indeed, there are a number of differences between the musical and natural sounds: The rustling of leaves has no definable pitch content; although there is certainly a temporal shape to the sound of leaves stirred by a breeze, that shape has none of the rhythmic specificity of Schubert's carefully constructed phrases; and while we might certainly attribute a kind of directedness to the boughs of a tree tossed by the wind—they are, after all, evidence of the movement of air from one place to another—rustling leaves by themselves offer none of the sense of anticipation created by Schubert's eight-measure introduction.

The notion of analogical reference offers one way to account for music's often-observed capacity to imitate natural sounds (which was the basis for the notion of musical mimesis used in the early modern period to explain how music could have meaning; see, for instance, Engel, 1998/1780). It also makes it possible to connect musical utterances with a range of dynamic processes that have proven to be important for human cultures, including the spontaneous gestures that accompany speech (Zbikowski, 2011), the patterned movements of dance (Zbikowski, 2012a), and the psychological and physical processes associated with the emotions (Zbikowski, 2010). Finally, and perhaps most importantly, it offers a way to distinguish between the resources humans employ for linguistic and musical communication. Language makes almost exclusive use of symbolic reference as a basis for communication (Deacon, 1997, pp. 69–101); music, by contrast, makes almost exclusive use of analogical reference (Zbikowski, 2017).

## Summary

There is now abundant evidence that analogical thought is a basic and characteristic feature of human intelligence. As such, it is not surprising that analogies would play a part in reasoning processes associated with musical practice, from the imitation of various natural sounds through sequences of musical events, to involved and highly analytical observations about musical organization, to drawing connections between a theme and its variations. Building upon such evidence, the notion of analogical reference (in contrast to symbolic reference) provides one way to capture the distinctiveness of musical utterances and to explain why every known human culture has developed the resources of both language and music.

## Metaphor

### Conceptual Metaphor Theory

Although there are any number of similarities between analogy and metaphor—enough that Dedre Gentner and her colleagues could give the ironical title "Metaphor is like analogy" (Gentner, Bowdle, Wolff, & Boronat, 2001) to a chapter on the relationship between the two—the exploration of metaphor from a cognitive perspective began only with George Lakoff and Mark Johnson's 1980 book *Metaphors We Live By*. On the view developed by Lakoff and Johnson, metaphor was not simply a manifestation of literary creativity but was in fact an extremely common way of structuring thought. They pointed out that expressions like "I'm feeling *up*" or "My spirits *sank*" are concerned not with a literal orientation of an individual in space but are instead evidence of a consistent pattern of thought in which emotional states are correlated with orientation in space (Lakoff & Johnson, 1980, pp. 15–17). According to this pattern UP is correlated with an elevated emotional state ("happiness" or "joy") and DOWN is correlated with a depressed emotional state ("sadness" or "despair"). Patterns such as this, which Lakoff and Johnson called conceptual metaphors, provide the structure for manifold different linguistic expressions and also constrain the interpretation of these expressions: "My spirits *sank*" thus gives cues about a person's emotional state (including the person's physical appearance) but does not entail any belief in the actual buoyancy of inner emotional states.

This perspective on thought and language has ready applications to descriptions of musical organization. In my initial account of the music represented by Figure 41.1, for instance, I observed that the pitches of the right-hand figuration of the introduction rise and fall; had I been interested in a somewhat richer account of the music, I might have noted that the sonorities of measure 7 possess a certain warmth. Of course, neither of these characterizations is true in a simple way: Although we conventionally describe pitch relationships with reference to vertical space, the pitches are not literally rising and falling. Indeed, were one to observe the actual trajectory traced by the pianist's hand it would not be up and down, but rightwards and leftwards. And as for the warmth of the sonorities in measure 7, the temperature associated with these chords would not be significantly greater or lesser than the "icy shivers" commentators have found elsewhere in *Winterreise*. Both of these characterizations—and, indeed, almost all non-technical accounts of music—can be seen to have their basis in conceptual metaphors, a point I shall explore in more detail below.

It should be noted that the characterizations I have just discussed also reflect correspondences between perceptual information drawn from different modes. Such correspondences connect with an important question raised by Lakoff and Johnson's research, which is the ultimate basis for the process of mapping knowledge between different domains. Even if we grant that we understand a target domain (such as pitch relationships) in terms of a source domain (such as orientation in vertical space), how is it that we understand the source domain in the first place? One explanation—considered in more detail in the concluding section—is that this understanding is based on cross-modal correspondences. For their part, metaphor theorists—and, in particular, Mark Johnson—took the position that conceptual metaphors had their basis in repeated patterns of bodily experience, patterns that Johnson called image schemata. As Johnson conceived it, an image schema was a dynamic cognitive construct that functioned somewhat like the abstract structure of an image and thereby connected together a vast range of different experiences that manifested this same recurring structure (Johnson, 1987, p. 2). Consider, for instance, the VERTICALITY schema, which captures the recurring structure manifested in experiences such as perceiving a tree, our felt sense of standing upright, the activity of climbing stairs, and watching the level of water rise in the bathtub. The VERTICALITY schema is the abstract structure of such experiences, images, and perceptions. Our concept of verticality is based on this schema, and this concept is in turn invoked by the various conceptual metaphors that use vertical space as a source domain through which to structure such target domains such as emotions, and musical pitch (Zbikowski, 2002, pp. 63–74).

For Johnson the image schema was a theoretical construct motivated both by the research on metaphor he did with Lakoff and by a philosophical perspective on knowledge that borrowed heavily from that developed by Immanuel Kant in his *Critique of Pure Reason* (Johnson, 1987, pp. 144–166). Although empirical evidence supporting the notion of image schemata is still inconclusive, over the past three decades researchers from a broad range of disciplinary traditions have shown that human cognitive processes are shaped by bodily experiences such as those that informed Johnson's theoretical approach. This has led to a disciplinary perspective that has come to be called grounded cognition (Barsalou, 2008) which is, to a certain extent, complementary to research on cross-modal correspondences.

## Recent Research on Music and Metaphor

Applications of conceptual metaphor theory to music have resulted in two different strands of research. The first strand was initiated almost immediately after Lakoff and Johnson set out their ideas about metaphor and has focused on the way the conceptual metaphors made explicit by language shape the understanding of music. The second strand is of more recent vintage, and has provided empirical studies—informed by metaphor theory—of the conceptualization of music.

*Music, language, and metaphor.* One of the earliest applications of conceptual metaphor theory to musical understanding is perhaps the most instructive. In his analysis of the musical thought of the Kaluli of Papua New Guinea, Steven Feld proposed that the metaphorical descriptions they used were a reflection of key aspects of their everyday experience. The Kaluli describe melodic intervals—whether in their own music or in the music of others—with the same terms they use to characterize features of waterfalls. For instance, in the language of the Kaluli *sa* means "waterfall," and a *mogan* is a still or lightly swirling waterpool; *sa-mogan* is the flow of a waterfall into a level waterpool beneath it. *Sa-mogan* is also used to describe a melodic line that descends to a repeated note, the contour of which replicates that of a waterfall flowing into a pool (Feld, 1981, pp. 30–31). The system of metaphorical relationships upon which such characterizations draw offers a rich description of musical events, but one that also has its limitations: The Kaluli do not, for example, have specific names for ascending intervals, which nonetheless do occur in their music.

As did Feld's work, most of the research on music and metaphor in the decades that followed the publication of Lakoff and Johnson's study has focused on the conceptual metaphors that guide and constrain the understanding of music. One branch of this research has explored the role of metaphor in the theorization and practice of novel repertoires, including heavy metal, musical multimedia, the music of the Grateful Dead, the music of Neil Young, and music from Java and Azerbaijan. Another branch has focused on recognized but not clearly understood conceptual models within music theory, including those pertaining to musical invariance, modulation theory, and hierarchical structures in music. (A summary of the research on music and metaphor that draws on conceptual metaphor theory is provided in Zbikowski, 2008, pp. 510–12.) Although there has been some speculation on the image-schematic basis of conceptual metaphors often applied to music (Brower, 2000), most of the focus has been on evidence provided by descriptions of musical materials and practices.

***Empirical studies bearing on music and metaphor.*** Empirical work that reflects the influence of conceptual metaphor theory is somewhat more limited and has developed only over the last ten years or so. One of the first published studies was by Zohar Eitan and Roni Granot, who investigated the visual and kinetic imagery summoned by sequences of musical sounds (2006). Eitan and Granot found that listeners drew on their knowledge of a variety of domains, including that related to objects moving through space, to characterize such sequences. One of the surprising findings was of asymmetries in such characterizations. As Eitan and Granot observed:

> Imagined musical space proves to be asymmetrical in diverse domains, as listeners who associate a musical stimulus with a particular kinetic quality often *do not* associate the inverse stimulus with the opposite kinetic quality. Thus . . . diminuendi descend, but crescendi do not ascend. Crescendi, however, speed up, while diminuendi (in faster tempi) do not slow down. Correspondingly, when pitch rises it moves faster (as well as further), but as it falls, it does not slow down or draw nearer. Pitch fall, however, moves strongly to the left, while pitch rise is only weakly related to motion rightward.
>
> *(2006, p. 238)*

In brief, then, Eitan and Granot's results suggest that listeners mapped knowledge from a variety of domains to characterize musical events, and that while such mappings are consistent they do not reflect straightforward cross-modal correlations. Further research Eitan conducted with Renee Timmers (first presented in 2006 and published in 2010) confirmed these results. Participants in this study were able to use a range of contrasting terms (such as "crocodile"—which, among the Shona of Zimbabwe, corresponds with low pitch—and "those who follow crocodiles"—which corresponds with high pitch) to categorize pitch differences, a capacity which suggested that they were able to recruit knowledge from novel source domains to structure their understanding of musical relationships (2010; see also Dolscheid, Shayan, Majid, & Casasanto, 2013). Similar results were obtained by Mihail Antović in a study of the ways Serbian and Romani children characterized musical relationships; these descriptions proved to be overwhelmingly metaphorical and to draw on visual and spatial knowledge (2009).

A slightly different perspective on the role of conceptual metaphors in musical understanding was provided by experiments which included blind participants. Eitan, Granot, and Ornoy found that congenitally or early blind participants characterized basic pitch relationships in terms of visual metaphors similar to those used by sighted participants (2012). These results suggest that descriptions of musical relationships by blind participants reflect language-based semantic associations rather than cross-modal perceptual information, something confirmed in a separate study by Antović, Bennett, and Turner (2013).

### *Summary: Music and Metaphor*

To the extent that it involves the correlation of structural features proper to two different domains, metaphor is indeed like analogy. Research on these cognitive processes suggests, however, that where analogy is primarily concerned with using knowledge about one domain to reason about another, metaphor more typically involves using correlations between domains to construct meaning. In consequence, metaphors demonstrate a directionality that is not as prominent in analogies: While one might use an analogy between a dancer and an elephant as the basis for a variety of inferences, the metaphor "The elephant is a ballerina" (which uses knowledge about a lithe dancer to characterize a ponderous pachyderm) is quite different from the metaphor "The ballerina is an elephant." This directionality points to a substantive difference between analogy and metaphor: It *means* one thing to say that an elephant is a ballerina, and it *means* something different to say a ballerina is an elephant.

One issue raised by applications of conceptual metaphor theory to descriptions of musical organization is whether music can serve as a source domain for a metaphorical mapping. The issue is of marked significance for research on musical knowledge: If it is the case that music cannot be an originary source domain—that is, if metaphorical mappings are always *from* language *to* music, and never *from* music *to* language—it would suggest that human conceptual knowledge is first codified through the resources offered by language, and only subsequently used to structure the understanding of music. Musical concepts, to the extent such exist, would of necessity be derivative of linguistic concepts.

### Conclusion: Analogy, Metaphor, and Cross-modal Correspondences

Work by a wide range of researchers has demonstrated that the ability to draw complex analogies is a basic and characteristic feature of human intelligence. Inasmuch as music is a product of human intelligence, it stands to reason that analogical thought would play a role in musical understanding. Such thought is not only demonstrated by writing about music—which, in many cases, is explicitly analogical—but also in musical imitations of natural sounds, in variation techniques, and in correspondences between music and other human activities (such as gesture and dance). Further, the role of analogy in musical understanding can be used as support for a notion of reference—analogical reference—uniquely exploited by music. There is also a body of research which suggests that a cognitive process closely allied with analogy—metaphor—is a fundamental structure of human thought. This research has led to thoughtful descriptions of the role conceptual metaphors play in musical understanding as well as empirical research that demonstrates humans' ability to use knowledge drawn from a variety of domains to structure their understanding of music.

A persistent question raised by research on descriptions of music that reflect conceptual metaphors is the extent to which such descriptions are influenced by correlations between perceptual modes. On the one hand, cross-modal descriptions by congenitally blind individuals would seem to argue against such influence. On the other hand, there is a substantial body of research suggesting that cross-modal characterizations of pitch relationships are independent from language (Casasanto, 2010, pp. 473–474; Walker, et al., 2010; Parkinson,

Kohler, Sievers, & Wheatley, 2012; Eitan, Schupak, Gotler, & Marks, 2014; Palmer, Langlois, & Schloss, 2016). One way to approach this contradictory evidence is through distinctions between three classes of cross-modal correspondences: structural correspondences, statistical correspondences, and semantically mediated correspondences (Spence, 2011, pp. 988–989). Thus descriptions of musical pitch by congenitally blind individuals that make recourse to visual information can be taken as evidence for semantically mediated correspondences; correlations of visual and sonic information by pre-verbal children, by contrast, reflect structural or statistical correspondences. This perspective can be expanded by taking into account the way analogical thought informs descriptions of musical relationships, especially where such descriptions reflect not only how modes are similar but also how they are different. Indeed, such an approach would conform with emerging research on predictive processing (Clark, 2016), through which top-down processes (such as analogy) shape bottom-up processes (such as those that drive structural and statistical cross-modal correspondences).

One can envision three research streams related to analogy and metaphor that might inform future work in music cognition. First, research could seek to expand our understanding of the role analogy plays in musical understanding, and the extent to which sequences of musical sound can be correlated with dynamic processes. Second, although there has been important work on music and metaphor, we have only begun to understand how conceptual metaphors inform musical understanding. Third, existing work on cross-modal correspondences could be placed in dialog with the perspectives on musical understanding provided by research on analogy and metaphor, the better to understand how processes of reasoning and meaning construction shape—and are shaped by—perceptual information.

## Core Reading

Eitan, Z., & Granot, R. Y. (2006). How music moves: Musical parameters and listeners' images of motion. *Music Perception, 23*(3), 221–247.

Gentner, D., Bowdle, B. F., Wolff, P., & Boronat, C. (2001). Metaphor is like analogy. In D. Gentner, K. J. Holyoak, & B. N. Kokinov (Eds.), *The analogical mind: Perspectives from cognitive science* (pp. 199–253). Cambridge, MA: MIT Press.

Spence, C. (2011). Crossmodal correspondences: A tutorial review. *Attention, Perception, & Psychophysics, 73*(4), 971–995.

Zbikowski, L. M. (2008). Metaphor and music. In R. Gibbs, Jr. (Ed.), *The Cambridge handbook of metaphor and thought* (pp. 502–524). Cambridge: Cambridge University Press.

## Further References

Antović, M., Bennett, A., & Turner, M. (2013). Running in circles or moving along lines: Conceptualization of musical elements in sighted and blind children. *Musicæ Scientiæ, 17*(2), 229–245.

Antović, M. (2009). Musical metaphors in Serbian and Romani children: An empirical study. *Metaphor and Symbol, 24*(3), 184–202.

Barsalou, L. W. (2008). Grounded cognition. *Annual Review of Psychology, 59*, 617–645.

Bar-Yosef, A. (2007). A cross-cultural structural analogy between pitch and time organizations. *Music Perception, 24*(3), 265–280.

Brower, C. (2000, Fall). A cognitive theory of musical meaning. *Journal of Music Theory, 44*(2), 323–379.

Call, J., & Tomasello, M. (2005). Reasoning and thinking in nonhuman primates. In K. Holyoak & R. G. Morrison (Eds.), *The Cambridge handbook of thinking and reasoning* (pp. 607–632). Cambridge: Cambridge University Press.

Casasanto, D. (2010). Space for thinking. In V. Evans, & P. A. Chilton (Eds.), *Language, cognition and space: The state of the art and new directions* (pp. 453–478). Advances in Cognitive Linguistics. London: Equinox Publishing, Ltd.

Chen, Z., Sanchez, R. P., & Campbell, T. (1997). From beyond to within their grasp: The rudiments of analogical problem solving in 10- and 13-month-olds. *Developmental Psychology, 33*(5), 790–801.

Clark, A. (2016). *Surfing uncertainty: Prediction, action, and the embodied mind.* Oxford: Oxford University Press.

Deacon, T. W. (1997). *The symbolic species: The co-evolution of language and the brain.* New York, NY: W.W. Norton & Company.

Dolscheid, S., Shayan, S., Majid, A., & Casasanto, D. (2013). The thickness of musical pitch: Psychophysical evidence for linguistic relativity. *Psychological Science, 24*(5), 613–621.

Eitan, Z., & Granot, R.Y. (2007). Intensity changes and perceived similarity: Inter-parametric analogies. *Musicæ Scientiæ, 11*(1 suppl), 39–75.

Eitan, Z., Granot, R.Y., & Ornoy, E. (2012). Listening in the dark: Congenital and early blindness and cross-domain mappings in music. *Psychomusicology: Music, Mind, & Brain, 22*(1), 33–45.

Eitan, Z., Schupak, A., Gotler, A., & Marks, L. E. (2014). Lower pitch is larger, yet falling pitches shrink. *Experimental Psychology, 61*(4), 273–284.

Eitan, Z., & Timmers, R. (2010). Beethoven's last piano sonata and those who follow crocodiles: Cross-domain mappings of auditory pitch in a musical context. *Cognition, 114*(3), 405–422.

Engel, J. J. (1998 [1780]). On painting in music. In L. Treitler (Gen. Ed.), O. Strunk (Ed.), *Source readings in music history* (Rev. ed., pp. 954–965). New York, NY: W. W. Norton & Company.

Fauconnier, G., & Turner, M. (2002). *The way we think: Conceptual blending and the mind's hidden complexities.* New York, NY: Basic Books.

Feld, S. (1981). Flow like a waterfall: The metaphors of Kaluli musical theory. *Yearbook for Traditional Music, 13,* 22–47.

Gentner, D., & Markman, A. B. (1994). Structural alignment in comparison: No difference without similarity. *Psychological Science, 5*(3), 152–158.

Gentner, D., & Markman, A. B. (1997). Structure mapping in analogy and similarity. *American Psychologist, 52*(1), 45–56.

Gentner, D. (2003). Why we're so smart. In D. Gentner, & S. Goldin-Meadow (Eds.), *Language in mind: Advances in the study of language and thought* (pp. 195–235). Cambridge, MA: MIT Press.

Goswami, U. (2001). Analogical reasoning in children. In D. Gentner, K. J. Holyoak, & B. N. Kokinov (Eds.), *The analogical mind: Perspectives from cognitive science* (pp. 437–470). Cambridge, MA: MIT Press.

Hofstadter, D., & Sander, E. (2013). *Surfaces and essences: Analogy as the fuel and fire of thinking.* New York, NY: Basic Books.

Holyoak, K. J., & Thagard, P. (1995). *Mental leaps: Analogy in creative thought.* Cambridge, MA: MIT Press.

Johnson, G., & Wigmore, R. (2014). *Franz Schubert: The complete songs.* New Haven, CT: Yale University Press.

Johnson, M. L. (1987) *The body in the mind: The bodily basis of meaning, imagination, and reason.* Chicago, IL: University of Chicago Press.

Kielian-Gilbert, M. (1990). Interpreting musical analogy: From rhetorical device to perceptual process. *Music Perception, 8*(1), 63–94.

Lakoff, G., & Johnson, M. L. (1980). *Metaphors we live by.* Chicago, IL: University of Chicago Press.

Lewin, D. (1987). *Generalized musical intervals and transformations.* New Haven, CT: Yale University Press.

Medin, D. L., Goldstone, R. L., & Gentner, D. (1993). Respects for similarity. *Psychological Review, 100*(2), 254–278.

Palmer, S. E., Langlois, T. A., & Schloss, K. B. (2016). Music-to-color associations of single-line piano melodies in non-synesthetes. *Multisensory Research, 29*(1–3), 157–193.

Parkinson, C., Kohler, P. J., Sievers, B., & Wheatley, T. (2012). Associations between auditory pitch and visual elevation do not depend on language: Evidence from a remote population. *Perception, 41*(7), 854–861.

Peirce, C. S. (1955). *Philosophical writings of Peirce*, Justus Buchler (Ed.). New York, NY: Dover.

Walker, P., Bremner, J. G., Mason, U., Spring, J., Mattock, K., Slater, A., et al. (2010). Preverbal infants' sensitivity to synaesthetic cross-modality correspondences. *Psychological Science, 21*(1), 21–25.

Zbikowski, L. M. (2002). *Conceptualizing music: Cognitive structure, theory, and analysis.* AMS Studies in Music. New York, NY: Oxford University Press.

Zbikowski, L. M. (2010). Music, emotion, analysis. *Music Analysis, 29*(i–iii), 37–60.

Zbikowski, L. M. (2011). Musical gesture and musical grammar: A cognitive approach. In A. Gritten, & E. King (Eds.), *New perspectives on music and gesture* (pp. 83–98). SEMPRE studies in the psychology of music. Farnham, Surrey, UK: Ashgate Publishing Ltd.

Zbikowski, L. M. (2012a). Music, dance, and meaning in the early nineteenth century. *Journal of Musicological Research, 31*(2/3), 147–165.

Zbikowski, L. M. (2012b). Music, language, and what falls in between. *Ethnomusicology, 56*(1), 125–131.

Zbikowski, L. M. (2017). *Foundations of musical grammar.* Oxford Studies in Music Theory. New York, NY: Oxford University Press.

# 42

# MUSICAL AESTHETICS
# AND VALUES

*Elizabeth Hellmuth Margulis*

The study of musical aesthetics has been complicated by the difficulty of articulating what listening experiences are really like. People can be powerfully moved by music, yet almost entirely incapable of describing their percepts and sensations. Philosophers have grappled with this resistance to verbalization, characterizing aspects of music listening as ineffable (Raffman, 1993) or nonconceptual (DeBellis, 1995), or pointing to the primacy of attentive engagement within the perceptual present over explicit awareness of larger-scale structural relationships (Levinson, 1998). Yet it is precisely this resistance to articulation that makes psychology such a powerful method for investigating musical aesthetics. By designing thoughtful and sensitive experiments, researchers can coax out implicit evidence of the processing involved in aesthetic perception, without relying on participants' ability to verbalize them. In this way, not only can philosophical theories make aesthetic experiences more susceptible to empirical investigation, but also empirical investigation can provide insights that inform new philosophical theories in aesthetics. This interplay between theory and experimentation is particularly crucial for domains—like musical aesthetics—where scientific understanding is at a relatively early stage.

## Historical Approaches to the Psychology of Musical Aesthetics

Experimental approaches to aesthetics arose in the late nineteenth-century in Germany with the work of Gustav Fechner and Wilhelm Wundt. These authors shared a commitment to what might now be thought of as ahistoricism—a conviction that it should be possible to specify rules that link the stimulus properties of artworks to associated aesthetic responses. In their view, these rules might be understood to apply universally. Despite that subsequent scholars would highlight the mediating role of enculturation, this early work established methodologies and framing ideas that made the experimental study of aesthetics possible. Fechner, for example, in his pursuit to document the allegedly enhanced aesthetic resonance of the Golden Section—proportions that amounted to approximately 1:0.618—presented people with various stimuli and asked them to choose which one they preferred, or asked people to create an object using the features that they preferred, or examined pre-existing objects of different levels of supposed quality to assess whether they featured the Golden

Section. All of these approaches—from forced-choice preference judgments to corpus studies—continue to be used in contemporary approaches to aesthetic perception, although research using these methods now tries to avoid prejudgments about an object's intrinsic aesthetic merit.

A resurgence of interest in the psychology of aesthetics occurred in the 1970s, well represented by the work of Daniel Berlyne (1971). He developed a new emphasis on listener response, using information theory to understand the relationship between stimulus features and aesthetic experiences. He adapted an inverted-U curve that originated in the work of Wundt to trace how preference can initially rise but subsequently decline as the arousal potential of a stimulus increases. For Berlyne, arousal potential includes such features as familiarity and complexity. For example, if the X-axis represents complexity, the inverted U's left-hand rise captures the intuition that people prefer a stimulus more as it becomes increasingly complex, but the inverted U's right-hand fall captures the intuition that past a certain point, increases in complexity actually result in decreased preference. According to this view, there is an optimal sweet spot at which preference is greatest, lying not at the minimum or the maximum amount of arousal potential, but rather somewhere in between.

## Optimal Complexity

Berlyne's notion of optimal complexity provided the seed for many more recent studies (see also Vuoskoski, this volume). Smith and Melara (1990) operationalized complexity as syntactic prototypicality, presenting harmonic progressions that ranged from highly prototypical to highly deviant to both expert and novice listeners. Only expert listeners preferred deviant progressions; novice listeners favored simple, prototypical ones. This difference points to the fact that listener background and experience can impact complexity; a stimulus that seems complex to one person might seem simple to someone well versed in its style. North and Hargreaves (1995) played people pop songs and asked them to rate both subjective complexity and preference, as well as their familiarity with the excerpt. As familiarity increased, so did liking, but preference showed an inverted-U relationship with subjective complexity ratings. Szpunar, Schellenberg, and Pliner (2004) showed that the effect of repeated exposure on preferences was modulated by attention, as well as by complexity. Complex, ecologically valid stimuli drawn from commercially available recordings engendered liking ratings that followed the typical inverted U, but simpler, less ecologically valid stimuli did not. In Margulis (2013), participants without prior experience in the style heard excerpts of challenging contemporary art music either in their original form, or in versions that had been digitally altered to feature more repetition. They rated the repetitive versions more enjoyable, more interesting, and more likely to have been crafted by a human artist rather than randomly generated by a computer.

Although many of the studies investigating the role of complexity on aesthetic response use explicit preference ratings as the dependent measure, recent work has attempted to address the topic using more implicit measures. For example, Hurley, Martens, and Janata (2014) varied the number of concurrent instrument parts as well as whether they entered simultaneously or in a staggered pattern—one after another—and both recorded the spontaneous movements participants made while listening, and assessed continuous ratings of the degree to which participants thought the music grooved. When the complexity increased gradually because the entrances were staggered, people moved more and reported higher perceived groove. To the extent that moving along with music can be taken as an indication of increased preference and affiliation—or connectedness to the music—these experiments might be understood to imply that not only baseline complexity, but also the dynamics with which this complexity unfolds across a piece contribute to enjoyment. In forthcoming work, Janata and colleagues presented similar stimuli, but used listening time as a measure of preference.

A key finding from all of these studies is that stimulus properties themselves do not predict aesthetic response; rather, the way these stimulus properties fit into a person's "listening biography"—the sum total of the music they've experienced, and in what form and context—influences perception and evaluation. Enculturation contributes to how simple or complex a particular piece sounds, and this perceived simplicity or complexity in turn contributes to aesthetic response. Additionally, experience shapes the kind of aesthetic orientation people bring to what they're hearing. Grunge music might seem like an invitation to moshing for one listener, or an inscrutable intrusion to another. Not only previous experience, but also personality can modulate response (see Vuoskoski, this volume, for further discussion). Rentfrow and Gosling (2003) found that preference for reflective and complex music correlated with individual traits such as openness to new experiences, self-perceived intelligence, and political liberalism. Armed with sufficient knowledge about a person's listening biography and personality, then, it should be possible to make reasonable predictions about their preference for a particular piece. This position, midway between an objectivist stance (according to which aesthetic experience arises from properties of an object), and a subjective stance (according to which aesthetic experience is idiosyncratic and varies from listener to listener), was termed by Reber, Schwarz, and Winkielman (2004) the interactionist stance—and it is the dominant perspective in contemporary empirical work on aesthetics.

## What Is an Aesthetic Response?

Preference is not the only kind of aesthetic response. Experiences ranging from emotional reactions to interest to a sense of being transported to a perception of successful communication to awe to appreciation of beauty have all been characterized, at various times, as aesthetic. For the purposes of music psychology, an aesthetic response can be thought of as a state of mind or experience that occurs in relation to a musical stimulus. This definition encompasses all kinds of things, from cognitive assessments, to autobiographical memory, to feelings and emotions, but there's a special emphasis on experiences that remain unaccounted for once well-understood categories have been examined. In other words, work on aesthetic response often tries to probe aspects of the phenomenology of music listening that are not straightforwardly captured elsewhere.

Several scales have been developed to probe these residual aspects of music listening. Sometimes, studies ask people directly to report on "aesthetic response," without providing further clarification of the term. For example, Diaz (2011) had people use a slider to continuously rate their "aesthetic response" while listening to a ten-minute excerpt of music. Remarkably, participants seemed to harbor an intuitive sense of what this term meant, and did not report difficulty with the task. In the same study, participants used continuous response methodology to capture the degree to which the music had put them in a state of "flow," or pleasurable immersion—despite that it would seem contradictory to a flow state to be required to continuously report on it; they also responded to a series of questions about their attentional state. More commonly, participants are asked to rate how interesting they find particular pieces (c.f. Margulis, 2013), the idea being that the degree to which a person is gripped by the music, or feels committed to following its course, is a critical component of aesthetic response not reducible simply to enjoyment.

A related notion is absorption—the capacity to attend sustainedly to a particular stimulus. Sandstrom and Russo (2011) developed a measure that assesses how successfully music tends to draw an individual into emotional experiences of it. Participants rate their agreement with a number of items such as "When I listen to music I can get so caught up in it that I don't notice anything" and "Sometimes when listening to music I feel as if my mind can understand the whole world," producing a composite score representative of the degree to which music tends to absorb them. People vary in their susceptibility to different types of aesthetic experiences, as well as in the degree to which they value these experiences; measures like Sandstrom and Russo's attempt to characterize some of these individual differences.

Similar to absorption, but more affectively charged is the state of being moved (for example, by a piece of music), a condition examined by Winfried Menninghaus and colleagues (2015). According to the psychological construct they developed, being moved entails coactivation of both sadness and joy, can manifest itself in tears or chills, elicits a tendency to approach and attend, and promotes social bonding. Not only works of art, but also critical personal, political, or natural events can elicit this state. Only in recent years have psychologists begun attempting to probe aesthetic states such as absorption and being moved, and it is not yet clear whether these dimensions are distinct, or whether and how they might overlap. Yet they constitute an important first step into a realm of human experience that is both widespread and generally construed as deeply meaningful, yet little understood.

More intense than absorption or being moved, but still fairly common in response to the arts (Gabrielssohn, 2011; Nusbaum & Silvia, 2014) is the aesthetic state of awe. According to the little existing work on this subject, awe depends first on the appraisal of something as vast, but second on the capacity to accommodate, or assimilate it into normal conceptual structures (Keltner & Haidt, 2003). Music can seem vast by virtue of a metaphoric sense of expansiveness, through for example timbre, dynamics, or rhythm (Nusbaum & Silvia, 2014). A signature harmonic gambit often associated with cinematic moments of wonder is the chromatic mediant (Huron, 2006), in which every note in one chord moves to a note in the next by no more than a step, yet the resultant harmony ends up startlingly far from the preceding one in tonal pitch space. Motion back and forth between two chords related this way can generate a distinct impression of vastness and has been known to trigger frisson, or chills, in some listeners. The seeming paradox of moving so little in voice-leading space to get somewhere so remote in tonal pitch space conjures up a vastness that at the same time works out—is capable of being accommodated—leading to awe or chills. Although chills are a common response to music, they won't be treated in this chapter, since they are normally categorized as an emotional, rather than an aesthetic response. But the link between the inducement of awe and the inducement of chills points to the difficulty not only of disentangling various aesthetic states, but also of discriminating aesthetic from emotional states.

A classic aesthetic response—although comparatively neglected in music research, where liking and interest have received more attention—involves experiencing something as beautiful. When people were shown a variety of visual stimuli and asked to describe their aesthetic experiences, they used the word "beautiful" more than any other (Augustin, Wagemans, & Carbon, 2012). Some lines of research have examined what characteristics lead to judgments of beauty—finding, for example, that more average faces were rated as more attractive; Repp

(1992) introduced ways of measuring "averageness" in performer microtiming, making it possible to investigate whether more average or more eccentric performances tended to be most prized by listeners.

There are other dimensions of musical experience that might be considered aesthetic. For example, emotional responses to music can seem sufficiently special to warrant the postulation of a distinct set of aesthetic emotions (cf. Scherer & Zentner, 2008). In addition, the sense of communion (Herbert, 2011), or successful communication (Hawkins, Cross, & Ogden, 2013), social bonding (Rabinowitch, Cross, & Burnard, 2013), or moving beyond ordinary boundaries to adopt a subjective stance with the music (Margulis, 2014) all might be considered aesthetic responses. Many of these states seem phenomenologically familiar, but difficult to measure, raising the question of how best to study aesthetic experience.

## How Can Aesthetic Responses Be Studied?

Researchers investigate aesthetic response most commonly by playing excerpts and asking participants to rate them along some aesthetic dimension after they conclude. For example, a study might play listeners ninety-second excerpts and after each ask them to rate on a Likert-like scale how much they enjoyed it, or how beautiful they found it, or interesting it was, or how much it absorbed them. While this method has produced many interesting results over the years, and has the advantage of simplicity and directness, it also suffers from several drawbacks. First, it relies on explicit characterizations, and might miss the more elusive aspects of aesthetic experience that seem resistant to verbal report. Second, it can expose the experiment's aims, leaving responses subject to demand characteristics. Third, it requires people to report on aesthetic experiences after they happen, rather than accessing them as they are ongoing. Fourth, the dimensions measured (for example, beauty or interest or enjoyment) might seem like imperfect approximations of the underlying experience.

An alternative is to measure responses not after excerpts conclude, but rather in real time, as they progress. Continuous response methodologies use sliders, dials, or joysticks to allow participants to register ratings of perceived tension, enjoyment, interest, or other dimensions dynamically, as a piece progresses. This approach allows insights into the moment-by-moment experience of music, and reveals linkages between specific occurrences in an excerpt and responses that might be tied to it. On the negative side, it does not permit an unmediated experience of music, since the participant has to continually monitor and report on his or her own perceptions as the piece progresses. Additionally, since it relies on explicit self-report, it suffers from some of the same drawbacks as post-excerpt responses.

Rather than rely on ratings of dimensions designated by experimenters, some studies invite free responses. For example, Alf Gabrielssohn (2011) asked people to describe their peak experiences of music in free prose, and subsequently examined the responses for commonalities. This design avoids biasing listeners in favor of a certain kind of experience, but depends even more critically on a capacity to verbalize. Moreover, it can be difficult to subject the responses to quantitative analysis, making it more useful for exploratory studies.

Implicit measures of aesthetic response are more rare. One option involves physiological measures, either of heart rate, respiratory frequency, galvanic skin response, listening time, or others. These measures have the advantage of circumventing explicit report, but often seem to possess only a crude connection to the underlying aesthetic experiences of interest (cf. Rickard, 2004).

Other implicit approaches use methods drawn from cognitive neuroscience; the burgeoning research area devoted to this kind of inquiry is termed "neuroaesthetics" (Chatterjee, 2013). In a classic study, people were scanned using fMRI while they looked at paintings they had previously categorized as beautiful or ugly. Activity in the orbito-frontal region and the motor cortex differentiated the two conditions (Kawabata & Zeki, 2004). Studies using music listening instead of the viewing of art confirm the role of the orbitofrontal cortex in making aesthetic judgments (Ishizu & Zeki, 2011). To date, studies in neuroaesthetics have often been limited to providing information about where in the brain known aesthetic responses take place, but the avoidance of explicit responses in neuroscientific approaches possesses the potential to illuminate deep questions about aesthetic experience in the future.

Another possible criticism of the methodologies used to study aesthetic experience invokes ecological validity; it might be harder to have an experience we would ordinarily call aesthetic when sitting in a sound-attenuated booth under fluorescent lighting in a laboratory, or when lying in a scanner. To address this concern, some studies distribute diaries or phones that buzz at certain times of day and ask participants to answer various questions about their aesthetic experiences. These more naturalistic studies often sacrifice elements of experimental control to allow for gains in ecological validity.

Motion-tracking technology might make possible additional methods of studying aesthetic response in the future. To the extent that overt movements provide evidence of an intensifying bodily affiliation with a musical stimulus, measuring them can provide insight into this dimension of aesthetic experience. Rhimmon Simchy-Gross and I asked people to explicitly rate the musicality of random tone sequences. During debriefing afterwards, when we asked participants what criteria they used to evaluate musicality, the most common response was that they thought about how much the sequences made them want to move or sing along (Margulis & Simchy-Gross, 2016). If this tendency seems to define what some people think about as "musical," it is potentially useful as a measure of a certain kind of aesthetic response.

## Modeling Aesthetic Experience

Leder, Belke, Oeberst, and Augustin, (2004) propose a model of aesthetic experience built around visual art, but transferrable to other artistic domains. According to this model, before an aesthetic experience can occur, a person needs to adopt an "aesthetic attitude." This attitude might be triggered by entering a concert hall or an art museum, for example, and be shaped by cultural notions of what constitutes an aesthetic experience. Next, the artwork is analyzed perceptually, both in a bottom-up fashion, largely governed by the attributes of the piece itself, and in a top-down fashion, with processing constrained by the experience and expertise of the perceiver. Following this analysis, a feedback loop between stages referred to as "cognitive mastering" and "evaluating" occurs, during which the listener builds models to understand the artwork, continually revisiting their quality through an evaluation process. The model's output takes two forms: aesthetic judgments and aesthetic emotions.

In general, models of aesthetic experience seek to provide a theoretical account of how aesthetic experience transpires, and what factors are relevant in generating it. Specifying these factors can lay the groundwork for an agenda of work in empirical aesthetics. For substantive progress to occur, clear and comprehensive models of aesthetic experience will need to be developed.

## Cross-Cultural Influences on Musical Aesthetics and Values

Ethnomusicologist Peter Manuel notes that

> restrictive modern concepts of "art" or "music" as denoting entities produced solely for disinterested aesthetic pleasure, free from any overt social function, would tend to eliminate from consideration a vast realm of expressive activities or products that we might otherwise well consider to be "artistic" or "musical."
>
> *(2011, pp. 535–536)*

He goes on to quote Alan Merriam's (1964) attempt to define the Western notion of the aesthetic in order to determine whether it applies to other cultures. Merriam's criteria include psychic distance, the manipulation of form for its own sake, the attribution of emotion-producing qualities to music conceived strictly as sound, the attribution of beauty to the art product or process, the purposeful intent to create something aesthetic, and the presence of a philosophy of the aesthetic. According to this definition, the construct of the aesthetic applies only quite narrowly. An alternative definition, however—as Manuel observes—might instead identify elements that define the aesthetic of particular cultures. For example, a person could study a culture's evaluative criteria for music, or the way it connects sound structures to broader value systems or epistemologies. According to this view, an aesthetic still entails a conscious, explicit way of thinking and talking about music.

Yet music cognition has often used the term aesthetic to talk about perceptions and experiences of music that are not particularly amenable to this kind of verbal capture. Some ethnomusicologists have adopted this perspective. David McAllester used the term "unvoiced aesthetic" (1954) to think about Navajo musical attitudes, and Chernoff (1979) argued that non-verbal behaviors should count as evidence for aesthetic perspectives. If music cognition took a cross-cultural approach to musical aesthetics seriously in the future—as indeed it should—the questions would probably pursue the lines of reasoning articulated by McAllester and Chernoff, trying to understand not only overt aesthetic responses, but also implicit ones.

Manuel observes that even the category of "music" can be problematic to assert cross-culturally, since some cultures possess words for individual actions like drumming or song, but not for an overarching category that includes them both. Indeed, the speech-to-song illusion (Deutsch, Henthorn, & Lapidis, 2011) reveals that even within a particular culture—even within a particular individual—a stimulus that is initially conceptualized as speech can come to be conceptualized as music. In the case of this illusion, the impetus for the transformed perception comes from a string of repeated exposures to the utterance, but it can also come from familiarity with the language at hand. Margulis, Simchy-Gross and Black (2015) demonstrated that not only do utterances in unfamiliar languages transform to song more readily than utterances in familiar languages, but they also start out sounding more song-like. In other words, the less familiar a language, the more music-like it may sound. This means that whether something is apprehended as music or not depends not just on context, but also on long-term enculturation. Listening to the speech-to-song illusion reveals that the phenomenological shift from hearing something as speech to hearing it as music is significant and distinctive: It seems to involve closer attention to temporal and pitch-based characteristics, and seems to invite a more participatory kind of orientation—such as imagined or overt singing along. Although these responses do not amount to an explicit aesthetic, they are certainly revealing of underlying aesthetic processes, and cross-cultural investigation of them would seem particularly illuminating. Sensitive studies could expose the intersection between explicit categorization as speech or music and the implicit responses involved in aesthetic processing.

Not only cross-cultural context, but also situational context can impact aesthetic perception. In *Howards End*, E.M. Forster famously chronicles the different aesthetic orientations to a performance of Beethoven's Fifth Symphony sustained by various characters:

> It will be generally admitted that Beethoven's Fifth Symphony is the most sublime noise that has ever penetrated into the ear of man. All sorts and conditions are satisfied by it. Whether you are like Mrs. Munt, and tap surreptitiously when the tunes come—of course, not so as to disturb the others—or like Helen, who can see heroes and shipwrecks in the music's flood; or like Margaret, who can only see the music; or like Tibby, who is profoundly versed in counterpoint, and holds the full score open on his knee; or like their cousin, Fraulein Mosebach, who remembers all the time that Beethoven is echt Deutsch; or like Fraulein Mosebach's young man, who can remember nothing but Fraulein Mosebach: in any case, the passion of your life becomes more vivid, and you are bound to admit that such a noise is cheap at two shillings.
>
> *(Forster, 1910)*

While Helen sees dramatic scenes play out before her eyes, Tibby buries his head in the score, and Fraulein Mosebach ponders the cultural associations of the music. What knocked each of them down these diverse paths? Probably not only personality, but also enculturation—what music they've encountered before, and in what circumstances, and embedded within what value system. Audience research has tried to get a holistic sense of these processes using audience interviews and surveys.

Numerous studies demonstrate that factors outside the boundaries of the acoustic content of the music itself influence the way it is apprehended aesthetically. For example, the presence and nature of associated visual stimuli can impact the perceived expressive intent (Davidson, 1993), and the presence and nature of relevant verbal information can impact enjoyment (Margulis, 2010), real-time judgments of performance expressivity (Silveira & Diaz, 2014), and preference (Kroger & Margulis, 2017).

## Future Prospects

Given the accruing evidence for the role of factors beyond "the notes themselves" in aesthetic experiences of music, it seems likely that future research will employ models that extend beyond a straightforward stimulus-response characterization, where elements of music structure mingle with the perceptual tendencies of listeners enculturated a particular way, and predictable results ensue. Rather, future studies will likely examine the way that the setting and context of a performance do or do not favor an aesthetic mode of attending, and the way these factors constrain or influence the possible aesthetic readings. They might think about the media involved in transmitting the performance, the information to which listeners have been exposed, and the social context of the experience.

Additionally, new institutions, tools, and journals are liable to build research communities that significantly accelerate progress on these questions. The Max Planck Institute for

Empirical Aesthetics opened in Frankfurt, Germany in 2015. Two relevant journals have recently been founded or reinvigorated: the APA journals *Empirical Studies of the Arts* and *Psychology of Aesthetics, Creativity, and the Arts*. Special concert halls wired for data collection as performances progress, such as the McMaster LiveLab, are making possible more ecologically valid studies, with more real-world factors included, and multiple simultaneous measures (for example, EEG, physiological readings, motion capture, and continuous response).

Yet even with new tools and new collaborations among relevant disciplines, for progress to occur, there must be much more thoughtful specification of what constitutes an aesthetic response in the first place. The likeliest path to advancement on this front seems liable to come from some combination of perceptive introspection, the design of clever experiments that expose implicit processes, and careful theorizing.

## Core Reading

Berlyne, D. E. (1971). *Aesthetics and psychobiology.* New York, NY: Appleton-Century-Crofts.
Margulis, E.H. (2014). *On repeat: How music plays the mind.* New York, NY: Oxford University Press.

## Further references

Augustin M. D., Wagemans, J., & Carbon, C.C. (2012). All is beautiful? Generality vs. specificity of word usage in visual aesthetics. *Acta Psychologica, 139,* 187–201.

Chaterjee, A. (2013). The aesthetic brain: How we evolved to desire beauty and enjoy art. New York, NY: Oxford University Press.

Chernoff, J. M. (1979). *African rhythm and African sensibility: Aesthetics and social action in African musical idioms.* Chicago, IL: University of Chicago Press.

Davidson, J. W. (1993) Visual perception of performance manner in the movements of solo musicians. *Psychology of Music, 21,* 103–113.

DeBellis, M. (1995). *Music and conceptualization.* Cambridge, UK: Cambridge University Press.

Deutsch, D., Henthorn, T., & Lapidis, R. (2011). Illusory transformation from speech to song. *Journal of the Acoustical Society of America, 129,* 2245–2252.

Diaz, F. M. (2011). Mindfulness, attention, and flow during music listening: An empirical investigation. *Psychology of Music, 41,* 42–58.

Forster, E. M. (1910). *Howards End.* London, UK: Edward Arnold and New York, NY: G. P. Putnam's Sons.

Gabrielsson, A. (2011). *Strong experiences with music: Music is much more than just music* (R. Bradbury, Trans.). New York, NY: Oxford University Press.

Hawkins, S., Cross, I., & Ogden, R. (2013). Communicative interaction in spontaneous music and speech. In M. Orwin, C. Howes, & R. Kempson (Eds.), *Music, language and interaction* (pp. 285–329). London, UK: College Publications.

Herbert, R. (2011). *Everyday music listening: Absorption, dissociation and trancing.* Aldershot, UK: Ashgate.

Hurley, B.K., Martens, P. A., & Janata, P. (2014). Spontaneous sensorimotor coupling with multipart music. *Journal of Experimental Psychology: Human Perception and Performance, 40,* 1679–1696.

Huron, D. (2006). *Sweet anticipation: Music and the psychology of expectation.* Cambridge, MA: MIT Press.

Ishizu, I., & Zeki, S. (2011). Toward a brain-based theory of beauty. *PloS ONE, 6,* e21852. doi:10.1371/journal.pone.0021852

Kawabata, H. and Zeki, S. (2004). Neural correlates of beauty. *Journal of Neurophysiology, 91,* 1699–1705.

Keltner, D., & Haidt, J. (2003). Approaching awe, a moral, spiritual, and aesthetic emotion. *Cognition and Emotion, 17,* 297–314.

Kroger, C., & Margulis, E. H. (2017). "But they told me it was good": Extrinsic factors in the evaluation of musical performance. *Psychology of Music, 45,* 49–64.

Leder, H., Belke, B., Oeberst, A. and Augustin, D. (2004). A model of aesthetic appreciation and aesthetic judgements. *British Journal of Psychology, 95,* 489–508.

Levinson, J. (1998). *Music in the moment*. Ithaca, NY: Cornell University Press.

Manuel, P. (2011). Ethnomusicology. In T. Gracyk, & A. Kania (Eds.), *The Routledge companion to philosophy and music* (pp. 535–546). New York, NY: Routledge.

Margulis, E. H. (2010). When program notes don't help: Music descriptions and enjoyment. *Psychology of Music, 38*, 285–302.

Margulis, E. H. (2013). Aesthetic responses to repetition in unfamiliar music. *Empirical Studies of the Arts, 31*, 45–57.

Margulis, E. H., Simchy-Gross, R., & Black, J. L. (2015). Pronunciation difficulty, temporal regularity, and the speech-to-song illusion. *Frontiers in Psychology, 6*, doi: 10.3389/fpsyg.2015.00048.

Margulis, E. H., & Simchy-Gross, R. (2016). Repetition enhances the musicality of randomly generated tone sequences. *Music Perception 33*, 509–514.

McAllester, D. P. (1954) Enemy way music: A study of social and esthetic values as seen in Navaho music. *Papers of the Peabody Museum of American Archaeology and Ethnology, Harvard University, 41*, no. 3. Cambridge, MA: Peabody Museum of American Archaeology and Ethnology.

Menninghaus, W., Wagner, V., Hanich, J., Wassiliwizky, E., Kuehnast, M., & Jacobsen, T. (2015). Towards a psychological construct of being moved. *Plos One, 10*: e0128451.

Merriam, A. (1964). *The anthropology of music*. Chicago, IL: Northwestern University Press.

North, A. C., & Hargreaves, D. J. (1995). Subjective complexity, familiarity, and liking for popular music. *Psychomusicology, 14*, 77–93.

Nusbaum, E. C., & Silvia, P. J. (2014). Unusual aesthetic states. In P. P. L. Tinio, & J. K. Smith (Eds.), *The Cambridge handbook of the psychology of aesthetics and the arts* (pp. 519–539). Cambridge, UK: Cambridge University Press.

Rabinowitch, T.-C., Cross, I., & Burnard, P. (2013). Long-term musical group interaction has a positive influence on empathy in children. *Psychology of Music, 41*, 484–498.

Raffman, D. (1993). *Language, music, and mind*. Cambridge, MA: MIT Press.

Reber, R., Schwarz, N., & Winkielman, P. (2004). Processing fluency and aesthetic pleasure: Is beauty in the perceiver's processing experience? *Personality and Social Psychology Review, 8*(4), 364–382.

Rentfrow, P. J., & Gosling, S. D. (2003). The do re mi's of everyday life: The structure and personality correlates of music preferences. *Journal of Personality and Social Psychology, 84*, 1236–1256.

Repp, B. (1992). Diversity and commonality in music performance: An analysis of timing microstructure in Schumann's "Traumerei." *Journal of the Acoustical Society of America, 92*, 2546–2568.

Rickard, N. S. (2004). Intense emotional responses to music: A test of the physiological arousal hypothesis. *Psychology of Music, 32*, 371–388.

Sandstrom, G. M., & Russo, F. A. (2013). Absorption in music: Development of a scale to identify individuals with strong emotional responses to music. *Psychology of Music, 41*, 216–228.

Scherer, K. R., & Zentner, M. (2008). Music-evoked emotions are different—more often aesthetic than utilitarian. *Behavioral and Brain Sciences, 31*, 595–596.

Silveira, J. M., & Diaz, F. M. (2014). The effect of subtitles on listeners' perceptions of expressivity. *Psychology of Music, 42*, 233–250.

Smith, J. D., & Melara, R. J. (1990). Aesthetic preference and syntactic prototypicality in music: 'Tis the gift to be simple. *Cognition, 34*, 279–298.

Szpunar, K. K., Schellenberg, E., & Pliner, P. (2004). Liking and memory for musical stimuli as a function of exposure. *Journal of Experimental Psychology: Learning, Memory, and Cognition, 30*, 370–381.

# 43

# MUSIC'S MEANINGS

*Eric F. Clarke*

## Introduction

Questions about whether music is meaningful, or has meaning, what kinds of meaning it has, and how it has those meanings, have preoccupied writers on music for two and a half millennia. Plato and Aristotle wondered and worried about the effects of music on people—and in some sense were therefore concerned with what music meant to people. Since then a huge volume and diversity of thinking and writing has grappled with this most fundamental and still elusive question about music, from perspectives that range from neuroscience through psychology, linguistics, semiotics, sociology and anthropology, to the very large volume of philosophical writing. Given this very diverse literature, and in the context of the overall focus of this *Companion*, the aim of this chapter is to consider those approaches that are broadly psychological, or which in one way or another are connected with psychological methods or considerations. Since even this narrowing of the terrain leaves a potentially huge array of fascinating ideas, what follows will be selectively thematic rather than in any sense encyclopedic.

Anticipating the discussions of specific approaches that follow, four underlying distinctions thread their way through this chapter. First, there is the distinction between music considered as substance (or thing), and as process. In the roughly sixty-year period with which this chapter is concerned, there has been a significant shift from substance-based towards process-based conceptions of music, signaling an increasing recognition that music's meanings are dynamic and time based, and are experienced in the course of musical action (playing, listening, dancing, improvising, composing). Second, there is a recurrent tension between what might be termed introversive and extroversive accounts of music's meanings—meanings that are associated with the dynamics of musical materials themselves (the unfolding of musical structures in time); and those that point beyond musical materials to a wider world. The distinction is itself questionable, with many musicologists quick to point out that music is "worldly, through and through"; but either by loose analogy with syntax and semantics in language, or sometimes by virtue of claims of direct parallelism, it persists. Third, there is a distinction between those approaches that have advocated tackling meaning in "music alone" (music devoid of lyrics/texts and drama, free of still or moving images and uncontaminated, to put it tendentiously, by interpretive discourse); as against those that have claimed that music is never "alone"—that it is always encountered in variously multimedia and socially embedded circumstances, and that this is central to how its meanings must be understood. And finally, there is the distinction between those approaches that understand music's meanings as fundamentally symbolic and representational; and those that view them as primarily perceptuo-motor—*presentational*, as opposed to *representational*.

## Cooke, Francès, Meyer: A 1950s Trilogy and Its Legacy

Three books that appeared within three years of each other in the middle of the last century stand as representative and influential treatments of the topic: Leonard Meyer's *Emotion and Meaning in Music* from 1956, Robert Francès' *La perception de la musique* from 1958, and Deryck Cooke's *The Language of Music* from 1959. Music is almost universally recognized as not having the denotational and propositional capacities of natural language, and is widely proposed as a "language of the emotions" that functions as a complement to the instructional and propositional capacities of natural language. This is essentially the perspective that Cooke adopted, stating that "[W]hatever else the mysterious art known as music may eventually be found to express, it is primarily and basically a language of the emotions, through which we directly experience the fundamental urges that move mankind, without the need of falsifying ideas and images–words or pictures" (Cooke, 1959, p. 272). He attributed this emotionally communicative capacity to two closely related and intertwined general principles: intrinsic properties of musical materials (primarily, but not solely, the harmonic series); and culturally contingent conventions of use. The intrinsic component is based on the principle that intervals lower in the harmonic series (the octave, fifth, major third) are perceptually more stable and anchored, and are associated with positive emotions; while intervals higher in the harmonic series (minor third, major and minor second) are more unstable and therefore associated with negative emotions. Melodic and harmonic processes are therefore imbued with emotional trajectories that directly reflect those stability gradients.

The culturally convened component of Cooke's theory focused on the association of particular musical materials with dramatic, narrative and verbal contexts that explicitly define the emotional message with which the music is associated. So when, for example, the text of a song is concerned with loss and grief, Cooke pointed to the associated music as demonstrating properties (based primarily on intervallic and rhythmic attributes) that convey that emotional message. He cited the consistency with which composers have used the same musical devices as evidence for the stability of the cultural conventions, implying considerable trans-historical and cross-cultural commonality.

Only a small amount of work (Gabriel, 1978; Kaminska & Woolf, 2000) has tried to test Cooke's theory empirically—with mixed outcomes. But the approach has also been critiqued on a range of theoretical grounds (see e.g. Cook & Dibben, 2010): the claim that music constitutes some kind of unmediated language that is "free of ideas" seems untenable, and furthermore, in Cooke's account, music is a "language" that seems to consist of little more than a lexicon; it is based on a historically and culturally narrow concept of emotion that is uncritically applied across a range of historical and cultural contexts; and in associating specific musical materials with particular textual and narrative/dramatic contexts, it seems to assume a mirroring relationship between words or drama and music, when a whole range of ironic or deliberately contradictory relationships are also evident. Nonetheless, despite these problems, Cooke's theory is one of the earlier examples of an approach that has taken a more sophisticated and historically nuanced form in the work of so-called topic theorists (Agawu, 1991, 2009; Monelle, 2000; Tagg, 2013), whose work is based on semiotic principles. Topic theory dispenses both with the focus on emotion as the sole domain of musical meaning, and with the principle that properties of the harmonic series endow musical materials with intrinsic meanings; and in a much more culturally and historically specific way develops the idea that musical meanings arise from the association of musical materials with social functions: galloping rhythms with equestrianism of a particular kind, and all that might be in turn associated with that (Monelle, 2006); horn calls with the "call to arms" and thus masculine heroism more generally (Tagg, 2013); or ostentatious contrapuntalism with compositional sophistication or "learnedness." As discussed elsewhere (Clarke, 2005) there are questions about whose listening topic theory is intended to represent (historical or contemporary, actual or idealized), but there is some empirical evidence (Krumhansl, 1998) that supports the perceptual reality of topics in the experience of ordinary listeners.

While Cooke is unabashedly theoretical and historical in his approach, Francès—the only psychologist among these three authors—adopts a broadly empirical approach complemented by an astute historical and cultural awareness. Rather than setting out a grand theory, he undertook a number of empirical studies to investigate the generality and specificity of listeners' broadly semantic and embodied responses to a range of musical materials, using methods ranging from verbal and graphical responses to physiological measures. The result is a sophisticated and sensitive account of listeners' perceptions of music's meanings, in which three aspects of more contemporary approaches are prefigured. First, Francès recognized the importance of a physical and embodied component, drawing attention to spatiality, muscular tension and vocality in how listeners perceive musical materials. Second, he observed the multi-modal and analogical character of listeners' perceptions, and in many cases the difficulty or impossibility of expressing these in language—a primary motivation for his use of graphical methods as one type of response. And third, he discussed at some length the complex intertwining of different degrees of acculturation (or perceptual tuning) and explicit knowledge of musical conventions (including sensitivity to musical "topics") in determining listeners' experiences of musical meaning. These are issues that remain central to current thinking.

Francès recognized the dynamic and evolving nature of musical materials, but made no systematic attempt to integrate this element into his account. By contrast, Meyer's (1956) central insight was that a range of musical phenomena, including meaning, can be understood as arising from processes that elicit, confirm or thwart expectations—an idea that continues to play a central role in music research. Distinguishing between what he identified as absolute (introversive) and referentialist (extroversive) meaning in music, and focusing his efforts on the former, Meyer drew important distinctions between a number of temporal phases (predicted, actual and retrospective) in the experience of musical meaning, and in both the 1956 book and its successors (Meyer, 1967, 1973) made significant progress in identifying some of the detailed musical processes that generate and shape expectations. The publication of David Huron's (2006) *Sweet Anticipation*, fifty years after Meyer's first book, arguably represents the "coming of age" of expectation theory in music. Huron identifies a more refined sequence of expectational phases (summarized with the abbreviation ITPRA, standing for Imagination, Tension, Prediction, Reaction, and Appraisal responses) that are used to account for a much richer repertoire of meaningful experiences, ranging from intimations of the future to the relatively settled sense of hindsight, and providing novel explanations for musically significant phenomena such as humor, shock, surprise and irony. There is also considerable empirical evidence for expectation as a central thread in music perception and cognition, formulated in various ways including priming (e.g., Bharucha, 1987) and predictive coding (Vuust & Witek, 2014), although it is not always clear that the level at which these phenomena take place is consistent with the experience of meaning. If the predictive coding process, for example, is a fundamental aspect of neuronal function (as argued by e.g. Clark, 2013), it seems unlikely that we could have any conscious access to it. By contrast, attending to the famous repeated harmonic sequence that saturates the Prelude to *Tristan and Isolde* gives rise to a powerful sense of incomplete harmonic and rhythmic processes, whose meaning demands to be understood through completion—in the same way that traversing a twisting, rising path promises arrival at a vantage point that will "make sense" of the whole journey.

## Links with Language

Expectation theory places musical meaning in a predominantly introversive domain even if it does not exclude the possibility of extroversive reference: Musical materials set up expectations for future *musical* events which are met, manipulated, thwarted, or diverted in all the variety of ways that Meyer and Huron explore. The introversive/extroversive distinction is analogous to that to which the philosopher Frege (1980 [1892]) first drew attention in language with the terms sense (*Sinn*) and reference (*Bedeutung*): A proposition in language has a sense that stems from its linguistic structure, which can be distinguished from what it might refer to (its reference). This specific parallel is one aspect of a more general resemblance between music and language: Both occur in sounded and written forms; and in their sounded forms, both involve manipulations of pitch, timing, timbre, dynamics and articulation, organized into units at a number of hierarchical levels. While attempts to develop a theory of music's meanings that directly parallels language (e.g. Bernstein, 1976) have not met with success, the similarities between language and music (e.g. Rebuschat et al., 2010) have led to investigations of other more specific parallelisms that arguably contribute to an understanding of music's meanings. Prominent among these is Lerdahl and Jackendoff's (1983) *Generative Theory of Tonal Music* which, while distancing itself from engaging with musical meaning, nonetheless constitutes a significant attempt to formalize the principles according to which suitably enculturated and experienced listeners make sense of tonal music. Seen in this way, the book is a theory of musical "sense," and one that has had a significant and long-lasting influence on research in music cognition.

A rather different approach to music's meanings, strongly connected with language but moving much closer to directly perceptual experience, is the approach based on the conceptual metaphor theory of Lakoff and Johnson (e.g. Lakoff & Johnson, 1980). Very influential in cognitive linguistics, conceptual metaphor theory broadly argues that much of our everyday understanding of ourselves and our world is based on mapping primary sensory-motor experiences onto more abstract domains. As in a literary metaphor, in which the attributes of a "source" domain are mapped onto a "target" domain ("All the world's a stage . . .," in which the attributes of the source domain "stage" serve to interpret the target domain "world"), our primary sensory-motor experiences act as the source domain for a whole range of target domains. Some of the more common mappings to which Lakoff and Johnson drew attention are those of CONTAINER as applied to our emotions ("bursting with joy," "holding back grief") and PATH in relation to life ("approaching puberty," "looking back on childhood," etc.), pointing out that in these and other such examples it is the body and its engagement with its immediate environment that forms the primary source domain.

Brower (2000) makes extensive use of this approach in her cognitive theory of musical meaning, as does Larson (2012), drawing on earlier work with Mark Johnson (Johnson, & Larson, 2003). Musical meaning is thus conceived as having a strongly embodied quality, and is experienced in terms of spatial and force-dynamic attributes in the domains of pitch, rhythm, loudness, texture and timbre, involving both local (within the piece) and more general (musical conventions, and cross-domain mappings) relationships. A musical motif, for example, that reappears in more or less literal or transformed ways elsewhere in the piece may be heard to articulate meaningful relationships of recurrence and development, but will also map onto a sense of tension and release, of moving away from a center of gravity or falling back to it; of pushing forward with more or less energy, smoothness or control. In this way, musical materials (e.g. motivic elements) and musical meanings (recurrence/ development, and embodied tension/release/motion etc.) become closely coordinated and intertwined, allowing quite detailed accounts of musical "actions"—moving by step or by leap, from thick texture to thin, or in rhythmically even or uneven ways—to be rather directly mapped onto corresponding embodied experiences.

In a number of publications, Zbikowski (e.g. Zbikowski, 2002, 2015; see also this volume) has also used conceptual metaphor theory, the related theory of conceptual integration networks (Fauconnier & Turner, 2002), and Peircian semiotic principles to offer a persuasive account of the ways in which listeners understand musical materials. Cross-domain mappings, and analogies between the dynamics of musical materials and dynamic processes in other fields of human experience (such as bodily movement, imagined narratives, the flux of emotions), constitute the basis on which "music within human cultures [can] provide sonic analogs for dynamic processes" (Zbikowski, 2015, p. 148). So the opening octave leap in the melody of "Somewhere over the rainbow" opens up a metaphorical space, and in doing so conveys (by analogy) a strong and assertive character or attitude on the part of the singer/ protagonist. Through a process of conceptual blending these attributes both engage with and are engaged by the words that the character Dorothy (in *The Wizard of Oz*) sings to this melody, creating a more complex meaning that is a blend of the assertive musical materials and the rather naïve and childish lyrics. The process can be understood as a specific example of music's tendency to attach itself to other media, or to have other media attach themselves to it—a perspective that Cook (2002) has explored in an approach that recognizes music's meanings "as at the same time irreducibly cultural *and* intimately related to its structural properties" (pp. 173–4). It is the affinities between music and its domain-crossing surroundings that constitute the lifeblood of musical meaning, since as he points out, music is almost never encountered in anything but a multimedia context: accompanied by speech, program notes, blogposts, cover art, videos, analytical commentaries, in films and advertisements, on YouTube and in videogames. Music both participates in the meanings of those other media, conferring cultural status (in an advertisement), anxious fear (in a movie soundtrack), or emergence into a new reality (in a videogame) on the words or images with which it blends; and it in turn takes on and transforms the meanings with which it comes into contact by structuring their dynamic and bodily trajectories.

Those approaches to music's meanings that stem from conceptual metaphor theory, conceptual blending and multimedia theory all recognize the mediating role of language—a position that is emphatically adopted by Lawrence Kramer (e.g., Kramer, 2001). But as Kramer acknowledges, this engagement with language and image is Janus-faced: Music is always both "interrelationship, something readily intermixed with other media and with social occasions both public and private," and is "organized sound independent of textual and circumstantial involvements" (Kramer, 2003, p. 8). The intertwining of music with other media is central to an understanding of music's meanings, but is certainly not the whole story: there is a domain of musical meaning that arguably sits prior to or outside the domain of language, and which is continuous with the more general field of auditory perception and ecological understanding, and it is to this that I now turn.

## Ecological Approaches

As observed above, Robert Francès was in many ways prescient in bringing together semiotic and more directly perceptual-motor perspectives to questions of expression and meaning in music. Over half a century later, that more directly perceptual-motor approach is flourishing, based on embodied and situated psychological principles. One such strand takes its lead from the work of the psychologist James Gibson (1966; 1979) and the ecological approach more generally. Clarke (2005), Dibben (2001), Krueger (2014), and Windsor (2000; Windsor & de Bézenac, 2012) have all made use of ecological principles to frame discussions of how listeners make sense of music. Central to this approach is a more inclusive notion of meaning than might be encountered in either the semiotic or the expectation-based literature—one that lies at the heart of ecological theory. For any sentient organism the most pressing concern in an environment full of opportunities and threats is to grasp what's going on and what to do about it (Clarke, 2012). Gibson (1966) coined the term "affordance" for this relationship between an organism's needs and capacities and the available environmental opportunities, and regarded it as capturing a sense of value (for the organism), and thus an important kind of meaning. For simple organisms, these affordances may in turn be relatively simple (e.g. good to eat, or important to avoid). For human societies, with all the complexity of their cultural elaboration, affordances can become hugely ramified and elaborated, even if the more basic affordances are never left behind. A Stradivarius violin, for example, is a complex and multivalent object in its social embedding, and affords (among other things) high monetary value to an auctioneer, expressive performance possibilities to a violinist, and pride in national excellence to an Italian cultural ambassador, even as it also affords starting a fire for a desperate person with a box of matches. Social affordances do not displace "practical" affordances: they co-exist.

What music means, then, according to this view, is what music affords, or—to put it another way—what people perceive they can do with, or make of, the music that they encounter, whether as performers or listeners. Because affordances capture the reciprocal relationships between object properties and perceiver capacities, this is a powerful and economical way to explain the extremely varied but not entirely unconstrained meanings/affordances of music. To a suitably stylistically attuned and able-bodied listener in an appropriate social context, the 2013 dance hit "Get Lucky" by Daftpunk affords pleasurable dancing, in part due to properties of tempo and moderate syncopation that have been shown to optimize the inclination to dance and the experience of pleasure (Witek et al., 2014). Those perception–action attributes are, however, embedded within a musical style (specified by instrumental, textural and tonal/rhythmic properties) that already specifies "dance music" to a suitably enculturated listener. A person who is unsympathetic to this music may hear the music's potential "danceability" but be entirely unmoved by it, and a person enculturated in a radically different musical tradition the music may hear the music as dull or bewildering rather than "danceable."

This approach to theorizing musical meaning sees music not as an autonomous domain separated from the practical and social realities of the everyday world, but as continuous with it. As I sit working on this chapter, I hear from the particular sound of a floorboard on the stairs that someone is about to enter the room, and I get ready to turn around and greet them. My apparently immediate grasp of what those sounds mean, and how to act in relation to them (to turn to greet the visitor) is a function of an attuned sensitivity to those specific sounds in that environment, and of appropriate social behavior, born of many years of inhabiting that particular niche. Likewise, the soloist sitting quietly at the piano in the first movement of Beethoven's Third Piano Concerto, who hears the orchestra approach the emphatic cadence that affords her initial entry, prepares to play the parallel octave c minor scales with which she begins, her attention finely tuned to the "risks and opportunities" of that moment. And so too the person on the phone waiting to get through to customer services, who perhaps unconsciously readies himself for a particular manner of conversation on the basis of the company's telephone hold music (Bach's Third Brandenburg Concerto, rather than a cheap jingle). Sounds—"everyday" and musical—specify a limitless variety of objects, events and circumstances, from the practical and tangible (Is someone approaching? What instrument is making that sound?), to the structural (cadence—get ready to play), and the ideological (classical music—class assumptions).

The sounds of music afford a huge range and variety of phenomena, from young children's rhythmic synchronization (Kirschner & Tomasello, 2009), and the mediation of emotions (DeNora, 2000); to enhancing the capacity to endure physical pain and distress (Edwards, 1995), or as an instrument of torture (Cusick, 2008). People become highly attuned to the musics in which they are enculturated, and pick up their meanings with astonishing immediacy and speed. A number of studies have demonstrated that listeners are able to pick up important and so-called abstract attributes of musical excerpts from extremely brief "slices" of sound: Gjerdingen and Perrott (2008) found that as little as 250 msec is enough for a listener to identify a musical genre (rock, classical, dance, latin, etc.; see also Krumhansl, 2009; Plazak & Huron, 2011). Contrary to the more conventional view that musical meaning is a high-level and abstract property of music that might therefore appear rather late in the whole perceptual process, these studies suggest that listeners identify what *kind* of music they're hearing—to what "cultural world" it belongs, and what it affords—extremely early. In most circumstance it is much more important to know that this is "funeral music," "classical concert music," or "dance music" than to hear that it is in compound triple meter or uses octatonic scales.

## Music's Meanings and Social Process

This leads directly to the final theme in this chapter—the idea that music's meanings are to be understood in terms of the social functions that music performs. It is important first to dispel the idea that this is a category of meaning that is relevant only to some musics (usually the music of another and distant culture)—and that there are musics that are somehow free of social function. All music is culturally embedded, and performs a social function however abstract and rarefied (or normalized) that may sometimes be. An excerpt of Schoenberg's piano music, used by a musicologist at a conference as an illustrative example, performs a number of social functions (contributing to academic discourse, supporting a claim in music theory, conferring music-historical gravitas on the speaker) no less than the ceremonial Nepali music (marking a seasonal festival, orchestrating/choreographing a procession around the town of Bhaktapur, expressing satire and burlesque) that Richard Widdess (2012) describes. It is ethnomusicologists and sociologists of music who have, understandably, been prominent in articulating music's social meanings, but as has already been evident, there is considerable overlap and engagement with psychological concerns.

Tia DeNora has made particularly significant contributions in this respect, *Music in Everyday Life* (DeNora, 2000) kick-starting a now burgeoning interest in the detailed examination of the function and meaning of music in people's lives from a combination of sociological and psychological perspectives. As DeNora has demonstrated with acutely observed case studies, people use music in complex socially embedded ways as a "technology of the self" that articulates or constructs a whole range of meanings in more or less familiar everyday circumstances. A woman uses a recording of a Schubert Impromptu that is strongly associated with the memory of her deceased father and childhood home to bring order and meaning to a stressful house move; an aerobics instructor compiles a playlist of music to provide the right sequence of warm-up, drive, sustain, and cool-down for the members of an exercise class; and a shopper attends to the music issuing from different clothes shops on a high street to "guide" him towards an outlet where he might find suitable clothes. In each of these cases what the music means (or affords—a term also used by DeNora) is the consequence of a complex conjunction of musical-material attributes (most obviously tempo and dynamics in the case of the aerobics music), social context and function, and the motivations and needs of the users (see Dibben, this volume).

Arguably the most significant domain in which music's meanings are seen in accounts such as DeNora's is in the construction, articulation, and maintenance of the sense of self (see Vuoskoski, this volume). Contemporary theories emphasize subjectivity and identity as life-long dynamic and constructive *processes*, rather than timeless or transcendent states; and for many people music is a powerful and persistent technology by means of which such self-making and maintaining is accomplished. The long association of music with affective states and people's inner lives (as well as with public displays of identity) has the consequence that music's meanings are often powerfully experienced as transformations or narratives of the self. In texted music, and particularly music in a singer-songwriter tradition, listeners may often hear themselves as being directly addressed by the music/musician, hearing the music's meanings as being paradoxically publicly enunciated—often on a massive scale—and at the same time intimately and personally targeted (Moore, 2012; Dibben, 2013).

## Conclusion

As Martin Clayton (2001) observes, understanding music's meanings has been hampered by regarding music as a thing—a structure to which meanings somehow become attached, rather than a process within and out of which meanings emerge. But hampered or not, the literature on music's meanings is an extremely rich and diverse body of work, drawing attention to the extraordinary way in which music's affordances are encountered across experiential domains. In the most direct and palpable manner, we hear musical sounds as specifying people, objects and actions (blowing and hitting and strumming and scraping) in spaces and places both real and virtual. And at the same time, we hear in those sounds structural processes and wordless narratives that engage with the dynamic attentional mechanisms that have been explored by expectation theorists. But music is less passive and contemplative than this might suggest, even in the peculiar circumstances of the Western concert hall, and a third domain of music's meanings engages the powerful corporeality that for a time seemed to be forgotten by both musicology and music cognition. In our throats, faces, limbs, torsos and viscera, we engage with and make music's meanings with our bodies, in overt and manifestly participatory fashion (dancing, gesturing, singing and playing along), as well as in ways that are discreet to the point of invisibility (the "internal choreography" of recumbent headphone listening). We perceive and *enact* music's meanings, even if we also have the capacity to contemplate and reflect upon the infinitely ramified connections and engagements of which musical processes are capable.

Overwhelmingly, the approaches discussed in this chapter have been concerned with *how* music means rather than with *what* music means—as is appropriate for a contribution to a volume concerned with music cognition, rather than hermeneutics. The multiplicity of music's meanings, the dependency of those meanings on the perceptual capacities and specific orientations of individual listeners, their momentary and accumulated "state of readiness" and how they are poised to respond, and the circumstances of listening mean that it is impossible to predict exactly *what* any specific musical process might mean to a listener. But this is not a recipe for total relativism. In all the ways that have been explored here, there is now a powerful and varied toolkit for investigating the constraints and opportunities that musical processes afford, and thus a principled basis on which to understand music's meanings. It may also provide the grounds on which to propose the specific meanings of specific musical circumstances, and appreciate or contest those that others may propose—but that is a different enterprise.

## Core Reading

Clarke, E. F. (2005). *Ways of listening. An ecological approach to the perception of musical meaning.* New York, NY: Oxford University Press.

Clarke, E. F. (2012). What's going on: Music, psychology and ecological theory. In M. Clayton, T. Herbert, and R. Middleton (Eds.), *The cultural study of music. A critical introduction* (2nd ed., pp. 333–42). London: Routledge.

Cook, N. (2002). Theorizing musical meaning. *Music Theory Spectrum, 23*(2), 170–95.

DeNora, T. (2000) *Music in Everyday Life.* Cambridge: Cambridge University Press

Huron, D. (2006). *Sweet anticipation. Music and the psychology of expectation.* Cambridge, MA: MIT Press.

Kramer, L. (2001) *Musical meaning: Toward a critical history.* Berkeley, CA: University of California Press.

## Further References

Agawu, K. (1991). *Playing with signs.* Princeton, NJ: Princeton University Press.

Agawu, K. (2009). *Music as discourse: Semiotic adventures in Romantic music.* New York, NY: Oxford University Press.

Bernstein, L. (1976). *The unanswered question.* Cambridge, MA: Harvard University Press.

Bharucha, J. J. (1987). Music cognition and perceptual facilitation: A connectionist framework. *Music Perception, 5*(1), 1–30.

Brower, C. (2000). A cognitive theory of musical meaning. *Journal of Music Theory, 44*(2), 323–379.

Clark, A. (2013). Whatever next? Predictive brains, situated agents and the future of cognitive science. *Behavioral and Brain Science, 36*(3), 181–204.

Clayton, M. (2001). Introduction: Towards a theory of musical meaning (in India and elsewhere). *British Forum for Ethnomusicology, 10*(1), 1–17.

Cook, N., & Dibben, N. J. (2010). Emotion in culture and history: Perspectives from musicology. In P. Juslin, & J. Sloboda (Eds.), *Handbook of music and emotion: Theory, research, applications* (pp. 45–72). Oxford: Oxford University Press.

Cooke, D. (1959) *The language of music.* Oxford: Oxford University Press.

Cusick, S. G. (2008). Musicology, torture, repair. *Radical Musicology, 3*(1), 1–9.

Dibben, N. (2001) What do we hear when we hear music? Music perception and musical material. *Musicae Scientiae, 5*(2), 161–94.

Dibben, N. (2013). Vocal performance and the projection of emotional authenticity. In D. Scott (Ed.), *The Ashgate research companion to popular musicology* (pp. 317–333). Aldershot, United Kingdom: Ashgate.

Edwards, J. (1995). "You are singing beautifully": Music therapy and the debridement bath. *The Arts in Psychotherapy, 22*(11), 53–5.

Fauconnier, G., & Turner, M. (2002). *The way we think: Conceptual blending and the mind's hidden complexities.* New York, NY: Basic Books.

Francès, R. (1988 [1958]). *The perception of music.* trans. W. J. Dowling. Hillsdale, NJ: Lawrence Erlbaum Associates. Originally *La perception de la musique.* Paris: J. Vrin, 1958.

Frege, G. (1980 [1892]) On sense and reference. In P. Geac, & M. Black (Eds. and trans.), Translations from the philosophical writings of Gottlob Frege (3rd ed., pp. 56–78). Oxford: Blackwell 1980. Originally Über Sinn und Bedeutung, Zeitschrift für Philosophie und philosophische Kritik, *100*, 25–50.

Gabriel, C. (1978). An experimental study of Deryck Cooke's theory of music and meaning. *Psychology of Music, 6*(1), 13–20.

Gibson, J. J. (1966). *The senses considered as perceptual systems.* Boston, NJ: Houghton Mifflin.

Gibson, J. J. (1979). *The ecological approach to visual perception.* Hillsdale, NJ: Lawrence Erlbaum Associates.

Gjerdingen, R., & Perrott, D. (2008). Scanning the dial: The rapid recognition of music genres. *Journal of New Music Research, 37*(2), 93–100.

Johnson, M., & Larson, S. (2003). "Something in the way she moves"—Metaphors of musical motion. *Metaphor and Symbol, 18*, 63–84.

Kaminska, Z., & Woolf, J. (2000). Melodic line and emotion: Cooke's theory revisited *Psychology of Music, 28*(2), 133–153.

Kirschner, S., & Tomasello, M. (2009). Joint drumming: Social context facilitates synchronization in preschool children. *Journal of Experimental Child Psychology, 102*(3), 299–314.

Kramer, L. (2003). Musicology and meaning. *The Musical Times, 144*(1883), 6–12.

Krueger, J. (2014). Affordances and the musically extended mind. *Frontiers in Psychology, 4*:1003. doi: 10.3389/fpsyg.2013.01003

Krumhansl, C. L. (1998). Topic in music: An empirical study of memorability, openness, and emotion in Mozart's String Quintet in C major and Beethoven's String Quartet in A minor. *Music Perception, 16*(1), 119–134.

Krumhansl, C. L. (2009). "Thin slices" of music. *Music Perception, 27*(5), 337–54.

Lakoff, G., & Johnson, M. (1980). *Metaphors we live by.* Chicago, IL: University of Chicago Press.

Larson, S. (2012). *Musical forces: Motion, metaphor, and meaning in music* Bloomington, IN: Indiana University Press.

Lerdahl, F., & Jackendoff, R. (1983). *A generative theory of tonal music.* Cambridge, MA: MIT Press.

Meyer, L. B. (1956). *Emotion and meaning in music.* Chicago, IL: University of Chicago Press.

Meyer, L. B. (1967). *Music, the arts, and ideas. Patterns and predictions in twentieth-century culture.* Chicago, IL: University of Chicago Press.

Meyer, L. B. (1973). *Explaining music. Essays and explorations.* Berkeley, CA: University of California Press.

Monelle, R. (2000). *The sense of music: Semiotic essays.* Princeton: Princeton University Press.

Monelle, R. (2006). *The musical topic. Hunt, military and pastoral.* Bloomington, IN: Indiana University Press.

Moore, A. (2012). *Song means. Analysing and interpreting recorded popular song.* Farnham, UK: Ashgate.

Plazak, J., & Huron, D. (2011). The first three seconds: Listener knowledge gained from brief musical excerpts. *Musicae Scientiae, 15*(1), 29–44.

Rebuschat, P., Rohrmeier, M., Cross, I., & Hawkins, J. (2010) (Eds.) *Language and music as cognitive systems.* Oxford: Oxford University Press.

Tagg, P. (2013). *Music's meanings. A modern musicology for non-musos.* New York, NY and Huddersfield, UK: The Mass Media Music Scholars' Press.

Vuust, P., & Witek, M. A. G. (2014). Rhythmic complexity and predictive coding: A novel approach to modeling rhythm and meter perception in music. *Frontiers in Psychology 5*: 1111. doi: 10.3389/fpsyg.2014.01111

Widdess, R. (2012). Music, meaning and culture. *Empirical Musicology Review, 7*(1–2), 88–94.

Windsor, W. L. (2000) Through and around the acousmatic: The interpretation of electroacoustic sounds. In S. Emmerson (Ed.), *Music, electronic media and culture* (pp. 7–33). Aldershot, UK: Ashgate Press.

Windsor W. L., & de Bézenac, C. (2012). Music and affordances. *Musicae Scientiae. 16*(1), 102–120.

Witek, M. A. G., Clarke, E. F., Wallentin, M., Kringelbach, M. L., & Vuust, P. (2014). Syncopation, body-movement and pleasure in groove music. *PloS ONE, 9*(4), e94446

Zbikowski, L. (2002) *Conceptualizing music: Cognitive structure, theory, and analysis.* New York, NY: Oxford University Press.

Zbikowski, L. (2015). Words, music, and meaning. In P. A. Brandt, & J. R. do Carmo, Jr. (Eds.), *Sémiotic de la musique / Music and Meaning. Signata: Annals of Semiotics 6* (pp. 143–164). Liège, Belgium: Presses universitaires de Liège–Sciences humaines.

# GLOSSARY

***Absolute pitch:*** (A P, also called *perfect pitch*) A rare cognitive ability that enables listeners to identify any frequency by its pitch name (e.g., F-sharp) without reference to an external standard like a musical instrument. A P possessors are also able to produce a pitch when given its name. Identification of pitches is typically rapid, effortless, and accurate for most A P possessors.

***Absolute timing:*** Sometimes referred to as *duration-based timing, interval-based timing,* or *non-beat-based timing.* Measurement and comparison of the absolute durations of isolated time intervals or time intervals organized into sequences that do not afford comparison against a relative metric (a *beat* or *metric grid*).

***Accents:*** Emphasis that is perceived on certain tones in a rhythm. Accents can be based on acoustical features, such as intensity, timing, or pitch, or can be *phenomenal*, arising due to a specific tone's temporal position within and between groups.

***Accompaniment systems:*** Intelligent music systems that enable the user to control the playback of music in order to synchronize to a live instrumentalist, much as a traditional accompanist would.

***Acousmatic:*** Without a visible source; a term introduced by Pierre Schaeffer to describe music or other sounds intended for listening lack a visible source.

***Action simulation:*** The internal enactment of others' actions using one's own action-planning system, enabling prediction of others' behaviors and coordination of one's own actions with the actions of others.

***Adaptive timing:*** The change in the speed and timing of one person's movements to allow coordination or synchronization with the changing movements of another person.

***Aesthetic response:*** A response to an artistic expression dealing with its beauty or artistic value; may include, *inter alia*, affective and cognitive responses.

***Affordance:*** a) In James J. Gibson's theory of ecological perception, a feature of an object or environment resulting from the dialectic between the properties of this object or environment and the needs and capacities of its perceiver. b) The risks and opportunities for action in relation to the perceiver's capacities that are perceived in an object or event.

***AIRS (Advancing Interdisciplinary Research in Singing):*** Major collaborative international research initiative, supported by the Social Sciences and Humanities Research

Council of Canada and directed by Annabel Cohen, aimed at understanding individual, cultural, and universal influences on singing (how it develops, how it is or should be taught), and the influence of singing on individuals and their societies (how singing can impact well-being).

***AIRS Test Battery of Singing Skills (ATBSS):*** Testing protocol, developed through the AIRS collaboration, for acquiring information about the role of age, gender, culture, and levels of musical training on a range of singing abilities.

***Amusia:*** Acquired or congenital disorder of music perception and production which cannot be explained by peripheral hearing loss or general cognitive impairments.

***Analogical reference:*** A system of reference based on structural similarities between tokens and the objects or phenomena for which they stand.

***Analogy:*** A reasoning process based on similarities between two apparently different objects or phenomena.

***Animal song:*** Animal vocalizations which are learned (rather than innate) and relatively complex. Animal songs are generally associated with territorial defense and courtship. Apart from humans, animal song is observed mainly in birds and cetaceans (whales).

***Anterior:*** Directional term, meaning close to the front.

***Anticipation:*** Process by which one person prepares for or adjusts their movement so as to coordinate or synchronize with another person's movements or with some other external signal, sounding or visual.

***Anticipatory imagery:*** Process by which people construct mental representations of the perceptual effects that they expect their overt actions to have.

***Aphasia:*** Language disorder characterized by an inability to produce or comprehend language due to brain injury. Lesions to the left hemisphere, specifically Wernicke's area, affect the ability to comprehend language, whereas damage to Broca's area affects the production of speech.

***Appraisal:*** Evaluation of stimuli, environment, and their relevance for an individual. This evaluation may typically concern a number of dimensions, including novelty, pleasantness, goal-relevance, and coping capability.

***Approach notes:*** A brief note, a quarter note or less in duration, which moves by step to a chord tone.

***Arousal potential:*** The capacity of music (or other stimuli) to induce arousal. Music's arousal potential is positively associated with its complexity, intensity, and novelty.

***Auditory image:*** When referring to a heard auditory percept, a single gestalt percept of a sound or combination of sounds.

***Augmented instrument:*** A familiar instrument, often but not always acoustic, whose capabilities have been extended with sensors, actuators, and computation.

***Aural copying:*** Learning to play specific musical passages or compositions by copying them via listening, either in a live setting or through a recording, or through aural memory.

***Automaticity:*** As a result of extensive practice, the ability to execute a specific perceptual-motor task without focused attention or deliberate control.

***Background music:*** Music that is heard or listened to concurrently with some other task, usually from recordings.

***Basic emotions:*** A set of emotions evolved to prepare humans to be "action ready" in situations crucial for survival. These include joy, sadness, anger, fear, disgust, and surprise.

**Basilar membrane:** A part of the inner ear where vibrations are transduced to neural signals. More specifically, a membrane lining the inside of the cochlea, with hair cells which respond to frequencies according to a tonotopographic organization, with the lowest frequencies at one end of the membrane and the highest frequencies at the other.

**Beat-based rhythms:** Rhythms comprising intervals that are related to one another by integer ratios (i.e., 1:2:3:4, where 1 corresponds to the duration of the base, or smallest, inter-onset-interval), and for which individual stimulus events align with on-beat locations.

**Beat-based timing:** Sometimes referred to as *relative timing*, where measurement and comparison of time intervals are made with respect to an underlying regularity that can be internally generated or explicitly emphasized (i.e., beat or metrical grid).

**Bebop:** A style of jazz characterized by fast tempo, instrumental virtuosity, and improvisation based on the combination of harmonic structure and melody, developed in the early and mid-1940s.

**Big Five personality traits:** A five-factor model that is used to measure and represent stable individual differences in personal characteristics, behavior, and emotions. The five traits included in the model are extraversion, neuroticism, agreeableness, conscientiousness, and openness to experience. The five-factor model does not categorize people into different personality "types"; instead, each of the five traits are presumed to be present in every individual to a greater or lesser degree.

**Biomusicology:** The study of the biological basis of human musicality, viewed from a comparative perspective (see *cross-species comparisons*).

**Broca's area:** A region in the left inferior frontal lobe of the brain, first identified by neurologist Paul Broca as being linked to language.

**Cadence:** a) A punctuation of a musical phrase, in which a melodic and harmonic progression comes to a rest. b) The end of a phrase or section in music that traditionally affirms the local key.

**Categorization:** A cognitive process through which discrete objects or phenomena are grouped together into a single class, such that each exemplar of the category is treated or regarded as functionally equivalent to other exemplars.

**CHILDES (Child Language Data Exchange System):** Online database comprised of annotated transcripts of children's speech, used by researchers since the 1980s to investigate the development and learning of language in children, developed by Brian Mac-Whinney and Catherine Snow.

**Choir:** Organized group of singers who perform vocal works as an ensemble.

**Clinical improvisation:** Improvisation in a therapeutic music therapy setting.

**Cochlea:** The snail-shaped organ of hearing housed inside the inner ear that transduces sound waves into electrochemical signals, which are sent to the brain via the auditory nerve for interpretation.

**Coefficient of variation:** A normalized measure of temporal variability, commonly used as a dependent measure to index tapping performance; computed as the standard deviation of inter-tap intervals divided by mean inter-tap interval.

**complex Auditory Brainstem Response (cABR):** Brain electrical activity measured in response to complex sounds (such as speech and music) and originating from subcortical areas of the auditory pathway, mainly located in the auditory midbrain.

**Complexity:** The opposite of simplicity; defined in music, for example, as the degree of structuring in a composition or the amount of effort required by a listener to follow and comprehend the music.

**Comprovisation:** A composition for improvisers.

**Conductor programs:** Computer systems that enable users to control expressive parameters such as tempo, timing, and dynamics.

**Conserved universals:** In the terminology introduced by Brown and Jordania (2013), the term "conserved universals" refers to characteristics that are universal to all musical utterances or phenomena. These may include the use of discrete pitches, octave equivalence, transposability, and the presence of common sound-based arousal-inducing parameters such as tempo, amplitude, and register.

**Consonance:** a) "Pleasant" or "good" sounding tones or their combinations, b) The combination of tones that are in simple frequency ratios, e.g., 1:1, 2:1.

**Cooperative principle:** In the work of the philosopher H. Paul Grice, the notion that communication is founded on mutual recognition of the communicative intent and goodwill of one's partners in communication, toward the accomplishment of mutual goals.

**Corpus study:** The analysis of a representative sample of musical works, typically encoded to facilitate statistical tests.

**Cortectomy:** Removal of part of the cerebral cortex.

**Cortex:** The outer layer of the brain.

**Counterpoint:** From the Latin *punctus contra punctum*: setting one note (*punctus*) against another so as to create simultaneously sounding auditory streams. Often refers to musical styles that showcase the independence of voices and the interplay of melodic figures between different voices.

**Critical period:** Age period during which the development of certain skills is enhanced.

**Crossmodal correspondences:** Correspondences between discrete perceptual modalities (e.g., hearing and vision) that underlie invariant associations between those modalities.

**Cross-species comparisons:** In the realm of music, a comparative approach across species that studies music-like behaviors associated with sound production and perception in non-human animals from a phylogenetic and evolutionary standpoint.

**Culture:** The practices and beliefs of a group of people, including artistic activities and products.

**Deaf:** Referring to the greatest measurable hearing loss or a profound hearing loss of 90 dB HL or greater.

**Default mode network:** A network of brain areas that activate together under certain conditions.

**Deliberate practice:** A structured activity with the explicit goal of improving performance.

**Development:** A process of growth or advancement, which usually corresponds with maturation.

**Diegetic music:** Music presented as if originating from a source inside the fictional world of film, such as music that the characters produce themselves, or control as by switching on a gramophone, or should be able to hear because it is supposedly playing within their environment. (See also *non-diegetic music*.)

**Digital Musical Instruments (DMIs):** Musical instruments created using computers or other digital electronics; DMIs typically include sensor inputs, a mapping layer, and sonic outputs.

**Digital Repository:**   Virtual system used to manage and store digital content, usually for multiple users.

**Dissonance:**   a) "Unpleasant" or "grating" sounding tones or their combinations, b) The combination of tones that are in complex frequency ratios, e.g., 45:32, 15:8.

**Dominant:**   In diatonic (scale-based) musical practice, the fifth note of the scale and, by extension, harmonies built upon that note. In C major, G is the dominant.

**Dopamine:**   A central neurotransmitter in the brain, well known for its association with motor control (e.g. as seen in Parkinson's disease). In the reward system, it is involved in the regulation of motivation and goal-directed behavior as well as in prediction and learning processes, related to future rewards.

**Dorsal:**   Directional term, meaning close to the back of an animal.

**DPMC (Dorsal premotor cortex):**   The upper part of the motor cortex lying within the frontal lobes of the brain and just anterior to the primary motor cortex.

**DLPFC (Dorsolateral prefrontal cortex):**   An area in the prefrontal cortex of the brain known for its involvement in executive functioning.

**Double dissociation:**   A medical condition in which one patient shows impaired processing in capacity A (e.g., pitch processing), but intact processing in capacity B (e.g., temporal processing), while another patient shows the reverse pattern.

**Ear-playing:**   Playing music that is learned through the activity of listening as distinct from reading notation.

**Ecological constraints:**   Perceptual bias resulting from living organisms' long-term experiences with nature and culture, such as, for example, acoustic laws and live music.

**Electroencephalography (EEG):**   A noninvasive research procedure for investigating brain activity by placing electrodes on the scalp and measuring changes in the minute electrical signals being produced by the brain. The signals so recorded may be interpreted as event-related potentials (ERPs) or in terms of energy in various frequency bands (alpha, delta, etc.)

**Electrode:**   Device for measuring neural signals, which in cochlear implants are composed of a noble metal platinum-irridium alloy. When arranged along an array in a cochlear implant each electrode emits electrical pulses to nearby tissue inside the cochlea, intending to stimulate any remaining neural tissue in individuals with severe-to-profound sensorineural hearing loss.

**Emotional arousal:**   The level of physiological arousal associated with the experience of an emotion. Some emotions are high in arousal, such as anger and ecstasy, while others are low in arousal, for example, depression and boredom. The intensity of an emotion (sadness or grief) may influence the associated physiological arousal.

**Empathy:**   A process through which we can understand and feel what another person is experiencing. True empathy entails experiencing the same emotion as observed in another, and being aware of the cause of one's emotional reaction. There are stable, dispositional differences in people's tendency and ability to experience empathy across different situations; this inter-individual variability is called *trait empathy*.

**Enculturation:**   The gradual process of learning the range of behaviors and conventions that, in practice, define a musical culture.

**Ergonomic effects:**   Effects (of music) that optimize human performance of physical tasks, such as in exercise and sport.

**Evaluative space model:**   Model of evaluative processes that allows for a coupled, as well as uncoupled, relationship between positive and negative evaluations of stimuli. If coupled, this does not need to be coupling in a reciprocal manner. Positive and negative evaluations can be co-activating under certain circumstances.

***Event-related brain potential (ERP):*** Analysis of the EEG signal that allows the experimenter to quantify time-locked brain electrical activity to particular stimulus events.

***Evidence-based treatment:*** Treatment based on approved principles derived from scientific evidence.

***Evoked responses:*** Brain responses that are time- and phase-locked to the onset of a stimulus; also referred to as *event-related potentials* (*ERPs*).

***Evolutionary musicology:*** The discipline that which studies the origins and possible biological or social functions of music and musicality from the perspective of evolutionary theory.

***Experience sampling study:*** Investigative method in which participants are asked to report their experiences at certain times during the day. A text alert may be sent to participants to prompt them to fill out a brief questionnaire. This questionnaire may, for example, ask them about their current situation and the music that is present in it.

***Expressive variation:*** Performers' changes in musical parameters such as loudness (dynamics) or speed (tempo) for purposes of musical expression.

***Expressive timing:*** Non-notated micro-variations of duration (rhythm) introduced in performance to highlight notes, harmonies, beginnings or ends of sections, and so on; such variations can cause delay or anticipation of note onsets or grouping of notes into gestures. Typical examples include non-synchrony between accompaniment and melody and instances when the first of four even notes under a slur is held slightly longer while the others are hurried over, or when the first of two even notes under a slur are played by leaning on the first and shortening the second (i.e. in a slightly long-short or swung manner).

***Fasciculus:*** Major pathway of white matter in the brain.

***Figured bass:*** Notated bass notes with numbers and signs above or below that indicate the intervals at which additional pitches should be sounded. These additional pitches create harmony together with the melody pitches. This short-hand notation was common during the Baroque period (ca. 1600–1750).

***Form, musical:*** The overall or large-scale design or plan of a piece of music, based on features such as its *formal design* relative to its melodic or thematic content or its *tonal design* relative to its harmonic content.

***Formal design:*** The overall plan or pattern of a piece of music, frequently understood in terms of its deployment of different thematic or melodic materials; often symbolized with letters, such as AABA.

***Formal function:*** The role played by a musical event in the overall structure of a musical composition, including but not limited to beginning, middle, or end.

***Formal education:*** The provision of teaching designed to effect learning under the auspices of institutional control and/or accreditation.

***Frontal lobe:*** One of the major lobes of the cerebral cortex located towards the front of the head. This area of the brain is responsible for higher-order mental processes, such as thinking and planning.

***Fronto-central negative component:*** A negative variation of the evoked potential with maximum amplitude over the frontal and central regions of the scalp.

***Functional neuroimaging:*** The process of observing brain activity over time.

***fMRI (functional Magnetic Resonance Imaging):*** A safe and non-invasive brain-scanning technique for measuring and mapping brain activity.

**Gene–environment correlation:**  Also called genotype–environment correlation; the influence that an individual's genotype can have on their environmental conditions, by generating behavior that selects features of the environment.

**GENEPLORE model:**  A model of the creative process that which employs a repeated cycle of generating, exploring, refining, and selecting materials or solutions.

**Generative music systems:**  Automatic music systems that apply serial procedures to seed material.

**Genetic pleiotropy:**  The phenomenon where one gene influences multiple phenotypic traits.

**Gestalt principles of organization:**  Psychological explanations for how humans make sense of complex perceptual inputs, for example in audition or vision. These include the principles of similarity (similar events or items are grouped together), proximity (events or items close to one another are grouped together), and good continuation (a shape or line will continue in its current direction).

**Grey matter:**  The darker tissue of the brain and spinal cord, mostly composed of nerve cell bodies and inputs.

**Gyrus:**  Outward fold of the brain.

**Harmonics:**  An overtone in a series whose cycles per second are whole integer multiples of the frequency of the fundamental; for example, the frequencies of the first three harmonics of 100 Hz (fundamental tone) are 200 Hz, 300 Hz, and 400 Hz.

**Harmony:**  A word originally referring to a reconciliation of diverse elements. When applied to music it can mean both the quality of individual multi-voice sonorities (e.g., "a major chord") and the general style of how chords are constructed and concatenated.

**Heritability:**  An estimate of the variation in a phenotypic trait within a population that is due to genetic variation among individuals within that same population. That is, heritability is the proportion of phenotypic variance that is attributable to genetic variance. More informally, heritability is the extent to which genetic differences contribute to differences in observed behavior within a population.

**Historical treatises:**  Books written by music theoreticians and practitioners on the rules and effects of composing and performing in a given historical period. These treatises, including instrumental tutors, offer practical advice on how to play particular instruments (e.g. the flute, violin, keyboard, or voice) and how to convey expression in composition or performance. They are helpful for modern musicians in their endeavor to recreate historical performing practices and to gain an understanding of a period's aesthetic preferences and concerns.

**Hypermeter:**  The recurring pattern of strong and weak bars in music.

**Hyperscanning:**  Measuring brain-to-brain couplings with various brain-imaging methods.

**Ice-breaker effect:**  The evidence discovered by Eiluned Pearce, Jacques Launay, and Robin Dunbar that singing mediates faster social bonding in groups of relative strangers than other group activities such as crafts or creative writing.

**Imagery, constructive:**  Use of internal mental models for perceptual organization and stimulus interpretation.

**Imagery, sensory:**  Mental simulation of a sensory event for any of the sensory modalities (i.e., visual, auditory, olfactory, gustatory, haptic/cutaneous, proprioceptive/kinesthetic), or any combination of these.

***Implicit learning:*** A type of learning that occurs spontaneously, unconsciously, and without explicit attention or effort. Implicit learning occurs when we are exposed to the language or music of our culture, for example; as we track phonemes or pitches, we learn which sounds are likely to follow other sounds to form words or musical motives. Implicit learning is typically contrasted with explicit learning, which occurs in school or music lessons with teacher and student focused on knowledge or skill acquisition.

***Improvisation:*** Playing music with a greater or lesser degree of freedom to create, add, or change parameters.

***Improvisation systems:*** Computer music systems that generate music "on the fly," often in response to and in the style of a human player, resulting in a collaborative performance.

***Infant:*** A term often used to describe a child younger than 12 months of age.

***Inferior frontal gyrus (IFG):*** A gyrus of the frontal lobe which includes language areas, also known as *Broca's area*.

***Informal learning:*** Learning that takes place aside from institutional control or accreditation.

***Information processing framework:*** In psychology, a conceptual framework for understanding human cognition as proceeding through several stages (perceptual, short-term, and long-term) of processing and memory, with information being transformed as it moves from stage to stage.

***Instrument paradigm music systems:*** Computer music systems that produce performances that are considered to be solo performances.

***Integer ratios:*** Ratios formed with the use of two integers (whole numbers). With regard to rhythm, time intervals that result from multiplication of a base inter-onset-interval by an integer. For example, a rhythm with a base inter-onset-interval of 250 ms would have possible integer-ratio intervals equal to 250 ms, 500 ms, 750 ms, 1000 ms, etc.

***Inter-onset-interval (IOI):*** The time between the beginning of one musical event (note) and another; one measurement of rhythmic duration and frequently used in the study of timing in musical performance.

***Intelligent music systems:*** Music systems that incorporate human-like intelligence to assist in music performance, either as instrument or musical partner.

***Interval-based timing:*** See *absolute timing*.

***Introversive vs. extroversive semiosis:*** Meanings arising from within some material itself, vs. meanings arising from reference beyond the material.

***Irrelevant Sound Effect (ISE):*** A phenomenon whereby serial recall of information is disrupted in the presence of task-irrelevant background sound. It derives from the *Irrelevant Speech Effect*, in which recall of information is hindered by concurrent irrelevant speech even when the list items are presented visually.

***Isochronous sequence:*** A sequence composed from strict repetition of a single *inter-onset-interval*.

***Kairos:*** Greek for the "right moment," right time to act; time concept related to bio-rhythm and individual psychophysiological condition.

***Kinematics:*** The motion of points or objects through space, typically quantified in terms of position change over time, velocity (movement speed), and acceleration (rate of change of movement speed).

***Kinesthesia:*** The perception of the movement of one's body in space.

***Lateral:*** Directional term, meaning close to the left or right sides (compare with medial).

***Licks:*** Stock melodic phrases used in jazz improvisation.

**Lifelong learning:** Learning that continues either informally and/or by virtue of formal or non-formal provision throughout the life-cycle into old age.

**Listening skills:** Skills developed by musicians to aid ear-playing, aural copying, playing along, and improvisation as well as other skills associated more closely with notationally transmitted music.

**Literacy:** Proficiency in a specific field of knowledge, generally used to describe the ability to read and write one's native language.

**Longitudinal study:** A research method in which data is gathered for the same subjects in separate sessions over a period of time.

**Lyrics:** The words produced by a vocalist during a song, which can be spoken or transcribed in the absence of pitch.

**Lyrics intelligibility:** Term used to describe how well a listener can correctly understand the words produced by a vocal performer.

**Mapping:** Correspondence between two or more continua, e.g. auditory-motor mapping.

**Mapping layer:** A set of programmed relationships linking sensor input to sonic or other output in a digital musical instrument.

**Markov model:** A mathematical model used to describe probabilistically changing systems; in musical research, frequently a *first-order model,* where it is assumed that future states depend only on the current state, not on the states that occurred before it.

**Medial:** Directional term, meaning close to the midline.

**Melodic contour:** The shape of a melodic event, including ascending, descending, arc-shaped, or inverted arc-shaped melodic lines.

**Melodic intonation therapy:** Music therapy treatment used to help patients with Broca's aphasia produce speech through singing, by activating areas of the brain still capable of language production.

**Metaphor:** In conceptual metaphor theory, a process through which structure from a source domain is mapped on to a target domain to construct new meaning.

**Meter:** The recurring pattern of strong and weak beats in music, grouped into bars, as traditionally indicated with a time signature.

**Microanalysis:** A detailed analysis of moments, events, and episodes within a selected timeframe or series of timeframes (such as a music therapy session).

**MIDI (Musical Instrument Digital Interface):** An industry standard protocol commonly used to allow synthesizers and musical controllers to send data to one another.

**Modes (diatonic):** A family of seven scales, each of which uses the same seven notes in the same order as the major scale but assigns the tonic to a different starting note.

**Monochord:** One-stringed musical instrument used not for performance but for investigation of intervals based on ratios of vibrating strings' lengths.

**MPFC:** Medial prefrontal cortex.

**Multimodality:** In music cognition, the various dimensions of experience and perception that might contribute to our understanding of musical structures and forms received through various sensory systems, or modalities, such as aural, sensorimotor, or visual.

**μ-opioid receptor system:** A physiological system highly involved in pain and stress reduction and reward processes through its interaction with the dopamine neurotransmitter.

**Musical chills:** A strong engagement with and emotional response to music, characterized by shivers down the spine or goosebumps (piloerection), often associated with intense pleasure. Sometimes referred to as *frisson.*

**Musicality:** The ability to perceive, produce, and appreciate musical sounds.

***Musical tension:*** The sense that the state of a piece of music is not at rest. Harmonic, melodic, and rhythmic structures, as well as psychoacoustic features, can be employed to create a sense of tension and relaxation. For example, within a tonal context, non-chord tones increase tension and induce an expectation for the non-chord tones to resolve to chord tones.

***Music grammar:*** see ***music syntax.***

***Music syntax:*** The regularities of patterning in a musical style that help to establish frames of reference and listener expectations. Often used to refer to structured successions of chords, as in a cadence.

***Music theory:*** As understood by beginners, the rudiments of music, including the notation of pitches, durations, and simple chords. As understood by researchers, the systematic and/or scientific study of musical repertories, especially as regards their style and syntax.

***Musical controller:*** A subclass of digital musical instruments which features inputs and a mapping layer, but leaves the sound generation to another system.

***Myelin:*** Fatty tissue that forms around axonal connections (nerve fibers), thus aiding their conduction.

***Naturalization:*** The process by which clearly unnatural or surreal sounds come to be perceived as natural, despite clearly breaking the acoustic laws of natural sonic environments.

***Neuroplasticity:*** The ability of the neural system, especially the brain, to change as a result of experience.

***Neurotransmitter:*** Brain chemical that aids in the communication of neural systems.

***New Interfaces for Musical Expression (NIMEs):*** Also known as *digital musical instruments.*

***Non–beat–based rhythms:*** Rhythms comprising intervals that are not related to one another by integer ratios (e.g., 1:2.3:2.7:3.8, where 1 corresponds to the duration of the base inter-onset-interval), and thus do not give rise to a sense of beat.

***Non–beat–based timing:*** See *absolute timing.*

***Non–diegetic music:*** Music which accompanies a scene but is external to the fictional world of the film, such as music that usually accompanies a chase scene; also called *dramatic score.* (See also *diegetic music.*)

***Non–formal learning/education/provision:*** Learning or the provision of activities by professionals, designed to effect learning and/or enjoyment under the auspices of institutional control but usually not accredited.

***Nonlinear resonance:*** Oscillations with amplitudes that are not predictable based on a linear transformation of the stimulus (input). From the perspective of rhythm and beat perception, enhanced oscillation strength at a subharmonic of the base inter-onset-interval; the subharmonic corresponds to the beat frequency.

***Octave equivalence:*** The phenomenon whereby tones separated by one or more octaves exhibit strong perceptual similarity and are perceived to be musically equivalent.

***Oral tradition:*** In music, the systematic transmission of musical performance conventions and repertoire through face-to-face teaching and learning.

***Ornamental tones:*** Notes in a melodic line that primarily serve elaborative or decorative (i.e. "non-structural") functions.

***Oscillatory coupling:*** Coupling of brain oscillations, measured using EEG with various dimensions such as coherence, phase synchronisation, asymmetry, and phase lag.

***Ostensive:*** Carried out in a manner indicating to another person that a communicative intention is involved.

**Oxytocin:**   A neuropeptide involved in affiliative/aggressive social behaviors, social stress, and social memory. Oxytocin promotes approach, affiliative behavior, and attachment, and influences pair bonding and parental care.

**Perceptual present:**   The time span during which perceptual events are directly perceived all at once or as a whole, without requiring access to memory; estimates of its duration vary but often lie in the range of 3–8 seconds.

**Performance cues (in rehearsal and performance):**   The features to which a performer attends during rehearsal and performance that guide the performer's attention and serve as cues for memory retrieval during performance (associated with the work of Richard Chaffin, Mary Crawford, Jane Ginsborg, and Gabriela Imreh).

**Performance-driven music systems:** Intelligent music systems that are capable of responding to performed elements.

**Perisylvian:**   Surrounding the Sylvian fissure, a deep fold of the brain that separates the temporal lobe from the frontal and parietal lobes.

**Phase–amplitude coupling:**   Coupling of the amplitude fluctuations of a relatively high-frequency neural oscillation with the phase of a relatively low-frequency neural oscillation.

**Pitch discrimination threshold:** The smallest pitch difference perceived by an individual.

**Playing along:**   Learning to play specific musical passages or compositions by mirroring it simultaneously, either in a live setting or alongside a recording.

**Playing by ear:**   a) Playing music that is learned through the activity of listening as distinct from reading notation; b) Performance of music which has been committed to memory aurally, without reference to musical notation.

**Pointillism (musical):**   A style of 20th-century composition which deliberately separates individual musical notes of a musical line, as by employing a change of timbre on each pitch.

**Polyphony:**   Music with two or more independently acting vocal or instrumental melodic lines. Used in opposition to homophony, where melodic lines act in synchrony.

**Portamento:**   An audible sliding between pitches; a common expressive device in singing and string playing throughout the common practice period, which in Western art music performance went out of fashion during the first half of the 20th century.

**Posterior:**   Directional term, meaning close to the back.

**Postlingual:**   Occurring after learning language.

**Preferential looking paradigm:**   Experimental method where a young child's interest in or attention to a phenomenon is measured by when and how long she looks toward a stimulus; longer looking indicates that the child is responding to novelty.

**Preference rule (PR):**   In an analytical system, a heuristic or rule of thumb that selects one more preferred interpretation of a musical event or passage from a set of possible, alternative interpretations.

**Prelingual:**   Occurring before learning language.

**Pre-literacy:**   A period of time in which infants and toddlers are susceptible to influences that facilitate the later development of literacy.

**pre-SMA (pre-supplementary motor area):**   A brain area anterior to the proper supplementary motor area which is located on the midline surface of the hemisphere just in front of the primary motor cortex leg representation.

**Prolongation:** The compositional expansion of an underlying structure (melodic, contrapuntal, or harmonic) through processes of elaboration or ornamentation.

**Propositional content:**   The underlying facts or assertions about states of affairs in an utterance.

***Prototypical gestures:*** In conducting, gestures typically and often used by various conductors.

***Psychophysical performance:*** Performance on a task that is designed to measure perceptual thresholds or to maintain near-threshold performance.

***Qualia:*** The perceptual quality or qualities of a sound.

***Quasi-AP:*** The ability to identify frequencies by their pitch names (e.g., F-sharp) at a much higher rate than chance would predict, yet not with the near-perfect accuracy of absolute-pitch (AP) possessors. Quasi-AP listeners may have particular pitches that they can identify with ease (but others with difficulty), or they may consistently misidentify pitches by a small margin of error, such as a semitone.

***Rallentando:*** Gradual slowing down; becoming slower.

***Random number generation:*** The generation of a sequence of numbers or symbols that cannot be reasonably predicted better than by a random chance.

***Relative pitch:*** a) The ability to identify or produce pitches in relation to other pitches, for example, recognizing or singing the next note of a familiar melody or identifying intervals (precise distances between two pitches). b) A cognitive strategy for encoding and retrieving music based upon perceived relationships between pitches. For example, pitches of a melody may be heard in relation to an underlying musical scale (e.g., scale degrees in major or minor). Relative-pitch processing allows listeners to hear transposed melodies as "the same" even when they share no pitches in common. Transposed melodies instead share their contour, intervals, and scale degrees. This strategy contrasts with absolute pitch, an ability to identify individual pitches by name (such as B-flat).

***Reward system:*** A physiological system incorporating a number of subcortical and cortical brain functions, involving motivation, pleasure, and learning, geared towards behaviors that ensure survival, such as feeding, social communication, and reproduction. This system is also activated by secondary rewards, such as monetary rewards, humor, and music.

***Rhythmic entrainment:*** The ability to synchronize movement or sound production to an externally produced isochronous pulse. Long seen as a uniquely human ability, rhythmic entrainment has now been shown in a few other species such as parrots and sea lions.

***Ritenuto:*** Held back in time, usually by only a note or beat, in which underlying base tempo is not affected, only duration (rhythm).

***Roman Jacobson's model of verbal communication:*** A model of communication in which a *message* is sent from sender to receiver through a channel in a certain code in a certain context.

***Rubato:*** Also called *tempo rubato*. The changing of speed or tempo during a musical performance; such changes in the timing of notes, interpreted as expressive on the part of musicians, are a frequent topic for empirical investigation.

***Schemas:*** Patterns or Gestalts that recur frequently in a given musical repertory. In classical European music, schemas (or schemata) are characterized by conventionalized pairings of basses and melodies used to structure small phrases and cadences.

***Schizophonia:*** The discontinuity characterizing the relationship between original and reproduced sounds (*schizo* is "split" and *phonia* is "sound" in Greek); a term introduced by R. Murray Schafer.

***Score-driven music systems:*** Intelligent music systems capable of aligning incoming events to score representations.

***Second language acquisition:*** The process of learning to speak a second language, different from one's native language.

***Semantic congruence:*** In film, correspondence between a moving image and the meaning of the accompanying music (e.g., emotion expressed by the music, or a learned association). This perceived correspondence often draws the viewers' attention to matching parts of the dynamic scene. (See also *temporal congruence.*)

***Semantics:*** The study of meaning, in language or other domains.

***Semiotics/Semiology:*** The study of sign systems.

***Sensitive periods:*** Phases of life or states of the brain when exposure or training generates maximally effective or enduring learning.

***Sensorimotor synchronization:*** The ability to align movements to rhythmic patterns heard or seen, as in dancing or clapping to the beat of music or to the movement of others.

***Sensorineural hearing loss:*** Loss of or reduced hearing due to damage or alteration of the sensory mechanism of the cochlea and/or the neural structures that lie more centrally to it.

***Sequenced playback music systems:*** Automatic music systems that play back sequenced output in response to incoming material.

***Shared Syntactic Integrated Resource Hypothesis (SSIRH):*** The proposal of Aniruddh Patel that mental representation of language and music requires the use of the same neural resources to activate the stored associative networks where domain-specific (i.e., linguistic and musical) representations reside.

***Singing acquisition:*** The long-term process by which an individual develops the capacity to sing and control the voice so as to match the intended performance.

***Situated cognition:*** Meaning, knowing, and learning generated in the situation of doing something bound to a temporal social, cultural, and physical context.

***Skills transfer:*** Achievement of skills in a different context than the original learning situation.

***Social bonding:*** The process of developing interpersonal connections and attachments between people, which typically develops through interactive and cooperative acts.

***Solfège:*** A system of naming pitches that remains in use in the French nomenclature (do-re-mi-fa-sol-la-ti-do meaning c-d-e-f-g-a-b-c). Since solfège originates in vocal music, outside of the French system (also called *fixed-do* solfège), the syllables can be transposed to any pitch-making notation relative to the performer's choice of pitch and is thus possible without staves, clefs, or key signatures.

***Sonata-allegro form:*** An important category of musical form in the Western art music tradition, typically built on the pattern of first presenting differing musical materials (such as first and second themes) in contrasting keys in the exposition, following this with a period of tonal and thematic development, and finally presenting the original materials in the main key of the movement in the recapitulation. Also called *sonata form* or *first movement form.*

***Sound box:*** Analytical three-dimensional model depicting height, width, and depth of the virtual space projected by recorded stereo sound. See also *space-form.*

***Source-bonded sounds:*** Sounds that are perceived as coming from a specific and recognizable source.

***Source-filter model of vocal production:*** Associated with the early work of Gunnar Fant for speech and Johan Sundberg for voice, vocal production is modeled as a combination of a sound source, such as the vocal cords (providing a wide range of fundamental periodic impulses), and the acoustic filter, the vocal tract having infinitely variable natural resonances.

***Space-form:*** A created sonic spatial environment. Term introduced by Dennis Smalley to describe the virtual space projected by electro-acoustic music. For a parallel notion from the field of popular musicology, see *sound box*.

***Spectrum:*** The range of frequency components which comprise a sound.

***Statistical learning:*** A type of implicit learning that occurs as our brains track probabilities in the environment. Without conscious effort, we register how often objects or events are seen or heard, and how often two or more things are seen or heard together. These observations allow us to make inferences about the probability of what will be seen or heard next. In music, for example, statistical learning allows us to predict that scale-degree 7 is likely to be followed by scale-degree 1 (because this succession happens relatively often in music repertoire).

***Structural tones:*** Notes in a melodic line or harmony that serve more than a superficial or decorative function. They might be thought of as the necessary "pillars" of a musical composition.

***Structural Equation Modeling (SEM):*** A statistical method used to infer causality from hidden, latent variables to observed, dependent variables.

***Structural neuroimaging:*** The process of obtaining and producing pictures of the brain.

***Sulcus:*** Inward fold of the brain.

***Symbolic reference:*** A system of reference based on arbitrary yet consistent correlations between tokens and the objects or phenomena for which they stand.

***Synesthesia:*** Non-volitional correspondences between discrete perceptual modalities.

***Synchronization/Desynchronization:*** In the neural system, increase (synchronization) or decrease (desynchronization) in the coordination, or phase locking, between neural oscillations.

***Tans:*** Melodic and rhythmicall constrained phrases rehearsed systematically in practice and incorporated into improvisations in classical Indian performance.

***Technology-mediated performance:*** Music performance conducted with the intervention of computers or electronics.

***Temporal congruence:*** In film, time-based (i.e., temporally synchronized) correspondences between some aspect of the moving image and the structure of the music, which often draws our attention to particular parts of the dynamic scene that correspond with the music. (See also *semantic congruence*.)

***Temporal envelope:*** Change in sound features over time (including features such as attack, decay, and sustain).

***Texture (musical, auditory):*** The simultaneous combination of many musical parts or auditory streams.

***Time series analysis:*** Analysis of a series of measurement points over time.

***Toddler:*** A term often used to describe a child from the age of 12 to 36 months.

***Tonal design:*** The large-scale harmonic plan or sequence of a composition.

***Tonic:*** a) The note in a collection of notes that generates the greatest sense of rest and repose. b) In diatonic (scale-based) musical practice, the first note of the scale and, by extension, harmonies built upon that note. In C major, C is the tonic.

***Tonotopic:*** The spatial organization of frequency encoding in the auditory system. Refers to the spatial configuration present in the inner ear (basilar membrane in the cochlea) all the way up the neuronal pathways of the auditory system.

***Tractography from diffusion tensor imaging:*** Representations of neural fiber tracks based on a methodology using magnetic resonance imaging.

***Transformative music systems:*** Automatic music systems that apply transformations to input events.

***Transposability:*** The ability of a melody to be perceived as invariant when transposed to a different pitch while preserving the intervallic relationships between successive tones. Transposability is associated with *relative pitch*.

***Ubiquitous music:*** Music that occurs in everyday life across a large variety of settings.

***Vasopressin:*** Neuropeptide involved in affiliative/aggressive social behaviors, social stress, and social memory. Vasopressin leads to higher arousal, anxiety, stress, and aggression and influences pair bonding and parental care.

***Ventral:*** Directional term, meaning close to the stomach of an animal.

***Ventricles:*** Fluid-filled spaces in the brain.

***Vibrotactile:*** The perception of sound waves via vibration on the surface of the skin.

***Visual dominance:*** The phenomenon whereby visual input often overrides information from other senses when stimuli are presented in more than one sense modality.

***Vocal learning:*** The ability to learn and imitate new vocalizations. This capacity, which is necessary for the acquisition of speech, is only found in a few animal clades (among mammals, humans, cetaceans, pinnipeds, elephants, and bats, and among birds, parrots, hummingbirds, and oscine songbirds).

***Vocal pedagogy:*** The study of Western music voice instruction, which is used to teach proper vocal technique and practice.

***Vocal tract:*** The open area (cavity) from the larynx to the lips that shapes the acoustic characteristics of sound produced by the vocal folds. Includes the oral and nasal tracts.

***Voxel-based morphometry:*** Neuroimaging analysis technique used to compare the volume of specific brain structures, and investigate the potential impact of age, environment influences, and disease.

***Well-being:*** A subjective and meaningful state of one's own happiness or overall welfare.

***White matter:*** The lighter tissue of the brain and spinal cord, mostly composed of nerve fibers and their fatty sheaths.

***Working memory capacity (WMC):*** A cognitive system of limited capacity, responsible for holding, processing, and manipulating information.

***Working narrative:*** As described in Annabel Cohen's Congruence-Association Model (CAM), the working narrative refers to the viewer's conscious, moment-to-moment, multimodal experience of the film as it is unfolding.

***Zoomusicology:*** The study of the music-like aspects of sound communication among non-human animals. An interdisciplinary field, it draws on a variety of scientific, musicological, and philosophical methods of inquiry.

# INDEX

Made in the USA
Las Vegas, NV
22 December 2022